Ethics and the Conduct of Business

Ethics and the Conduct of Business

John R. Boatright
John Carroll University

PRENTICE HALL, ENGLEWOOD CLIFFS, NEW JERSEY 07632

Library of Congress Cataloging-in-Publication Data

Boatright, John Raymond,
    Ethics and the conduct of business / John R. Boatright,
      p.   cm.
    Includes bibliographical references and index.
    ISBN 0-13-292723-3
    1. Business ethics. 2. Social responsibility of business,
I. Title.
HF5387.B6 1993
174' .4--dc20   92-20960
                                          CIP

Acquisitions Editor: **Ted Bolen**
Editorial and production supervision:
  Mary McKinley and John Rousselle
Editorial Assistant: **Diane Schaible**
Copy Editor: **B. Torjusson**
Prepress Buyer: **Herb Klein**
Manufacturing Buyer: **Patrice Fraccio**
Cover Design: **Ben Santora**
Cover art: **G. Gove/The Image Bank**

Credits and copyright acknowledgments appear on p. xv,
which constitutes an extension of the copyright page.

© 1993 by Prentice-Hall, Inc.
A Simon & Schuster Company
Englewood Cliffs, NJ 07632

Printed in the United States of America
10 9 8 7 6 5 4 3

ISBN 0-13-292723-3

Prentice-Hall International (UK) Limited, *London*
Prentice-Hall of Australia Pty. Limited, *Sydney*
Prentice-Hall Canada, Inc., *Toronto*
Prentice-Hall Hispanoamericana, S.A., *Mexico*
Prentice-Hall of India Private Limited, *New Delhi*
Prentice-Hall of Japan, Inc., *Tokyo*
Simon & Schuster Asia Pte. Ltd., *Singapore*
Editora Prentice-Hall Do Brasil, Ltda., *Rio de Janeiro*

To Claudia

Contents

Preface

In little more than a decade, the field of business ethics has grown from the interest of a few philosophers into an interdisciplinary area of study that has found a secure niche in both the liberal arts and the standard business curriculum. Credit for this development belongs to many individuals—both philosophers and business scholars—who have succeeded in relating ethical theory to the various problems of ethics that arise in business. They have shown not only that business is a fruitful area for philosophical exploration but also that practicing managers in the world of business can benefit from the results.

Ethics and the Conduct of Business is a relatively comprehensive and up-to-date discussion of the most prominent issues in the field of business ethics and the major positions and arguments on these issues. There has been no attempt to develop a distinctive ethical system or to offer a supposed "right answer" in every instance. The field of business ethics is marked by diversity and reasonable disagreement, and a good text should reflect this.

The focus of the book is primarily on ethical issues that corporate decision makers face in developing policies about employees, customers, and the general public. The positions on these issues and the arguments for them are taken from a wide variety of sources, including economics and the law. The study of ethical issues in business is neither confined to a single academic discipline, nor is it limited to the academic world. The issues selected for discussion are widely debated by legislators, judges, government regulators, business leaders, journalists, and, indeed, virtually everyone with an interest in business. Hence, readers wholly unacquainted with ethical theory will find most of the material in this book familiar and accessible.

An underlying assumption of this book, however, is that ethical theory is essential for a full understanding of the arguments commonly offered for positions on virtually every issue in business ethics. Fortunately, the amount of theory is relatively small, and its purpose is to clarify and further develop positions and arguments presented primarily by nonphilosophers. Part One provides a reasonably comprehensive survey of the relevant ethical theory. Readers wishing to tackle the substantive ethical problems in the remaining chapters need only refer to the basic material on utilitarianism and Kant's ethics. Instructors may want to assign only this material initially and return periodically to pick up more theory.

The book contains a subtantial amount of legal material. The reason is twofold. First, most issues in business ethics have been addressed by the law, and the resulting legal framework is part of the "reality" that must be considered by any decision maker. It is pointless to discuss what a manager ought to do in a discrimination case, for example, without knowing the relevant law. Second, and more important, the law incorporates a large body of settled moral opinion about business practice. A close examination of the wording of certain laws, their legislative history, and relevant judicial decisions yields many valuable ethical insights. Questions of ethics often arise when the law is not yet fully formed or is in a state of transition so that we are forced to consider what the law ought to be, and a resolution of legal uncertainty often represents a consensus on the ethical issues involved. Business ethics and business law thus have a great deal in common.

An attempt has been made, whenever possible, to incorporate material from the functional areas of business and the actual practice of corporations. If the discussion of ethical issues in business is to have any relevance for management decision-making, it must take into account the outlook of people in business and the environment in which they operate. And as the field of business ethics becomes increasingly more interdisciplinary, it is essential that a text cross the boundary between philosophy on the one hand and economics, management, marketing, finance, and accounting on the other. Although maintaining a strong philosophical orientation, this book is designed to be used both as a text in a strictly philosophical business ethics course and in one taught in a school of business.

Many people have aided me by their patient encouragement and thoughtful advice. The following people have read one or more chapters and provided me with much useful criticism: Norman E. Bowie, the University of Minnesota; Thomas Donaldson, Georgetown University; Robert E. Frederick, Bentley College; Kenneth E. Goodpaster, College of St. Thomas; Lisa H. Newton, Fairfield University; Lynn Sharp Paine, Harvard Business School; and Patricia H. Werhane, Loyola University Chicago. Jan Willem Bol and John Walton in the marketing department at Miami University gave me the benefit of their work in marketing ethics. I also received help from Robert Lawry, Edward Mearns, Jr., and Todd Smith of the Case Western Reserve University Law School. My thanks go to colleagues in the department of philosophy at John Carroll University—William Langenfus and Paul Thomson—and to Jonathan Smith and William N. Bockanic in the School of Business. I was greatly helped by the comments of anonymous reviewers engaged by Prentice Hall.

I owe a special debt of gratitude for the encouragement and support of Robert D. Sweeney, chair of the department of philosophy at John Carroll University, Frederick F. Travis, dean of the College of Arts and Sciences, and Frank J. Navratil, dean of the School of Business. The writing of the book was facilitated by release time provided by a George E. Grauel Faculty Fellowship awarded by John Carroll University. The strong commitment of John Carroll University to business ethics is due in large measure to the president, Michael J. Lavelle, S.J., one of the few presidents to teach the subject. Finally, my deepest expression of gratitude must go to my wife, Claudia, whose affection, patience, and support was essential for the completion of this book. To her it is dedicated.

Acknowledgments

I would like to acknowledge my gratitude for permission to use material from the following published sources:

A. Carl Kotchian, "The Payoff: Lockheed's 70-Day Mission to Tokyo," *Saturday Review Magazine*, July 9, 1977, © 1977, reprinted by permission of *Saturday Review Magazine*.

Milton Friedman, "The Social Responsibility of Business Is to Increase Its Profits," *The New York Times Magazine*, September 13, 1970, © 1970, reprinted by permission of The New York Times Company.

Richard A. Wasserstrom, "Preferential Treatment," in *Philosophy and Social Issues*, © 1980, reprinted by permission of Notre Dame University Press.

George Sher, "Groups and Justice," *Ethics*, 87 (1977), © 1977, reprinted by permission of University of Chicago Press.

John R. Boatright, "Ethics and the Role of the Manager," *Journal of Business Ethics*, 7 (1988), © 1988, reprinted by permission of Kluwer Academic Publishers.

I would also like to thank the Campbell Soup Company for permission to publish the statement *Our Principles*.

CHAPTER ONE

Introduction: Ethics in the World of Business

A sales representative for a struggling computer supply firm has a chance to close a multimillion-dollar deal for an office system to be installed over a two-year period. The machines for the first delivery are in the company's warehouse, but the remainder would have to be ordered from the manufacturer. Because the manufacturer is having difficulty meeting the heavy demand for the popular model, the sales representative is not sure that subsequent deliveries could be made on time. Any delay in converting to the new system would be costly to the customer; however, the blame could be placed on the manufacturer. Should the sales representative close the deal without advising the customer of the problem?

The director of research in a large aerospace firm recently promoted a woman to head an engineering team charged with designing a critical component for a new plane. She was tapped for the job because of her superior knowledge of the engineering aspects of the project, but the men under her direction have been expressing resentment at working for a woman by subtly sabotaging the work of the team. The director believes that it is unfair to deprive the woman of advancement merely because of the prejudice of her male colleagues, but quick completion of the designs and the building of a prototype are vital to the success of the company. Should he remove the woman as head of the engineering team?

The vice-president of marketing for a major brewing company is aware that college students account for a large proportion of beer sales and that people in this age group form lifelong loyalties to particular brands of beer. The executive is personally uncomfortable with the tasteless gimmicks used by her competitors in the industry to encourage drinking on campuses, including beach parties and beer-drinking contests. She worries about the company's contribution to underage drinking and alcohol abuse among college students. Should she go along with the competition?

Finally, the CEO of a mid-size producer of a popular line of kitchen appliances is approached about merging with a larger company. The terms offered by the suitor are very advantageous to the CEO, who would receive a large severance package. The shareholders of the firm would also benefit, since the offer for their stock is substantially above the current market price. The CEO learns, however, that plans call for closing a plant which is the major employer in a small town. The firm has always taken its social responsibility seriously, but the CEO is now unsure of how to balance the welfare of the employees who would be thrown out of work and the community where the plant is located against the interests of the shareholders. He is also not sure how much to take his own interests into account. Should he bail out in order to enrich himself?

These four hypothetical examples give some idea of the ethical issues that arise at all levels of business. The individuals in these cases are faced with questions about ethics in their relations with customers, employees, and members of the larger society. Frequently the ethically correct course of action is clear, and people in business act accordingly. Exceptions occur, however, when there is uncertainty about ethical obligations in particular situations or when considerations of ethics come into conflict with the practical demands of business. The sales representative might not be sure, for example, about the extent to which he is obligated to provide information about possible delays in delivery. And the director of research, although convinced that discrimination is wrong, might still feel that he has no choice but to remove the woman as head of the team in order to get the job done.

In deciding on an ethical course of action, we can rely to some extent on the rules of right conduct that we employ in everyday life. Deception is wrong, for example, whether we deceive a friend or a customer. And corporations no less than persons have an obligation not to discriminate or to cause harm. Unfortunately, business activity also has some features that limit the applicability of our ordinary ethical views. What we ought to do depends to some extent on our situation and on the particular roles we occupy, and slightly different rules or codes of ethics are needed to guide us in the different departments of our lives. The CEO, by virtue of his position, has responsibilities to several different constituencies, and his problem is, in part, to find the proper balance.

One of the features that distinguishes business activity is its *economic* character. In the world of business, we interact with each other not as family members, friends, or neighbors but as buyers and sellers, employers and employees, and the like. Trading, for example, is often accompanied by hard bargaining, in which both sides conceal their full hand and perhaps engage in some bluffing. And a skilled salesperson is well-versed in the art of arousing a customer's attention (sometimes by a bit of puffery) to clinch the sale. Still, there is an "ethics of trading" that prohibits the use of false or deceptive claims and tricks such as "bait-and-switch" advertising.

Employment is also recognized as a special relation with its own standards of right and wrong. Employers are generally entitled to hire and promote whomever they wish and to lay off or terminate workers without regard for the consequences. (This right is being increasingly challenged, however, by those who hold that employers ought to fire only for cause and to give employees an opportunity to defend themselves.) Employees also have some protections, such as a right not to be discriminated against or to be exposed to workplace hazards. There are many controversies in the workplace, such as the rights of employers and employees with regard to drug testing.

The ethics of business, then, is at least in part the ethics of economic relations—such as those involving buyers and sellers and employers and employees. So we need to ask, what are the rules that ought to govern these kinds of relations? And how do these rules differ from those that apply in other spheres of life?

A second distinguishing feature of business activity is that it typically takes place in large, impersonal *organizations*. An organization, according to organizational theory, is a hierarchical system of functionally defined positions designed to achieve some goal or set of goals. Consequently, the members of a business organization, in assuming a particular position—such as sales representative or vice-president for marketing or CEO—take on new obligations to pursue the goals of the firm. Thus, the marketing executive is not free to act solely on her own standards of good taste and social responsibility at the expense of sales for the brewing company. Nor can the CEO rightfully ignore the interests of shareholders and consider only the impact of the merger on one group of employees of the company and their community any more than he can consider only his self-interest.

The organizational nature of work does not require individuals to abandon their view of right and wrong. However, jobs in business organizations carry an additional set of obligations that must be balanced against those of everyday life. Engineers working on the Ford Pinto project, for example, were aware of defects in the design of the car that caused it to explode in rear-end collisions, and they have been widely criticized for not warning the public. Richard T. DeGeorge defends them by arguing that *this* is not what they were being paid to do.[1] The job required them to report their concerns about the safety of the Pinto to Ford management, which then had the responsibility to make a final decision on whether to proceed with production. And as employees, they had an obligation to be loyal to the company and not to divulge confidential information except under carefully specified conditions.

Whistle-blowing is a classic example of a conflict between two kinds of obligations: the general obligations of morality that all people have, such as the obligation to protect others from harm by warning them of a danger, and the specific obligations that people assume as part of a particular role. Obligations of both kinds also come into conflict with organizational imperatives. Ford executives were under tremendous pressure, for example, to have a subcompact car in dealers' showrooms in time for the 1971 season to compete with Japanese imports. Balancing the demands of morality with the pursuit of the goals of an organization creates difficult situations for managers.

This book is about the ethical issues that arise for managers—and, indeed, for all people, including employees, consumers, and members of the public. Corporate activities affect us all, and so the conduct of business is a matter of concern for everyone with a stake in ethical management. The ethical issues we will be examining are those considered by managers in the ordinary course of their work, but they are also issues that are discussed in the pages of the business press, debated in the halls of Congress, and scrutinized by the courts. This is because ethical issues in business are closely tied to important matters of public policy and to the legislative and judicial processes of government. They are often only part of a complex set of issues.

Decision-making in business, moreover, involves many factors, of which ethics is only one. Economic and legal considerations, along with political realities and technological developments, play a central role. In order to gain an understanding of the relevance of ethics for the conduct of business, it will be useful to begin with a description of three points of view from which decisions in business can be made: the moral, the economic, and the legal. Then we can see how these points of view can be integrated to form an approach to business decision-making that can aid people facing the kinds of issues described at the beginning of this chapter.

THE MORAL POINT OF VIEW

A decision can be made from many different points of view. Closing the deal for the sale of an office computer system is good from a strictly economic or business point of view, as long as there are no repercussions. The quick completion of the design for the airplane component and increasing beer sales among college students are good for the same reason. The individuals involved might also evaluate different courses of action from the point of view of their own careers and ask, what is best for me? What should I do from the point of view of self-interest? Or the individuals involved might consider the law and take a legal point of view. Would removing the woman from her job as head of the engineering team be considered illegal sexual discrimination? Would it be legal to oppose the merger merely to avoid closing the plant? Finally, the individuals involved might consider the moral point of view when making their decisions. Morally speaking, what is the best thing to do?

In order to understand what it means to decide something from the moral point of view, let us consider the case of the sales representative. In deciding whether to disclose the possible delays in delivery, he might ask: What is accepted business practice? What would my boss expect me to do? What would other sales representatives in my company or the industry do? What kind of conduct is generally regarded as legally permissible? To proceed in these ways is to seek guidance from what is conventionally thought by one's peers or society at large to be right or wrong. Unable to find an answer, or perhaps wanting to make sure that he had found the correct one, the sales representative might push further and ask for the reasons that he ought to act in one way rather than another. Three reasons readily suggest themselves.

First, informing the customer about the possibility of a delay might result in losing the sale and a handsome commission. Judged purely by considerations of benefit to himself, he ought to close the deal, unless, of course, he would suffer greater harm if the company is unable to fulfill the contract. If benefit and harm to himself are reasons for acting in some way, why should he not consider the benefit and harm for the customer as well? The fact that the customer might suffer substantial losses would seem to be a morally relevant reason for revealing the possible delivery problems. But the sales representative might think, "I have no obligation to look out for this customer's welfare. If he suffers a loss, that's his problem, not mine; I am not going to pass up a sale to protect him."

On further reflection, however, he might realize that trust is essential in his line of work. If he and the company acquire a reputation for dishonesty, doing business will be more difficult in the future. In addition, if trust is lost in business as a whole—if buyers and sellers can no longer rely on each other's word in their dealings, then everyone suffers. Full disclosure in trade is of value because, on the whole, it helps everyone. In terms of benefit and harm for all concerned, therefore, it is a good policy to inform a customer of matters such as the possibility of delays.

Second, insofar as not revealing the information is misrepresenta-tion, it is a form of lying; and we have been taught since childhood that lying is wrong. Misrepresentation does not require that something false actually be said. If the sales representative assures the customer that there will be no problem with the deliveries, then he is lying. But a person can lie by remaining silent or even saying something true. Con-sider a person selling a used car who says that the transmission was checked by a mechanic only last week but fails to add that the mechanic found serious problems. Since the seller's words would lead a hearer to conclude that the transmission is in sound condition, misrepresentation has occurred.

If we wish to push the matter further, we can ask, what is morally wrong with lying or misrepresentation? If we appeal to the harm done, so that the rule Do not lie is itself based on benefit and harm, then this second reason is no different from the first. However, a different line of reasoning can be sketched as follows. To intentionally bring about a false belief so that another person cannot make a rational decision about some matter of importance is to manipulate that person. Manipulating, or using, another person is morally objectionable because it involves treating people as "things" for satisfying our desires and preventing them from acting to satisfy their own desires. In short, manipulation shows a lack of respect for the essential humanity of others. And the idea of respect for persons is an important moral consideration—different from benefit and harm—that supports the commonly accepted view that lying is wrong.

Third, the sales representative might ask, how would my action appear to the customer were he to know the full facts? Or how would I view it if I were in the customer's place? Would I want to be treated in the same way? These questions suggest a line of reasoning that is com-monly expressed by the Golden Rule: Do unto others as you would have them do unto you. Part of the force of this rule is its insistence on equality, which is an important element of fairness or justice. To treat others in ways that we would not like to be treated is to make exceptions for ourselves and hence to depart from strict equality. The point is also expressed in the familiar slogan, "What's fair for one is fair for all." Assuming that the sales representative would not want to have impor-tant information withheld from him, then it would be wrong for him to withhold the information from the customer.

Features of the Moral Point of View

The moral point of view has two important features.[2] First is a willingness to seek out and act on *reasons*. The best action, according to one writer, is "the course of action which is supported by the best reasons."[3] This does not get us very far without some account of what are the best reasons, but it indicates a commitment to use reason in deliberating about what to do and to construct moral arguments that are persuasive to ourselves and others. Moral rules should not be accepted merely because they are a part of the prevailing morality. Rather, we should attempt to justify the rules we act on by means of the most general and comprehensive kind of reasons available.

Second, the moral point of view requires us to be *impartial*. We must regard the interests of everyone, including ourselves, as equally worthy of consideration and give all interests equal weight in deciding what to do. The moral point of view is the opposite of being purely self-interested. The idea of a personal morality—that is, a morality to be followed only by ourselves—is absurd. Morality by its very nature is public, in the sense that it involves a shared set of rules that can be observed by everyone.[4] A good test of the moral point of view is whether we would feel comfortable if our colleagues, friends, and family were to know about a decision we had made. Would we be willing to have an article on it appear on the front page of the local newspaper, for example? A decision made from the moral point of view can withstand and even invites this kind of openness and scrutiny.

Merely taking the moral point of view does not solve ethical disputes, of course. It is only the beginning of an arduous process of deliberation that involves more than a commitment to the impartial consideration of reasons. Determining what are good reasons requires substantive principles of ethics, such as those discussed in Part I. Our reasoning must also meet the conditions for critical thought of any kind. Of particular importance to ethical reasoning are the following:

1. Definitional clarity. Many ethical issues involve value-laden terms, and it is essential to define them carefully to clear up any confusion about their meaning. For example, bribery is generally regarded as morally wrong, but there are many gray areas. "Grease payments" are necessary in some parts of the world in dealing with balky bureaucrats, and sometimes payments are demanded by corrupt government officials as a condition for doing business. Are there any morally relevant differences between bribery, facilitating payments, and extortion? Other examples of value-laden terms are *discrimination, conflict of interest,* and *deceptive advertising.*

2. Adequate information. No ethical issue can be profitably discussed without knowing the relevant facts. Controversies over the treatment of people with AIDS in the workplace, for example, or the need to restrict program trading in the stock market require a great amount of technical information that can be provided only by experts. Many debates, such as those over proposals to require companies to give notice of plant closings or to give employees leave for the care of newborn children, revolve around predictions of consequences that are difficult to prove or refute.

The Relevance of the Moral Point of View in Business

Taking the moral point of view is easier said than done. Many people in business are apt to say, "I am able to take the moral point of view to determine what ought to be done in my personal life. But in business, decisions simply are not made that way. There is no place in business for the moral point of view." According to this response, the only relevant rules in business regard economic competition and the law. The sole purpose of business is to turn out some product or service at a profit. Every decision, therefore, must be made with an economic point of view. What is most profitable, not what is morally right, must be the overriding consideration—although what is legal must also be taken into account.

The people who say this do not mean that business is an immoral activity; rather, that business is an *a*moral activity, meaning that it is an activity conducted by rules of its own, so that moral considerations are not relevant.[5] According to those who take the *a*moral view of business, the law provides all the rules necessary for engaging in economic competition. Is it profitable and is it legal are the only two questions appropriate for making a business decision. Outside critics can, of course, take the moral point of view, and even people within an organization might pause to consider the morality of what they are doing. But the moral evaluation of business activity is not—and many would say, cannot be—a part of the business decision-making process.

Since a premise of this book is that the moral point of view is essential for business decision-making along with the economic and legal points of view, the thesis that business is an amoral activity needs to be met head on. The problem with the thesis is that it does not recognize the extent to which moral evaluation is already an integral part of business activity. Like Molière's famous bourgeois gentleman who discovers that he has been speaking prose all his life, managers and others frequently "speak ethics." This is not to say that ethics does not need to be made more prominent and incorporated more explicitly into the corporate decision-making process. Still, the commonly held position that business decisions are and ought to be made solely from the economic and legal points of view is not an adequate description of business as it is currently practiced. Managers employ all three points of view—the economic and legal points of view, as well as the moral—and all three are absolutely essential for successfully managing a business firm.

In order to understand the relevance of the moral point of view in business, then, let us examine the other two points of view more fully.

THE ECONOMIC POINT OF VIEW

We are constantly reminded that businesses are profit-making organizations. They also provide us with valuable goods and services. In order to achieve this result, however, it is essential that business firms be operated primarily with profit in mind.

According to economic theory, firms in a free market utilize scarce resources or factors of production (labor, raw materials, and capital) in order to produce an output (goods and services). The demand for this output is determined by the preferences of individual consumers who select from among the available goods and services so as to maximize their own satisfaction. Firms seek to increase their output up to the point where the amount received from the sale of goods and services equals the amount spent for labor, raw materials, and capital—that is, where marginal revenues equal marginal costs. Under fully competitive conditions, the result is economic efficiency, which means the production of the maximum output for the least amount of input. Elaborate techniques have been developed by economists to determine the equilibrium point between marginal revenues and marginal costs that represents the most efficient utilization of resources for producing goods and services.

In order for business activity to result in benefit to the members of society, economic theory requires that certain conditions be satisfied. These include the observance of minimal moral restraints to prevent theft, fraud, and the like. Also, all costs of production must be reflected in the prices that firms and consumers pay. But as long as these conditions are satisfied, business managers need to be concerned only with maximizing profit. Profit maximization, according to some, is the only "morality" needed for managing a business enterprise.

In practice, this concern for profit maximization translates into taking the economic point of view in making decisions about virtually every aspect of a company's operations—from marketing and personnel matters to corporate strategy and long-range planning. And the decision-making process in most companies incorporates this point of view through the use of sophisticated techniques such as management by objectives (MBO), incentive plans tied to performance, and mathematical models for production and operations management and the evaluation of corporate financial performance. Given the extent to which decision-making in the modern corporation has been refined and formalized, using elaborate management information systems and the latest theories of management consultants, it is not surprising that many people in business look upon the moral point of view as a potentially disruptive element in a rationally organized, smoothly functioning system.

Difficulties with the Economic Point of View

The difficulty with taking only the economic point of view, however, is that it is not and cannot be a complete guide to business decision-making. This is so for three reasons. First, the economic theory underlying the economic point of view itself contains some ethical requirements for people's behavior, and the theory also makes many assumptions about perfect competition, the internalization of costs, and so on, which are not satisfied in the actual world. As a result, business activity cannot exclude moral considerations entirely; individuals in business need to observe certain moral standards, and firms must consider harmful consequences of their actions. Second, companies are not merely the abstract firms of economic theory but large-scale organizations that coordinate the activities of flesh-and-blood human beings. The task of organizing work so that people interact with each other productively requires some attention to ethics. The ethical climate of a workplace has a significant bearing on economic performance. Third, business firms operate in a complex environment with many constituencies to which they must constantly justify their activities. In recent years, oil companies, for example, have faced the wrath of consumers and the public over charges of price gouging at the gasoline pump, oil spills from ruptured supertankers, plans for offshore drilling, illegal political campaign contributions, and support for apartheid in South Africa. A tarnished reputation from unethical conduct is a liability in doing business, not least because of the greater government regulation that it brings. Each of these reasons calls for some comment.

1. Ethics is required by the market system. The need for ethics in business goes far beyond the obvious rules against theft and fraud. Bribery and kickbacks, conflict of interest, insider trading, and misappropriation of trade secrets are all practices that interfere with the efficient operation of a free market and hence cannot be permitted. Such matters are typically covered by corporate ethics codes—and, to a great extent, the law—but there are many gray areas where employee conduct cannot be adequately policed by rules, and judgment must be exercised.

Consider ethics in pricing. Under conditions of perfect competition, decisions concerning the price of products can be left to market forces. To the extent that markets are imperfect, however, other factors, including ethics, come into play. This point is illustrated by the controversy over the price of AZT, an experimental drug for the treatment of

AIDS, which is manufactured by only one company, Burroughs Wellcome. As a result of the lack of competition, advanced victims of AIDS were being forced to pay around $8,000 a year for AZT. After months of mounting protests and charges of price gouging, Burroughs Wellcome finally agreed to lower the wholesale price by 20 percent. In explaining the company's decision, a spokesperson said, "We are certainly mindful of the needs of the patients and the desire for a price change in the medical community."[6]

Other examples are provided by such unintended consequences of business activity as job-related accidents, injuries to customers by defective products, and harm to the general public through pollution and the destruction of the environment. In economic theory, these are costs of production, and if they are factored into the prices that companies pay—that is, if they are internalized—then, economists argue, the market itself takes care of the problem. Forced to pay the true cost of pollution, for example, instead of being able to use air and water as free resources, companies have an incentive to stop polluting. However, the costs of pollution control are often not internalized but passed on to workers, consumers, and the public as spillover effects or *externalities.* When externalities are present, the economic point of view is inadequate to provide the needed protection, and the problem of environmental damage must be addressed directly in business decision-making. Many of the problems of business ethics, as well as government regulation, concern situations involving externalities.

Finally, many social problems, including unemployment, urban decay, racial strife, malnutrition, and inadequate education and health care, stem from the distribution of income and wealth in this country—which is largely determined by the workings of the economy. Economists generally regard these matters as the responsibility of government. The only responsibility of business is to operate efficiently. If the result is inequality, then it is up to government to manage the equity/efficiency tradeoff through tax-supported programs. To a great extent, this division of responsibility is appropriate for a free market system operating in a democracy, but questions remain about whether business can operate with no concern for the problems generated by our economic system.

2. Ethics is required for organizations. Economists tend to view business firms as a web of contractual relations, but working in an organization involves more than providing a service in return for a paycheck. Firms are groupings of human beings who must be motivated to cooperate with others in a mutual endeavor. Large modern corporations, in particular, are incredibly complex organizations with a largely hierarchical structure and a myriad of rules, procedures, and customs. Organizational theorists stress the need for a moral code to guide the behavior of individuals in an organization. In one of the classics of organizational theory literature, *The Functions of the Executive*, Chester I. Barnard describes the manager as the creator and maintainer of values in an organization. According to Barnard, "The distinguishing mark of executive responsibility is that it requires not merely conformance to a complex code of morals but also the creation of moral codes for others."[7] The main function of the executive is to communicate a common purpose which is not that of any individual alone.[8]

On a more practical level, Thomas J. Peters and Robert H. Waterman, Jr., the writers of the popular book *In Search of Excellence*, contend that making a profit requires that a corporation have a strong sense of values.[9] The best run companies in their study do not concentrate solely on financial goals but have an obsession with quality that leads them to take a strong interest in the needs and interests of consumers and to show a respect for the dignity and worth of their own employees. They have written:

> Some colleagues who have heard us expound on the importance of values and distinctive cultures have said in effect, "That's swell, but isn't it a luxury? Doesn't the business have to make money first?" The answer is that, of course, a business has to be fiscally sound. And the excellent companies are among the most fiscally sound of all. But their value set *integrates* the notions of economic health, serving customers, and making meanings down the line. As one executive said to us, "Profit is like health. You need it, and the more the better. But it's not why you exist."[10]

3. Ethics is required by corporate constituencies. As a major institution in our society, the corporation is subject to demands from many diverse groups, and the ability to make a profit often depends on how well the managers handle the conflicting pressures. In *A Behavioral Theory of the Firm*, James G. March and Richard M. Cyert argue that corporations are coalitions of many constituencies which must be accommodated so as to avoid disruptive conflicts. Instead of pursuing some overriding goal, such as making a profit, managers give "sequential attention" to a variety of problems, solving them one at a time, in the manner of a politician who first satisfies one group then another.[11] Success consists in maintaining the organization against threats to its survival.

Not all the demands on corporations involve moral issues, of course, but many do. Some of the strongest pressure in recent years has come from organized campaigns to stop American investments in South Africa. Beginning in the 1970s, religious groups, such as the Interfaith Center on Corporate Responsibility, and other organized shareholders urged major U.S. corporations to withdraw entirely or at least to adopt a set of principles drawn up in 1977 by an African-American minister, Leon Sullivan, from Philadelphia. The so-called Sullivan Code requires, among other things, that companies doing business in South Africa desegregate working facilities, pay equal wages for black and white workers performing similar work, advance blacks into higher level positions, and improve living conditions for black workers.

The fact that ethical issues are raised by the constituencies of corporations does not require that managers consider them *as ethical issues*. They may respond to shareholder resolutions and consumer boycotts as problems to "get around" by any means available. However, some companies address ethical issues directly and incorporate ethics into the decision-making process. A few have established an ethics committee of the board of directors to monitor the corporation's ethical performance. Although the task of institutionalizing ethics in corporations is in its infancy, the movement is definitely growing.[12]

THE LEGAL POINT OF VIEW

Business activity takes place within an extensive framework of law, so that all business decisions need to be made from the legal as well as the economic point of view. Some people hold, however, that the law is *all* that is morally required in business. Their motto is, If it's legal, then it's morally okay.[13] This cannot be accepted as an adequate guide. It is necessary to take the moral point of view along with the economic and legal in making business decisions. In short, the law is not enough.

Why the Legal Point of View Is Inadequate

First, the law is inappropriate for regulating certain aspects of business activity. Not everything that is immoral is illegal. Murder, theft, and fraud are both immoral and illegal, and for good reason. But cheating at cards, although immoral, is not usually a legal offense. The main reason is that there is no pressing need for a law against it. Not only are the stakes seldom high enough to warrant the cost of legal enforcement, but cheating at cards is probably more effectively restrained by the informal actions of cardplayers themselves. For similar reasons, laws against adultery, where they still exist, are rarely enforced. Adultery is generally agreed to be immoral, but the law is simply not a suitable instrument for regulating people's extramarital sexual behavior.

Some ethical issues in business are like these examples in that they concern interpersonal relations between co-workers or between employees and their superiors, which would be difficult to regulate by law. Taking credit for someone else's work, making unreasonable demands on subordinates, and unjustly reprimanding an employee are all ethically objectionable practices, but, as with cheating at cards, they are best left outside the law. More serious matters, such as lying on employment applications and padding expense accounts, are also usually not dealt with by the law, except when the stakes are very high. Generally, legislatures and the courts are reluctant to intervene in ordinary business decisions unless significant rights and interests are at stake. They rightly feel that outsiders should not second-guess the business judgment of people closer to a problem and impose broad rules for problems that require a more flexible approach. Companies also prefer to handle many problems without outside interference. Still, just because it is not illegal to take credit for someone else's work or to lie on a job application form does not mean that it is morally okay.

Second, the law is often slow to develop in new areas of concern. Christopher D. Stone points out that the law is primarily reactive, responding to problems that people in the business world can anticipate and deal with long before they come to public attention.[14] The legislative and judicial processes themselves take a long time, and meanwhile much damage can be done. He concluded:

> Thus, there is something grotesque—and socially dangerous—in encouraging corporate managers to believe that, until the law tells them otherwise, they have no responsibilities beyond the law. . . . We do not encourage human beings to suppose so. And the dangers to society seem all the more acute where corporations are concerned.[15]

This is true not only for unknown problems, such as those created by new technologies, but also for long-recognized problems where the law has lagged behind public awareness. For example, racial and sexual discrimination was legal—and widely practiced in business—before the passage of the Civil Rights Act of 1964. It should not take a major piece of legislation to make corporate managers aware that discrimination is wrong. They should have recognized this and changed their discriminatory practices long before Congress finally got around to passing a law. The motto If discrimination is legal, then it's morally okay cannot serve to defend employers who discriminated before 1964. At the present time, legal protection for employees who blow the whistle and those who are unjustly dismissed is just beginning to develop. Employers should not wait until they are forced by law to act on such matters of growing concern.

Third, the law itself often employs moral concepts which are not precisely defined, so that it is impossible in some instances to take the legal point of view without also considering matters of morality. Norman E. Bowie argues that the motto If it's legal, then it's morally okay does not express a minimal conception of morality at all but, in fact, commits the holder to a very extensive set of moral standards.[16] The requirement of *good faith*, for example, is ubiquitous in law. The National Labor Relations Act requires employers and the representatives of employees to bargain "in good faith." One defense against a charge of price discrimination is that a lower price was offered in a good faith attempt to meet the price of a competitor. Yet the notion of good faith is not precisely defined in either instance. Abiding by the law, therefore, requires decision makers to have an understanding of this key moral concept.

The *fiduciary duty* of a person, such as a trustee, to act in the best interests of a third party is another example. The classic statement of this duty was given by Justice Benjamin Cardozo in the case *Meinhard* v. *Salmon*:

> Many forms of conduct permissible in a workaday world for those acting at arm's length, are forbidden to those bound by fiduciary ties. A trustee is held to something stricter than the morals of the market place. Not honesty alone, but the punctilio of an honor the most sensitive, is then the standard of behavior.[17]

A person in a fiduciary relation, then, must act with reference to a very high standard that is properly a part of morality. As a final example, the law holds that a trade secret cannot be acquired by *improper* means, but this crucial notion is not itself defined. A court ruled, however, that flying over a plant under construction and taking aerial photographs to discover the method developed by DuPont for producing methanol was an improper means. According to the opinion in the case:

> "Improper" will always be a word of many nuances, determined by time, place, and circumstance. We therefore need not proclaim a catalogue of commercial improprieties. Clearly, however, one of its commandments does say, "Thou shalt not appropriate a trade secret deviously under circumstances in which countervailing defenses are not reasonably available."[18]

A fourth argument, closely related to the one preceding, is that the law itself is often unsettled, so that whether some course of action is legal must be decided by the courts. And in making a decision, the courts are often guided by moral considerations. Many people have thought that their actions, although perhaps immoral, were still legal, only to discover otherwise. To illustrate this point, Ronald Dworkin cites an 1889 New York case in which a young man who killed his grandfather was named in the will as the legal heir of the estate. The court acknowledged that a literal reading of the will entitled the grandson to the inheritance. Still, the court reasoned:

> . . . all laws as well as contracts may be controlled in their operation and effect by general, fundamental maxims of the common law. No one shall be permitted to profit by his own fraud, or to take advantage of his own

wrong, or to found any claim upon his own iniquity, or to acquire property by his own crime.[19]

The courts often refuse to interpret the law literally when doing so gives legal sanction to blatant immorality. Judges have some leeway or discretion in making decisions. In exercising this discretion, judges are not necessarily substituting morality for law but rather expressing a morality that is embodied in the law. Instead of the motto If it's legal, it's morally okay, another motto is perhaps more accurate: If it's morally wrong, it's probably also illegal. Where there is doubt about what the law is, morality is a good predictor of how the courts will decide.

Fifth, a pragmatic argument is that the law is a rather inefficient instrument, and an exclusive reliance on the legal point of view invites legislation and litigation where it is not necessary. Many landmark enactments, such as the Civil Rights Act of 1964, the National Environment Policy Act of 1969, the Occupational Safety and Health Act of 1970, and the Consumer Protection Act of 1972, were passed by Congress in response to public outrage over the well-documented failure of American businesses to act responsibly. Although business leaders lament the explosion of product liability suits by consumers injured by defective products, for example, consumers are left with little choice but to use the legal system when manufacturers themselves hide behind If it's legal, it's morally okay. Adopting this motto, then, is often shortsighted, and businesses may often advance their self-interest more effectively by considering the moral point of view in the making of decisions.

Reasons for Doing Only What the Law Requires

Despite these objections to the motto If it's legal, then it's morally okay, there are still good reasons for using the law as a guide for moral action and adhering closely to its requirements. The law provides a moral minimum, which sometimes is not very minimal! (Consider, for example, the extensive obligations imposed by antidiscrimination legislation or the Occupational Safety and Health Act.) And corporations sometimes go beyond the moral minimum of legality at their peril.

First, the law embodies many of our common moral beliefs and is often an adequate guide to right action. There is scarcely an ethical issue in business that has not been addressed at one time or another by a legislature, a regulatory agency, or the courts. These bodies have duly considered the moral arguments and come, in a great many instances, to well-thought-out conclusions. The law reflects the results of a sustained public discussion of most of the ethical issues that arise in business. The law has also benefited from a wealth of practical experience. Almost every conceivable problem that could arise with a contract, for example, has already occurred and been adjudicated. As a result, contract law has a richness of detail that could never be achieved by armchair theorizing.

Second, the law provides a clearly defined set of rules. Morality alone could never adequately regulate business activity because it lacks the means to formulate rules precisely and settle disputes over their interpretation. Laws for the sale of property, securities transactions, and the like are exceedingly detailed and complex, as they must be. Since so much is often at stake in business dealings, it is also essential that there be some authoritative means for resolving disagreements. In a dispute over a contractual matter, therefore, the law is more likely to yield a satisfactory resolution.

Third, the law consists of enforceable rules that apply to everyone. In a highly competitive activity such as business, it is important that everyone play by the same rules and that no one be disadvantaged by obeying the rules while others do not. If standards for deceptive advertising, for example, were left to individual judgment, without the Federal Trade Commission (FTC) or some other authoritative body, then ethical advertisers would be at a disadvantage. With the FTC, however, advertisers can refrain from using deceptive ads, knowing that their competitors cannot take unfair advantage. Legally enforceable rules prohibiting deceptive advertising, moreover, give advertisers some justification for adhering only to the letter of the law, because they would be at a disadvantage if they voluntarily adopted a higher standard. If a higher standard is warranted, then Congress or the FTC should act, so that everyone is held to the same rules. The same kind of argument can be used to justify using the law as a guide in matters concerning workplace hazards, product safety, pollution, and the like.

A fourth argument is that the law represents a consensus arrived at through long experience and extensive deliberation. On some issues, people hold sharply differing moral views, and a manager wanting to act morally has to question whose view to accept. Differences exist, for example, about the morality of advertising tobacco products. Enough of a consensus exists to support a legal ban on cigarette advertising on television and a law requiring warning labels. Opinion is divided, however, on whether all tobacco advertising should be prohibited. Until there is sufficient support for a complete advertising ban, tobacco manufacturers and the advertising industry may continue current practices.

Finally, the law is not wholly impartial. The political process by which laws are created and enforced is an arena of powerful competing forces, and business executives occasionally feel, perhaps not without some justification, that the law is an enemy to be fought whenever possible and obeyed with reluctance. On issues such as consumer protection, worker health and safety, and the environment, many groups lobby for legislation and more stringent regulations to achieve their own ends.

Politicians and bureaucrats have interests that they attempt to advance as well. While an "us versus them" mentality is unfortunate, it is not wholly unwarranted in the response business takes to the law.

AN INTEGRATED APPROACH

The approach advocated in this book is that decision-making in business should involve an integration of all three points of view: the economic, the legal, and the moral. Business ethics is simply the attempt to think clearly and deeply about ethical issues in business and to arrive at conclusions that are supported by the strongest possible arguments. An integrated approach requires that we give proper weight to the economic and legal aspects of a problem, but to think that sound business decisions could be made solely from a perspective that excludes ethics is just as wrongheaded as it is to think that they could be made on the basis of ethical reasoning alone.

Integrating different points of view is nothing new; we do it all the time. Managers must juggle financial, production, marketing, personnel, and a host of other factors in taking just the economic point of view. Inevitably, there is tension between the three points of view, but the ideal resolution is not a tradeoff between ethics and other considerations. The outcome, instead, should be a decision that is ethically defensible while at the same time satisfying the legitimate demands of economic performance and a company's legal obligations.

An illustration of an integrated approach is provided by Procter & Gamble's swift action in a controversy over the safety of a new product, the Rely tampon.[20] Superabsorbent tampons were first linked to a rare and fatal disease known as toxic shock syndrome (TSS) by a study of the Centers for Disease Control (CDC) in June 1980. A two-month survey of TSS cases completed by the CDC in September showed that 71 percent of the 42 women in the sample had been using Rely. Procter & Gamble executives were not convinced that enough data existed to implicate Rely as the cause and thought that extensive publicity had biased the results. They could have dug in their heels and done nothing. Instead, on September 22, 1980, Procter & Gamble announced that the sale of Rely tampons was being suspended, a move that the company estimated would cost $75 million after taxes. A few days later, Procter & Gamble agreed to an FDA request to take all packages of the product off retailers' shelves and buy back all Rely tampons still in the hands of consumers, including $10 million in promotional samples. The company also agreed to conduct an informational advertising campaign warning women not to use Rely and to exercise care in the use of other tampons.

These actions were not undertaken entirely for reasons of ethics, of course. Economic and legal considerations also played a large role. The FDA had the power to require warning labels on packages of Rely and to order the product off the market if the evidence continued to mount. A number of multimillion-dollar product liability suits had already been filed, and more were sure to come. Even the $2 million that Procter & Gamble earmarked for continued research on TSS could serve to reassure consumers of the integrity of the company's products and also to facilitate the reentry of the company into the lucrative menstrual products market if subsequent findings showed Rely not to be related to the disease. Still, Procter & Gamble executives gave ethical concerns a high priority in arriving at their decision. The chairman of Procter & Gamble, Edward G. Harness, commented afterward:

> Company management must consistently demonstrate a superior talent for keeping profit and growth objectives as first priorities. However, it also must have enough breadth to recognize that enlightened self-interest requires the company to fill any reasonable expectation placed upon it by the community and the various concerned publics. Keeping priorities straight and maintaining the sense of civic responsibility will achieve important secondary objectives of the firm. Profitability and growth go hand in hand with fair treatment of employees, of direct customers, of consumers, and of the community.[21]

Integrating the three points of view requires an understanding of the ethical point of view in making decisions about problems that typically arise in business. Managers receive training in making decisions on the basis of purely economic considerations from their formal education and long years of experience. If they are unfamiliar with the law, company lawyers are there to give advice on the legal aspects of any problem. Many people assume, however, that taking the moral point of view requires nothing more than what we learned at home or the morality that we practice in our everyday life. Like the major functional areas in business education, philosophical ethics provides a set of concepts and theories for understanding and resolving complex issues. The first part of this book, therefore, covers important concepts and theories that form an essential foundation for the discussion of the specific ethical issues in business that follows.

MORALITY, ETHICS, AND ETHICAL THEORY

Before proceeding further, we need to clarify the meaning of the key terms *morality* and *ethics* and the cognates *moral* and *ethical* and *morally* and *ethically*. Generally, *morality* and *ethics*, *moral* and *ethical*, and so on are interchangeable. The presence of two words in the English language with the same meaning is due to the fact that they derive from different roots; *morality*, from the Latin word *moralitas*, and *ethics*, from the Greek *ethikos*. There is no difference, therefore, between describing discrimination as a moral issue or as an ethical issue, or between saying that discrimination is morally wrong or that it is ethically wrong. There are some subtle differences, however, between *morality* and *ethics*.

Morality is generally used to describe a sociological phenomenon; namely, the existence in a society of rules and standards of conduct. Every society has a morality, since this constitutes the basis for mutually beneficial interaction. Without such fundamental rules as Do not kill and Do not steal, for example, stable communities would be impossible. Not all rules and standards are part of morality, of course. Eating peas with a knife, for example, is a breach of etiquette but not a moral wrong, and the rule Look both ways before crossing the street is a rule of prudence, not morality. Etiquette and prudence, therefore, constitute sets of nonmoral rules and standards. Morality also has many complex ties to the law, as we have already observed.

Moralities are also specific to societies and exist at certain times and places. Thus, we can speak of the morality of the Trobriand Islanders or the colonial settlers. The morality of Americans in the 1990s is different from that in the 1950s or the 1850s. We can even speak, as Karl Marx did, of the morality of different classes in society. In a highly developed society such as our own, morality also includes a complex vocabulary and patterns of reasoning that permit the members of the society to engage in moral discourse for the purpose of evaluating the actions of individuals and the practices and institutions of the society. *Ethics* is roughly a synonym for *morality*, but it is often restricted to the rules and norms of specific kinds of conduct or the codes of conduct for specialized groups. Thus, we talk about the ethics of stockbrokers or the code of ethics for the accounting profession but usually not about the morality of these groups.

The term *ethics* also has another, quite different, use, which is to denote the field of *moral philosophy*. Ethics, along with logic, epistemology, and metaphysics, is a traditional area of philosophical inquiry that dates back to the time of the ancient Greeks. Ethics as a philosophical endeavor is concerned largely with the possibility of justification. It takes morality as its subject matter and asks such questions as: Are there any means for showing that the rules and standards of our morality are the right ones? Are there any ultimate moral principles that can be used to resolve inconsistencies or conflicts? Ethics is not a substitute for morality; rather, it seeks to organize our ordinary moral beliefs and render them precise and consistent.[22]

The Possibility of Justification

A long philosophical tradition holds that ultimately no justification of morality is possible. There are many different versions of this thesis, and it is important to understand exactly which one is being asserted. The thesis known as *cultural relativism* holds that morality varies from one culture to another, since practices that are regarded as right in some cultures are regarded as wrong in others. As an observation about the moralities of different cultures, this is undeniably true, although differences in practices do not necessarily indicate ultimate moral disagreement. Different family arrangements or sexual mores, for example, might be means of achieving the same end under different conditions.[23] The fact of cultural relativism has no bearing, however, on the possibility of justification, since *regarding* practices as right (or wrong) does not necessarily make them so. The fact that culture X practices cannibalism, for example, and regards it as right does not exclude the possibility of demonstrating conclusively that cannibalism is wrong and that the beliefs of culture X are mistaken.[24]

One thesis that does deny the possibility of justification is *ethical relativism*, which is distinct from cultural relativism. The latter thesis asserts a fact about cultures whereas the former is a philosophical assertion. What ethical relativism asserts is that there is no standard of right or wrong apart from the morality of a culture and that whatever is held to be right in a culture really is right for that culture.[25]

Although many people *think* they are ethical relativists, a clear understanding of what this position entails is often sufficient to convince them otherwise. Mary Midgely cites as an example the custom in feudal Japan that required a Samurai warrior to try out a new sword on a passing stranger on the road.[26] The warrior had to take care only that the wayfarer be cut cleanly in two with a single stroke; otherwise, he committed an offense against his own honor, that of his ancestors, and even the honor of the emperor. Ethical relativism, if true, would deny us the possibility of morally appraising this custom. "But, that's wrong!" has no meaning for the ethical relativist, because there is no standard outside the Japanese culture of the time. Similarly, if the Nazis sincerely believed that Jews should be exterminated, then their belief has as much claim to validity as our own. They simply had a different morality.

Once we accept as equally valid the morality of different cultures, there is no reason to stop there. If groups in our own society have moral beliefs different from our own, then why are the practices they sanction not right for those people? Many people who believe that abortion is wrong, for example, are not content to hold that abortion is wrong only for *themselves*; they hold that abortion is wrong for anyone, including women who hold different moral beliefs. Further, if one lone individual holds a moral belief, no matter how abhorrent, we have no basis on which to maintain the mistakenness of that person's belief, if we hold ethical relativism to be true. The ultimate logic of ethical relativism, as Midgely points out, is that we are reduced to an uncritical acceptance of all beliefs as equally valid and any rational discussion is impossible.

Understanding and Tolerating Moral Differences

If ethical relativism is so implausible, why would anyone accept it? One answer is that the thesis is often confused with two other positions, both quite reasonable. These are

1. We ought to refrain from criticizing a practice of others until we have tried to understand that practice fully.
2. We ought to be tolerant of practices different from our own.

Suppose that before condemning the practice of *tsujigiri* or "trying out one's new sword" on a hapless passerby, we attempt to understand it in the context of Japanese culture at the time. Midgely suggests that a defender might justify the Sumurai's seemingly barbarous behavior in the following way:

> He will try to fill in the background, to make me understand the custom, by explaining the exalted ideals of discipline and devotion which produced it. He will probably talk of the lower value which the ancient Japanese placed on individual life generally. . . . He may add, too, that the wayfarers did not seriously mind being bisected, that in principle they accepted the whole arrangement.[27]

This justification assumes that if we sensitively seek to understand a practice of another culture, we will come to see its justification in terms of our own norms or values, even if we are not wholly convinced. The argument that the acceptance of the practice even by the victims themselves constitutes a kind of justification is based on a more general ethical principle that the defender assumes we share. The defender, therefore, is attempting to engage us in a rational discussion of the kind that ethical relativism precludes us from having. Having tried to find an acceptable justification and failed, moreover, we are in a position to condemn the practice as immoral.

The point that we ought to understand a practice of another culture before criticizing it can also be applied to business practices in different contexts. We believe bribery to be wrong in the United States; however, in some countries of the world, bureaucrats are underpaid and bribes are regarded as part of their compensation. In such circumstances, some people argue, bribery is morally permissible. Similarly, Albert Z. Carr created a storm in the *Harvard Business Review* a number of years ago by arguing that bluffing, which is immoral in everyday life, is acceptable and even expected in some areas of business. Drawing an analogy with bluffing in poker, Carr wrote:

> Poker's own brand of ethics is different from the ethical ideals of civilized human relationships. The game calls for distrust of the other fellow. It ignores the claim of friendship. Cunning deception and concealment of one's strength and intentions, not kindness and openheartedness, are vital in poker. No one thinks any the worse of poker on that account. And no one should think any the worse of the game of business because its standards of right and wrong differ from the prevailing traditions of morality in our society.[28]

These examples do not support ethical relativism, however. They have, in fact, quite the opposite effect, because they admit the possibility of justification apart from the beliefs of a culture or a group of individuals. If bribery is justified in Thailand but not in the United States, the reason is not a difference in the beliefs of people in the two countries but a difference in the contexts. If conditions X, Y, and Z exist in Thailand and justify bribery there, then everyone, Americans included, should agree that bribery *under those conditions* is justified. And bribery would be justified in the United States if conditions X, Y, and Z were to exist here. By the same line of reasoning, if bluffing is justified in labor negotations, then that is because of conditions which would lead most people to recognize bluffing as justified *under those conditions*. That actions may be right in one context and wrong in another is an obvious point that can be admitted without denying the possibility of justifying our moral beliefs about the rightness or wrongness of actions in different contexts. Tolerance is not the same as uncritical acceptance.

Turning now to the second position, anyone holding the thesis of ethical relativism is required to adopt an extreme form of tolerance for the practices of others. Merely being tolerant, however, does not commit a person to being an ethical relativist, because there are good reasons for taking a tolerant attitude apart from the thesis of ethical relativism. Tolerance is amply justified by the high value we place on individual freedom—and also by a proper humility about the possibility of being mistaken in our own moral beliefs. As long as the social fabric can withstand a diversity of practices, allowing people to act in accord with their own moral beliefs—even those we consider to be wrong—promotes freedom. Because we might be wrong in our moral beliefs, tolerance allows us to engage in rational discussion with people who hold contrary views, thus allowing everyone an opportunity to correct any mistaken beliefs. Tolerance has its limits, of course, and one merit of the justification for tolerance just sketched is that it still allows us to be critical of the moral beliefs of others and to oppose those we regard as abhorrent.

These considerations do not disprove ethical relativism, however. They show only that two reasonable positions which many people mistakenly identify with ethical relativism are not the same as ethical relativism and do not commit us to the thesis. The obligations to understand a practice before condemning it and to be tolerant are wholly compatible with the possibility of justification in ethics. The main obstacle to laying ethical relativism to rest once and for all is the difficulty of justifying our moral beliefs. Although moral philosophers have made great progress, ethics as a field of philosophy does not consist of a body of generally accepted moral truths in the same way that sciences such as chemistry and physics contain a large core of accepted scientific truths.

The Differences Between Ethical Theories

In the next few chapters, two major theories of ethics are presented as the basis for our beliefs about moral obligations, rights, and justice, and they are applied in discussions of a number of issues concerning the rights and obligations of employees in a firm, employee relations, the protection of employees and consumers, and the responsibility of corporations to the public at large. We will discover a large measure of agreement between these two ethical theories in their content and in the results of applying them to specific cases. This should come as no surprise since both are theories of the same thing; namely, the morality of everyday life. Something would be amiss if an ethical theory did not reflect our accepted moral beliefs. The extent of the agreement is often obscured by differences in approach or emphasis, but when these are stripped away, we see that rival theories often express the same point in different ways.

The amount of agreement between these two ethical theories should not blind us, however, to the fact that there are substantial differences between them. Again, this should not be surprising, because there are profound differences between people's moral outlooks as a result of differences in experiences, social class, cultural conditions, and the like. Differences in outlook are also due to progress in morality. Great thinkers, religious teachers, and social reformers have increased our awareness and provided us with new concepts and ideals. The Greek concept of a universal moral law that applies to all human beings and the biblical ideal of universal love were both very radical at one time. More recently, the civil rights struggle and the women's movement have made us more aware of issues of race and gender. Highly technical work in cost-benefit analysis, risk assessment, and social choice theory has also greatly expanded the methods available for reasoning about ethical issues

The differences between theories should not lead us to despair of resolving ethical issues or to conclude that one resolution is as good as another. Nor should we be discouraged by the fact that agreement on complex ethical issues is seldom achieved. (Disagreement is also a feature of science and such business-related fields as economics and finance.) Unanimity in ethics is an unreasonable expectation. The best we can do is to analyze the issues as fully as possible, which means getting straight on the facts and achieving definitional clarity, then to develop the strongest and most complete arguments we can for what we consider to be the correct conclusions.

NOTES

1. RICHARD T. DeGEORGE, "Ethical Responsibilities of Engineers in Large Organizations," *Business and Professional Ethics Journal*, 1 (1981), 1–14.
2. The concept of the moral point of view is developed in KURT BAIER, *The Moral Point of View: A Rational Basis of Ethics* (Ithaca: Cornell University Press, 1958). A similar account is offered in JAMES RACHELS, *The Elements of Moral Philosophy* (New York: Random House, 1986), chap. 1.
3. BAIER, *The Moral Point of View*, 88.
4. BAIER, *The Moral Point of View*, 195–96.
5. For a fuller discussion of this point, see RICHARD T. DeGEORGE, *Business Ethics*, 3rd ed. (New York: Macmillan, 1990).
6. Quoted in PHILIP J. HILTS, "AIDS Drug's Maker Cuts Price by 20%," *The New York Times*, September 19, 1989, sec. 1, p. 1.
7. CHESTER I. BARNARD, *The Functions of the Executive* (Cambridge: Harvard University Press, 1968), 279.
8. BARNARD, *The Functions of the Executive*, 217–27.
9. THOMAS J. PETERS and ROBERT H. WATERMAN, JR., *In Search of Excellence* (New York: Harper and Row, 1982).
10. PETERS and WATERMAN, *In Search of Excellence*, 103.
11. RICHARD M. CYERT and JAMES G. MARCH, *A Behavioral Theory of the Firm* (Englewood Cliffs, NJ: Prentice Hall, 1963), 118. Similar accounts are given in HERBERT A. SIMON and JAMES G. MARCH, *Organizations* (New York: Wiley, 1958); JEFFREY PFEFFER and GERALD SALANCIK, *The External Control of Organizations* (New York: Harper and Row, 1978); and from a public policy perspective, CHARLES E. LINDBLOM, *The Public Policy Process* (Englewood Cliffs, NJ: Prentice Hall, 1968).
12. See Center for Business Ethics, "Are Corporations Institutionalizing Ethics?" *Journal of Business Ethics*, 5 (1986), 85–91. An overview is provided by The Business Roundtable, *Corporate Ethics: A Prime Business Asset*, February 1988.
13. This phrase is taken from NORMAN E. BOWIE, "Fair Markets," *Journal of Business Ethics*, 7 (1988), 89–98.
14. CHRISTOPHER D. STONE, *Where the Law Ends: The Social Control of Corporate Behavior* (New York: Harper and Row, 1975), 94.
15. STONE, *Where the Law Ends*, 94.

16. BOWIE, "Fair Markets." Much of the argument on this point is derived from Bowie's article.

17. *Meinhard* v. *Salmon*, 164 N.E. 545 (1928).

18. *E. I. du Pont de Nemours & Co.* v. *Christopher*, 431 F.2d 1012 (5th Cir. 1970).

19. *Riggs* v. *Palmer*, 115 N.Y. 506 (1889). Discussed in RONALD DWORKIN, *Taking Rights Seriously* (Cambridge: Harvard University Press, 1978), 23.

20. Material on this case is taken from ELIZABETH GATEWOOD and ARCHIE B. CARROLL, "The Anatomy of Corporate Social Response: The Rely, Firestone 500, and Pinto Cases," *Business Horizons*, 24 (September–October 1981), 9–16; "Managing Product Safety: The Procter and Gamble Rely Tampon," Harvard Business School, reprinted in JOHN B. MATTHEWS, KENNETH E. GOODPASTER, and LAURA L. NASH, eds., *Policies and Persons: A Casebook in Business Ethics*, 2nd ed. (New York: McGraw-Hill, 1991), 377–83; and "Procter & Gamble's Rely Tampons," in TOM L. BEAUCHAMP, ed. *Case Studies in Business, Society, and Ethics* (Englewood Cliffs, NJ: Prentice Hall, 1989), 87–94.

21. EDWARD G. HARNESS, "Views on Corporate Responsibility," *Corporate Ethics Digest*, 1 (September–October 1980), cited in GATEWOOD and CARROLL, "The Anatomy of Corporate Social Response."

22. For a further discussion of justification in ethics, see "Ultimate Moral Principles, Their Justification," in *The Encyclopedia of Philosophy*, vol. 8.

23. This is argued by RICHARD B. BRANDT, *Ethical Theory* (Englewood Cliffs, NJ: Prentice Hall, 1959), chap. 5.

24. Two good discussions by philosophers are CARL WELLMAN, "The Ethical Implications of Cultural Relativity," *The Journal of Philosophy*, 62 (1954), 169–84; and KAI NIELSEN, "Ethical Relativism and the Facts of Cultural Relativity," *Social Research*, 33 (1966), 531–51.

25. For a fuller statement of the thesis, see "Ethical Relativism," *The Encyclopedia of Philosophy*, vol. 3. A collection of critical essays is JOHN LADD, ed., *Ethical Relativism* (Belmont, CA: Wadsworth, 1973).

26. MARY MIDGELY, *Heart and Mind* (New York: St. Martin's Press, 1981), chap. 5.

27. MIDGELY, *Heart and Mind*, 72–73.

28. ALBERT Z. CARR, "Is Business Bluffing Ethical?" *Harvard Business Review*, 46 (January–February 1968), 145.

CHAPTER TWO
Utilitarianism

When Carl Kotchian, president of Lockheed Aircraft Corporation, made a trip to Japan in August 1972, the company he headed was in a very precarious financial situation. Lockheed had failed to get contracts with several major European carriers. Cost overruns on the C5A Galaxie transport plane and performance problems with the Cheyenne helicopter had caused the Defense Department to cancel its orders for these aircraft. And Lockheed had avoided bankruptcy in 1971 only with a $250 million loan guarantee from the federal government. The survival of Lockheed as a company was riding on the effort to sell the new L-1011 TriStar passenger jet to All Nippon Airways.

Shortly after landing in Tokyo, Kotchian asked a representative of the Marubeni Corporation, a trading company that Lockheed had engaged to aid in negotiations with All Nippon Airways (ANA), to arrange a meeting with Kakuei Tanaka, the prime minister of Japan.[1] Kotchian knew that Tanaka would be meeting with President Richard Nixon in Hawaii in a few days and that Nixon would ask him to improve the U.S. balance of payments by buying more American products. He felt that it was important for the prime minister to be informed beforehand about the merits of the TriStar.

The representative of Marubeni, Toshiharu Okubo, informed Kotchian that a "pledge" of five hundred million yen (about $1.6 million) would be required to set up such a meeting. Without specifically being told the destination of the money, Kotchian assumed that it was intended for the prime minister's office. Kotchian was hesitant about making an irregular payment of this size to the highest official in the Japanese government, but he knew that refusing to do so would hamper Lockheed's efforts and that the blame for any failure would rest squarely on his shoulders. So he agreed to pledge the amount requested, and a meeting was held at seven thirty the next morning. At the meeting, which Kotchian did not attend, the president of Marubeni allegedly secured Tanaka's help on behalf of Lockheed with an offer of five hundred million yen.

After more than two months of complex negotiations, executives of ANA were on the verge of placing an order for six planes with an option to buy eight more. Late in the evening of Sunday, October 29, Carl Kotchian received a telephone call from Okubo informing him that the sale was assured if he would do three things. Two of them were minor, but the third was a bombshell. Kotchian was asked to have $400,000 in Japanese yen ready the next morning. Of this amount, $300,000, or ninety million yen, was to be paid to Tokuji Wakasa, the president of All Nippon Airways. This figure was based on $50,000 for each of the six planes ordered. The remaining $100,000, or thirty million yen, was to be divided among six Japanese politicians. When Kotchian protested that it would be impossible to raise that much cash so quickly, he was told the thirty million yen for the politicians was essential; the rest could wait. By ten o'clock the next morning, thirty million yen in cash was delivered to Okubo, and the ninety million yen payment to the president of ANA was made a week later.

Kotchian returned to the company's headquarters in Burbank, California, amid general celebration and apparently forgot about the pledge of five hundred million yen for Prime Minister Tanaka. Eight months later, though, Okubo called Kotchian to say that now was the time to follow through. Kotchian asked whether the payment was necessary since the deal had been concluded such a long time ago. Okubo assured him that if he did not honor the pledge, Lockheed would never be able to do business in Japan again, and he hinted darkly that the president of Marubeni, who had made the offer to Tanaka, would have to leave the country. In an account of his experiences, Kotchian wrote:

> After hanging up the telephone, I went home and thought about the matter overnight. I decided on the basis of what Okubo had told me that we could not possibly risk any retaliation against Lockheed or against Marubeni. If we did not make the payment on this matter, Hiyama [the president of Marubeni] would be forced into exile, Lockheed might not be able to sell anything in Japan again, and our relations with Marubeni might be completely disrupted. Consequently, the more I thought about it, the more I was convinced that there was no alternative but to make the

payment. In the end, after talking it over with other Lockheed executives, I called Okubo and told him we would honor the pledge.[2]

Later, when All Nippon exercised the option to buy eight more TriStar planes, Okubo requested $400,000, based on $50,000 per plane. Kotchian again felt that he had no choice but to comply and ordered that the payment be made. In all, Lockheed paid about $12.5 million in bribes and commissions to sell twenty-one TriStars in Japan.

Kotchian explained his decision to approve the first payments to the president of ANA and the six politicians in the following way:

> If some third party had heard this conversation, he could ask why I responded to this request for secret payments. However, I must admit that it was extremely persuasive and attractive at that time to have someone come up to me and confidently tell me, "If you do this, you will surely get ANA's order in twenty-four hours." What businessman who is dealing with commercial and trade matters could decline a request for certain amounts of money when that money would enable him to get the contract? For someone like myself, who had been struggling against plots and severe competition for over two months, it was almost impossible to dismiss this opportunity.[3]

And he justified all the payments for the sale of the TriStar by making three points:

> The *first* is that the Lockheed payments in Japan, totaling about $12 million, were worthwhile from Lockheed's standpoint, since they amounted to less than 3 percent of the expected sum of about $430 million that we would receive from ANA for 21 TriStars. Further, as I've noted, such disbursements *did not violate American laws*. I should also like to stress that my decision to make such payments stemmed from my judgment that the TriStar payments to ANA would provide Lockheed workers with jobs and thus redound to the benefit of their dependents, their communities, and stockholders of the corporation.
>
> *Secondly*, I should like to emphasize that the payments to the so-called "high Japanese government officials" were all requested by Okubo and were *not brought up from my side*. When he told me "five hundred million yen is necessary for such sales," from a purely ethical and moral standpoint I should have declined such a request. However, in that case, I would *most certainly* have sacrificed commercial success.
>
> *Finally*, I want to make it clear that I never discussed money matters with Japanese politicians, government officials, or airline officials. . . . From my experience in international sales, I knew that if we wanted our product to have a chance to win on its own merits, we had to follow the functioning system. . . . [W]e understood that we would have to pay, or pledge to pay, substantial sums of money in addition to the contractual sales commissions. We never *sought* to make these extra payments. We

would have preferred not to have the additional expenses for the sale. But, always, they were recommended by those whose experience and judgment we trusted and whose recommendations we followed.[4]

Do these arguments serve to justify the actions of Lockheed in Japan? Although bribery is morally wrong in most situations, Lockheed officials contended that it is an accepted practice in many parts of the world and a necessity in a competitive climate where other companies do the same. If Lockheed had refused to make the requested payments, the company would quite possibly have lost the Japanese market to less scrupulous competitors. The arguments used by Carl Kotchian appeal primarily to *consequences*. Tens of thousands of jobs were saved, thereby benefiting Lockheed workers, their families, and the communities in which they lived. The cost to the company was negligible given the size of the deal. Stockholders were saved from the loss that would have resulted from the collapse of the company. And the sale benefited the country as a whole by reducing the U.S. balance of payments problem. Kotchian insists that Lockheed violated no American law.[5] Besides, some people argue, no one really got hurt. The cost of the bribes would eventually be passed on to consumers and taxpayers, but these losses, they feel, are not significant when compared to the gains for Lockheed.[6]

The appeal to consequences is not conclusive, however. Lockheed was competing for sales with two other American companies: Boeing with its 747 and McDonnell Douglas and the DC 10. So the jobs that were saved in Burbank, California, were lost in Seattle, St. Louis, and elsewhere, and the workers for these two companies, their families, subcontractors, and the stockholders of Boeing and McDonnell Douglas were all harmed as a result. Lockheed's success in taking business away from other American companies does nothing, moreover, to improve the balance of payments for the United States. In the aftermath of the Lockheed affair, many careers were destroyed. Carl Kotchian resigned from Lockheed. Prime Minister Tanaka was forced from office and prosecuted along with other Japanese officials. Many Japanese feel that the country itself was hurt because of the distrust of political institutions that the revelations created in Japan. Although the scandal prompted a movement toward reform, some observers believe that it also increased the strength of right-wing elements who think that Japan has been corrupted by modern life and ought to abandon parliamentary democracy and return to the old imperial system.

Consequences aside, some people hold that bribery is wrong because of the violation of *duty* it involves. Officials both in the Japanese government and at All Nippon Airways hold positions of trust, in which they are pledged to serve the interests of the people of Japan. They betrayed this trust by accepting the bribes, and Lockheed, by paying the bribes, is guilty of complicity in their betrayal. Even if bribery has no adverse consequences, it is still wrong according to ethical theories based on the notion of duty because of the betrayal of trust that it involves.

Carl Kotchian has attempted to defend himself against such a position by denying that his actions constituted bribery. Bribery, he seems willing to concede, is wrong, but in this case, Kotchian contends, Lockheed was an innocent victim of extortion demands made by the Japanese. In Senate hearings, Daniel J. Haughton, the chairman of Lockheed, insisted that the payments were not bribes, which are illegal in most countries, but kickbacks, the legal status of which is less clear. Lockheed's motive in making the payments, moreover, was not to make a sale by corrupting Japanese officials; the company was simply trying to do business in an atmosphere tainted by the corruption of others. In addition, the payments were actually offered by the middlemen of the Marubeni Corporation, who were apparently well-versed in the ways of decision-making Japanese style.[7]

This defense is not entirely successful. The Marubeni Corporation was chosen by Lockheed officials to help conduct negotiations, so they were acting on Lockheed's behalf. In addition to Marubeni, Lockheed had also hired as an agent Yoshio Kodama, a notorious *kuromaku*, or "fixer," with known connections to organized crime. Kodama also served Lockheed in 1958 when the company beat out the Grumman Corporation for the sale of jet fighters to the Japanese Air Force, reportedly through the use of bribery. According to Japanese sources, Kodama was hired after Lockheed fired its previous agent, Dai Ichi Bussan, for resisting suggestions that payments be made.

Japan was not the only country in which Lockheed had made payments. A scandal erupted in Italy when a president, Giovanni Leone, and two prime ministers, Aldo Moro and Mariano Rumor, were accused of accepting bribes from Lockheed for aiding in the sale of aircraft in that country. And Prince Bernhard, the husband of Queen Juliana of the Netherlands, was greatly embarrassed by the disclosure of a "gift" of more than $1 million for assisting in the sale of 138 F-104 Starfighter jets to the Dutch Air Force. Lockheed admitted to making questionable payments in a number of countries, totaling more than $30 million. Lockheed, it appears, was no stranger to the bribery game.

Who is correct in this case? What is the best way to reason about these kinds of ethical issues? Are there any theories of ethics that can aid us in handling cases such as those faced by Carl Kotchian? This chapter examines one major ethical theory, known as utilitarianism, which looks for justification to the consequences of actions. In subsequent chapters we will look at other important theories, including some that base right action on the notion of duty. It will also be useful in this chapter and the next to clarify the distinction already made between two types of ethical theories; namely, those based on consequences and on duty—or teleological and deontological theories, to use their technical names.

TELEOLOGICAL THEORIES

It is customary to divide ethical theories into two groups, usually called teleological and deontological. The most prominent historical examples of a teleological and a deontological theory are utilitarianism and the ethical theory of Immanuel Kant, respectively. An important third kind of ethical theory that is not further discussed in this book is one based on the concept of virtue. Aristotle's ethics is the best example of a theory of this kind.[8]

Teleological theories hold that the rightness of actions is determined solely by the amount of good consequences they produce. The word *teleological* is derived from the Greek word *telos,* which refers to an end. Actions are justified on teleological theories by virtue of the end they achieve, rather than some feature of the actions themselves. Thus, the concept of goodness is fundamental in teleological theories, and the concepts of rightness and obligation, or duty, are defined in terms of goodness. According to utilitarianism, our obligation, or duty, in any situation is to perform the action that will result in the greatest possible balance of good over evil.

Obviously, a great deal depends on what is regarded as good and as evil. In classical utilitarianism, pleasure is taken to be ultimately the only good, and evil is the opposite of pleasure, or pain. But utilitarianism can be understood more broadly, so that goodness is human well-being. Whatever makes human beings generally better off or provides some benefit is good, and whatever makes them worse off or harms them is evil. Differences of opinion exist, of course, on what constitutes benefits and harms, or being better or worse off. Generally, utilitarianism does not attempt to resolve these differences but accepts each person's own conception of what being better off means for him or her.

The Strengths of Teleological Theories

Teleological theories have many strengths. One is that they are in accord with much of our ordinary moral reasoning. The fact that an action would provide some benefit or inflict some harm is generally a morally relevant reason for or against performing it. So utilitarianism is able to explain why such actions as lying, breaking a promise, stealing, and assault are wrong and their opposites—truth-telling, promise-keeping, respect for property, and the like—are right. Lying, for example, creates false beliefs that often lead people to make disadvantageous choices, and if lying were to become common, then trust would be eroded, with a resulting decline in welfare for everyone. Having true beliefs, by contrast, is generally beneficial, and a society that values truth-telling will have a higher level of welfare. Utilitarianism can also explain why lying in some circumstances is the right thing to do. It would be wrong to tell a murderer the location of an intended victim, for example, because the harm that would be done in this instance outweighs any benefit from telling the truth.

Second, teleological theories provide a relatively precise and objective method for moral decision-making. Assuming that the goodness of consequences can be easily measured and compared, a teleological decision maker need only determine the possible courses of action and calculate the consequences of each one. For this reason, utilitarianism is attractive not only for matters of individual choice but also for decisions on issues of public policy. In writing a tax code, constructing a health care system, or regulating the airline industry, for example, planners in government and the private sector generally rely on such tools as cost-benefit analysis and risk assessment, which are refinements of utilitarian reasoning. Utilitarian reasoning has also found favor among economists, who use the assumption that individuals seek to maximize their own utility or welfare to explain and predict a wide range of economic phenomena, such as prices and the allocation of resources. The ethical theory underlying classical economic theory is broadly utilitarian.

Teleological theories do not require that we actually calculate consequences in deciding what to do. Consequences are ultimately what make actions right or wrong, but the good might be achieved more effectively by cultivating people with good moral character or training them to follow the rules of a well-designed social system. In these ways, the utilitarian end might be achieved more effectively than by aiming at good consequences directly. The test of a good moral character or a well-designed social system, however, is whether people, acting accordingly, produce good consequences.

The Weaknesses of Teleological Theories

The weaknesses of teleological theories derive from the same features that constitute their strengths. Although much of our ordinary moral reasoning is teleological, some of it is decidedly nonteleological in character. Generally, we have an obligation to keep our promises, even when more good might be achieved by breaking them. If we promise another person to store some food that belongs to them, for example, it would be wrong to give the food away to hungry beggars merely because doing so would have better consequences. Indeed, in deciding whether to keep a promise, the consequences seem to be morally irrelevant, although there might be stronger obligations that override the keeping of a promise. If the food is needed to save the life of a person, for example, then we might have an obligation to provide it—not because of the good consequences, however, but because of a stronger obligation to save a life.

Role obligations, which occupy a prominent place in business, often seem to be nonteleological. Parents have obligations to their children, for example, that are created by the special relation of parenthood. There is nothing wrong with parents providing for their children—even when the money could be better spent on orphan relief. Indeed, parents who contribute to the good of more children by their donations to orphan relief while neglecting their own children would be properly regarded as failing to fulfill their duty as parents. Also, a night watchman might be faulted for dereliction of duty in leaving a plant unguarded to prevent a break-in elsewhere, since this is not what he is being paid to do.

The concepts of rights and justice pose an especially difficult challenge for teleological theories. The right of free speech, for example, generally entitles us to speak freely—even when restricting this right might produce better consequences. The right of free speech protects not only the discussion of ideas that are essential to democracy and scientific progress but also the expression of views that are socially disruptive or deeply offensive to some people. A controversial issue in business is whether employees have the right to criticize their employers in public without fear of retaliation. Public criticism can do much harm to an employer, but if employees have an unrestricted right of free speech, then harm to the employer is not a morally relevant consideration.

Similarly, we believe that justice ought to be done regardless of consequences. This view is reflected in the ancient maxim, "Let justice be done though the heavens may fall." Even if it could be shown that discrimination against women or racial minorities, on balance, produces better consequences, discrimination is morally wrong and ought not to be practiced, simply because it involves the violation of a basic principle of justice; namely, that equals ought to be treated alike. This principle of equal treatment, as with the right of free speech, seems to be nonteleological in character.

The difficulties that role obligations, rights, and justice pose for teleological theories are not fatal. However, ways need to be found to show that, despite appearances, these concepts can be accounted for by appealing to consequences. Utilitarians have ways of justifying role obligations, and there are well-developed utilitarian theories of rights and justice that deserve careful consideration. Teleological theories cannot be rejected out of hand, therefore, but we need to understand their problems and make sure that they are satisfactorily resolved.

In order to assess fully the strengths and weaknesses of teleological theories, let us now examine in detail the most developed and influential theory of this kind: utilitarianism.

CLASSICAL UTILITARIANISM

Different parts of the utilitarian doctrine were advanced by philosophers as far back as the ancient Greeks, but it remained for two English reformers in the nineteenth century to fashion them into a single coherent whole.[9] The creators of classical utilitarianism were Jeremy Bentham (1748–1832) and John Stuart Mill (1806–1873). In their hands, utilitarianism was not an ivory tower philosophy but a powerful instrument for social, political, economic, and legal change. Bentham and Mill used the principle of utility as a practical guide in the English reform movement.

Jeremy Bentham

Bentham's version of utilitarianism is set forth in the following passage:

> By the principle of utility is meant that principle which approves or disapproves of every action whatsoever, according to the tendency which it appears to have to augment or diminish the happiness of the party whose interest is in question: or, what is the same thing in other words, to promote or to oppose that happiness.

So stated, the principle requires that consequences be measured in some way so that the pleasure and pain of different individuals can be added together and the results of different courses of action compared. Bentham assumed that a precise quantitative measurement of pleasure and pain was possible, and he outlined a procedure that he called the *hedonistic calculus* ("hedonistic" is derived from the Greek word for pleasure). The amount of pleasure and pain, according to Bentham, is determined by six factors. These include not only the intensity of a pleasure or a pain and its duration but also such matters as the likelihood of its occurring and its nearness in time. Thus, an immediate specific pleasure has more value than a less certain pleasure in the distant future. Bentham's procedure is to begin with any one individual whose interest is affected:

> Sum up all the values of all the *pleasures* on the one side, and those of all the pains on the other. The balance, if it be on the side of pleasure, will give the *good* tendency of the act upon the whole, with respect to the interests of that *individual* person; if on the side of pain, the *bad* tendency of it upon the whole.

If this process is repeated for all other individuals whose interests are affected, the resulting sums will show the good or bad tendency of an action for the whole community. The inference from the good of each individual to the good of the community is possible because of another fundamental assumption in Bentham's thought, which is that a community is nothing over and above its members. "The interest of the community then is what?—the sum of the interests of the several members who compose it."

Bentham's theory is open to some rather obvious objections. Among them is the longstanding opposition of many philosophers to the thesis of *hedonism*: that pleasure and pleasure alone is good. Both Plato and Aristotle presented strong arguments against this view, and critics at the time complained that pleasure is too low to constitute the good for human beings. The fact that even pigs are capable of pleasure led to the charge that utilitarianism is a "pig philosophy," a doctrine fit only for swine. One absurd consequence of Bentham's view, according to critics, is that it would be better to live the life of a satisfied pig than that of a dissatisfied human being such as Socrates.

John Stuart Mill

John Stuart Mill was aware of the objections to Bentham's theory, and in his major work on ethics, *Utilitarianism* (1863), he attempted to develop a more defensible version of the utilitarian position. His initial statement of the principle of utility is indistinguishable, however, from that of Bentham:

> The creed which accepts as the foundation of morals, Utility, or the Greatest Happiness Principle, holds that actions are right in proportion as they tend to promote happiness, wrong as they tend to produce the reverse of happiness. By happiness is intended pleasure, and the absence of pain; by unhappiness, pain, and the privation of pleasure.

Mill departed from Bentham's strict quantitative treatment of pleasure by introducing the idea that pleasures also differ in their *quality*. The charge that utilitarianism is a "pig philosophy" can be met, Mill claimed, by holding that human beings are capable of enjoying higher pleasures than those experienced by swine.

First, the thesis of hedonism does not deny that many things are good; it asserts only that ultimately what makes anything good is the pleasure it produces. Thus, intellectual pursuits, such as the enjoyment of poetry or fine music, are good, but they are valued not for themselves but for the pleasure they bring.

Second, Mill adopted the same defense used by the followers of Epicurus, an ancient Greek philosopher who also believed that pleasure alone is good.

When thus attacked, the Epicureans have always answered, that it is not they, but their accusers, who represent human nature in a degrading light; since the accusation supposes human beings to be capable of no pleasures except those of which swine are capable. . . . The comparison of the Epicurean life to that of beasts is felt as degrading, precisely because a beast's pleasures do not satisfy a human being's conception of happiness. Human beings have faculties more elevated than the animal appetites, and when once made conscious of them, do not regard anything as happiness which does not include their gratification. . . . But there is no known Epicurean theory of life which does not assign to the pleasures of the intellect, of the feelings and imagination, of the moral sentiments, a much higher value as pleasures than those of mere sensation.

For these reasons, Mill felt entitled to assert:

It is better to be a human being dissatisfied than a pig satisfied; better to be Socrates dissatisfied than a fool satisfied. And if the fool, or the pig, are of a different opinion, it is because they know only their side of the question.

Even if some pleasures are better than others, this insight does not succeed in saving the thesis of hedonism or the utilitarian principle that we ought to produce the greatest possible amount of pleasure. First, the higher pleasures enjoyed by a few people with elevated tastes are unlikely, in any actual society, to outweigh the total sum of the low pleasures enjoyed by the bulk of the population. As long as the number of people who prefer trashy television shows, for example, greatly exceeds the number who appreciate fine drama on television, a utilitarian decision maker would be forced, most likely, to give preference to soap operas and situation comedies over the plays of Shakespeare. In any event, Mill's writings give us no guidance for comparing the quality with the quantity of pleasure.

A second, deeper problem concerns how we know which pleasures are higher. Mill's answer is, consult competent judges! "Of two pleasures, if there be one to which all or almost all who have experience of both give a decided preference, irrespective of any feeling of moral obligation to prefer it, that is the more desirable pleasure." This answer confronts Mill with a dilemma. If higher pleasures mean that which is preferred by those who have experience of both, then either they desire them because they contain a greater amount of pleasure or for some other reason. In the former case, quality adds nothing to the quantity of pleasure; in the latter, Mill is abandoning his hedonism. As Henry Sidgwick remarked, "it is hard to see in what sense a man who of two alternative pleasures chooses the less pleasant on the ground of its superiority in quality can be affirmed to take '*greatest*' happiness or pleasure as his standard of preference."[10]

Utilitarianism does not require the thesis of hedonism, however, and many things besides pleasure have been regarded as good by utilitarian theorists. G. E. Moore, for example, held that in addition to pleasure, friendship and aesthetic enjoyment are goods that are not reducible to pleasure.[11] The term *ideal utilitarianism* has been coined to describe theories such as Moore's that, in contrast to hedonistic utilitarianism, recognize a plurality of goods as the source of our obligations.[12] In his famous essay *On Liberty*, Mill moves close to the position that the development of our critical faculties and the capacity for autonomous action are worthwhile ends in themselves. Although Mill officially adhered to the thesis of hedonism, then, his recognition of its problems seems to have pushed him toward some version of ideal utilitarianism.

More than two hundred years have elapsed since Bentham's formulation of the principle of utility, and in that time many refinements have been made. Contemporary utilitarianism takes many different forms that are more adequate than the classical theory. The next section deals with some of these forms of contemporary utilitarianism.

THE FORMS OF UTILITARIANISM

Classical utilitarianism can be stated formally as follows:

AN ACTION IS RIGHT IF AND ONLY IF IT PRODUCES THE GREATEST BALANCE OF PLEASURE OVER PAIN FOR EVERYONE.

So stated, the utilitarian principle involves four distinct theses:

1. **Consequentialism**. The principle holds that the rightness of actions is determined solely by their consequences. It is by virtue of this thesis that utilitarianism is a teleological theory.
2. **Hedonism**. Utility in this statement of the theory is identified with pleasure and the absence of pain. Hedonism is the thesis that pleasure and only pleasure is ultimately good.
3. **Maximalism**. A right action is one that has not merely some good consequences but the greatest amount of good consequences possible when the bad consequences are also taken into consideration.
4. **Universalism**. The consequences to be considered are those of everyone.

The first two theses have already been explained, but the last two call for some comment.

Virtually every action produces both pleasure and pain, and the principle of utility does not require that only pleasure and no pain result from a right action. An action may produce a great amount of pain and still be right from the utilitarian view as long as the amount of pleasure produced is, on balance, greater than the amount produced by any other action. Both Bentham and Mill assumed that the amount of pain produced by an action can be subtracted from the amount of pleasure to yield the net amount of pleasure—in the same way that an accountant subtracts debts from assets to determine net worth. Theories in which we are obligated merely to produce more pleasure than pain or a certain positive balance of pleasure over pain are possible forms of utilitarianism, but usually the principle is stated in the "maximalist" form, which obligates us to produce the *greatest* net amount of pleasure. It is possible for two actions to have exactly the same balance of pleasure over pain, in which case they are morally indistinguishable. A more adequate statement of the principle of utility, therefore, is that a right action is one that produces at least as much pleasure over pain as any other action open to a person at the time. This last qualification is necessary, since people can be obligated to perform only actions that are within their power.

The thesis of universalism requires us to consider the pleasure and pain *of everyone alike*. Thus, we are not following the principle of utility by considering the consequences only for ourselves, for our family and friends, or for an organization of which we are a part. Utilitarianism does not require us to ignore our own interest, but we are permitted to place it no higher and no lower than the interest of anyone else. As Mill expressed the point:

> . . . [T]he happiness which forms the utilitarian standard of what is right in conduct, is not the agent's own happiness, but that of all concerned. As between his own happiness and that of others, utilitarianism requires him to be as strictly impartial as a disinterested and benevolent spectator.

The utilitarian principle does not insist that the interest of everyone be *promoted*, though. In deciding whether to close a polluting plant, for example, we need to consider the citizens of the community who suffer from the pollution, the workers who will lose their jobs if the plant is shut down, the owners of the company that operates the plant, and, possibly, consumers as well. No matter what decision is made, the interests of some people will be harmed. Utilitarian reasoning obligates us only to include the interests of everyone in our calculations, not to act in a way that advances every individual interest.

The Greatest Happiness for the Greatest Number

The principle of utility is sometimes stated as, The greatest happiness for the greatest number. This formulation has the merit of addressing a recognized problem with the classical theory. Consider the following two distributions of utility for three individuals, A, B, and C, assuming that utility can be expressed in units.

	I			II	
A	10		A	14	
B	10		B	8	
C	10		C	8	
	30			30	

States I and II have the same total amount of utility, but they differ in the way that the utility is *distributed*. Some critics contend that utilitarianism considers only the total amount of utility and not the pattern of the distribution.[13] Assuming, however, that distribution matters and that an equal distribution is morally preferable to an unequal distribution—everything else being the same—then the statement of the utilitarian principle as, The greatest good for the greatest number gives us the "right" result; namely, the selection of I.

The two parts of the principle, "the greatest good" and "the greatest number," can produce conflicting results in some instances, however.[14] The conflict is shown by considering a third possible distribution.

	I			III	
A	10		A	16	
B	10		B	9	
C	10		C	7	
	30			32	

State III is superior to state I in terms of "the greatest good," but it is inferior to state I when judged by the criterion of "the greatest number," because B and C are worse off in III than they are in I. Use of the principle, The greatest good for the greatest number, therefore, is inconclusive in deciding between states I and III.

Moreover, the criterion "the greatest number" does not even serve to ensure equality in distribution. This point is shown by considering a choice between II and III.

	II			III	
A	14		A	16	
B	8		B	9	
C	8		C	7	
	30			32	

Both parts of the principle, The greatest good for the greatest number agree that III is morally preferable to II. State III has more total utility, and two people, A and B, are better off than they would be in II. Yet, III involves a more unequal distribution of utility! Therefore, The greatest good for the greatest number is a faulty formulation of utilitarianism.[15]

Act- and Rule-Utilitarianism

There is another formulation of the utilitarian principle that is significantly different and, in the view of some philosophers, more defensible. Based on the principle, as stated, an action is judged to be right by virtue of the consequences of performing *that action*. As a result, telling a lie or breaking a promise is right if it has better consequences than any alternative course of action. Utilitarian morality thus seems to place no value on observing rules, such as, Tell the truth or Keep your promises, except perhaps as "rules of thumb"; that is, as distillations of past experience about the tendencies of actions that eliminate the need to calculate consequences in every case. This result can be avoided if we consider the consequences of performing not just particular actions but *actions of a certain kind*. Although some instances of lying have consequences that are better than telling the truth, lying in general does not. As a kind of action, then, truth-telling is right by virtue of the consequences of performing actions of that kind, and any instance of truth-telling is right because actions of that kind are right.

This suggestion leads to a version of utilitarianism in which rules are primary. Whether an action is right is determined by appealing to the relevant rule of morality, which is justified in turn by the consequences of observing that rule. Individuals, for the most part, do not need to calculate the consequences of specific actions in order to decide what they ought to do. A familiarity with common morality is generally sufficient. Some interpreters attribute this view to Mill, although it is unlikely that Mill was fully aware of the distinction.[16] This revised version of the theory is known as rule-utilitarianism (RU), and the principle of utility, as stated at the beginning of this section, is called act-utilitarianism (AU). Both may now be expressed formally in the following way:

(AU)   AN ACTION IS RIGHT IF AND ONLY IF IT PRODUCES THE GREATEST BALANCE OF PLEASURE OVER PAIN FOR EVERYONE.

(RU)   AN ACTION IS RIGHT IF AND ONLY IF IT CONFORMS TO A SET OF RULES THE GENERAL ACCEPTANCE OF WHICH WOULD PRODUCE THE GREATEST BALANCE OF PLEASURE OVER PAIN FOR EVERYONE.[17]

Act- and rule-utilitarianism each has its merits, and there is no consensus among philosophers about which is correct.[18] Act-utilitarianism is a simpler theory and provides an easily understood decision procedure. Rule-utilitarianism seems to give firmer ground, however, to the rules of morality and to role obligations, which are problems for all teleological theories. Society works better, rule-utilitarians argue, if individuals, for the most part, fulfill their assigned role and do not violate a role obligation—even if more good could be achieved in particular instances by doing so. A further advantage of rule-utilitarianism, according to its proponents, is that it eliminates the difficult task of calculating the consequences of each individual act.

Applying the Two Principles

When applied to bribery in international business, act- and rule-utilitarianism seem to yield different results. Carl Kotchian was reasoning as an act-utilitarian when he defended Lockheed's expenditure of more than $12 million in Japan to secure the sale of twenty-one TriStar aircraft to All Nippon Airways. Let us suppose for the sake of argument that the benefit to Lockheed workers, their families and communities, Lockheed shareholders, and the American public was sufficient to outweigh the harm done to Japanese society, the consumers of ANA, Lockheed competitors, and others. If Kotchian saved Lockheed Aircraft Corporation from financial ruin, his otherwise unethical behavior might be justified on act-utilitarian grounds. Bribery as a general practice, though, is commonly recognized as having harmful consequences. It usually results in higher prices and reduced quality, since people are led by personal advantage to make decisions on considerations other than the value of the goods and services being offered. A widespread system of bribery would lead to less competitive conditions and a resulting decline in efficiency. On rule-utilitarian grounds, therefore, bribery is properly regarded as morally wrong.

One of Lockheed's defenses was, "We don't make the rules. And if we don't go along with the game as it's played, we only hurt ourselves and accomplish nothing." In a world in which others bribe, what should a utilitarian do? This question points up the fact that the consequences of our actions often depend on the actions of others. Garrett Hardin dramatically illustrates the problem of ethical decision-making under such conditions with a case in which there is no restriction on grazing sheep on a commons. If everyone sends their sheep out to graze, the land will become barren and useless.

> Asking everyone to use it with discretion will hardly do, for the considerate herdsman who refrains from overloading the commons suffers more than a selfish one who says his needs are greater. If everyone would restrain himself, all would be well; but it takes only one less than everyone to ruin a system of voluntary restraint.[19]

The root of the problem is the well-recognized need for cooperation in ethics, and the solution is not to do what everyone else is doing but to change the system. Lockheed alone cannot eliminate bribery in the sale of planes abroad, of course, but by engaging in the practice so readily, they perpetuate it and encourage others to do the same. (Officials of the Northrop Corporation who set up a special subsidiary in Switzerland to handle payments told a Senate investigative committee that "they learned how to do that from Lockheed.")[20] Moreover, Lockheed could take small steps to work with others who will cooperate to remove corruption wherever possible.[21] In short, rule-utilitarianism draws attention to the need to create a mutually beneficial set of moral rules, and the obligation of each individual and business firm is to follow these rules.

Problems with Calculating Utility

Differences among utilitarians also occur as a result of problems with calculating utility. Classical utilitarianism requires that we be able to determine: (1) the amount of utility (that is, the balance of pleasure over pain) for each individual affected by an action, and (2) the amount of utility for a whole society. Whether we can measure utility in the way that utilitarianism requires has been a concern not only of philosophers but also of economists, since utility has been generally accepted as a basis for economic theory. Because of the need in economics for precise calculations of utility—and misgivings about Bentham's simplistic hedonistic calculus—economists have introduced a number of important refinements into the theory of utilitarianism.

There is little difficulty in calculating that some actions produce more pleasure for us than others. A decision to spend an evening at a concert is usually the result of a judgment that listening to music will give us more pleasure at that time than any available alternative. Confronted with a range of alternatives, we can usually rank them in order from the most pleasant to the least pleasant. A problem arises, however, when we attempt to determine exactly how *much* pleasure each course of action will produce. We can sense that one day is hotter than another, for example, and by using a thermometer, we can measure the temperature of each day and express the magnitude and the corresponding difference in units. But we lack any meaningful units of pleasure and the means for measuring pleasure as a precise quantity. In the jargon of science, a comparative ranking, such as, "Today is hotter than yesterday," produces an *ordinal* value (that is, a ranking from least warm to the warmest), whereas the measurement of magnitudes, such as, "Today the temperature was 87 degrees Fahrenheit," results in a *cardinal* value (that is, one expressible in unit values). One problem with utilitarian calculations can be expressed, then, by saying that amounts of pleasure can be measured only with ordinal and not with cardinal values.[22]

Utilitarianism requires that we calculate the pleasure of alternative courses of action not only for ourselves but for everyone. Some critics contend that this requirement imposes an information burden on utilitarian decision makers that is difficult to meet. In order to buy a gift for a friend that will produce the greatest amount of pleasure, for example, we need to know something about that person's desires and tastes. Knowledge about others is more problematical than knowledge about ourselves, but we are usually able to buy gifts for family members and close friends, at least, with reasonable confidence. Consider, however, the task faced by a utilitarian legislator who must decide whether to permit logging in a public park. This person must identify all the people affected, determine the amount of pleasure and pain for each one, and then compare the pleasure that hiking brings to nature lovers versus the pain that would be caused to loggers if they lost their jobs. The abilities of ordinary human beings are inadequate, critics complain, to acquire and process the vast amount of relevant information in such a case.

The response of utilitarians to this problem is that we manage in practice to make educated guesses by relying on past experience and limiting our attention to a few aspects of a situation. Management theorists have long noted that decision makers do not approach tasks as strict utility-maximizing calculators but as pragmatic problem solvers. Similarly, chess players typically do not calculate long sequences of moves, as might be expected, but utilize themes and patterns learned from playing countless games. And grandmasters are still able to beat computers that can calculate millions of variations in a few seconds! This result suggests that human thought processes, although different from those assumed by utilitarianism, might even be superior in achieving the goal of the theory.

The Interpersonal Comparison of Utility

Comparing the pleasure and pain of different people raises a further problem about the *interpersonal comparison of utility*. Imagine two people who each insist after attending a concert that he or she enjoyed it more. In the absence of cardinal values for pleasure, there seems to be no way in principle to settle this dispute. Some philosophers and economists consider this problem to be insoluble and a reason for rejecting utilitarianism both as an ethical theory and as a basis for economics.[23] Others argue for the possibility of interpersonal comparisons on the basis that regardless of whether we can make such comparisons precisely, we do make them in everyday life with reasonable confidence.[24] We may give away an extra ticket to a concert, for example, to the friend we believe will enjoy it the most. Also, we assume that members of the Sierra Club who spend their leisure time hiking value parks highly, and we weigh their feelings about logging accordingly.

In conclusion, the problem of the interpersonal comparison of utility, although it raises serious conceptual difficulties for utilitarianism, is not insuperable. As long as rough comparisons are sufficient for utilitarian calculation, pleasure is adequate as an interpretation of utility. Other interpretations of utility are possible, however. One of these is involved in the method of cost-benefit analysis, which is considered next.

COST-BENEFIT ANALYSIS

Bentham's ideal of a precise quantitative method for decision-making is most fully realized in *cost-benefit analysis*. This method differs from Bentham's hedonistic calculus primarily in the use of monetary units to express the benefits and drawbacks of various alternatives. Any project in which the dollar amount of the benefits exceeds the dollar amount of the damages is worth pursuing, according to cost-benefit analysis, and from among different projects, the one that promises the greatest net benefit, as measured in dollars, ought to be chosen.[25]

From an economic point of view, cost-benefit analysis is simply a means for achieving an efficient allocation of resources. Business decisions that evaluate investment opportunities in terms of their return are thus instances of cost-benefit analysis. However, there is an important difference between business decision-making and what is usually described as cost-benefit analysis. Companies usually calculate the anticipated costs and benefits only for *themselves*, whereas legislators, social planners, regulators, and other users of cost-benefit analysis generally ask what the costs and benefits are for *everyone* who is affected.[26]

The chief advantage of cost-benefit analysis is that the price of many goods is set by the market, so that the need to have knowledge of people's pleasures or preference rankings is largely eliminated. And the value of different goods is easily totaled to produce a figure that reflects the costs and benefits of different courses of action for all those concerned. Money also provides a common denominator for allocating resources among projects that cannot easily be compared otherwise. Would scarce resources be better spent on a Head-Start program, for example, or on the development of new sources of energy? In cost-benefit analysis, decision makers have an analytic framework that enables them to decide among such disparate projects in a rational, objective manner.

Because of the narrow focus on economic efficiency in the allocation of resources, cost-benefit analysis is not commonly used as a basis for personal morality but as a means for making major investment decisions and decisions on broad matters of public policy. It is not a complete ethical theory, therefore, but a utilitarian form of reasoning with a limited but important range of application. Cost-benefit analysis is also not necessarily intended to be the *only* means for making decisions. Vincent Vaccaro wrote:

> . . . [C]ost-benefit analysis is "a formal procedure for comparing the costs and benefits of alternative policies." The words are clear—the purpose of this procedure is to compare only one aspect of alternative policies, not the policies themselves. For this reason, it is inappropriate to expect this analytical tool to serve as *the* basis for comparing alternative policies.[27]

Utilitarians generally favor efficiency on the ground that it increases the welfare of society as a whole. But the rights of consumers in matters of product safety and the goal of protecting the environment, for example, sometimes override considerations of efficiency and lead to the adoption of regulations in which the costs exceed the immediate benefits. Still, determining the appropriate level of product safety or environmental protection requires an awareness of the costs and benefits of different regulatory schemes and of the tradeoffs being made. Cost-benefit analysis, therefore, is an important tool that may be used even by nonutilitarian decision makers to provide one kind of morally relevant information.

A distinction is commonly made, moreover, between cost-benefit analysis and cost-effectiveness analysis. *Cost-effectiveness analysis* assumes that we already have some agreed-upon end, such as reducing injuries from defective products or protecting the environment, so that the only remaining question is, what is the most efficient means for achieving this end? *Cost-benefit analysis,* by contrast, is used to select both the means to ends and the ends themselves.[28] Nonutilitarians who reject the use of cost-benefit analysis to settle questions about ends, such as the rights of consumers and the value of environmental protection, should have no quarrel with a requirement that we pursue morally justified ends in the most efficient manner possible. The use of cost-effectiveness analysis is wholly compatible, therefore, with the recognition of other morally relevant considerations.

The Problems of Assigning Monetary Values

Cost-benefit analysis is criticized on many different grounds. First, not all costs and benefits have an easily determined monetary value. The value of the jobs that are provided by logging on public land can be expressed precisely in dollars, as can the value of the lumber produced. But because the opportunity for hikers to enjoy unspoiled vistas and fresh-smelling air is not something that is commonly bought and sold, it has no fixed market price. There is also no market to determine the price of peace and quiet, the enjoyment of the company of family and friends, and freedom from the risk of physical injury and death.

And the same is true of many public goods, such as police protection, roads and bridges, and public health programs.

In addition, the market for some goods is distorted by various factors so that the price of these goods does not reflect their "true" value. In economic terms, the market price of goods does not always correspond to their opportunity cost, as determined by consumers' marginal rates of substitution, which economists regard as the proper measure of value. The fact that a yacht costs more than a college education, for example, does not entail that consumers value yachts more highly than education. It would be a mistake, therefore, to use cost-benefit analysis to support policies that foster the ownership of yachts by the rich while making it more difficult for the poor to attend college. Critics complain, however, that noneconomic goods and mispriced goods tend to be left out of cost-benefit analyses entirely or else are assigned arbitrary values.

Some applications of cost-benefit analysis require that a value be placed on human life. Although this may seem cold and heartless, it is necessary if cost-benefit analysis is to be used to determine how much to spend on prenatal care to improve the rate of infant mortality, for example, or on reducing the amount of cancer-causing emissions from factories. The Ford Motor Company was widely criticized in the 1970s for using a cost-benefit analysis to determine whether to make a design change at a cost of $11 per vehicle to reduce the likelihood of fire in a collision.[29] However, the number of safety improvements that can be made in a car are unlimited, and some means must be found to decide which are worth making. Similarly, reducing infant mortality or the death rate from cancer justifies the expenditure of some funds, but how much? Would further investment be justified if it reduced the amount available for education or medical care for the elderly? No matter where the line is drawn, some tradeoff must be made between saving lives and securing other goods.

Experts in cost-benefit analysis attempt to overcome the problem of assigning a dollar figure to noneconomic goods with a technique known as *shadow pricing*. This consists of determining the value reflected by people's market and nonmarket behavior. For example, by comparing the prices of houses near airports, busy highways, and the like with the prices of similar houses in less noisy areas, it is possible to infer the value that people place on peace and quiet. The value of life and limb can be similarly estimated by considering the amount of extra pay that is needed to get workers to accept risky jobs. Several methods exist, in fact, for calculating the value of human life for purposes of cost-benefit analysis.[30] Among these are the discounted value of a person's future earnings over a normal lifetime, the value that existing social and political arrangements place on the life of individuals, and the value that is revealed by the amount that individuals are willing to pay to avoid the risk of injury and death. When people choose through their elected representatives not to spend additional amounts to improve traffic safety, for example, they implicitly indicate the value of the lives that would otherwise be saved. Similarly, people who refuse to wear seat belts or who drive too fast show how much value they place on their own life.

There are some pitfalls in using the technique of shadow pricing, especially when human life is involved. Many people buy houses in noisy areas or accept risky jobs because they are unable to afford decent housing anywhere else or to secure safer employment. Some homebuyers and job seekers may not fully consider or appreciate the risks they face, especially when the hazards are unseen or speculative. Also, the people who buy homes near airports or accept work as steeplejacks are possibly less concerned with noise or danger than is the general population. We certainly do not want to assume, however, that workplace safety is of little value simply because a few people are so heedless of danger that they accept jobs that more cautious people avoid.[31] Finally, people's individual and collective decisions are not always rational. People who drive without seat belts are probably aware of their benefit *for other people* but are convinced that nothing will happen *to them* because they are such good drivers.[32] As a result, they (irrationally) expose themselves to risks that do not accurately reflect the value they place on their own life. Mark Sagoff observes further that the choices we make as consumers do not always correspond to those we make as citizens. He cites as examples the fact that he buys beverages in disposable containers but urges his state legislators to require returnable bottles and that he has a car with an Ecology Now sticker that leaks oil everywhere it is parked.[33]

Should All Things Be Assigned a Monetary Value?

A second criticism of cost-benefit analysis is that even if all the technical problems of shadow pricing could be solved, there are still good reasons for not assigning a monetary value to some things. Steven Kelman argues that placing a dollar value on some goods reduces their perceived value, since they are valued precisely because they cannot be bought and sold in a market. Friendship and love are obvious examples. "Imagine the reaction," Kelman observes, "if a practitioner of cost-benefit analysis computed the benefits of sex based on the price of prostitute service."[34] In *The Gift Relationship: From Human Blood to Social Policy*, Richard M. Titmuss very perceptively compares the American system of blood collection with that of the British. In the United States, about half of all blood is purchased from donors and sold to people who need transfusions.[35] The British system, by contrast, is purely voluntary. No one is paid for donating blood, and it is provided without charge to anyone in need. As a result, the giving of blood and blood itself have an entirely different significance. Peter Singer expressed this point very eloquently:

> If blood is a commodity with a price, to give blood means merely to save someone money. Blood has a cash value of a certain number of dollars, and the importance of the gift will vary with the wealth of the recipient. If blood cannot be bought, however, the gift's value depends upon the need of the recipient. Often, it will be worth life itself. Under these circumstances blood becomes a very special kind of gift, and giving it means providing for strangers, without hope of reward, something they cannot buy and without which they may die. The gift relates strangers in a manner that is not possible when blood is a commodity.[36]

Although some things are cheapened in people's eyes if they are made into commodities and traded in a market, the same consequences do not follow if goods are assigned a value merely for purposes of comparison. It is the actual buying and selling of blood that has the consequences Singer describes, not performing a cost-benefit analysis. (In fairness to Singer, it should be pointed out that he does not present his point as an objection to cost-benefit analysis.) Moreover, Titmuss himself argues in favor of the British system on the grounds that the system in the United States is (1) highly wasteful of blood, resulting in chronic acute shortages; (2) administratively inefficient because of the large bureaucracy that it requires; (3) more expensive (the price of blood is five to fifteen times higher); and (4) more dangerous, because there is a greater risk of disease and death from contaminated blood.[37] In short, a cost-benefit analysis shows that it is better not to have a market for blood.

Moreover, the fact that there are some things that cannot be meaningfully valued does not eliminate the need to make comparisons when these goods come into conflict with hard economic realities. Instead of being a defect, it is a virtue of cost-benefit analysis that it forces us to consider exactly how much we do value things that have no market price. A respondent to Kelman's article noted:

> There are many things one specially values—in the sense that one would find the effort to assign a market price to them ridiculous—which are nonetheless affected by economic factors. I may specially value a family relationship, but how often I phone is influenced by long-distance rates. I may specially value music, but be affected by the price of records or the cost of tickets to the Kennedy Center.[38]

Kelman's objection also involves a confusion about *what* is being valued. Although many relationships are "priceless," so that we would go to any lengths to preserve them, we typically do compare them with other goods. When we ask whether the cost of a telephone call is worth the benefit we receive, what we are valuing is not the relationship itself but the marginal utility of the enjoyment of the telephone call. To this a price can easily be assigned without detracting in any way from the value of the relationship.

Other Values in Cost-Benefit Analysis

Cost-benefit analysis, according to its critics, is heavily value laden, despite its appearance of objectivity. Alasdair MacIntyre argues that values are presupposed in cost-benefit analysis in five different ways.[39] These may be summarized as follows:

1. It is impossible for analysts to consider all possible alternatives, and so the range of alternatives must be limited by some nonutilitarian principle before cost-benefit analysis can even begin.
2. Cost-benefit analysis requires some prior commitment to what counts as a cost and a benefit and to some ranking of their importance. Loud outdoor rock concerts, for example, are a benefit to fans of that kind of music, but they are a cost for lovers of classical music who are forced to endure the noise. Similarly, a new electric generating plant which is regarded as a benefit by most users of electrical energy is apt to be viewed by environmentalists as a step in the wrong direction and hence a cost.
3. Since people consider different things to be either costs or benefits, some decision must be made about *whose* values are to be taken into consideration. In comparing the relative importance of cheap electric power and a clean environment, for example, should the values of consumers and business interests be dominant or those of environmentalists? Analysts who answer this question differently will produce different policy recommendations.
4. Analysts must further decide what is to count as a *consequence* of a particular course of action. Should the costs and benefits of various packaging materials be calculated only up to the time that the product reaches consumers, for example, or should the calculations continue to include the costs of disposing of the materials? If better packaging encourages people to eat more fast food to the detriment of their health, should this also be included as a consequence in the analysis? In economic terms, the question is, to what extent should "spillover effects" or externalities be considered?
5. Finally, how far into the future should consequences be calculated? Applying cost-benefit analysis presupposes some commitment to a time frame for calculating the consequences of alternatives for future generations.

To this latter point can be added the objection that cost-benefit analysis considers the values held by consumers at the present time. Thus, it has no way of anticipating future shifts as a result of changed conditions. A cost-benefit analysis done in the 1950s, for example, would most likely not have considered environmental concerns, the women's movement, and the globalization of the U.S. economy.

Defenders of cost-benefit analysis, such as Vaccaro and Tom L. Beauchamp, reply that any theory is "value laden," and an advantage of cost-benefit analysis is that it makes its value commitments explicit, so that they can be properly taken into account. According to Beauchamp:

> What is important, morally speaking, is that one conscientiously projects the most acceptable action based on the best available data, and then with equal deliberateness attempts to perform it. . . . MacIntyre's problems about restricting the range of alternatives, as well as his difficulties over specifying relevant consequences of actions . . . seem to me far less troublesome than he would admit. While he is correct in insisting that some "arbitrariness" in selecting variables and principles is bound to creep into human calculation, this problem is no greater for utilitarianism than for other moral theories.[40]

And Vaccaro has argued:

> . . . [A] good cost-benefit analyst will always include discussions of alternatives or assumptions that cannot be assessed by cost-benefit procedures. The exclusion of such alternatives or factors, rather than eliminating them from consideration by the policy-maker, in fact, flags them as alternatives or factors that must be considered simply because they have not been adequately evaluated in the analysis. It is because cost-benefit theory is sensitive to identifying and clarifying critical non-economic issues that it is a valuable tool for those who must establish and implement our public policies and goals.[41]

Critics contend, however, that even if unexamined alternatives and debatable assumptions are "flagged" for further consideration, cost-benefit analysis still encourages a reliance on the numbers. However, no method can be better than the people who use it. To quote Vaccaro again:

> I think that it should be obvious by now that cost-benefit analysts must be innovative and creative thinkers who can deal effectively with economic and non-economic issues and not mere self-serving or obsequious, number-crunching drones. . . . My last point is that all the work of the economic theorists, data gatherers, and cost-benefit analysts is useless if the policy-maker either cannot or does not take the time to read and understand the analysis.[42]

An Assessment of Cost-Benefit Analysis

Most of the objections to the theoretical adequacy of cost-benefit analysis can be met. Properly done, a cost-benefit analysis is capable of identifying and representing a broad range of morally relevant considerations in a way that permits alternatives to be rationally compared and evaluated. The crucial phrase, of course, is "properly done." The validity of any particular cost-benefit analysis depends on the thoroughness and objectivity of the people who conduct it. We must also have an understanding of the proper role of cost-benefit analysis in public decision-making. It is not intended to be the sole means for arriving at the choices we make as a society. Efficiency in the allocation of resources is not our only value. We also want a society that seeks to prevent suffering, fosters a respect for life, promotes learning and the arts, preserves our cultural heritage, and protects the environment. For this reason, we insist that decisions about such matters as consumer protection, worker health and safety, and the environment be made through open debate and the political process. The key question is, what matters should be turned over to the analysts? And this question cannot itself be decided by a cost-benefit analysis. A more comprehensive ethical framework is needed.

Conclusion

Utilitarianism is a powerful and widely accepted ethical theory that has special relevance to problems in business. Not only does it enable us to justify many of the obligations of individuals and corporations, such as to refrain from bribery in the case of Lockheed in Japan, but the principle of utility, as we will see in subsequent chapters, provides a strong foundation for various rights and also for our most deeply held views about justice. Utilitarianism fits in easily, moreover, with the emphasis on results in business decision-making.

Act-utilitarianism provides a relatively straightforward decision procedure for determining the best course of action in any given situation: Make a list of all the available alternatives, follow the consequences of each one as far into the future as possible, and select the alternative with the greatest balance of pleasure over pain for everyone. The theory does not require that decisions actually be made in this manner, however, and we have noted that the actual reasoning of managers is often very different. Still, this version of utilitarianism provides a test of right action for evaluating results, no matter what the process.

Most of the ethical obligations of people in business are expressed in terms of codes of conduct and the responsibility of a company toward employees, competitors, consumers, and the public at large. Professional ethics also plays a part in regulating the behavior of professionals in business, such as accountants, legal counsels, and the like. This framework of rules and generally accepted practices can be grounded in a number of different ways. Both teleological and deontological theories serve to demonstrate the evils of discrimination, for example. We will find in this book that utilitarianism, either in its act- or rule-utilitarian form, is relevant to most of the topics considered. Utility arguments occur in just about every chapter, and they provide a relatively firm and coherent basis for business ethics. Regardless of our estimate of the theoretical adequacy of utilitarianism, these arguments are worthy of serious and careful consideration.

NOTES

1. The most complete source of information on this case is ROBERT SHAPLEN, "Annals of Crime: The Lockheed Incident," *The New Yorker*, January 23, 1978, 48–74; and January 30, 1978, 74–91. Kotchian's own reflections are contained in A. CARL KOTCHIAN, "The Payoff: Lockheed's 70-Day Mission to Tokyo," *Saturday Review*, July 9, 1977, 7–12. This article is adapted from a memoir, *Lockheed Sales Mission: Seventy Days in Tokyo*, published in Japan. Two case studies are "A Japanese Bribe," in MANUEL G. VELASQUEZ, *Business Ethics: Concepts and Cases*, 3rd ed. (Englewood Cliffs, NJ: Prentice Hall, 1992), 207–9; and "Selling the Lockheed TriStar," in MILTON SNOEYENBOS, ROBERT ALMEDER, and JAMES HUMBER, eds. *Business Ethics: Corporate Values and Society* (Buffalo: Prometheus Books, 1983), 138–44.
2. KOTCHIAN, "The Payoff," 11.
3. KOTCHIAN, "The Payoff," 10.
4. KOTCHIAN, "The Payoff," 12.
5. Although the payments were legal under U.S. law at the time, Lockheed was found guilty in 1979 of four counts of fraud and four counts of making misleading statements for deducting payments from their taxes as "marketing cost" in violation of Section 162C of the Internal Revenue Code.
6. For a defense of Lockheed on these grounds, see MARK PASTIN, *The Hard Problems of Management* (San Francisco: Jossey-Bass, 1986), 119–21.
7. For the distinctions between bribery, kickbacks, and extortion, see MICHAEL PHILLIPS, "Bribery," *Ethics*, 94 (1984), 621–36; THOMAS L. CARSON, "Bribery, Extortion, and the 'Foreign Corrupt Practices Act'," *Philosophy and Public Affairs*, 14 (1985), 66–90; JOHN DANLEY, "Towards a Theory of Bribery," *Business and Professional Ethics Journal*, 2 (1983), 19–39; and KENDALL D'ANDRADE, JR., "Bribery," *Journal of Business Ethics*, 4 (1985), 239–48. A comprehensive study is NEIL JACOBY, PETER NEHEMKIS, and RICHARD EELLS, *Bribery and Extortion in World Business: A Study of Corporate Political Payments Abroad* (New York: Macmillan, 1977).
8. For a defense of an Aristotelian virtue-based ethical theory, see ALASDAIR MACINTYRE, *After Virtue* (Notre Dame: Notre Dame University Press, 1981).
9. For a brief account of the historical origins of utilitarianism, see ANTHONY QUINTON, *Utilitarian Ethics* (New York: St. Martin's Press, 1973).
10. HENRY SIDGWICK, *Outlines of the History of Ethics*, 6th ed. (London: Macmillan, 1931), 247.
11. G. E. MOORE, *Principia Ethica* (Cambridge: Cambridge University Press, 1903), 188–202.
12. The term is due to HASTINGS RASHDALL, *The Theory of Good and Evil*, 2nd ed. (Oxford: Oxford University Press, 1928).
13. See, for example, JOHN RAWLS, *A Theory of Justice* (Cambridge: Harvard University Press, 1971), 26.

14. This point is developed by NICHOLAS RESCHER, *Distributive Justice* (Indianapolis: Bobbs-Merrill, 1966), 25–28.
15. Another complication in developing a formulation of utilitarianism is whether to consider *total* or *average* utility. A society with more people sharing the same resources is apt to result in a greater total amount of utility but a lower average amount of utility. Do we have an obligation, therefore, to increase the number of people as long as the total amount of utility is increased or to seek the population level with the greatest average amount of utility? The first person to consider these questions within the context of the utilitarian theory seems to have been HENRY SIDGWICK, *The Methods of Ethics*, 7th ed. (Chicago: University of Chicago Press, 1907), 415–16. Sidgwick's views are criticized in JAN NARVESON, *Morality and Utility* (Baltimore: The Johns Hopkins Press, 1967), 46–50. See also NARVESON, "Utilitarianism and New Generations," *Mind*, 76 (1967), 62–72. The terms "total" and "average" are due to J.J.C. SMART, *An Outline of a System of Utilitarian Ethics* (Melbourne: Melbourne University Press, 1961), 18.
16. This view is attributed to Mill in J. O. URMSON, "The Interpretation of the Moral Philosophy of J. S. Mill," *The Philosophical Quarterly*, 3 (1953), 33–39. For criticism of Urmson's interpretation, see J. D. MABBOTT, "Interpretations of Mill's *Utilitarianism*," *The Philosophical Quarterly*, 6 (1956), 115–20; and MAURICE MANDELBAUM, "Two Moot Issues in Mill's *Utilitarianism*," in J. B. SCHNEEWIND, ed., *Mill: A Collection of Critical Essays* (Garden City, NY: Anchor Books, 1968), 206–33.
17. This formulation of RU follows that given by David Lyons for what he calls ideal rule-utilitarianism. DAVID LYONS, *Forms and Limits of Utilitarianism* (Oxford: Oxford University Press, 1965), 140. There is considerable controversy over the correct formulation of RU and the relation between AU, RU, and another principle usually called utilitarian generalization. In addition to the discussion in LYONS, *Forms and Limits of Utilitarianism*, see MARCUS G. SINGER, *Generalization in Ethics* (New York: Knopf, 1961), chap. 7; NARVESON, *Morality and Utility*, 129–40; and R. B. BRANDT, *A Theory of the Good and the Right* (Oxford: Oxford University Press, 1979), 278–85. Early discussions of the distinction between AU and RU are R. F. HARROD, "Utilitarianism Revised," *Mind*, 45 (1936), 137–56; JONATHAN HARRISON, "Utilitarianism, Universalization, and Our Duty to Be Just," *Proceedings of the Aristotelian Society*, 53 (1952–53), 105–34; J.J.C. SMART, "Extreme and Restricted Utilitarianism," *The Philosophical Quarterly*, 6 (1956), 344–54. Perhaps the most ambitious attempt to formulate an adequate statement of RU is R. B. BRANDT, "Toward a Credible Form of Utilitarianism," in HECTOR-NERI CASTAÑEDA and GEORGE NAKHNIKIAN, eds., *Morality and the Language of Conduct* (Detroit: Wayne State University Press, 1963), 107–43. Criticism of Brandt is contained in ALAN DONAGAN, "Is There a Credible Form of Utilitarianism?" in MICHAEL BAYLES, ed., *Contemporary Utilitarianism* (Garden City, NY: Anchor Books, 1968), 187–202. Brandt's fullest statement of a roughly rule-utilitarian position that he calls "a pluralistic welfare-maximizing moral system" is in *A Theory of the Good and the Right*.
18. Some philosophers hold that there is no difference between the two formu-

lations. See LYONS, *Forms and Limits of Utilitarianism*, chap. 3. Also, R. M. HARE, *Freedom and Reason* (Oxford: Oxford University Press, 1963), 130–36; and ALAN F. GIBBARD, "Rule-Utilitarianism: Merely an Illusory Alternative?" *Australasian Journal of Philosophy*, 43 (1965), 211–20.

19. GARRETT HARDIN, "Lifeboat Ethics: The Case against Helping the Poor," *Psychology Today*, 8 (1974). Reprinted in WILLIAM AIKEN and HUGH LA FOL-LETTE, eds., *World Hunger and Moral Obligation* (Englewood Cliffs, NJ: Prentice Hall, 1977), 14.

20. Cited in SHAPLEN, "The Lockheed Incident."

21. This idea is developed in DONALD H. REGAN, *Utilitarianism and Co-operation* (Oxford: Oxford University Press, 1980), as a new theory called co-operative utilitarianism.

22. For a clear introduction to the problems of measuring utility, see DONALD DAVIDSON, J.C.C. MCKINSEY, and PATRICK SUPPES, "Outlines of a Formal Theory of Value, I" *Philosophy of Science*, 22 (1955), 140–60. Two important discussions are ARMEN A. ALCHIAN, "The Meaning of Utility Measurement," *American Economic Review*, 43 (1953), 26–50; and ROBERT M. MCNAUGHTON, "A Metrical Conception of Happiness," *Philosophy and Phenomenological Research*, 14 (1954), 172–83. A good philosophical discussion of pleasure is GILBERT RYLE, *Dilemmas* (Cambridge: Cambridge University Press, 1954), chap. 4. For a good analysis by a psychologist, see KARL DUNCKER, "Pleasure, Emotion, and Striving," *Philosophy and Phenomenological Research*, 1 (1940), 391–430.

23. See, for example, LIONEL ROBBINS, *An Essay on the Nature and Significance of Economic Science* (London: Macmillan, 1932), 140; and KENNETH ARROW, *Social Choice and Individual Values*, 2nd ed. (New York: Wiley, 1963), 9.

24. A defense of interpersonal comparisons of utility by a prominent economist is I.M.D. LITTLE, *A Critique of Welfare Economics*, 2nd ed. (Oxford: Oxford University Press, 1957), chap. 4. For attempts to develop a means for interpersonal comparisons, see JOHN C. HARSANYI, "Cardinal Welfare, Individualistic Ethics, and Interpersonal Comparisons of Utility," *Journal of Political Economy*, 63 (1955), 309–21; reprinted in *Essays in Ethics, Social Behaviour, and Scientific Explanation* (Dordrecht: Reidel, 1976). And ILMAR WALDNER, "The Empirical Meaningfulness of Interpersonal Utility Comparisons," *The Journal of Philosophy*, 70 (1972), 87–103.

25. For an authoritative exposition, see E. J. MISHAN, *Cost-Benefit Analysis* (New York: Praeger, 1976).

26. RICHARD T. DEGEORGE, *Business Ethics*, 3rd ed. (New York: Macmillan, 1990), 44.

27. VINCENT VACCARO, "Cost-Benefit Analysis and Public Policy Formulation," in NORMAN E. BOWIE, ed., *Ethical Issues in Government* (Philadelphia: Temple University Press, 1981), 148. The definition used by Vaccaro is from HENRY M. PESKIN and EUGENE P. SESKIN, "Introduction and Overview," in PESKIN and SESKIN, eds., *Cost-Benefit Analysis and Water Pollution Policy* (Washington, DC: Urban Institute, 1975), 1.

28. MICHAEL S. BARAM, "Cost-Benefit Analysis: An Inadequate Basis for Health, Safety, and Environmental Regulatory Decision Making," *Ecological Law Quarterly*, 8 (1980), 473.

29. See MARK DOWIE, "Pinto Madness," *MotherJones* (September–October 1977). Reprinted in MARK GREEN, ed., *The Big Business Reader* (New York: Pilgrim Press, 1983), 32–45.

30. See M. W. JONES-LEE, *The Value of Life: An Economic Analysis* (Chicago: University of Chicago Press, 1976). Also, MICHAEL D. BAYLES, "The Price of Life," *Ethics*, 89 (1978), 20–34. For trenchant criticism of these methods, see STEVEN E. RHOADS, "How Much Should We Spend to Save a Life?" in RHOADS, ed. *Valuing Life: Public Policy Dilemmas* (Boulder, CO: Westview Press, 1980), 285–311.

31. These points are made by STEVEN KELMAN, "Cost-Benefit Analysis: An Ethical Critique," *Regulation*, January–February 1981, 33–40.

32. ROSEMARY TONG, *Ethics in Public Policy Analysis* (Englewood Cliffs, NJ: Prentice Hall, 1986), 20.

33. MARK SAGOFF, "At the Shrine of Our Lady of Fatima, or Why Political Questions Are Not All Economic," *Arizona Law Review*, 23 (1981), 1283–98.

34. KELMAN, "Cost-Benefit Analysis: An Ethical Critique," 39.

35. RICHARD M. TITMUSS, *The Gift Relationship: From Human Blood to Social Policy* (London: George Allen & Unwin, 1971).

36. PETER SINGER, "Rights and the Market," in JOHN ARTHUR and WILLIAM H. SHAW, eds., *Justice and Economic Distribution* (Englewood Cliffs, NJ: Prentice Hall, 1978), 213.

37. TITMUSS, *The Gift Relationship*, 246.

38. JAMES V. DeLONG, *Regulation* (March–April 1981), 40.

39. ALASDAIR MACINTYRE, "Utilitarianism and Cost-Benefit Analysis: An Essay on the Relevance of Moral Philosophy to Bureaucratic Theory," in KENNETH SAYRE, ed., *Values in the Electric Power Industry* (Notre Dame: University of Notre Dame Press, 1977), 217–37.

40. TOM L. BEAUCHAMP, "Utilitarianism and Cost/Benefit Analysis: A Reply to MacIntyre," in TOM L. BEAUCHAMP and NORMAN E. BOWIE, eds., *Ethical Theory and Business*, 1st ed. (Englewood Cliffs, NJ: Prentice Hall, 1979), 279.

41. VACCARO, "Cost-Benefit Analysis and Public Policy Formulation," 148–49.

42. VACCARO, "Cost-Benefit Analysis and Public Policy Formulation," 153–54.

CHAPTER THREE

Kantian Ethics and Rights

Those who argue that the actions of Lockheed in Japan were wrong not because of their *consequences* but because we have a *duty* not to bribe are taking a deontological rather than a teleological approach to ethical reasoning. Bribery, some say, is wrong by its very nature, regardless of the consequences. Other examples of nonconsequentialist reasoning in ethics include arguments based on principles such as the Golden Rule (Do unto others as you would have them do unto you) and those that appeal to basic notions of human dignity and respect for other persons. The Golden Rule asks us to consider our actions from the point of view of the person affected and thereby keeps us from making unjustified exceptions for ourselves. Discrimination, for example, runs counter to the Golden Rule (no person would want to be denied opportunities because of race or sex), and it is also incompatible with a respect for the intrinsic worth of all human beings. To treat people equally, without regard for race or sex, is an elemental obligation, or duty, that does not seem to depend on consequences.

Our reasoning may take a decidedly nonteleological or nonconsequentialist turn, and when it does, we need to be prepared to state and defend the principles involved. Some philosophers have attempted to do this, and the result is a number of deontological theories of ethics. The most significant and influential of these is the theory of Immanuel Kant, which we will examine in some detail. First, though, it will be useful to examine the nature of deontological theories at greater length in order to understand their strengths and weaknesses. Deontological theories are also closely linked with rights, and so this chapter contains a discussion of various theories of rights, including those provided by Kantian ethics as well as utilitarianism.

DEONTOLOGICAL THEORIES

Deontological theories, in contrast to teleological theories such as utilitarianism, deny that consequences are relevant to determining what we ought to do. Deontologists typically hold that certain actions are right not because of some benefit to ourselves or others but because of the nature of these actions or the rules from which they follow. Obligation, or duty, is the fundamental moral category in deontological theories, and goodness and other concepts are to be defined in terms of obligation, or duty. (The word *deontological* derives, in fact, from *deon*, the Greek word for duty.)

An example of a deontological theory consisting of a set of absolute moral rules is that presented by the twentieth-century British philosopher W. D. Ross. The seven rules in Ross's system are the following:

1. **Duties of fidelity**—to keep promises, both explicit and implicit, and to tell the truth.
2. **Duties of reparation**—to compensate people for injury that we have wrongfully inflicted on them.
3. **Duties of gratitude**—to return favors that others do for us.
4. **Duties of justice**—to ensure that goods are distributed according to people's merit or deserts.
5. **Duties of beneficence**—to do whatever we can to improve the condition of others.
6. **Duties of self-improvement**—to improve our own condition with respect to virtue and intelligence.
7. **Duties of nonmaleficence**—to avoid injury to others.[1]

One virtue of deontological theories such as Ross's is that they make sense of cases in which consequences seem to be irrelevant. Especially in justifying the obligations that arise from *relations*, such as contracts and roles, it is more plausible to appeal to the relations themselves than to the consequences. Thus, a manufacturer has an obligation to honor a warranty on a defective product even if the cost of doing so exceeds the benefit of satisfying a consumer. And an employee has an obligation to an employer to be loyal and to do his or her job. The obligation of the manufacturer arises from an actual or implied contract, and the obligation of an employee begins when a job is accepted. Another example is a duty of gratitude for past service, as when a supplier shows a special commitment to a client by designing a product to meet that client's needs, working overtime to meet unanticipated demands, or acting promptly to resolve problems. Such an obligation is similar to that of an individual to return a favor.

Another strength of deontological theories is the way they account for the role of *motives* in evaluating actions. Intuitively, we feel that a person who steals a few thousand dollars in small amounts from people who scarcely notice and one who steals millions and leaves the victims destitute have performed actions with very different consequences, but their actions are equally immoral. On the other hand, two people who give large amounts to charity—one out of genuine concern to alleviate suffering and the other to impress friends and associates—produce the same amount of good, yet we evaluate the two actions differently. These two examples show that our evaluation of actions is sometimes based on motives rather than on consequences. The role of motives in evaluating actions is easily explained if we accept the belief of most deontologists that the rightness of actions depends wholly or in part on the motives from which they are performed and not on consequences.

Teleological theorists typically respond by arguing that motives are relevant to some judgments but not to those about the rightness of actions. G. E. Moore, for example, argued that there is no inconsistency with teleological theories in judging motives to be good or bad as long as the rightness of actions does not depend on the goodness or badness of the motives. Also, motives are relevant for making judgments about whether people deserve moral praise and blame, but these judgments, too, are consistent with the teleological view.[2] John Stuart Mill wrote in *Utilitarianism*, ". . . utilitarian moralists have gone beyond almost all others in affirming that the motive has nothing to do with the morality of the action, though much to do with the worth of the agent." Thus, we judge that a person who gives to charity to impress his friends has performed a good *action* but is not necessarily a good *person*.

The Weaknesses of Deontological Theories

The main weakness of deontological theories lies in the failure to provide a plausible account of how we can know our moral obligations and resolve problems of moral conflict. Although the rules in Ross's theory are plausible, no reason is offered for accepting these rules and not others. Ross's rules are also open to the charge of ethnocentrism; that is, of erroneously accepting the rules of our own society as though they were universal. People at different times and in different places might reject Ross's rules and regard others as being equally worthy. Worse, he suggests no order of priority among the rules, so that we have no guidance in cases where they conflict. For example, should we keep a promise or tell the truth, when doing so will harm someone? Or should gratitude for a past favor alter in some way a distribution of goods according to merit or desert?

Ross attempted to solve the problem of conflict among rules by making a distinction between *actual* and *prima facie* obligations. All rules have exceptions. Thus, the rule Tell the truth does not necessarily rule out harmless falsehoods or so-called white lies. In most cases of rule conflict, however, we do not make exceptions to rules, Ross claims. Rather, a rule that is overridden by another still applies and would be our actual duty if the other rule did not intervene. If we lie to save a person's life, for example, this case is not an exception to the rule Tell the truth. But the obligation that a rule creates is only a prima facie obligation. That is, it is an obligation that we ought to perform unless another prima facie obligation overrides it. In any given situation, we may have several prima facie obligations. Our actual obligation, though, is what we ought to do "on balance," or "all things considered."[3]

Although Ross's distinction provides a useful way to understand cases of conflict, it does nothing to solve the main problem with his theory. Instead of determining which rule applies, we now have to ask, which of our prima facie duties is our actual duty? Ross correctly refused to recognize any priority among the rules. Sometimes justice takes precedence over beneficence, for example; sometimes it does not. As a result, though, we are left with no guidance on how to apply the rules when they conflict. The response of some deontologists is that our moral life is too complex to admit of easy solutions. Ross believed that he had given the fullest account possible of our system of moral reasoning and that no further means exist for determining our obligations in hard cases.

The most common response of deontologists to the problem of conflict is to invoke a faculty of *intuition*. Some eighteenth-century deontologists held that moral rules and principles are like mathematical truths in that they are obvious to any rational person who considers them.[4] That we ought to tell the truth is known in the same way as $2 + 2 = 4$ has not proved to be very persuasive among philosophers. Most deontologists in the nineteenth and twentieth centuries abandoned the mathematical analogy but have not managed to provide a convincing explanation for how a supposed faculty of intuition enables us to know our moral obligations.[5] To some skeptics, the idea of a faculty of intuition is merely a high-sounding way of covering up the fact that deontologists can offer no further support for their moral rules.[6]

Conclusion

Ross and other intuitionists are unsuccessful, then, in providing an adequate foundation for a deontological ethical theory. The main stumbling block is the difficulty of explaining how if not by consequences the rules of morality are justified. Their key insight is that morality is based in some way on reason, but their explanation of the role of reason in morality is not very persuasive. Immanuel Kant offers a radically different alternative, which many consider more satisfactory.

KANT'S ETHICAL THEORY

Immanuel Kant (1724–1804) wrote his famous ethical treatise *Foundations of the Metaphysics of Morals* (1785) before the rise of English utilitarianism, but he was well-acquainted with the idea of founding morality on the feelings of pleasure and pain, rather than on reason. Accordingly, Kant set out to restore reason to what he regarded as its rightful place in our moral life. Specifically, he attempted to show that there are some things that we ought to do and others that we ought not to do merely by virtue of being rational. Moral obligation thus has nothing to do with consequences, in Kant's view, but arises solely from a moral law that is binding on all rational beings. Although Kant was not entirely successful in realizing his aim of founding morality on pure reason, his ethical theory contains some important insights about morality, which have exercised a tremendous influence on subsequent thought.

The main features of the ethical theory presented in the *Foundations* can be illustrated by considering one of Kant's own examples:

> . . . [A] man finds himself forced by need to borrow money. He well knows that he will not be able to repay it, but he also sees that nothing will be loaned him if he does not firmly promise to repay it at a certain time. He desires to make such a promise, but he has enough conscience to ask himself whether it is not improper and opposed to duty to relieve his distress in such a way.

What (morally) ought this man to do? A teleological theory would have us answer this question by determining the consequences of each alternative course of action. Making a promise that he knows he cannot keep might enable the man to extricate himself from his immediate troubles, but more likely the long-term consequences of being in debt and losing the trust of others would outweigh any possible gain. No rule that would make such an action morally right could possibly be justified, moreover, by the consequences of everyone's acting in that way. According to both act- and rule-utilitarianism, therefore, the man probably ought to refrain from making the untruthful promise.

Kant regarded all such appeals to consequences as morally irrelevant. As a deontologist, he held that the duty to tell the truth when making promises arises from a rule that ought to be followed without regard for consequences. Even if the man could do more good by borrowing money under false pretenses—by using it to pay for an operation that would save a person's life, for example—the action would still be wrong. Kant denied, furthermore, that any consequence, such as pleasure, could be good. In a deontological theory, duty rather than good is the fundamental moral category. As a result, the only thing that can be good without qualification, according to Kant, is what he called a *good will*, performing an action solely because it is our duty. This, he believed, is in accord with our ordinary moral views, since it offends our sense of justice to see a wicked person enjoying a life of uninterrupted pleasure. A good will, he said, "seems to constitute the indispensable condition even of worthiness to be happy."

The Problem of Knowing Which Rules to Follow

The main difficulty of deontological theories that include a list of absolute moral rules is the lack of any convincing answer to the question, How do we know that these are the rules we should follow? Intuitionists, such as Ross, assume that somehow we just "see" that certain rules are correct. Kant posed the question in a different way by seizing on a difference between the moral and nonmoral senses of the word *ought*. Consider the following examples:

1. If you want to improve your serve, then you ought to take lessons from a tennis pro.
2. If you want to lower your cholesterol level, then you ought to eat less red meat.

Kant called these *hypothetical imperatives*, because they tell us to do something only on the condition that we have the relevant desire. They have the form, If you want _____, then do _____. If we do not care about improving our serve, though, or lowering our cholesterol level, then there is nothing that we *ought* to do. In neither case does the use of the word *ought* express a moral obligation.

Kant characterized moral rules as imperatives that express what we ought to do *categorically* rather than hypothetically. That is, they are uses of the word *ought* that tell us what to do regardless of our desires. Imperatives that command categorically are of the form Do _____ (period). Thus, we cannot evade the force of the moral rule Tell the truth merely by saying, for example, "But I don't care about being trusted." The question of how we can know which rules to follow was posed by Kant, then, as follows: How is it possible for there to be imperatives that command categorically; that is, that command us to perform actions no matter what desires we happen to have? His answer is that they follow from a principle, called the *categorical imperative*, which he believed every rational being must accept.

Kant's own turgid statement of the categorical imperative is

Act only according to that maxim by which you can at the same time will that it should become a universal law.

Rendered into more comprehensible English, Kant's principle is, act only on rules (or maxims) that you would be willing to see everyone follow.[7] The categorical imperative suggests a rather remarkable "thought experiment" to be performed whenever we deliberate about what to do. Suppose, for example, that every time we accept a rule for our own conduct, that very same rule would be imposed, by some miracle, on everybody. Under such conditions, are there some rules that we, as rational beings, simply could not accept (that is, will to become universal law)?

Let us see how this would apply to Kant's example. If the man were to obtain the loan under false pretenses, the rule on which he would be acting would be something like, Whenever you need a loan, make a promise to repay the money, even if you know that you cannot do so. Although such a rule could easily be acted on by one person, the effect of its being made a rule for everyone—that is, of becoming a universal law—would be, in Kant's view, self-defeating. No one would believe anyone else, and the result would be that the words "I promise to do such-and-such" would lose their meaning. Kant wrote:

> For the universality of a law which says that anyone who believes himself to be in need could promise what he pleased with the intention of not fulfilling it would make the promise itself and the end to be accomplished by it impossible; no one would believe what we promised to him but would only laugh at any such assertion as a vain pretense.

Kant has sometimes been accused of being a "closet utilitarian" by slipping in an appeal to consequences. To Kant's own way of thinking, however, the objection to the rule just stated is not that everyone's following it would lead to undesirable consequences but that everyone's following it describes an impossible state of affairs. Willing that everyone act on this rule is analogous to a person making plans to vacation in two places, say Acapulco and Aspen, *at the same time.* Both are desirable vacation spots, but willing the metaphysical impossibility of being in two places at once is not something that can be done by a rational person.

Evaluating the Categorical Imperative

If Kant is correct, then immoral conduct is also irrational. But is he correct? Not many philosophers have been persuaded by any of the four examples that Kant presents in the *Foundations.*[8] If everyone were to make untruthful promises, then promise-making as a practice could not exist. Similarly, if everyone cheated at bridge, then the game as we know it would cease to be played. A world without promises (or bridge) would be less desirable than our own, but there is no impossibility lurking in the description of such a world.

Some writers maintain that this objection involves a misunderstanding of Kant's point, which is rather that as beings who act to achieve certain ends, we could not "will" a world in which essential means for achieving our ends would be lacking.[9] It is irrational, in other words, to act in ways that we know will thwart the realization of our own ends. An appropriate analogy on this interpretation is a person who makes vacation plans but steadfastly refuses to make airline or hotel reservations. This interpretation is no better, however, since we do many things that prevent us from achieving our ends. And though behavior of this kind is unfortunate and often foolish, it is not necessarily irrational. People on diets sometimes eat foods that they know they should avoid, for example, and some students drop out of college, even though they realize that a diploma is essential for their goals in life.

Kant is unsuccessful, then, in his attempt to show how it is possible for some imperatives to command categorically and not merely hypothetically. Still, many philosophers find a kernel of truth in Kant's principle of the categorical imperative, which they express as the claim that all moral judgments must be *universalizable*. That is, if we say that an act is right for one person, then we are committed to saying that it is right for all other relevantly similar persons in relevantly similar circumstances. By the same token, if an act is wrong for other people, then it is wrong for any one person unless there is some difference that justifies making an exception. This *principle of universalizability* expresses the simple point that, as a matter of logic, we must be consistent in the judgments we make. A professor who gives a grade of A to a student with an examination score of 90 and a B to another with exactly the same score, for example, is being inconsistent, and the recipient of the B is unlikely to be satisfied with an explanation such as, "Well, the handwriting on the other examination is *so* much neater!" because this is an irrelevant difference.[10]

The Principle of Universalizability

The principle of universalizability has immense implications for moral reasoning. First, it counters the natural temptation to make exceptions for ourselves or to apply a double standard. Consider a job applicant who exaggerates a bit on a résumé but is incensed to discover, after being hired, that the company misrepresented the opportunity for advancement. The person is being inconsistent to hold that it is all right for him to lie to others but wrong for anyone else to lie to him, or that there is nothing wrong with lying if it is necessary to get a job, but companies ought to be completely truthful in their dealings with potential employees. An effective move in a moral argument is to challenge people who hold such positions to cite some morally relevant difference. What is so special about you specifically or job applicants in general? If they can give no acceptable answer, then they are forced by the laws of logic to give up one or the other of the inconsistent judgments.

Second, the universalizability principle can be viewed as underlying the common question, "What if everyone did that?"[11] The consequences of a few people cheating on their taxes, for example, are negligible. If everyone were to cheat, however, the results would be disastrous. The force of "What if everyone did that?" is to get people to see that since it would be undesirable for everyone to cheat, no one ought to do so. This pattern of ethical reasoning involves an appeal to consequences, but it differs from standard forms of utilitarianism in that the consequences are hypothetical rather than actual. That is, whether anyone else actually cheats is irrelevant to the question "What if everyone did that?" The fact that the results would be disastrous *if everyone did* is sufficient to entail the conclusion that cheating is wrong.[12]

Let us now consider the force of the principle of universalizability in the case of bribery. If it was right for Lockheed to make payments to government officials, for example, then it is also right for McDonnell Douglas, Boeing, and every other manufacturer to do the same. However, little reflection is needed to see that if everyone in the industry were to act as Lockheed did, then the manner in which planes are sold would be radically transformed. No longer would selling take place in a free market, with competition among sellers to offer the best product at the lowest price. Agreements would be reached, instead, by Byzantine maneuverings through intermediaries, with bundles of cash furtively exchanged at prearranged meeting spots. In short, bribery, if universally practiced, would destroy the market as a means for economic exchange, and with the destruction of the market would go all the benefits the market brings.

Furthermore, if bribery were the norm, then no advantage could be obtained by offering a bribe. Bribery is effective in a free market, because a company that offers a bribe gains an (unfair) advantage over competitors that play by the rules of the economic system. Their situation is like that of a football team which tries to win in the usual way while their opponents bribe the referees. If both teams bribe the referees, though, then no advantage can be gained. The game then becomes transformed from an athletic to a financial contest. The winner is the team that *pays* best rather than the team that *plays* best. Bribery also has its intended effect only when it is kept secret. Once a company's competitors become aware of bribe offers, then they can seek to neutralize the advantage by offering bribes of their own.

These points do not show that universal bribery is self-defeating or impossible in some way. In parts of the world today, bribery pervades all business and government dealings. What they do show, however, is that people who deplore such corruption cannot consistently hold that it is still all right for *them* to bribe. They must either admit that bribery is wrong for them as well or else justify their actions by citing some relevant difference; otherwise, their position is logically inconsistent.

Problems with Universalizability

Although this kernel of truth in Kant's categorical imperative is of great importance, it is too limited to serve as the basis for a complete ethical theory.[13] First, people accused of wrongdoing can insist that significant differences exist between their actions and those of others. Carl Kotchian, for example, pointed to the fact that Lockheed never offered to pay officials of the Japanese government or All Nippon Airways and that the demands for money were made by the recipients themselves. Lockheed did not engage in bribery, in Kotchian's view, but was instead a victim of extortion. Thus, we can imagine Kotchian arguing that although bribery is wrong because the consequences of everyone offering bribes is clearly undesirable, giving in to extortion demands is not, especially when tens of thousands of jobs and perhaps the survival of the company are at stake. To be consistent, Kotchian would have to hold not only that it was right for Lockheed to make payments under such circumstances but that it would be right for any company to act in the same way under the same circumstances. He would probably have no hesitation in universalizing his action in this way, though. So the results of applying the principle of universalizability to the Lockheed case are inconclusive. Whether people are being inconsistent in the judgments they make often depends on what are relevant differences, and the principle of universalizability alone gives us no guidance in such matters.

Second, the principle of universalizability is incapable of refuting fanatics who would be content for everyone to act as they do. John Stuart Mill wrote that Kant:

> . . . fails, almost grotesquely, to show that there would be any contradiction. . . in the adoption by all rational beings of the most outrageously immoral rules of conduct. All he shows is that the consequences of their universal adoption would be such as no one would choose to incur.

Although this objection rests on a misunderstanding of the categorical imperative, it is valid against the principle of universalizability. R. M. Hare asks us to consider the case of a Nazi who is so convinced of the rightness of the ideal of a pure Aryan race that even evidence proving him to be a Jew does not change his mind. We can also imagine an unscrupulous businessperson who when asked, "Would you be willing to live in a world in which everyone else attempted to cheat and steal as you do?" replies, "That'd be fine with me. No one can take advantage of me, and I'd come out even further ahead." Most people are unlikely to accept such repugnant consequences. But as long as there are fanatics who are willing for everyone else to act in the same way, their positions—no matter how immoral—cannot be refuted by appealing merely to the principle of universalizability.

Fortunately, there are few fanatics in this world; most of us are not willing to live in a world in which everyone performed actions that we consider to be wrong. Attempts to find relevant differences between our situation and that of others is often revealed to be special pleading. The universalizability principle, therefore, although not always conclusive, is a valuable, practical guide. In a wide variety of cases, to ask ourselves or others, "Would you be willing for everyone to act in the same way?" is enough to settle the question of rightness.

RESPECT FOR PERSONS

The *Foundations* contains a second formulation of the categorical imperative which Kant expressed as follows:

> *Act so that you treat humanity, whether in your own person or in that of another, always as an end and never as a means only.*

These words are usually interpreted to mean that we should respect other people (and ourselves!) as human beings. The kind of respect that Kant had in mind is compatible with achieving our ends by enlisting the aid of other people. We use shop clerks and taxi drivers, for example, as a means for achieving our ends, and the owners of a business use employees as a means for achieving their ends. What is ruled out by Kant's principle, however, is treating people *only* as a means, so that they are no different, in our view, from mere "things." The most extreme case of treating people in this way is slavery, in which human beings become forms of property, subject entirely to the control of their "owners."

The moral importance of human beings is not unique to Kant's theory, of course. Virtually all systems of ethics require that we respect other persons. The distinctiveness of Kant's contribution lies in his view of what it means to be a human being and what we are respecting when we have respect for persons. For utilitarians, human beings are creatures capable of enjoying pleasure, and so we are morally obligated to produce as much pleasure as possible, taking into consideration the pleasure of everyone alike. What is morally objectionable about slavery is that slaves lead miserable lives, and the suffering they endure is not offset by an increase in the amount of pleasure enjoyed by others. (Utilitarians also point to the corrupting effect that slavery has on the whole of society, including slave owners.) Kant holds, by contrast, that the morally significant feature of human beings is not their capacity for enjoying pleasure but their *rationality*. Lower animals are capable of enjoying pleasure, too; what distinguishes human beings, for Kant, is their capacity for using reason. To respect persons, therefore, is to respect them as rational creatures.

Rationality is what gives persons a greater moral value than anything else in creation, including pleasure. Indeed, rational beings are the only things that ultimately have value, according to Kant; other things have value only because we place a value on them as means to our ends. Books, music, fine food, travel, and the company of friends, for example, have value as a result of our enjoyment of them. Apart from rational beings who want them and act to obtain them, they have no value at all. Kant expressed this point by saying that their value is *conditional*. The only thing which has *unconditional* value and is an end in itself is that which gives value to other things; namely, human beings. In Kant's own words:

> Now, I say, man and, in general, every rational being exists as an end in himself and not merely as a means to be arbitrarily used by this or that will. In all his actions, whether they are directed to himself or to other rational beings, he must always be regarded at the same time as an end.

From this follows the second formulation of the categorical imperative.

Our account of the second formulation is not complete, however, without an explanation of how Kant understood reason. Reason, in Kant's view, is what enables human beings to act freely. Every event in nature other than the actions of human beings is rigidly determined by antecedents. The ringing of a doorbell, for example, follows inevitably once the button is pushed. Human beings are exempt, however, from the determinism that prevails in the rest of the natural world. We alone have a free will. Thus, we are free to push a doorbell button—or not to push it, as we choose. Freedom of this kind is possible, according to Kant, because we are able to create the rules that govern our conduct. His conception of rationality can be expressed roughly by saying that we are rule-making beings. This idea of acting on rules of our own devising is also conveyed by the term *autonomy*, which is derived from two Greek words meaning "self" and "law." To be autonomous is quite literally to be a lawgiver to oneself, or self-governing. A rational being, therefore, is a being who is autonomous.

To respect other people, then, is to respect their capacity for acting freely; that is, their autonomy. More specifically, it is to respect them as beings, with their own wants, hopes, and aspirations, who have the capacity to engage in purposeful action to achieve their various ends. What is morally objectionable about slavery from a Kantian perspective, then, is not the pain and loss of pleasure that it involves but the fact that slavery deprives persons of the feature that makes them rational beings; namely, their freedom of will, their autonomy.

The difference between Kant's conception of respect for persons and utilitarianism is vividly illustrated by a dilemma that medical practitioners often face. Should patients be fully informed about their condition—even if the knowledge upsets them and perhaps interferes with medical treatment—or is it permissible to withhold information for the patients' own good? Utilitarians consider the welfare of patients, including their peace of mind and the effectiveness of their treatment, to be the determining factors. (Some utilitarians argue, though, that a policy of full disclosure still has the best consequences, all things considered.) Kantians hold, by contrast, that lying to patients—even when doing so is in their best interest—involves a lack of respect, since, without adequate information, they are unable to make decisions about matters that profoundly affect them. Full disclosure is necessary, in other words, for patient autonomy.

Business Applications of the Principle

The principle of respect for persons has many applications in business. Companies show a lack of respect in the Kantian sense when they regard employees as so many interchangeable parts in the production process and make no attempt to address their needs or desires, encourage their personal development, or provide meaningful and rewarding work. Industrial psychologists have long told managers that their workers will be more productive if they are treated as human beings. In 1960, Douglas McGregor in *The Human Side of Enterprise* coined the phrase Theory X to describe a management style in which workers need to be closely supervised and coerced into obedience.[14] He suggested replacing this approach with Theory Y, in which workers are encouraged to be self-directed, to accept responsibility, and to find fulfillment in their jobs. More recently, the success of the Japanese style of management has been attributed to their emphasis on treating employees with respect. Management specialist William G. Ouchi has labeled this approach Theory Z in his bestselling book *Theory Z: How American Business Can Meet the Japanese Challenge.*[15] One American company that has made respect for employees a key part of its business is Johnson & Johnson. Its statement *Our Credo* reads in part:

> We are responsible to our employees, the men and women who work with us throughout the world. Everyone must be considered as an individual.

We must respect their dignity and recognize their merit. They must have a sense of security in their jobs. Compensation must be fair and adequate, and working conditions clean, orderly and safe. We must be mindful of ways to help our employees fulfill their family responsibilities. Employees must feel free to make suggestions and complaints. There must be equal opportunity for employment, development and advancement for those qualified.

Respect for persons is not confined to employee relations, however. The principle also applies to the way in which companies treat consumers and members of the communities in which they are located. Whether products are marketed solely with a view to what sells or with the interests of consumers in mind says a lot about the respect that companies have for consumers. Also, advertisements that educate consumers so that they can made rational informed choices show respect, whereas deceptive and misleading advertisements and advertisements that manipulate and create desires for unnecessary products do not. Companies treat members of a community solely as ends to their profit-making activity when they expose them to hazardous pollutants without any warning or fail to give notice before closing a factory that is vital to the well-being of the community.

Strengths and Weaknesses of the Principle

The principle of respect for persons has some significant strengths and weaknesses. The main weakness is that it does not lend itself to a precise method for decision-making. Certainly, slavery and gross exploitation of labor are forbidden by the principle, but utilitarianism judges these practices to be immoral as well. Respect for persons is likely to yield different results, though, in cases where utilitarians would sacrifice the interests of a few individuals to increase the overall welfare of society. Kant's principle lays a greater stress on the welfare of every person, thereby providing greater protection for the claims of individuals over those of society at large. However, it does not tell us where to draw the line.

For example, any company that claims to treat its employees with respect must assure them of reasonable job security. Lifetime employment is a frequently cited feature of Japanese management. Job security involves a certain loss of efficiency, though, since companies are less able to adapt to changing conditions, and the cost is borne by consumers in higher prices or by the employees themselves in lower wages. If job security increases unemployment, it protects those workers who already have a job while harming those who are unemployed. Respect for persons supports *some* level of job security, then, but it provides little help in managing the inevitable tradeoffs. Utilitarianism, although perhaps too ready to sacrifice the interests of individuals, is better suited to this task.

Respect for persons is also likely to yield different results in cases where the welfare of individuals comes into conflict with their freedom to choose. In matters of occupational health and safety, for example, utilitarians tend to favor government regulations to protect workers. An alternative that is more compatible with Kant's principle is to inform workers of the dangers and allow *them* to decide whether to assume the risk. Regulation, according to some critics, is *paternalistic*; that is, it treats workers as a parent treats a child. It is demeaning, they contend, for bureaucrats in Washington to tell workers what conditions they can work under, even if the regulation is for their own good. Utilitarians argue in reply that a lack of regulation leaves workers vulnerable to exploitation by employers, so that outlawing unsafe working conditions shows greater respect for workers as persons than leaving the choice to them. Regulation is justified, they say, because workers cannot effectively exercise individual choice in this case.

Conclusion

Despite shortcomings, Kant's ethical theory yields at least two important results. The principles of universalizability and respect for persons, although not sufficient for deciding all questions of ethics, are still important avenues of ethical reasoning that serve as valuable correctives to the utilitarian approach. Kantianism also provides a strong foundation for rights, which is another part of morality.

THE CONCEPT OF A RIGHT

Rights play an important role in business ethics—and, indeed, in virtually all moral issues. Both employers and employees are commonly regarded as having certain rights. Employers have the right to conduct business as they see fit, to make decisions about hiring and promotion, and to be protected against unfair forms of competition. Employees have the right to organize and engage in collective bargaining and to be protected against discrimination and hazardous working conditions. Consumers and the general public also have rights in such matters as marketing and advertising, product safety, and the protection of the environment.

Beyond business, the debate over abortion, the use of life support systems, access to medical care, and discrimination in housing and education all involve the rights of different parties. Each side in the abortion debate, for example, appeals to a supposed right: the right to life of the fetus or the right of a woman to choose whether to bear a child.

There is growing support for the recognition of the right of the terminally ill to choose to die, the right of people to a minimal level of health care, and so on. Many of our constitutional protections in the Bill of Rights arouse controversy. Does the First Amendment right of free speech, for example, protect obscenity or flag-burning?

Rights are also prominent in the Western political tradition and the present-day international order. The Virginia Declaration of Rights (1776), for example, mentions as inherent rights "the enjoyment of life and liberty, with the means of acquiring and possessing property, and pursuing and obtaining happiness and safety." Other important documents that proclaim rights are the French Declaration of the Rights of Man and of Citizens (1787), the Bill of Rights in the American Constitution (1791), and the Universal Declaration of Human Rights of the United Nations (1948). Among the rights included in this latter document are

> **Article 3** Everyone has the right to life, liberty and security of person.
>
> **Article 4** No one shall be held in slavery or servitude. . . .
>
> **Article 5** No one shall be subjected to torture or to cruel, inhuman or degrading treatment or punishment.
>
> **Article 9** No one shall be subjected to arbitrary arrest, detention or exile.

The introduction of rights into the discussion of ethical issues is often confusing. First, the term *rights* is used in many different ways, so that the concept of a right and the various kinds of rights must be carefully distinguished. Second, many rights come into conflict. The right of an employee to leave his or her employer and join a competitor conflicts with the legitimate right of employers to protect trade secrets, for example, so that some balancing is required. And the traditional rights of employers in personnel matters are being increasingly challenged by employees who claim a right to privacy in the workplace and a right to due process in the event of discipline or dismissal. Whether employees should have these rights is hotly debated.

Because of the moral significance that we attach to rights, there is a tendency to stretch the concept in ways that dilute its meaning. For example, the rights to receive adequate food, clothing, and medical care, mentioned in the Universal Declaration of Human Rights, are perhaps better described as political goals rather than rights. Often the dispute is not over the existence of the rights in question, such as the right to life or the right of women to control their own childbearing capacities, but over the extent of these rights and their relative weight when they come into conflict. For all these reasons, the claim of a right is frequently the beginning of an ethical debate rather than the end.

The Nature and Value of Rights

In order to understand the nature and value of rights, consider the following case.

In thirty-two years with the Sees Candy Company, Wayne Pugh worked his way up from washing pots and pans to a vice-presidency and membership on the board of directors of one of Sees's major subsidiaries.[16] During the Christmas and Valentine's Day season, his sales in the San Francisco area set new records, and the March issue of the company newsletter contained two pictures of Pugh along with congratulations on his excellent performance. He thought that he was in line for a promotion when he was summoned to the office of the president. Instead, he was handed a letter informing him of his immediate dismissal. He was ordered not to return to his office or to contact any of his former colleagues during working hours. No reason was given for the dismissal except for the cryptic suggestion of the president to "look within himself."

Although being fired is never pleasant, the experience is especially galling when there is no explanation of the reasons and no opportunity to respond. In 1982, the International Labour Organization (ILO) adopted a convention which lists the rights that every nation ought to recognize in the dismissal of employees.[17] Article 4 of the ILO convention states:

> The employment of a worker shall not be terminated unless there is a valid reason for such termination connected with the capacity or conduct of the worker based on the operational requirements of the undertaking, establishment, or service.

Employees are accorded the right in Article 7 to be notified of the charges against them, and Article 8 provides that employees who believe they have been unjustly dismissed have a right to a review by an impartial body.

These rights, which embody the essentials of due process, provided no protection for Wayne Pugh, since the United States cast the only vote against the ILO convention and lags behind virtually all other major industrial countries in implementing its provisions. There is no comprehensive federal legislation covering unjust dismissal, and only a few states have passed laws in this area. The only substantial protection for workers in the private sector is an employment contract that specifies grounds for termination and the procedures to be followed.[18] Still, we can ask whether employees have a moral right to due process.

The concept of a right can be explained by imagining a company that treats employees fairly but does not recognize due process as a right.[19] In this company, employees are dismissed only for good reasons after a thorough and impartial hearing, but there is no contract, statute, or other provision establishing a right of due process for all employees. Something is still missing, since the fair treatment that the employees enjoy results solely from the company's voluntary acceptance of certain personnel policies. If the company were ever to change these policies, then employees dismissed without due process would have no recourse. Contrast this with a company in which due process is established as a right. Employees in this company have something that was lacking in the previous company. They have an independent basis for challenging a decision by the company to dismiss them. They have something to stand on; namely, their rights.

Rights can be understood, therefore, as *entitlements*.[20] To have rights is to be entitled to act on our own or to be treated by others in certain ways without asking permission of anyone or being dependent on other people's goodwill. Rights entitle us to make claims on other people either to refrain from interfering in what we do or to contribute actively to our well-being—not as beggars, who can only entreat others to be generous, but as creditors, who can demand what is owed to them. This explanation of rights in terms of entitlements runs the risk of circularity (after all, what is an entitlement but something we have a right to?), but it is sufficiently illuminating to serve as a beginning of our examination.

Legal and Moral Rights

A distinction needs to be made at the outset between legal rights and moral rights. *Legal rights* are rights that are recognized and enforced as part of a legal system. In the United States, these consist primarily of the rights set forth in the Constitution, including the Bill of Rights, and those created by acts of Congress and state legislatures. Thus, Americans have a constitutional right to freedom from government interference in matters of speech and religion, to protection from unreasonable searches and seizures, and to equal protection of the laws. There are some rights not specifically mentioned in the Constitution that have been held by the Supreme Court to be a part of it. The Court has interpreted the right of free speech, for example, to protect pornography and symbolic "speech" such as flag-burning. The right to due process means that suspects must be advised of their right to counsel and provided with a lawyer if they cannot afford one. Among the rights created by legislative acts are the many rights that business firms have under the Uniform Commercial Code, the right of workers to form a union and to engage in collective bargaining (established by the National Labor Relations Act of 1935), and the rights of consumers under the Consumer Product Safety Act (1972).

Moral rights, by contrast, are rights that do not depend on the existence of a legal system. They are rights that we (morally) *ought* to have, regardless of whether they are explicitly recognized by law. Moral rights derive their force not from being part of a legal system but from more general ethical rules and principles. Thus, people ought to have a right to free speech even if in some countries such a right is not a part of the legal system. Moral rights of this kind provide an ethical justification for some legal rights and a means for ethically evaluating legal systems that lack them. The justification for including the right of free speech in the Constitution, for example, is that it is a moral right, and a legal system that lacks a right of free speech is, in that respect, morally deficient.

Not every moral right is a legal right, of course, and some perhaps ought not to be. The United States has not implemented Article 23 of the Universal Declaration of Human Rights, which holds that everyone has the right to work, on the grounds that the level of employment ought to be left to the workings of the labor market and not legislated. There are other moral rights, such as a right to respect as an equal, that are simply not capable of being secured by law. Although our legal and moral rights overlap considerably, they are conceptually distinct and rest on different foundations.

The Correlativity of Rights and Duties

A widely held analysis of both legal and moral rights is that they are closely correlated with obligations, or duties. Specifically, one person can have a right only if another person has an obligation to perform a certain action. All rights, in other words, presuppose a corresponding obligation, although not all obligations entail a right. This analysis is commonly called the *correlativity thesis*.[21] A simple example of the correlativity thesis is the following: If A has loaned ten dollars to B, then A has a claim on B for the repayment of the loan. But this is to say that B has an obligation or duty to pay A ten dollars. Rights and obligations in this analysis are simply two ways of describing the same normative relation, distinguished only by the use of the active and passive voice.[22]

If the correlativity thesis is correct, then there is nothing mysterious about rights. They are explainable in terms of obligations, and a justification of rights requires nothing more than a theory of obligation. Unfortunately, the analysis does not fit all legal rights. In his classic treatise *Fundamental Legal Conceptions*, Wesley Newcomb Hohfeld holds that rights and duties are correlated in the case of *claim rights*.[23] Rights of this kind, which are exemplified by the case of a loan, are regarded by Hohfeld as rights in the proper sense of the term. But some rights, such as the right to free speech, are *liberty rights*, which do not impose a correlative obligation on others, except not to interfere. Hohfeld also distinguishes rights that are legal *powers*, such as the right to get married or to make a will and the right of police officers to make an arrest, and legal *immunities*, such as the right not to be compelled to testify against ourselves or to be tried twice for the same crime. Using some ingenuity, we might be able to find obligations that correlate with these rights. David Lyons suggests, for example, that the right of free speech imposes an obligation on Congress not to pass laws limiting speech. The power of police officers is correlated with certain rights and duties of motorists, so that the power of an officer does not extend to interfering when motorists are exercising their rights (making a U-turn where permitted, for example) but does include cases where motorists have a duty to obey (for example, an order to stop).[24] Still, the correlation of rights and obligations in the law is not as neat and tidy as the loan example suggests.

Turning now to moral rights, the correlation is also not perfect. First, insofar as moral rights have the diversity of legal rights, so that some moral rights are also liberties, powers, and immunities,[25] then the analysis does not easily fit. Second, if rights are entitlements, then we may be entitled to something without anyone else having an obligation to provide it. Joel Feinberg, who analyzes rights as valid *claims* against others, holds that rights typically involve two elements: a claim *to* something and a claim *against* someone.[26] Thus, in the loan example, A has a claim *to* the ten dollars and a claim *against* B to repay it. H. J. Mc-Closkey points out, however, that we can have some rights, such as the rights to education, adequate nutrition, minimal medical care, and decent housing, even though no one else is obligated to provide these things.[27]

Despite these difficulties, the correlativity thesis is a valuable reminder that many (if not all) rights are correlated with obligations, or duties. If any person has rights, then there are things that other people ought to do or refrain from doing. Rights are part of the web of moral relations that bind us together. No one can have a right in isolation.

Some Other Distinctions Between Rights

Some rights are *specific* in that they involve identifiable individuals. In the loan example, it is A and no one else who has a right to the ten dollars, and the obligation to repay it rests on B alone. In law, these are called *in personam* rights. A major source of specific, or *in personam*, rights is contracts, since these ubiquitous intruments create a set of mutual rights as well as duties for the individuals who are parties to them. Other rights are *general*, or *in rem*, rights, since they involve claims against everyone, or humanity in general. Thus, the right of free speech belongs to everyone, and the obligation to enforce this right rests with the whole community. Similarly, a right to education or medical care is a right that entitles us to make a claim on our common resources. A major objection to the correlativity thesis can be expressed in this form: All specific, or *in personam*, rights are closely correlated with obligations, but some general, or *in rem*, rights are not.[28]

Another common distinction exists between *negative* and *positive* rights. Generally, negative rights are correlated with obligations on the part of others to refrain from acting in certain ways; that is, to act negatively by not interfering with our own freedom of action. Positive rights, by contrast, impose obligations on other people to provide us with some good or service and thereby to act positively on our behalf.[29] The right to property, for example, is largely a negative right, since no one else is obligated to provide us with property, but everyone has an obligation not to use or take our property without permission. The rights mentioned in the Bill of Rights are negative rights insofar as they serve to limit the extent to which government can encroach on the sphere of individual liberty. Some of the rights enumerated in the Universal Declaration of Human Rights, however, are positive rights. Article 25 states, for example:

> Everyone has the right to a standard of living adequate for the health and well-being of himself and of his family, including food, clothing, housing and medical care and necessary social services, and the right to security in the event of unemployment, sickness, disability, widowhood, old age or other lack of livelihood in circumstances beyond his control.

Implementation of these rights requires extensive action by the state to ensure that basic goods, such as food, clothing, and shelter, are available and to provide a range of social services, such as unemployment insurance, workers' compensation, and old age and survivors' benefits. Joel Feinberg notes that, typically, general, or *in rem*, rights are negative, whereas specific, or *in personam*, rights (contract rights, for example) are positive,[30] but the correspondence is very rough, since the positive rights mentioned in the Universal Declaration are mostly *in rem* rights.

Although it is useful for understanding the concept of a right, the distinction between negative and positive rights is not entirely clear, since the underlying distinction between acting and not acting, or between an action and an omission, is often a matter of interpretation.[31] The right of due process, for example, requires employers *not* to fire employees without good reasons and a fair hearing; but it also requires that employers *do* certain things as well, such as notifying employees of the reasons for their dismissal and conducting hearings. Similarly, the rights of employees in matters of occupational health and safety sometimes involve *not* ordering workers to perform their jobs on unsafe equipment or in unsafe areas. But it also involves taking active steps to make the workplace safer by installing guards on equipment or rails on elevated walkways, for example.

The Foundation of Rights

With this examination of the concept of a right now complete, let us turn to the more difficult and controversial matter of the foundation of rights. Are rights fundamental moral categories with their own source of support? Or are rights part of some more general ethical theory, such as utilitarianism or Kantian ethics? We begin by considering the natural rights tradition, which offers a historically influential account of rights separate from these other possible grounds.

NATURAL RIGHTS THEORY

One prominent foundation for rights focuses on what are called *natural* rights or, more recently, *human* rights. Rights of this kind, which are prominent in historical documents such as the Virginia Declaration of Rights, the Declaration of the Rights of Man and of Citizens, and the Universal Declaration of Human Rights, are rights that belong to all persons purely by virtue of their being human.[32] They are characterized by two main features: *universality* and *unconditionality*.

Universality means that they are possessed by *all* persons, without regard for race, sex, nationality, or any specific circumstances of birth or present condition. Unconditionality means that natural or human rights do not depend on any particular practices or institutions in society. The right of U.S. citizens to vote, for example, depends on the specific form of government and the election laws of this country and so cannot be a natural, or human, right. The unconditionality of rights also means that there is nothing we can do to relinquish them or to deprive ourselves or others of them. This feature of natural, or human, rights is what is usually meant by the term "inalienable."[33]

The Theory of John Locke

The idea of natural rights has a long and distinguished history going back to the ancient Greeks, who held that there is a "higher" law which applies to all persons everywhere and serves as a standard for evaluating the laws of states.[34] Both Roman law and the medieval church adopted this idea and developed it into a comprehensive legal theory. Perhaps the most influential natural rights theory, though, is that presented by John Locke (1633–1704) in his famous *Second Treatise of Government* (1690).[35]

Locke, like Thomas Hobbes before him, began with the supposition of a state of nature, which is the condition of human beings in the absence of any government. Their idea is to imagine what life would be like if there were no government, and then to justify the establishment of a political state to remedy the defects of the state of nature. Hobbes's state of nature is devoid of any moral restrictions, with the result that the state of nature is a state of war in which life is "solitary, poor, nasty, brutish, and short." Locke held, on the contrary, that human beings have rights, even in the state of nature, and that the justification for uniting into a state is to protect these rights.

The most important natural right for Locke is the right to property, which he justified in the following way:

> God, who has given the world to men in common, has also given them reason to make use of it to the best advantage of life and convenience. The earth and all that is therein is given to men for the support and comfort of their being. And though all the fruits it naturally produces and beasts it feeds belong to mankind in common. . . ; yet being given for the use of men, there must of necessity be a means to appropriate them some way or other before they can be of any use or at all beneficial to any particular man.

The means by which people are able to take goods out of the common storehouse of nature and make them their own is by the use of labor, which is also a form of property. "Every man has property in his own person," according to Locke, and so "The labor of his body and the work of his hands . . . are properly his."

Locke's theory of natural rights represents a significant advance over the traditional theory in at least two respects. First, it clearly distinguishes between a right as an entitlement and right action, which are run together in Greek and medieval theories. Rights, in particular, are protections against the encroachment of the state in certain spheres of our lives, so that individuals have moral standing as persons independent of their role as citizens. Second, the particular rights listed by Locke, especially the right to property, are precisely those required for the operation of a free market. Thus, Locke's theory is important in the rise of modern capitalism.

Conclusion

Natural rights theory, in its traditional form or the version offered by Locke, fails to provide a wholly satisfactory basis for the full range of rights in our modern society. A number of contemporary philosophers have attempted to resurrect the notion of natural rights with only limited success.[36] This result is no cause for alarm, however, since many philosophers hold that rights are not fundamental but are properly part of a more comprehensive ethical system. So perhaps the foundation we are seeking can be found in one of two major theories; namely, utilitarianism and Kantian ethics.

UTILITY AND RIGHTS

Any attempt to found rights on utility might seem to be doomed from the start, since a standard objection against utilitarianism is that the theory is incapable of accounting for rights. Bentham's hostility to rights is well-known, but his rejection extended only to moral rights as standards separate from a legal system and not to legal rights, for which he thought utilitarianism provided the only possible foundation. In contrast, Mill recognized moral rights as a necessary part of a complete utilitarian theory, and he presented a well-developed account of them. Other utilitarian writers have offered justifications of moral rights as well.[37] Whether utilitarianism is capable of providing a foundation for both moral and legal rights, then, is an open question that needs to be explored and not dismissed out of hand.

The major stumbling block for the utilitarian theory is that rights often serve to protect individual interests against claims based on general welfare. For example, the right of due process entitles employees to a fair hearing *even if more good could be achieved by firing employees without one.* Similarly, the right of free speech protects unpopular and dangerous opinions that society might be better off without. Ronald Dworkin characterizes rights as "trumps" that override otherwise conclusive utilitarian arguments.[38] Just as a trump card in bridge takes precedence over a card in any other suit, so rights take precedence over considerations of welfare. A government is justified in making a street one way, for example, in order to achieve some overall benefit, despite the inconvenience to some motorists, since no rights are involved. But the right of free speech, Dworkin contends, denies authority for a government to limit people's expression merely on the grounds of general welfare.[39] In Dworkin's view, rights are nonutilitarian by definition.

However, a tough-minded utilitarian such as Bentham can respond by simply denying that rights are "trumps." We have a right to due process and free speech insofar as respecting these rights usually has good consequences, but if more utility can be achieved in certain instances by denying them, then these rights no longer provide us with any protection.

Mill's Theory of Rights

Mill's writings suggest a different kind of response, however.[40] The ultimate test of a system of morality, for Mill as for Bentham, is whether it maximizes utility. But the greatest amount of utility is apt to be achieved, in Mill's view, not by *direct* pursuit—that is, by selecting in each instance the action that has the best outcome—but *indirectly*, by developing practices and institutions that lead people to act in socially beneficial ways. In contemporary terms, Mill was a rule- rather than an act-utilitarian. The main reason for the superiority of the indirect pursuit of utility or rule-utilitarianism is that we do not know all the consequences of our actions, so that attempts to achieve the utilitarian optimum directly, by using act-utilitarian reasoning, occasionally backfire.

Rights facilitate the indirect pursuit of utility in special kinds of situations where (1) substantial considerations of human welfare are at stake, and (2) the connection between right action and the consequences for human welfare are difficult to see and we are strongly tempted to act in the wrong way. When these two features are present, it is especially urgent that people not reason as act-utilitarians but, in fact, suppress any inclination to do so. Since claims of rights have a stronger moral force than mere rules of obligation, people are induced by them to disregard utilitarian considerations and act on the basis of rights—thereby achieving the greatest good from the utilitarian point of view.

The only foundation for rights, Mill insists, is utility. In Chapter 5, "On the Connection Between Justice and Utility," he wrote:

> When we call anything a person's right, we mean that he has a valid claim on Society to protect him in the possession of it, either by the force of law, or by that of education and opinion.

And later:

> To have a right, then, is, I conceive, to have something which society ought to defend me in the possession of. If the objector goes on to ask, why it ought? I can give him no other reason than general utility.

But not all rules supported by the utilitarian principle are rules setting forth rights—only those concerned with justice. The difference between justice and other moral obligations is the existence of a right, which enables us to compel a person in the way that "one exacts a debt."

> Justice implies something which it is not only right to do and wrong not to do, but which some individual person can claim from us as his moral right.

Right claims are distinguished, further, by the importance of the conduct they regulate. According to Mill:

> Justice is a name for certain classes of moral rules, which concern the essentials of human well-being more nearly, and are therefore of more absolute obligation, than any other rules for the guidance of life; and the notion which we have found to be of the essence of the idea of justice, that of a right residing in an individual, implies and testifies to this more binding obligation.

He continued:

> It appears from what has been said, that justice is a name for certain moral requirements, which, regarded collectively, stand higher in the scale of social utility, and are therefore of more paramount obligation, than any other; though particular cases may occur in which some other social duty is so important, as to overrule any one of the general maxims of justice.

Mill on Free Speech

Mill's analysis neatly fits the right of free speech. At first glance, it is difficult to understand how a utilitarian could justify unbridled liberty for inflammatory racist diatribes or sordid pornographic works. The principle of utility would seem to support some restrictions on the expression of socially undesirable views. Mill contends, however, in his famous defense of free speech in Chapter 2 of *On Liberty*, that by denying a right to free speech we run the risk of suppressing the truth along with error, and to suppose that we can distinguish between the two is to make an assumption of infallibility. History is full of examples of the persecution of people holding unpopular opinions, including Socrates, Jesus, and the early Christians. Even the expression of false beliefs ought to be allowed, since by public discussion their falsity is all the more clearly revealed. Mill presented his argument in the form of a dilemma:

> . . . [T]he peculiar evil of silencing the expression of an opinion is, that it is robbing the human race; posterity as well as the existing generation; those who dissent from the opinion, still more than those who hold it. If the opinion is right, they are deprived of the opportunity of exchanging error for truth; if wrong, they lose what is almost as great a benefit, the clearer perception and livelier impression of truth, produced by its collision with error.

Also, the absence of a right of free speech creates an atmosphere in which thinkers are afraid to challenge prevailing orthodoxies and to entertain new and unfamiliar ideas. "The greatest harm done," Mill said, "is to those who are not heretics and whose whole mental development is cramped, and their reason cowed, by the fear of heresy."

The justification for a right to free speech, then, is that once we start restricting people's expression, we lose much of the benefit of the open exchange of ideas. The utilitarian optimum would be to permit only beneficial speech, while suppressing speech that is socially undesirable; but this ideal is unattainable. And since the utility of suppressing unpopular views is often immediate and evident, while the utility of permitting them distant and speculative, there is a great temptation to deny freedom of speech. Giving free speech the status of a right, therefore, serves to keep us from being shortsighted and acting precipitously.

Conclusion

Mill's theory provides a plausible utilitarian foundation for rights. In order to justify them, he found it necessary to abandon the direct pursuit of utility in favor of pursuing utility indirectly. That is, Mill held that we should disregard all consequences and consider only rights and the other rules that make up our system of morality.[41] Still, the justification that Mill offers for various rights is very strong, and in subsequent chapters, we will find utilitarian arguments well-represented in the discussion of many different rights. Although the success of these arguments varies, it is certainly wrong to charge that utilitarianism is incapable of accounting for rights.

A KANTIAN FOUNDATION FOR RIGHTS

Kant himself did not give a great deal of attention to rights, but subsequent philosophers in the Kantian tradition have developed a number of justifications based on the concepts of rational agency and respect for persons.

Kant observed that although rights are correlated with duties, they are further distinguished by the fact that we are justified in using coercion to enforce them.[42] He defined a right, accordingly, as a "moral capacity to bind others."[43] This is similar to Mill's description of a right as something that can be exacted from another as a debt. Rights are divided by Kant into innate and acquired. Innate rights are those that belong to everyone "by nature, independently of any juridical act"; that is, any explicit human convention. These are what other writers call natural, or human, rights. Acquired rights, by contrast, depend on some human convention or "juridical act."

Innate rights are founded by Kant on his conception of humans as rational agents; that is, as beings who are capable of acting autonomously. In order to be agents of this kind, it is necessary for us to be free from limitations imposed by the will of others. Complete freedom is impossible, however, since one person can be free only if others are constrained in some way. We are free to speak, for example, only if everyone else is prevented from interfering. Being rational, autonomous agents requires, therefore, that we be justified in placing restrictions on what others can do, which is to say that we have rights.

Our rights must be in accord with universal law, however. That is, we have rights that justify our limiting the freedom of others only to the extent that others have these same rights to limit us. (This is the requirement of universality contained in the first formulation of the categorical imperative.) It follows that there is only one fundamental innate right, according to Kant, and that is the right to be free from the constraint of the will of others insofar as this is compatible with a similar freedom for all. From this fundamental right follow several subsidiary rights, including the right to equal treatment, equality of opportunity, and the ownership of property.

Some contemporary philosophers have also attempted to found rights on the concept of rational agency, or autonomy.[44] Others have proceeded from the Kantian concepts of dignity and respect for persons. The following passage sketches an argument of this kind:

> Rights, we are suggesting, are fundamental moral commodities because they enable us to stand up on our own two feet, "to look others in the eye, and to feel in some fundamental way the equal of anyone. To think of oneself as the holder of rights is not to be unduly but properly proud, to have that minimal self-respect that is necessary to be worthy of the love and esteem of others." Conversely, to lack the concept of oneself as a rights bearer is to be bereft of a significant element of human dignity. Without such a concept, we could not view ourselves as beings entitled to be treated as not simply means but ends as well.[45]

The writers of this passage conclude, "In our view, human or natural rights are those rights that must be acknowledged if human dignity, self-respect, and respect for persons as ends in themselves are to be secure."[46]

Difficulties with the Kantian Foundation

One criticism of the Kantian foundation for rights is that the fundamental right it supports—namely, the right to freedom—is excessively narrow.[47] In particular, Kant argues primarily for negative rights to noninterference and not for positive rights to welfare. Thus, many of the rights in the Universal Declaration of Human Rights—to education, health care, adequate nutrition, housing, and the like—are not supportable in Kant's theory.

A further difficulty is that Kantian theory provides few resources for determining what rights we do have. Without a doubt, slavery and torture are wrong because they violate the minimal conditions for rational action or dignity and respect. But the minimal conditions in other instances are less clear. Exactly how much freedom and well-being must we have to be rational, or autonomous, agents? Kantian rights theorists are often vague on whether rights are minimal conditions for rational action or dignity and respect, or whether they are maximal conditions.

If they are minimal conditions, then their theories run the risk of justifying too little. But if rights are maximal conditions, then these theorists are in danger of justifying too much, since full autonomy and human dignity are ideals that go beyond the obligations that can reasonably be imposed on people.

Conclusion

This concludes our discussion of the two major theories of ethics considered in this book, along with the foundation they provide for rights. As theories about the ultimate justification of our moral judgments (that is, about what makes right actions right), they are very different. To the extent that they suggest patterns of moral reasoning, however, they are not wholly incompatible. For example, a utilitarian can also accept the principle of universalizability and even combine it with the principle of utility to form a hybrid ethical system.[48] Utilitarians no less than Kantians consider the principle of respect for persons and the concepts of dignity and autonomy as essential elements of morality, although they offer different reasons for their importance.

Ultimately, the success of any rights theory depends on the arguments it enables us to construct for specific rights. Both utilitarianism and Kant's ethics provide powerful justifications for this important ethical concept. In the course of this book, many arguments about the rights of employees, consumers, the public, and others are developed, using both theories as grounds. Thus, we will have ample opportunity to evaluate both the utilitarian and Kantian foundations for rights. Our treatment of ethical theory would not be complete, however, without a consideration of one remaining concept—namely, justice—which is the subject of the next chapter.

NOTES

1. W. D. Ross, *The Right and the Good* (Oxford: Oxford University Press, 1930), 21.
2. G. E. Moore, *Ethics* (Oxford: Oxford University Press, 1912), 77–80.
3. For a thorough examination of the distinction, see H. J. McCloskey, "Ross and the Concept of Prima Facie Duty," *Australasian Journal of Philosophy*, 41 (1964), 336–45.
4. For a brief survey of eighteenth-century intuitionism, see W. D. Hudson, *Ethical Intuitionism* (New York: St. Martin's Press, 1967). A classic study of intuitionism is contained in Henry Sidgwick, *The Methods of Ethics*, 7th ed. (Chicago: University of Chicago Press, 1907).
5. For a brief account of twentieth-century intuitionism, see Mary Warnock, *Ethics since 1900*, 3rd ed. (Oxford: Oxford University Press, 1978), chap. 2.
6. See, for example, W. D. Hudson, *Modern Moral Philosophy* (Garden City, NY:

Anchor Books, 1970), 100–105. A more detailed criticism of intuitionism is presented in J. KEMP, *Reason, Action and Morality* (London: Routledge and Kegan Paul, 1964), chap. 10.

7. As might be expected, there is considerable controversy over the exact interpretation of Kant's principle. A very good starting point for those unfamiliar with the *Foundations* is FRED FELDMAN, *Introductory Ethics* (Englewood Cliffs, NJ: Prentice Hall, 1978), 97–134. Reprinted in CHRISTINA HOFF SOMMERS, ed. *Right and Wrong: Basic Readings in Ethics* (San Diego: Harcourt Brace Jovanovich, 1986), 18–43. A helpful commentary on the *Foundations* is ROBERT PAUL WOLFF, *The Autonomy of Reason* (New York: Harper & Row, 1973). For a full-length study of the categorical imperative, see ONORA NELL, *Acting on Principle: An Essay on Kantian Ethics* (New York: Columbia University Press, 1975).

8. For objections to Kant's examples, see JONATHAN HARRISON, "Kant's Examples of the First Formulation of the Categorical Imperative," *The Philosophical Quarterly*, 7 (1957), 50–62. A response is J. KEMP, "Kant's Examples of the Categorical Imperative," *The Philosophical Quarterly*, 8 (1958), 63–71; and HARRISON replies in "The Categorical Imperative," *The Philosophical Quarterly*, 8 (1958), 360–64. All three articles are reprinted in ROBERT PAUL WOLFF, ed. *Kant: A Collection of Critical Essays* (Garden City, NY: Anchor Books, 1967).

9. This is the position taken by KEMP in "Kant's Examples of the Categorical Imperative." See also KEMP, *Reason, Action and Morality*, 75–91.

10. For a further development of the logical basis for the principle of universalizability, see R. M. HARE, *Freedom and Reason* (Oxford: Oxford University Press, 1963), chap. 2; and *Moral Thinking: Its Levels, Method and Point* (Oxford: Oxford University Press, 1981), chap. 6. This principle is also called the generalization principle and is closely related to the principle of utilitarian generalization. See MARCUS G. SINGER, *Generalization in Ethics* (New York: Knopf, 1961), chap. 2.

11. For a discussion of the logical force of this question, see COLIN STRANG, "What If Everyone Did That?" *Durham University Journal*, 53 (1960), 5–10. This article is widely reprinted. One source is SOMMERS, *Right and Wrong*, 51–62.

12. For Singer, this is the generalization argument, which utilizes the generalization principle but also requires the support of a utilitarian principle that he calls the principle of consequences. See SINGER, *Generalization in Ethics*, chap. 4.

13. An ambitious attempt to develop the principle of universalizability into a complete ethical theory is ALAN GEWIRTH, *Reason and Morality* (Chicago: University of Chicago Press, 1978).

14. DOUGLAS MCGREGOR, *The Human Side of Enterprise* (New York: McGraw-Hill, 1960).

15. WILLIAM G. OUCHI, *Theory Z: How American Business Can Meet the Japanese Challenge* (Reading, MA: Addison-Wesley, 1981).

16. The material for this case is taken from DAVID L. NYE, "Fire at Will—Careful, Now, Careful," *Across the Board*, 19 (November 1982), 37–40.

17. The full title is "The ILO Convention concerning Termination of Employ-

ment at the Initiative of the Employer." Reprinted in *International Labour Conference, Provisional Record of Sixty-Eighth Session*, No. 30A (June 21, 1982).

18. Government employees, but not those in the private sector, are protected not only by substantially more legislation but also by the due process clause of the Fifth Amendment.

19. This method of explaining rights is derived from JOEL FEINBERG, "The Nature and Value of Rights," *The Journal of Value Inquiry*, 4 (1970), 243–57. Reprinted in JOEL FEINBERG, *Rights, Justice, and the Bounds of Liberty* (Princeton: Princeton University Press, 1980), 143–55, and in DAVID LYONS, ed., *Rights* (Belmont, CA: Wadsworth, 1979), 78–91.

20. This term is used in H. J. MCCLOSKEY, "Rights," *The Philosophical Quarterly*, 15 (1965), 115–27, and also in RICHARD A. WASSERSTROM, "Rights, Human Rights, and Racial Discrimination," *The Journal of Philosophy*, 61 (1964), 628–41. This latter article is reprinted in LYONS, *Rights*, 46–57. For a useful survey of different accounts, see REX MARTIN and JAMES W. NICKEL, "Recent Work on the Concept of Rights," *American Philosophical Quarterly*, 17 (1980), 165–80.

21. The correlativity thesis goes back at least as far as Bentham. See DAVID LYONS, "Rights, Claimants, and Beneficiaries, *American Philosophical Quarterly*, 6 (1969), 173–85, reprinted in LYONS, *Rights*, 58–77; and H.L.A. HART, "Bentham on Legal Rights," in A.W.B. SIMPSON, ed., *Oxford Essays in Jurisprudence* (Oxford: Oxford University Press, 1973), 171–203, reprinted in LYONS, *Rights* 125–48, and (under the title "Legal Rights") in H.L.A. HART, *Essays on Bentham: Jurisprudence and Political Theory* (Oxford: Oxford University Press, 1982), 162–93. It is mentioned in JOHN AUSTIN'S *The Province of Jurisprudence Determined* (1832). Early discussions of the thesis are F. H. BRADLEY, *Ethical Studies*, 2nd ed. (Oxford: Oxford University Press, 1927), 207–13; and ROSS, *The Right and the Good*, 48–56. More recent statements are S. I. BENN and R. S. PETERS, *Social Principles and the Democratic State* (London: George Allen & Unwin, 1959), 101–4; and RICHARD B. BRANDT, *Ethical Theory* (Englewood Cliffs, NJ: Prentice Hall, 1959), 434–41. Two good critical examinations are JOEL FEINBERG, "Duties, Rights, and Claims," *American Philosophical Quarterly*, 3 (1966), 137–44, reprinted in FEINBERG, *Rights, Justice, and the Bounds of Liberty*, 130–55; and DAVID LYONS, "The Correlativity of Rights and Duties," *Noûs*, 4 (1970), 45–55. Lyon's article is criticized in DAVID BRAYBROOKE, "The Firm But Untidy Correlativity of Rights and Obligations," *Canadian Journal of Philosophy*, 1 (1972), 351–63; and MARCUS G. SINGER, "The Basis of Rights and Duties," *Philosophical Studies*, 23 (1972), 48–57. See also ALAN R. WHITE, *Rights* (Oxford: Oxford University Press, 1984), chap. 5.

22. This way of explaining the distinction is due to BRANDT, *Ethical Theory*, 434.

23. WESLEY NEWCOMB HOHFELD, *Fundamental Legal Conceptions* (New Haven: Yale University Press, 1923). For a clear exposition, see ARTHUR L. CORBIN, "Legal Analysis and Terminology," *Yale Law Journal*, 29 (1919), 163–73.

24. LYONS, "The Correlativity of Rights and Duties."

25. This is maintained by CARL WELLMAN, "A New Conception of Human Rights," in E. KAMENKA and A.E.S. TAY, eds., *Human Rights* (New York: St. Martin's Press, 1978), 48–58.

26. JOEL FEINBERG, "The Rights of Animals and Unborn Generations," in *Justice, Rights, and the Bounds of Liberty*, 159.

27. See MCCLOSKEY, "Rights," 118–19.

28. Feinberg avoids this objection by countering that general, or *in rem*, rights which are only claims *to* but not claims *on* are "manifesto" rights, that is, rights that are put forth as desirable social goals but are not sufficiently accepted at the present time to generate specific rights. FEINBERG, "The Nature and Value of Rights," in *Rights, Justice, and the Bounds of Liberty*, 153.

29. Closely related is a distinction between negative and positive liberty. A poor man is free (in a negative sense) to buy a loaf of bread, for example, as long as no one stands in his way, but he is not free (in a positive sense) unless he has the means to buy the bread. Compare these two senses in the case of "fee for service" medical care, which secures free *choice*, and socialized medicine, which provides free *access*. Which system of medical care is more "free"? The classic discussion of this distinction is ISAIAH BERLIN, "Two Concepts of Liberty," in *Four Essays on Liberty* (Oxford: Oxford University Press, 1969), 118–72.

30. JOEL FEINBERG, *Social Philosophy* (Englewood Cliffs, NJ: Prentice Hall, 1973), 59.

31. See JUDITH LICHTENBERG, "The Moral Equivalence of Action and Omission," *Canadian Journal of Philosophy*, supp. vol. 8 (1982), 19–36; and HENRY SHUE, *Basic Rights: Subsistence, Affluence, and U.S. Foreign Policy* (Princeton: Princeton University Press, 1980), 37–40.

32. Among the many works describing natural or human rights are: MAURICE CRANSTON, *What Are Human Rights?* (New York: Basic Books, 1963); B. MAYO, "What Are Human Rights?" in D. D. RAPHAEL, ed., *Political Theory and the Rights of Man* (Bloomington: Indiana University Press, 1967), 68–80; D. D. RAPHAEL, "Human Rights, Old and New," in RAPHAEL, *Political Theory and the Rights of Man*, 54–67; MAURICE CRANSTON, "Human Rights, Real and Supposed," in RAPHAEL, *Political Theory and the Rights of Man*, 43–53; FEINBERG, *Social Philosophy*, 84–97; and A. I. MELDEN, *Rights and Persons* (Berkeley and Los Angeles: University of California Press, 1977), 166–69.

33. See STUART M. BROWN, Jr., "Inalienable Rights," *The Philosophical Review*, 64 (1955), 192–211; and B. A. RICHARDS, "Inalienable Rights: Recent Criticism and Old Doctrine," *Philosophy and Phenomenological Research*, 29 (1969), 391–404.

34. A good survey of the early history of natural rights is RICHARD TUCK, *Natural Rights Theories: Their Origin and Development* (Cambridge: Cambridge University Press, 1979).

35. Locke's theory of natural rights is the subject of great controversy. Two articles that provide a good introduction are W. VON LEYDEN, "John Locke and Natural Law," *Philosophy*, 21 (1956), 23–35; and WILLIAM J. WAINWRIGHT, "Natural Rights," *American Philosophical Quarterly*, 4 (1967), 79–84. The thesis that Locke was not a natural rights theorist is developed in LEO STRAUSS, *Natural Right and History* (Chicago: University of Chicago Press, 1953). One response is CHARLES H. MONSON, JR., "Locke and His Interpreters," *Political Studies*, 6 (1958), 120–35.

36. For a survey, see TIBOR R. MACHAN, "Some Recent Work in Human Rights Theory," *American Philosophical Quarterly*, 17 (1980), 103–15. Two important

articles are MARGARET MACDONALD, "Natural Rights," *Proceedings of the Aristotelian Society* 47 (1947–1948), reprinted in A. I. MELDEN, ed., *Human Rights* (Belmont, CA: Wadsworth, 1970), 40–60; and H.L.A. HART, "Are There Any Natural Rights?" *The Philosophical Review*, 64 (1955), 175–91, also reprinted in MELDEN, *Human Rights*, 61–75.

37. One notable work is L. W. SUMNER, *The Moral Foundation of Rights* (Oxford: Oxford University Press, 1987).

38. RONALD DWORKIN, *Taking Rights Seriously* (Cambridge: Harvard University Press, 1978). See also RONALD DWORKIN, "Rights as Trumps," in JEREMY WALDRON, ed., *Theories of Rights* (Oxford: Oxford University Press, 1984), 153–81. This article is adapted from RONALD DWORKIN, "Is There a Right to Pornography?" *Oxford Journal of Legal Studies*, 1 (1981), 177–212.

39. DWORKIN, *Taking Rights Seriously*, 191.

40. The account that follows is one developed by DAVID LYONS in several articles, most notably "Human Rights and the General Welfare," *Philosophy and Public Affairs*, 6 (1977), 113–29; but see also "Mill's Theory of Morality," *Noûs*, 10 (1976), 101–20; "Mill's Theory of Justice," in A. I. GOLDMAN and J. KIM, eds., *Values and Morals: Essays in Honor of William Frankena, Charles Stevenson, and Richard Brandt* (Dordrecht: Reidel, 1978), 1–20; and "Benevolence and Justice in Mill," in HARLAN B. MILLER and WILLIAM H. WILLIAMS, eds., *The Limits of Utilitarianism* (Minneapolis: University of Minnesota Press, 1982), 42–70. Lyons is doubtful, however, of the account presented in these articles. See "Utility and Rights" in J. ROLAND PENNOCK and JOHN W. CHAPMAN, eds., *Ethics, Economics and the Law,* (New York: New York University Press, 1982), 107–38, reprinted in WALDRON, *Theories of Rights*, 110–36. Criticism of Lyons is contained in ALAN GEWIRTH, "Can Utilitarianism Justify Any Moral Rights?" in PENNOCK and CHAPMAN, *Ethics, Economics and the Law*, 158–93, reprinted in GEWIRTH, *Human Rights* (Chicago: University of Chicago Press, 1982), 143–62.

41. LYONS, "Utility and Rights," 134.

42. An examination of Kant's account of rights, on which the following discussion is largely based, is BRUCE AUNE, *Kant's Theory of Morals* (Princeton: Princeton University Press, 1979), 141–52.

43. IMMANUEL KANT, *The Metaphysical Elements of Justice: Part I of the Metaphysics of Morals*, trans. JOHN LADD (Indianapolis: Bobbs-Merrill, 1965), 37.

44. The fullest account is GEWIRTH, *Reason and Morality*, discussed below. See also GEWIRTH, "The Basis and Content of Human Rights," in J. ROLAND PENNOCK and JOHN W. CHAPMAN, eds., *Human Rights* (New York: New York University Press, 1981), 119–47, reprinted in GEWIRTH, *Human Rights*, 41–67; and DAVID A. J. RICHARDS, "Rights and Autonomy," *Ethics*, 92 (1981), 3–20.

45. NORMAN E. BOWIE and ROBERT L. SIMON, *The Individual and the Political Order: An Introduction to Social and Political Philosophy*, 1st ed. (Englewood Cliffs, NJ: Prentice Hall, 1977), 78. The quoted passage is from FEINBERG, "The Nature and Value of Rights," in *Rights Justice, and the Bounds of Liberty*, 151.

46. BOWIE and SIMON, *The Individual and the Political Order*, 78.

47. See AUNE, *Kant's Theory of Morals*, 151.

48. This is proposed by R. M. HARE in *Moral Thinking*.

CHAPTER FOUR

Justice and the Market System

Justice, like rights, is an important moral concept with a wide range of applications. We use it to evaluate not only the actions of individuals but also social, legal, political, and economic practices and institutions. Although the word *just* is sometimes used interchangeably with *right* and *good,* it generally has a more restricted meaning that is closer to *fair.* Questions of justice often arise when there are conflicting interests. If there is a shortage of organ donors, for example, we ask, what is a just, or fair, way of deciding who gets a transplant? And if there is a burden, such as taxes, we want to make sure that everyone bears a fair share. Justice is also concerned with the righting of wrongs. It requires, for example, that a criminal be punished for a crime and that the punishment fit the crime by being neither too lenient nor too severe. To treat people justly is to give them what they deserve, which is sometimes the opposite of generosity and compassion. Indeed, we often speak of tempering justice with mercy.

The concept of justice is relevant to business ethics primarily when a wrong has been done and we want to know what can be done to make amends. Justice requires that something be done to compensate the victims of discrimination, for example. But whether affirmative action programs are an appropriate response or merely discrimination in reverse is a difficult question that tests our understanding of the nature of justice. Justice is also at the center of controversies concerning the obligations of businesses in matters of product safety and industrial accidents. What is a just resolution of the claims of workers whose lives have been destroyed by exposure to asbestos, for example? What does Exxon owe for the environmental damage caused by the massive oil spill from the tanker *Valdez*? And what does Union Carbide owe for the disastrous leak of deadly gas at the company's plant in Bhopal, India, that killed thousands of sleeping residents? Since justice is also an important concept in evaluating institutions and various forms of social organization, we can also ask about the justice of the economic system in which business activity takes place.

In succeeding sections, four theories of justice are examined; namely, Aristotle's principle of proportionate equality, the utilitarian theory, and the prominent contemporary theories of John Rawls and Robert Nozick. One important kind of justice is economic justice, and a system of free markets is both criticized and defended on grounds of justice. This chapter includes, therefore, a discussion of the justification of the market system.

ARISTOTLE'S ANALYSIS OF JUSTICE

The first thorough analysis of the concept of justice is still the best. Aristotle observed in Book V of the *Nicomachean Ethics* that the word *justice* has a double meaning. In one sense it applies to the whole of virtue. A just or morally upright person is one who always does what is morally right and obeys the law. Justice in this sense is called *universal justice* by Aristotle. The other sense of justice, which he called *particular justice,* is concerned with virtue in specific situations. More precisely, particular justice consists in taking only a proper share of some good. An unjust person is thus a grasping person who takes too much wealth, honor, or other benefit that society offers, or a shirker who refuses to bear a fair share of some burden. Aristotle divided particular justice into:

1. **Distributive justice,** which deals with the distribution of benefits and burdens.
2. **Compensatory justice,** which is a matter of compensating persons for wrongs done to them.
3. **Retributive justice,** which involves the punishment of wrongdoers.

Both compensatory and retributive justice are concerned with correcting wrongs. Generally, compensating the victims is the just way of correcting wrongs in private dealings, such as losses resulting from accidents and the failure to fulfill contracts, whereas retribution—that is, punishment—is the just response to criminal acts, such as assault or theft.[1]

Questions about distributive justice arise mostly in the evaluation of our social, political, and economic institutions, where the benefits and burdens of engaging in cooperative activities must be spread over a group. In some instances, a just distribution is one in which each person shares equally; but in others, unequal sharing is just if the inequality is in accord with some principle of distribution. Thus, in a graduated income tax system, ability to pay and not equal shares is the principle for distributing the burden. Generally, distributive justice is *comparative*, in that it considers not the absolute amount of benefits and burdens of each person but each person's amount relative to that of others.[2] Whether income is justly distributed, for example, cannot be determined by looking only at the income of one person but requires us, in addition, to compare the income of all people in a society.

The rationale of compensatory justice is that an accident caused by negligence, for example, upsets an initial moral equilibrium by making a person worse off in some way. By paying compensation, however, the condition of the victim can be returned to what it was before the accident, thereby restoring the moral equilibrium. Similarly, a person who commits a crime upsets a moral equilibrium by making someone else worse off. The restoration of the moral equilibrium in cases of this kind is achieved by a punishment that "fits the crime." Both compensatory and retributive justice are *noncomparative*. The amount of compensation owed to the victim of an accident or the punishment due a criminal is determined by the features of each case and not by a comparison with other cases. (Unequal punishment of people who commit the same crime is prima facie evidence of unjust sentencing, but the injustice would not be removed merely by giving everyone the same excessive punishment, for example.)

Just Procedures and Just Outcomes

A useful distinction not discussed by Aristotle is that between just *procedures* and just *outcomes*.[3] In cases of distributive justice, we can distinguish between the procedures used to distribute goods and the outcome of those procedures; that is, the actual distribution achieved. A similar distinction can be made between the procedures for conducting trials, for example, and the outcomes of trials. If we know what outcomes are just in certain kinds of situations, then just procedures are those that produce or are likely to produce just outcomes. Thus, an effective method for dividing a cake among a group consists of allowing one person to cut it into the appropriate number of slices with the stipulation that that person take the last piece. Assuming that an equal division of the cake is just, a just distribution will be achieved, since cutting the cake into equal slices is the only way the person with the knife is assured of getting at least as much cake as anyone else. Similarly, just outcomes in criminal trials are those in which the guilty are convicted and the innocent are set free. The complex procedures for trials are those that generally serve to produce those results.

John Rawls further distinguishes perfect and imperfect procedural justice. Perfect procedural justice always produces a just outcome, whereas imperfect procedural justice does so only to some extent. The method of having the person who slices the cake take the last piece is an example of the former (assuming, of course, a steady hand), and trial by jury is an example of the latter.[4] In some situations, which John Rawls calls "pure procedural justice," there is no independent criterion of a just outcome; a just outcome is, instead, whatever results from following a given procedure.[5] Gambling provides a good example. As long as the rules of wagering are strictly observed, any distribution of a betting pool that results is just. Sometimes there are good reasons to follow proven procedures even when they are imperfect and fail occasionally. Trial by jury, for example, is not a perfect procedure, but any alternative is worse. So unless we are willing to accept the verdicts of juries—even when the outcome is the conviction of an innocent person or the exoneration of a guilty one—the result is likely to be even more unjust outcomes.

Aristotle on Distributive Justice

Aristotle observed in the *Politics* that, "All men think justice to be a sort of equality," but what sort of equality justice is remains a source of controversy to the present day.[6] The extreme egalitarian position that everyone should be treated exactly alike has found few advocates, and most who call themselves egalitarians are concerned only to deny that certain differences ought to be taken into account.[7] A more moderate egalitarianism contends that we ought to treat like cases alike. That is, any difference in the treatment of like cases requires a moral justification.

Aristotle expressed the idea of treating like cases alike in an arithmetical equation that represents justice as an equality of ratios.[8] Let us suppose that two people, A and B, each receive some share of a good, P. Any difference in their relative shares must be justified by some relevant difference, Q. Thus, a difference in pay, P, is justified if there is a difference in some other factor, Q, that justifies the difference in P—such as the fact that one person worked more hours or was more productive. Aristotle added the further condition that the difference in each person's share of the good must be *proportional* to the difference in their share of the relevant difference. If one person worked twice as many hours as another, then the pay should be exactly twice as much—no more and no less. Aristotle's principle of distributive justice can be stated in the following manner.[9]

$$\frac{\text{A'S SHARE OF P}}{\text{B'S SHARE OF P}} = \frac{\text{A'S SHARE OF Q}}{\text{B'S SHARE OF Q}}$$

This account of Aristotle's principle of distributive justice is obviously not complete until the content of both P and Q are fully specified. What are the goods in question? What features justify different shares of these goods? Among the goods distributed in any society are material goods—such as food, clothing, and housing—and income and wealth, which enable the people to purchase material goods. There are many nonmaterial goods, including economic power, participation in the political process, and access to the courts, which are also distributed in some manner. Finally, Aristotle counted honor as a good, thereby recognizing that society distributes status and other intangibles. This multiplicity of goods has led philosophers to speak of many different kinds of justice, such as economic justice, legal justice, political justice, and social justice. It is unclear whether Aristotle's principle is intended to be an account of all these or only some.

Justifying Features

Among the many different justifying features that have been proposed are ability, effort, accomplishment, contribution, and need.[10] In setting wages, for example, an employer might award higher pay to workers who have greater training and experience or greater talent (*ability*); to workers who apply themselves more diligently, perhaps overcoming obstacles or making great sacrifices (*effort*); to workers who have produced more or performed notable feats (*accomplishment*) or who provide more valued services (*contribution*); or, finally, to workers who have large families to support or who, for other reasons, have greater *need*.

Each of these justifying features has some merits and some defects. Ability alone is not a suitable criterion since it rewards workers with great ability who exert little effort and consequently do not accomplish much. The criterion of effort rewards people with less ability who must try harder to make the same contribution. We also use different justifying features in different contexts. Thus, ability is an appropriate criterion for selecting budding tennis players for a training program, whereas invitations to a tournament ought to be based on accomplishment. The socialist slogan, From each according to his abilities, to each according to his needs holds that different criteria are relevant to determining what a person ought to contribute to society and what a person ought to receive in return. Finally, more than one criterion may be relevant to a single decision. College scholarships, for example, are often awarded on the basis of a combination of ability, effort, achievement, contribution, and need. Disagreements are possible, therefore, over the relevant justifying feature and, if there is more than one, their relative weight.

In a competitive labor market, wages are determined by none of the features listed above but by supply and demand. Is Aristotle's principle applicable to the determination of wages in a capitalist economy? Some argue that it is not. The distribution of income, these philosophers contend, is an outcome of a system of pure procedural justice. That is, the economy is a kind of game played according to certain rules, and as long as the rules are followed, any distribution of economic goods that results is just. (This is roughly the view of Robert Nozick, which is examined later in this chapter.) Another answer, however, is that the distribution of income by means of a competitive labor market is an example of imperfect procedural justice. Under capitalism, wages ought to be distributed in proportion to contribution, which is to say, productivity, and a competitive labor market is a procedure that achieves this outcome, albeit imperfectly.

A final difficulty is that the arithmetical form of Aristotle's principle suggests more precision than is possible. If Q is quantifiable (the number of hours worked, for example), then it is possible to say that A worked twice as many hours as B and hence ought to be paid twice as much. There is no reason, however, for insisting on strict ratios. A pay scale with higher wages for overtime might result in A's being paid *more* than twice as much; and a system in which workers are paid a bonus for exceeding a production quota might result in A's being paid more than B but *less* than twice as much. Some relevant differences are not quantifiable in ways that permit meaningful ratios. Education, for example, is a legitimate criterion for evaluating job applicants, and, other things being equal, an employer is justified in selecting an applicant with a 4.0 average over one with an average of 2.0. It does not follow, however, that the 4.0 applicant is twice as able and ought to be paid twice as much. And many relevant differences are simply incapable of being quantified and hence cannot be expressed in ratios at all. On what scale, for example, can we compute people's needs?

Conclusion

Despite these difficulties, Aristotle's principle of distributive justice contains much of value. The main shortcoming of the theory is that it is a purely *formal* principle; that is, the statement of the principle contains variables with no specified content. Aristotle's principle lays down a logical requirement of consistency and thus provides a necessary condition for distributive justice but not a sufficient condition. A sufficient condition could be provided only by a principle that fully specifies, among other things, the relevant features that justify different treatment. The value of the principle lies chiefly in its insistence that different treatment be justified by citing relevant differences and that difference in treatment be in proportion to these differences.

UTILITY AND JUSTICE

Justice, along with rights, is commonly regarded as a stumbling block for utilitarianism.[11] One problem that distributive justice poses for utilitarianism has already been discussed. It is that the principle of utility seems to favor any redistribution that increases the total amount of utility, without regard for how it is distributed. Thus, in the following three distribution schemes, I and II are morally indistinguishable, as judged by the total amount of utility; and III is preferable to both I and II, despite the apparent inequality.

I		II		III	
A	10	A	14	A	16
B	10	B	8	B	9
C	10	C	8	C	7
	30		30		32

We have seen, however, that justice does not require complete equality. In Aristotle's principle of justice, certain departures from I are justified *if* there are morally relevant differences between A, B, and C. So it might be that II and III are more just than I and that III is the most just distribution of all. This would be the case if A were more talented and hard-working, for example, and hence deserved more. The possibility of justified inequalities provides no defense for utilitarianism, however, because it might also be the case that there are no relevant differences between A, B, and C, so that the inequality is unjustified.

The problem that justice poses for utilitarianism, then, is not merely that the theory seems to place no value on equality but that it seems to make no allowance for justified claims for unequal treatment. According to Nicholas Rescher:

> ... [T]he *decisive and fatal* objection to any straightforward adoption of the classical principle of utility as a rule of distribution is this: it leaves wholly out of account that essential reference to claims, merit, and desert without which no theory of distributive justice fulfills the requisite for serious consideration.[12]

Bentham's Theory of Justice

Utilitarians generally respond that any conflict between utility and justice is only apparent and that utilitarianism, properly understood, is capable of providing a wholly adequate foundation for our judgments about what is just and what is unjust.[13] One position taken by Bentham and his followers consists of the assertion that the principle of utility, consistently applied, results in outcomes that fit with our ordinary views about justice. A society with the greatest amount of utility, in other words, is also a just society, as justice is commonly understood.[14] The concepts of equality and desert, however, are not part of the meaning of utility; rather, the connection between them is purely a matter of fact, and if utility should ever conflict with equality or desert, the latter would have to give way. Utilitarians such as Bentham believe that conflicts of this kind rarely if ever occur, though.[15]

The Arguments for Convergence

The main argument used by utilitarians to account for the convergence of utility and justice is that a system of maximizing utility has a tendency toward equality in distribution because of the phenomenon of *diminishing marginal utility*.[16] A basic tenet of economics is that the amount utility we receive from a good decreases as the amount of the good increases. The first cookie in a box, for example, gives us much pleasure, especially if we are hungry; the second cookie, less so; and by the time we reach the last cookie, we are likely to be so full that it gives us no pleasure at all. The marginal utility of income is similar. We use the first few dollars we earn to satisfy our most basic needs and our strongest desires, with a great increase in utility. Succeeding dollars satisfy lesser felt needs and more ephemeral desires, and so they bring us correspondingly less utility. Each additional (marginal) dollar of a person's income, therefore, "buys" less utility than the one before it. A utilitarian decision maker with a dollar to give away would thus produce a greater amount of utility by giving it to a poor person than a rich one. Similarly, practices and institutions that redistribute wealth from the rich to the poor, thereby moving a society toward greater equality, at the same time increase utility.

Although this argument is plausible, it has proven difficult in practice to verify the effect of income redistribution on the amount of utility—mainly because of the problem of measurement. Some economists argue that the marginal utility of income increases and decreases in stages, so that a person coming into great wealth might suddenly have a burning desire for a yacht and French Impressionist paintings, which he did not have before.[17] Further, some inequality increases utility. A stock argument for putting money in the hands of the wealthy is that they will put it to more productive use than the poor and thereby increase the wealth of the whole society. The tendency of utilitarianism toward equality is offset, therefore, by a countertendency toward inequality, and the optimal level of equality (or inequality) is not easily determined. An additional complication is that diminishing marginal utility constitutes a powerful argument for satisfying the basic needs of all members of society, but it is less persuasive as an argument for equality once everyone attains a certain minimal level of welfare—that is, the wealthier a society becomes, the greater the inequality permitted by the principle of utility (as long as the basic needs of everyone are met).

A second argument for the convergence of utility and justice is that a system for maximizing utility also tends to reward people according to desert. The reason why it is considered just to distribute goods in proportion to ability, effort, accomplishment, or contribution is that doing so encourages people to develop their abilities, exert greater effort, accomplish more, and perform more valued services—all of which promote the welfare of society. We do not reward all abilities or efforts, for example, but only those that contribute to human well-being, and we do the same with accomplishments and contributions. The social benefit of these criteria can be obtained, moreover, only in a stable social order in which people are treated according to their deserts *consistently*. A company that discriminates against women, for example, is unlikely to motivate female employees to develop their abilities and put forth their best efforts; it is also not likely to attract the best female applicants. A utilitarian objection to discrimination of all kinds, then, is that it reduces the overall level of utility.

Mill's Theory of Justice

Mill's position on the connection between justice and utility is, at first glance, different from that of Bentham. Although Bentham held that the standards of equality and desert are conceptually distinct from the utilitarian principle, Mill contended that they are involved "in the very meaning of Utility." This position is much less plausible than Bentham's, and Mill's arguments for it are marred by confusions.

One argument that can be quickly dismissed is the following:

> That principle [the principle of utility] is a mere form of words without rational signification, unless one person's happiness. . . is counted for exactly as much as another's. Those conditions being supplied, Bentham's dictum, "everybody to count for one, nobody for more than one," might be written under the principle of utility as an explanatory commentary.

What Mill apparently failed to see is that considering each person's happiness equally in the calculation of utility is very different from securing for each person an equal share of happiness.[18] A utilitarian assessment of slavery "counts" the amount of pleasure and pain to the slave even as the slave is consigned to a life without happiness.

A second argument presented by Mill can be sketched as follows. One sense of equality, which is expressed in Aristotle's principle of justice, is a presumptive right of equal treatment that requires any inequalities in treatment to be justified. In Mill's words, "All persons are deemed to have a *right* to equality of treatment, except when some recognised social expediency requires the reverse." Mill characterized impartiality, which is a part of justice closely related to equality, as an obligation not to be swayed by irrelevant considerations in treating others. And this obligation, in turn, is part of "the more general obligation of giving to every one his right." Mill's argument, in short, is that justice includes treating people according to their rights unless utility dictates otherwise, and that this obligation of justice is implicit in the meaning of the utilitarian principle.

Mill further supported his argument by noting that equality is incapable of providing a complete account of justice and must be supplemented by another criterion of just action, such as utility. On the question of whether justice requires paying workers on the basis of effort or productivity, there are two conflicting considerations. From the point of view of what individuals deserve, wages ought to be determined by effort, since productivity is often due to accidents of birth over which an individual has little control. Productivity is the appropriate criterion, however, from the point of view of society, which is paying for the labor of individuals. The principle of treating workers equally is compatible with either criterion and so cannot be used to decide between them; only another principle of justice can settle the question.[19]

Mill thus held that equality is a part of the meaning of utility—all the while contending that it can be overridden by considerations of utility. "Each person maintains," Mill wrote, "that equality is a dictate of justice, except where he thinks that expediency requires inequality." This position is not contradictory, as some have argued.[20] But it does make equality superfluous. The meaning of, Treat people equally except where utility requires unequal treatment can be fully expressed by the simple, Treat people as utility requires.

Conclusion

Mill did not succeed, then, in showing that equality and desert are involved in "the very meaning of Utility," and his position, in the end, is little different from Bentham's. The arguments for the convergence of justice and utility have some plausibility, however, and so it may be possible for utilitarianism to provide a foundation for justice after all, despite the skepticism of many philosophers. One of these skeptics is John Rawls, who offers a highly influential egalitarian theory of justice as an alternative to utilitarianism.

THE EGALITARIAN THEORY OF JOHN RAWLS

In *A Theory of Justice* (1971), the contemporary American philosopher John Rawls argues for two principles that he thinks express our considered views about justice. Although his arguments and the principles themselves are rather complex, the basic outlines of his theory, which were first presented in a 1958 article "Justice as Fairness," are relatively easy to understand.[21]

Rawls's aim is to give an account of justice that embodies a Kantian conception of equality. His objection to utilitarianism, as we have already seen, is that it does not give adequate attention to the way in which utility is distributed among different individuals. "Utilitarianism," Rawls charges, "does not take seriously the difference between persons."[22] As an alternative to the utilitarian ideal of a society with the highest level of welfare, Rawls proposes a society that recognizes its members as free and equal moral persons, a concept he attributes to Kant.[23] For Rawls, questions of justice arise primarily when free and equal persons attempt to advance their own interests and come into conflict with others pursuing their self-interests.

The key to a well-ordered society is the creation of institutions that enable individuals with conflicting ends to interact in mutually beneficial ways. The principles of justice assist in this effort by assigning rights and duties in the basic institutions of society and distributing the benefits and burdens of mutual cooperation.[24] The focus of Rawls's theory, then, is on *social* justice; that is, on a conception of justice that is suited to a well-ordered society. Once we have determined what constitutes a just society, however, we can then apply the results to questions of justice in the political, legal, and economic spheres.

Rawls's Method

Rawls begins by asking us to imagine a situation in which free and equal persons, concerned to advance their own interests, attempt to arrive at unanimous agreement on principles that will serve as the basis for constructing the major institutions of society. He does not assume that these individuals already have some conception of the principles of justice and that their task is to come to an agreement about what these principles are. Rather, he describes persons in this imaginary situation as self-interested agents, who evaluate principles according to whether they help or hinder them in achieving their ends. These people favor principles that enable them to get more of what they want and oppose principles that hinder them. Thus, Rawls's theory is based on the notion of pure procedural justice; that is, any principles on which everyone would agree are for that reason just—no matter what their content.[25] He assumes, moreover, that the people he is describing are rational in the sense that they conceive ends and act purposefully to achieve them and that they are willing to cooperate with others when this is possible and to abide by any agreements made.[26]

The approach taken by Rawls in *A Theory of Justice* is similar to the traditional contract theories of Hobbes, Locke, Rousseau, and Kant. The main difference is that the object of the agreement is not to establish a particular society but to arrive at principles of justice applicable to any society.[27] The assumption underlying most contract theories, including Rawls's, is that if individuals in some hypothetical precontract situation would unanimously accept certain terms for governing their relations, then those terms are just and all people have an obligation to abide by them.

A crucial part of any contract theory is a description of the precontract situation, which is called the state of nature by Hobbes, Locke, and others and the *original position* by Rawls. A distinctive feature of the original position, as described by Rawls, is the *veil of ignorance.*[28] The individuals who are asked to agree on the principles of justice must do so without knowing many facts about themselves and their situation. They do not know their social status or class, their natural assets or abilities, their intelligence or physical strength, their race or sex, or even their own conception of the good life. However, they have enough general knowledge about human psychology, social organization, political affairs, and the like to make informed choices about the principles of justice.

The purpose of the veil of ignorance is to ensure that agreement is possible. Rawls conceives of the process as a "bargaining game," in which people are free to offer proposals of their own and to reject those of others until unanimity is achieved.[29] If people in the original position know too much about themselves and how proposed principles would affect them personally, they might become deadlocked and prefer no agreement to one that puts them at a disadvantage. Behind the veil of ignorance, they are forced to be impartial and to view proposed principles from the perspective of all persons at once. Without any knowledge of their race or sex, for example, they are unlikely to advocate or support discriminatory principles, since they could be among the victims of discrimination. Certainly, no one could rationally choose a system of slavery without knowing who would be the masters and who, the slaves.

The Principles of Justice

Now, what principles would rational, self-interested persons freely agree to in a position of equality behind a veil of ignorance? Rawls thinks that there are two, which he states as follows:

1. Each person is to have an equal right to the most extensive total system of basic liberties compatible with a similar system of liberty for all.
2. Social and economic inequalities are to be arranged so that they are both:
   a. to the greatest benefit of the least advantaged, and
   b. attached to offices and positions open to all under conditions of fair equality of opportunity.[30]

The two principles are arranged by Rawls in order of priority. The task of ensuring that everyone has basic rights (the first principle) ought to be completed before any inequalities based on the second principle are permitted.[31] Further, liberty ought not to be traded for welfare; that is, no one following these principles would give up liberties for the sake of an increase in welfare.

The Reasoning Behind the Two Principles

The reasoning behind the first principle is that an equal share of whatever goods are available is the most that any person could reasonably expect, given the requirement of unanimous agreement.[32] No one would voluntarily accept less than an equal share if it were possible to share equally, since to do so would make that person comparatively worse off. Also, no one would be able to get more than an equal share by pressing for some special advantage, since someone else would have to agree to receive less than an equal share; and that, we have already seen, no one would voluntarily do. Like the person who cuts the cake knowing that he will get the last piece, persons in the original position would opt for equal shares. As Rawls remarks, "Indeed, this principle is so obvious that we would expect it to occur to anyone immediately."[33]

Both of Rawls's principles apply to the distribution of what he calls *primary goods*.[34] Behind the veil of ignorance, no one knows what particular things he or she values; however, there are certain goods that every rational person can be presumed to want because they are of use no matter what life plan is adopted. These primary goods include rights and liberties, powers and opportunities, income and wealth, and self-respect.[35] No matter what a person wants in life, more rather than fewer opportunities and more rather than less income and wealth would be preferred. Basic liberties are among the most important of these primary goods. They include, according to Rawls, the right to vote and hold public office, freedom of thought and expression, the right of assembly, the right to own property, and freedom from unlawful arrest and detention.[36] So essential are basic liberties to our well-being that only equal shares and the most extensive system possible would be accepted by persons in the original position.

The second principle recognizes, however, that there are conditions under which rational, self-interested persons would make an exception to the first principle and accept less than an equal share of some primary goods. One such condition is that everyone would be better off with the inequality than without it.[37] If it is possible to increase the total amount of income, for example, but not possible to distribute it equally, then the resulting distribution is still just, according to Rawls, as long as the extra income is distributed in such a way that everyone benefits from the inequality.

To illustrate, consider the following distribution schemes:

I		II		III		IV	
A	10	A	14	A	16	A	14
B	10	B	8	B	9	B	11
C	10	C	8	C	7	C	11
	30		30		32		36

We have already seen that from the utilitarian point of view, I and II are morally indistinguishable; and III is superior to both I and II, despite the inequality, because of the increase in the total amount of utility. For Rawls, however, people in the original position would prefer I over II, since two people, B and C, are worse off in II. For the same reason, they would reject III, despite the greater amount of utility, since B and C are still worse off than they are in I. However, IV would be unanimously favored by people in the original position over I, because everyone is better off. Only people influenced by envy at the prospect of someone's being better off than they would opt for I instead of IV. Since envy of this kind makes everyone worse off and, hence, is irrational, Rawls stipulates that people in the original position must be nonenvious.[38]

The Difference Principle

In principle 2(a), commonly known as the *difference principle*, Rawls states another condition under which persons in the original position would be willing to accept inequalities. The condition is not that everyone be better off but that the *least advantaged person* be better off.[39] What Rawls has in mind here is that in every distribution there is a worst-off person—although this is not necessarily the same person in each possible scheme. For example:

IV		V		VI		VII	
A	14	A	14	A	12	A	10
B	11	B	12	B	10	B	12
C	11	C	10	C	14	C	14
	36		36		36		36

The least advantaged person in V, VI, and VII is C, B, and A, respectively. In V, VI, and VII, at least one person is better off than in IV. Still, IV is preferable, according to Rawls, since the worst-off persons, namely B and C, are better off than the worst-off person in each of V, VI, and VII. (A person in the original position would also choose IV over I, II, or III for the reason that the worst off person in IV is still better off than the worst-off person in I, II and III.)

Rawls's argument for these claims is that under conditions of uncertainty, a rational person would "play it safe" and choose the alternative in which the worst possible outcome is still better than the worst possible outcome of any other alternative. His argument thus employs a rule of rational choice drawn from game theory known as "maximin," which holds that it is rational to *maxi*mize the *min*imum outcome in choosing between different alternatives.[40] This is a rational rule to follow when, as Rawls says, your place will be determined by your worst enemy.

The Principle of Equal Opportunity

Principle 2(b), the principle of equal opportunity, is similar to the view that careers should be open to all on the basis of talent. Whether a person gets a certain job, for example, ought to be determined by competence in that line of work and not by skin color, family connections, or any other irrelevant characteristic. Rawls is careful, however, to distinguish his principle from allocative efficiency. Utilitarians also favor equal opportunity for the reason that filling jobs with the best qualified applicants makes the most efficient use of human resources, with a corresponding increase in welfare for the whole of society. When the efficient matching of people with jobs is achieved by rewarding people for ability, effort, contribution, and so on, the result is often considerable inequality. In Rawls's view, however, it is unjust to reward (or penalize) people for their natural endowments or for accidental features of their circumstances. From the moral point of view, these are no more relevant to the distribution of income and wealth than a person's sex or race.[41]

In a just society, therefore, every effort should be made to eliminate differences that result from the accidents of birth and social conditions, in order to give people roughly equal prospects to fill positions in society. Thus, the principle of equal opportunity would lead to a heavy inheritance tax, child-care support, comprehensive free education, training programs for the unskilled, and effective measures to prevent discrimination. Natural differences that cannot be eliminated ought to be regarded, Rawls says, as "a common asset," to be used for the benefit of everyone.[42]

The Application of Rawls's Principles

Rawls's two principles are more abstract than Aristotle's principle of justice or the principle of utility. In *A Theory of Justice*, though, he discusses some problems of creating social institutions that are in accord with his theory. And so it is possible to sketch roughly how the two principles are to be applied in practice. The first question we need to ask is, does everyone in a society have the full range of basic liberties? If the answer is no, then we need to find ways of altering the basic institutions of society so as to ensure that they do. Insofar as people are discriminated against on the basis of race or sex, for example, we can pass laws against discrimination and set up affirmative action programs, taking care not to reduce the liberties of other members of society.

Once basic liberties are secured for everyone, then we need to ask, is there any institutional arrangement that would raise the well-being of the least advantaged member of society under that arrangement above the level of the least advantaged person under any alternative arrangement? And finally, we need to ask, does each person have the greatest possible opportunity to occupy any particular position in society? Only when all these questions have been answered satisfactorily can we say that a society is just.

The Maximin Rule

Whether Rawls's theory is superior to utilitarianism depends in large part on his success in defending maximin as a rule of rational choice. Persons who have to choose principles behind a veil of ignorance might well "play it safe" and give exclusive priority to improving the condition of a representative "least advantaged" person out of fear that they might be that person. But why is it not also rational for them to opt for a principle of maximizing average utility, especially if they have a propensity for risk?[43] By choosing the principle of maximum average utility, the chances of being better off are greater than under Rawls's principles. Further, they just might be one of the best off people in the society that results.

If people in the original position are acquainted with the phenomenon of diminishing marginal utility, they might conclude that the principle of maximum average utility would prevent anyone from falling below a utility floor that represents a minimal standard of living. Or they might also adopt a twofold utilitarian principle that would establish a floor below which no one would be permitted to fall and then use utility as a criterion for improvements above that floor.[44] It is far from certain, therefore, that maximin is justified as a rule for rational choice for persons behind the veil of ignorance.[45]

Congruence with Our Beliefs About Justice

Ultimately, the justification for Rawls's theory of justice is its congruence with our most deeply held beliefs about justice. Some of the consequences of the two principles fit better than those of utilitarianism, others do not fit as well. Although Rawls's list of basic liberties is relatively uncontroversial, he provides no priority among them when not all basic liberties can be realized or when they come into conflict with one another. There are other liberties, moreover, that might be added to the list, and Rawls provides no justification for excluding them. In addition, the priority of liberties over other primary goods is criticized for reflecting the bias of a well-to-do society whose material needs are already satisfied.[46] People in a struggling third world country might prefer to sacrifice some liberties in order to improve their standard of living.

The difference principle accounts for our intuitive judgment that it would be wrong to enslave a portion of society even if the result were a vast increase in the total amount of utility. At the same time, it bars even the smallest sacrifice on the part of the least advantaged person, no matter how great the increase in welfare to the rest of society. The difference principle is also compatible with a redistribution that considerably worsens the condition of people not too far above the least advantaged person, as long as it improves the condition of the person at the bottom, even if only slightly. Thus, although protecting the least advantaged from a worsening of their position, Rawls's theory provides no corresponding protection to the more advantaged members of society.

UTILITY AND THE MARKET SYSTEM

In a capitalist economy, such as we have in the United States, major decisions about what goods and services to produce, how to manufacture and sell them, and so on are made primarily through the impersonal forces of supply and demand in the marketplace. The principal aim of business firms in this system is to maximize the return on investment, or to make a profit. Although the market system operates largely without any explicit consideration of what is right or just, it does not follow that the system itself lacks an ethical justification. Indeed, we value our capitalist economy and hold it to be superior to other forms of economic organization, not only because of its ability to provide an abundance of goods and services at low prices but also because *we believe it to be morally justified.*

The market system is characterized by three main features: (1) *private ownership* of resources and the goods and services produced in an economy; (2) *voluntary exchange,* in which individuals are free to enter into mutually advantageous trades; and (3) the *profit motive*, whereby people engage in trading solely to advance their own well-being. In the market system described by Adam Smith and other classical economic theorists, individuals trade with each other, giving up things they own in exchange for other things they need or want. The motive of these economic actors is to improve their lives. This simple picture of the market is considerably complicated by neoclassical economics, in which the firm is the major unit of analysis. Business organizations of various kinds mobilize the productive resources of society, including labor, and transform them into goods and services to be sold in a mass market. Corporations are owned by tens of thousands or millions of shareholders. Still, all three features are present in the description of the market system offered by neoclassical economists.

The arguments justifying the market system can be conveniently reduced to two: a utilitarian argument that a market system produces the highest possible level of welfare for society and a rights-based argument that a market system best protects our liberty, especially with respect to private property.[47] The first of these is derived from Adam Smith and his notion of an invisible hand that leads self-seeking individuals to promote a collective good. The second argument originated with John Locke's defense of property as a fundamental right, which today is generally advanced by conservative economists and libertarians. The utilitarian argument is examined in this section, and the rights-based argument is considered in the one following.

Adam Smith's "Invisible Hand"

Adam Smith (1723–1790) is generally regarded as the founder of modern economics, and his major work, *An Inquiry into the Nature and Causes of the Wealth of Nations*, published in 1776, is a landmark in the history of Western thought. One of Smith's key insights is the importance of trading in an economy. A central problem for any economic system is how to enlist the aid of others in satisfying our basic needs. Trading solves this problem by appealing to other people in terms of their own advantage. According to Smith:

> . . . [M]an has almost constant occasion for the help of his brethren, and it is in vain for him to expect it from their benevolence only. He will be more likely to prevail if he can interest their self-love in his favour, and shew them that it is for their own advantage to do for him what he requires of them. Whoever offers to another a bargain of any kind, proposes to do this. Give me that which I want, and you shall have this which you want, is the meaning of every such offer; and it is in this manner that we obtain from one another the far greater part of those good offices which we stand in need of. It is not from the benevolence of the butcher, the brewer, or the baker, that we expect our dinner, but from their regard

to their own interest. We address ourselves, not to their humanity but to their self-love, and never talk to them of our own necessities but of their advantages.

If two people want the same thing, conflict is inevitable; but if they want different things, and each person has what the other wants, then a trade is to the advantage of both. Trading is an instance, therefore, of mutually advantageous cooperation. And whenever a trade takes place voluntarily, we can be sure that both parties believe themselves to be better off (or, at least, not worse off), since, by assumption, no one willingly consents to being worse off.

In an economy built on free trade, the same beneficial effects occur. Laborers, in search of the highest possible wages, put their efforts and skill to the most productive use. Buyers seeking to purchase needed goods and services at the lowest possible price force sellers to compete with each other by making the most efficient use of the available resources and keeping prices at the lowest possible level. The resulting benefit to society as a whole is due not to any concern with the well-being of others but solely to the pursuit of self-interest. By seeking only personal gain, each individual is, according to a famous passage in *The Wealth of Nations*, "led by an invisible hand to promote an end which was no part of his intention." He continued, "Nor is it always the worse for the society that it was no part of it. By pursuing his own interest he frequently promotes that of the society more effectually than when he really intends to promote it."

The invisible hand argument was developed further by the successors of Adam Smith. Using refined mathematical techniques, economic theorists are able to demonstrate that in a free market, individuals will continue to trade up to a point of equilibrium where no further mutually advantageous trades are possible. Thus, a system of free trades results in maximum efficiency. The details of this argument can be found in virtually any introductory economics textbook.[48]

Problems with the "Invisible Hand" Argument

There are many problems with the utilitarian argument in both the invisible hand version offered by Adam Smith and the more technical formulation of modern economic theory. First, the argument, strictly speaking, does not prove that free markets maximize *utility*; only that they are *efficient*, which is to say that they produce the greatest amount of output for the least amount of input. It stands to reason that a more productive economy has a higher level of utility, since more goods and services are available. But the connection is not assured unless the economy produces the goods and services that people want and manufactures and distributes them in ways that meet these needs. At a minimum, holders of the invisible hand argument need to clarify the relation between efficiency and utility.

Second, the argument that free markets are efficient presupposes *perfect competition*. This condition is satisfied when there are many buyers and sellers who are free to enter or leave the market at will and a large supply of relatively homogeneous products that buyers will readily substitute one for another. In addition, each buyer and seller must have complete knowledge of the goods and services available, including prices. In a market with these features, no firm is able to charge more than its competitors, since customers will purchase the competitors' products instead. Also, in the long run, the profit in one industry can be no higher than that in any other, since newcomers will enter the field and offer products at lower prices until the rate of profit is reduced to a common level.

Competition in actual markets is always imperfect to some degree. One reason is the existence of monopolies and oligopolies, in which one or a few firms dominate a market and exert an undue influence on prices. Competition is also reduced when there are barriers to market entry, when products are strongly differentiated, when some firms have information that others lack (about new manufacturing processes, for example), and when consumers lack important information. Thus, the automobile industry in the United States before the advent of foreign competition was dominated by the "Big Three"—General Motors, Ford, and Chrysler—which chose to act in concert instead of engaging in all-out competition. Rivals were shut out by the high start-up costs of new car production, and each company turned out highly differentiated products, so that similarly priced Chevrolets and Fords were not the same in consumers' eyes. The inability of consumers to obtain relevant information also contributed to the lack of competition in the American automobile industry.

Competition is also reduced by *transaction costs*; that is, the expense required for buyers and sellers to find each other and come to an agreement. Transaction costs in most instances are substantial and strongly affect the efficiency of trading in a free market. Great expense is involved, for example, merely in making and enforcing contracts, so that manufacturers with superior resources have a decided advantage in dealing with consumers about such matters as sales agreements and warranties.

Third, the argument that free markets are efficient makes certain assumptions about human behavior. It assumes, in particular, that the individuals who engage in economic activity are fully rational and act to maximize their own utility.[49] This construct, commonly called *economic man*, is faulty for at least two reasons. One is that people lack the ability to make all the calculations required to act effectively in their own interests. Consequently, they are unable to act as rational utility maximizers even when they are motivated to do so. The other reason is that human motivation is much more complex than the simple view of economic theory. People often give money to the poor or return a lost wallet, for example, with no expectation of gain. Altruism and moral commitment play a prominent role in our economic life, along with self-interest, and yet economic theory gives them scant regard.[50]

Also, firms do not always act in the ways predicted by economic theory. Because of limitations on the ability of human beings to acquire and process the amount of information needed for corporate decision-making, managers have what is described as *bounded rationality*. To compensate for these limitations, business organizations develop rules and procedures for decision-making that substitute for the direct pursuit of profit. Also, firms do not necessarily seek optimal outcomes, as economists assume, but, in the view of some organizational theorists, they settle for merely adequate solutions to pressing problems through a process known as *satisficing*. The immediate aim of firms, according to these theorists, is to achieve an *internal* efficiency; which is to say, the well-being of the firm, rather than *external* efficiency in the marketplace.[51]

Fourth, the invisible hand argument disregards the possibility of spillover effects or *externalities*. It assumes that all costs of production are reflected in the prices of goods and services and are not passed on to others. An externality is present when the manufacturer of a product is permitted to pollute a stream, for example, thereby imposing a cost on businesses downstream and depriving people of the opportunity to fish and swim in the stream. Other examples of externalities in present-day markets include inefficient use of natural resources (automobile drivers do not pay the full cost of the gasoline they use), occupational injuries, and accidents from defective products.

The task of dealing with externalities falls mainly to governments, which have many means at their disposal.[52] Polluters can be forced to internalize the costs of production, for example, by regulations that prohibit certain polluting activities (the use of soft coal, for example), set standards for pollution emissions, create tax incentives for installing pollution control devices or switching to less polluting technologies, and so on. Some free market theorists have proposed solutions to the problem of externalities that make use of market mechanisms. Allowing firms that exceed pollution standards to "sell" the rights to pollute to those whose emissions violate the standards is one example.

A fifth and final objection to the "invisible hand" argument concerns the problem of *collective choice*.[53] In a market system, choices that must be made for a whole society—a transportation policy, for example—are made by aggregating a large number of individual choices. Instead of leaving to a central planner a decision about whether to build more roads or more airports, we allow individuals to decide for themselves whether to drive a car or to take an airplane to their destination, and through a multitude of such individual decisions, we arrive at a collective choice. The underlying assumption is that if each individual makes rational choices—that is, choices that maximize his or her own welfare—then the collective choice that results will also be rational and maximize the welfare of society as a whole.

The Problem of Public Goods

The validity of the assumption about collective choice is open to question, most notably, in the case of *public goods*. A market economy has a well-known bias in favor of private over public consumption; that is, the production of goods that can be owned and used by one person as opposed to goods that can be enjoyed by all.[54] Automobiles are an example of a private good. Roads, by contrast, are a public good in that their use by one person does not exclude their use by others. As a result of this bias in favor of private consumption, people spend large sums on their own cars but little to build and maintain a system of roads. Public parks, a free education system, public health programs, and police and fire protection are all examples of public goods that are relatively underfunded in an otherwise affluent society.[55]

The reason for this bias is simple: There is no profit in public goods. Since they cannot be packaged and sold like toothpaste, there is no easy way to charge for them. And although some people are willing to pay for the pleasure of a public park, for example, others, who cannot be excluded from enjoying the park as well, will be *free riders*; that is, they will take advantage of the opportunity to use a public good without paying for it. Indeed, if we assume a world of rational economic agents who always act in their own interest, then everyone would be a free rider, given the chance. To act otherwise would be irrational.[56] Consequently, public goods are ignored by the market and left for governments to provide, usually in a grudging manner. As the economist Joan Robinson has observed:

> When you come to think of it, what can easily be charged for and what cannot, is just a technical accident. Some things, such as drainage and street lighting, are so obviously necessary that a modicum is provided in spite of the fact that payment has to be collected through the rates, but it is only the most glaring necessities that are met in this way, together with some traditional amenities, like flower-beds in the parks, that are felt to be necessary to municipal self-respect.[57]

The Prisoners' Dilemma

The assumption that rational individual choices always result in rational collective choices is also brought into question by another problem illustrated by the well-known *prisoners' dilemma*.[58] Suppose that two guilty suspects have been apprehended by the police and placed in separate cells where they cannot communicate. Unfortunately, the police have only enough evidence to convict them both on a minor charge. If neither one confesses, therefore, they will receive a light sentence of one year each. The police offer each prisoner the opportunity of going free if he confesses and the other does not. The evidence provided by the suspect who confesses will then enable the police to convict the other suspect of a charge carrying a sentence of twenty years. If they both confess, however, they will each receive a sentence of five years.

Obviously, the best possible outcome—one year for each prisoner—is obtained when both do not confess. Neither one can afford to seek this outcome by not confessing, however, since he faces a twenty-year sentence if the other does not act in the same way. Confessing, with the prospect of five years in prison or going scot-free, is clearly the preferable alternative. The rational choice for both prisoners, therefore, is to confess. But by doing so, they end up with the second-best outcome and are unable to reach the optimal solution to their problem.

The dilemma in this case would not be solved merely by allowing the prisoners to communicate, since the rational strategy for each prisoner in that case would be to agree not to confess and then turn around and break the agreement by confessing. The prisoners' dilemma is thus like the free rider problem discussed earlier. If each prisoner has the opportunity to take advantage of the other's cooperation without paying a price, then it is rational to do so.[59] The true lesson of the prisoners' dilemma is that to reach the best possible outcome, each must be *assured* of the other's cooperation. The prisoners' dilemma is thus an assurance problem.[60] It shows that a rational collective choice can be made under certain circumstances only if each person in a system of cooperative behavior can be convinced that others will act in the same way.

The prisoners' dilemma is not an idle intellectual puzzle. Many real-life situations involve elements of this problem.[61] Consider the following example. The factories located around a lake are polluting the water at such a rate that within a few years none will be able to use the water and they will all be forced to shut down or relocate. The optimal solution would be for each factory to install a water-purification system or take other steps to reduce the amount of pollution. It would not be rational for any one factory or even a few to make the investment required, however, since the improvement in the quality of the water would be minimal and their investment wasted. Without assurance that all will bear the expense of limiting the amount of pollution, each factory will continue to pollute the lake and everyone will lose in the end. The most rational decision for each factory individually will thus result in a disastrous collective decision.

The usual solution to prisoners' dilemma cases—along with those involving externalities and public goods—is government action. By ordering all the factories around the lake to reduce the amount of pollution and backing up that order with force, a government could assure each factory owner that the others will bear their share of the burden. As a result, they could achieve an end that they all desire but could not seek without this assurance. Regulation of this kind is not necessarily incompatible with the operation of a free market. Thomas C. Schelling points out that voluntarism versus coercion is a false dichotomy because coercion can enable firms to do what they want to do but could not do voluntarily.[62] Firms are not always averse to internalizing costs and providing public goods, Schelling observes, as long as they are not penalized more than their competitors.[63] This condition can also be secured by government regulation.

Conclusion

We have seen that the utilitarian argument for the market system, expressed primarily in Adam Smith's famous invisible hand metaphor, has a number of significant problems. These do not show that free markets are unjustified but only that they have limitations, or shortcomings. The proper response, therefore, is not to scrap the market system but to find ways of correcting the problems and helping markets to achieve the goal of providing for our well-being. With an understanding of the problems of the utilitarian argument, we are in a better position to adopt measures that enable the market system to operate in a morally justified manner.

THE LIBERTARIAN JUSTIFICATION OF THE MARKET SYSTEM

Present-day libertarians are the intellectual successors to the laissez-faire tradition in economics. The distinctive feature of the libertarian philosophy is a commitment to individual liberty, conceived in the Lockean sense of a right to own property and to live as much as possible free from the interference of others. Two of the most prominent exponents of libertarianism are the Austrian-born economist Friedrich von Hayek and the American economist Milton Friedman, both of whom are strong defenders of the classical free market as the economic system that most fully supports their conception of individual liberty. The fullest state-

ment of libertarianism by a contemporary philosopher is Robert Nozick's *Anarchy, State, and Utopia*, published in 1974.[64] The discussion that
follows is mainly concerned, therefore, with the theory of justice that
Nozick calls the entitlement theory.

Nozick's Entitlement Theory

The principles of justice in Nozick's theory differ from the principle of utility and Rawls's principles in two major respects. First, they are
historical principles as opposed to nonhistorical or *end-state* principles.[65]
Historical principles, he explains, take into account the process by which
a distribution came about, whereas end-state principles evaluate a distribution with regard to certain structural features at a given time. A
utilitarian judges between two alternatives solely in terms of the amount
of utility present, and a Rawlsian compares only the relative well-being
of the least advantaged persons in each case. Nozick asserts that we
often consider how a distribution came about.

> If some persons are in prison for murder or war crimes, we do not say
> that to assess the justice of the distribution in the society we must look
> only at what this person has, and that person has, . . . at the current time.
> We think it relevant to ask whether someone did something so that he
> *deserved* to be punished, deserved to have a lower share.[66]

Similarly, we want to know what workers have done in order to determine how much they ought to be paid.[67]

Second, the principles of justice in both utilitarianism and Rawls's
theory are *patterned*.[68] A principle is patterned if it specifies some feature in a particular distribution and evaluates the distribution according
to the presence or absence of that feature. Any principle of the form,
Distribute according to _____, such as, Distribute according to IQ
scores, is a patterned principle. Both Aristotle's principle and the principle of utility are patterned principles, as is the socialist formula, From
each according to his abilities, to each according to his needs. Rawls's
two principles might appear at first glance to be nonpatterned because
they are based on pure procedural justice; that is, any principle that is
agreed to in the original position is, for that reason, just. However,
Nozick argues that Rawls allows a process of bargaining to determine
the principles of justice, but once these are determined, no agreement is
just unless the result is a distribution that conforms to the pattern in the
principles.[69]

Nozick thinks that any acceptable principle of justice must be nonpatterned because any particular pattern of distribution can be achieved
and maintained only by violating the right to liberty. Upholding the
right to liberty, in turn, upsets any particular pattern of justice. He

argues for this point by asking us to consider a case in which there is a perfectly just distribution, as judged by some desired pattern, and also perfect freedom. Now suppose that a famous athlete—Nozick suggests Wilt Chamberlain—will play only if he is paid an additional twenty-five cents for each ticket sold and that many people are so excited to see Wilt Chamberlain play that they will cheerfully pay the extra twenty-five cents for the privilege. Both Wilt Chamberlain and the fans are within their rights to act as they do, but at the end of the season, if one million people pay to see him play, then Wilt Chamberlain will have an additional income of $250,000, which is presumably more than he would be entitled to on a patterned principle of justice. By exercising their right to liberty, though, Wilt Chamberlain and the fans have upset the just distribution that formerly prevailed. In order to maintain the patterned distribution, it would be necessary to restrict the freedom of Wilt Chamberlain or the fans in some way, such as prohibiting the extra payment or taxing away the excess.

Nozick has observed:

> The general point illustrated by the Wilt Chamberlain example . . . is that no end-state principle or distributional patterned principle of justice can be continuously realized without continuous interference with people's lives. Any favored pattern would be transformed into one unfavored by the principle, by people choosing to act in various ways; for example, by people exchanging goods and services with other people, or giving things to other people, things the transferrers are entitled to under the favored distributional pattern. To maintain a pattern one must either continually interfere to stop people from transferring resources as they wish to, or continually (or periodically) interfere to take from some person the resources that others for some reason chose to transfer to them.[70]

The entitlement theory can be stated very simply. A distribution is just, Nozick says, "if everyone is entitled to the holdings they possess."[71] Whether we are entitled to certain holdings is determined by tracing their history. Most of what we possess comes from others through transfers, such as purchases and gifts. Thus, we might own a piece of land because we bought it from someone, who in turn bought it from someone else, and so on. Proceeding backward in this fashion, we ultimately reach the original settler who did not acquire it through a transfer but by clearing the land and tilling it. As long as each transfer was just and the original acquisition was just, then our present holding is just. "Whatever arises from a just situation by just steps is itself just," Nozick writes.[72] In his theory, then, particular distributions are just not because they conform to some pattern (equality or social utility, for example) but solely because of antecedent events.

Just Transfer and Original Acquisition

Nozick's theory requires at least two principles: a principle of just transfer and a principle of just original acquisition. Since holdings can be unjustly appropriated by force or fraud, a third principle, a principle of rectification, is also necessary, in order to correct injustices by restoring holdings to the rightful owners. If we rightfully possess some holding—a piece of land, for example, either by transfer or original acquisition—then we are free to use or dispose of it as we wish. We have a right, in other words, to sell it to whomever we please at whatever price that person is willing to pay, or we can choose to give it away. As long as the exchange is purely voluntary, with no force or fraud, the resulting redistribution is just. Any attempt to prevent people from engaging in voluntary exchanges in order to secure a particular distribution is a violation of liberty, according to the entitlement theory.

Nozick's principle of just original acquisition is similar to Locke's theory of property rights.[73] Every person has a right to his or her own labor, Locke held, and whatever we "mix" our labor with and remove from "the common state nature placed it in" is rightfully ours. A person who clears and tills previously unowned land, for example, thereby establishes a right to it. A major problem for both Locke and Nozick arises when there is not enough in nature for everyone. Would one person be justified in laying claim to the only water hole in a desert? Or how much of the world's oil supply is the United States justified in consuming? Locke added the famous proviso, "at least where this is enough, and as good left in common for others." In Nozick's theory, an original acquisition is unjust "if the position of others no longer at liberty to use the thing is thereby worsened."[74] Obviously, taking anything worsens the positions of others, since there is now one thing they are no longer free to take themselves. This is not what Nozick has in mind, however. A system of ownership in accord with the principle of just acquisition also allows other people to take things they would not be able to take otherwise. So a person is made worse off by someone's taking something only if they are worse off than they would be without a system of ownership. To be worse off means, in other words, to be worse off than they would be in a state of nature.[75] Thus, the first finder of a water hole in the desert cannot lay claim to it and charge what the market will bear if the other goods remaining to be claimed are insufficient to compensate other people for their loss of the water hole.[76]

A world consisting only of just acquisitions and just transfers would be just, according to Nozick, no matter what the pattern of distribution. Some people, through hard work, shrewd trades, or plain good luck, would most likely amass great wealth, while others, through indolence, misjudgment, or bad luck, would probably end up in poverty. However, the rich in such a world would have no obligation to aid the poor,[77] nor would it be just to coerce them into doing so. Each person's share would be determined largely through his or her choices and those of others. Nozick suggests that the entitlement theory can be expressed in the form of a patterned theory of justice as follows:

> From each according to what he chooses to do, to each according to what he makes for himself (perhaps with the contracted aid of others) and what others choose to do for him and choose to give him of what they've been given previously (under this maxim) and haven't yet expended or transferred.[78]

Or more simply: *From each as they choose, to each as they are chosen.*

Justice and Free Markets

A market system with only the absolute minimum of government intervention would be just, in Nozick's theory, as long as the principles of just acquisition and just transfer are satisfied. The reason is that a system in which we have complete freedom to acquire property and engage in mutually advantageous trades (without violating the rights of another person, of course) is one in which our own rights are most fully protected. To critics who fear that unregulated markets would lead to great disparities between rich and poor and a lowering of the overall welfare of society, Nozick has a reply. The point of justice is not to promote human well-being or to achieve a state of equality; it is to protect our rights. Since a market system does this better than any other form of economic organization, it is just.

Difficulties with Nozick's Theory

The main difficulty with Nozick's theory is the lack of argument for the key assumption that liberty, conceived as the unhindered exercise of property rights, is a paramount value. First, there are rights, such as a right to a minimal level of welfare, that some consider to be at least as important as the rights of property owners. Yet, in Nozick's view, it would be unjust to provide for the well-being of the members of society if doing so involved forcing the well-to-do against their will to aid the poor. Taxation for this purpose, according to Nozick, is on a par with forced labor.[79] What is the justification, though, for allowing the poor to starve merely to protect the rich against being coerced in this way?

Nozick suggests that the value of property rights derives from the second formulation of Kant's categorical imperative: treat others "always as an end and never as a means only." To force people to act without their consent is to use them solely as a means to the satisfaction of someone else's ends. Certainly, slavery is an example of coercion that treats people as means for the benefit of others. But it does not follow that all forms of treating people without their consent is tantamount to forced labor or slavery—or that respecting property rights never involves coercing others.

To take the second objection first, Nozick seems to overlook the point that not all restrictions of liberty are due to interference by the state. By exercising their property rights, people sometimes effectively restrict the choices of others. Suppose that Wilt Chamberlain uses his wealth to buy the only factory in town and immediately cuts all wages. Libertarians hold that it would be an unjustified violation of property rights for the state to tax an individual $500, say, to finance a social security system; but according to Nozick, the liberty of the workers in the factory is not restricted by Wilt Chamberlain's action even if they are deprived by the same amount. James P. Sterba asks:

> But how can requiring a person to pay $500 into a social security program, under threat of greater financial loss, infringe upon the person's liberty when requiring a person to take a job that pays $500 less, under threat of greater financial loss, does not infringe upon the person's liberty? Surely, it would seem that if one requirement restricts a person's liberty, the other will also.[80]

Nozick's answer is that Wilt Chamberlain is acting within his rights as the owner of the factory. The workers, moreover, are free to quit and seek work elsewhere at whatever wages they can command. Hence, no one's rights are being violated. Since wealth breeds even greater wealth, however, a system of unlimited property rights is likely to produce a situation in which a few people own most of the available property and are able to force everyone else to work for them. But such a result is a paradigm of treating people only as a means! Nozick's defense of property rights thus involves a contradiction that one writer calls "the fallacy of libertarian capitalism."[81]

The first objection—that forcing people to act without their consent is not always tantamount to forced labor or slavery—rests on the point that people can justly be required by Kant's categorical imperative to contribute to the well-being of others. Respecting people as ends does not involve merely refraining from interference but involves actively assisting others to some extent in setting goals and acting to achieve them.[82] This is especially true when a person benefits from a system that disadvantages others. Is it unjust for a computer programmer who lands a high-paying job to be taxed to provide unemployment compensation for a steelworker thrown out of work? Both the computer programmer and the steelworker owe their respective conditions to forces largely beyond their control. People also can be justly taxed to bear a fair share of a system of mutual cooperation from which they benefit, even though they have not consented to it.

Finally, justice in transfers and original acquisition depends on conditions that are scarcely ever satisfied in the actual world. Transfers are just, according to Nozick, if each person is entitled to the holdings he or she possesses. The present distribution of holdings is heavily determined, however, by forced takings—fraud, theft, wars, and the like. And the original acquisition of much of the earth's land and resources scarcely left "enough, and as good" for others. Correcting such injustices is a task for the principle of rectification, which is applied by attempting to predict what would have happened had the injustice not occurred and then enforcing the result. Although isolated injustices can be rectified in this manner,[83] what is the possibility of determining the course of events if American Indians had not been deprived of their land, slavery had never occurred, and so on?[84] An adequate theory of justice should be capable of leading us from an unjust world to one a little more just, a test that Nozick's theory fails.

Conclusion

In this chapter, we have examined four theories of justice; namely, those of Aristotle, Mill, Rawls, and Nozick. The purpose of these theories is primarily to provide a means for evaluating existing and proposed institutional arrangements. They are intended, in other words, to be applied not to relatively small-scale decisions, such as pay increases in an office, but rather to larger questions—about the way in which wages are determined in an economy, for example. Rawls is especially clear on this point when he says of the principles of justice, "they provide a way of assigning rights and duties in the basic institutions of society and they define the appropriate distribution of the benefits and burdens of social cooperation."[85] We should not be concerned, therefore, if these four theories of justice have little immediate practical use. They come into play mainly when we seek to justify our social, political, and economic forms of organization.

On the question of the organization of our economic system, utilitarianism and libertarianism both support a system of free markets.[86] Insofar as the market system promotes utility *and* protects rights, it is doubly justified, so to speak. Some proponents of free markets employ both justifications. The two are not wholly compatible, however, and in practice we often face tradeoffs between utility or welfare on the one hand and liberty or property rights on the other. When such situations occur, the holders of these two justifications are forced to choose between them. Typically, libertarians cast their lot with unregulated markets, whereas utilitarians favor limited regulation to correct what they see as market failures.

NOTES

1. Aristotle makes the distinction between compensatory and retributive justice in terms of voluntary and involuntary relations. A contract is a voluntary arrangement between two people, whereas the victim of an assault enters into the relation involuntarily. Many commentators have found this a rather awkward way of making the distinction.

2. The distinction between comparative and noncomparative justice is discussed in JOEL FEINBERG, "Comparative Justice," *The Philosophical Review*, 83 (1974), 297–338. Reprinted in JOEL FEINBERG, *Rights, Justice, and the Bounds of Liberty* (Princeton: Princeton University Press, 1980), 265–306. See also JOEL FEINBERG, *Social Philosophy* (Englewood Cliffs, NJ: Prentice Hall, 1973), 98–99.

3. The distinction is discussed in BRIAN BARRY, *Political Argument* (London: Routledge and Kegan Paul, 1965), 97–100. See also FEINBERG, *Social Philosophy*, 117–19.

4. JOHN RAWLS, *A Theory of Justice* (Cambridge: Harvard University Press, 1971), 85–86.

5. RAWLS, *A Theory of Justice*, 86.

6. For a discussion of the connection, see GREGORY VLASTOS, "Justice and Equality," in RICHARD B. BRANDT, ed., *Social Justice* (Englewood Cliffs, NJ: Prentice Hall, 1962), 31–72.

7. For a discussion of egalitarianism, see S. I. BENN and R. S. PETERS, *Social Principles and the Democratic State* (London: George Allen & Unwin, 1959), chap. 5. Also, H. J. MCCLOSKEY, "Egalitarianism, Equality, and Justice," *Australasian Journal of Philosophy*, 44 (1966), 50–69.

8. For a discussion of Aristotle's principle, see HANS KELSEN, "Aristotle's Doctrine of Justice," in KELSEN, *What is Justice* (Berkeley and Los Angeles: University of California Press, 1957), 117–36; and RENFORD BAMBROUGH, "Aristotle on Justice," in BAMBROUGH, ed., *New Essays on Plato and Aristotle* (London: Routledge and Kegan Paul, 1965), 159–74.

9. Taken from WILLIAM K. FRANKENA, "Some Beliefs about Justice," in JOHN BRICKE, ed., *Freedom and Morality* (Lawrence: University of Kansas, 1976), 56.

10. For a discussion of this list, see NICHOLAS RESCHER, *Distributive Justice* (Indianapolis: Bobbs-Merrill, 1966), chap. 4.

11. Mill opened the chapter on justice in *Utilitarianism* with the observation: "In all ages of speculation, one of the strongest obstacles to the reception of the doctrine that Utility or Happiness is the criterion of right and wrong, has been drawn from the idea of Justice."

12. RESCHER, *Distributive Justice*, 48.

13. For a discussion of utilitarian responses, see D. C. EMMONS, "Justice Reassessed," *American Philosophical Quarterly*, 4 (1967), 144–51.

14. For an account of Bentham's theory of justice, see HUGO A. BEDAU, "Justice and Classical Utilitarianism," in CARL J. FRIEDRICH and JOHN W. CHAPMAN, eds., *Justice* (New York: Atherton Press, 1963), 284–305.

15. Contemporary philosophers who take this position are JAN NARVESON, *Morality and Utility* (Baltimore: Johns Hopkins University Press, 1967), 210–19; ROLF E. SARTORIUS, *Individual Conduct and Social Norms* (Encino, CA: Dick-

inson, 1975), 130–33; J.J.C. SMART, "Distributive Justice and Utilitarianism," in JOHN ARTHUR and WILLIAM H. SHAW, eds., *Justice and Economic Distribution* (Englewood Cliffs, NJ: Prentice Hall, 1978), 103–15; and R. M. HARE, "Justice and Equality," in ARTHUR and SHAW, *Justice and Economic Distribution*, 116–31. RICHARD B. BRANDT argues for a convergence of justice with his version of utilitarianism as a pluralistic welfare-maximizing moral system in *A Theory of the Good and the Right* (Oxford: Oxford University Press, 1979), chap. 16.

16. A good statement of this argument is given in RICHARD B. BRANDT, *Ethical Theory* (Englewood Cliffs, NJ: Prentice Hall, 1959), 415–19. A more extended discussion is BRANDT, A *Theory of the Good and the Right*, 311–16.

17. On this point, see BRANDT, *Ethical Theory*, 416–17; and C. DYKE, *The Philosophy of Economics* (Englewood Cliffs, NJ: Prentice Hall, 1981), 38–39.

18. WILLIAM K. FRANKENA, *Ethics*, 2nd ed. (Englewood Cliffs, NJ: Prentice Hall, 1973), 42.

19. Henry Sidgwick discusses the bearing of the principle of equality on wages and reaches a similar conclusion, that the principle must be supplemented by other considerations. See HENRY SIDGWICK, *The Methods of Ethics*, 7th ed. (Chicago: University of Chicago Press, 1907), 285–90.

20. See BEDAU, "Justice and Classical Utilitarianism," 303.

21. A good exposition is ROBERT PAUL WOLFF, *Understanding Rawls: A Reconstruction and Critique of A Theory of Justice* (Princeton: Princeton University Press, 1977). For a critical study, see BRIAN BARRY, *The Liberal Theory of Justice* (Oxford: Oxford University Press, 1973). Among the many collections of articles are NORMAN DANIELS, ed., *Reading Rawls: Critical Studies of A Theory of Justice* (New York: Basic Books, 1975); and H. GENE BLOCKER and ELIZABETH H. SMITH, eds., *John Rawls's Theory of Social Justice* (Athens: Ohio University Press, 1980).

22. RAWLS, *A Theory of Justice*, 27.

23. See JOHN RAWLS, "A Kantian Conception of Equality," *Cambridge Review*, February 1975, 94.

24. RAWLS, *A Theory of Justice*, 4.

25. RAWLS, *A Theory of Justice*, 136.

26. RAWLS, *A Theory of Justice*, 142–45.

27. RAWLS, *A Theory of Justice*, 11.

28. RAWLS, *A Theory of Justice*, 136–42.

29. The term "bargaining game" is derived from game theory, which Rawls employs in *A Theory of Justice*. The classic work on game theory is R. D. LUCE and HOWARD RAIFFA, *Games and Decisions* (New York: John Wiley and Sons, 1957).

30. RAWLS, *A Theory of Justice*, 302.

31. RAWLS, *A Theory of Justice*, 243–51, 541–48.

32. The reasoning behind both principles is discussed in RAWLS, *A Theory of Justice*, 150–61.

33. RAWLS, *A Theory of Justice*, 151.

34. RAWLS, *A Theory of Justice*, 62, 90–95.

35. On self-respect as a primary good, see RAWLS, *A Theory of Justice*, 440.

36. RAWLS, *A Theory of Justice*, 61.

37. Rawls's formulation of the second principle in "Justice as Fairness" is, "Inequalities are arbitrary unless it is reasonable to expect that they will work out for everyone's advantage." RAWLS, "Justice as Fairness," *The Philosophical Review*, 67 (1958), 165. And his initial statement in *A Theory of Justice* is that "social and economic inequalities are to be arranged so that they are both (a) reasonably expected to be to everyone's advantage, and (b) attached to positions and offices open to all." RAWLS, *A Theory of Justice*, 60.

38. RAWLS, *A Theory of Justice*, 143–44.

39. The reasons for the shift in the formulation of the difference principle involve rather technical problems concerning the comparison of alternatives. For an explanation, see WOLFF, *Understanding Rawls*, 42–47, 63–65.

40. RAWLS, *A Theory of Justice*, 152–56. For a full explanation, see LUCE and RAIFFA, *Games and Decisions*, chap. 13.

41. RAWLS, *A Theory of Justice*, 104.

42. RAWLS, *A Theory of Justice*, 102.

43. Some critics of Rawls argue that a principle of maximum average utility is the only possible choice in the original position. See JOHN C. HARSANYI, "Can the Maximin Principle Serve as a Basis for Morality? A Critique of John Rawls' Theory," *American Political Science Review*, 69 (1975), 594–606. Also, HARSANYI, "Morality and the Theory of Rational Behavior," in AMARTYA SEN and BERNARD WILLIAMS, eds., *Utilitarianism and Beyond* (Cambridge: Cambridge University Press, 39–62).

44. This is suggested in SARTORIUS, *Individual Conduct and Social Norms*, 126. BARRY, *The Liberal Theory of Justice*, 93–94, suggests another possibility.

45. For further objections to the justification of maximin in the original position, see THOMAS NAGEL, "Rawls on Justice," *The Philosophical Review*, 82 (1973), 229–32.

46. On this problem, see BARRY, *The Liberal Theory of Justice*, 59–82; and H.L.A. HART, "Rawls on Liberty and Its Priority," *University of Chicago Law Review*, 40 (1973), 534–55.

47. A comprehensive survey of the economic and ethical arguments for and against the market system is ALLEN BUCHANAN, *Ethics, Efficiency, and the Market* (Totowa, NJ: Rowman and Littlefield, 1988). See also the collection of essays in GERALD DWORKIN, GORDON BERMANT, and PETER G. BROWN, eds., *Markets and Morals* (Washington, DC: Hemisphere Publishing Co., 1977); and VIRGINIA HELD, ed., *Property, Profits, and Economic Justice* (Belmont, CA: Wadsworth, 1980.)

48. A good explanation is contained in DYKE, *Philosophy of Economics*. A more detailed account is presented in A. FELDMAN, *Welfare Economics and Social Choice Theory* (Dordrecht: Martinus Nijhoff, 1980).

49. For a brief discussion of this assumption, see AMARTYA SEN, *On Ethics and Economics* (Oxford: Basil Blackwell, 1987), 10–28.

50. Some economists and behavioral scientists recognize the role of altruism and moral commitment and attempt to incorporate them into economic theory. See, for example, E. S. PHELPS, ed., *Altruism, Morality, and Economic Theory* (New York: Russell Sage, 1975); HARVEY LEIBENSTEIN, *Beyond Economic Man* (Cambridge: Harvard University Press, 1976); DAVID COLLARD, *Altruism and Economy: A Study in Non-Selfish Economics* (New York: Oxford University

Press, 1978); HOWARD MARGOLIS, *Selfishness, Altruism, and Rationality: A Theory of Social Choice* (Cambridge: Cambridge University Press, 1982); AMITAI ETZIONI, *The Moral Dimension: Towards a New Economics* (New York: The Free Press, 1988); and ROBERT H. FRANK, *Passions Within Reason: The Strategic Role of the Emotions* (New York: W. W. Norton, 1988).

51. On the concepts of bounded rationality and satisficing, see HERBERT A. SIMON, *Administrative Behavior: A Study of Decision Making Processes in Administrative Organization*, 3rd ed. (New York: The Free Press, 1976), originally published in 1947; JAMES G. MARCH and HERBERT A. SIMON, *Organizations* (New York: Wiley, 1958); and RICHARD M. CYERT and JAMES G. MARCH, *A Behavioral Theory of the Firm* (Englewood Cliffs, NJ: Prentice Hall, 1963).

52. See BUCHANAN, *Ethics, Efficiency, and the Market*, 24–25.

53. For an insightful study of this problem, see AMARTYA SEN, *Collective Choice and Social Welfare* (San Francisco: Holden Day, 1970). Also, KENNETH ARROW, *Social Choice and Individual Values*, 2nd ed. (New York: Wiley, 1963).

54. JOAN ROBINSON, *Economic Philosophy* (London: C. A. Watts, 1962), 132.

55. The disparity between private and public consumption in the United States is the major theme in JOHN KENNETH GALBRAITH, *The Affluent Society* (Boston: Houghton Mifflin, 1958).

56. If everyone attempts to be a free rider, however, then certain kinds of collective choices are impossible unless people are coerced in some way. See MANCUR OLSON, *The Logic of Collective Action* (Cambridge: Harvard University Press, 1965), 44.

57. ROBINSON, *Economic Philosophy*. 132–33.

58. For discussion of the prisoners' dilemma see any book on game theory, such as LUCE and RAIFFA, *Games and Decisions*.

59. This point is made by RUSSELL HARDIN, "Collective Action as an Agreeable n-Person Prisoners' Dilemma," *Behavioral Science*, 16 (1971), 472–79.

60. C. FORD RUNGE, "Institutions and the Free Rider: The Assurance Problem in Collective Action," *Journal of Politics*, 46 (1984), 154–81. Cited in IAN MAITLAND, "The Limits of Business Self-Regulation," *California Management Review*, 27 (Spring 1985), 134.

61. For the empirical significance of the prisoners' dilemma, see ANATOL RAPOPORT and ALBERT M. CHAMMAH, *The Prisoner's Dilemma* (Ann Arbor: University of Michigan Press, 1965); and ROBERT AXELROD, *The Evolution of Cooperation* (New York: Basic Books, 1984).

62. THOMAS C. SCHELLING, "Command and Control," in JAMES W. MCKIE, ed., *Social Responsibility and the Business Predicament* (Washington, DC: The Brookings Institution, 1974), 103–5.

63. SCHELLING, "Command and Control," 103.

64. ROBERT NOZICK, *Anarchy, State, and Utopia* (New York: Basic Books, 1974).

65. NOZICK, *Anarchy, State, and Utopia*, 153–55.

66. NOZICK, *Anarchy, State, and Utopia*, 154. Ellipses in original.

67. For a critical assessment of the distinction, see LAWRENCE C. BECKER, "Against the Supposed Difference between Historical and End-State Theories," *Philosophical Studies*, 41 (1982), 267–72.

68. NOZICK, *Anarchy, State, and Utopia*, 155–60.

69. NOZICK, *Anarchy, State, and Utopia*, 207–10.

70. NOZICK, *Anarchy, State, and Utopia*, 163.
71. NOZICK, *Anarchy, State, and Utopia*, 151.
72. NOZICK, *Anarchy, State, and Utopia*, 151.
73. NOZICK, *Anarchy, State, and Utopia*, 174–78.
74. NOZICK, *Anarchy, State, and Utopia*, 178.
75. THOMAS SCANLON, "Nozick on Rights, Liberty, and Property," *Philosophy and Public Affairs*. 6 (1976), 5. For further discussion, see ROBERT EHMAN, "Nozick's Proviso," *The Journal of Value Inquiry*, 20 (1986), 51–56.
76. On Nozick's theory, a person is still justified in owning the water hole as long as others are compensated to the extent of their loss, so that they are no longer worse off. The provision for compensation creates numerous problems for Nozick's theory. See HILLEL STEINER, "The Natural Right to the Means of Production," *The Philosophical Quarterly*, 27 (1977), 41–49; and "Nozick on Appropriation," *Mind*, 87 (1978), 109–10.
77. Individuals could voluntarily agree with others to contribute to the relief of poverty, in which case an obligation would exist. See NOZICK, *Anarchy, State, and Utopia*, 265–68.
78. NOZICK, *Anarchy, State, and Utopia*, 160.
79. NOZICK, *Anarchy, State, and Utopia*, 169.
80. JAMES P. STERBA, *The Demands of Justice* (Notre Dame: University of Notre Dame Press, 1980), 113.
81. JEFFREY H. REIMAN, "The Fallacy of Libertarian Capitalism," *Ethics*, 92 (1981), 85–95. Reiman considers and rejects attempts by libertarians to avoid this contradiction.
82. ALAN H. GOLDMAN, "The Entitlement Theory of Distributive Justice," *The Journal of Philosophy*, 73 (1976), 829. A more general argument for the right of a state to compel individuals to contribute to the welfare of others is presented in THOMAS NAGEL, "Libertarianism without Foundations," *Yale Law Journal*, 85 (1975), 136–49.
83. For a discussion of some of the problems, see LAWRENCE DAVIS, "Comments on Nozick's Entitlement Theory," *The Journal of Philosophy*, 73 (1976), 839–42.
84. For one answer, see DAVID LYONS, "The New Indian Claims and Original Rights to Land," *Social Theory and Practice*, 4 (1977), 249–72.
85. RAWLS, *A Theory of Justice*, 4.
86. Rawls's theory also justifies the market system, although he distinguishes between free markets as a method of allocation and distribution and capitalism as an economic system that includes private ownership. Markets, according to Rawls, can be a feature of either capitalism or socialism, and whether an economic system with free markets is just depends a great deal on other background institutions. See RAWLS, *A Theory of Justice*, 270–74.

CHAPTER FIVE
Whistle-blowing

In 1969, A. Ernest Fitzgerald testified before a committee of Congress about a $2 million cost overrun on the C-5A cargo plane. At the time, he was a dedicated, hard-working financial analyst for the Defense Department. His cost-cutting zeal was highly valued, even though his outspoken criticism of procurement practices in internal reports irritated some of his superiors. Instead of correcting the cost overrun, his employer reacted by retaliating against Fitzgerald for revealing the embarrassing truth. First he was demoted to insignificant assignments, including the cost problems of bowling alleys in Thailand, and then his position was eliminated in a reorganization undertaken for reasons of "economy." It took Fitzgerald thirteen years and more than $60,000 of his own money for legal expenses to be restored to his original position. As a result of these experiences, Fitzgerald has become a highly vocal in-house whistle-blower, and his testimony is often solicited in congressional hearings. He keeps a close watch on defense spending, even offering to leak information for others so that they can avoid the kind of trouble he encountered.

There have always been informers, or snitches, who reveal information to enrich themselves or to get back at others. But a whistle-blower, by contrast, is generally thought of as a conscientious person who exposes some wrongdoing, often at great personal risk. The term *whistle-blower* was applied first to government employees, such as Ernest

Fitzgerald, who "go public" with complaints of corruption or mismanagement in federal agencies. It is now used in connection with similar
activities in the private sector.[1]

TWO WHISTLE-BLOWERS

As examples of whistle-blowing in the private sector, consider the experiences of these two employees.

Chuck Atchinson

At the age of forty, Charles (Chuck) Atchinson had achieved a
measure of success.[2] His job as a quality control inspector for Brown &
Root, a construction company building a nuclear power plant for the
Texas Utilities Electric Company, paid more than $1,000 a week. This
was enough to provide a comfortable house for his wife and thirteen-
year-old daughter, along with new cars, vacation trips, and a bounty of
other luxuries. Four years later, the family was six months behind on the
rent on a trailer home on a gravel street in Azle, Texas, near Fort
Worth. Chuck Atchinson had been fired by Brown & Root and was
unable to find work. The house was repossessed, and most of the family's furniture and other possessions had been sold to cover living expenses and mounting legal bills.

The source of Chuck Atchinson's misfortune was his inability to
get his superiors at Brown & Root to observe safety regulations in the
construction of the Comanche Peak nuclear power plant being built in
Glen Rose, Texas, and to correct a number of potentially dangerous
flaws. When his repeated complaints to the company got no response,
he brought the situation to the attention of government regulators.
Soon after that he was dismissed from his job. Brown & Root justified
the dismissal on the grounds of poor performance as a safety inspector,
and the company attempted to downplay the credibility of his charges.
Around the time that he was testifying to government regulators, he
received threatening anonymous telephone calls warning him to keep
quiet, and he suspected that he was being followed and his telephone
monitored

Finding a new job was not easy. He worked for a while driving a
wrecker, and out of desperation he even gathered cans along the highway for sale as scrap aluminum. After finally landing a job as an inspector at a plant in New Orleans, Chuck Atchinson was on the job for only
a week before he was subpoenaed to give further testimony about the
Comanche Peak plant. According to his own account, "When I got back,
my boss called me in and fired me. He said I was a troublemaker." He
was not even given the chance to assume a new job at a power plant in

Clinton, Illinois. "Two days before I was to leave," he said, "they called and said they wouldn't take me, because I was a troublemaker. I tried other plants and I found that I was blacklisted."

Chuck Atchinson eventually found stable employment doing quality control work for the aerospace division of LTV, and he is finally getting back on his feet financially. But the psychic scars still remain. Especially disturbing to the family was the loss of friends. "The whistle-blower has about the same image as the snitch does," he said. "Everyone thinks you're slime." Still he expresses few regrets for blowing the whistle and asserts that he would do it again if he had to. "I've got absolutely nothing in my hand to show as a physical effect of what I've done, except the losses I've had. But I know I was the cutting edge of the knife that prevented them from getting their license and sent them back to do repairs. I know I did right. And I know I'll always sleep right. I'll sleep like a baby."

Joseph Rose

A similar tale is related by Joseph Rose.[3] In the course of his work as an in-house attorney for the Associated Milk Producers Incorporated (AMPI), Joseph Rose became aware of illegal political contributions to the Nixon reelection campaign. He knew that the confidentiality of the attorney-client relation barred him from voluntarily releasing information about past contributions, even if they constituted a criminal conspiracy. At the same time, his legal training told him that his present activity—helping to cover up illegal activity—made him a co-conspirator in a crime. He first contacted the president of AMPI, a Wisconsin dairy farmer, and told him that he would not approve certain payments. Warned that he was now as guilty as anyone else, he concluded that there was no point in going to the other executives of AMPI, who were all deeply implicated in the illegal scheme. So he decided that he had to collect the incriminating evidence and present it to the board of directors. In his own words:

> I was never allowed to do that. My attempt [to talk to the board] happened on a weekend during their convention in Minneapolis. Labor Day followed, and then Tuesday I went to work. I found a guard posted at my door; locks had been changed. The general manager demanded to see me. My services had become very, very unsatisfactory. After I was fired, I felt virtually a sense of relief. I was glad to be out of it, and I planned to keep my mouth shut. Then I had a call from one of the lawyers involved in an antitrust case against AMPI. He said, "They are really slandering you—making some very vicious attacks on you." I had indicated to AMPI executives that if the board would not listen to me, I would go right to the dairy farmers and they obviously felt my career and credibility had to be completely destroyed to protect their own tails.

In the end, AMPI was fined $35,000 and forced to pay $2.9 million in back taxes. Two executives were convicted, and one received a prison sentence. (The other executive died while he was waiting to be sentenced.) Joseph Rose also paid a price in terms of the disruption of his career. Despite the fact that he had been compelled by law to testify before Congress and to the grand jury led by the Watergate special prosecutor, Joseph Rose was regarded by potential employers as someone who had been disloyal and was unreliable as an employee.

Like Chuck Atchinson, Joseph Rose has put his life back together. He has been able to establish a successful practice in San Antonio, Texas, and some of his clients come to him because of his reputation for integrity and toughness in the face of adversity. However, the experience has left him with a cynical view of American business.

> . . . [A]ll of the public utterances of corporations and indeed of our own government concerning "courage, integrity, loyalty, honesty, and duty" are nothing but the sheerest hogwash that disappear very rapidly when it comes to the practical application of these concepts by strict definition. The reason that there are very few . . . [whistle-blowers] is that the message is too clearly out in this society that white-collar crime, or nonviolent crime, should be tolerated by the public at large, so long as the conduct brings a profit or a profitable result to the institution committing it. . . .

Questions About Whistle-blowing

As these examples show, whistle-blowers often pay a high price for their acts of dissent. Retaliation is common and can take many forms—from poor evaluations and demotion to outright dismissal. Some employers seek to blacklist whistle-blowers, so that they cannot obtain jobs in the same industry. Many whistle-blowers suffer career disruption and financial hardship resulting from the job dislocation and legal expenses, and there is severe emotional strain on whistle-blowers and their families as co-workers, friends, and neighbors turn against them. Given the high price that whistle-blowers sometimes pay, should people really be encouraged to blow the whistle? Is the exposure of corruption and mismanagement in government and industry the best way to correct these faults? Or are there more effective ways to deal with them without requiring individuals to make heroic personal sacrifices? Should whistle-blowers be protected, and if so, how can this best be done?

In addition to these practical questions, there are more philosophical issues about the ethical justification of whistle-blowing. Do employees have a right to blow the whistle? Although they usually act with the laudable aim of protecting the public by drawing attention to wrongdoing on the part of their organization, whistle-blowers also run the risk of violating genuine obligations that employees owe to employers. Employees have an obligation to do the work that they are assigned, to be loyal to their employer, and generally to work for the interest of the company, not against it. In addition, employees have an obligation to preserve the confidentiality of information acquired in the course of their work, and whistle-blowing sometimes involves the release of this kind of information. Cases of whistle-blowing are so wrenching precisely because they involve very strong conflicting obligations. It is vitally important, therefore, to understand when it is morally permissible to blow the whistle and when whistle-blowing is, perhaps, not justified.

Our first task, though, is to develop a definition of whistle-blowing.

WHAT IS WHISTLE-BLOWING?

As a first approximation, whistle-blowing can be defined as the release of information by a member or former member of an organization that is evidence of illegal and/or immoral conduct in the organization or conduct in the organization which is not in the public interest. There are several points to observe in this definition.

First, blowing the whistle is something that can be done only by a member of an organization. It is not whistle-blowing when a witness of a crime notifies the police and testifies in court. It is also not whistle-blowing for a reporter who uncovers some illegal practice in a corporation to expose it in print. Both the witness and the reporter have incriminating information, but they are under no obligation that prevents them from making it public. The situation is different for employees who become aware of illegal or immoral conduct in their own organization. Whistle-blowing, therefore, is an action that takes place *within* an organization.

The difference is due to the fact that an employee is expected to work only as directed, to go through channels, and, especially, to act in all matters for the well-being of the organization. Also, the information involved is typically obtained by an employee in the course of his or her employment, as a part of the job. Such information is usually regarded as confidential, so that an employee has an obligation not to reveal it, especially to the detriment of the employer. To "go public" with information that is damaging to the organization is generally viewed as violating a number of obligations that an employee has as a member of the organization.

Second, there must be information. Merely to dissent publicly with an employer is not in itself to blow the whistle; whistle-blowing necessarily involves the release of nonpublic information. According to Sissela Bok, "The whistleblower assumes that his message will alert listeners to something they do not know, or whose significance they have not grasped because it has been kept secret."[4] A distinction can be made between *blowing the whistle* and *sounding the alarm*. Instead of revealing new facts, as whistle-blowers do, dissenters who take a public stand in opposition to an organization to which they belong can be viewed as trying to arouse public concern, to get people alarmed about facts that are already known.

Third, the information is generally evidence of some significant kind of misconduct on the part of an organization or some of its members. The term *whistle-blowing* is usually reserved for matters of substantial importance. The illegal campaign contributions that AMPI funneled to the Nixon reelection campaign provide a good example, since information about the contributions constituted grounds for legal action against the organization and several executives. An employee could also be said to blow the whistle about other practices that are legal but contrary to the public interest, such as a lobbying effort for maintaining artificially high prices for milk products. Information of this kind could alert the public and aid consumers and other interest groups in counteracting the lobbying effort, for example. However, merely exposing incompetent or self-serving management or leaking information to influence the course of events is not commonly counted as whistle-blowing. Lacking in these kinds of cases is a serious wrong that could be averted or rectified by whistle-blowing.

Fourth, the information must be released outside normal channels of communication. In most organizations, employees are instructed to report instances of illegal or improper conduct to their immediate superiors, and other means often exist for employees to register their concerns. Some corporations have an announced policy of encouraging employees to submit any suspicions of misconduct in writing to the CEO, with an assurance of confidentiality. Others have a designated official—often called an *ombudsman*—for handling employee complaints. Whistle-blowing does not necessarily involve "going public" and revealing information outside the organization. There can be *internal* as well as *external* whistle-blowing. However, an employee who follows established procedures for reporting wrongdoing is not a whistle-blower. Joseph Rose, by contrast, saw that it would be futile to confront the executives of AMPI with his evidence of their illegal campaign contributions and decided to go over their heads to the board of directors, thereby blowing the whistle.

A definition of whistle-blowing also needs to take into account *to whom* the whistle is blown. In both internal and external whistle-blowing, the information must be revealed in ways that can reasonably be expected to bring about a desired change. Merely passing on information about wrongdoing to a third party does not necessarily constitute whistle-blowing. Chuck Atchinson testified before a regulatory agency, for example, and Joseph Rose testified before a committee of Congress and the Watergate grand jury. Going to the press is often effective because the information ultimately reaches the appropriate authorities. Reporting to a credit-rating agency that a person faces bankruptcy, by contrast, would not usually be an instance of whistle-blowing but of ordinary snitching.

Fifth, the release of information must be something that is done voluntarily, as opposed to being legally required, although the distinction is not always clear. Joseph Rose did not volunteer his evidence of illegal campaign contributions outside the organization, for example; he had to be subpoenaed and legally forced to testify. And some of Chuck Atchinson's testimony was also the result of court orders. One thing that confuses the distinction is that whistle-blowers are often required by law to reveal information, but the call to testify comes only after they volunteer that they have incriminating evidence. However, in a state supreme court case, *Petermann* v. *International Brotherhood of Teamsters*, a treasurer for a union had no desire to be a whistle-blower, but he refused to perjure himself before a California state legislative body as he had been ordered to do by his employer.[5] Although Petermann acted with considerable courage, it is not clear whether he should be called a whistle-blower, since he had little choice under the circumstances.

A sixth point is that whistle-blowing must be undertaken as a moral protest; that is, the motive must be to correct some wrong and not to seek revenge or personal advancement. This is not to deny that a person with incriminating evidence could conceivably be justified in coming forth, whatever the motive. People "go public" for all sorts of reasons—a common one being fear of their own legal liability—and by doing so, they often benefit society. Still, it is useful to draw a line between the genuine whistle-blower and corporate malcontents and intriguers. Because the motives of whistle-blowers are often misperceived in the organization, employees considering the act must carefully examine their own motivation.

A Final Definition

Putting all these points together, a more adequate (but unfortunately long-winded) definition of whistle-blowing is as follows: Whistle-blowing is the voluntary release of nonpublic information, as a moral protest, by a member or former member of an organization outside the normal channels of communication to an appropriate audience about illegal and/or immoral conduct in the organization or conduct in the organization that is opposed in some significant way to the public interest.

With a definition of whistle-blowing out of the way, we can now proceed to the central question of the conditions for justified whistle-blowing. Can this act ever be justified?

THE JUSTIFICATION OF WHISTLE-BLOWING

The ethical justification of whistle-blowing might seem to be obvious in view of the laudable public service that whistle-blowers provide—often at great personal risk. However, whistle-blowing has the potential to do great harm to both individuals and organizations.

This view is given vigorous expression in a widely cited passage from a 1971 speech by James M. Roche, who was chairman of the board of General Motors Corporation at the time:

> Some critics are now busy eroding another support of free enterprise— the loyalty of a management team, with its unifying values of cooperative work. Some of the enemies of business now encourage an employee to be disloyal to the enterprise. They want to create suspicion and disharmony, and pry into the proprietary interests of the business. However this is labelled—industrial espionage, whistle blowing, or professional responsibility—it is another tactic for spreading disunity and creating conflict.[6]

A more temperate statement along the same lines is given by Sissela Bok:

> Furthermore, the whistleblower hopes to stop the game; but since he is neither referee nor coach, and since he blows the whistle on his own team, his act is seen as a violation of loyalty. In holding his position, he has assumed certain obligations to his colleagues and clients. He may even have subscribed to a loyalty oath or a promise of confidentiality. Loyalty to colleagues and to clients comes to be pitted against loyalty to the public interest, to those who may be injured unless the revelation is made.[7]

As these remarks indicate, the main stumbling block in justifying whistle-blowing is the duty of loyalty that employees have to the organization of which they are a part. The public service that whistle-blowers provide has to be weighed against the disruptive effect that the disclosure of information has on bonds of loyalty. Does a person in a position to blow the whistle have a greater obligation to the public or to the organization? Where does the greater loyalty lie?

That we have an obligation to the public is relatively unproblematic; it is the obligation to prevent serious harm to others whenever this is within our power. An obligation of loyalty to an organization is more complex, involving, as it does, questions about the basis of such an obligation and the concept of loyalty itself. What does an employee owe an employer, and, more to the point, does the employment relation deprive an employee of a right to reveal information about wrongdoing in the organization? In order to answer these questions, let us begin with a commonly used argument against the right of an employee to blow the whistle.

The Loyal Agent Argument

According to one argument, an employee is an *agent* of an employer.[8] An agent is a person who is engaged to act in the interests of another person (called a *principal*) and is authorized to act on that person's behalf. This relation is typical of professionals, such as lawyers and accountants, who are called upon to use their skills in the service of a client. Employees are also considered to be agents of an employer in that they are hired to work for the benefit of the employer. Specifically, an employee, as an agent, has an obligation to work as directed, to protect confidential information, and, above all, to be loyal. All these are seemingly violated when an employee blows the whistle.

The loyal agent argument receives considerable support from the law, where the concept of agency and the obligations of agents are well-developed. Although our concern is with the *moral* status of employees, the law of agency is a rich source of relevant insights about the employment relation.[9] According to one standard book on the subject, "an agent is a person who is authorised to act for a principal and has agreed so to act, and who has power to affect the legal relations of his principal with a third party."[10] Agents are employed to carry out tasks that principals are not willing or able to carry out for themselves. Thus, we hire a lawyer to represent us in legal matters, where we lack the expertise to do the job properly.

The main obligation of an agent is to act in the interests of the principal. We expect a lawyer, for example, to act as we would ourselves, if only we had the same ability. This obligation is expressed in the *Second Restatement of Agency* as follows: ". . . an agent is subject to a duty to his principal to act solely for the benefit of the principal in all matters connected with his agency."[11] The ethical basis of the duty of agents is a contractual obligation or an understood agreement to act in the interests of another person. Lawyers agree for a fee to represent clients, and employees are similarly hired with the understanding that they will work for the benefit of an employer.

At first glance, a whistle-blower is a disloyal agent who backs out of an agreement that is an essential part of the employer-employee relation. A whistle-blowing employee, according to the loyal agent argument, is like a lawyer who sells out a client—clearly a violation of the legal profession's code of ethics. Closer examination reveals that the argument is not as strong as it appears. Athough employees have an obligation of loyalty that is not shared by a person outside the organization, the obligation is not without its limits. Whistle-blowing is not something to be done without adequate justification, but at the same time, it is not something that can never be justified.

First, the law of agency does not impose an absolute obligation on employees to do whatever they are told. Rather, an agent has an obligation, in the words of the *Second Restatement*, to obey all *reasonable* directives of the principal. This is interpreted to exclude illegal or immoral acts; that is, employees are not obligated as agents to do anything illegal or immoral—even if specifically instructed by a superior to do so. Questions can arise, of course, about the legal and moral status of specific acts. Is an agent free to disobey an order to do something that is suspect but not clearly illegal or immoral, for example? Borderline cases are unavoidable, but in situations where a crime is being committed or people are exposed to the risk of serious injury and even death, the law of agency is clear: an employee has no obligation to obey.

The law of agency further excludes an obligation to keep confidential any information about the commission of a crime. Section 395 of the *Second Restatement of Agency* reads in part: "An agent is privileged to reveal information confidentially acquired . . . in the protection of a superior interest of himself or a third person." The *Restatement* does not define what is meant by a "superior interest" except to note that there is no duty of confidentiality when the information is about the commission of a crime. ". . . [I]f the confidential information is to the effect that the principal is committing or is about to commit a crime, the agent is under no duty not to reveal it."[12] Protecting oneself from legal liability can reasonably be held to be a "superior interest," as can preventing some serious harm to others.

Second, the obligations of an agent are confined to the needs of the relation. In order for a lawyer to represent a client adequately, it is necessary to impose a strong obligation of loyalty, but the obligation of loyalty required for employees to do their job adequately is less stringent. The obligation of agents to follow orders exactly stems, in part, from the fact that they may be binding the principal to a contract or exposing the principal to tort liability. The duty of confidentiality is justified by the legitimate right of an employer to maintain the secrecy of certain vital information. Thus, a quality control inspector, such as Chuck Atchinson, has an obligation to perform his work as directed so that nuclear power plants are built safely, and he has an obligation of confidentiality since certain information could benefit a competitor. These obligations are essential to a quality control inspector's job.

Employees are hired for limited purposes, however. As Alex Michalos points out, a person who has agreed to sell life insurance policies on commission is committed to performing *that* activity as a loyal agent. "It would be ludicrous," he continues, "to assume that the agent has also committed himself to painting houses, washing dogs, or doing anything else that happened to give his principal pleasure."[13] Similarly, a quality control inspector is not hired to overlook defects, falsify records, or do anything else that would permit a dangerous plant to go into operation. Information about irregularities in safety matters is also not the kind that the employer has a right to keep confidential, since it is not necessary to the normal operation of the business of constructing nuclear power plants.

To conclude, the loyal agent argument does not serve to show that whistle-blowing can never be justified. The obligations that employees have as agents of an organization are of great moral importance, but they do have limits. Specifically, the agency relation does not require employees to engage in illegal or immoral activities or to give over their whole life to an employer.

The Meaning of Loyalty

The concept of loyalty itself raises some questions. One is whether whistle-blowing is always an act of disloyalty or whether it can sometimes be done out of loyalty to the organization. The answer depends, in part, on what we mean by the term *loyalty*. If loyalty means merely following orders and not "rocking the boat," then whistle-blowers are disloyal employees. But loyalty can also be defined as a commitment to the true interests or goals of the organization, in which case whistle-blowers are often very loyal employees. Thus, whistle-blowing is not necessarily incompatible with loyalty, and, indeed, in some circumstances, loyalty may require employees to blow the whistle on wrongdoing in their own organization.

All too often, the mistake of the whistle-blower lies not in being disloyal to the organization as such but in breaking a relation of trust with a few key members of an organization or with associates and immediate superiors. Insofar as an employee has a duty of loyalty, though, it cannot be merely to follow orders or to go along with others. Loyalty means serving the interests and goals of an organization, which can sometimes lead to divided loyalties and uncertainties about what is best for an organization.

Sociological and Economic Evidence

Some evidence for the claim that whistle-blowers are often loyal—perhaps even too loyal—to the organizations they serve is provided by Myron Glazer, a sociologist who interviewed fifty-five whistle-blowers in depth. One of his findings is that:

> Virtually all of the ethical resisters . . . had long histories of successful employment. They were not alienated or politically active members of movements advocating major changes in society. On the contrary, they began as firm believers in their organizations, convinced that if they took a grievance to superiors, there would be an appropriate response. This naiveté led them into a series of damaging traps. They found that their earlier service and dedication provided them with little protection against charges of undermining organizational morale and effectiveness.[14]

The irony of this finding is that whistle-blowers are often loyal employees who take the first steps toward whistle-blowing in the belief that they are doing their job and acting in the best interests of the company. This is true of Joseph Rose, who has written:

> I never set out to be a whistleblower; I merely tried to alert the appropriate officials at AMPI to the misconduct I became aware of—I felt that was my duty as AMPI's in-house counsel. Even though AMPI fired me abruptly for attempting to discharge my duty . . . , my personal set of ethics dictated that I attempt to shield the company because of the unsettled question of our attorney-client relationship. If I was a whistleblower, I became one reluctantly.[15]

As further evidence that the relation between whistle-blowing and loyalty is far more complex than it first appears, the economist Albert O. Hirschman argues in a book entitled *Exit, Voice, and Loyalty* that members of organizations and people who deal with organizations, such as customers of a firm, can respond to dissatisfaction either by leaving the organization and having no further dealings with it (exit) or by speaking up and making the dissatisfaction known in the hope of bringing about change (voice). Loyalty is a factor that keeps people from exiting an organization; but, at the same time, it activates the voice option. According to Hirschman:

> . . . the likelihood of voice increases with the degree of loyalty. In addition, the two factors are far from independent. A member with a considerable attachment to a product or organization will often search for ways to make himself influential, especially when the organization moves in what he believes is the wrong direction; conversely, a member who wields (or thinks he wields) considerable power in an organization and is therefore convinced that he can get it "back on the track" is likely to develop a strong affection for the organization in which he is powerful.[16]

On Hirschman's analysis, exit is a more extreme form of dissent than voice, but business firms do not usually regard an employee's departure as a form of disloyalty. In fact, whistle-blowers are often treated in ways designed to get them to leave voluntarily. It may benefit an organization in the short run to get rid of troublemakers, but Hirschman argues that in the long run, encouraging employees to use the exit option will harm the organization by depriving it of those people who can bring about healthy change.

> As a result of loyalty, these potentially most influential customers and members will stay on longer than they would ordinarily, in the hope or, rather, reasoned expectation that improvement or reform can be achieved "from within." Thus loyalty, far from being irrational, can serve the so-

cially useful purpose of preventing deterioration from becoming cumulative, as it so often does when there is no barrier to exit.[17]

The Problem of Conflicting Loyalties

A further complication is the fact that employees typically have a number of loyalties, both inside and outside an organization, which can come into conflict. This point is well made by Daniel Ellsberg, the Defense Department employee who finally decided to disclose the so-called Pentagon Papers to the press.

> I think the principle of "company loyalty," as emphasized in the indoctrination within any bureaucratic structure, governmental or private, has come to sum up the notion of loyalty for many people. This is not a healthy situation, because the loyalty that a democracy requires to function is a somewhat varied set of loyalties which includes loyalty to one's fellow citizens, and certainly loyalty to the Constitution and to the broader institutions of the country. Obviously, these loyalties can come into conflict, and merely mentioning the word "loyalty" doesn't dissolve those dilemmas that one faces.[18]

Even if we limit loyalty to a specific employer, such as a government agency or a corporation, questions about what loyalty means still arise. The Code of Ethics for Government Service, for example, contains the following instruction for federal employees: "Put loyalty to the highest moral principles and to country above loyalty to persons, party, or government department." This lofty statement is a prescription for confusion when employees of an administration or an agency are called upon to be team players. Instructions were given in a government handbook issued during the Nixon era to reassign "undesirable" employees— those who were not in sympathy with the administration's philosophy and policies—to "undesirable" positions, from which they would resign. Ernest Fitzgerald would seem to typify the model government employee who puts "loyalty to the highest moral principle and country" above all other loyalties. But the view of Mr. Fitzgerald in the White House was revealed in the following remark by a Nixon aide:

> Fitzgerald is no doubt a top-notch cost expert, but he must be given very low marks for loyalty, and after all loyalty is the name of the game. Only a basic "nogoodnik" would take his official grievances so far from normal channels. We should let him bleed for a while at least.[19]

(The remark was made by Alexander Butterfield, who became a famous whistle-blower of sorts by revealing the existence of the White House tapes, which played a critical role in unraveling the Watergate scandal.)

Can People Be Disloyal to Organizations?

Philosophers have attempted to clarify the concept of loyalty by asking what kinds of things can be the *object* of loyalty? Some argue that we can be loyal only to people and not to organizations. Organizations, according to those who hold this position, are merely the people who compose them and not an entity over and above the members. John Ladd calls this the "social atomist" view—to refer to society is to refer in a shorthand way to the individuals (atoms) who make up society. He continues:

> . . . in our common moral language, as well as historically, "loyalty" is taken to refer to a relationship between persons—for instance, between a lord and his vassal, between a parent and his children, or between friends. Thus, the object of loyalty is ordinarily taken to be a person or group of persons.
>
> Loyalty is conceived as interpersonal, and it is also always specific; a man is loyal to *his* lord, *his* father, or *his* comrades. It is conceptually impossible to be loyal to people in general (to humanity) or to a general principle, such as justice or democracy.[20]

The social atomist view is characteristic of utilitarianism, especially as formulated by Bentham. Opposing it is the idealist view, held by the successors of Kant in the German idealist tradition, most notably Hegel. According to this view, the state and other forms of human association assume a reality of their own apart from specific individuals.

One philosopher, Ronald Duska, has seized on the social atomist view to argue that an organization such as a corporation is not the kind of entity to which one can be disloyal, any more than one can be disloyal to the moon or to the color red. It simply does not make sense.[21] John Ladd criticizes the social atomist view for failing to recognize the fact that loyalty to persons in organizations still depends on relations that depend for their existence on organizations.

> The social atomist fails to recognize the special character and significance of the ties that bind individuals together and provide a basis for loyalties. Loyalty is not founded on just any casual relationship between persons, but on a specific kind of relationship or tie. The special ties involved arise from the twofold circumstance that the persons so bound are comembers of a specific group (community) distinguished by a specific common background and sharing specific interests, and are related in terms of some sort of role differentiation with that group. . . . Special ties of this sort provide both the necessary and sufficient conditions for a person to be a proper object of loyalty.[22]

Duska recognizes the force of this criticism and admits that certain kinds of groups or organizations can be objects of loyalty—but not business firms. A large corporation, such as General Motors or IBM, is not a community in the requisite sense. Duska argues, "Loyalty depends on ties that demand self-sacrifice with no expectation of reward. Business functions on the basis of enlightened self-interest. . . . I am not devoted to it at all, nor should I be. I work for it because it pays me."[23] He continues:

> The cold hard truth is that the goal of profit is what gives birth to a company and forms that particular group. Money is what ties the group together. But in such a commercialized venture, with such a goal, there is no loyalty, or at least none need be expected. An employer will release an employee and an employee will walk away from an employer when it is profitable for either one to do so.[24]

The conclusion that Duska draws from his analysis of corporations as an object of loyalty is that worry over the permissibility of whistle-blowing is misconceived. Whether the whistle-blower violates a duty of loyalty is not an issue at all, because there is no such duty.

This analysis has some merit. Business firms are different from other forms of human association in ways that affect their claims upon our loyalty. The picture that Duska paints is unduly pessimistic, however. Employees often have a great deal of loyalty to a company, and it is doubtful that businesses could operate if everyone took the attitude Duska describes. Duska's mistake is to look in the wrong place for the basis of an employee's duty of loyalty. In the agency argument, an employee has a duty of loyalty not by virtue of the nature of the organization but by virtue of an agreement to act as an agent of the organization. The lawyer-client relation is no less commercial than that of employer and employee (perhaps even more so), yet lawyers have a very strong obligation of loyalty as well as of obedience and confidentiality. These obligations are not deserved by virtue of any ongoing relation but exist primarily by mutual agreement. The obligations of a parent to a child and a neighbor in a community, by contrast, are deserved by virtue of the relation in which the parties find themselves. Corporations may not *deserve* our loyalty, but it is *owed* to them if, in voluntarily becoming an employee, we commit ourselves to the role of loyal agent.

The proper conclusion, then, is that it makes sense to speak of an obligation of loyalty to an organization by virtue of an agreement to serve as an employee. But we have also seen that the obligation of loyalty is not incompatible with whistle-blowing. Being loyal to an organization can, in fact, require an employee to blow the whistle in order to better serve the true interests or goals of an organization, and sometimes whistle-blowing can be justified by appealing to a higher loyalty. Merely because employees have an obligation of loyalty to an organization, therefore, it does not follow that whistle-blowing is never justified. The conditions for justified whistle-blowing must be satisfied, however. To these we now turn.

THE CONDITIONS FOR JUSTIFIED WHISTLE-BLOWING

The following are some questions that should be considered in deciding whether to blow the whistle in a specific case.[25]

Is the situation of sufficient moral importance to justify whistle-blowing? A coverup of lethal side effects in a newly marketed drug, for example, is an appropriate situation for disclosure because people's lives are at stake. But situations are not always this clear. Is whistle-blowing warranted if the side effects are not lethal or debilitating but capable of causing temporary discomfort or pain? What if the drug is the most effective treatment for a serious medical problem, so that the harm of the side effect is outweighed by the benefit of using the drug? We need to ask, in such a case, how serious is the potential harm compared to the benefit of the drug and the trouble that would be caused by blowing the whistle? The less serious the harm, the less appropriate it is to blow the whistle.

In addition to the moral importance of the situation, consideration should also be given to the extent to which harm is a direct and predictable result of the activity that the whistle-blower is protesting. For example, a toy that might be hazardous under unusual circumstances warrants whistle-blowing less than one that poses a risk under all conditions. Sissela Bok contends that the harm should also be imminent. According to her, an alarm can be sounded about defects in a rapid-transit system that is already in operation or is about to go into operation, but an alarm should not be sounded about defects in a system that is still on the drawing boards and is far from being operational.[26]

Do you have all the facts and have you properly understood their significance? Whistle-blowing usually involves very serious charges that can cause irreparable harm if they turn out to be unfounded or misinterpreted. A potential whistle-blower, therefore, has a strong obligation to the people who are charged with wrongdoing to make sure that the charges are well founded. The whistle-blower should also have as much documentation and other corroboration as possible. A whistle-blower's case is stronger when the evidence consists of verifiable facts and not merely hunches or rumors. Since whistle-blowing cases often end up in court, the proof should also be strong enough to stand up under scrutiny. The support for the charges need not be overwhelming, but it should meet the ordinary legal standard of a preponderance of evidence.

Employees often have access to only some of the facts of a case and are liable, as a result, to form false or misleading impressions. Would-be whistle-blowers must be careful, therefore, not to jump to conclusions about matters that higher level managers, with a fuller knowledge of the situation, are in a better position to judge. Typically, employees have only one kind of expertise, so they are not able to make an accurate judgment when different kinds of knowledge are needed.

Have all internal channels and steps short of whistle-blowing been exhausted? Whistle-blowing should be a last rather than a first resort. It is justified only when there are no morally preferable alternatives. The alternatives available to employees depend to a great extent on the provisions an organization makes for dissent, but virtually every organization requires employees to take up any matter of concern with an immediate superior before proceeding further—unless that person is part of the problem. Courts will generally not consider a complaint unless all possible appeals within an organization have been exhausted. Some progressive corporations have recognized the value of dissent in bringing problems to light and have set up procedures that allow employees to express their concern through internal channels. Steps of this kind reduce the need for whistle-blowing and the risks that external whistle-blowers take. It is possible to justify not using internal channels, however, when the whole organization is so mired in the wrongdoing that there is little chance that using them would succeed.

Another justification for "going public" before exhausting internal channels is if there is a need for a quick response and internal whistle-blowing would be too slow and uncertain. Two engineers at Morton Thiokol expressed concern to their superiors about the effects of low temperature on the O-rings on the booster rockets for the *Challenger* spacecraft, but their warning never reached the officials at NASA who were responsible for making the decision to go ahead with the launch. The engineers spoke out after the *Challenger* explosion—for which they were disciplined by Morton Thiokol—but their whistle-blowing was too late to avert the disaster. To be effective, they would have had to blow the whistle before the decision was made to launch the spacecraft. This would have required them to go outside the company and contact the officials at NASA directly.

What is the best way to blow the whistle? Once a decision is made to "go public," a host of other questions have to be answered. To whom should the information be revealed? How much information should be revealed? Should the information be revealed anonymously or accompanied by the identity of the whistle-blower? Often an anonymous complaint to a regulatory body, such as the Environmental Protection Agency or the Securities and Exchange Commission, is sufficient to spark an investigation. The situation might also be handled by contacting the FBI or a local prosecuting attorney or by leaking information to the local press. The less information that is revealed, the less likely an employee is to violate any duty of confidentiality. Employees can also reduce conflicts by waiting until they leave an organization to blow the whistle.

Whistle-blowing is also more likely to be effective when an employee presents the charge in an objective and responsible manner. It is especially important that a whistle-blower stick to the important issues and refrain from conducting crusades or making personal attacks on the persons involved. Organizations often seek to discredit whistle-blowers by picturing them as disgruntled misfits or crazy radicals; intemperate, wide-ranging attacks undermine the whistle-blower's own credibility. Many whistle-blowers recommend developing a clear plan of action. Do not blow the whistle impulsively, they advise, but think out each step and anticipate the possible consequences.[27]

What is my responsibility in view of my role in the organization? The justification for blowing the whistle depends not only on the wrongdoing of others but also on the particular role that a whistle-blower occupies in an organization. Thus, an employee is more justified in blowing the whistle—and may even have an obligation to do so— when the wrongdoing concerns matters over which the employee has direct responsibility. Chuck Atchinson, for example, was not merely an employee of Brown & Root; he was a quality control inspector, and so the irregularities in the construction of the nuclear power plant involved matters that were part of his job. A company such as Brown & Root employs quality control inspectors in order to be sure that nuclear power plants are built to certain standards of safety. The welfare of the company and the public alike depend on people such as Chuck Atchinson doing their job conscientiously. In order to operate a nuclear power plant, moreover, a company must file an application under oath with the Nuclear Regulatory Commission (NRC), and it is a criminal offense for any employee to participate knowingly in the submission of an application that contains false information. Had Chuck Atchinson been called upon to verify that the work on the plant had been performed according to specifications, he would have faced the choice of refusing or becoming an accomplice in a crime.

When an employee is a professional, the question of whether to blow the whistle must be considered in the context of professional ethics. Professionals, such as lawyers, accountants, and engineers, have a greater obligation to blow the whistle under some circumstances and are restricted or prohibited from whistle-blowing under others. For example, Joseph Rose, the staff lawyer for the Associated Milk Producers Incorporated, realized that he had an obligation as a lawyer for AMPI to seek to recover the missing funds, which is an obligation that an employee in a different position would not necessarily have. Yet, at the same time, he planned after leaving his position to keep quiet about what he knew, because he had also discharged his legal responsibility by informing his superiors. In addition, he had to be careful about violating the guarantee of confidentiality inherent in the lawyer-client relation. His situation was thus substantially different from that of other employees at AMPI.

What are the chances for success? Insofar as whistle-blowing is justified because of some good to the public, it is important to blow the whistle only when there is a reasonable chance of achieving that good. Whistle-blowing may be unsuccessful for many reasons. Sometimes the fault lies with the whistle-blower, who fails to make a case that attracts widespread concern or to devise an effective plan of action; other times it is simply that the organization is too powerful or the public not sufficiently responsive. Ernest Fitzgerald took on a powerful organization in protesting the procurement practices of the Department of Defense, but he was probably fortunate in his timing, since the turmoil of the Vietnam War created a willingness in Congress and the public at large to question military spending. In other circumstances he might have had less success.

IS THERE A RIGHT TO BLOW THE WHISTLE?

Even though whistle-blowing can be justified in some situations, the sad fact remains that courageous employees who perform a valuable public service are often subjected to harsh retaliation. Our reaction when this occurs is, "There ought to be a law!" and, indeed, many have been proposed in Congress and various state legislatures.[28] Few have passed, however, and there are some strong arguments against providing legal protection for whistle-blowers. In this section we will examine the debate over the moral justification of laws to protect whistle-blowers against retaliation. It will be useful, first, to survey the existing legal protection.

Existing Legal Protection

President Reagan vetoed the Whistleblower Protection Act of 1988, which would have created an independent agency to investigate claims of retaliation against federal employees who report instances of waste and corruption in government. Such retaliation was already prohibited, however, by the Civil Service Reform Act of 1978, which also set up the Merit System Protection Board (MSPB) to receive and act on complaints of retaliation.[29] Some protection for whistle-blowers in both the public and private sectors exists in the antiretaliation provisions of various pieces of federal legislation. The National Labor Relations Act of 1935

(NLRA) forbids employers to retaliate against any employee who files a charge with the National Labor Relations Board (NLRB). Title VII of the 1964 Civil Rights Act protects employees who file a charge of discrimination, participate in an investigation or proceeding connected with a charge, or oppose an activity of a company that the employee believes is discriminatory. The Occupational Safety and Health Act of 1970 also prohibits retaliation against any employee who files a complaint with the Occupational Safety and Health Administration or testifies in a proceeding.

Other federal acts with antiretaliatory provisions are the Surface Mining Act, the Railway Safety Act, the Surface Transportation Safety Act, the Safe Drinking Water Act, the Toxic Substance Control Act, the Clear Air Act, the Water Pollution Control Act, and the Energy Reorganization Act. Also, the once moribund Federal False Claims Act of 1863 (amended 1986), which allows private citizens who report fraud by government contractors to share in the financial recovery and to sue for damages if they lose their jobs or suffer in their career, is now being used by whistle-blowers.[30]

At least thirty states have passed laws designed to protect whistle-blowers. Most of these apply only to government employees, but a few—Michigan's Whistle Blowers Protection Act, for example—extend more widely. A significant source of protection for whistle-blowers comes from state court decisions limiting the traditional right of employers to fire at will. These decisions protect workers against retaliation for many reasons besides whistle-blowing, but they leave some whistle-blowers unprotected. A further discussion of the issues in this kind of protection is contained in Chapter 10, "Unjust Dismissal."

The Arguments Against Whistle-blower Protection

There are many problems with drafting legislation for protecting whistle-blowers. First, a law recognizing whistle-blowing as a right is open to abuse. Whistle-blowing might be used by disgruntled employees to protest company decisions or to get back at their employers. Employees might also find an excuse to blow the whistle in order to cover up their own incompetence or inadequate performance. Alan F. Westin notes, "Forbidding an employer to dismiss or discipline an employee who protests against illegal or improper conduct by management invites employees to take out 'antidismissal insurance' by lodging a whistle-blowing complaint."[31]

Second, legislation to protect whistle-blowers would encroach on the traditional right of employers to conduct business as they see fit and would add another layer of regulation to the existing legal restraints on business, thereby making it more difficult for managers to run a company efficiently. The courts would be called upon to review and possibly reverse a great many personnel decisions. And the likely increase in employee litigation could also, according to Westin, "create an informer ethos at work that would threaten the spirit of cooperation and trust on which sound working relationships depend."[32]

Third, if whistle-blowing were protected by law, what should be the legal remedy for employees who are unjustly dismissed? Reinstatement in the workplace, which is the usual remedy in union contract grievance procedures, may not be feasible in the case of employees who are perceived as being disloyal. As an alternative to reinstatement, though, whistle-blowers could be offered a monetary settlement to compensate them for the losses suffered by being wrongly dismissed. An award could be arrived at by negotiation or arbitration, or it could result by allowing dismissed employees to sue for tort damages.

The Arguments for Whistle-blower Protection

The main argument in defense of a law to protect whistle-blowers is a utilitarian one that rests on the contribution whistle-blowers make to society. There is a direct benefit in having instances of illegal corporate conduct, gross waste and mismanagement, and dangers to the public brought to light. This benefit can be achieved, the argument goes, only if whistle-blowers are encouraged to come forward and make their information known. Ralph Nader makes the further point that allowing employees greater freedom to speak out makes it easier to enforce existing laws and to bring about desirable changes in corporate behavior. He has observed:

> Corporate employees are among the first to know about industrial dumping of mercury or fluoride sludge into waterways, defectively designed automobiles, or undisclosed adverse effects of prescription drugs and pesticides. They are the first to grasp the technical capabilities to prevent existing product or pollution hazards. But they are very often the last to speak out, much less to refuse to be recruited for acts of corporate or governmental negligence or predation. Staying silent in the face of a professional duty has direct impact on the level of consumer and environmental hazards.[33]

These benefits must be balanced against the undeniable harm that a greater incidence of whistle-blowing would have on business firms. Insofar as companies are less efficient—either because of the greater regulation or the loss of loyalty within organizations—a right to blow the whistle is not justified on utilitarian grounds.

A second argument for providing legal protection for whistle-blowers appeals to the First Amendment right of freedom of speech. A distinction needs to be made, though, between the appeal to freedom of speech as a legal argument and as a moral argument. Our rights under the Constitution protect us for the most part only against acts of government and not against those of private employers. Consequently, the freedom of speech that we have as a matter of legal right does not necessarily prevent corporations from retaliating against whistle-blowers, although it does confer some protection on government employees who speak out as citizens.

A teacher in Illinois, for example, wrote a letter to the editor of a local newspaper criticizing the school board for favoring athletics at the expense of the academic program. The teacher, named Pickering, was fired on the grounds that writing the letter was "detrimental to the efficient operation and administration of the schools of the district." Pickering charged in reply that writing the letter was an exercise of the First Amendment right of free speech that cannot be denied citizens just because they are government employees. The U.S. Supreme Court agreed with Pickering and thereby established whistle-blower protection for government employees.[34] The Court, in a 1978 decision *Holodnak v. Avco Corporation*, extended the precedent set by *Pickering* to private employers who do extensive work for the federal government.[35] The plaintiff, Michael Holodnak, charged in a letter to a local newspaper that the company and the union had undermined the employee grievance procedure at Avco. Although admitting that *Pickering* did not apply to employees in private industry, the Court ruled that the fact that 80 percent of Avco's business was with the federal government justified extending the right of free speech to its employees.[36]

Although the First Amendment right of free speech cannot be used as a *legal* argument for holding that whistle-blowing is a protected activity in the private sector, it can still be maintained that there is a *moral* right to freedom of speech and that (morally) there ought to be a law extending this right to whistle-blowers.[37] At least one writer has urged that we recognize a right that is broader than merely freedom of speech—namely, a right to follow one's own conscience. Whistle-blowers are often led to speak out not by a desire to serve the public good but to do what they feel is morally required of them. "Thus," this writer concludes, "the interests that weigh in favor of providing legal protection to the external whistleblower are not those embodied in an employee's obligation to society, but rather those embodied in his interest as an individual to act in accordance with the dictates of conscience."[38]

Conclusion

Whether to blow the whistle on misconduct in an organization is the most difficult decision that some people ever have to make. The decision is wrenching personally because the stakes are so high. The lives of Ernest Fitzgerald, Chuck Atchinson, and Joseph Rose were irreparably damaged, and yet many whistle-blowers say that they could not have lived with themselves if they had stayed silent. The decision is also difficult ethically, since whistle-blowing involves a conflict between two competing duties: to protect the public and to be loyal to an organization. And although loyalty is not always overriding, as the loyal agent argument holds, neither is it inconsequential. Deciding between these duties often requires that an employee exercise very careful judgment.

The one certain conclusion of this chapter is that whistle-blowing is ethically permissible under certain carefully specified conditions. (Whether it can ever be ethically required is a different question that seldom arises. Everyone has an obligation not to be a part of illegal and immoral activity, but exposing it at great risk to oneself is usually regarded as beyond what duty requires.) Blowing the whistle is only one response that an employee can make to corporate misconduct, however, and the act of whistle-blowing itself can take many different forms. So in addition to *whether* to become a whistle-blower, employees are faced with the further question of *how* to blow the whistle in a justified manner.

Finally, it is evident that employees who are justified in blowing the whistle ought not to suffer retaliation. What ought to be done to protect whistle-blowers from this fate is less clear. A plausible case can be made for legislation in this area, but the difficulty is drafting laws that achieve the desired result without interfering unduly in the legitimate conduct of business.

NOTES

1. For a discussion of the etymology of the word, see WILLIAM SAFIRE, *Safire's Political Dictionary*, 3rd ed. (New York: Random House, 1978), 790.
2. The material for this case is taken from N. R. KLEINFIELD, "The Whistle Blowers' Morning After," *The New York Times*, November 9, 1986, sec. 3, p. 1.
3. Material for this case is taken from MYRON GLAZER, "Ten Whistleblowers and How They Fared," *The Hastings Center Report*, 13 (December 1983), 33–41; and from ALAN F. WESTIN, ed., *Whistle Blowing! Loyalty and Dissent in the Corporation* (New York: McGraw-Hill, 1981), 31–38.
4. SISSELA BOK, "Whistleblowing and Professional Responsibility," in TOM L. BEAUCHAMP and NORMAN E. BOWIE, eds., *Ethical Theory and Business*, 3rd ed. (Englewood Cliffs, NJ: Prentice Hall, 1988), 295.
5. *Petermann* v. *International Brotherhood of Teamsters*, 174 Cal. App. 2d 184, 344, P. 2d 25 (1959). This case is discussed further in the chapter on unjust dismissal, since Petermann was fired for testifying.
6. JAMES M. ROCHE, "The Competitive System to Work, to Preserve, and to Protect," *Vital Speeches of the Day*, May 1971, 445.
7. BOK, "Whistleblowing and Professional Responsibility," 294.
8. One form of this argument is examined in ALEX C. MICHALOS, "The Loyal Agent's Argument," in NORMAN E. BOWIE and TOM L. BEAUCHAMP , eds.,

Ethical Theory and Business, 1st ed. (Englewood Cliffs, NJ: Prentice Hall, 1979), 338–48.

9. The concept of agency is not confined to law but occurs in economics (especially the theory of the firm) and organizational theory. For a useful collection of articles exploring the ethical relevance of agency theory, see NORMAN E. BOWIE and R. EDWARD FREEMAN, eds., *Agency Theory and Ethics* (New York: Oxford University Press, forthcoming).

10. R. POWELL, *The Law of Agency* (London: Pitman and Sons, 1965), 7.

11. *Second Restatement of Agency*, Sec. 387. A Restatement is not a statute passed by a legislature but a summary of the law in a given area, written by legal scholars, which is often cited in court opinions. Other important Restatements are those on contracts and torts.

12. *Second Restatement of Agency*, Sec. 358, Comment f.

13. MICHALOS, "The Loyal Agent's Argument," 344.

14. MYRON PERETZ GLAZER and PENINA MIGDAL GLAZER, "Whistleblowing," *Psychology Today*, August 1986, 39. See also MYRON PERETZ GLAZER and PENINA MIGDAL GLAZER, *The Whistle-Blowers: Exposing Corruption in Government and Industry* (New York: Basic Books, 1989).

15. WESTIN, *Whistle Blowing!* 36.

16. ALBERT O. HIRSCHMAN, *Exit, Voice, and Loyalty* (Cambridge: Harvard University Press, 1970), 77.

17. HIRSCHMAN, *Exit, Voice, and Loyalty*, 79.

18. CHARLES PETERS and TAYLOR BRANCH, *Blowing the Whistle: Dissent in the Public Interest* (New York: Praeger, 1972), 269.

19. Media Transcripts Incorporated, Program *20/20*. December 18, 1980, p. 14. Quoted by GLAZER in "Ten Whistleblowers and How They Fared," 39.

20. JOHN LADD, "Loyalty," in *The Encyclopedia of Philosophy*, vol. 5, 97.

21. RONALD DUSKA, "Whistleblowing and Employee Loyalty," in BEAUCHAMP and BOWIE, *Ethical Theory and Business*, 3rd ed., 299–303.

22. LADD, "Loyalty," 97.

23. DUSKA, "Whistleblowing and Employee Loyalty," 302.

24. DUSKA, "Whistleblowing and Employee Loyalty," 302.

25. For similar lists, see RICHARD T. DEGEORGE, *Business Ethics*, 3rd ed. (New York: Macmillan, 1990), 208–11; GENE G. JAMES, "Whistle Blowing: Its Moral Justification," in W. MICHAEL HOFFMAN and JENNIFER MILLS MOORE, eds., *Business Ethics: Readings and Cases in Corporate Morality*, 2nd ed. (New York: McGraw-Hill, 1990), 332–44.

26. BOK, "Whistleblowing and Professional Responsibility," 294–95.

27. For a more thorough discussion of the practical aspects of whistle-blowing see PETER RAVEN-HANSEN, "Dos and Don'ts for Whistleblowers: Planning for Trouble," *Technology Review*, 83 (May 1980), 34–44.

28. See MARTIN H. MALIN, "Protecting the Whistleblower from Retaliatory Discharge," *Journal of Law Reform*, 16 (Winter 1983), 277–318; and DOUGLAS MASSENGILL and DONALD J. PETERSEN, "Whistleblowing: Protected Activity or Not?" *Employee Relations Law Journal*, 15 (Summer 1989), 49–56.

29. Two studies of the MSPB in 1980 and 1983 showed that it had done little to encourage employees to report waste and corruption or to prevent retaliation against those who did. See ROSEMARY CHALK, "Making the World Safe for Whistleblowers," *Technology Review*, 91 (January 1988), 55.

30. See RICHARD W. STEVENSON, "Workers Who Turn in Bosses Use Law to Seek Big Rewards," *The New York Times*, July 10, 1989, sec. 1, p. 1.
31. WESTIN, *Whistle Blowing!* 134.
32. WESTIN, *Whistle Blowing!* 136. All the points in this paragraph are made by WESTIN.
33. NADER, PETKAS, and BLACKWELL, *Whistle Blowing*, 4.
34. *Pickering v. Board of Education*, 391 U.S. 563 (1968).
35. *Holodnak v. Avco Corporation*, 423 U.S. 892 (1975).
36. In other Supreme Court decisions, the right to speak out on matters of public concern was upheld in cases involving a police officer, a firefighter, and a public health nurse. *Muller v. Conlisk*, 429 F.2d 901 (7th Cir. 1970). *Dendor v. Board of Fire and Police Commissioners*, 11 Ill. App.3d 582, 297 N.E.2d 316 (1973). *Rafferty v. Philadelphia Psychiatric Center*, 356 F. Supp. 500 (E.D.Pa. 1973).
37. This is advocated by PATRICIA H. WERHANE, "Individual Rights in Business," in TOM REGAN, ed., *Just Business: New Introductory Essays in Business Ethics* (New York: Random House, 1984), 114–18.
38. MARTIN H. MALIN, "Protecting the Whistleblower from Retaliatory Discharge," *Journal of Law Reform*, 16 (Winter 1983), 309.

CHAPTER SIX
Trade Secrets and Conflict of Interest

In 1968, C. Lester Hogan resigned as executive vice-president of Motorola and general manager of its semiconductor division and assumed the post of president and chief executive officer of Fairchild Camera and Instrument Company, taking six other Motorola executives with him.[1] Motorola went to court but was unsuccessful in its attempt to prevent Mr. Hogan and the six other executives from working for Fairchild and from disclosing any of Motorola's trade secrets.[2] About the same time, the Telex Corporation lured several executives away from IBM to bolster its efforts to design and develop peripheral equipment that would be compatible with IBM computers. In this case, the former employer prevailed in court, and Telex was ordered to pay $21,900,000 in compensation for damages caused by the wrongful acquisition of IBM trade secrets.[3]

It is not surprising that corporations such as Motorola and IBM attempt to protect themselves against the loss of trade secrets when departing employees join a competitor or go into business for themselves. Information is a valuable business asset that generally provides companies with a significant advantage over competitors who lack it. We need to ask, however, what rights do companies have in maintaining the secrecy of valuable information? And also, what corresponding obligations do employees have not to disclose company trade secrets to outsiders or use them for their own advantage?

There is considerable justification for holding that companies have some rights with respect to trade secrets and other intellectual property, such as patents, copyrights, and trademarks. In general, employees have an obligation of confidentiality not to disclose or use information acquired during their employment. On the other hand, employees, including Mr. Hogan and the six other Motorola executives, have the right to change jobs or to start up a business of their own using some of the skill and knowledge they have acquired while working for a former employer.

In addition, businesses have a right to compete using trade secrets of other companies as long as the information is acquired legitimately. Thus, a manufacturer, such as Telex, is generally free to use nonpatented discoveries that are made independently or result from examining a competitor's product, a process known as "reverse engineering." The Telex Corporation, however, offered one IBM employee a $500,000 bonus to switch employers and doubled the salary of an IBM engineer. Such unusually large payments smack of bribery, which is not a legitimate way of acquiring information from another company.

Trade secrets, then, pose a complex set of problems about the rights and obligations of companies possessing valuable information as well as the rights and obligations of employees and competitors. The courts have long struggled with these problems without much success. Even what information constitutes a trade secret is a source of contention.

A rough definition of a trade secret is that it is information which is used in the conduct of a business and is not commonly known by others. Section 757 of the *Restatement of Torts* defines a trade secret as follows:

> A trade secret may consist of any formula, pattern, device or compilation of information which is used in one's business, and which gives him an opportunity to obtain an advantage over competitors who do not know or use it.

Examples of trade secrets include the ingredients or chemical composition of a product, the design of a machine, the details of a manufacturing process, methods of quality control, results of marketing surveys, financial projections, and lists of customers and suppliers.

A distinction is made in the *Restatement* between trade secrets and confidential business information. The latter is information concerning specific matters, such as the salary of an employee, which is kept secret but not actually used to manufacture anything or provide a service. The amount of a specific bid is also not a trade secret, but the procedure of a company for calculating bids might be. A former employee who is knowledgeable about the bidding procedure of a company, for example, might be able to use that information to enter lower bids.

The *Restatement* admits that an exact definition is not possible, but it lists six factors that can be used to determine what information is protectable as a trade secret. These are

> (1) the extent to which the information is known outside his business; (2) the extent to which it is known by employees and others involved in his business; (3) the extent of measures taken by him to guard the secrecy of the information; (4) the value of the information to him and his competitors; (5) the amount of effort or money expended by him in developing the information; (6) the ease or difficulty with which the information could be properly acquired or duplicated by others.

One reason why Motorola lost its suit against the employees who left to join Fairchild, for example, was the failure of the company to make any real effort to keep sensitive information secret.

Unlike patents, trade secrets need not involve any particular originality. They often involve only an application of well-known techniques or a combination of common elements. However, minor changes in manufacturing methods and materials or the composition or design of a product can sometimes make the difference between profit and loss. Two former employees of the Head Ski Company, for example, defended themselves against charges of misappropriating trade secrets by arguing that the construction technology in Head skis was common knowledge among aeronautical engineers and the materials could be determined by simple tests.[4] The court ruled against them, however, on the grounds that applying the principles of airplane construction to the manufacture of skis is a novelty. In the words of the court, ". . . a knowledge of the particular process, method or material which is most appropriate to achieve the desired result may *itself* be a trade secret." Furthermore, knowing what tests would reveal the materials used in the skis is information that the former Head employees possessed by virtue of their work for the company. It would take some time for an outsider to determine the composition of Head skis and to reproduce the method for constructing them by trial and error, and time is often a crucial element in a competitive business.

THE ARGUMENTS FOR PROTECTING TRADE SECRETS

There are three major arguments for trade secret protection. One argument views trade secrets as a kind of *property* and attempts to apply common-law principles of property rights to them. In the second argument, cases involving trade secrets are considered in terms of the right to compete and the principles of *fair competition*. The third argument holds that employees who disclose trade secrets to others or who use them for their own gain violate an obligation of *confidentiality* that is part of the employer-employee relation.

The Property Rights Argument

Trade secrets, along with patents, copyrights, and trademarks, are commonly regarded in the law as intellectual property that can be said to belong to an owner. Patents, copyrights, and trademarks, in particular, are like tangible property in that the owner has a right of exclusive use and the right to sell, license, or otherwise assign ownership to others. This right does not depend on keeping the information secret. Ownership of a trade secret, by contrast, does not confer a right of exclusive use but only a right not to have the secret misappropriated or wrongfully acquired by others. And once the information is widely known, it ceases to be a protectable trade secret. All forms of intellectual property are unlike tangible property, however, in that they are not inherently exclusive; that is, their use by one person does not preclude their use by another. As one writer observes, "If someone borrows your lawn mower, you cannot use it, nor can anyone else. But if someone borrows your recipe for guacamole, that in no way precludes you, or anyone else, from using it."[5]

According to the decision in a landmark case, *Wexler* v. *Greenberg*, an employer has the burden of showing two things: "(1) a legally protectable trade secret; and (2) a legal basis, either a covenant or a confidential relationship, upon which to predicate relief."[6] Information is protectable as a trade secret, in other words, only as long as it meets certain conditions, one of which is that it is genuinely a secret. Furthermore, the owner of a trade secret is protected against the use of this information by others only when it is disclosed by an employee in violation of an obligation of confidentiality, for example, or when a competitor obtains it by theft, bribery, industrial espionage, or some other impermissible means.

One source for the argument that patentable ideas, trade secrets, and the like are a form of property is the Lockean view that we own the results of our own labor.[7] Patent and copyright laws are based in part on the premise that inventors and writers who work with their minds and turn out such products as blueprints and novels should have the same rights of ownership that is accorded to creators of more tangible objects. Insofar as intellectual property is created by individuals who have been hired by a company for that purpose and paid for their labor, then it follows, in the Lockean view, that the company is the rightful owner. Just as the products made on an assembly line belong to the company and not to the workers who make them, so too do inventions made by people who are hired to invent. The company has paid them for their efforts and provided them with the wherewithal to do their work.

In addition, there are good utilitarian reasons for holding that companies have property rights to certain kinds of information. First, society generally benefits from the willingness of companies to innovate, but without the legal protection provided by patent and trade secret laws, companies would have less incentive to make the costly investments in research and development that innovation requires. Second, patent and copyright laws encourage a free flow of information, which leads to additional benefits. Patent holders are granted a period of seventeen years in which to capitalize on their discoveries; but even during the period of the patent, others can use the information in their research and perhaps make new discoveries.

The existence of legal protection for trade secrets, patents, and other forms of intellectual property also has its drawbacks. A patent confers a legal monopoly for a fixed number of years, which raises the price that the public pays for the products of patent holders during that time. Trade secrets permit a monopoly to exist as long as a company succeeds in keeping key information out of the hands of competitors. Since there is no requirement that patents be used, a company could conceivably patent a large number of processes and products which rival its own and thereby prevent competitors from using them.[8] And the owner of copyrighted material can prevent the wide dissemination of important information either by denying permission to print it or by charging an exorbitant price.

These drawbacks can be minimized by the optimal tradeoff between the advantages and disadvantages of providing legal protection for patents, trade secrets, and the like. This tradeoff is achieved, in part, by the limits on what can be patented or copyrighted or protected as a trade secret. Other means for achieving the optimal tradeoff include placing expiration dates on patents and copyrights and defining what constitutes infringements of patents and copyrights. Thus, the Copyright Act of 1976 includes a provision for "fair use" that permits short quotations in reviews, criticism, and news reports.

Fair Competition

The second argument holds that companies are put at an unfair competitive disadvantage when information they have expended resources in developing or gathering can be used without cost by their competitors. Even when the information is not easily classifiable as property and there is no contract barring disclosure or use of the information, it may still be protected on grounds of fairness in trade.

A good illustration of this argument is provided by a 1918 case in which the Associated Press complained that a news service was rewriting its stories and selling them to newspapers in competition with the Associated Press.[9] The defendant, International News Service, argued in reply that although the specific wording of a news story can be regarded as a form of property, like a literary work, which belongs to the writer, the content itself cannot belong to anyone. Further, there is no contract between the parties that International News Service had breached. In the words of Justice Louis D. Brandeis:

> An essential element of individual property is the legal right to exclude others from enjoying it. . . . But the fact that a product of the mind has cost its producer money and labor, and has a value for which others are willing to pay, is not sufficient to insure to it this legal attribute of property. The general rule of law is, that the noblest of human productions— knowledge, truths ascertained, conceptions, and ideas—become, after voluntary communication to others, free as the air to common use.

In this view, information which cannot be patented or copyrighted has the same legal status as trade secrets, so that a plaintiff must show that there is a breach of contract or some other wrongful means of acquisition. Accordingly, Brandeis continued:

> The means by which the International News Service obtains news gathered by the Associated Press is . . . clearly unobjectionable. It is taken from papers bought in the open market or from bulletins publicly posted. No breach of contract, or of trust and neither fraud nor force, are involved. The manner of use is likewise unobjectionable. No reference is made by word or act to the Associated Press. . . . Neither the International News Service nor its subscribers is gaining or seeking to gain in its business a benefit from the reputation of the Associated Press. They are merely using its product without making compensation. That, they have a legal right to do; because the product is not property, and they do not stand in any relation to the Associated Press, either of contract or trust, which otherwise precludes such use.

A majority of the justices of the Supreme Court sided with the Associated Press, however, arguing that the case should be decided not on grounds of property rights or breach of contract but on considerations of fair competition. Although the public may make unrestricted use of the information contained in news stories, the two parties were direct competitors in a business in which the major stock in trade is news, a product that requires the resources and efforts of a news gathering organization. In selling news stories based on dispatches from the Associated Press, the International News Service was, in the words of the majority opinion, "endeavouring to reap where it has not sown, and

. . . appropriating to itself the harvest of those who have sown." The opinion further held:

> We need spend no time, however, upon the general question of property in news matter at common law, or the application of the Copyright Act, since it seems to us the case must turn upon the question of unfair competition in business. . . . The underlying principle is much the same as that which lies at the base of the equitable theory of consideration in the law of trusts—that he who has fairly paid the price should have the beneficial use of the property. It is no answer to say that complainant spends its money for that which is too fugitive or evanescent to be the subject of property. That might . . . furnish an answer in a common-law controversy. But in a court of equity, where the question is one of unfair competition, if that which complainant has acquired fairly at substantial cost may be sold fairly at substantial profit, a competitor who is misappropriating it for the purpose of disposing of it to his own profit and to the disadvantage of complainant cannot be heard to say that it is too fugitive and evanescent to be regarded as property. It has all the attributes of property necessary for determining that a misappropriation of it by a competitor is unfair competition because contrary to good conscience.

The Confidentiality Argument

The third argument—that employees who disclose trade secrets to others or use them themselves are guilty of violating an obligation of confidentiality—is based on the view that employees agree as a condition of employment to become agents of an employer and be bound by the duty that agents have to preserve the confidentiality of certain information.[10] Section 395 of the *Restatement of Agency* states that an agent has an obligation:

> . . . not to use or to communicate information confidentially given him by the principal or acquired by him during the course of or on account of his agency . . . to the injury of the principal, on his own account or on behalf of another . . . unless the information is a matter of general knowledge.

The obligation of confidentiality does not end with the employment relation but continues to exist after an employee leaves one job for another. And employees who sign an explicit confidentiality agreement may be bound by more stringent contractual obligations than those contained in the agency relation.

Companies can also have an obligation of confidentiality that prohibits them from misappropriating trade secrets. A company that inveigles trade secrets from another company under the guise of negotiating a license agreement or a merger, for example, might be charged with a violation of trade secret law, since the process of negotiation creates a relation of confidentiality. (They might also be charged with failing to negotiate in good faith.) It is also not uncommon for companies to reject ideas brought to them by outsiders, only to adopt them later as their own. The courts have ruled in many such instances that inventors and others have a right to expect that their ideas will be received in confidence and not misappropriated.

These arguments—from the standpoints of property rights, fair competition, and an obligation of confidentiality—uphold the right of companies to some trade secret protection. This right is not unlimited, however, and the same arguments can also be used to establish rights for employees and competing companies. Let us turn first to the property rights argument to see what rights employees and competitors have.

TRADE SECRETS AS PROPERTY

Imagine a lone inventor who, after years of hard work, develops an improved process for manufacturing a common product and builds a factory to turn out the product using the new process. Even if the innovations are not sufficiently original to be patentable, we can accept that he owns the results of his creative efforts, at least to the extent that it would be wrong for a worker in the factory to disclose the details of the manufacturing process to a competitor, especially if the employee had been sworn to secrecy.[11]

The question of who owns what becomes more complicated if the inventor is himself employed by a manufacturer of the product in question. As long as he gets his ideas while performing unrelated work for his employer, however, and conducts the experiments on his own time using his own materials and facilities, then it seems only right that he be recognized as the sole owner of the improved manufacturing process and be permitted—perhaps after leaving his present employer—to sell the secrets of the process to another manufacturer or to go into business for himself, as in the original example. If, on the other hand, he is hired as an inventor to develop improved methods of manufacture or if he does his creative work on his employer's time with the resources of his employer, then some or all the rights of ownership could reasonably be claimed to belong to the employer.

In determining the ownership of information protectable as a trade secret, it is necessary, then, to consider a number of factors. Chief among them are the scope of an employee's responsibility and the relative contribution of the employer and the employee to the development of the information. These factors are not without problems, however, so let us examine them further.

The "Hired-to-Invent" Test

First, employees who are charged with a specific task, such as solving a problem, designing a product, or compiling data, are merely doing what they are being paid to do. In the view of the courts, they have been "hired to invent."[12] So the results of their creative talents and efforts rightly belong to the employer who has paid for the inventions and assumed the risk of investment. The employees are compensated for their contribution by the wages they receive.

Application of the hired-to-invent test is complicated when there is disagreement as to what an employee has specifically been hired to do. Dr. Robert J. Cade, for example, was hired as an associate professor of medicine at the University of Florida to teach and conduct research. In the course of doing research on electrolytes (substances in the bloodstream that control the balance of fluids) Dr. Cade hit upon the formula for Gatorade, which is now marketed by the Stokely-Van Camp Company as a popular thirst quencher for athletes. Both the University of Florida and the Department of Health, Education, and Welfare, which had funded Dr. Cade's research, claimed the rights to the product. Dr. Cade contended that he owned Gatorade because he had developed the formula using his own funds. Furthermore, inventing the drink was not what he was paid to do—either by the university or the federal government. (The dispute ended in a private settlement, and royalties from the sale of Gatorade are now placed in a special trust.)

The "Shop-Right" Concept

Second, when employees who have not been hired to invent nevertheless make some innovation on company time with materials or equipment provided by an employer, fairness to both parties requires that the rights of ownership be divided in some equitable way. The courts have attempted to arrive at a fair division of rights by giving employers a "shop right," which allows them to make use of innovations by their employees without paying the employees for them. Thus, although employees are recognized as the owners of an invention, they must allow their employers use of it free of charge. The shop-right concept, like the hired-to-invent test, raises the problem of determining the extent to which an employer contributes to the development of an innovation.

In the early 1930s, for example, two scientists employed by the U.S. Bureau of Standards developed a radio-controlled guidance system for bombs and torpedos. They patented their system and turned over the rights to the Dubilier Condenser Corporation for commercial exploitation. The Bureau of Standards claimed ownership of the invention on the ground that the two scientists made their discovery while working for the federal government. Using the hired-to-invent test, the Supreme

Court found that developing the system was not one of their assigned tasks and that the patent rights to the invention belonged to the employees.[13] Still, the government was granted a permanent license to use the guidance system without paying any royalties, since the scientists made their discovery during working hours using the facilities of the U.S. Bureau of Standards. The employer, in other words, was recognized as having a "shop right" in the invention.

The Employee's Own Property

Third, it is often difficult to draw a line between the skill and knowledge of employees, which they are free to carry with them from one job to another, and proprietary information that rightfully belongs to an employer. All employees have an educational background that they bring to their first job, and once on the job, they acquire a greater familiarity with the particulars of a certain line of work. The experience of workers constitutes part of their set of qualifications, which in turn determines their value to employers. So even when employers pay workers for their contribution and bear other costs associated with the acquisition of commercially valuable information, it does not belong to them alone. This information also constitutes part of the skill and knowledge of employees, which is a kind of property that employees own.

The case *Wexler* v. *Greenberg* is instructive in this regard. Alvin Greenberg was employed as chief chemist for the Buckingham Wax Company, which manufactured floor cleaners, polishes, and other maintenance materials. One of his tasks as chief chemist was to analyze the products of competitors and to use the results to develop new formulas. After eight years with the company, Greenberg left to join Brite Products, which had previously purchased exclusively from Buckingham. With the formulas that Greenberg had developed while working for Buckingham, Brite was able to dispense with Buckingham as a supplier and become a manufacturer itself, whereupon Buckingham sued to prevent Greenberg and his new employer from using the formulas, on the grounds that they were trade secrets which Greenberg had misappropriated.

In overturning a lower court ruling which held that Greenberg had an obligation of confidentiality not to disclose the formulas, the Supreme Court of Pennsylvania cited the fact that the supposed trade secrets had not been disclosed to Greenberg by his employer but had been developed by Greenberg himself.

> The usual situation involving misappropriation of trade secrets in violation of a confidential relationship is one in which an employer *discloses to his employee* a pre-existing trade secret (one already developed or formulated) so that the employee may duly perform his work. . . . It is then that a

pledge of secrecy is impliedly extracted from the employee, a pledge which he carries with him even beyond the ties of his employment relationship. Since it is conceptually impossible, however, to elicit an implied pledge of secrecy from the sole act of an employee turning over to his employer a trade secret which he, the employee, has developed, as occurred in the present case, the appellees must show a different manner in which the present circumstances support the permanent cloak of confidence cast upon Greenberg. . . .

The formulas, moreover, were not significant discoveries on Greenberg's part but were merely the result of routine applications of Greenberg's skill as a chemist. As such, they were, in the court's view, the kinds of technical knowledge that any employee acquires by virtue of being employed. Even though the formulas are trade secrets, which the Buckingham Wax Company is permitted to use, they properly belong to Greenberg, who has a right to use them in his work for a new employer.

Society also makes an investment in the development of information; it is not the exclusive property of an individual or a firm. Because patentable ideas and other innovations are generally built on foundations that have been laid by others, even companies that have spent a great deal for research cannot claim sole right of ownership. Richard T. DeGeorge has presented this argument in a very forceful manner.

> Whatever new knowledge a company produces is always an increment to past knowledge which has been developed by society in years past, and passed from one generation to the next. Any new invention is made by people who learned a great deal from the general store of knowledge, before they could bring what they knew to bear on a particular problem. Though we can attribute inventions and discoveries to particular efforts of individuals or teams, they are also the result of those people who developed them and passed on their knowledge to others. In this way, every advance in knowledge is social, and belongs ultimately to society, even though for practical purposes we can assign it temporarily to a given individual or firm.[14]

An illustration of this argument is provided by the case of an aerospace engineer, Roderick Koutnik, who was a specialist in the design of valves for guided missiles and rockets.[15] After Koutnik left the Futurecraft Corporation to work for a competitor, the Clary Corporation, his former employer went to court to seek compensation for the wrongful acquisition of Futurecraft's trade secrets and an injunction to prevent Clary from using them. Koutnik worked for Futurecraft part time from 1949 to 1951 while he was also employed by the Jet Propulsion Laboratory at the California Institute of Technology, and he returned to work at the Jet Propulsion Laboratory from April 28, 1952, to January 25, 1953, between periods of work for Futurecraft. Consequently, the trial court found that when Koutnik began working for Futurecraft, he carried with him a great amount of knowledge concerning valve design and manufacture, most of which had probably been acquired at the laboratory of a major university that is dependent on a mixture of private philanthropy and government grants. The trade secrets that Futurecraft attempted to protect as its exclusive property, therefore, were in some measure the result of research supported by society as a whole.

Clarifying the Ownership of Ideas

Many companies attempt to clarify the ownership of patentable ideas by requiring employees to sign an agreement turning over all patent rights to the employer. Such agreements are morally objectionable, however, when they give companies a claim on discoveries that are outside the scope of an employee's responsibilities and make no use of the employer's facilities and resources.[16] Courts in the United States have often invalidated agreements that force employees to give up the rights to inventions which properly belong to them. The law in most of the other industrialized countries of the world provides for sharing the rights to employee inventions or providing additional compensation to employees, especially for highly profitable discoveries.[17]

The ownership of ideas is a difficult area, precisely because the contributions of employers and employees are so difficult to disentangle. Arguably, the law in the United States has tended to favor the more powerful party, namely, employers. Contracts or other agreements that spell out in detail the rights of employers and employees are clearly preferable to ambiguous divisions that often land in the courts. These arrangements must be fair to all concerned, however, and granting employees a greater share of the rewards might be a more just solution— and also one that benefits corporations in the long run, by motivating and retaining talented researchers.

FAIR COMPETITION AND CONFIDENTIALITY

In *Wexler* v. *Greenberg*, the court considered not only who owns the formulas that Greenberg developed for the Buckingham Wax Company but also whether placing restrictions on Greenberg's use of the formulas in his work for another company unfairly deprived him of a right to compete with his former employer. According to the decision in *Wexler*:

> . . . any form of post-employment restraint reduces the economic mobility of employees and limits their personal freedom to pursue a preferred course of livelihood. The employee's bargaining position is weakened because he is potentially shackled by the acquisition of alleged trade secrets; and thus, paradoxically, he is restrained because of his increased expertise,

from advancing further in the industry in which he is most productive. Moreover . . . society suffers because competition is diminished by slackening the dissemination of ideas, processes and methods.

The problem of trade secrets, in the view of the court, is one of accommodating the rights of both parties: "the right of a businessman to be protected against unfair competition stemming from the usurpation of his trade secrets and the right of an individual to the unhampered pursuit of the occupations and livelihoods for which he is best suited."

The courts have generally been reluctant to grant the request of employers to place legal restraints on former employees after they have left to work for a competitor, except when the employees have competed while still working for the former employer and taken company documents and other materials with them. When Steve Jobs, a cofounder of Apple Computer, resigned as chairman and started a new venture, Next, Inc., that competed directly with Apple for the lucrative educational market, the board of directors did not deny that he had a right to leave Apple and found a rival company.[18] They charged in a suit, however, that Jobs had secretly begun laying plans and recruiting Apple employees while he was still working for the company and that he had schemed to get his hands on the designs for Apple's newest computer. (Jobs hotly denied all the charges.)

C. Lester Hogan was also charged by his former employer with recruiting Motorola executives before he left the company to join Fairchild. He responded that he had only sought the advice of his colleagues at Motorola and that those who expressed an interest in joining his management team were referred to an official at Fairchild, with whom they negotiated their new positions. The court accepted Mr. Hogan's version of events and ruled that he had not conspired with the other executives while he was still employed by Motorola.

Noncompetition Agreements

Because of the difficulty of imposing legal restraints on employees after they leave, many companies require employees to sign a noncompetition agreement when they are hired. These agreements typically restrict an employee from working for a competitor for a certain period of time or within a given geographical territory after leaving a company. Agreements not to compete are a common feature of the sale of a business, and the courts have generally not hesitated to enforce them. But there is little justification for restricting employees in this way. Noncompetition agreements are almost entirely for the benefit of the employer and inflict a burden on employees that is out of proportion to any gain. At least twelve states consider them so unfair that they are prohibited entirely.[19]

Where noncompetition agreements are permitted by law, the courts have generally imposed a number of tests to determine whether they are justified.[20] These tests are that the restrictions contained in an agreement: (1) must serve to protect legitimate business interests, (2) must not be greater than that which is required for the protection of these legitimate interests, (3) must not impose an undue hardship on the ability of an employee to secure gainful employment, and (4) must not be injurious to the public. Legitimate business interests include the protection of proprietary information or customer relations, but the purpose of an agreement cannot be merely to protect an employer against competition.

In determining whether restrictions are greater than those required to protect the legitimate interests of an employer, three factors are important. These are the time period specified, the geographical area, and the kind of work that is excluded. The value of trade secrets is reduced over time, so that a noncompetition agreement designed to protect trade secrets can justifiably restrain an employee only during the time that they have value. Without a time limit on an agreement, an employee could be prevented from working for a competitor even after former proprietary information becomes common knowledge. Similarly, an employer with a legitimate interest in protecting the customers it serves in New York City, for example, might be justified in preventing a sales representative from working for a competitor in that area but not elsewhere.

Noncompetition agreements that specify the kind of work too broadly also run the risk of hampering an employee unduly. In one case, a woman in Georgia signed a contract with an employment agency in which she agreed not to work in any capacity for a period of one year for any competitor within a twenty-five mile radius. The Supreme Court of Georgia ruled that the time period and the area were reasonable but that the phrase "in any capacity" was unreasonably broad, since it would bar her from doing any work for a competitor and not merely the work that she had done for her former employer.[21] Generally, agreements prohibiting employees from working on a particular project or soliciting specific clients, for example, are less likely to be objectionable than vague restrictions such as writing computer programs or selling insurance.

Examples of Unfair Competition

The suit by the Associated Press against a rival news service suggests that considerations of fair competition are more appropriate than those of property rights in determining the rights and obligations of other companies with respect to the trade secrets of their rivals. Using the argument of fair competition, there is no need to show that information is a protectable trade secret that has been disclosed in violation of a relation of confidentiality. All that needs to be shown is that the information was acquired through an unfair competitive practice, such as through fraud or deception.

For example, useful bits of information are sometimes picked up during job interviews with a competitor's employees, and so some companies have advertised and conducted interviews for positions that do not exist, in the hope that some applicants would inadvertently reveal trade secrets of their present employer.[22] Other devious practices include asking consulting firms to solicit information from competitors under the guise of doing a study of the industry and getting friendly customers to make phony requests for bids from competitors, since bids often contain confidential technical information about the bidder's products. Requesting tours of a competitor's facility while posing as a potential customer or supplier is unethical, although the evaluation of such a practice is less clear when employees take public tours and do not attempt to disguise their identity. (Procter & Gamble accused several rivals of picking up information by touring plants where its patented Duncan Hines cookies were made, and the enterprising college-age son of one employee sent to spy succeeded in obtaining an unbaked dough sample.)[23] Although some forms of corporate intelligence gathering are fair, any that involve misrepresentation are ethically objectionable.[24]

The Confidentiality Argument

The argument for an obligation of confidentiality provides strong support for the right of employers to trade secret protection, but it too has a number of shortcomings. It assumes, for example, that the information was received from the employer and was not, as in the case of Alvin Greenberg, developed by the employee. And the obligation of confidentiality is also limited by the right of employees to use their skill and knowledge in the pursuit of a trade or occupation.

Many employees sign a confidentiality agreement which creates an explicit contractual obligation that is often more stringent than the obligation of confidentiality that employees ordinarily have as agents. Although confidentiality agreements have some advantages for both employers and employees, they are open to the same objections as agreements to assign patent rights to employers and to refrain from post-employment competition. Since they are usually required as a condition of employment, employees are effectively coerced into giving up rights to which they might otherwise be entitled.

By relying on an enforceable obligation of confidentiality, companies often place unnecessary restraints on employee mobility and career prospects. Michael S. Baram contends that litigation rarely preserves either the secrecy of company information or the liberty of employees and that both of these are better served by more sophisticated management.[25] Among the policies he suggests are improving security procedures in the workplace; securing the legal protection of patents, copyrights, and trademarks whenever possible; segmenting information so that fewer people know the full scope of a trade secret; limiting information to those with a need to know; and using increased pensions and post-employment consulting contracts to keep employees from taking competitive employment.

In addition, the incentive for employees to leave with valuable trade secrets can be reduced by greater recognition of employees for their contributions. Not infrequently, employees go to a competitor or set up a business of their own because of a feeling that they have not been fairly treated. Baram concludes that the key to protecting trade secrets lies in improved employee relations, in which both employers and employees respect the rights of the other and take their obligations seriously. And a key element in improving employee relations is an ethical climate of fair play. Employers might find that treating employees fairly provides more protection for trade secrets than relying on the law.

CONFLICT OF INTEREST

In April 1984, a reporter for *The Wall Street Journal* was fired for violating the newspaper's policy on conflict of interest. The firing occurred after R. Foster Winans, a contributor to the influential stock market column "Heard on the Street," admitted to his employer and investigators from the Securities and Exchange Commission (SEC) that he conspired over a four-month period, beginning in October 1983, with two stockbrokers at Kidder, Peabody & Company, to trade on the basis of advance information about the content of the column. Since the publicity generated by "Heard on the Street" often caused short-run price swings, Mr. Winans and his co-conspirators were able to make a profit of $690,000 by buying stock or call options when a column contained favorable news about a stock and by selling short or buying put options when the news was unfavorable.

Just as employees have an obligation to respect trade secrets and confidential business information generally, they also have an obligation to avoid *conflict of interest* of the kind illustrated by the Winans case. Virtually all corporate codes of ethics address conflict of interest, since it interferes with the ability of employees to act in the best interests of an employer. The acceptance of gifts or lavish entertainment from suppliers, for example, is generally prohibited or strictly limited for the simple reason that the judgment of employees is apt to be compromised. Company codes usually contain guidelines on investing in customers, suppliers, and competitors of an employee's firm for the same reason.

Prohibitions on conflict of interest cannot be so extensive, however, as to prevent employees from pursuing unrelated business opportunities, taking part in community and political affairs, and generally acting as they see fit in matters outside the scope of their employment. One problem with conflict of interest is in drawing a line between legitimate and illegitimate activities of employees in the pursuit of their personal interests. A further problem is the large gray area that surrounds conflict of interest situations. Perhaps no other ethical concept in business is so elusive and subject to dispute. Many people charged with conflict of interest see nothing wrong with their behavior. It is important, therefore, to define the concept clearly and to understand the different kinds of conflict of interest.

What Is Conflict of Interest?

The case of R. Foster Winans involved a personal interest that came into conflict with the interests of his employer, *The Wall Street Journal*. It would be inaccurate, however, to define a conflict of interest as merely a clash between conflicting or competing interests. A report prepared for the Twentieth Century Fund Steering Committee on Conflict of Interest in the Securities Markets asserts, for example, that the term *conflict of interest* denotes "a situation in which two or more interests are legitimately present and competing or conflicting."[26] This definition is too broad, since it could be extended to cover virtually every business relation. In the relation between buyer and seller, for example, each party strives to advance his or her own interest at the expense of the other, but neither party faces a conflict of interest as the term is commonly understood.[27]

Although the Twentieth Century Fund report (mistakenly) describes the relation between buyer and seller as a conflict of interest, it further notes that conflict of interest arises in the securities market—which is the concern of the report—when a person or an institution operates as a fiduciary with an obligation to a client.

> It is important to distinguish the relation between fiduciary and client from that between ordinary buyer and seller. A used car salesman has much narrower obligations to his customers than a fiduciary has to his client. Of course, sellers have obligations of truthfulness—for example, the used car dealer has a duty not to set back the odometer—and in some situations sellers may have special duties, such as when a buyer relies upon a seller to select an article for particular use. But except for such limited duties, neither party is obligated to serve the other's interests.[28]

The key to understanding conflict of interest is in the last sentence. The conflict in a conflict of interest is not merely a conflict between conflicting interests, although conflicting interests are involved. The conflict occurs when a personal interest comes into conflict with an obligation to serve the interests of another. More precisely, we can say that a conflict of interest is a conflict that occurs when a personal interest interferes with a person's acting so as to promote the interests of another *when the person has an obligation to act in that other person's interest.* This obligation is stronger than the obligation merely to avoid harming a person and can arise only when the two persons are in a special relation, such as employer and employee.

Specifically, the kind of obligation described in this definition is that which characterizes an agency relation, in which one person (an agent) agrees to act on behalf of another (the principal) and to be subject to that person's control. This fact explains why conflict of interest is most often encountered by professionals—lawyers, doctors, and accountants, for example—and among fiduciaries, such as executors and trustees. Employees of business firms are also in an agency relation in that they have a general obligation to serve the interests of an employer.

An important feature of an agency relation is its open-endedness. An agent is obligated to perform not merely this or that act but, in the words of the *Restatement of Agency*, "to act solely for the benefit of the principal *in all matters concerned with his agency.*"[29] The duties of an agent are not determined solely by a list of moral rules but by the nature of the interests to be served. This open-ended character of the agency relation explains why it is a conflict of interest for an agent to acquire *any* interest that is contrary to that of a principal, since the kinds of situations in which an agent might be called upon to act in the interest of another are not easily anticipated.

To complete the definition of conflict of interest, some account should also be given to a personal interest. Roughly, a person has an interest in something when the person stands to gain a benefit or an advantage from that thing. "Having an interest" is not the same as "taking an interest." A person can take an interest in someone else's interest, especially when that person is a family member or a close associate. In that case, however, the benefit or advantage accrues to someone else—although the person taking an interest in the well-being of another might also gain in some way. The benefit or advantage is usually restricted to a financial gain of some kind and should be limited to something tangible. Merely satisfying a desire, for example, would not seem to be enough, for otherwise a lawyer who detests a client and secretly hopes that the client will be convicted would face a conflict of interest, as would a lawyer who prefers to play golf instead of spending the time adequately representing a client. The benefit or advantage would also have to be substantial enough to interfere significantly with a person's performance of an obligation.

SOME RELEVANT DISTINCTIONS

All instances of conflict of interest are morally suspect, but some are more serious than others. In their rules on conflict of interest, company codes of ethics and codes for professionals, such as lawyers and accountants, contain a number of relevant distinctions that can aid us in understanding the concept of conflict of interest.

Actual and Potential Conflict of Interest

There is a distinction between *actual* and *potential* conflict of interest.[30] A conflict is actual when a personal interest leads a person to act against the interests of an employer or another person whose interests the person is obligated to serve. A situation constitutes a potential conflict of interest when there is the possibility that a person will fail to fulfill an obligation to act in the interests of another, even though the person has not yet done so.[31]

R. Foster Winans was clearly in an actual conflict-of-interest situation by virtue of the fact that he engaged in stock trading based on information that was to appear in forthcoming columns. All reporters face a potential conflict of interest, though, in writing stories that could have an impact on their own financial holdings. Many newspapers avoid such potential conflict of interest by prohibiting reporters from writing about companies in which they have stock or from buying stock in a company immediately before or after writing an article about it. A policy of this kind serves the dual purpose of removing the temptation for reporters to compromise their standards and assuring readers of the journalistic integrity of the reporting in the newspaper.

Obviously, the categories of actual and potential conflict of interest involve subjective elements. A dedicated reporter might honestly claim that he or she is able to write objectively about events that could adversely affect his or her personal interests. Merely having these interests creates a potential conflict of interest, but determining whether an actual conflict of interest exists would require us to make a judgment about the reporter's objectivity. Similarly, whether an interest creates a potential conflict depends on the strength of the influence it exerts on a person. Owning a small amount of stock in a company, for example, is unlikely to influence anyone's conduct, and so most employers do not impose an absolute prohibition on investments. More often they place a dollar limit on outside financial interests, or else they require a disclosure of stock ownership so that the potential for conflict of interest can be evaluated in each case.

Personal and Impersonal Conflict of Interest

A second distinction can be made between *personal* and *impersonal* conflict of interest. The definition developed in the preceding section is phrased in terms of a personal interest that comes into conflict with the interests of another. A conflict can also arise when a person is obligated to act in the interests of two different persons or organizations whose interests conflict. Thus, a lawyer who represents two clients with conflicting interests may not stand to gain personally from favoring one or the other, and yet, according to Rule 1.7(a) of the American Bar Association's "Model Rules of Professional Conduct," such an arrangement constitutes a conflict of interest.[32] A lawyer who has a personal interest that conflicts with the interests of a client has a personal conflict of interest, whereas a lawyer who represents two clients with conflicting interests faces an impersonal conflict of interest.

It is necessary to qualify the category of an impersonal conflict of interest to avoid cases of the following kind. Lawyers are regarded in the law not only as agents of a client but also as agents of the court. In this dual role, a lawyer might find that delaying a trial unnecessarily, for example, would be to the advantage of a client but doing so would be an abuse of the court system and, hence, a violation of the lawyer's duty to the court. Public accountants face a similar conflict as a result of being simultaneously agents of the companies being audited and public servants who have an obligation to ensure the integrity of financial information. It seems inappropriate to speak of such cases as involving conflict of interest, since doing so generally implies that a person has done something wrong. The conflicts in these cases, however, involve systematic features of situations that professionals such as lawyers and accountants individually cannot alter. We can avoid labeling cases of this kind conflict of interest by excluding from the definition conflicts which arise from systematic features of situations that are not easily altered. These kinds of conflicts present difficult moral dilemmas for individuals, however, and they need to be addressed in the structure and codes of ethics of the professions in question.

Individual and Organizational Conflict

Third, conflict of interest can be either *individual* or *organizational*. In the agency relation, the agent is typically a person acting in the interests of a principal, which may be another person or an organization; however, organizations can be agents as well and hence parties to conflicts of interest. Many large accounting firms, for example, provide management services to companies they also audit, and there is great concern in the profession that this dual function endangers the independence and objectivity of accountants—even when the work is done by different divisions of a firm.[33] Advertising agencies whose clients have competing products face a similar kind of conflict of interest. And investment banking houses have also been accused of conflict of interest for financing takeovers of companies with which they have had long-standing relations. Further, large law firms face the possibility of conflicts of interest when they have clients with competing interests—even when the work is done by different lawyers in the firm.

For an accountant to provide management services to a company that he or she also audits—or for an individual ad person, banker, or lawyer to accept clients with conflicting interests—is a clear conflict of interest. But why should it be a conflict when these functions are performed by different persons in different departments of a firm? The answer is that an accounting firm, for example, also has an interest that is shared by every member of the organization, and the interests of the firm can affect decisions about individual clients. When management services are more lucrative than auditing, for example, firms may have an incentive to concentrate on them to the detriment of other functions. They may also be tempted to conduct audits in ways that favor the clients to whom they provide management services.

Similarly, the creative work for competing advertising accounts is generally done by independent groups, but there is an incentive to commit greater resources and talent to more valuable accounts. In addition, when an organization such as an advertising agency takes on a client, there is an organizational commitment of loyalty that goes beyond merely delivering agreed upon services. For an organization to work for and against a client at the same time is incompatible with this kind of organizational commitment. In addition, advertising campaigns involve sensitive information about product development and marketing strategies that is not easily kept confidential. Banking houses and large law firms encounter similar challenges to their ability to serve the interests of all clients to the fullest.

Organizations, then, can encounter conflicts of interest that are genuinely organizational in nature and not merely an instance of individuals within an organization facing a conflict of interest. This fact raises no difficulty for the definition that has been developed, since organizations as well as individuals can be agents and can have organizational obligations and interests which are not necessarily the same as those of the individuals who comprise an organization. They can also have obligations to serve the interests of two or more parties with conflicting interests, so that the distinction between personal and impersonal conflict of interest applies to organizations as well. Organizational conflict of interest can be accommodated in the definition merely by expanding the term *person* to include organizations.

THE KINDS OF CONFLICT OF INTEREST

The concept of conflict of interest is complex in that it covers several distinct moral failings which are often run together. It is important to separate them, though, in order to have a full understanding both of the definition of conflict of interest and of the reasons that it is morally wrong for a person to be in a conflict-of-interest situation. Briefly, there are four kinds of conflict of interest: (1) exercising biased judgment, (2) engaging in direct competition, (3) misusing a position, and (4) violating confidentiality. Each of these calls for some explanation.

Biased Judgment

The exercise of judgment is characteristic of professionals, such as lawyers, accountants, and engineers, whose stock in trade is a body of specialized knowledge that is used in the service of clients. Not only are professionals paid for using this knowledge to make judgments for the benefit of others but part of the value of their services lies in the confidence that can be placed in a professional's judgment. Accountants do not merely examine a company's financial statement, for example, they also attest to the accuracy of that statement and to its compliance with generally accepted accounting principles, or GAAP. The National Society of Professional Engineers' *Code of Ethics for Engineers* stipulates that engineers shall not submit plans or specifications that are unsafe or not in conformity with accepted engineering standards.[34] So an engineer's signature on a blueprint is also a warrant of its quality.

Judgment is not exclusively a feature of professional work, however. Most employees are called upon to exercise some judgment in the performance of their jobs. Purchasing agents, for example, often have considerable latitude in choosing among various suppliers of a given product. The judgment of purchasing agents in all matters, however, should be used to make decisions that are in the best interests of the employing firm. For a purchasing agent to accept a bribe or kickback in return for placing an order constitutes a clear conflict of interest.

The reason is simple. Bribes and kickbacks are usually intended to induce an employee to grant some favor for a supplier at the expense of the employer. Other factors that could influence the judgment of an employee include outside business interests, such as stock or other investments in companies which have a business relation with the employee's company as a competitor, supplier, or customer or which are possible targets for merger or acquisition. Conflict of interest also occurs when an employee is in a position to make decisions that affect family members, relatives, or close associates. A purchasing agent would be in a conflict-of-interest situation if one of the suppliers submitting a bid were owned by a brother-in-law, for example, since there is a personal interest that is liable to influence the judgment of the purchasing agent in selecting the best bid.

Whether it is a potential conflict of interest for a purchasing agent to accept a gift from a supplier who expects favorable treatment in the future is less clear. An answer to this question depends largely on the value of the gift, the circumstances under which it is offered, the practice within the industry, and whether the gift violates any law. The code of ethics of a large bank, for example, states that employees should not accept gifts where the purpose is "to exert influence in connection with a transaction either before or after that transaction is discussed or consummated. Gifts, for any other purposes, should be limited to those of nominal value." "Gifts of nominal value," the code continues, "generally should be limited to standard advertising items displaying a supplier's logo." A maximum value of twenty-five dollars is suggested as a guideline.

Direct Competition

For an employee to engage in direct competition with his or her employer is a conflict of interest. One reason, of course, is that an employee's judgment is apt to be impaired by having another interest. In addition, the quality of the employee's work might be reduced by the time and effort devoted to other activities. Unlike other kinds of outside business interests, however, direct competition is generally prohibited by companies even when it is disclosed and there is no danger of impaired judgment or diminished work performance. Consider this case, which is taken from a policy statement issued by the Xerox Corporation:

> The wife of a Xerox tech rep inherits money. They decide it would be profitable to open a copy shop with her money and in her name in a suburban city. The territory they choose is different from his. However, there are several other copy shops and an XRC in the vicinity. She leases equipment and supplies from Xerox on standard terms. After working hours, he helps his wife reduce costs by maintaining her equipment himself without pay. He also helps out occasionally on weekends. His job performance at Xerox remains as satisfactory as before. One of the nearby competitive shops, also a lessee of Xerox equipment, writes to his manager complaining that the employee's wife is getting free Xerox service and assistance.

The conflict of interest in this case consists mainly in the fact that the employee's investment and work outside of his employment at Xerox place him in direct competition with the company. The territory is different from his own, and so he would never have to make decisions on the job that could be influenced by his wife's business. And the outside interest has no effect on the quality of his work for Xerox. Still, on the assumption that the husband benefits from his wife's business venture, he is competing directly with his employer, since Xerox operates an XRC in the area.

In addition, by maintaining the equipment in the wife's shop himself, the employee harms the company by depriving it of the potential for additional business. It would be a conflict of interest for the tech rep to do service for any copy shop using equipment of any make, as long as he is employed by Xerox. His skill as a technician, which is in part the result of company training, belongs in a sense to the company, and he would be free to exercise these skills only upon leaving the employment of Xerox. And finally, the employee is indirectly harming the interests of Xerox by upsetting the relations between the company and other lessees of Xerox equipment.

Misuse of Position

Misuse of position constitutes a third kind of conflict of interest. One of the charges against R. Foster Winans was that he misused his position as a *Wall Street Journal* reporter to enrich himself, in violation of a provision in the newspaper's code of ethics that reads as follows:

> It is not enough to be incorruptible and act with honest motives. It is equally important to use good judgment and conduct one's outside activities so that no one—management, our editors, an SEC investigator with power of subpoena, or a political critic of the company—has any grounds for even raising the suspicion that an employee misused a position with the company.[35]

Or consider the hypothetical case of a bank manager who, in the course of arranging home improvement loans, makes it a point to ask customers whether they have lined up a contractor. She casually drops the name of her brother who operates a general contracting business and mentions that a number of bank customers have been very satisfied with the work of his company.

The bank manager's mention of her brother is clearly improper if she misuses her power to grant or deny a loan to induce customers to use him as a contractor. A conflict of interest is still present, though, even if she does not allow her personal interest to have any effect on the decisions she makes on behalf of her employer. There is no conflict between the interests of the manager and those of the bank, and the bank is not harmed in any significant way. Still, the manager has taken the opportunity to advance her personal interests while acting in her capacity as an official of the bank. Holding a position with a company or other organization gives a person powers and opportunities that would not be available otherwise, and an employee has an obligation not to use these powers and opportunities for personal gain.

Extortion also constitutes a misuse of position. Unlike bribery, with which it is often confused, extortion does not involve the use of a payment of some kind to influence the judgment of an employee. Rather, extortion in a business setting occurs when a person with decision-making power for a company demands a payment from another party as a condition for making a decision favorable to that party. For example, a purchasing agent who threatens a supplier with a loss of business unless the supplier agrees to give a kickback to the purchasing agent is engaging in extortion. Extorting money from a supplier in this way is a conflict of interest, even if the company is not directly harmed, since the purchasing agent is violating an obligation to act in the position solely for the interests of the employer.

Violation of Confidentiality

Finally, violating confidentiality constitutes, under certain circumstances, a conflict of interest. The duty of lawyers, accountants, and other professionals, for example, precludes the use of information acquired in confidence from a client to advance personal interests—even if the interests of the client are unaffected. Similarly, because a director of a company is privy to much information, it would be wrong to use it for personal gain or other business interests.

The case of R. Foster Winans also illustrates a conflict of interest involving a breach of confidentiality. A reporter with information prior to publication who attempts to capitalize on the expected results is using that information for his or her own personal gain. Specifically, the courts found Mr. Winans guilty of *misappropriating* confidential information that properly belonged to his employer. In the Supreme Court decision affirming the conviction of Mr. Winans, Justice Byron White observed:

> Confidential business information has long been recognized as property. "Confidential information acquired or compiled by a corporation in the course and conduct of its business is a species of property to which the corporation has the exclusive right and benefit. . . ."[36]

Justice White further noted:

> The District Court found, and the Court of Appeals agreed, that Winans had knowingly breached a duty of confidentiality by misappropriating prepublication information regarding the timing and the contents of the "Heard" columns, information that had been gained in the course of his employment under the understanding that it would not be revealed in advance of publication and that, if it were, he would report it to his employer.

In one analysis, insider trading constitutes a conflict of interest.[37] The typical case of insider trading occurs when an executive makes stock trades based on information about the company that has not yet been made public, such as an unexpected change in earnings or an anticipated takeover. The position of the SEC is that insider trading involves a misappropriation of information acquired during the course of employment and hence is a violation of a duty to use that information solely for the interests of the employer.[38]

One difficulty with this argument, however, is that if the only moral argument against insider trading is that it involves the taking of information that properly belongs to another, then the "owner" of the information—that is, the employer—could give permission for employees to use it.[39] What is morally objectionable about insider trading, according to its critics, though, is not the misappropriation of a company's information but the harm done to the investing public. Merely giving employees permission to use information would not address this concern. So the breach of confidentiality in insider trading cannot be the sole reason for prohibiting it. Most arguments against insider trading, therefore, center on fairness to other traders and harm to investors.

Conclusion

Like whistle-blowing, trade secrets and conflict of interest involve a delicate balancing of the rights and interests of employers and employees, as well as the public at large. Especially in the case of trade secret protection, we see how different kinds of arguments—for property rights, fair competition, and a duty of confidentiality—underlie the law in this area and support our views about what is morally right. For the most part, the language of rights and the obligations of agents have dominated our discussion, although utilitarian considerations about the harm and benefit of protecting trade secrets have been introduced. In the next chapter we examine another right, namely, the right of employees to privacy in the workplace, in which strongly utilitarian and Kantian arguments are used to explain the concept of employee privacy and provide a foundation for it. Unlike trade secrets and conflict of interest, privacy is an area where the law has yet to develop very far, and so we can focus mainly on ethical issues.

NOTES

1. This case and the one following are described in STANLEY H. LIEBERSTEIN, *Who Owns What Is in Your Head?* (New York: Hawthorn Books, 1979), 1–2.
2. See *Motorola, Inc.* v. *Fairchild Camera & Instrument Corp.*, 366 F. Supp. 1173.
3. *Telex Corp.* v. *International Business Machines Corp.*, 510 F.2d 894 (1975). The

amount of the award was reduced on appeal, though, and the two companies eventually negotiated a private settlement.

4. *Head Ski Company* v. *Kam Ski Company*, 158 F. Supp. 919 (1958).
5. EDWIN C. HETTINGER, "Justifying Intellectual Property," *Philosophy and Public Affairs*, 18 (1989), 34.
6. *Wexler* v. *Greenberg*, 160 A.2d 430 (1960).
7. For a discussion of the Lockean view as well as the utilitarian argument discussed below, see HETTINGER, "Justifying Intellectual Property," 36–51.
8. This point is made by ROBERT E. FREDERICK and MILTON SNOEYENBOS, "Trade Secrets, Patents, and Morality," in *Business Ethics* (Buffalo: Prometheus Books, 1983), 165–66.
9. *International News Service* v. *Associated Press*, 248 U.S. 215 (1918).
10. All employees are regarded in law as agents, at least while acting within the scope of their assigned responsibilities, but their specific obligations, including those with respect to confidentiality, are determined by the amount of trust placed in them and any understandings, such as company policies or professional ethics.
11. These are essentially the facts in the classic case *Peabody* v. *Norfolk*, 98 Mass. 452 (1868).
12. For a discussion of the "hired to invent" test, see LIEBERSTEIN, *Who Owns What Is in Your Head?* 9–14. Much of the following is drawn from this discussion.
13. *United States* v. *Dubilier Condenser Corp.*, 289 U.S. 178 (1933).
14. RICHARD T. DEGEORGE, *Business Ethics*, 3rd ed. (New York: Macmillan, 1990), 246.
15. *Futurecraft Corp.* v. *Clary Corp.*, 205 C.A.2d 279 (1962).
16. For a discussion of the ethical issues, see MARK MICHAEL, "Patent Rights and Better Mousetraps," *Business and Professional Ethics Journal*, 3 (1983), 13–23.
17. For a summary of the law in other countries, see LIEBERSTEIN, *Who Owns What Is in Your Head?*, 225–32.
18. See "Sour Apples: His Old Company Sues Jobs," *Time*, October 7, 1985, 51.
19. See KEVIN MCMANUS, "Who Owns Your Brain?" *Forbes*, June 6, 1983, 178.
20. See HARLAN M. BLAKE, "Employee Covenants Not to Compete," *Harvard Law Review*, 73 (1960), 625–91.
21. *Dunn* v. *Frank Miller Associates, Inc.*, 237 Ga. 266 (1976). The case is cited by LIEBERSTEIN, *Who Owns What Is In Your Head?* 50–51.
22. Much of the material in this paragraph and the one following is contained in STEVEN FLAX, "How to Snoop on Your Competitors," *Fortune*, May 14, 1984, 28–33. For a discussion of the ethics of intelligence gathering, see LYNN SHARP PAINE, "Corporate Policy and the Ethics of Competitor Intelligence Gathering," *Journal of Business Ethics*, 10 (1991), 423–36.
23. "Cookie Cloak and Dagger," *Time*, September 10, 1984, 44. The rival company destroyed the dough without examining and apologized to Procter & Gamble.
24. For a fuller discussion of fair and unfair tactics, see PAINE, "Corporate Policy and the Ethics of Competitor Intelligence Gathering."
25. MICHAEL S. BARAM, "Trade Secrets: What Price Loyalty?" *Harvard Business Review*, 46, November–December 1968, 66–74.

26. *Abuse on Wall Street: Conflicts of Interest in the Securities Markets* (Westport, CT: Quorum Books, 1980), 4.
27. Norman E. Bowie has also characterized a conflict of interest as the presence of conflicting legitimate interests with the further stipulation that only one of the interests can be fulfilled as opposed to "competing interests," which permit the balancing and partial satisfaction of different interests. NORMAN E. BOWIE, *Business Ethics* (Englewood Cliffs, NJ: Prentice Hall, 1982), 103. BOWIE continues to hold this view in a more recent paper "Accountants, Full Disclosure, and Conflicts of Interest," *Business and Professional Ethics Journal*, 5, nos. 3–4, 59–73.
28. *Abuse on Wall Street*, 5.
29. *Second Restatement of Agency*, Sec. 385. Emphasis added.
30. This distinction is made in THOMAS M. GARRETT and RICHARD J. KLONOSKY, *Business Ethics*, 2nd ed. (Englewood Cliffs, NJ: Prentice Hall, 1986), 55; and in MANUAL G. VELASQUEZ, *Business Ethics: Concepts and Cases*, 3rd ed. (Englewood Cliffs, NJ: Prentice Hall, 1992), 377–78.
31. MICHAEL DAVIS, in "Conflict of Interest," *Business and Professional Ethics Journal*, 1 (1982), 17–27, makes a threefold distinction between actual, latent, and potential conflicts of interest. Latent conflict of interest involves conflict situations that can reasonably be foreseen, whereas potential conflict of interest involves conflict situations that cannot reasonably be foreseen.
32. The rule reads: "A lawyer shall not represent a client if the representation of that client will be directly adverse to another client unless: (1) the lawyer reasonably believes the representation will not adversely affect the relationship with the other client; and (2) each client consents after consultation."
33. See ABRAHAM J. BRILOFF, "Do Management Services Endanger Independence and Objectivity?" *CPA Journal*, 57 (August 1987), 22–29.
34. National Society of Professional Engineers, *Code of Ethics for Engineers*, 1987, III, 2(b).
35. "Media Policies Vary on Preventing Employees and Others from Profiting on Knowledge of Future Business Stories," *The Wall Street Journal*, March 2, 1984, p. A12.
36. *Carpenter et al.* v. *U.S.*, 484 U.S. 19 (1987).
37. For an analysis of insider trading and an examination of the arguments against it, see JENNIFER MOORE, "What Is Really Unethical about Insider Trading?" *Journal of Business Ethics*, 9 (1990), 171–82.
38. This analysis is controversial, and the Winans case was expected to be a legal test of it. However, the Supreme Court split 4–4 on the insider-trading charge and so failed either to accept or to reject the SEC analysis. The Court ruled 8–0 to convict Mr. Winans of mail and wire fraud, and the result of the deadlock on the charge of insider trading (which is technically securities fraud in violation of SEC Rule 10(b)5) left standing a lower court conviction.
39. See MOORE, "What Is Really Unethical about Insider Trading?" 174–76.

CHAPTER SEVEN
Privacy in the Workplace

Early in the century, the Ford Motor Company set up a "Sociological Department" in order to make sure that workers, in Henry Ford's words, were leading "clean, sober, and industrious" lives.[1] Company inspectors checked bank accounts to keep Ford employees from squandering their munificent five-dollars-a-day wages. They visited employees' living quarters to see that they were neat and healthful, and they interviewed wives and acquaintances about the handling of finances, church attendance, daily diet, drinking habits, and a host of other matters. Workers who failed to live up to Henry Ford's standards of personal conduct were dismissed.

Employers today would scarcely dare to intrude so openly into the private lives of their employees, but they possess less obvious means for acquiring the information sought by Ford's teams of snooping inspectors—and some information that Henry Ford could not have imagined! Among the tools available to present-day employers are quick and inexpensive drug tests, polygraph machines and pencil-and-paper tests for assessing honesty and other personality traits of employees, extensive computer networks for storing and retrieving information about employees, and sophisticated telecommunication systems and concealed cameras and microphones for supervising employees' work activities. In addition, employers can now do genetic testing to screen employees for genes that make them more vulnerable to chemicals in the workplace.

Although privacy is a cherished value, we recognize that we must give some personal information to others. We volunteer a great many details of our lives to employers, and businesses know a great deal about us as consumers. Still, there are limits beyond which business, government, and others are not entitled to go.

The danger of invading the privacy of employees is vividly illustrated by the case of John J. O'Brien, whose ten-year career with a New England restaurant chain came to an abrupt end in 1982 over an unproven charge of drug use.[2] As an area supervisor for Papa Gino's of America, he was in charge of 28 restaurants and about 500 workers. He felt that he was in line for a vice-presidency with the company until he was informed by his boss that he had been seen taking drugs at a party. He was given an ultimatum: take a polygraph test or be fired. He took the test but was fired anyway when the company claimed that the machine proved he was lying. The company never revealed the name of the informant, but Mr. O'Brien suspects that it was the son of a director of Papa Gino's whom he had refused to promote, despite repeated requests. After losing his $50,000-a-year job, he had difficulty finding work, and he feels that the false charge of drug use will always haunt him. "People in the company avoided me like the plague when they spread that around," he says, "and I think I'll always carry the stigma."

One way of protecting workers from abuses of corporate power of the kind experienced by Mr. O'Brien is by recognizing an employee's right to privacy. Concern about employee privacy is a relatively recent occurrence. However, a 1979 public-opinion survey conducted by Louis Harris for the Sentry Insurance Company revealed that three out of four respondents believe that privacy should be regarded as a fundamental right akin to life, liberty, and the pursuit of happiness and that half of them fear that American corporations do not adequately safeguard the personal information they gather on individuals.[3] More than 90 percent of those who responded said that they favored safeguards to prevent the disclosure of personnel and medical files to outsiders. A law granting employees access to the information collected about them was favored by 70 percent, and 62 percent wanted Congress to pass a law regulating the kind of information that corporations may collect about individuals.

There are many reasons that privacy has become a major issue in government and business in recent years. One is simply the vast amount of personal information that is collected by government agencies. The need to protect this information became especially acute after the passage of the Freedom of Information Act (FOIA) in 1966. Intended by Congress to make government more accountable for its actions, the act had the unforeseen consequence of compromising the confidentiality of information about private individuals. The Privacy Act of 1974 was designed in large part to resolve the conflict between government accountability and individual privacy. So great were the problems that Congress created the Privacy Protection Study Commission to investigate and make recommendations about further action. The National Labor Relations Board has long faced a similar problem with union demands for access to personnel files and other employee records. Unions claim that they need the information in order to engage in fair collective bargaining, but allowing unions to have unlimited access to this information without consent violates the employees' right of privacy.[4]

Government is not the only collector of information. A great amount of data is required by corporations for the hiring and placement of workers, for the evaluation of their performance, and for the administration of fringe benefit packages, including health insurance and pensions. Private employers also need to compile personal information about race, sex, age, and handicap status in order to document compliance with the law on discrimination, and the law on workers' compensation and occupational health and safety requires employers to maintain extensive medical records. Alan F. Westin, an expert on privacy issues, observes that greater concern with employee rights in matters of discrimination and occupational health and safety has had the ironic effect of creating greater dangers to employees' right of privacy.[5]

Monitoring the work of employees is an essential part of the supervisory role of management, and new technologies enable employers to watch more closely than ever before, especially when the work is done on telephones or computer terminals. Supervisors can eavesdrop on the telephone conversations of employees, for example, and call up on their own screens the input and output as it appears on the terminals of the operators.[6] Hidden cameras and microphones can also be used to observe workers without their knowledge. A computer record can be made of the number of telephone calls, their duration, and their destination. And the number of keystrokes made by a data processor, the number of errors and corrections made, and the amount of time spent away from the desk can also be recorded for use by management. Even the activities of truck drivers can be monitored by a small computerized device attached to a vehicle which registers speed, shifting, and the time spent idling or stopped.

Companies claim that they are forced to increase the monitoring of employees with these new technologies as a result of the changing nature of work. More complex and dangerous manufacturing processes require a greater degree of oversight by employers. And the electronic systems for executing financial transactions and transferring funds used by banks and securities firms have a great potential for misuse and costly errors. In addition, employers are increasingly concerned about the use of drugs by workers and the high cost of employee theft, including the stealing of trade secrets. Employers also claim to be acting on a moral and a legal obligation to provide a safe workplace in which employees are free from the risk of being injured by drug-impaired co-workers.[7]

Ethical questions about employee privacy are unavoidable, since obtaining and using personal information about employees and monitoring their work performance is essential for the conduct of business. But employees also have a legitimate interest in maintaining a private life that is free from unwarranted intrusion by employers and in preventing employers from using personal information against them. Finding the right balance between the rights of employers and employees in matters of privacy is not a simple task. A set of guidelines or a company code on privacy must address an immense number of different questions. Before we make the attempt to find a balance between these competing rights, though, it is necessary for us to inquire into the meaning of privacy as an ethical concept.

THE CONCEPT OF EMPLOYEE PRIVACY

A definition of the concept of privacy has proven to be very elusive. After two years of study, the members of the Privacy Protection Study Commission were still not able to agree on one. Much of the difficulty is due to the diverse nature of the many different situations in which claims of a right of privacy are made. Even the narrower concept of employee privacy is applied in such dissimilar circumstances that it is not easy to find a common thread running through them.

History of the Concept

As a legal concept, privacy dates only from the late nineteenth century. There is no mention of privacy in the original Constitution or the Bill of Rights. Although a number of rights related to privacy have long been recognized in American law, they have generally been expressed in terms of freedom of thought and expression, the right of private property, protection from "unreasonable searches and seizures," and other constitutional guarantees. The first sustained discussion of privacy occurred in an 1890 article in the *Harvard Law Review* written by two young attorneys, Samuel Warren and Louis Brandeis (who later became a famed Justice of the Supreme Court).[8]

The theory of privacy presented by Warren and Brandeis was slow to gain acceptance. It was rejected by the courts in a number of cases around the turn of the century in which the names and pictures of prominent persons were used to advertise products. The public uproar over one of these cases prompted the New York legislature to enact a law prohibiting the commercial use of a person's name or likeness without permission.[9] Gradually, most states followed the lead of New York in granting persons a right to be free of certain kinds of intrusion into their private life. But it was not until 1965 that the Supreme Court declared privacy to be a constitutionally protected right. The decision came in *Griswold* v. *Connecticut*, which concerned the right of married couples to be free of state interference in the use of contraceptives.[10]

Some philosophers and legal theorists have argued that the concept of privacy does not introduce any new rights into the law but merely expresses several traditional rights in a new way. William L. Prosser, in an influential 1960 article, offers an account of the latter kind in which the concept of privacy encompasses four ways a person can be wronged. These are

1. Intrusion upon the plaintiff's seclusion or solitude, or into his private affairs.
2. Public disclosure of embarrassing private facts about the plaintiff.
3. Publicity which places the plaintiff in a false light in the public eye.
4. Appropriation, for the defendant's advantage, of the plaintiff's name or likeness.[11]

The first two wrongs involve the infliction of mental distress; the third wrong is a form of defamation of character; and the fourth wrong constitutes the misappropriation of a kind of property. Our legal system already contains the resources to protect individuals against these wrongs without creating a distinct right of privacy.

The Warren and Brandeis Definition

The literature contains many attempts to elucidate privacy as an independent right that is not reducible to any other commonly recognized right. Three definitions in particular merit examination. One, which derives from Warren and Brandeis and finds expression in *Griswold* v. *Connecticut*, holds that privacy is the right to be left alone. Warren and Brandeis were concerned mainly with the publication of idle gossip in sensation-seeking newspapers. The aim of privacy laws, they thought, should be to protect "the privacy of private life" from unwanted publicity, and their proposals all deal with limits on the publication of information about the private lives of individuals. Brandeis applied his definition of privacy to a 1928 case concerning the constitutionality of telephone wiretapping. In his celebrated dissenting opinion in that case, *Olmstead* v. *United States*, Brandeis wrote that the right of privacy is "the right to be let alone—the most comprehensive of rights and the right most valued by civilized men."[12]

A similar view of privacy was expressed by the majority in *Griswold*. Laws governing the use of contraceptives intrude into an area of the lives of individuals where they have a right to be left alone. Justice

William J. Brennan expressed the view in a subsequent birth control case that:

> If the right to privacy means anything, it is the right of the individual, married or single, to be free from unwarranted government invasion into matters so fundamentally affecting a person as the decision whether to bear or beget a child.[13]

Many critics have pointed out that the phrase "to be left alone" is overly broad.[14] Individuals have a right "to be left alone" in matters of religion and politics, for example, but legal restrictions on religious practices, such as snake handling, or on political activity, such as the making of political contributions, do not involve violations of privacy. At the same time, the Warren and Brandeis definition is too narrow, since some violations of privacy occur in situations where there is no right to be left alone. Workers have no right to be free of supervision, for example, even though it can be claimed that their privacy is invaded by the use of hidden cameras to monitor their activity secretly.

These objections, in the view of critics, are merely symptoms of a deeper source of error in the Warren and Brandeis definition, which is the confusion of privacy with liberty. These examples show that a loss of liberty is neither a necessary nor a sufficient condition for a loss of privacy. Perhaps greater clarity is achieved by limiting the concept of privacy to matters involving information and not stretching the concept to include all manner of intrusions into our private lives.

Privacy as Control Over Personal Information

This suggestion is reflected in a second definition in which privacy is expressed in terms of control over information about ourselves.[15] The following definition by Alan F. Westin is typical: "Privacy is the claim of individuals . . . to determine for themselves when, how, and to what extent information about them is communicated to others."[16] This definition is open to the same charge: that it is at once too broad and too narrow. Richard B. Parker observes, "Not every loss or gain of control over information about ourselves is a gain or loss of privacy."[17] For example, a student whose poor performance on an examination reveals a lack of preparation has not suffered a loss of privacy. Furthermore, all definitions of privacy as exercising control flounder on the fact that individuals can relinquish their own privacy by voluntarily divulging all sorts of intimate details themselves.[18] There is a loss of privacy under such circumstances but not a loss of control. Indeed, the loss of privacy occurs as a result of the way in which control over personal information is exercised by these individuals. Therefore, privacy cannot be identified with control.

A More Adequate Definition

A third, more adequate definition of privacy holds that a person is in a state of privacy when certain facts about that person are not known by others. W. A. Parent in an important 1983 article, "Privacy, Morality, and the Law," defines privacy as "the condition of not having undocumented personal knowledge about one possessed by others."[19] By the phrase "personal knowledge," Parent does not mean all information about ourselves but only those facts "which most individuals in a given society at any given time do not want widely known."[20] It is necessary that the definition be restricted to *undocumented* personal information, since some facts that individuals commonly seek to conceal are a matter of public record and can be known without prying into their private lives. A person does not suffer a loss of privacy, for example, when a conviction for a crime becomes known to others, since court records are public documents. Similarly, there is no loss of privacy when an easily observable fact, such as a person's baldness, is known to others, even though the person is sensitive about it and prefers that others not be aware of it.

In the remaining discussion, the concept of privacy is limited to matters involving information and, in particular, to the access of others to undocumented personal information, as described by Parent. The two other definitions—as a right to be left alone and to have control over information about ourselves—confuse privacy with other values. The Parent definition, we will discover, encompasses all the situations in which a threat to employee privacy is charged. Having gained some understanding of the concept of privacy, we can now turn to the question of why privacy is a value.

THE VALUE OF PRIVACY

Why do we value privacy so highly and hold that it ought to be protected as an employee right? Certainly, we desire to have a sphere of our life in which others do not possess certain information about us. But the mere fact that we have this desire does not entail that we have a right of privacy. Nor does it tell us how far a right of privacy extends. Some arguments are needed, therefore, to establish the value of privacy and the claim that we have a right to it.

Most of the arguments developed by philosophers and legal theorists fall into one of two categories. One category consists of utilitarian arguments that appeal to consequences, and the second is Kantian arguments that link privacy to being a person or having respect for persons. To a great extent, these two different kinds of arguments express a few key insights about privacy in slightly different ways.

Utilitarian Arguments

One of the consequences cited by utilitarians is that great harm is done to individuals when inaccurate or incomplete information collected by an employer is used as the basis for making important personnel decisions. The lives of many employees have been tragically disrupted by groundless accusations in their personnel record, for example, and the results of improperly administered polygraph and drug tests. Even factual information that ought not to be in an employee's file, such as the record of an arrest without a conviction, can cause needless harm. And the harm from these kinds of practices is more likely to occur and to be repeated when employees are unable to examine their files and challenge the information (or misinformation) in them.

A drawback to this argument is that it rests on an unproved assumption that could turn out to be false. It assumes that on balance more harm than good will result when employers amass files of personal information, use polygraph machines, conduct drug tests, and so on. Whatever harm is done to employees by invading their privacy has to be balanced, in a utilitarian calculation, against the undeniable benefits that these practices produce for both employers and employees.

Furthermore, the argument considers only the possible harmful consequences of privacy invasions. However, some practices, such as observing workers with hidden cameras and eavesdropping on business conducted over the telephone, are generally considered to be morally objectionable in themselves, regardless of their consequences. One objection to drug testing is that the way in which samples are collected is embarrassing and demeaning. Honest workers, for example, have nothing to fear from surveillance that is designed to protect against employee theft, and indeed the use of hidden cameras in a warehouse can even benefit those who are honest by reducing the possibility of false accusations. Still, workers have a right to complain that secret surveillance of their activities on the job violates the right of privacy. It is the fact that they are subjected to constant observation and not the possible consequences of being observed that is morally objectionable. Similarly, the mere existence of certain kinds of information in company files or the fact that unauthorized people may have access to legitimately acquired information is morally objectionable, even when there is no actual misuse or even the potential for misuse.[21]

These objections are avoided by more sophisticated utilitarian arguments that do not locate the harmful consequences solely in the harm that occurs when information is misused. According to these arguments, a certain amount of privacy is necessary for the enjoyment of some activities, so that invasions of privacy change the character of our experiences and deprive us of the opportunity for gaining pleasure from them. Monitoring and surveillance in the workplace, for example, affect job satisfaction and the sense of dignity and self-worth of all workers. They send a message to employees that they are not trusted and respected as human beings, and the predictable result is a feeling of resentment and a decline in the satisfaction of performing a job.

An illustration of this point is provided by a truck driver with forty years experience with the Safeway Company who reports that he used to love his job because "you were on your own—no one was looking over your shoulder. You felt like a human being." After the company installed a computerized monitoring device on his truck, he decided to take early retirement. He complains, "They push you around, spy on you. There's no trust, no respect anymore." And a directory-assistance operator reported, "I've worked all those years before monitoring. Why don't they trust me now? I will continue to be a good worker, but I won't do any more than necessary now."[22]

Some writers argue that privacy is of value because of the role it plays in developing and maintaining a healthy sense of personal identity. According to Alan F. Westin, privacy enables us to relax in public settings, release pent-up emotions, and reflect on our experiences as they occur—all of which are essential for our mental well-being. A lack of privacy can result in mental stress and even a nervous breakdown.[23] Another common argument appeals to the importance of privacy in promoting a high degree of individuality and freedom of action among the members of a society. Critics of these arguments object, however, that there is little evidence that privacy has the benefits claimed for it or that the predicted harm would follow from limiting people's privacy.[24] Many societies function very well with less room for solitude than our own, and the experiences of human beings in prisons and detention camps are cited by critics to refute these arguments.

Kantian Arguments

Two Kantian themes that figure prominently in defense of a right to privacy are those of autonomy and respect for persons. Stanley I. Benn, for example, notes that utilitarian arguments for a right of privacy are not able to show what is morally wrong when a person is secretly observed without any actual harm being done. "But respect for persons," Benn claims, "will sustain an objection even to secret watching, which may do no actual harm at all." He continues:

> Covert observation—spying—is objectionable because it deliberately deceives a person about his world, thwarting . . . his attempts to make a rational choice. One cannot be said to respect a man . . . if one knowingly and deliberately alters his conditions of action, concealing the fact from him.[25]

Benn's argument thus appeals to both Kantian themes by arguing that invading a person's privacy violates the principle of respect for persons *and* prevents a person from making a rational choice as an autonomous being.

Hyman Gross argues in a similar vein that what is morally objectionable about being observed unawares through a hidden camera or having personal information in a data bank is that a person loses control over how he or she appears to others. He has written:

> A good reason for objecting is that a data bank is an offense to self-determination. We are subject to being acted on by others because of conclusions about us which we do not know and whose effect we have no opportunity to counteract. There is a loss of control over reputations which is unacceptable because we no longer have the ability to try to change what is believed about us. We feel entitled to know what others believe, and why, so that we may try to change misleading impressions and on occasion show why a decision about us ought not be based on reputation even if the reputation is justified.[26]

Control of the kind Gross describes is valuable because without it we no longer have the opportunity for autonomous or self-directed activity, which is a characteristic of human beings. Hence, invasions of privacy diminish an essential condition for being human.

In a very influential discussion, Charles Fried argues that privacy is of value because it provides a "rational context" for some of our most significant ends, such as love, friendship, trust, and respect, so that invasions of privacy destroy our very integrity as a person.[27] What makes this argument different from utilitarian arguments is that privacy, in Fried's view, is not merely a means for attaining these ends but is conceptually tied to them—that is, it is impossible even to *conceive* of relations of love, trust, and so on without the existence of privacy. Fried has explained his argument in the following way:

> To respect, love, trust, or feel affection for others and to regard ourselves as the objects of love, trust, and affection is at the heart of our notion of ourselves as persons among persons, and privacy is the necessary atmosphere for these attitudes and actions, as oxygen is for combustion.[28]

The reason that privacy is essential for respect, love, trust, and so on is that these are intimate relations, and intimacy is created by the sharing of personal information about ourselves which is not known by other people. In a society without privacy, we could not share information with other people (because they would already know it), and hence we could not establish intimate relations with them.

Thus, monitoring, in Fried's view, "destroys the possibility of bestowing the gift of intimacy, and makes impossible the essential dimension of love and friendship."[29] Similarly, trust cannot exist where there is monitoring or surveillance, since trust is the expectation that others will behave in a certain way without the need to check up on them. To check up on a person you trust is a contradiction in terms, according to Fried.

The arguments of Benn, Gross, Fried, and others seize upon important insights about the value of privacy, but many critics have found flaws in the details of their arguments. Jeffrey H. Reiman, for one, objects that it is too strong to assert that *all* instances of watching a person unawares result in deceiving a person and depriving that person of a free choice. Otherwise, we would be violating a person's right of privacy by observing him or her strolling down a street or riding a bus. If the claim in the argument is limited to observation in more personal matters, then we need to ask, what is the justification for limiting the principle in this way? And if the justification is provided by a principle to the effect that the more personal the information, the more we have a right that it not be known by others, then the argument begs the question, since this is a roundabout way of asserting that we have a right to privacy, which is what is to be proved.[30]

A frequently cited objection to Fried's argument and those similar to it is that intimate relations such as love and friendship do not consist solely in the sharing of information. They also involve, as one writer says, "the sharing of one's total self—one's experiences, aspirations, weaknesses, and values."[31] Consequently, these relations can exist and even flourish in the absence of an exclusive sharing of information. Also, although trust might no longer be necessary if a person's thoughts and actions could be known by privacy-invading techniques, some critics contend that trust would still be possible.[32]

A Third Kind of Argument

Several philosophers have suggested that the key to a more satisfactory theory of privacy can be constructed by understanding the way in which individuals are socialized in our culture.[33] Privacy, in the view of these philosophers, is neither a necessary means for realizing certain ends nor conceptually a part of these ends. Nevertheless, we are trained from early childhood to believe that certain things are shameful (for example, public nudity) and others strictly our own business (such as annual income). There is no intrinsic reason why our body or our financial affairs should be regarded as private matters. People at different times and places have been socialized differently with regard to what belongs to the sphere of the private, and we might even be better off if we had been socialized differently. Still, we have been socialized in a certain way. And in our culture, certain beliefs about what ought to be private play an important role in the process by which a newborn child develops into a person and by which we continue to maintain a conception of ourselves as persons. In the words of Jeffrey H. Reiman:

> Privacy is an essential part of the complex social practice by means of which the social group recognizes—and communicates to the individual—that his existence is his own. And this is a precondition of personhood. To be a person, an individual must recognize not just his actual capacity to shape his destiny by his choices. He must also recognize that he has an exclusive moral right to shape his destiny. And this in turn presupposes that he believes that the concrete reality which he is, and through which his destiny is realized, belongs to him in a moral sense.[34]

This argument is broadly utilitarian. The consequences that it appeals to, however, are not the simple pleasures and pains of classical utilitarianism or even the notions of mental health and personal growth and fulfillment of more sophisticated utilitarian arguments. The argument goes deeper by appealing to the importance of privacy for personhood, which is a concept that is more commonly used by Kantian theorists. Unlike Kantian arguments, though, this one recognizes that privacy is not necessary for all people in all times and places but is merely a value specific to our late twentieth-century Western culture. There are societies that function very well with less privacy than we are accustomed to; however, given the role privacy plays in our socialization process, a certain amount is needed for us to develop as persons and have a sense of dignity and well-being.

Both utilitarian and Kantian arguments point to a key insight: that privacy is important in some way to dignity and well-being. They claim too much, however; privacy is not absolutely essential to either one, except insofar as we have come to depend on it. For better or worse, privacy has become an important value in our culture, and now that it has, it needs to be maintained. Privacy is like the luxury that soon becomes a necessity, but "necessary luxuries" are not less valuable just because we could formerly get by without them. The justification of privacy just offered is thus the most adequate one we have.

JUSTIFYING A RIGHT OF EMPLOYEE PRIVACY

The arguments in the preceding section show that privacy is of sufficient value that it ought to be protected. There are many instances, however, in which other persons and organizations are fully justified in having personal information about us and thereby in intruding into our private lives. The task of justifying a right of employee privacy, then, consists not only in demonstrating the value of privacy but also in determining which intrusions into the private lives of employees are justified and which are not.[35]

A number of different issues must be addressed in developing the case for a right of privacy in employment—and in formulating a company privacy protection plan or a law on employee privacy. Among these are:

1. The kind of information which is collected.
2. The use to which the information is put.
3. The persons within a company who have access to the information.
4. The disclosure of the information to persons outside the company.
5. The means used to gain the information.
6. The steps taken to ensure the accuracy and completeness of the information.
7. The access that employees have to information about themselves.

The Purpose for Gathering Information

The first three issues are closely related, since the justification for an employer's possessing any particular kind of information depends, at least in part, on the purpose for which the information is gathered. Some information is simply of no conceivable use in company decision-making and constitutes a gratuitous invasion of employee privacy. It is more often the case, however, that an employer has a need or interest that provides some justification for intruding into the private lives of employees. An invasion of employee privacy is justified, however, only when the information is used for the intended purpose by the individuals who are responsible for making the relevant decisions.

Companies are generally justified in maintaining medical records on employees in order to administer benefit plans, for example, and to monitor occupational health and safety. If these are the purposes for which a company gathers this kind of information, then it follows that: (1) only medical information that is essential for these purposes can be justifiably collected; (2) only those persons who are responsible for administering the benefit plans or monitoring the health and safety of employees are justified in having access to the information; and (3) these persons must use the information only for the intended purposes. There are three corresponding ways in which employees' right of privacy can be violated. These are when: (1) personal information is gathered without a sufficient justifying purpose; (2) it is know by persons who are not in a position that is related to the justifying purpose; and (3) persons who are in such a position use the information for other, illegitimate purposes.

Obviously, the notion of a justifying purpose plays a critical role in determining the exact scope of the right of privacy in employment.

There is considerable room for disagreement on the questions of whether any given purpose is a legitimate one for a business firm to pursue, whether a certain kind of information is essential for the pursuit of a particular purpose, and whether the information is in fact being used for the intended purpose. Companies have an interest and, indeed, an obligation to ensure that employees are capable of performing physically demanding work and are not subjected to undue risk, for example. The purposes for which Henry Ford created the Sociological Department, however, went beyond this concern to include a paternalistic regard for the general welfare of his employees, which is not a legitimate purpose. Even to the extent that the work of the inspectors from the Ford Motor Company was justified by a legitimate purpose, there could still be an objection to the excessive amount of information they sought. Information about the handling of finances, church attendance, and eating and drinking habits is more than the company needs to know.

Determining the purpose for which information is being used can raise difficult questions about intentions. A controversy was sparked in 1980, for example, when it became publicly known that the Du Pont Company was routinely screening black applicants at a plant in New Jersey for signs of sickle cell anemia. The company asserted that the purpose for conducting the screening was to protect black workers, since carriers of the disease, who are mostly black, were thought to be more vulnerable to certain chemicals used at the plant. Such a purpose is arguably legitimate, but some critics of Du Pont charged that the company was actually using genetic screening for another purpose, namely to prevent liability suits and to avoid having to protect workers from dangerous chemicals.[36]

Resolving Disagreements About Purpose

Is there any way in which the notion of a justifying purpose can be clarified so that such disagreements can be resolved? One possibility is to specify the conditions necessary for a business to conduct normal operations. In order to do this, a company must be able to assess the suitability of applicants for employment, supervise their work-related behavior, administer fringe benefit plans, and so on. In addition, employers must be left free to acquire the information necessary for complying with legal requirements about taxes, social security, discrimination, health and safety, and the like. As a result, employers are justified in asking potential employees about their educational background, past employment, and so on, but not, for example, about their marital status, since this information is not necessary in order to make a decision about hiring. Once employees are hired, a company may have a need to inquire about marital status in order to determine eligibility for medical benefits, but only if the employee in question chooses to participate in a medical insurance plan. And even then, this information should be used only for the purpose of determining eligibility for medical benefits.

Joseph R. DesJardins suggests that questions about the extent of the right of privacy in the workplace can be settled by appealing to a contract model of the employer-employee relation.[37] Viewing employment as a contractual relation between an employer and an employee provides a basis for granting a set of rights to both parties, since the validity of contracts requires that certain conditions be satisfied. Contracts are valid, first, only if they are free of force and fraud. As a result, an employer has a right to require applicants to provide enough information to make an informed decision about hiring and to submit to tests for measuring relevant aptitudes and skills. Once hired, employees have an obligation to permit employers to monitor work performance, for example, and to gather whatever information is necessary to maintain an ongoing contractual relation.

Second, valid contracts also require mutual voluntary consent, so that a contract model of employment would not permit employers to collect information without the knowledge and permission of the employees affected. Covert searches, surveillance by hidden cameras, the use of private investigators, and so on would be incompatible with the view of employment as a contractual relation. Similarly, objections could be raised to employer demands that employees either submit to drug tests and interrogation with a polygraph machine or be dismissed, because an employee has little choice but to comply. Union contracts in which employees are able to exercise effective choice often contain provisions prohibiting such practices.

Disclosure to Outsiders

The fourth issue—concerning the disclosure of personal information to persons outside a company—arises because of the practice, once very common, of employers sharing the content of personnel files with landlords, lending agencies, subsequent employers, and other inquiring persons without the consent of the employees involved. Even when there is a legitimate purpose that would justify these various parties having the information, it can be argued that an employer has no right to provide it, since the employer is justified in collecting and using information only for purposes connected with the employer-employee relation. What is morally objectionable about an employer's disclosing personal information to an outside party, in other words, is not necessarily that the outside party is not justified in having it but that the employer has no justification for giving it to them.

Thus, medical records collected by a former employer ought not to be passed along to a subsequent employer without the employee's consent. The former employer presumably had a purpose that justified the gathering of that information, and the new employer might also have a similar purpose in gathering the same information. The justification in the case of the former employer, however, is related to *that* employment relation, and the information gathered can be justifiably used only for purposes connected with it. The subsequent employer, although perhaps justified in gathering the same information, must proceed in the same way as the former employer.

This argument points up an important difference between personal information and other kinds of corporate records. Databases of various kinds are generally regarded as resources which are *owned* by a company. Ownership, however, generally entails an exclusive and unrestricted right of access and control, which employers do not have with respect to personal information. A mailing list, for example, is a kind of property that a company can use in any way it pleases, with no restrictions. Medical records, by contrast, can be compiled by a company only for a specific purpose, and any use unrelated to this purpose is prohibited. The fact that employers bear a burden of proof for justifying the collection and use of personal information shows that the notion of ownership is inappropriate in this case.[38]

It is also not appropriate to describe the information in personnel files as belonging to employees either, since they relinquish some rights to it by virtue of entering into the employment relation. Neither an employer nor an employee, therefore, can be said to own the information in a company's personnel files. Such information is simply not property in the usual sense, unlike other kinds of data gathered by corporations. It is necessary, therefore, to develop a conceptual model for personal information other than that of ownership.

The Means Used to Gather Information

Justifying the means used to gather information, which is the fifth issue, involves a different set of considerations. Use of certain means may violate an employee's right of privacy, even when the information gathered is of a kind that an employer is fully justified in possessing. Examples of impermissible means are polygraph-testing and pretext interviews. (Pretext interviews are inquiries made under false pretenses, as when an employer seeks information from an applicant's family while posing as a market researcher.) Even if employers are justified in asking certain questions on a job application, they are not, for that reason, justified in using a polygraph machine or a pretext interview to verify the accuracy of a person's responses.

A major consideration in evaluating the means used to gather information is whether less intrusive means are available. In general, less intrusive means are morally preferable to those that are more intrusive. Employers are justified in seeking information about drug use by employees in the workplace, for example, but such means as searches of lockers and desks, hidden cameras in restrooms, random drug tests, and the like are not justified when sufficient information could be gathered by less intrusive means, such as closer observation of work performance and testing only for cause. (Some means are not justified, of course, even if less intrusive means are not available. Hidden cameras and random drug tests are possible examples.)

What makes some means more intrusive than others depends on several factors. Such practices as conducting strip searches and watching while a urine sample is produced involve an affront to human dignity. An objection to constant monitoring, personality tests, and the use of polygraph machines is that they collect more information than is necessary and that they collect it indiscriminately. Honesty tests, for example, often inquire into personal habits and interests, family relations, and sexual adjustment—matters that are extraneous to the ostensible purpose.[39] Improperly administered polygraph tests can easily become "fishing expeditions," which result in the revelation of information that an employer is not justified in having.

Another reason why some practices such as monitoring and surveillance by hidden cameras and polygraph-testing are unusually intrusive is that they deprive persons of an opportunity to exercise control over how they appear to others, which is essential for being an autonomous individual. An employee who is unaware of being observed, for example, might be unwittingly led to reveal facts that he or she would otherwise keep from others. George J. Brenkert argues, very perceptively, that since a polygraph machine measures physical characteristics such as breathing rate, perspiration, and blood pressure over which we have little or no control, it "circumvents the person" and undercuts the "way by which we define ourselves as autonomous persons."[40] As a person, we can shape how we appear to others and create an identity for ourselves. A machine that registers our involuntary responses denies us the power to do that.

Accuracy, Completeness, and Access

The last two issues are concerned primarily with matters of fairness. If the information in personnel files and other corporate databases is going to be used to make critical decisions about wage increases, promotions, discipline, and even termination of employment, then it is only fair that the information be as accurate and complete as possible and that employees have access to their personnel files so that they can challenge the contents or at least seek to protect themselves from adverse treatment based on the information in them.

Employers who maintain inaccurate or incomplete files and deny employees access to them are not invading the privacy of their employees, as the concept of privacy is commonly defined. What is at issue is not the possession of personal information by an employer but its use in ways that are unfair to employees. The right that employers violate is a right of fair treatment, which is not the same as a right of privacy. Still, since these are issues involved in the handling of personal information, they must be considered in devising policies or laws dealing with employee privacy.

Vindictive employers have been known to slip highly damaging false reports into personnel files and to make groundless charges in references for former employees. One employer reported to a Chicago retailer that a security guard who was seeking employment was a problem drinker who had deliberately wrecked a company car and was being investigated for forgery. None of these charges was repeated, however, when the employer was hauled into court and forced to testify under oath.[41] Employees can also be unfairly harmed by true reports that are still misleading in some way, as when a person's file contains poor evaluations during a period of illness, for example, but not the excellent evaluations that the person received at other times.

Another objection to drug tests and polygraph machines is their unreliability. A number of factors, including the use of prescription drugs and careless laboratory work, can result in false positives, especially in simpler, less expensive drug tests. Polygraph machines are inherently unreliable, since they register only bodily responses and not the mental experience that triggers them. An investigator might conclude that a subject is lying when the responses recorded by the machine are actually due to a different kind of association. One study, in which 14 polygraphers were asked to evaluate the charts of 207 criminal suspects, found that 50 percent of the experts thought that innocent suspects gave deceptive answers and 36 percent of them considered the guilty suspects to be telling the truth.[42] After a review of the studies to date, the U.S. Office of Technology Assessment concluded in 1983 that polygraph-testing was useless for screening in preemployment contexts.[43]

Conclusion

In summary, determining the exact limits of the right of employees to privacy in the workplace requires that we address a number of issues. Questions about four of these issues—those concerning the kind of information collected, the use to which it is put, and the persons both inside and outside the company who have access to it—can be answered largely by appealing to the notion of a legitimate purpose. The issue of the means used to gain information involves different questions about whether some means are inherently objectionable and whether others are objectionable because less intrusive means are available. Finally, the remaining issues involve the fair treatment of employees, which is not, strictly speaking, part of a right of privacy but is still related to the handling of personal information.

NOTES

1. For information on the Sociological Department, see ROBERT LACEY, *Ford: The Men and the Machine* (Boston: Little, Brown and Company, 1986), 117–25.
2. See *O'Brien v. Papa Gino's of America, Inc.*, 780 F.2d 1067 (1st Cir., 1986). The case is also described in "Privacy," *Business Week*, March 28, 1988, 63.
3. See AL NOEL, "Privacy: A Sign of Our Times," *Personnel Administrator*, 26 (March 1981), 59–62.
4. For a discussion of this problem see KARL J. DUFF and ERIC T. JOHNSON, "A Renewed Employee Right to Privacy," *Labor Law Journal*, 34 (1983), 747–62.
5. ALAN F. WESTIN, "The Problem of Privacy Still Troubles Management," *Fortune*, June 4, 1979, 120–26. See also JOYCE ASHER GILDEA, "Safety and Privacy: Are They Compatible?" *Personnel Administrator*, 27 (February 1982), 80–83.
6. These new technologies are described in GARY T. MARX and SANFORD SHERIZEN, "Monitoring on the Job: How to Protect Privacy as Well as Property," *Technology Review*, 89 (November–December 1986), 63–72. See also GARY T. MARX, "The New Surveillance," *Technology Review*, 88 (May–June 1985), 42–48.
7. See JOHN C. NORTH, "The Responsibility of Employers for the Actions of Their Employees: Negligent Hiring Theory of Liability," *Chicago-Kent Law Review*, 53 (1977), 717–30; and MARIAN M. EXTEJT AND WILLIAM N. BOCKANIC, "Theories of Negligent Hiring and Failure to Fire," *Business and Professional Ethics Journal*, 8 (Winter 1989), 21–34.
8. SAMUEL WARREN and LOUIS D. BRANDEIS, "The Right to Privacy," *Harvard Law Review*, 4 (1890), 193–220. Two earlier discussions are in JAMES FITZ-JAMES STEPHEN, *Liberty, Equality, and Fraternity* (New York: Henry Holt and Co., 1873), and E. L. GODKIN, "Rights of the Citizen, Part IV—To His Own Reputation," *Scribner's Magazine*, 8 (1890), 58–67.
9. The case is *Robertson v. Rochester Folding Box Co.*, 171 N.Y. 538 (1902).
10. *Griswold v. Connecticut*, 381 U.S. 479 (1965).
11. WILLIAM L. PROSSER, "Privacy," *California Law Review*, 48 (1960), 389. Other writers who argue that privacy is a complex of rights are FREDERICK DAVIS, "What Do We Mean by 'Right to Privacy'?" *South Dakota Law Review*, 4 (1959), 1–24; and JUDITH J. THOMSON, "The Right to Privacy," *Philosophy and Public Affairs*, 4 (1975), 295–315. For criticism of Prosser, see EDWARD J. BLOUSTEIN, "Privacy as an Aspect of Human Dignity: An Answer to Dean Prosser," *New York University Law Review*, 39 (1964), 962–1007.
12. *Olmstead v. United States*, 277 U.S. 438 (1928).
13. *Eisenstadt v. Baird*, 405 U.S. 438 (1972).
14. See W. A. PARENT, "Privacy, Morality, and the Law," *Philosophy and Public*

Affairs, 12 (1983), 269–88; H. J. McCLOSKEY, "Privacy and the Right to Privacy," *Philosophy*, 55 (1980), 17–38; and JOSEPH R. DESJARDINS, "Privacy in Employment," in GERTRUDE EZORSKY, ed., *Moral Rights in the Workplace* (Albany: State University of New York Press, 1987), 127–39.

15. See CHARLES F. FRIED, *An Anatomy of Values* (Cambridge: Harvard University Press, 1970), 141; RICHARD A. WASSERSTROM, "Privacy," in WASSERSTROM, ed., *Today's Moral Problems*, 2nd ed. (New York: Macmillan, 1979), 393; ELIZABETH L. BEARDSLEY, "Privacy: Autonomy and Selective Disclosure," in J. ROLAND PENNOCK and JOHN W. CHAPMAN, eds., *Privacy* (New York: Atherton Press, 1971), 65; and ARTHUR MILLER, *The Assault on Privacy* (Ann Arbor: University of Michigan Press, 1971), 25.

16. ALAN F. WESTIN, *Privacy and Freedom* (New York: Atheneum, 1967), 7.

17. RICHARD B. PARKER, "A Definition of Privacy," *Rutgers Law Review*, 27 (1974), 279.

18. This point is made by PARENT, "Privacy, Morality, and the Law," 273.

19. PARENT, "Privacy, Morality, and the Law," 269.

20. PARENT, "Privacy, Morality, and the Law," 269–70.

21. This point is made by STANLEY I. BENN, "Privacy, Freedom, and Respect for Persons," in PENNOCK and CHAPMAN, *Privacy*, 12.

22. Both of these cases are contained in MARX and SHERIZEN, "Monitoring on the Job," 67.

23. WESTIN, *Privacy and Freedom*, 31–42.

24. For criticisms of these arguments see MCCLOSKEY, "Privacy and the Right to Privacy," 34–35; and PARENT, "Privacy, Morality, and the Law," 275–76.

25. BENN, "Privacy, Freedom, and Respect for Persons," 10–11.

26. HYMAN GROSS, "Privacy and Autonomy," in CHAPMAN and PENNOCK, *Privacy*, 174.

27. FRIED, *An Anatomy of Values*, 9. A similar account is given in JAMES RACHELS, "Why Privacy Is Important," *Philosophy and Public Affairs*, 4 (Summer 1975), 295–333.

28. FRIED, *An Anatomy of Values*, 140.

29. FRIED, *An Anatomy of Values*, 148.

30. See JEFFREY H. REIMAN, "Privacy, Intimacy, and Personhood," *Philosophy and Public Affairs*, 6 (1976), 26–44.

31. PARENT, "Privacy, Morality, and the Law," 275. A similar point is expressed by REIMAN, "Privacy, Intimacy, and Personhood," 33.

32. See MCCLOSKEY, "Privacy and the Right to Privacy," 36.

33. Arguments of this kind are presented in WASSERSTROM, "Privacy," and REIMAN, "Privacy, Intimacy, and Personhood."

34. REIMAN, "Privacy, Intimacy, and Personhood," 39.

35. This point is made by PARENT, "Privacy, Morality, and the Law," 280. Much of the argument in this section is derived from Parent's analysis of wrongful invasion of privacy.

36. See THOMAS H. MURRAY, "Thinking the Unthinkable about Genetic Screening," *Across the Board*, 20 (June 1983), 34–39.

37. DESJARDINS, "Privacy in Employment."

38. This point is made by DONALD HARRIS, "A Matter of Privacy," *Personnel*, 64 (February 1987), 38.

39. See ANNE E. LIBBIN, SUSAN R. MENDELSSOHN, and DENNIS P. DUFFY, "The Right to Privacy, Part 5: Employee Medical and Honesty Testing," *Personnel*, 65 (November 1988), 47.
40. GEORGE J. BRENKERT, "Privacy, Polygraphs and Work," *Business and Professional Ethics Journal*, 1 (1981), 30.
41. *Geyer* v. *Steinbronn*, 506 A.2d 901 (Sup. Ct. PA 1985).
42. DAVID T. LYKKEN, "Polygraphic Interrogation," *Nature*, February 23, 1984, 681.
43. "Scientific Validity of Polygraph Testing: A Research Review and Evaluation," Technical Memorandum OTA-TM-H-15 (Washington, DC: Office of Technology Assessment, November 1983).

CHAPTER EIGHT
Discrimination in Employment

Clara Watson felt fortunate in 1976 to be one of the few blacks ever employed as a teller by the Fort Worth Bank and Trust. Her ambition, though, was to become a supervisor in charge of other tellers at the bank, despite the fact that only one other black person had ever held this position.[1] She applied to be a supervisor on four separate occasions, and each time she was denied the position. The bank claimed that all promotion decisions were based strictly on evaluations of fitness for the job and that race was not a factor in filling any of the vacancies for which Clara Watson applied. However, a study showed that during a four-year period, white supervisors at the bank hired 14.8 percent of the white applicants and only 3.5 percent of the black applicants. The same supervisors rated black employees 10 points lower than white employees on a scale used for annual salary evaluations. As a result, blacks were promoted more slowly from one salary grade to another and earned less. In 1981, Clara Watson left the bank, but not before she went to the Equal Employment Opportunity Commission and filed a charge of racial discrimination.

Before the civil rights movement of the 1960s, it was unlikely that Clara Watson would have been hired even as a teller by the bank, much less as a supervisor. Rigid segregation in American society confined blacks mostly to menial labor and prevented their entry into jobs traditionally held by whites. This kind of discrimination is now against the law. Although the barriers have fallen in one area after another, however, the advancement of blacks into more desirable occupations is still hampered by subtle forms of discrimination that are difficult to confirm. How can it be determined, for example, whether Clara Watson was a victim of discrimination or simply less qualified than the whites who were promoted ahead of her? Is the statistical under-representation of blacks employed at the bank sufficient evidence to charge the bank with discrimination? These are difficult questions that separate cases such as that of Clara Watson from blatant discri-mination.

Of course, blacks are not the only racial group in this country to suffer from discrimination in employment. American Indians, Hispan-ics, and Orientals have long been kept out of certain lines of work by deep-seated racial prejudice. Prejudice has also existed at various times in America's history against many European ethnic groups, including the Irish, Italians, and Poles, and against members of certain religious groups, such as Catholics and Jews. The treatment of women by Ameri-can business constitutes another prominent form of discrimination. Historically, women have been confined to unpaid labor in the home and to low-paying, low-status jobs that are stereotyped as "women's work."

Discrimination is not simply a matter of the number of women, blacks, and other groups who are hired by an employer. In the early 1970s, for example, more than one half of the employees of American Telephone & Telegraph Company (AT&T) were women, and racial mi-norities constituted more than 10 percent of the AT&T work force.[2] Women employees were largely concentrated in low-paying clerical and telephone operator jobs, however; and blacks, Hispanics, and members of other racial minorities were employed chiefly in unskilled job catego-ries, such as maintenance workers and janitors. The skilled-craft cate-gory, by contrast, covering workers who install and repair telephone lines, consisted almost entirely of white males. Women and blacks were also conspicuously absent from higher level managerial positions and the executive ranks. As a result, AT&T was charged with discriminating against women and racial minorities by using sex and race as factors in making job assignments. Eventually, the company agreed to increase the representation of these groups in job categories from which they had previously been excluded.

This chapter is concerned primarily with the ethical arguments against discrimination in employment. Because of the controversial na-ture of these issues, it will be helpful to begin with a definition of discrimination in employment and to discuss some of the forms it can take.

WHAT IS DISCRIMINATION?

The term *discrimination* describes a large number of wrongful acts in employment, housing, education, medical care, and other important areas of public life. Although discrimination in each of these areas takes different forms, what they have in common is that a person is deprived of some benefit or opportunity because of membership in some group toward which there is substantial prejudice. Racial minorities and women are the principal groups targeted for discrimination, but discrimination also occurs against other groups, such as the elderly and the handicapped.

Discrimination in employment, which is our concern here, generally arises from the decisions employers make about hiring, promotion, pay, fringe benefits, and the other terms and conditions of employment that directly affect the economic interests of employees. Employers make these kinds of decisions every day, and it is inevitable that some employees and applicants for employment will be treated differently from others. There is nothing unjust about such decisions as long as they are made for reasons that are reasonably job-related. But when a person's race or sex is not relevant to the performance of a job (which is almost always), it ought not to be taken into consideration. For an employer to single out a person for adverse treatment merely because that person is black or a woman, for example, is generally an act of discrimination.

A simple example of discrimination in employment is paying men and women different wages for performing the same work. This practice was the first to be addressed by federal nondiscrimination legislation. The Equal Pay Act of 1963 forbids an employer to offer different wages to men and women who perform the same or substantially similar work unless the difference is based on some valid factor other than sex, such as seniority or productivity. One ethical justification for the Equal Pay Act is the Aristotelian principle of justice. Paying employees differently is justified only if there is some relevant difference between them.

Although discrimination is a form of unequal treatment, not all unequal treatment is discrimination. An employer who shows favoritism in deciding on promotions, for example, is guilty of violating the principle of equality in dealing with employees but not necessarily of discriminating against them. Two further elements are necessary. First, discrimination involves decisions that directly affect the employment status of individuals or the terms and conditions of their employment; that is, discrimination occurs in what are generally regarded as *personnel* decisions, such as those involving hiring and firing, promotion, pay, advancement opportunities, and the like. Second, the unequal treatment results from prejudice or some other morally unjustified attitude against members of the group to which an individual belongs. In cases of discrimination, individuals are not treated on the basis of individual merit but on the basis of group characteristics or what are believed (often wrongly) to be characteristics of certain groups.

The 1964 Civil Rights Act

These two elements can be observed in Title VII of the 1964 Civil Rights Act. Section 703(a) reads as follows:

> It shall be an unlawful employment practice for an employer—(1) to fail or refuse to hire or to discharge any individual with respect to his compensation, terms, conditions, or privileges of employment, because of such individual's race, color, religion, sex, or national origin; or (2) to limit, segregate, or classify his employees or applicants for employment in any way which would deprive or tend to deprive any individual of employment opportunities or otherwise adversely affect his status as an employee, because of such individual's race, color, religion, sex, or national origin.[3]

Notice that Title VII first describes the kinds of employment decisions that are governed by the statute and then lists five factors—race, color, religion, sex, and national origin—that employers are not legally permitted to take into consideration. These factors define groups that are called in law *protected classes*. In subsequent legislation, Congress extended the list of protected classes in order to prevent discrimination against older people (Age Discrimination in Employment Act of 1967), the handicapped (Rehabilitation Act of 1973), and pregnant women (Pregnancy Discrimination Act of 1978).

The prejudice involved in discrimination is of several different kinds. One kind of prejudice behind much racial and ethnic discrimination consists of strong feelings of antipathy and intolerance. Some prejudice is based not on strong feelings but on misunderstandings, such as stereotypes about women, older workers, and the handicapped. Finally, some prejudice is due primarily to economic considerations. Employers are sometimes deterred from hiring pregnant women, older workers, and the handicapped merely because of the higher cost.

Among the questions to be addressed in defining discrimination is whether there must be an *intent* to discriminate. A charge of discrimination requires that the adverse treatment of a person be related in some way to membership in a certain group, but what is the nature of this relation? Section 703(a) of Title VII states that it is illegal for an employer to make decisions about hiring, discharge, compensation, and so on because of an individual's race, color, sex, religion, or national origin. The crucial phrase "because of" is not explained in the law, however.

One kind of discrimination occurs when there is an express intent to treat the members of certain groups differently. Thus, an employer who refuses to receive applications from blacks or has a policy of hiring blacks only for certain jobs would be guilty of discrimination of this kind. It would be discriminatory in a similar way for an employer to seek a "competent, experienced woman" for a secretarial position or a "recent college graduate" for an opening in sales. Such wording implies that sex and age will be considered in decisions about hiring.

In some cases, employers defend themselves against charges of discrimination by arguing that race, sex, or some other characteristic is relevant to the job. Although admitting an intent to treat their employees and applicants differently on the basis of some characteristic, these employers maintain that they are motivated not by racism or sexism or some other kind of prejudice but purely by business considerations. Some situations of this kind are relatively uncontroversial. Obviously, Catholic priests and Jewish rabbis must be of the religion that they serve. A woman's college could justifiably have a preference for a female president. A college for the deaf was forced by student protest to rescind the appointment of a new president and to seek a president who is deaf.[4] Airlines are legally permitted to force pilots to stop flying at the age of sixty.

Section 703(e) of Title VII allows exceptions for sex, religion, and national origin when these are a "bona fide occupational qualification [BFOQ] reasonably necessary to the normal operation of that particular business or enterprise." Race and color are not included in Section 703(e) as a BFOQ and thus cannot be used legally to make distinctions for purposes of employment. The courts have interpreted the BFOQ exception very narrowly, so that employers must show that the qualification is absolutely essential for the conduct of business and not merely useful. In a suit brought by an unsuccessful male applicant for a job as a flight attendant with Pan American World Airways, a federal appeals court rejected the employer's contention that women were superior to men in "providing reassurance to anxious passengers" and in "giving courteous personalized service."[5] Not only are these services that could be provided by men, but they are peripheral to Pan Am's main business of transporting passengers safely from one location to another.

One of the few cases in which the Supreme Court has held sex to be a BFOQ concerned a rule adopted by the Alabama Board of Corrections excluding women from positions in a maximum-security male prison requiring close contact with the inmates.[6] The majority opinion argued, first, that women employees are likely to be the victims of sexual assaults in a prison characterized by "rampant violence" and a "jungle atmosphere." Second, the likelihood of sexual assaults would reduce the ability of a woman to maintain order in the prison, which is the main function of a prison employee. The presence of women in a male prison poses a threat, therefore, "not only to the victim of the assault but also to the basic control of the penitentiary and protection of its inmates and other security personnel."

Several members of the Court disagreed. It is not clear, they said, that women are exposed to significantly greater risk of attack than men who are employed in the same positions at the prison. And even if a job is more dangerous for some individuals than others, it is less discriminatory to allow individuals to decide voluntarily the degree of risk to assume rather than bar those at greater risk. Also, Justice Thurgood Marshall observed, "It is women who are made to pay the price in lost job opportunities for the threat of depraved conduct by male prison inmates." A better solution, perhaps, would be to make the workplace safer for women instead of limiting their employment opportunities because of the threatened conduct of others.

Disparate Treatment and Disparate Impact

Employment policies that do not explicitly involve classifying employees by race, sex, or other impermissible characteristics can still serve to exclude members of these groups in disproportionate numbers. In interpreting Title VII, the courts have generally held that employers are guilty of discrimination in the absence of any intent *when the effects are the same as if there had been an intent to discriminate*. Discrimination is thus not solely a matter of intention but also of consequences. A distinction is made in law between *disparate treatment*, which is discrimination of the first kind, involving an express intention, and *disparate impact*, which is discrimination of the second kind.

A landmark case in discrimination law that illustrates the distinction between disparate treatment and disparate impact is *Griggs* v. *Duke Power Company*.[7] Before the passage of Title VII of the Civil Rights Act of 1964, Duke Power Company openly practiced discrimination against blacks. At the Dan River Plant in Draper, North Carolina, blacks were employed only in the labor department, which was the lowest paying of the five operating divisions. In order to comply with Title VII, the company revised its hiring and promotion policies in 1965 so as to eliminate distinctions between blacks and whites. For initial placement in any department except labor, all applicants, regardless of race, were now required to have a high school diploma and pass two standardized tests, the Wonderlic Personnel Test, which is designed to measure general intelligence, and the Bennett Mechanical Comprehension Test. Current employees in the labor department could qualify for promotion to a higher department by satisfying one of these requirements—that is, either by having a high school diploma or by passing the two tests.

Thirteen black employees in the labor department brought suit against Duke Power Company, contending that the education and test requirements were discriminatory for two reasons. First, according to the 1960 census, 34 percent of white males in North Carolina had graduated from high school as compared with a figure of only 12 percent for black males. The requirement of a high school diploma, therefore, served to exclude black applicants in proportionately greater numbers than white applicants. Second, the passing scores on the two standardized tests were set by the company at the national median of high school graduates, with the result that 58 percent of whites taking the test passed, whereas only 6 percent of the blacks succeeded in doing so. Again, a requirement imposed by the company had a disproportionate impact on blacks applying for employment.

The difference between blacks and whites in the percentages graduating from high school and the performance of the two groups on the standardized tests is largely attributable to the segregated school system in the state. Thus, the requirements, although ostensibly colorblind, served to perpetuate the effects of discrimination in schooling. Chief Justice Warren Burger asserted in the majority opinion that "practices, procedures, and tests neutral on their face, and even neutral in terms of intent, cannot be maintained if they operate to 'freeze' the status quo of prior discriminatory employment practices."

Duke Power Company responded to the charge of discrimination by holding that Title VII does not require employers to treat workers without regard for qualifications. The requirement of a minimal educational attainment is reasonable, and intelligence and aptitude tests are specifically sanctioned by Section 703(h) of the Civil Rights Act. This section authorizes the use of "any professionally developed ability test" that is not "designed, intended, or used to discriminate because of race."

The position of the Supreme Court is that neither requirement had been shown by the company to be related to successful job performance. According to the majority opinion:

> On the record before us, neither the high school completion requirement nor the general intelligence test is shown to bear a demonstrable relationship to successful performance of the jobs for which it was used. . . . The evidence, however, shows that employees who have not completed high school or taken the tests have continued to perform satisfactorily and make progress in departments for which the high school and test criteria are now used. The promotion record of present employees who would not be able to meet the new criteria thus suggests the possibility that the requirements may not be needed even for the limited purpose of preserving the avowed policy of advancement within the company. . . .

The decision in *Griggs* v. *Duke Power Company* interprets Title VII as prohibiting employment practices that involve no intent to discriminate (disparate treatment) but still operate to exclude members of protected classes unnecessarily (disparate impact). Companies are free to hire and promote workers on the basis of defensible requirements. But in the words of the Court:

> The touchstone is business necessity. If an employment practice which operates to exclude Negroes cannot be shown to be related to job performance, the practice is prohibited.

Moreover:

> . . . Congress has placed on the employer the burden of showing that any given requirement must have a manifest relationship to the employment in question.[8]

THE FORMS OF DISCRIMINATION

A definition cannot answer all the difficult and perplexing questions about discrimination that arise in the workplace. Aside from the question of intent, there are conceptual questions about who belongs to the groups regarded as protected classes and what acts constitute discrimination against members of these groups. It has fallen to the courts to answer many of these questions, since they concern the interpretation of Title VII and other legislation barring discrimination in employment, including the Age Discrimination in Employment Act and the Rehabilitation Act. Although our concern is not with the law as such, the positions taken by the courts in controversial cases have significant ethical implications.

Discrimination on the Basis of Race and Sex

In the United States, racial discrimination is generally directed against four groups: blacks, Hispanics, American Indians, and Orientals. Although Title VII lists race and color as protected classes, a distinction is not commonly made between them.

Sex discrimination is most commonly directed against women, although laws that give preference to women in such matters as alimony and child custody are being challenged by men as instances of sex discrimination. In the interpretation of Title VII, sex discrimination is discrimination based on the fact that a person is male or female and not on sex-related matters, such as sexual orientation or marital status. Although some local governments have passed laws barring discrimination in employment and other matters against homosexuals, discrimination of this kind is not covered by the Civil Rights Act of 1964. Employers are permitted by Title VII to treat married and single employees differently as long as no distinction is made between men and women. An employer can give a preference in hiring to married applicants, for example, but it would be discriminatory to prefer married men and single women in filling jobs.

Unlike race and color, sex can be a BFOQ. Many of the problems about what constitutes sexual discrimination arise in cases where a person's sex can arguably be taken into consideration, such as in hiring guards for a male prison or service in the armed forces. In some other cases, sex is not a BFOQ, but the stated qualifications serve to exclude virtually all women. Examples are tests for police officers and firefighters that require considerable strength and endurance. Whether the qualifications are discriminatory depends largely on whether they are absolutely necessary for the performance of the job.

The Special Case of Pregnancy

Does the Title VII prohibition against discrimination because of sex protect women who are pregnant? Congress passed the Pregnancy Discrimination Act in 1978 in order to resolve this question. The main impetus came from a case in which a woman challenged a policy at General Electric Company forcing her to take unpaid maternity leave with the loss of all fringe benefits.[9] After a miscarriage, the woman suffered a further medical problem unrelated to the pregnancy. Since she lost all fringe benefits because of her pregnancy, the company refused to cover the cost of the unrelated medical problem. The Supreme Court ruled that the policy at General Electric did not constitute sexual discrimination under Title VII but challenged Congress, if it disagreed, to clarify whether the law on sexual discrimination covers pregnancy. Congress accepted the challenge and declared it did.

The Pregnancy Discrimination Act amends the phrase in Title VII "because of sex" to include decisions made on the basis of "pregnancy, childbirth, or related medical conditions." The act mainly affects fringe benefits of two kinds: hospital and major medical plans and policies on temporary disability and sick leave. All such plans and policies are required by the act to treat pregnancy as any other condition. Employers are not required to grant maternity leaves or pay for the medical care associated with pregnancy. But if they allow an employee with a broken leg, for example, to have a paid leave of absence or they pay for the cost of a broken leg under the company's medical plan, then a woman's pregnancy must be treated in exactly the same way. Men are also protected by the Pregnancy Discrimination Act in that the medical coverage for the pregnant wife of a male employee must be the same as that provided for the husband of a female employee.[10]

Many questions remain about the extent of the protection that pregnant women morally and legally ought to have. For example, are men and women being treated equally if a father is not given a leave for delivery and the early months of care for the newborn? Should the time allowed for a maternity leave be based solely on the medical condition of the mother, or should the welfare of the child also be taken into account? Would it be permissible for a state to mandate maternity benefits greater than those provided for other conditions? (The Supreme Court has answered this last question by upholding a California law that requires employers to provide unpaid leaves of absence for up to four months and to allow women to return to the same or a similar job in the event of pregnancy.[11])

Sexual Harassment

Improper sexual conduct in the workplace—which includes lewd and suggestive comments, touching and fondling, persistent attention, and requests for sexual favors—has long been a problem for women, and occasionally men. All too often, such sexual harassment has been regarded by employers as a personal matter beyond their control, or as an unavoidable part of male–female relations. However, increased attention to the problem and developments in the law have made employers aware of their responsibilities—and women, of their rights!

That sexual harassment is morally wrong is not in dispute. The main questions are: What is sexual harassment? How serious is the problem? And who is responsible for preventing it? A further, legal question is whether sexual harassment is prohibited by the 1964 Civil Rights Act. Although Title VII does not mention sexual harassment, the courts have ruled that it is a form of discrimination and, hence, an illegal employment practice.

Surveys of employee attitudes reveal substantial agreement on some of the activities that constitute sexual harassment, and differences on others. In particular, most of the respondents in a 1980 poll conducted by *Harvard Business Review* and *Redbook* magazine consistently rated a supervisor's behavior as more serious than the same action by a co-worker, thereby recognizing that sexual harassment is mainly an issue of power.[12] Barbara A. Gutek has found that more than 90 percent of both men and women consider socializing or sexual activity as a job requirement to be sexual harassment. However, 84 percent of the women surveyed, but only 59 percent of the men, identified "sexual touching" as sexual harassment.[13] In general, women are more likely than men to label the same activity as sexual harassment.

In 1980, the EEOC issued guidelines on sexual harassment that included the following definition:

> Unwelcome sexual advances, requests for sexual favors, and other verbal or physical conduct of a sexual nature constitute sexual harassment when (1) submission to such conduct is made either explicitly or implicitly a

term or condition of an individual's employment, (2) submission to or rejection of such conduct by an individual is used as the basis for employment decisions affecting such individual, or (3) such conduct has the purpose or effect of unreasonably interfering with an individual's work performance or creating an intimidating, hostile, or offensive working environment.

This definition makes a distinction between two kinds of harassment. One is *quid pro quo* harassment, in which a superior, who is usually a man, uses his power to grant or deny employment benefits to exact sexual favors from a subordinate, who is usually a woman. The other kind is *hostile working environment* harassment, in which the sexual nature of the conduct of co-workers and others causes a woman (or a man) to be very uncomfortable.

Quid pro quo harassment clearly violates the Title VII provision that men and women should not be treated differently in their "compensation, terms, conditions, or privileges of employment." A woman who is promised a promotion or a raise—or threatened with demotion, termination, or loss of pay—based on whether she submits to the sexual demands of her boss is being held to a different standard, merely because of her sex.

Some observers contend that quid pro quo harassment, while unfortunate, is not sexual discrimination but merely a wrongful act committed by one employee against another. It is not uncommon for workers of both sexes to encounter personal problems on the job, and harassment, in this view, is one of these personal problems. However, Catharine A. MacKinnon has argued that sexual harassment in the workplace is more than "personal"; it has a connection to "the female condition as a whole."

> As a practice, sexual harassment singles out a gender-defined group, women, for special treatment in a way which adversely affects and burdens their status as employees. Sexual harassment limits women in a way men are not limited. It deprives them of opportunities that are available to male employees without sexual conditions. In so doing, it creates two employment standards: one for women that includes sexual requirements, one for men that does not.[14]

Initially, the courts were reluctant to recognize sexual harassment as discrimination unless a woman suffered some economic loss, such as a reduction in pay or the loss of her job. If this position is accepted, however, then any amount of harassment is legal as long as the woman's employment status is not affected. In 1981, though, a court held that sexual harassment is illegal even when there is no economic loss. No woman, the court declared, should be forced to endure the psychological trauma of a sexually intimidating workplace as a condition of employment.[15] Finally, in *Meritor Savings Bank* v. *Vinson* (1986), the U.S. Supreme Court declared that "without question" both quid pro quo harassment and hostile working environment harassment constitute sexual discrimination under Title VII.[16]

Hostile working environment harassment is both more pervasive and more difficult to prove. Studies have shown that quid pro quo harassment is relatively rare, but in surveys about one third of working women (33%) report incidents of sexual remarks and jokes and around a fourth cite staring and suggestive leers (27%) and unwanted sexual touching (24%).[17] Not all of this conduct is considered to be sexual harassment, however, even by the women who report it. Removing all sexual conduct from the workplace, moreover, is impractical—and, perhaps, even undesirable. Still, a line must be drawn somewhere.

One possibility is a *reasonable person* standard, whereby conduct that is offensive to a person of average sensibilities would be impermissible. However, one court has rejected this approach on the grounds that it "tends to be male-biased and tends to systematically ignore the experiences of women." This court has proposed, instead, a *reasonable woman* standard, which requires that the alleged harassment be judged from the recipient's point of view.[18]

In *Meritor*, the Court also considered the question of an employer's responsibility for harassment by a supervisor or co-worker. Although Mechelle Vinson charged that her supervisor, Sidney Taylor, made repeated sexual advances and raped her on several occasions, she did not report this to anyone at the bank or use the bank's formal complaint procedure. The bank held that it was not responsible, therefore, because of the lack of knowledge. The Supreme Court disagreed, however, and held that an employer has a responsibility to ensure that the workplace is free of sexual harassment.

Most corporations have accepted this responsibility and have established programs to deal with sexual harassment on the job. The major features of these programs are: developing a firm policy against harassment and communicating this policy to all employees; providing training, where necessary, to secure compliance; setting up a procedure for reporting violations; investigating all complaints thoroughly and fairly; and, finally, taking appropriate action against the offenders.

Religious Discrimination

Religious discrimination is substantially different from discrimination based on race or sex. There are instances, to be sure, of religious discrimination in which employers refuse to hire or promote individuals simply because of prejudice against members of certain religious groups, such as Catholics and Jews. Most charges of religious discrimination in employment, however, involve conflicts between the religious beliefs and practices of employees and workplace rules and routines. Suppose, for example, that an employee's religion requires strict observance of the Sabbath. Does an employer have an obligation to revise work schedules in order to accommodate the dictates of this employee's religion, especially if other employees are inconvenienced by having to work instead?

Employees often request time off with or without pay to observe religious holidays, to participate in religious ceremonies and observances, and to do religious work. Since Christians are usually not required to work on Christmas and Easter, is it discriminatory to deny similar release time for Jews on Rosh Hashanah or Yom Kippur? Members of some religious groups have special dress or grooming requirements, such as a yarmulke for Jewish men and a turban and a beard for Sikh men.[19] Some employees have religious objections to performing certain kinds of work. Two postal workers whose religious beliefs did not permit military conscription were fired for refusing to handle draft registrations, for example.[20] Other instances of conflict include employee requests for prayer breaks and special foods in the company cafeteria and refusals to undergo medical examinations.

Religious discrimination also involves the violation of a right not to be adversely affected because of the religious beliefs and practices of employers or other employees. For example, a Texas woman who was an atheist resigned her job at a savings and loan association in order to avoid compulsory monthly staff meetings that began with a religious service.[21] Aggressive proselytizing on the job has occurred in many companies. There are a growing number of "Christian" companies that attempt to do business according to certain principles and to impose these principles on their employees. These employers sometimes screen applicants by asking questions to determine whether they believe in God, attend church regularly, read the Bible, and engage in prayer, and whether they have been divorced or had premarital or extramarital sexual relations.

What makes these conflicts different from racial and sexual discrimination is that they are usually not motivated by prejudice or some other morally unjustified attitude toward members of certain groups. Employees who charge religious discrimination are often not being treated differently because of their religion. The problem is quite the opposite. They are being treated like everyone else *when they have a right to be treated differently because of their religion or lack of one.*

In 1972, Congress amended Title VII by adding Section 701(j), which states that there is no religious discrimination if "an employer demonstrates that he is unable to reasonably accommodate an employee's or prospective employee's religious observance or practice without undue hardship on the conduct of the employer's business." As a result of this amendment, the bulk of the court cases involving charges of religious discrimination raise questions about what constitutes "reasonable accommodation" and "undue hardship."

The landmark case that has guided the courts in answering these questions is *Trans World Airlines* v. *Hardison*.[22] Hardison belonged to the Worldwide Church of God, which prohibits work from sundown Friday to sundown Saturday. In order for him to avoid work during this period, it would have been necessary either for the union to force someone with greater seniority to work on the undesirable shift or for the company to pay an employee from another department overtime. The Supreme Court ruled that Title VII does not require other employees to give up their rights to choose work schedules based on collective-bargaining agreements and seniority; nor does it require the employer's expense to be more than *de minimus*, a minimal amount.

In addition, the courts have held that religious objections can be dismissed by an employer when they interfere with employee safety. A court ruled in favor of a company, for example, that required a Sikh man who worked around dangerous chemicals to be clean-shaven on the grounds that a beard would prevent the proper use of a respirator in the event of an accident, which could cause death or serious injury to the employee and possibly subject the company to penalties for being in violation of OSHA regulations.[23] However, the courts have insisted in a number of decisions subsequent to *Trans World Airlines* v. *Hardison* that companies have to make an active effort to accommodate an employee and must offer a reasonable alternative if one is available.[24]

National Origin Discrimination

National origin discrimination overlaps discrimination based on race, color, and, to some extent, religion. It is conceptually distinct, however, since an employer could have employment policies that exclude Mexican immigrants but not other Hispanics, or Vietnamese but not other Orientals. In the interpretation of Title VII, the phrase *national origin* refers not only to the country of an individual's birth but to that of his parents or more distant ancestors. Title VII is also interpreted so as to protect individuals from national origin discrimination because of an individual's foreign-sounding name or marriage to a person from another nationality or an association with a nationality group.

It is not discriminatory under Title VII for an employer to require U.S. citizenship as a condition for hiring or promotion as long as the requirement is reasonably job-related and is not a pretext for excluding members of some nationality group. However, an employer cannot make any distinction among citizens of other countries—by accepting Canadian citizens, for example, but excluding citizens of Mexico. Similarly, an employer is permitted by Title VII to impose a requirement that employees be fluent in English, even if it excludes recent immigrants, as long as the requirement is dictated by legitimate business reasons and is uniformly applied. Legal challenges to citizenship and fluency in English as requirements in employment are judged by the standards for disparate impact that are set forth in the *Griggs* decision.

A curious unresolved question is whether there can be national origin discrimination against American nationals. As more businesses in the United States come under the control of Japanese and European parent companies, there is a growing tendency for them to draw plant supervisors and higher level managers from their own countries. Is this discrimination on the basis of national origin against Americans by foreigners? In a 1982 case, the Supreme Court held that the American subsidiary of a Japanese company was subject to the Title VII provision concerning discrimination on the basis of national origin, although the Court left open the possibility that national origin can be a BFOQ. According to the decision in *Sumitomo Shoji America* v. *Avagliano*:

> There can be little doubt that some positions in a Japanese-controlled company doing business in the United States call for great familiarity with not only the language of Japan, but also the culture, customs, and business practices of that country.[25]

In another case, however, an official of a wholly Japanese-owned American subsidiary argued that Japanese were favored over Americans in management positions because only native Japanese possess *shosha*, which translates literally as "moving think tank."[26] Such a person has extensive knowledge of the organization and the industry and is able to collect and analyze information and to formulate and implement business decisions effectively. The idea that only native Japanese possess *shosha* is an unwarranted stereotype, however, and there was no effort by the company to train American employees in Japanese ways of doing business or to transfer them to Japan for experience.[27]

Discrimination Against the Handicapped and Older Persons

Age discrimination is one form of discrimination that we are all liable to face if we live long enough. It results largely from the benefits that employers perceive in shunting older employees aside to make room for younger employees who often have more up-to-date skills and innovative ideas. Younger employees are also less expensive to employ, since older employees generally have higher salaries and make more extensive use of fringe benefits. Youth is sometimes preferred by employers for marketing reasons. Three employees in their fifties were dismissed by I. Magnin Department Stores in 1978, for example, as part of what they claimed was a new strategy by the company to appeal to younger shoppers.[28] For many years, the nation's airlines enforced a maximum age for stewardesses in order to maintain an image of youthful attractiveness.

The Age Discrimination in Employment Act (ADEA), passed by Congress in 1967, follows the form of Title VII in prohibiting employers from discriminating in the hiring, promotion, discharge, compensation, or other terms and conditions of employment because of age. Originally, the act protected employees from the ages of forty to sixty-five, but the upper limit was raised to seventy in 1978 and eliminated altogether in 1986; however, employees can be forced to retire at the age of seventy. Exceptions to the ADEA are permitted when age is a bona fide occupational qualification. The courts have interpreted this exception very narrowly, however, and employers have been upheld largely for jobs such as that of airline pilot, where advancing age poses a safety hazard to the public at large. The act permits exceptions in cases where a company has a bona fide seniority system. And highly paid corporate executives are also generally excluded from protection under the ADEA.

Although some instances of age discrimination are obvious, others are more subtle. Even when age is a BFOQ for a particular job, employers must be careful not to use age for any purpose other than that for which it is justified. In particular, employers must take care that seemingly neutral criteria do not exclude a disproportionate number of older employees. The courts commonly use the standards developed in *Griggs* with regard to disparate impact. Thus, an early-retirement program at the Chrysler Corporation, which was part of a general work force reduction, was thrown out by a federal court because workers under fifty-five were laid off with a chance of recall, whereas workers over fifty-five were permanently discharged with no chance of being recalled.[29]

The analysis of discrimination that has been developed for race, sex, and so on can easily be extended to cover the handicapped. The extent of discrimination is difficult to determine precisely, since the career prospects and the earning potential of the handicapped are limited by their disabilities. One measure of the extent of discrimination against the handicapped, however, is the difference between the jobs and income they have compared with the jobs and income they would have if their abilities were taken into consideration. According to one study of discrimination in wages, approximately two thirds of the lower earnings of handicapped men is due to their lower productivity and the costs of employing them and is therefore justified. One third of the difference, however, can be accounted for only by unjustified discrimination on account of their handicapped status.[30]

In many respects, discrimination against the handicapped is like religious discrimination rather than discrimination on the basis of race or sex. Employing the handicapped often requires that they be treated differently in order to compensate for their disabilities. And it may be argued that employers ought to be willing to make reasonable accommodations for the impairments or disabilities of the handicapped just as they are obligated to make reasonable accommodations for the religious beliefs of their employees. One kind of discrimination occurs, then, when an employer, as a result of a prejudicial attitude, refuses to hire a handicapped person or places a person with a handicap in a lower paying position that does not utilize that person's true abilities. Discrimination of a second kind occurs when a handicapped person could perform satisfactorily in a job but is prevented from doing so by the unwillingness of an employer to make the necessary accommodations, by providing wheelchair access, for example.[31]

Conclusion

This section has covered a number of questions surrounding discrimination of different kinds. We have seen that defining key terms, such as *race* and *sex*, requires us to make some morally relevant distinctions (between gender and marital status, for example). More important is the fact that employers are permitted to treat protected groups differently (except those based on race and color) if there is sufficient reason. Gender-based classifications can be justified by law, for example, for jobs in which sex is a BFOQ. And policies with a disparate impact are legal if they serve a legitimate business purpose (the "business necessity" test). The burden that businesses can be justifiably expected to bear also varies for different kinds of discrimination. Employers are required by law to go to great lengths to accommodate pregnant women and the handicapped, for example, but employees' religious beliefs are to be accommodated only if the cost is minimal. As our discussion shows, what constitutes discrimination is not always easy to determine.

ETHICAL ARGUMENTS AGAINST DISCRIMINATION

That discrimination is wrong can be shown by a variety of arguments. There are, first, straightforward utilitarian arguments that cite the ways discrimination harms individuals, business firms, and society as a whole. A second kind of argument appeals to the Kantian notions of human dignity and respect for persons. Arguments of a third kind are based on various principles of justice. Any one of these arguments is sufficient to establish the point, but it is still worthwhile to examine them all, since each brings out some important aspects of the problem of discrimination.

The Economic Efficiency Argument

One standard utilitarian argument favored by economists is that discrimination creates an economically inefficient matching of people to jobs. The productivity of individual businesses and the economy as a whole is best served by choosing the most qualified applicant to fill any particular position. When applicants are evaluated on the basis of characteristics, such as race and sex, that are not job-related, productivity suffers. Similarly, it is economically disadvantageous for employees to discriminate by refusing to work with blacks or women and for customers to discriminate by refusing to patronize minority-owned businesses. Insofar as we value efficiency or productivity, then, discrimination should be eliminated from all economic relations.

There are a number of difficulties with this argument. First, not all forms of discrimination produce economic inefficiencies. This is especially true of religious discrimination and discrimination against the handicapped, because complying with the laws protecting these groups requires employers to make "reasonable accommodation," which imposes some cost. It is often cheaper for employers to dismiss employees with troublesome religious beliefs and practices and to avoid hiring handicapped people who have special needs. Age discrimination is a problem in our society precisely because of the economic incentives for employers to slight older employees. The economists' argument has been developed primarily with racial and, to some extent, sexual discrimination in mind, and so it is not equally effective against these other kinds of discrimination.

Second, it is not clear that even racial and sexual discrimination are always inefficient. Under the assumptions of classical economic theory, they *should* be, but the predictions of economic theory are not always borne out in practice. According to free market theory, employers who discriminate on the basis of race or sex are expressing a "taste for discrimination," which they pay for by imposing a higher cost on themselves.[32] For example, when a more productive black applicant is passed over by an employer who prefers to hire whites merely because of race, the output of that employer will be lower. The difference is a cost that the employer is presumably willing to assume in order to satisfy a preference for a white work force. In a free market, however, employers with a "taste for discrimination" are liable to be driven out of business, and so discrimination should be reduced over time.[33]

Some of the empirical implications of this analysis have been borne out. Discrimination has been found to be more prevalent under monopolistic conditions than in more competitive markets, for example. But wage differentials between men and women have not significantly decreased over time. There is much controversy among economists over how to account for this. Kenneth J. Arrow suggests that one reason for the persistence of discrimination is that although it might be less costly for an employer to have more blacks or women in the work force, currently employed white males who prefer not to work with them would demand more in wages. The shift to a nondiscriminatory hiring policy thus has an "adjustment cost" that might offset the savings that would result.[34] Another proposed reason is that in the absence of discrimination, employees would be hired solely on the basis of productivity, but since productivity is difficult to determine, employers "hedge their bets" by selecting white males in order to take advantage of statistical averages, on the assumption that white males are more productive.[35] Barbara R. Bergmann argues that the presence of blacks and women in traditionally segregated job categories can create counterproductive friction that is not taken into account by formal economic models.[36]

A Stronger Utilitarian Argument

A stronger utilitarian argument focuses on the harm that discrimination does to the welfare of society as a whole by perpetuating the effects of racism and sexism. When racial discrimination in employment is combined with discrimination in education, housing, medical care, and other areas of life, the result is poverty with all its attendant social ills. And although the situation of women is quite different from that of blacks in our society, sexism also serves to disadvantage women as a group and create social problems.

This argument is open to the objection that the harm that discrimination inflicts on individual blacks and women might be offset by a gain to society as a result of racist and sexist practices. Proving that this is not the case is rather difficult, since, as Richard A. Wasserstrom points out, little work has been done to develop a conception of what a thoroughly nonracist or nonsexist society would look like.[37] In an ideal utilitarian society, a person's race and sex would still play some role. But it is difficult to imagine that the utilitarian optimum would involve the systematic deprivation of benefits and opportunities to whole groups in society.

Racism, in particular, can scarcely be defended on utilitarian grounds. But sexism is more problematical. Some writers maintain that there is a utilitarian benefit in defining sex roles so as to take account of the biological differences between men and women.[38] This kind of argument is roundly criticized as sexist. And even if some difference in the treatment of women could be justified, it would surely be different from the discrimination that women have traditionally faced in the job market in the United States.

Despite these objections, though, the utilitarian argument is very strong. Racism, sexism, and other injustices have inflicted much harm on individuals and the social fabric of our society, and the welfare of society as a whole is surely increased by steps to reduce the amount of discrimination.

Kantian Arguments

From a nonconsequentialist point of view, discrimination can be shown to be wrong by appealing to the Kantian notions of human dignity and respect for persons. This is especially true of discrimination based on contempt or enmity for racial minorities or women. Discrimination of this kind typically involves a racist or sexist attitude that denies individuals in these groups the status of fully developed human beings who deserve to be treated as the equal of others. The victims of racial and sexual discrimination are not merely disadvantaged by being forced to settle for less desirable jobs and lower pay. They are also deprived of a fundamental moral right to be treated with dignity and respect.

This moral right is also denied when individuals are treated on the basis of group characteristics rather than individual merit. Much of the discrimination against women, older workers, and the handicapped does not result from the belief that they are less deserving of respect and equal treatment. It results instead from the stereotypes that lead employers to overlook significant differences among individuals. Stereotypes, which are a part of racism and sexism, clearly result in a denial of dignity and respect. But stereotyping by its very nature is morally objectionable since it leads employers to treat individuals only as members of groups.

Insofar as religious discrimination does not involve a prejudicial attitude toward the religious group in question, a different kind of argument is needed. The moral basis of an employer's obligation to respect the religious beliefs and practices of employees is similar to arguments concerning the right of free expression and the right to privacy in the workplace. These rights are sufficiently important that employees should not be required to relinquish them as conditions of employment. This claim can be supported on utilitarian grounds, but Kantian reasoning is singularly appropriate, since it can be argued that the freedom to hold a religion (or *not* to hold one) is vital to our dignity as human beings and should not be restricted except for very compelling reasons.

Arguments Based on Justice

Perhaps the strongest arguments against discrimination are those that appeal to some principle of justice. Fundamental to many principles of justice is the requirement that we be able to justify our treatment of other people by giving good reasons. James Rachels has expressed the point in the following way:

Consider the position of a white racist who holds, for, example, that it is right for the best jobs in society to be reserved for white people. He is happy with a situation in which almost all the major corporation executives, government officials, and so on, are white, while blacks are limited mostly to menial jobs, and he supports the social arrangements by which this situation is maintained. Now we can ask for reasons; we can ask why this is thought to be right. Is there something about white people that makes them better fitted for the highest-paying and most prestigious positions? Are they inherently brighter or more industrious? . . . Are they capable of benefiting more from the availability of such positions? In each case, the answer seems to be no—and if there is no good reason for treating people differently, discrimination is unacceptably arbitrary.[39]

A major objection to discrimination, then, is its arbitrariness. To discriminate is to treat people differently when there is no good reason for doing so.

By Aristotle's principle of justice as proportional equality—that like cases should be treated alike, and unlike cases should be treated differently in proportion to the relevant differences—discrimination is unjust because characteristics such as race and sex are generally irrelevant to the performance of a job. Even when the differences between individuals constitute genuinely job-related characteristics, the difference in pay, for example, should still be in proportion to that difference.

Among the difficulties with the Aristotelian case against discrimination is lack of clarity about what counts as a relevant characteristic. In the context of employment discrimination, it is generally a characteristic that has a bearing on productivity. But seniority is often considered to be relevant even though it is only marginally related to productivity. And preference for veterans after a war is generally considered justifiable despite the lack of any connection with productivity. Why should these not be considered relevant?

Further, why should productivity and not certain social goals be the appropriate determinant of what is relevant? Many firms are hiring more minorities and women not because they are necessarily more productive but because achieving a greater degree of integration in the workplace is considered to be a desirable social goal. Need is another characteristic that is not usually considered to be relevant to employment decisions, but why should it not also be taken into account as a justified difference?

A Rawlsian Argument Against Discrimination

The contract theory of John Rawls provides the basis for yet another argument against discrimination. One of the principles that would be adopted in the original position is described by Rawls as follows: "Social and economic inequalities are to be arranged so that they are . . .

attached to offices and positions open to all under conditions of fair equality of opportunity."[40] Rawls is careful to distinguish his principle from both utility-based arguments and the meritocratic ideal implicit in Aristotle's principle. Even if it were to the advantage of everyone to exclude some groups from certain positions, such a denial of opportunity could not be justified because individuals would be deprived of an important opportunity for self-development. In Rawls's words:

> ... if some places were not open on a basis fair to all, those kept out would be right in feeling unjustly treated even though they benefited from the greater efforts of those who were allowed to hold them. They would be justified in their complaint not only because they were excluded from certain external rewards of office such as wealth and privilege, but because they were debarred from experiencing the realization of self which comes from a skillful and devoted exercise of social duties. They would be deprived of one of the main forms of human good.[41]

Rawls's objection to a pure meritocracy, then, is that there is no reason in the original position to favor a system of rewards based on personal characteristics that does not allow for equal access to the full range of goods.[42]

AVOIDING DISCRIMINATION

Being a truly nondiscriminatory employer is not an easy task. In addition to good-faith compliance with the law, employers must be aware of some subtle and surprising sources of discrimination. This section discusses what is involved in pursuing a policy of nondiscrimination by examining three basic steps in the hiring and promotion process: analyzing the job to be performed, recruiting applicants, and assessing the applicants for suitability. Discrimination is not confined to hiring and promotion, of course, but the points made here can easily be applied to other kinds of personnel decisions.

Job Analysis

In order to ensure that decisions on hiring and promotion consider only job-related characteristics and result in finding the best person for the job, it is necessary to conduct a *job analysis*. A job analysis consists of two parts: (1) an accurate *job description* that details the activities or responsibilities involved in a position, and (2) a *job specification* listing the qualifications required to perform the job as described. Virtually every job in any present-day corporation has been analyzed in this way, since job analysis is a standard management tool for organizing work and appraising performance. The details can be found in almost any introductory management textbook.

Because a job description focuses on the specific activities or responsibilities of a position rather than on the people who have traditionally held it, certain kinds of work are less likely to be stereotyped as belonging to one group or another. Although most secretaries are women, for example, there is nothing in the description of the job that excludes men from this kind of work, and so there is no reason to list being a woman as a qualification in the job specification. Even when the qualifications for a job favor one sex over another, a job description that lists only the qualifications will not serve to exclude the members of the other sex who meet them. And since the qualifications must be related to the description, it is easier to determine whether they are really needed for the satisfactory performance of a job. The inability of the Duke Power Company to prove that a high school education is necessary for advancement, for example, led the Supreme Court to conclude that the requirement is discriminatory.

A job analysis need not be confined to traditional job categories. If a job is unnecessarily identified with one sex or another, it can be redesigned, perhaps by combining the activities of one or more other jobs, so that the newly created job is attractive to both men and women. The job of secretary, for example, previously held almost exclusively by women, is beginning to disappear in corporate America in favor of "executive assistant" and other euphemisms. These jobs include some responsibilities previously held by men, and they are now filled by both men and women. Jobs can also be narrowed so as to avoid excluding some groups unnecessarily. A desk job that involves some moving and lifting can be redesigned to exclude these tasks in order to accommodate the handicapped.

Recruitment and Selection

After a job analysis is done, a company is faced with the task of recruiting applicants in a nondiscriminatory manner. An obvious first step is to make sure that information about an opening is widely disseminated, especially to nontraditional groups. When information is spread by word of mouth or by advertisements in newspapers and trade magazines with limited circulation, many well-qualified individuals will not even learn about an opening. Employers who are serious about not discriminating will place listings of job opportunities with minority publications and educational institutions and employment agencies serving minorities. They can also maintain lists of previous applicants and contact them when positions open. Finally, applications from members of nontraditional groups are more likely to be received if significant numbers of minorities and women are involved in the company's recruitment effort and also if a number of nontraditional applicants are hired at one time.[43]

After a sufficient number of applicants have been recruited, the next task is to select the person who is best suited to fill the job. Discrimination can enter into this stage of hiring in many different ways. The selection process itself, which often includes a battery of tests and rounds of interviews, can be discouraging for many nontraditional applicants. Employers can address this problem by simplifying the application procedure or providing instruction on how to proceed. Small differences in treatment can also make racial minorities and women feel uncomfortable. In one study of women beginning a career, the researcher reports, "The young women said . . . that they expected to be treated in a professional manner when being interviewed for selection and promotion. But many of them felt that they had been subjected to questioning that men would not have experienced."[44]

One source of discrimination that affects promotion is the existence of lines of promotion in corporations. In the complex organizational hierarchy of the typical corporation, both horizontal and vertical promotion proceeds along fixed lines. So when minorities and women are initially placed in race- and sex-segregated job categories, their promotion possibilities are determined in advance. In many companies, a woman file clerk, for example, can aspire only to a few superior positions, with no chance of promotion to a position in a different line. In addition to placing nontraditional applicants in a greater range of initial positions, many companies have addressed this source of discrimination by reducing the number of promotion lines and increasing their flexibility so that minorities and women have more opportunities for advancement.

Objective Tests and Subjective Evaluations

Two other important sources of discrimination in both the hiring and promotion process are objective tests and subjective evaluations formed on the basis of personal interviews or the recommendations of supervisors. Three kinds of objective tests are commonly used to make decisions on hiring and promotion: (1) tests that measure specific knowledge and skills, such as those needed to be a bookkeeper or a typist; (2) tests that measure intelligence and general aptitude for performing certain kinds of work; and (3) tests that attempt to gauge an applicant's suitability for employment generally and the extent to which an applicant will fit into a specific work environment.

Objective tests of these kinds are ethically and legally permissible under certain conditions. Title VII of the 1964 Civil Rights Act, for example, includes the following provision:

... nor shall it be an unlawful employment practice for an employer to give and to act upon the results of any professionally developed ability test provided that such test, its administration or action upon the results is not designed, intended or used to discriminate because of race, color, religion, sex, or national origin.

One condition laid down in *Griggs* v. *Duke Power Company*, however, is that a test not unnecessarily exclude a disproportionate number of members of protected classes, which is to say that it should not have disparate impact. A second condition is that a test be *validated*; that is, an employer must be able to show that a test for any given job is a reliable predictor of successful performance in that job. Commenting on the Civil Rights Act, the writer of the majority opinion in *Griggs* stated:

Nothing in the Act precludes the use of testing or measuring procedures; obviously they are useful. What Congress has forbidden is giving these devices and mechanisms controlling force unless they are demonstrably a reasonable measure of job performance.

The two tests administered by Duke Power Company, the Wonderlic Personnel Test and the Bennett Mechanical Comprehension Test, are professionally prepared instruments that presumably provide an accurate measure of general intelligence and mechanical ability, respectively. What the company failed to prove, however, is that passing scores on these tests are closely correlated with successful job performance. They failed, in other words, to validate the tests that they used.

The Supreme Court has held employers to very high standards of proof in validating tests. It is not sufficient merely to show that employees who successfully perform a certain job also attain high scores on any given test. An employer must be able to show, further, that applicants with lower scores would not be capable of performing just as well. A biased test that results in the exclusion of a substantial percentage of blacks or women, for example, might still be a reliable predictor of successful performance for those who pass but not a reliable predictor of the lack of success of those who fail the test. Further, comparing the scores of employees who are currently performing a job successfully with the scores of inexperienced applicants is not sufficient proof of the reliability of a test. In order to draw a significant conclusion, it would be necessary to know how the current job holders would have scored on the test before they were hired.[45]

Objective tests are ethically and legally permissible, then, as long as they do not have disparate impact and are validated. Do the same two conditions apply to subjective evaluations based on personal interviews or the recommendations of supervisors? On the one hand, evaluations of this kind are made by experienced employees who are well-acquainted with the job to be filled and have an opportunity to assess qualities in an applicant that do not lend themselves to objective testing. On the other hand, the evaluations of interviewers and supervisors are apt to be influenced by irrelevant factors, such as a person's appearance or manner, and by conscious or unconscious prejudice. This is especially true when the evaluator is not well trained for the task.

Some of the pitfalls of a subjective evaluation system are illustrated by the practice of General Motors in the early 1970s.[46] Hourly paid assembly line workers in General Motors plants were eligible for promotion to a number of salaried positions, including foreman, clerk, accountant, and security guard, but only if they could obtain a recommendation from their immediate supervisor. This recommendation was the single most important factor in the promotion process, and it was based largely on the supervisor's subjective evaluation of an employee's "ability, merit, and capacity." The Fifth Circuit Court of Appeals found the promotion system at General Motors to be discriminatory on several counts. One is that the criteria of "ability, merit, and capacity" are unacceptably vague and subjective. Further, the supervisors who made the evaluations were given no written instructions on the specific qualifications for promotion to each position, thus leaving a great deal of room for personal preferences. Finally, there were no safeguards in the system to prevent supervisors who were so inclined from deliberately discriminating against blacks. Even supervisors who are not inclined to discriminate might still do so unconsciously because of closer social relations with other members of the same race. The opinion in the case expresses a skepticism that "Black persons dependent directly on decisive recommendations from Whites can expect non-discriminatory action."

The Clara Watson Case

The first opportunity for the Supreme Court to decide on the conditions for an acceptable subjective evaluation system came in 1988 with the suit of Clara Watson against the Fort Worth Bank and Trust Company, which opened this chapter. The statistical evidence of discrimination was not in dispute, and so the principal issue in this case is not whether the procedures used by the bank had disparate impact (they did) but whether the fact that they involved subjective evaluations rather than objective tests made a difference in the interpretation of Title VII. A related issue is whether the requirement of validation, which applies to objective tests, should be extended to subjective evaluations.

The Fort Worth Bank and Trust Company used three common types of subjective evaluation procedures: interviews, rating scales, and experience requirements. Rating scales differ from interviews in that they record evaluations derived from observations made over a long period of time while an employee is actively at work. Typically, an evaluator is asked to rank an employee on a numerical scale with respect to certain qualities, such as drive and dependability. Experience requirements involve an inventory of specific jobs performed that provide a basis on which to make judgments about future performance.

The American Psychological Association (APA) submitted an amicus curiae, or "friend of the court," brief in the Watson case in order to support the claim that these three types of subjective evaluation procedures are capable of validation.[47] Each procedure is open to bias. The most common bias in interviews and rating scales is the "halo effect," in which a single trait exercises an inordinate influence on an evaluator. Closely related to the halo effect is stereotyping, in which assumptions about members of certain groups influence an evaluator. Interviewers are also subject to the "similar-to-me" phenomenon, in which they are inclined to be more favorable to people who have the same traits as themselves. Among the problems with rating scales are the tendencies of evaluators to place persons toward the center of a scale, thereby avoiding the extremes, and to be lenient, scoring most people favorably. The APA brief also cites considerable evidence to show that scores on rating scales are affected by racial factors:

> White raters have been found to assign significantly higher ratings to white ratees than black ratees. These findings were noted in a comprehensive review of 74 studies involving 17,159 ratees in which the rater was white and 14 studies involving 2,420 ratees in which the rater was black. Race effects were more pronounced in real-life settings than in laboratory settings and more likely . . . when the proportion of blacks in the workforce was small.[48]

All these biases can be avoided by subjective evaluation procedures that are designed and carried out according to the APA's *Standards for Educational and Psychological Testing* and the *Principles for the Validation and Use of Personnel Selection Procedures*. The key in each type of procedure is to relate it to a thorough analysis of the job to be filled. The interview should be carefully structured with questions designed to elicit information that is relevant only to the qualifications and performance criteria of the job. The traits on the rating scale and the kinds of experience used as experience requirements should be similarly selected. As much as possible, the results of evaluation procedures should reflect the personal characteristics of the person being evaluated and not the person doing the evaluating, so that differences between evaluators is kept to a minimum. And interviewers, supervisors, and other persons involved in the process should be thoroughly trained in performing their roles in the hiring and promotion process.

The APA brief faults Fort Worth Bank and Trust for failing to meet the generally accepted standards for subjective evaluation procedures and for the lack of any validation of the procedures used. Interviews were conducted by only one person, a white male, and there is no evidence that the questions were carefully designed with job-related qualifications in mind. No job analysis was done in order to guide the selection of questions in the interview and the traits on the rating scales. Moreover, the traits on the rating scale were vaguely defined and not clearly related to job performance. The supervisors who performed the ratings were not specifically trained for that task, and no steps were taken to avoid the effect that race is known to have on the results of rating scales. Finally, it would be impossible without a job analysis of the position to determine what prior experience would enable her superiors to judge the success of Clara Watson in that position.

In a 8–0 decision, the Supreme Court found in favor of Clara Watson and established that the theory of disparate impact applied to subjective evaluation procedures as well as to objective tests of the kind at issue in *Griggs*.

NOTES

1. Material on the case is taken from "Bias Lawsuit May Have Wide Impact," *The New York Times*, January 18, 1988, sec. 1, p. 10; and from *Clara Watson* v. *Fort Worth Bank and Trust*, 487 U.S. 977 (1988).
2. The information on AT&T is taken from EARL A. MOLANDER, "Affirmative Action at AT&T," in *Responsive Capitalism: Case Studies in Corporate Conduct* (New York: McGraw-Hill, 1980), 56–70.
3. 42 U.S.C. 2000e-2.
4. "College for Deaf Is Shut by Protest over President," *The New York Times*, March 8, 1988, sec. 1, p. 20.
5. *Diaz* v. *Pan American World Airways, Inc.*, 442 F.2d 385 (1971).
6. *Dothard* v. *Rawlinson*, 433 U.S. 321 (1977).
7. *Griggs* v. *Duke Power Company*, 401 U.S. 424 (1970). Some material is also taken from a case prepared by NANCY BLANPIED and TOM L. BEAUCHAMP, in TOM L. BEAUCHAMP and NORMAN E. BOWIE, eds., *Ethical Theory and Business*, 3rd ed. (Englewood Cliffs, NJ: Prentice Hall, 1988), 383–85.
8. The precedent of *Griggs* was altered by several subsequent court decisions, most notably *Wards Cove Packing Co.* v. *Antonio*, 490 U.S. 642 (1988), which made it more difficult for employees to sue for discrimination. A 1991 civil rights bill largely restored the interpretation of *Griggs* that had prevailed before.
9. *General Electric Co.* v. *Gilbert*, 419 U.S. 125 (1976).
10. *Newport News Shipbuilding and Dry Dock Co.* v. *EEOC*, 462 U.S. 669 (1983). For a discussion, see MICHAEL A. MASS, "The Pregnancy Discrimination Act: Protecting Men from Pregnancy-Based Discrimination," *Employee Relations Law Journal*, 9 (1983), 240–50.
11. *California Federal Savings and Loan Association* v. *Guerra*, 479 U.S. 272 (1987).
12. ELIZA G. C. COLLINS and TIMOTHY B. BLODGETT, "Sexual Harassment:

Some See It . . . Some Won't," *Harvard Business Review*, 59 (March-April 1981), 76–95.

13. BARBARA A. GUTEK, *Sex and the Workplace* (San Francisco: Jossey-Bass, 1985), 43–44.

14. CATHARINE A. MACKINNON, *Sexual Harassment of Working Women* (New Haven: Yale University Press, 1979), 193.

15. *Bundy* v. *Jackson*, 641 F.2d 934 (D.C. Cir. 1981).

16. *Meritor Savings Bank* v. *Vinson*, 477 U.S. 57 (1986).

17. ROBERT C. FORD and FRANK MCLAUGHLIN, "Sexual Harassment at Work: What Is the Problem?" *Akron Business and Economic Review*, 20 (Winter 1988), 79–92.

18. *Ellison* v. *Brady*, 924 F.2d 872 (1991). See also HOWARD A. SIMON, "*Ellison* v. *Brady*: A 'Reasonable Woman' Standard for Sexual Harassment," *Employee Relations Law Journal*, 17 (Summer 1991), 71–80.

19. For a discussion of these and other problems, see JAMES G. FRIERSON, "Religion in the Workplace," *Personnel Journal*, 67 (July 1988), 60–67; and DOUGLAS MASSENGILL and DONALD J. PETERSEN, "Job Requirements and Religious Practices: Conflict and Accommodation," *Labor Law Journal*, 39 (July 1988), 402–10.

20. *American Postal Workers Union* v. *Postmaster General*, 781 F.2d 772 (1986).

21. *Young* v. *Southwestern S & L Association*, 509 F.2d 140 (5th Cir. 1975).

22. *Trans World Airlines* v. *Hardison*, 432 U.S. 63 (1977).

23. *Bhatia* v. *Chevron USA, Inc.*, 734 F.2d 1382 (9th Cir. 1984).

24. See *Protos* v. *Volkswagen of America*, 41 FEP Cases 598 (3rd Cir. 1986), and *Redmond* v. *G.A.F. Corp.*, 17 FEP Cases 208 (7th Cir. 1978). In an important case, *Ansonia Board of Education* v. *Philbrook*, 107 S.Ct. 367 (1986), the Supreme Court rejected a lower court contention that a company was required by Title VII to accept the alternative favored by the employee and held that the company was free to choose any alternative that meets the employee's need.

25. *Sumitomo Shoji America* v. *Avagliano*, 457 U.S. 176 (1982).

26. *Spiess* v. *C. Itoh & Co. (America), Inc.*, 457 U.S. 1128 (1982).

27. These points are made in ELIZABETH PICKAR GRAY, "The National Origin BFOQ under Title VII: Limiting the Scope of the Exception," *Employee Relations Law Journal*, 11 (1985), 311–21.

28. TONY MAURO, "Age Bias Charges: Increasing Problem," *Nation's Business* (April 1983), 46.

29. MAURO, "Age Bias Charges: Increasing Problem," 46.

30. WILLIAM G. JOHNSON and JAMES LAMBRINOS, "Wage Discrimination against Handicapped Men and Women," *The Journal of Human Resources*, 20 (1985), 264–77.

31. There are also hidden costs in hiring the handicapped, such as the increase in insurance premiums for employers. See FRANK BOWE, *Rehabilitating America* (New York: Harper & Row, 1980), 76–83.

32. This analysis and the phrase "taste for discrimination" are due to GARY S. BECKER, *The Economics of Discrimination*, 2nd ed. (Chicago: University of Chicago Press, 1971).

33. This point is also made in MILTON FRIEDMAN, *Capitalism and Freedom* (Chicago: Chicago University Press, 1962), 109–10. Ironically, Friedman uses the

analysis to argue *against* legislation curbing discrimination on the grounds that competition alone is sufficient to bring discrimination to an end.

34. KENNETH J. ARROW, "The Theory of Discrimination," in ORELY ASHENFEL-TER and ALBERT REES, eds., *Discrimination in Labor Markets* (Princeton: Princeton University Press, 1973), 3–33. A similar account is given by LESTER C. THUROW, *Generating Inequality* (New York: Basic Books, 1975).

35. See DENNIS J. AIGNER and GLEN G. CAIN, "Statistical Theories of Discrimination in Labor Markets," *Industrial and Labor Relations Review*, 30 (1977), 175–87.

36. BARBARA R. BERGMANN and WILLIAM DARITY, JR., "Social Relations, Productivity, and Employer Discrimination," *Monthly Labor Review*, 104 (April 1982), 47–49.

37. RICHARD A. WASSERSTROM, "Racism and Sexism," in *Philosophy and Social Issues* (Notre Dame: University of Notre Dame Press, 1980), 23.

38. See, for example, STEVEN GOLDBERG, *The Inevitability of Patriarchy* (New York: William Morrow & Co., 1973).

39. JAMES RACHELS, *The Elements of Moral Philosophy* (New York: Random House, 1986), 9–10.

40. JOHN RAWLS, *A Theory of Justice* (Cambridge: Harvard University Press, 1971), 83.

41. RAWLS, *A Theory of Justice*, 84.

42. RAWLS, *A Theory of Justice*, 100–108.

43. ROSABETH MOSS KANTER in *Men and Women of the Corporation* (New York: Basic Books, 1977), chap. 8, proposes "batch" promotions of two or more individuals from excluded groups so that they can support each other and break down barriers.

44. ESTELLE PHILLIPS, "Discrimination Still a Problem," *Personnel Management*, 20 (August 1988), 62.

45. These points are made in *Albemarle Paper Company* v. *Moody*, 422 U.S. 405 (1975).

46. The material on this case is taken from *Rowe* v. *General Motors Corporation*, 457 F.2d 348 (1972).

47. "In the Supreme Court of the United States: *Clara Watson* v. *Fort Worth Bank and Trust*," *American Psychologist*, 43 (1988), 1019–28. See also an accompanying explanation by DONALD N. BERSOFF, "Should Subjective Employment Devices Be Scrutinized? It's Elementary, My Dear Ms. Watson," *American Psychologist*, 43 (1988), 1016–18.

48. "In the Supreme Court of the United States: *Clara Watson* v. *Fort Worth Bank and Trust*," 1024.

CHAPTER NINE
Affirmative Action

After the passage of the 1964 Civil Rights Act, employers scrutinized their hiring and promotion practices and attempted to eliminate sources of discrimination. Even the best efforts of companies did not always succeed in increasing the advancement opportunities of women and racial minorities, however. In 1974, at a plant operated by the Kaiser Aluminum Company in Grammercy, Louisiana, for example, only five skilled craft workers (out of 273) were black. Kaiser had long sought out qualified black workers, but few met the requirement of five years of prior craft experience, in part because of the traditional exclusion of blacks from craft unions. In an effort to meet this problem, Kaiser Aluminum and the local union, the United Steelworkers of America, developed an innovative program to train the company's own employees to become skilled craft workers. The plan set up a training program that admitted blacks and whites in equal numbers based on seniority until the proportion of blacks in the skilled craft category equaled the percentage of blacks in the area work force, which was approximately 39 percent.

In 1978, Santa Clara County in California undertook a similar effort. Recognizing that women and racial minorities were underrepresented in some job categories and overrepresented in others, the county board adopted an Equal Employment Opportunity Policy that set broad goals and objectives for hiring and promotion in each agency. Specifically, the policy stated:

> It is the goal of the County and Transit District to attain a work force which includes in all occupational fields and at all employment levels, minorities, women and handicapped persons in numbers consistent with the ratio of these groups in the area work force.

According to the 1970 census, women constituted 36.4 percent of local workers. Only 22.4 percent of county employees were women, and these were concentrated in two areas: paraprofessionals (90 percent female) and office and clerical (75.9 percent female). Out of 238 skilled craft workers, not one was a woman. To carry out the board's policy, the Santa Clara Transportation Agency, the agency responsible for road maintenance in the county, developed a detailed plan for increasing the percentages of women and minorities in job categories where they were underrepresented. The director of the agency and division managers were specifically charged with implementing the plan.

The programs adopted by Kaiser Aluminum and Santa Clara County are examples of *affirmative action.* The idea behind affirmative action is that merely ceasing to discriminate is not enough. Employers, if they choose to do so, ought to be permitted to take more active steps to ensure a balanced work force, including plans that give preference to job applicants on the basis of race or sex. Although the goal of eliminating discrimination in employment has generally been accepted in business, people are still divided over the appropriate means. Affirmative action plans, in particular, have provoked an impassioned debate that has divided even the strongest supporters of the goal of nondiscrimination. This debate is of immense practical importance, since almost every person now working or preparing for a career is liable to be affected by affirmative action.

Advocates of affirmative action argue that special programs are required as a matter of "simple justice." Victims of discrimination, they say, deserve some advantage. Preferential treatment is necessary to ensure equality of opportunity. Opponents counter that if it is unjust to discriminate against racial minorities and women on account of their race or sex, then it is similarly unjust to give them preference for the same reason. People who are passed over in favor of a black or a woman are victims of discrimination in reverse. What justice requires, in the opponents' view, is equal opportunity for previously disadvantaged groups but not an additional advantage in order to produce equal results.

This debate raises a bewildering array of questions. What does it mean to treat people of different races equally or to assure that both men and women have equal opportunity? Is equal treatment the same as equality of opportunity, as when each runner starts from the same line, or does it entail equality of outcomes, so that all runners cross the finish line together? Are there any rights involved in affirmative action? Do blacks or women, for example, have a right to be given preference in hiring or promotion, or do white males have any rights that are violated when preference is given on the basis of race or sex?

These questions are raised in a number of important Supreme Court cases that have divided the justices and produced a series of conflicting decisions. In one case, an applicant, Allan Bakke, was refused admission to the medical school of the University of California at Davis, while less qualified minority applicants were admitted under an admissions program designed to give special consideration to disadvantaged students.[1] In response to the plan at Kaiser Aluminum, a white employee, Brian Weber, sued both the company and his own union.[2] Weber had insufficient seniority to be admitted as a white trainee, even though he had worked longer at the Kaiser plant than any of the blacks who were selected. He charged, therefore, that he himself was a victim of discrimination in violation of Title VII of the 1964 Civil Rights Act.

A suit also arose as a result of the plan adopted by the Transportation Agency of Santa Clara County when a white male, Paul Johnson, was passed over for promotion and the job went to a woman.[3] In December 1979, Paul Johnson and Diane Joyce applied along with ten other employees for promotion to the position of dispatcher for the road division of the transportation agency. Dispatchers, who assign road crews, equipment, and materials for road maintenance and keep records of the work done, are classified as skilled craft workers. Applicants for the position were required to have four years of dispatch or road maintenance experience with Santa Clara County. The eligible candidates were interviewed by two different boards. The first board, using a numerical scale, rated Johnson slightly above Joyce (75 to 73), and the second board, although rating both candidates "highly qualified," also recommended Johnson over Joyce. The director of the agency was authorized to select any eligible candidate, however, and in order to implement the affirmative action plan, he gave the nod to Joyce. Johnson, like Weber, believed himself to be a victim of discrimination and sued.

Another kind of affirmative action plan that has been challenged in the courts is a "set-aside" provision for minority contractors. The Public Works in Employment Act, passed by Congress in 1977, required that at least 10 percent of the funds granted to state and local governments for construction be set aside for "minority business enterprise" (MBE) contractors. An MBE is defined as a business in which minority group members (blacks, Hispanics, Orientals, or American Indians) have at least half ownership. Some municipalities have enacted similar legislation. The city of Richmond, Virginia, for example, adopted a Minority

Business Utilization Plan that required recipients of city construction contracts to subcontract at least 30 percent of the dollar amount of each contract to minority-owned businesses. Some white contractors have charged that set-aside provisions are an illegal form of discrimination.[4]

How should such cases be decided? Is affirmative action a justified response to the problem of discrimination in business and American society as a whole? Or is it a form of discrimination in reverse, as people such as Allan Bakke, Brian Weber, and Paul Johnson claim? The Supreme Court has ruled in these cases and established some precedents. Allan Bakke won his case, and the medical school of the University of California at Davis was ordered to admit him. In *Weber* v. *Kaiser Aluminum* and *Johnson* v. *Transportation Agency*, however, the Supreme Court held that the affirmative action plans in question were not discriminatory under Title VII. Both Brian Weber and Paul Johnson thus lost their suits. After approving set-asides for minority-owned contractors in a 1980 decision, *Fullilove* v. *Klutznick*, the Court cast all such programs into doubt in *City of Richmond* v. *J. A. Croson* (1989).

Both the legal and ethical issues in affirmative action remain a source of much controversy. This chapter is devoted to examining the main ethical arguments both for and against affirmative action plans of the kinds described above. The justification of affirmation action, we will see, depends a great deal on the specific features of each plan. To be justified, in other words, an affirmative action plan must be carefully designed and implemented to avoid violating the rights of employees who are adversely affected.

THE COMPENSATION ARGUMENT

One argument for giving preferential treatment to members of certain groups is that it is owed to them as *compensation* for the injustice done by discrimination directed against them personally or against other members of a group to which they belong.

Aristotle's Account of Justice in Compensation

The root idea in this argument is deeply ingrained in our thinking about justice. Aristotle, in his classic discussion in Book V of the *Nicomachean Ethics*, distinguished between justice in the distribution of goods (distributive justice) and justice where one person has wrongfully inflicted some harm on another (corrective justice). In the latter case, justice requires that the wrong be corrected by providing compensation. For example, if A, while driving carelessly, crashes into B's new car, then B suffers a loss which is A's fault. An injustice has been done. It can be corrected, though, if A compensates B for the amount of the loss, say the cost of repairs plus any inconvenience. In Aristotle's analysis, A has unfairly made B worse off, perhaps to A's advantage, and justice requires that the situation of A and B be restored as far as possible to what it was before the accident occurred. Similarly, if A has a right not to be discriminated against and B discriminates, thereby harming A unjustifiably, then it is only just that B compensate A to correct the harm done.

Six conditions must be satisfied before compensation is owed. First, there must be an identifiable person who is injured or made to suffer some loss. Second, there must be another person who has caused the injury or loss. Third, this person must have acted wrongfully or been at fault in some way. Fourth, there must be a form of compensation adequate to rectify or correct the injustice done. Fifth, the person who is obligated to provide the compensation must be the one who wrongfully inflicted the harm. And sixth, the compensation must be given to the person who is harmed. Thus, a person whose automobile is damaged by high winds, where no one can be blamed, does not have a right to be compensated; neither does a person who foolishly wrecks an automobile, since that person has only himself or herself to blame. Of course, it would be patently unjust for the owner of a damaged automobile to attempt to collect compensation from an innocent third party or for the compensation to be paid to someone other than the owner.

The payment of compensation is fully justified and indeed demanded by justice in many instances. Aristotle's analysis perfectly fits the situation, for example, of an employer who has been found guilty of discriminating against women or racial minorities by assigning them to lower paying jobs and bypassing them in promotions. Class action lawsuits in such cases are often settled by requiring the employer to pay the victims the difference between what they actually earned and what they would have earned had no discrimination taken place and advancing them to the positions that they would have attained. This was the case, for example, in the settlement with women employees of AT&T in the early 1970s.

It is easy to specify a just settlement in cases of this kind, since the parties involved can be readily identified and the nature and extent of the losses precisely determined. But consider the difficulty of trying to compensate workers who were never hired because of discrimination or who lacked the qualifications even to be considered because of the debilitating effects of discrimination in schooling. Which persons deserve to be compensated under such conditions? Who has an obligation to do the compensating? And how much compensation is owed?

Applying Aristotle's Account to Affirmative Action

Many critics charge that some affirmative action plans are not justified by the compensation argument for the reason that they do not satisfy the conditions required by Aristotle's analysis of corrective justice.

First, the individuals who are given preferential treatment are often not the same as those who are victims of discrimination. Affirmative action plans almost always single out persons as members of a group that has suffered discrimination without requiring any evidence that the persons themselves have been victimized in any way. A person may be a member of a disadvantaged group and yet lead a rather privileged life, relatively free of the effects of discrimination. Given the competing requirement of justice—that opportunities should go to those who are best qualified—the result is, ironically, to favor those members of disadvantaged groups who have suffered the effects of discrimination the least (or at least who have been most successful in overcoming the effects).

In response to this objection, Judith Jarvis Thomson notes that racial and sexual discrimination has subtle psychological effects on all blacks and women, despite the profound changes that have taken place in our society:

> Obviously the situation for blacks and women is better than it was . . . twenty-five years ago. But it is absurd to suppose that the young blacks and women now of an age to apply for jobs have not been wronged. . . . Even young blacks and women have lived through down-grading for being black or female. . . . And even those who were not themselves downgraded for being black or female have suffered the consequences of the down-grading of other blacks and women: lack of self-confidence, and lack of self-respect.[5]

Racial and sexual discrimination directed at individuals merely because they are members of a certain group inevitably affects all members of that group to some degree.

Bernard R. Boxill correctly observes that the critics' objection involves a non sequitur. From the premise that better qualified blacks or women are less deserving of compensation than some who have been more severely handicapped by discrimination, it does not follow that they do not deserve any compensation at all. He has written:

> Let us grant, that qualified blacks, for example, are less deserving of compensation than unqualified blacks, that those who most deserve compensation should be compensated first, and finally that preferential hiring is a form of compensation. How does it follow that preferential hiring of qualified blacks is unjustified? Surely, the assumption that unqualified blacks are more deserving of compensation than qualified blacks does not require us to conclude that qualified blacks deserve no compensation. Because I have lost only one leg, I may be less deserving of compensation than another who has lost two legs, but it does not follow that I deserve no compensation at all.[6]

It also does not follow, according to Boxill, that victims of discrimination who succeed in overcoming the harm done to them are any less deserving of compensation than those who are unable to succeed to the same degree.[7] Some blind people are better able to adjust than others who are blind, for example, but that is no reason why a person who proves to be very adept at reading Braille should be compensated less. The harm actually inflicted on a person who has been blinded is not diminished by the success of the person in overcoming the affliction. Boxill expresses this point by saying that "being harmed is not the only ground for deserving compensation. There is also the ground of simply being wronged."[8] These two different kinds of grounds are reflected in the tort law distinction between actual and punitive damages.

This response still does not answer the question, why should preference not be given to those who most deserve compensation, the people who have most suffered the effects of racial discrimination and who are consequently among the least qualified? One reply is that giving preference in hiring is only one way of compensating individuals for past discrimination, and it is a way that is of greater help to those who are better qualified for the jobs available. Those who have been more disadvantaged by discrimination may be less able to benefit from affirmative action and may derive greater benefit from other forms of help, such as job training programs.

A defender of affirmative action can also argue that claims of compensatory justice must be balanced against another principle of justice, the principle that hiring should be done on the basis of competence.[9] Giving preference to the best qualified of those who are deserving of compensation, according to this argument, is the best way of accommodating these two conflicting principles. Another argument cites the practical difficulty of evaluating each case to determine the extent to which an individual has been harmed by discrimination and hence deserves compensation. Giving preference to members of groups without regard for the particulars of individual cases, therefore, is a matter of administrative convenience.[10]

Can Compensation Be Owed to Groups?

The critics' objection that affirmative action plans often benefit undeserving individuals merely because they belong to a group that has been subjected to discrimination can be countered by a more radical response. This is the claim that compensation is owed not to specific individuals but to groups as a whole.[11] When individuals are wrongly treated merely because of membership in a racial or sexual group, the group itself is the victim of injustice and deserves to be compensated without any need to justify the benefit given to individual members of the group. Thus, compensation given to any blacks or Hispanics or women, regardless of whether they are victims of discrimination, benefits the group as a whole and redresses the wrong done to that group.

This response raises the thorny conceptual question of whether it makes any sense to speak of groups as the kind of entity that can be wrongly harmed and hence deserving of compensation. In an influential article, George Sher has argued that it does not make any sense to talk in this way.[12] A group is wronged, according to Sher, when it receives less than a fair share in the distribution of goods. In Aristotle's principle of distributive justice, unequal treatment of different persons can be justified, but the inequality must be in proportion to the possession of some relevant characteristic. Thus, it may be just to give more food to the hungry because of a greater need for food or to give higher wages to those who have greater ability or put forth greater effort. Needs, abilities, and effort, however, are characteristics possessed only by flesh-and-blood human beings and not by groups. The notion of a need, for example, is conceptually tied to the well-being of an organism and so cannot be applied to racial and sexual groups. Sher has written:

> Such groups, unlike their members, do not satisfy the preconditions for attaining any of the states of well-being with which we are familiar. They do not have single organized bodies, and so can neither sustain good bodily health nor suffer illness. They do not have nervous systems and so cannot experience the various states of comfort and discomfort that these systems make possible. They do not have consciousness, and so cannot experience either amusement, happiness, interest, or self-esteem, or the less pleasant states that stand opposed to these. They do not even have the degree of legal or conventional organization that is shared by corporations, clubs, and other legal persons. Hence, they cannot increase or decrease their wealth or holdings as these other composite entities can. Because racial and sexual groups lack the sorts of organization that alone confer capacities to attain states of well-being, they can hardly have the sorts of needs that presuppose these capacities.[13]

Similarly, the concepts of ability, effort, and the other characteristics that could justify unequal treatment in Aristotle's principle of distributive justice presuppose a capacity to act that is lacking in groups. According to Sher, "groups do not have the organization required to act at all. Hence, they cannot possibly perform the sorts of actions alone through which efforts are made, skills exercised, abilities demonstrated, and goods produced."[14] He continues:

> Hence, the proper conclusion is not merely that racial and sexual groups do not qualify for exemptions from equal treatment, but rather, and more radically, that such groups do not fall under the principle of distributive justice at all. There may indeed be circumstances in which justice dictates preference for each group member; but if there are, this must be because

each group member has suffered deprivation in the past. In any such case, it will be the affected individuals, and not the group itself, to whom the principle of distributive justice applies.[15]

Just as the principle of distributive justice cannot be applied to groups, neither can Aristotle's analysis of compensatory justice. First, the analysis requires that there be wrongful harm, but groups cannot be harmed for the same reason they cannot be given an unfair distribution of goods. Second, it makes no sense to speak of compensating groups by providing some kind of offsetting benefit to the harm suffered. Since they cannot be harmed, they also cannot be benefited. It does not seem, therefore, that the critics' first point can be countered by changing the unit of analysis from the individual to the group.

Who Pays the Price?

Turning now to the second objection to the compensation argument, in affirmative action the burden of providing compensation often falls on individuals who are not themselves guilty of acts of discrimination. In the competition for admission into colleges and universities and for hiring and promotion in jobs, it is largely white males—people such as Allan Bakke, Brian Weber, and Paul Johnson—who are asked to pay the price of correcting injustices that are not of their making. Critics ask, why should a few white males bear such a disproportionate burden?

One answer to this question is that white males, even when they are not themselves guilty of discrimination, are still the beneficiaries of discrimination that has occurred and thus are merely being asked to give back some ill-gotten gain. Judith Jarvis Thomson, for one, has responded in this way:

> No doubt few, if any, have themselves, individually done any wrongs to blacks and women. But they have profited from the wrongs the community did. Many may actually have been direct beneficiaries of policies which excluded or down-graded blacks and women . . . and even those who did not directly benefit in this way had, at any rate, the advantage in the competition which comes of confidence in one's full membership, and of one's rights being recognized as a matter of course.[16]

This response does not fully meet the critics' point. Even if Thomson is correct in her claim that all white males have benefited to some degree, it still needs to be shown that what is given up by the few white males who are passed over when preference is given to others is equal to the benefit they have obtained by living in a discriminatory society. Furthermore, it would still seem to be unjust to place the full burden in such an arbitrary manner on a few when so many other members of society have also benefited from discrimination.[17] More serious is the observation made by Robert L. Simon that Thomson's response involves the dubious assumption that "if someone gains from an unjust practice for which he is not responsible and even opposes, the gain is not really his and can be taken from him without injustice."[18]

Boxill further points out that white males are typically asked not to give up gains they have already made but to forego a future benefit to which no one has an undisputed right.[19] Brian Weber and Paul Johnson, for example, were not deprived of any gains they had made but only of an opportunity for advancement. Although this is a real loss, neither one had a right to be selected but only a right not to be discriminated against in the selection process. Whether they were discriminated against in the selection process is precisely the question addressed by the compensation argument.

If the compensation argument is correct, then those who were selected *deserved* the advantage given by their race or sex and hence no discrimination took place. (Ironically, the opportunity for Brian Weber to receive on-the-job training for a skilled craft position would not have existed had Kaiser Aluminum not adopted an affirmative action plan in order to hire more blacks.) Still, if the job prospects of white males are substantially reduced by affirmative action, then they have suffered a loss. And there is surely some limit on the amount of compensation any individual or group of individuals can justifiably be required to pay.

Accordingly, the courts have laid down three conditions for permissible affirmative action plans to protect those adversely affected by them. They are (1) that a plan does not create an absolute bar to the advancement of any group, (2) that the plan does not unnecessarily trammel the rights of others, and (3) that it be temporary. The training program in the Weber case was open to black and to white workers in equal numbers. Although Brian Weber failed to gain admittance to the first class, his seniority would have assured him a place eventually. In addition, he had other opportunities for realizing his ambition of becoming a skilled craft worker. Finally, the training program was scheduled to terminate when the proportion of black craft workers reached 39 percent, the percentage of blacks in the local work force.

Conclusion

The objections to the compensation argument examined in this section pose serious but not insurmountable problems for the compensation argument. Victims of discrimination deserve to be compensated in some way. But identifying the persons who are owed compensation and deciding how they will be compensated and who will bear the burden are not easy tasks. Certainly, the Aristotelian model of corrective justice does not comfortably fit the kinds of situations in which affirmative action is used as a form of corrective justice. However, the idea that compensation is owed in cases of wrongdoing is deeply entrenched in both morality and law, and many people in our society are undeniably victims of the moral wrong of discrimination. The law is also guided by the dictum, No right without a remedy, which is to say that a person cannot be said to have a right unless there is also some means of correcting a violation of that right. If we have a right not to be discriminated against, then the courts should be able to provide some remedy when that right is violated. Much of the case law on affirmative action is thus concerned with the righting of wrongs done by discrimination.

EQUALITY ARGUMENTS

We noted in Chapter 4 that, according to Aristotle, justice is a kind of equality. Whether affirmative action is just, therefore, can be decided, perhaps, by the principle that people ought to be treated equally, or as equals. Two quite different concepts of equality are relevant to the debate over affirmative action, however. These are *equality of opportunity* and *equality of treatment.*

Justice, in the first interpretation of equality, requires that everyone have an equal opportunity to succeed in life and that no one be held back by arbitrarily imposed restraints or barriers. Better enforcement of the laws against discrimination can help to equalize the opportunities for everyone, but the effects of past discrimination also need to be neutralized in some way.

President Lyndon B. Johnson expressed the argument graphically in a 1965 speech on an executive order requiring every federal contractor to be an "equal opportunity employer":

> Imagine a hundred yard dash in which one of the two runners has his legs shackled together. He has progressed 10 yards, while the unshackled runner has gone 50 yards. How do they rectify the situation? Do they merely remove the shackles and allow the race to proceed? Then they could say that "equal opportunity" now prevailed. But one of the runners would still be forty yards ahead of the other. Would it not be the better part of justice to allow the previously shackled runner to make-up the forty yard gap; or to start the race all over again? That would be affirmative action towards equality.[20]

The equal opportunity argument addresses not only the harm done to individuals from past discrimination but also the barriers posed by discrimination in present-day society. Many fully qualified blacks and women have not been disadvantaged by past discrimination but are still at a competitive disadvantage because of lingering racism and sexism on the part of employers. Giving preferential treatment may be necessary under such circumstances simply to ensure that people are considered equally. Whether this is true depends, in part, on what we mean by equal opportunity.

The Meaning of Equal Opportunity

What does equal opportunity mean? It should be noted, first, that this concept can be applied only within a specific context. To speak of equality of opportunity intelligibly we need to know, in particular, which persons are being compared (opportunity for whom?) and with respect to which opportunities they are being compared (opportunity to do what?).[21] There may be equal opportunity for all engineering graduates in the competition for positions in the research department of General Motors but not for journalism students (because they have not studied engineering), although they may have an equal opportunity in applying for jobs at *The Wall Street Journal*. And there may be equality of opportunity in a society with respect to jobs but not for positions of power or prestige or for access to medical care. In addition, we need to know what factors limit opportunity and ought to be eliminated. So we also have the further question, opportunity *from* what? Race and sex are the most frequently criticized factors, but advocates of equal opportunity have also attacked barriers such as noble birth, wealth, nationality, social status, religion, and so on.[22]

The word *opportunity* is itself ambiguous, with three distinct senses. One sense is employed in the sentence, "She has the opportunity to visit the Louvre while in Paris," which suggests she can visit the museum and has only to *choose* to do so. The opportunity is there, and whether she takes advantage of it is up to her. The claim that everyone has an equal opportunity to win the state lottery obviously involves a different sense of the word *opportunity*, since one cannot simply choose to win. What this claim means is that each ticket holder has an equal *chance* of winning the lottery. The chance can be expressed as some degree of probability. If there are N tickets, where N is some number, say one hundred, then the probability is one in N, or one in one hundred. Corresponding to these two senses of the word *opportunity* are two different meanings of the concept of equality of opportunity. Two or more people might be said to have equal opportunity in the first sense when they are able to choose among all the same possibilities. They have equal opportunity in the second sense when they have the same chance; that is, when the N in "one chance in N" is the same for each of them.

The claim that everyone has the opportunity to become a surgeon or a novelist or a figure skater suggests a third sense of opportunity. No one can merely choose one of these careers, nor does everyone have the same prospects of success. But the *means* for pursuing such goals are open to all.[23] Two people have an equal opportunity, then, when each has the same means available for achieving some goal. This is the sense that comes closest to Rawls's notion of "offices and positions open to all" and the French revolutionary ideal of "careers open to talent."

Equality of Prospects

It is obvious that the concept of equal opportunity employs only the latter two senses of the word *opportunity*, namely, having a chance or having the means. Following Douglas Rae in his book *Inequalities*, let us call these two possibilities the *prospect-regarding* and the *means-regarding* interpretations of the concept of equal opportunity.[24] Prospect-regarding equality aims at eliminating *all* factors affecting the distribution of goods in a society except for mere chance. Means-regarding equality, by contrast, is compatible with considerable inequality of prospects. The only requirement for equality of opportunity in this latter interpretation is that the results reflect only differences in personal attributes and not differences in the means available to persons.

Equality of prospects is an ideal of egalitarians who want to minimize the role of "accidents" of birth on people's success in life. Just as our race or sex should have no bearing on what we are able to achieve, so too should it not matter whether we are born into wealth or poverty or whether we are born with certain mental or physical endowments. The egalitarian ideal is not that everyone should have an equal chance to attain any particular job, such as that of a concert violinist or a college professor, for example, but that each person should have an equal chance for satisfying some significant portion of the desires that he or she has. The probability that a particular college professor might have been an accomplished violinist might be very low, and similarly a violinist might have had virtually no chance to become a college professor. But each had good prospects for careers of roughly equal desirability. Two people might be said to have equal opportunity, then, when their *total* prospects in life are comparable.[25]

There are a number of difficulties with the egalitarian's insistence that equal opportunity be interpreted to mean equality of prospects. First, because people begin life with vastly different prospects, steps must be taken to equalize these prospects. Should every possible means be used, or is there a limit to the remedies that society is morally required to take? If every person were to have an equal shot at becoming a Supreme Court Justice, for example, it would be necessary not merely to ensure that children from disadvantaged backgrounds receive an education comparable to that of more advantaged children—which is surely required by justice—but to provide them with additional remedial help, thereby allocating greater resources to schools with disadvantaged students. In an effort to equalize prospects, society might be expending resources that could be put to better use in other ways.

Second, how are we to know when unequal prospects have been offset? If members of disadvantaged groups are equally represented in the professions, managerial positions, and other desirable job categories, then this fact constitutes prima facie evidence of equality of prospects. Equality of prospects need not result in equal outcomes, however, if people make different choices. So there must be some way of determining when prospects are equal without looking at the outcomes.

Equality of Means

The interpretation of equal opportunity as equality of means entails that rewards should be distributed on the basis of some relevant criteria. Artificial barriers to advancement, such as racial or sexual characteristics, are irrelevant and should be removed, but justice does not require the removal of inequalities in prospects resulting from differences in a person's various physical and mental characteristics. Equal opportunity, on this view, means a chance to compete under fair conditions.

One difficulty with this interpretation is that it requires only that all discrimination cease; it does nothing to address President Johnson's concern about the head start provided by discrimination in the past. Is it a fair race if one runner has been shackled? If the only purpose of affirmative action is to prevent further discrimination from taking place, then those who have been harmed by past discrimination are still in an unfair competitive position. Equality of prospects may be too strong as an interpretation of equal opportunity, but the interpretation as equality of means seems to be too weak to serve as a justification for affirmative action aimed at overcoming the effects of past discrimination.

A further difficulty is that the conditions for fair competition are highly suspect. Talent, however it is understood, is not only a product of native endowments and individual initiative but also a product of the society into which a person is born. Social institutions determine to a great extent the conditions under which talent is recognized and allowed to develop and prosper. What is commonly called talent is largely the acquisition of the expertise and skills provided by education and certified through formal procedures. If access to education or certification is affected by racial or sexual discrimination, then we can scarcely be said to have equal access to the means for achieving success in life.

Accusations of bias have often been expressed, for example, over the use of standardized tests and, in particular, the Scholastic Aptitude Test (SAT) in college admissions. On the SAT, whites on average consistently achieve a higher score than blacks, and men a higher score than women. Some critics of standardized tests charge that many of the questions contain a cultural bias that discriminates against minority racial groups and a male bias that puts women at an unfair disadvantage. Experts also suggest that social pressures keep women from doing as well as men, especially in mathematics and science. Even if "talent" is the appropriate criterion for making decisions about admitting students to college and awarding scholarships, it is still necessary to show that the SAT and other standardized tests actually measure talent and not something else.

To conclude, equality of opportunity can be interpreted in at least two different ways: as equality of prospects and as equality of means. Equality of means comes closer to capturing what is most commonly meant by equality of opportunity, but even this weaker version of the concept does not clearly specify the extent to which means ought to be equal. Equality is still an important source of justification for affirmative action, but for many the relevant sense is equal treatment, not equal opportunity.

Equality of Treatment

When some people are selected for a job or are accepted into a professional school on the basis of race or sex, there are other people who are passed over because of *their* race or sex. If discrimination is wrong when directed against racial minorities and women, then it is equally wrong when the victims are white males.[26] Affirmative action does not eliminate discrimination, some critics charge, because it still involves making distinctions among people and treating them according to their differences. The concept of equality of treatment is often used, therefore, as an argument *against* affirmative action, although supporters of affirmative action maintain that it is compatible with treating people equally.

Ronald Dworkin, for one, uses the concept of equal treatment to defend against the charge of reverse discrimination and to argue *for* affirmative action. When we say that certain white males have been denied their right to equal treatment, he says, we might have in mind two different rights.[27]

> The first is the right to *equal treatment*, which is the right to an equal distribution of some opportunity or resource or burden. . . . The second is the right to *treatment as an equal*, which is the right, not to receive the same distribution of some burden or benefit, but to be treated with the same respect and concern as anyone else.[28]

The right to equal treatment in the sense of a right to receive an equal share applies only to a few things, such as the right that each person's vote shall count equally. In the distribution of most things, it is a right to the same respect and concern that is at stake. These two kinds of rights can come into conflict, and when they do, the second kind of right takes precedence over the first. In Dworkin's words, "the right to treatment as an equal is fundamental, and the right to equal treatment, derivative."[29] Dworkin uses the following example to support this point. "If I have two children, and one is dying from a disease that is making the other uncomfortable, I do not show equal concern if I flip a coin to decide which should have the remaining dose of drug."[30]

The Application to Allan Bakke

How does this distinction show that Allan Bakke, for example, was not deprived of a right to equal treatment in the medical school admission process? Those who call his treatment reverse discrimination hold that equal treatment of the fundamental kind—the right to equal respect and concern—is precisely what was denied when race was used as the basis for making the decision in this case. Dworkin makes a distinction between the rules for deciding any particular case, such as admitting applicants to medical school, and the application of those rules. Unequal treatment can occur in each of these two different places. Rules that single out blacks for exclusion purely by virtue of their race are morally objectionable even when they are equally applied. The equal application of immoral rules, such as the laws enforcing slavery, can even increase the moral wrong. On the other hand, fully justified rules can still be applied in morally objectionable ways.

In the application of the rules used by the medical school in deciding on admissions, Allan Bakke was treated in the same way as everyone else. The rules, which contained provisions for giving special consideration, were themselves applied impartially. Any fault, therefore, must be in the rules and not in the way they were applied. Now, the rules for admission to medical school necessarily affect applicants differently, but they cannot be said for this reason to discriminate against those who are less intelligent or lacking in preparation, for example, since a legitimate purpose of the rules is precisely to weed out those kinds of applicants. The rules themselves (as opposed to their application) fail to treat applicants equally, then, only when the criteria for selection are not justified by some overriding social good. Dworkin has written:

> Any standard will place certain candidates at a disadvantage as against others but an admission policy may nevertheless be justified if it seems reasonable to expect that the overall gain to the community exceeds the overall loss, and if no other policy that does not provide a comparable disadvantage would produce even roughly the same gain. An individual's right to be treated as an equal means that his potential loss must be

treated as a matter of concern, but that loss may nevertheless be out-weighed by the gain to the community as a whole.[31]

What makes race but not intelligence an objectionable basis for decision-making is that, historically, decisions based on race have been motivated by contempt and even hatred for those who were the victims of discrimination. In preferential treatment programs, there is no similar contempt or hatred for white males; the motivation is, rather, to achieve a social good that cannot be achieved in any other way. Dworkin concludes:

> In the past it made sense to say that an excluded black or Jewish student was being sacrificed because of his race or religion; that meant that his or her exclusion was treated as desirable in itself, not because it contributed to any goal in which he as well as the rest of society might take pride. Allan Bakke is being "sacrificed" because of his race only in a very artificial sense of the word. . . . [H]e is being excluded not by prejudice but because of a rational calculation about the socially most beneficial use of limited resources for medical education.[32]

In the decision to include a preference for disadvantaged applicants in the medical school admissions procedure, the welfare of Allan Bakke and other applicants like him was given the same respect and concern as that of every other person in society. Since this is all that the right to equal treatment requires, according to Dworkin, there was no violation of his rights and hence no discrimination, reverse or otherwise.

Objections to Dworkin's Argument

This argument is open to a serious objection.[33] In Dworkin's interpretation, the right to equal treatment is the right to equal respect and concern as rational calculations are made about the social good. According to Robert L. Simon, "So understood, the right to treatment as an equal looks suspiciously like the utilitarian requirement that everyone count for one and only one in computing social benefits and burdens."[34] If Simon is correct, then the right to equal treatment is compatible with institutional arrangements that discriminate on the basis of race or sex. If it could be shown, for example, that menial labor for blacks or household employment for women was the most beneficial arrangement for the whole of society—even with equal consideration being given to the welfare of the disadvantaged group—then the right of blacks or women to equal treatment would not be violated by the adoption of these arrangements. Such a result would show that Dworkin's interpretation is too weak to capture the sense of the right to equal treatment which is violated by discrimination.

Also, this interpretation is not wholly consistent with Dworkin's own description of rights as "trumps" that override purely utilitarian calculations of what is socially beneficial and prevent the sacrifice of individual welfare for the collective good.[35] Simon suggests that by placing more emphasis on *respect* for other persons rather than on *concern* that their welfare be given equal weight, a basis can be found for a nonutilitarian theory of rights. He finds the basis for such a theory in Dworkin's remark that humans should be respected as beings "who are capable of forming and acting on intelligent conceptions of how their lives should be lived."[36] If the right to equal treatment is interpreted to mean a right to equal respect in living a life according to our own conceptions, which is closer to a Kantian theory of rights than to a utilitarian theory, then it is less clear that preferential treatment is a benign form of discrimination that does not violate the rights of white males such as Bakke and Weber.

Conclusion

The conclusion to be drawn from the discussion in this section is that the concept of equal opportunity is too vague and ambiguous to provide conclusive support for any particular position on the justification of affirmative action. Those who favor preferential treatment programs and those who oppose them can find a meaning of "equal opportunity" to fit their particular position. Equality of treatment, by contrast, provides a more solid basis for affirmative action. This principle demands, however, that we think carefully about the reasons for affirmative action and make sure that the goals to be achieved are worthwhile and cannot be attained by means that do not involve taking race or sex into account. The compensation argument and the argument from equal opportunity both provide worthwhile goals for affirmative action, but the welfare of society is another. So let us now turn to this essentially utilitarian argument for affirmative action.

UTILITARIAN ARGUMENTS

Unlike the two previous arguments for affirmative action, arguments based on utility do not hold that programs of preferential treatment are morally *required* as a matter of justice but that we are morally *permitted* to use them as means for attacking pressing social problems. Richard A. Wasserstrom expresses the point by saying that programs of preferential treatment are instrumentalities rather than ideals. "Whenever they have been proposed and defended the fundamental justificatory claim is not that they should be made a part of the *ongoing* institutional life of the good society, but rather that they should be introduced because they are a way to help bring that society into being."[37]

The utilitarian arguments that follow are divisible into two groups. One group consists of arguments holding that preferential treatment programs are necessary to eradicate lingering racial and sexual discrimination and to accelerate the pace of integrating certain groups into the mainstream of American society. The second group of arguments cite the economic benefits of preferential treatment programs, which include alleviating poverty and its attendant social ills.

Combatting Racism and Sexism

Arguments in the first group begin with the assumption that racism and sexism are deeply embedded in the major social, political, and economic institutions of our society and in people's attitudes, expectations, and perceptions about social realities. If this assumption is correct, then antidiscrimination legislation addresses only the surface manifestations of racism and sexism and does not penetrate to the root causes. Action must be taken to change the institutions of society and the ways people think about themselves and their world. Otherwise, the goal of a discrimination-free society will come only slowly, if at all. This view has been expressed by Thomas Nagel with reference to race:

> When this society finally got around to moving against the caste system, it might have done no more than to enforce straight equality of opportunity, perhaps with the help of weak affirmative action, and then wait a few hundred years while things gradually got better. Fortunately it decided instead to accelerate the process by both public and private institutional action, because there was wide recognition of the intractable character of the problem posed by this insular minority and its place in the nation's history and collective consciousness. This has not been going on very long, but the results are already impressive, especially in speeding the advancement of blacks into the middle class. Affirmative action has not done much to improve the position of poor and unskilled blacks. That is the most serious part of the problem, and it requires a more direct economic attack. But increased access to higher education and upper-level jobs is an essential part of what must be achieved to break the structure of drastic separation that was left largely undisturbed by the legal abolition of the caste system.[38]

Preferential treatment programs may make more jobs available to blacks, Hispanics, women, and others, first, by lowering the stated qualifications and formal accreditation required for hiring and promotion, especially when these are not relevant to the job. Antidiscrimination laws prohibit requirements for jobs that have the *effect* of discriminating, even where there is no *intent* to discriminate.[39] The onus, therefore, is on an employer to show that the conditions imposed for employment are bona fide occupational qualifications (BFOQ). Some forms of preferential treatment go beyond nondiscrimination, however, by waiving certain requirements that are permissible under the law and hiring applicants for reasons of race or sex.

A second way in which opportunities are increased for groups subject to discrimination is by breaking down stereotypes in the eyes of employers and the rest of society and by creating role models for people who would not otherwise consider certain lines of work. The long history of sexual and racial stereotyping of jobs in this country has hampered the acceptance of women and members of some racial minorities in the professions, the upper levels of management, and most of the other desirable positions in our society. This history has also affected the very people who were excluded by limiting their career aspirations. A young black who has never seen a black doctor or college professor or corporate executive is less likely to aspire to any one of these roles or to undertake the serious preparation required to achieve them. Similarly, until recently, few women gave serious thought to applying to law school or seeking an MBA, even though many were fully qualified. A few black doctors and an occasional woman lawyer are not likely to have much impact; a substantial number of blacks and women need to enter nontraditional job categories for substantial changes to occur.

Affirmative action functions in a third way to increase opportunities by heightening awareness about discrimination and changing the hiring and promotion process. When business firms make a commitment to achieve a certain racial and sexual mix in their work force with established goals, the officials responsible for hiring and promoting employees cannot help but be sensitive to the issue of discrimination in every decision they make. Assigning a prominent role to a policy of nondiscrimination in the workplace through preferential treatment programs also serves as an official symbolic denunciation of racism and sexism.[40]

Relieving Poverty

The main economic argument in favor of affirmative action is that it serves to address the problem of poverty in this country. A far greater percentage of blacks than whites live in poverty, a fact largely attributable to continuing discrimination in society and to the cumulative effects of America's history of discrimination.[41] Color barriers in the job market have resulted in much higher unemployment rates for blacks and the concentration of blacks into jobs with low pay and few opportunities for advancement. The lack of education and skills that keep blacks from competing more effectively with whites can be traced to inadequate schooling in black communities and to other manifestations of racism. Insofar as preferential treatment programs are effective in reducing the level of poverty, they also help to alleviate the social problems associated with poverty.

One difficulty with this argument is that although preferential treatment programs have proven effective in reducing black unemployment and in enhancing the earning power of blacks as a group, the benefits have gone largely to blacks who were already employed and living above the poverty line. Thus, it has been questioned whether affirmative action is an effective tool in alleviating poverty in American society. According to sociologist Nathan Glazer:

> It seems clear that the main impact of preferential hiring is on the better qualified—the professional and technical, who are already the beneficiaries of an income bonus on the basis of their relative scarcity; the skilled worker already employed, upgraded through governmental pressures; the unskilled worker already regularly employed, also given opportunities of upgrading. Undoubtedly some of the benefit reaches down, but the lion's share must inevitably go to the better qualified portion of the black population.[42]

Some writers even argue that preferential treatment and similar programs have exacerbated the problems of the poor by deflecting attention away from more effective means of attacking poverty.[43]

Supporters of affirmative action attempt to get around this difficulty by arguing that programs which now benefit the members of the black community who already have more advantages will gradually improve the position of blacks generally in American society and will make it easier for those less well off to advance. Set-aside provisions in government contracts that favor minority-owned businesses, for example, will eventually provide more unskilled jobs for the black poor. More black doctors will eventually result in better health care for blacks and so on. The benefits accruing to those who are better able to take advantage of preferential treatment programs will thus "trickle down" to those less able. There is virtually no evidence, however, to support this version of the "trickle down" thesis.[44] But it can be argued more plausibly that preferential treatment is an essential part of a multipronged strategy for addressing poverty, a strategy that must also include job training and other programs that provide more direct help.[45]

Affirmative action also provides a direct economic benefit to corporations themselves by increasing the pool of job applicants and generally improving community relations. Discrimination introduces inefficiency into the job market by excluding whole groups of people on the basis of race or sex, some of whom are highly qualified. The result is that people in these groups tend to be "underutilized" in jobs that do not make full use of their abilities and training, and employers are deprived of the best possible work force. The following statement by an executive of Monsanto Corporation testifies to the benefit that affirmative action can have for employers: "We have been utilizing affirmative action plans for over 20 years. We were brought into it kicking and screaming. But over the past 20 years we've learned that there's a reservoir of talent out there, of minorities and women that we hadn't been using before. We found that it works."[46]

Some Problems with Affirmative Action

Affirmative action has some significant undesirable consequences that must be balanced against the undeniable utilitarian benefits of preferential treatment programs. Three arguments in particular are commonly used by opponents of affirmative action. These are (1) that affirmative action involves hiring and promoting less qualified people and lowering the quality of the work force, (2) that it is damaging to the self-esteem of employees who are favored because of race or sex, and (3) that it produces a race consciousness which promotes rather than fights discrimination. Let us examine these in turn.

The Quality Argument

The first argument—the quality argument—can be expressed in the following way. The most qualified person for a position has no need for special consideration. Therefore, a person who is given preference on the basis of race or sex cannot be the most qualified person and cannot perform as well in a job as someone who is more qualified. The result is a decline in the quality of goods and services, which has an adverse affect on the whole of society. This argument has a deceptive simplicity, for a close examination of the notion of a qualification leads to unexpected complications.

A supporter of affirmative action can question, first, how much quality is given up. Preferential treatment does not involve the hiring or promotion of people who are *un*qualified but who are (at worst) *less* qualified to some degree. And the degree can be so slight as to be of no significance. Many jobs require only minimal qualifications and can readily be mastered by persons of normal abilities. Even occupations requiring considerable ability and expertise involve many tasks that can be satisfactorily performed by people who are not the best available. For delicate brain surgery, for example, we might seek out the best specialist available, but for a common ailment, any competent doctor is as good as the best. Similarly, we want a competent mechanic to tune our automobile, but there is no advantage in having the work done by the best mechanic in town.

In many instances, "qualified" means "already trained," which brands as unqualified those people who are capable of being fully competent with some training. Critics complain that one consequence of government guidelines is to change the meaning of "qualified" to "qualified to train."[47] But why should this be a criticism? Training new hires imposes an additional cost on employers, but the result may be a black worker who is as fully qualified after training as a white was before. Affirmative action, therefore, imposes a cost on employers but need not impair the quality of work that demands only a low level of skill. Most college graduates are not "qualified" when they take their first job and need considerable on-the-job training.

Also, whether a person is qualified for a certain job depends on how qualifications are recognized or determined. Conventional measures, such as standardized tests and academic record, are often criticized for containing a bias against women and racial minorities. The credentials used to certify competence in various fields, such as licenses, certificates, union cards, diplomas, and the like, have been accused of containing a similar bias. Personal interviews, job evaluations, and recommendations all have an inescapable subjective element.

More complications emerge when we ask, what are the relevant qualifications for the performance of any given job? And can race or sex ever be relevant to the evaluation of qualifications? It is sometimes argued, for example, that a black police officer can be more effective in a black community and that an applicant's race is, therefore, a legitimate consideration in the hiring of a police force.[48] The same argument is used in education. A largely male college faculty may not provide a learning environment that is as beneficial to women students as one with a substantial number of female professors. Similarly, colleges consider the race and sex of their applicants in order to achieve balance and diversity in the student body.

The Injury Done by Affirmative Action

A second utilitarian argument against affirmative action is that it injures the very people it is designed to help. The effect of hiring and promoting blacks and women because of their race or sex is to draw attention to their lack of qualifications and create an impression that they could not succeed on their own. In a case concerning the admissions procedure of a law school, Justice William O. Douglas compared the effect to that of segregation:

> A segregated admissions process creates suggestions of stigma and caste no less than a segregated classroom, and in the end it may produce that result despite its contrary intention. One other assumption must be clearly disapproved, that Blacks or Browns cannot make it on their individual

merit. That is a stamp of inferiority that a State is not permitted to place on any lawyer.[49]

Another effect of affirmative action is to reduce the respect of society for the many hard won achievements of blacks and women and to undermine their own confidence and self-esteem. A black economist, Thomas Sowell, argues that the main result of preferential treatment programs has been:

> . . . to destroy the legitimacy of what had already been achieved, by making all black achievements look like questionable accomplishments, or even outright gifts. Here and there, this program has undoubtedly caused some individuals to be hired who would otherwise not have been hired—but even that is a doubtful gain in the larger context of attaining self-respect and the respect of others.[50]

The stigma attached by preferential treatment programs may even have the unintended consequence of impeding racial integration. This was discovered by the Detroit Symphony Orchestra, which had increased the number of black musicians in response to threats from Michigan legislators to cut off state funding unless more blacks were hired.[51] As a result, however, the orchestra lost several promising black applicants who did not want to appear unable to make it into a major orchestra on the basis of their own musical ability. James DePriest, a prominent black conductor, reportedly declined an offer of the top post of music director. "It's impossible for me to go to Detroit because of the atmosphere," he said. "People mean well, but you fight for years to make race irrelevant, and now they are making race an issue."

This is an argument to be taken seriously. Thomas Sowell's position, though, depends on the questionable assumption that programs of preferential treatment have not significantly helped blacks. Insofar as they have boosted some blacks into higher level positions of prestige and responsibility, there is bound to be an increase in their pride and self-respect. James W. Nickel has argued:

> . . . it seems to be an exaggeration to say, as Justice Douglas does, that programs designed to remedy injustices and overcome handicaps nevertheless stigmatize blacks no less than policies that required blacks to attend segregated schools. Indeed, if the stigmatizing effect of preferential programs were as great as that of segregated schools, one would expect to find blacks avoiding such programs, black organizations opposing them, and black leaders denouncing them. In practice, however, one finds nothing of the sort and indeed finds the opposite.[52]

Most people in our society recognize that success is not purely a matter of merit and that unearned advantage plays a large role. Children of wealthy parents have a tremendous advantage in life, but this fact does not seem to damage them psychologically. Manuel Velasquez wryly observes, "For centuries white males have been the beneficiaries of racial and sexual discrimination without apparent loss of their self-esteem."[53]

The Heightening of Race Consciousness

The third and final utilitarian argument against preferential treatment programs is that they increase rather than decrease the importance of race and other factors in American society. If the ideal of an equal society is one in which no one is treated differently because of color, ethnic origin, religion, or any other irrelevant factor, then preferential treatment defeats this ideal by heightening our consciousness of these differences. Nathan Glazer sees this development as a reversal of the success of the civil rights movement of the 1960s:

> In the phrase reiterated again and again in the Civil Rights Act of 1964, no distinction was to be made in the right to vote, in the provision of public services, the right to public employment, the right to public education, on the ground of "race, color, religion, or national origin." Paradoxically, we then began an extensive effort to record the race, color, and (some) national origins of just about every student and employee and recipient of government benefits or services in the nation; to require public and private employers to undertake action to benefit given groups; and school systems to assign their children on the basis of their race, color, and (some) national origins.[54]

To observers such as Glazer, all uses of racial, ethnic, and religious classifications are abhorrent and ultimately destructive of the fabric of a society.

One response by proponents of affirmative action is that the use of racial classifications is a temporary expedient, necessary only to eradicate the last vestiges of racism before we can realize the ideal of an equal society. In the *Bakke* case, Justice Harry Blackmun wrote:

> I suspect that it would be impossible to arrange an affirmative action program in a racially neutral way and have it successful. To ask that this be so is to demand the impossible. In order to get beyond racism, we must first take account of race. There is no other way. And in order to treat some persons equally, we must treat them differently.

The Supreme Court has long held that distinctions based on race and ethnic origin are "by their very nature odious to a free people whose institutions are founded upon the doctrine of equality."[55] Nevertheless, they are permissible when the conditions warrant their use.

Others argue that classifying people along racial and ethnic lines is itself morally neutral and what makes classifications wrong is the use to which they are put. There is a great difference between the racial distinctions that were an essential element of the institution of slavery and the race consciousness that is a part of the present-day attack on racism. The argument is forcefully presented by Richard A. Wasserstrom:

> A fundamental feature of programs that discriminated against blacks and women was that these programs were a part of a larger social universe which systematically maintained a network of institutions which concentrated power, authority, and goods in the hands of white male individuals. This same social universe contained a complex ideology which buttressed this network of institutions and at the same time received support from it. Practices which excluded or limited the access of blacks or women into the desirable institutions were, therefore, wrong both because of the direct consequences of these practices on the individuals most affected by them and because the system of racial and sexual superiority of which they were constituents was an immoral one in that it severely and without any adequate justification restricted the capacities, autonomy, and happiness of those who were members of the less favored categories.
>
> Whatever may be wrong with today's programs of preferential treatment, even those with quotas, it should be clear that the evil, if any, is simply not the same. . . . If preferential treatment programs are to be condemned or abandoned, it cannot, therefore, be because they seek either to perpetuate an unjust society in which all the desirable options for living are husbanded by and for those who already have the most, or to realize a corrupt ideal of distinct classes and grades of political, social, and moral superiority and inferiority. When viewed and offered as instrumentalities of social change they do neither.[56]

In Wasserstrom's position, there is nothing inherently wrong with consciousness and the awareness of sexual, religious, ethnic, and other differences. What makes any of these wrong is their use to degrade and oppress people with certain characteristics. Any utilitarian analysis of affirmative action must take into account the history of racial minorities, women, and other groups in this country and the present-day social realities. All things considered, he concludes, the race consciousness engendered by affirmative action is socially beneficial.

Conclusion

Affirmative action is an especially rich field for ethical exploration. Rights figure prominently in arguments both for and against preferential treatment programs—the rights, first, of people long victimized by pervasive and persistent discrimination and the rights of persons, mostly white males, who (arguably) bear a disproportionate burden in society's efforts to rectify past wrongs. Considerations of justice also play a large role. The compensation argument is based on the idea that justice requires that people who are wronged be compensated in some way, but what is just compensation for the wrongs of discrimination? Who ought to be compensated, and who ought to do the compensating? Justice further requires that people be treated equally, but we have seen how complicated are the concepts of equal opportunity and equal treatment. Finally, arguments based on utility provide strong support for affirmative action, although their force is vitiated to some extent by certain disutilities that deserve to be taken seriously. One advantage of utilitarian arguments, though, is that the relevant issues are clearly identified. What are the effects of preferential treatment programs? Do they do more good than harm? Do they foster or hinder the goal of a discrimination-free society? The many questions involved in the justification of affirmative action are among the most difficult we face as a society—and also among the most important.

NOTES

1. *University of California Regents* v. *Bakke*, 438 U.S. 265 (1978).
2. *United Steelworkers and Kaiser Aluminum* v. *Weber*, 443 U.S. 193 (1979).
3. *Johnson* v. *Transportation Agency, Santa Clara County*, 480 U.S. 616 (1987).
4. The landmark cases are *Fullilove* v. *Klutznick*, 448 U.S. 448 (1980); and *City of Richmond* v. *J. A. Croson Company*, 488 U.S. 469 (1989).
5. JUDITH JARVIS THOMSON, "Preferential Hiring," *Philosophy and Public Affairs*, 2 (1973), 381.
6. BERNARD R. BOXILL, "The Morality of Preferential Hiring," *Philosophy and Public Affairs*, 7 (1978), 247.
7. BOXILL, "The Morality of Preferential Hiring," 248.
8. BOXILL, "The Morality of Preferential Hiring," 249.
9. For a defense of this principle, see ALAN H. GOLDMAN, "Justice and Hiring by Competence," *American Philosophical Quarterly*, 14 (1977), 17–26.
10. For an argument of this kind, see JAMES NICKEL, "Classification by Race in Compensatory Programs," *Ethics*, 84 (1974), 147–48.
11. This is argued by PAUL W. TAYLOR, "Discrimination and Compensatory Justice," *Analysis*, 33 (1973), 177–82; and by MICHAEL D. BAYLES, "Reparations to Wronged Groups," *Analysis*, 33 (1973), 182–84.
12. GEORGE SHER, "Groups and Justice," *Ethics*, 87 (1977), 174–81.
13. SHER, "Groups and Justice," 175.
14. SHER, "Groups and Justice," 176.
15. SHER, "Groups and Justice," 176–77.
16. THOMSON, "Preferential Hiring," 383–84.
17. These points are made by GEORGE SHER, "Preferential Hiring," in TOM REGAN, ed., *Just Business: New Introductory Essays in Business Ethics* (New York: Random House, 1984), 48.
18. ROBERT L. SIMON, "Preferential Hiring: A Reply to Judith Jarvis Thomson," *Philosophy and Public Affairs*, 3 (1974), 318. For criticism of this assumption,

see ROBERT K. FULLINWIDER, "Preferential Hiring and Compensation," *Social Theory and Practice*, 3 (1975), 307–20.

19. BOXILL, "The Morality of Preferential Hiring," 266.
20. Quoted in LEWIS D. SOLOMON and JUDITH S. HEETER, "Affirmative Action in Higher Education: Towards a Rationale for Preference." *Notre Dame Lawyer*, 52 (October 1976), 67. The quotation also appears in ROBERT K. FULLINWIDER, *The Reverse Discrimination Controversy: A Moral and Legal Analysis* (Totowa, NJ: Rowman and Littlefield, 1980), 94–95.
21. Many points in this and the following paragraphs are made in ALISTAIR M. MACLEOD, "Equality of Opportunity," in JAN NARVESON, ed., *Moral Issues* (New York: Oxford University Press, 1983), 370–78; CHARLES FRANKEL, "Equality of Opportunity" *Ethics*, 81 (1971) 191–211; T. D. CAMPBELL, "Equality of Opportunity," *Proceedings of the Aristotelian Society*, 75 (1974–1975), 51–68; MICHAEL E. LEVIN, "Equality of Opportunity," *The Philosophical Quarterly*, 31 (1981), 110–25; and FULLINWIDER, *The Reverse Discrimination Controversy*, 93–123.
22. This point is made by S. I. BENN and R. S. PETERS, *Social Principles and the Democratic State* (London: George Allen & Unwin, 1959), 138.
23. This is pointed out by DOUGLAS RAE, *Inequalities* (Cambridge: Harvard University Press, 1981), 66–68.
24. RAE, *Inequalities*, 66–68.
25. More technically, there is equal opportunity when the sum of the probabilities of their achieving a range of goals are equal, with adjustment for the intrinsic desirability of these goals and for differences in each individual's desires. This is similar to the notion of a "competition curve," developed in LEVIN, "Equality of Opportunity."
26. For a statement of this point, see BARRY R. GROSS, *Discrimination in Reverse: Is Turnabout Fair Play?* (New York: New York University Press, 1978).
27. RONALD DWORKIN, *Taking Rights Seriously* (Cambridge: Harvard University Press, 1978), 223–39; and DWORKIN, *A Matter of Principle* (Cambridge: Harvard University Press, 1985), 293–331.
28. DWORKIN, *Taking Rights Seriously*, 227.
29. DWORKIN, *Taking Rights Seriously*, 227.
30. DWORKIN, *Taking Rights Seriously*, 227.
31. DWORKIN, *Taking Rights Seriously*, 227.
32. DWORKIN, *A Matter of Principle*, 301–2.
33. The discussion of this objection is derived largely from ROBERT L. SIMON, "Individual Rights and 'Benign' Discrimination," *Ethics*, 90 (1979), 88–97.
34. SIMON, "Individual Rights and 'Benign' Discrimination," 91.
35. See DWORKIN, *Taking Rights Seriously*, 184–205.
36. DWORKIN, *Taking Rights Seriously*, 272.
37. RICHARD A. WASSERSTROM, "Preferential Treatment," in *Philosophy and Social Issues: Five Studies* (Notre Dame: University of Notre Dame Press, 1980), 52–53.
38. THOMAS NAGEL, Testimony before the Subcommittee on the Constitution of the Senate Judiciary Committee, June 18, 1981. Reprinted in TOM L. BEAUCHAMP and NORMAN E. BOWIE, eds., *Ethical Theory and Business*, 3rd ed. (Englewood Cliffs, NJ: Prentice Hall, 1988), 347.

39. *Griggs et al.* v. *Duke Power Co.*, 401 U.S. 424 (1971); *Albemarle Paper Co.* v. *Moody*, 422 U.S. 405 (1975); *Franks* v. *Bowman Transportation Co.*, 401 U.S. 747 (1976).

40. HARDY E. JONES, "On the Justifiability of Reverse Discrimination," in GROSS, *Discrimination in Reverse*, 349.

41. This is the commonly accepted view that has guided much public policy over the past three decades, but it has been challenged by William Julius Wilson, who assigns a greater role at the present time to cultural forces in black communities and to structural changes in the American economy. See WILSON *The Declining Significance of Race* (Chicago: University of Chicago Press, 1978), and *The Truly Disadvantaged: The Inner City, the Underclass, and Public Policy* (Chicago: University of Chicago Press, 1987).

42. NATHAN GLAZER, *Affirmative Discrimination: Ethnic Inequality and Public Policy* (New York: Basic Books, 1975), 73. See also WILSON, *The Truly Disadvantaged*, 113–14.

43. See, for example, CHARLES MURRAY, *Losing Ground: American Social Policy 1950–1980* (New York: Basic Books, 1984).

44. See WILSON, *The Truly Disadvantaged*, 116.

45. WILSON, *The Truly Disadvantaged*, 154.

46. Quoted in PETER PERL, "Rulings Provide Hiring Direction: Employers Welcome Move," *The Washington Post*, July 3, 1986, p. A1. Cited by TOM L. BEAUCHAMP, "The Justification of Goals and Quotas in Hiring," in BEAUCHAMP and BOWIE, *Ethical Theory and Business*, 355.

47. THOMAS SOWELL, *Knowledge and Decisions* (New York: Basic Books, 1980), 251.

48. The example and much that follows is taken from ALAN WERTHEIMER, "Jobs, Qualifications, and Preferences," *Ethics*, 94 (1983), 99–112. A different kind of argument for the relevance of race as a qualification is presented by MICHAEL DAVIS, "Race as Merit," *Mind*, 42 (1983), 347–67. For a criticism of the kind of argument presented by Wertheimer, see FULLINWIDER, *The Reverse Discrimination Controversy*, 78–86; and ALAN H. GOLDMAN, *Justice and Reverse Discrimination* (Princeton: Princeton University Press, 1979), 167–68.

49. *DeFunis* v. *Odegaard*, 416 U.S. 312.

50. THOMAS SOWELL, " 'Affirmative Action' Reconsidered," *The Public Interest*, 42 (Winter 1976), 64.

51. "Discordant Notes in Detroit: Music and Affirmative Action," *The New York Times*, March 5, 1989, sec. 1, p. 1.

52. JAMES W. NICKEL, "Preferential Policies in Hiring and Admissions: A Jurisprudential Approach," *Columbia Law Review*, 75 (1975), 554–55.

53. MANUEL G. VELASQUEZ, *Business Ethics: Concepts and Cases*, 3rd ed. (Englewood Cliffs, NJ: Prentice Hall, 1992), 355.

54. GLAZER, *Affirmative Discrimination*, 4.

55. *Hirabayashi* v. *United States*, 320 U.S. 81 (1943).

56. WASSERSTROM, *Philosophy and Social Issues*, 64.

CHAPTER TEN
Unjust Dismissal

A woman employed as a machine operator by a small manufacturing firm for about a year was promoted to work on a machine carrying a higher rate of pay. She was demoted back to the lower paying machine, however, for unsatisfactory performance, and later she was demoted again to sweeping up the floors and cleaning the washrooms. Finally, she was dismissed for violating a rule against being absent for three consecutive days without notifying the company.

At first glance, there is nothing remarkable about this case. In the United States, employers are generally regarded as having the right to make decisions about hiring, promotion, and discharge, as well as wages, job assignments, and other conditions of work. Employees have a corresponding right to accept or refuse work on the terms offered and to negotiate for more favorable terms. But in the absence of a contract that spells out the conditions under which employment can be terminated, employees can be legally dismissed for any reason—or for no reason at all.

The moral and legal basis for this particular assignment of rights for employers and employees is a doctrine known as *employment at will*. Employment, according to this doctrine, is an "at-will" relation that comes into existence when two parties willingly enter into an agreement, and the relation continues to exist only as long as both parties will that it do so. Employers and employees both have the right to enter into any mutually agreeable arrangement without outside interference. Each party is also free to end an arrangement at any time without violating the rights of the other, as long as doing so is in accord with the terms which they have agreed on.

A closer look at the case just described raises some troubling questions about the doctrine of employment at will. The woman, Olga Monge, worked nights at the Beebe Rubber Company and attended college during the day. She requested a promotion, and her foreman, who was a friend of the personnel manager, secured the better paying job provided that she go out with him. When she refused his advances, she was demoted, with the concurrence of the personnel manager, to successively more undesirable jobs. One night she was found unconscious in a washroom and was taken to the hospital. She never returned to work and was fired ten days later.

In the resulting suit, *Monge* v. *Beebe Rubber Company*, the New Hampshire Supreme Court ruled in favor of Mrs. Monge and stated specifically that the doctrine of employment at will could not be used to justify such abusive treatment of an employee.[1] This decision represents a sharp departure from the precedent set by a 1938 Alabama Supreme Court decision that rejected the claim of a man who was fired because his wife refused to have sexual relations with the man's foreman on the grounds that he was an at-will employee who could be fired at any time without any reason being given.[2] The history of employment law in this country is replete with similar examples of unjust dismissals that have been sanctioned by courts in the name of employment at will.

Employment at will is a common-law doctrine long embodied in American labor practice. The first explicit statement that employment is an at-will relation occurred in an 1877 work by H. G. Wood entitled, *A Treatise on the Law of Master and Servant*.[3] The doctrine was first given legal force by an 1884 Tennessee Supreme Court decision in the case *Paine* v. *Western & A.R.R.* In an often quoted sentence, the court declared, "All may dismiss their employee(s) at will, be they many or few, for good cause, for no cause, or even for a cause morally wrong."[4] Other state courts followed the example of Tennessee, as did the U.S. Supreme Court, so that shortly after the turn of the century, the doctrine of employment at will was firmly established in American law.

A typical decision from the turn of the century is *Lochner* v. *New York* (1905).[5] At issue in this case was an 1897 New York statute limiting the work of bakers to ten hours a day and sixty hours a week. The law was intended to protect the health of bakers, which was being undermined by the long, exhausting hours that they were required to work. This piece of protective legislation was struck down, however, on the grounds that it violated the right of bakers and bakery owners alike to contract on mutually agreeable terms. According to the majority opinion, "the freedom of master and employee to contract with each other in relation to their employment . . . cannot be prohibited or interfered with, without violating the Federal Constitution." More specifically, the Court ruled that the law violated the due process clause of the Fourteenth Amendment, which stipulates that no state shall "deprive any person of life, liberty, or property, without due process of law."

The reasoning of *Lochner* was embraced in a long series of decisions extending into the 1930s, striking down worker protection legislation and minimum wage laws as similar violations of the due process clause. But in the changed climate of the Depression and the New Deal, the Court abruptly reversed itself, for reasons that are described later in this chapter. The doctrine of employment at will, however, remained firmly entrenched, and it has been only in the past thirty years that some state courts have begun to make exceptions to it.

The task of this chapter is to examine the justification of this doctrine in order to determine the rights that employees have against unjust dismissal and other adverse treatment at the hands of employers. Three arguments are commonly used to justify employment at will. One argument holds that the doctrine is entailed by the rights of property owners; the second argument appeals to the notion of freedom of contract; and the third argument is based on considerations of efficiency. Each of these arguments upholds certain rights for employers, but they can also be used to make a strong case for the rights of employees and to provide greater protection from unjust dismissal than the prevailing legal interpretation of employment at will.

PROPERTY RIGHTS AND EMPLOYMENT AT WILL

One argument for employment at will—the property rights argument—begins with the assumption that both employers and employees have property of some kind. The owner of a factory, for example, owns the machinery and raw materials for the manufacture of a product, along with a certain amount of money for wages. The only resource lacking is labor for operating the machinery and turning the raw materials into a finished product. Labor, or more precisely the productivity of labor, thus has an economic value and can be said to be a kind of "property" that is "owned" by the worker. Employment can be described, therefore, as an exchange of a worker's productive power for the wages that are given out in return by the factory owner.

In this exchange, both parties are free to exercise the rights of property ownership. The owner of the factory is free to utilize the productive resources of the factory and to pay out money as wages in any way that workers are willing to accept. And the workers are free to accept work under the conditions and at the wages offered or to seek work elsewhere on more favorable terms. It follows that any restriction on the kinds of agreements that employers and employees can make is a violation of the property rights of one or both parties. Just as consumers are under no obligation to continue buying a product, employers are free to stop "buying" the labor of an employee. Although the loss of a job may create some hardship for the person dismissed, no rights are violated.

The historical roots of the property rights argument are contained in John Locke's idea that there is a *natural* right to property, by which he meant a morally fundamental right that exists apart from any particular legal system. Accepting the biblical belief that God gave the bounty of the earth to all persons in common for the purposes of life, Locke went on to observe that we can make use of this bounty only by appropriating it and making it our own. The fruit of a tree cannot nourish us, for example, until we pluck and eat it; but when one person eats a piece of fruit, that person deprives another of its use. Locke's argument for property as a natural right is based, therefore, on the role that property, including labor, plays in satisfying human needs.

How Important Are Property Rights?

The property rights argument seems to confer a right on the owners of businesses to hire and fire at will. All rights are limited, however, for the simple reason that they inevitably come into conflict with each other and with important societal interests. Government is permitted under the Constitution to place legal restrictions on the use of property as long as "due process" is observed. The doctrine of employment at will is supported by the property rights argument, then, only when it is further assumed that the right to property is of such importance that it takes precedence over all other competing values.

This was the view of the Supreme Court in the decisions of the *Lochner* era, when considerations of adequate pay, worker health and safety, the right to organize, and the like were held to be of little account. The *Lochner* era came to an end in 1937 with the decision in *West Coast Hotel* v. *Parrish*, which upheld the constitutionality of a Washington State law setting a minimum wage for women and children.[6] In the majority opinion, Chief Justice Charles Evans Hughes observed that:

> . . . the Constitution does not recognize an absolute and uncontrollable liberty. Liberty in each of its phases has its history and connotation. But the liberty safeguarded is liberty in a social organization which requires the protection of law against the evils which menace the health, safety, morals and welfare of the people.

He continued:

> In dealing with the relation of employer and employed, the legislature has

necessarily a wide field of discretion in order that there may be suitable protection of health and safety, and that peace and good order may be promoted through regulations designed to insure wholesome conditions of work and freedom from oppression.[7]

Problems with Locke's Theory

A further objection to an unlimited right to property can be constructed using Locke's own premises. Property rights are fundamental in Locke's political theory because of the role they play in satisfying our basic needs and securing liberty. It can be argued, however, that instead of serving these Lockean ends, the doctrine of employment at will has the opposite effect: namely, the impoverishment of a substantial portion of society and their subjugation to the will of others. Philip J. Levine has observed, for example:

> The notion of an absolute right to property, although originally conceived of as the basis of liberty, has resulted in the subjugation of the working class. It has allowed employers to exercise dominion over their employees, without any corresponding protection of the employee's interests. This freedom from governmental restraint has enabled employers to place unconscionable conditions on employment.
>
> The seriousness of the situation is compounded by the importance of employment to the individual employee. The essential elements of his life are all dependent on his ability to derive income. His job is the basis of his position in society, and, therefore, may be the most meaningful form of wealth he possesses.[8]

If this argument is correct, then something has gone seriously wrong. The explanation, according to C. B. Macpherson, is to be found in two factors, neither of which was anticipated by Locke. One is a change in the conception of property.

> As late as the 17th century, it was quite usual for writers to use the word in what seems to us an extraordinarily wide sense. John Locke repeatedly and explicitly defined men's properties as their lives, liberties, and estates. . . . One's own person, one's capacities, one's rights and liberties were regarded as individual property. They were even more important than individual property in material things and revenues, partly because they were seen as the source and justification of individual material property.
>
> That broad meaning of property was lost in the measure that modern societies became fully market societies. Property soon came to have only the narrower meaning it generally has today: property in material things or revenues.[9]

The second factor is the unequal distribution of property which prevails in modern society. A certain amount of inequality is justified by Locke insofar as it reflects the differing efforts of individuals. What Locke failed to anticipate is that those who have only their labor to "sell" accelerate the process of transferring the wealth of society to those who are in a position to employ them.

As a result of these two factors, Macpherson has claimed:

> Those who have to pay for access to the means of using their capacities and exerting their energies, and pay by making over to others both the control of their capacities and some of the product of their energies—those people are denied equality in the use and development and enjoyment of their own capacities. And in a modern market society, that amounts to most people. . . .[10]

Property Rights and Democracy

In holding that property rights enable individuals to be free and equal members of a state, Locke failed to recognize another aspect of property rights, pointed out in a classic essay, "Property and Sovereignty," by Morris R. Cohen. Property makes it possible for individuals to be citizens in a democracy, in Locke's view, by providing them with a base of individual power that enables them to stand up against the sovereign power of the state. Without a right to the means for making a living by developing and exercising our own capacities, human beings would be in the position of supplicants who receive the necessities of life as gifts from the state. What Cohen observed is that property gives individuals not only power against the state but also power against each other. The owner of property has not only a right to the exclusive use of some material thing but also a means for gaining control over fellow human beings. Property itself thus constitutes a kind of sovereignty in addition to that of the state.

According to Cohen:

> The extent of the power over the life of others which the legal order confers on those called owners is not fully appreciated by those who think of the law as merely protecting men in their possession. Property law does more. It determines what men shall acquire. Thus, protecting the property rights of a landlord means giving him the right to collect rent, protecting the property of a railroad or a public-service corporation means giving it the right to make certain charges. . . .
>
> From this point of view it can readily be seen that when a court rules that a gas company is entitled to a return of 6 per cent on its investment, it is not merely protecting property already possessed, it is also determining that a portion of the future social produce shall under certain conditions go to that company. Thus not only medieval landlords but the owners of all revenue-producing property are in fact granted by the law certain powers to tax the future social product. When to this power of taxation there is added the power to command the services of large num-

bers who are not economically independent, we have the essence of what historically has constituted political sovereignty.[11]

Because of the many problems with Locke's theory, there is ample reason to limit property rights—and with them the doctrine of employment at will—by recognizing counterbalancing rights of employees in the employment relation. If the justification for property rights is the securing of liberty, and if these rights, when applied to the employment relation, fail to do that, then we are no longer justified in holding property rights as absolute.

Property Rights in a Job

For some philosophers and legal theorists, the problem lies not with the notion of property rights but with the limited way property is conceived. Employees, according to Locke, have property in their own labor, but it is argued that they also have property rights in a job and in the education and special skills that they put at the service of an employer. If employees have property rights of this kind, then the right of an employer to dismiss "at will," instead of being a right entailed by the employer's property rights, should be viewed as a violation of the property rights of an *employee*. The property rights argument can thus be turned on its head to undermine rather than to support the doctrine of employment at will. Before jumping to this conclusion, however, it is necessary to defend the claim that employees can be said to have property rights in a job.[12]

Consider the case of Robert Sindermann, who had been a teacher for ten years with the Texas state college system, rising to the position of professor of government and social science at Odessa Junior College. After four years in this position, he was not offered a contract for the next academic year. The reason cited by the college's board of regents was Sindermann's "insubordination." But no specific reasons were given, and his request for a hearing to challenge the dismissal was refused by the regents. During the past academic year, however, Sindermann had served as president of the Texas Junior College Teachers Association, and in this capacity he left the classroom on several occasions to testify before committees of the Texas State Legislature. His name also appeared in a newspaper advertisement that was highly critical of the board of regents.

In the resulting lawsuit, *Perry* v. *Sindermann*, Sindermann claimed that in addition to violating his right to freedom of speech, the board of regents had violated his rights under the Fourteenth Amendment by depriving him of property without due process of law.[13] Since the college did not have a tenure system, Sindermann had no contractual guarantee of continued employment. The college had nevertheless given assurances that any faculty member with seven or more years of service "may expect to continue in his academic position unless adequate cause for dismissal is demonstrated in a fair hearing, following established procedures of due process." Sindermann contended that this promise of continued employment constitutes property, so that he was at least entitled to a hearing of the charges against him.

What Is Property?

A crucial issue in evaluating Sindermann's claim is, what is property? As Morris R. Cohen noted, "Any one who frees himself from the crudest materialism readily recognizes that as a legal term 'property' denotes not material things but certain rights."[14] In a famous passage, R. H. Tawney wrote:

> Property is the most ambiguous of categories. It covers a multitude of rights which have nothing in common except that they are exercised by persons and enforced by the State. Apart from these formal characteristics, they vary indefinitely in economic character, in social effect, and in moral justification. They may be conditional like the grant of patent rights, or absolute like the ownership of ground rents, terminable like copyright, or permanent like a freehold, as comprehensive as sovereignty or as restricted as an easement, as intimate and personal as the ownership of clothes and books, or as remote and intangible as shares in a gold mine or rubber plantation.[15]

The economic assets of most employees do not consist of land, machines, and the like, which are commonly thought of as productive property. Rather, they consist in the possession of an education and certain specialized skills, which are often certified by a diploma or a license of some kind. The most valuable economic asset of a medical doctor is likely to be the MD degree and the license from a state, which permit the doctor to practice. Charles A. Reich has observed that government bestows many entitlements and that these are steadily taking the place of more traditional forms of property.[16] Unless we recognize that the wealth of many employees consists of their education, skills, and government entitlements, these valuable assets will not be protected as well as traditional forms of property.

In *Perry* v. *Sindermann*, the Supreme Court ruled for the first time that a job is a form of property for purposes of the Fourteenth Amendment, so that Sindermann and employees in a similar situation are entitled by the due process clause to a fair hearing. In the majority opinion, Justice Potter Stewart, wrote:

> We have made it clear . . . that "property" interests subject to procedural due process protection are not limited by a few rigid, technical forms.

Rather, "property" denotes a broad range of interests that are secured by "existing rules or understandings." A person's interest in a benefit is a "property" interest for due process purposes if there are such rules or mutually explicit understandings that support his claim of entitlement to the benefit and that he may invoke at a hearing.

There are some legal obstacles, however, to the claim that the due process clause applies to cases of private employment where an employee is dismissed without a just cause or a fair hearing. *Perry* v. *Sindermann* and similar cases have involved only government and not private employment. The due process clause protects an individual only when deprivation of property occurs by the action of a state, not by a private employer. Furthermore, there must be some basis other than the Constitution for asserting that a property right exists. The Supreme Court has clearly stated that the Constitution does not create property rights but merely extends "various procedural safeguards" to protect them.[17]

Still, a powerful moral argument can be constructed to support the claim that employees such as Sindermann have interests in a job that (morally) ought to be protected. If we accept such an argument, then these moral rights of employees must be weighed against the property rights that have traditionally been accorded to the owners of a business. The right of employees to be protected from unjust dismissal cannot be denied merely by appealing to the property rights of corporations. Employees have property rights, too, and these are just as deserving of protection as the property rights of employers.

THE FREEDOM OF CONTRACT ARGUMENT

Employment can be viewed as a contractual arrangement between employers and employees. This arrangement arises in some instances from an *explicit* contract, a legal document signed by both parties, in which a business firm states the terms under which it is willing to hire a person and that person signifies by his or her acceptance a willingness to work under those terms. Union employees are typically covered by a company-wide contract that is agreed to by both the management of a company and the union rank and file. In the absence of an explicit contract, we can still understand the employment relation as involving an *implicit* contract insofar as the conditions of employment are understood and tacitly accepted by both parties.

To place a limit, then, on the kinds of agreements that can be made between an employee and an employer is to limit the right of contract of both parties. Just as it would be a violation of rights to force an employee to remain in a job, so it would be a violation of rights to prevent an employer from terminating an employee who voluntarily entered into an at-will employment relation. This was the reasoning of the Supreme Court in *Lochner*. A more explicit statement of employment at will as a consequence of freedom of contract occurs in a decision upholding the right of an employer to fire an employee for belonging to a labor organization. The majority opinion in this case, *Adair* v. *United States* (1907), held:

> . . . [I]t is not within the functions of government—at least in the absence of contract between the parties—to compel any person, in the course of his business and against his will, to accept or retain the personal services of another, or to compel any person, against his will to perform personal services for another. The right of a person to sell his labor upon such terms as he deems proper is, in its essence, the same as the right of the purchaser of labor to prescribe the conditions upon which he will accept such labor from the person offering to sell it. So the right of the employee to quit the service of the employer for whatever reason is the same as the right of the employer, for whatever reason, to dispense with the services of such employee. . . . In all such particulars the employer and the employee have equality of right, and any legislation that disturbs that equality is an arbitrary interference with the liberty of contract which no government can legally justify in a free land.[18]

In another case the Court held, "This right is as essential to the laborer as to the capitalist, to the poor as to the rich; for the vast majority of persons have no other honest way to begin to acquire property, save by working for money."[19]

The Philosophical Basis for Freedom of Contract

In the British and American legal traditions, the philosophical basis for the freedom of contract argument, as for the property rights argument, derives from John Locke, who considered the exercise of property rights to be only one part of a more general freedom of action. On the Continent, however, the philosophical basis for freedom of contract derives not from Locke but from Immanuel Kant and his concept of autonomy.

The Kantian argument can be sketched briefly as follows. Autonomy involves the capacity and opportunity to make meaningful choices about matters that bear most significantly on our lives. That is, we are autonomous insofar as it is *we* who make the important decisions affecting our lives and not *others*. An essential part of acting autonomously in this sense is the possibility of making mutually binding voluntary agreements. Therefore, autonomy entails freedom of contract.

A contemporary version of Kant's argument is given by Charles Fried in his book *Contracts As Promises*. Contracts, in Fried's view, are a kind of promise, and promises in turn constitute a convention whereby we are able to realize our aims by creating expectations about one another's conduct. The convention of promising depends on our being able to trust each other and on showing respect. Thus Fried concludes, "By virtue of the basic Kantian principles of trust and respect, it is wrong to invoke that convention in order to make a promise, and then to break it."[20]

Problems with the Freedom of Contract Argument

Use of the freedom of contract argument to support the doctrine of employment at will is problematic because of the immense difference in bargaining power.that usually prevails between employers and employees. Bargaining almost always takes place between parties of different strengths, and the stronger side usually gains at the expense of the weaker. The outcome need not be unjust for this reason. But is there some point at which employers ought not to be permitted to take advantage of their superior bargaining position?

The decision in *Lochner* v. *New York* denied that there was any morally significant difference in bargaining strength between bakery workers and their employers. The majority opinion held, "There is no contention that bakers as a class are not equal in intelligence and capacity to men in other trades . . . or that they are not able to assert their rights and care for themselves without the protecting arm of the state." As mentioned earlier, the *Lochner* era came to an end in 1937 with the decision in *West Coast Hotel* v. *Parrish*. Chief Justice Hughes, who delivered the majority opinion, cited "an additional and compelling consideration which recent economic experience has brought into a strong light." This consideration is the "exploitation of a class of workers who are in an unequal position with respect to bargaining power and are thus relatively defenceless against the denial of a living wage." The doctrine of employment at will cannot be justified by a right to freedom of contract, according to Chief Justice Hughes, when the result is to deprive employees of the ability to protect their most vital interests. This decision was followed by a series of federal and state worker protection laws that addressed the most serious abuses of employment at will.

Restrictions on Freedom of Contract

Freedom of contract, like the right to property, is not absolute. Outside the employer-employee relation, there are a number of moral and legal limits on the right of individuals to enter into contractual relations. Children and people who are mentally incompetent cannot be parties to a contract, for example. Contracts can be invalidated by showing that they were made under duress or under threats of harm or that they involve misrepresentation or fraud. And the courts sometimes refuse to recognize contracts that exploit people's inexperience or ignorance.

The reason for these restrictions is that contracts are valid only when they are made with the genuine consent of both parties. Children and the retarded and insane, for example, do not have the mental or emotional capacity to understand the terms of a contract. Hence, they are not able to give their consent in a meaningful way. A person who is coerced into accepting the terms of a contract through the use of intimidation or force "consents" only in a very artificial sense of the term, since the person lacks any significant degree of choice. And when a contract is secured by misrepresentation or fraud—as is the case when a buyer of a house is not told about hidden structural defects or termite damage—the victim's "consent" is also not consent in the full meaning of the term, since the person lacks full knowledge of what is being agreed to.[21] These restrictions are compatible with, and indeed even required by, Locke's conception of freedom.

The same restrictions on freedom of contract are justified when freedom of contract is based on Kant's conception of autonomy. Children and the mentally incompetent lack the capacity for autonomous action to a sufficient degree. And when a person is coerced into agreeing to the terms of a contract—whether it be by physical compulsion or deception of some kind—that person cannot be said to be acting autonomously. Autonomy, along with Lockean freedom, requires that our consent be voluntarily given.

An Autonomy Argument

Although autonomy can be used to support freedom of contract— and with it the doctrine of employment at will—the same concept can also serve as the basis for an argument *against* employment at will.[22] A sketch of the argument is as follows:

If people are to have autonomy, then they must have not only the capacity for autonomous action but also an acceptable range of alternatives from which to choose. What makes us autonomous is not the mere fact that we are able to make a choice, no matter what the alternatives are. A meaningful account of autonomy must also consider the number and desirability of alternatives available to us. When we choose to do one thing and not another, the alternatives are largely fixed by a social, political, and economic order over which we have little control. A student who wants to become a doctor, for example, cannot merely *choose* to do so. For some, a career in medicine is not a viable alternative. The student may be limited by his or her own abilities and education in comparison with those who are also competing for entry into a medical school. Once trained, a doctor must practice within a system of medical care that is constrained by the resources available, by the demand for services, and by the priorities of the society.

Some people have more alternatives from which to choose than others. A person with few skills and limited resources might "choose" to accept menial, exhausting, and dangerous work at low pay when the alternative is no work at all. But the choices these people make are scarcely the ones they would *like* to make. They would like to be able to choose from a more desirable list of alternatives. To some extent the degree of freedom of choice each of us has is a matter of our own endowments, but it is also due to forces outside ourselves. Complete freedom of choice, in the sense that we are free to make any choice we please from an unlimited list of alternatives, is an unrealistic ideal. And this cannot be what autonomy requires. At the other extreme, it would be absurd to say that slaves are free simply because they can choose to obey their master or accept the consequences. There must be some point between these two extremes where we are justified in saying that a person is acting autonomously.

Once we recognize that the autonomy of a person cannot be separated from the alternatives available to that person, it becomes obvious that employment cannot be analyzed merely as a contractual arrangement between two parties. Any agreement between an employer and an employee takes place in a larger setting that profoundly influences the relative bargaining strength of the two parties and consequently the outcome of their negotiations. Among people with relatively equal bargaining strength with respect to employment, there might be no need for any restrictions on the agreements that are made. But this is seldom the case. To require employees to negotiate a contract with regard to the terms of their employment under conditions of decidedly unequal bargaining strength, then, is not to enhance their autonomy but to diminish it.

How should the employment relation be constructed in a society that values and wishes to advance the autonomy of its members? Adina Schwartz suggests, "A crucial implication is that respecting people as autonomous is not equivalent, as commonly assumed, to leaving them as free as possible from social influences. Instead, a society respects all its members as autonomous to the extent that it assists them in leading a certain kind of life."[23] A kind of life that embodies a realistic view of autonomy, according to Schwartz, is one that allows for "shaping one's circumstances by planning rationally to achieve some over-all conception of one's goals" and "shaping one's goals by rationally criticizing and changing one's over-all conception."[24] In short, a society fosters autonomy to the extent that it makes it possible for people to decide for themselves how they want to live and enables them to implement their decisions effectively.

Conclusion

The two arguments for freedom of contract discussed in this section lead to the same conclusion. Whether the right of employers and employees to contract freely is based on a Lockean conception of freedom or a Kantian conception of autonomy, certain conditions must be satisfied in order for the resulting agreements to be just. There is ample room for controversy over what these conditions are. But to the extent that the necessary conditions are not satisfied, the doctrine of employment at will cannot be supported by the freedom of contract argument.

EFFICIENCY AND EMPLOYMENT AT WILL

The third argument for employment at will is a utilitarian one that relies not on property rights or the freedom of contract but on the importance of this doctrine for the efficient operation of business. The success of any business enterprise depends on the efficient use of all resources, including the resource of labor. For this reason, employers are generally accorded considerable leeway to determine the number of workers needed, to select the best workers available, to assign them to the jobs for which they are best suited, and to discipline and dismiss workers who perform inadequately. The intrusion of factors other than the most efficient allocation of resources into business decision-making can only impair efficiency, according to this argument, and thereby harm everyone concerned. Furthermore, legal limitations on the commonly accepted prerogatives of employers puts legislatures and courts in the position of making vital business decisions.

Although employment at will has undeniable benefits, most of these go to employers. A utilitarian justification does not allow us to look merely at the consequences of this doctrine for employers but requires that we also consider the consequences for workers and for the whole of society. One of the objections made by Chief Justice Hughes in *West Coast Hotel* v. *Parrish* is that the exploitation of workers which the doctrine of employment at will makes possible is "not only detrimental to their health and well-being but casts a direct burden for their support upon the community. What these workers lose in wages the taxpayers are called upon to pay." When the benefits to employers are balanced against the cost to workers and the other members of society, it may be that employment at will is not an efficient but a very inefficient way of using human resources.

The case of Olga Monge is instructive here. That the foreman's conduct was reprehensible is not in dispute. The relevant question from the utilitarian point of view is whether the protection of women from sexual harassment in the workplace is a sufficiently important social good to override the traditional prerogatives of employers with regard to discipline and dismissal. Would the welfare of society as a whole be better served by maintaining the doctrine of employment at will, even though it is open to abuse, or by making an exception in cases such as that of Mrs. Monge? The New Hampshire Supreme Court ruled that it is in the best interests of society and businesses themselves to make an exception. According to the court:

> . . . in all employment contracts whether at will or for a definite term the employer's interest in running his business as he sees fit must be balanced against the interest of the employee in maintaining his employment and the public's interest in maintaining a balance between the two.

Further, the court held:

> We hold that a termination by the employer of a contract of employment at will which is motivated by bad faith and malice or based on retaliation is not in the best interest of the economic system or the public good and constitutes a breach of the employment contract.

Monge v. *Beebe Rubber Company* was among the first of many cases in which the courts have made exceptions to the doctrine of employment at will based on considerations of *public policy*. In a West Virginia case, an employee was dismissed for complaining to his superiors and other employees about apparent violations by the bank of state and federal consumer protection laws. In finding for the employee, the state supreme court also appealed to the matter of public policy at stake in the case:

> . . . [T]he rule giving the employer the absolute right to discharge an at will employee must be tempered by the further principle that where the employer's motivation for the discharge contravenes some substantial public policy, then the employer may be liable to the employee for damages occasioned by the discharge.[25]

The case of Dr. Grace Pierce provides another illustration of a public policy exception. As an employee of the Ortho Pharmaceutical Corporation, she was forced to resign after she refused to proceed with tests of a new drug containing what she considered to be a dangerously high level of saccharin. In remanding the case for trial, an appeals court judge ruled that there was a clear and well-defined public policy at issue. Members of the public have a right to be protected against the testing of potentially unsafe drugs, and the public interest is not served by allowing the company to pressure Dr. Pierce to act against her best professional judgment. The trial judge stated that it may be that:

... public policy will develop to a degree that professionals, even though employees at will, will be permitted to resist what they consider to be a professionally unsound and unethical decision without fear of demotion or discharge.

Dr. Pierce eventually lost her case in the New Jersey Supreme Court, however.[26]

The efficiency argument, then, not only provides some grounds for justifying employment at will but also justifies some limitations for reasons of public policy. Merely admitting that there are some limits, however, does not enable us to determine exactly what these limits are. There are still some good reasons for proceeding cautiously in this area. These are well-expressed by the appeals judge in *Pierce* v. *Ortho Pharmaceutical Corporation*:

> We note that a public policy exception would represent a departure from the well-settled common law employment-at-will rule. If such a departure is to be made, care is required in order to insure that the reasons underlying the rule will not be undermined. Most notably in this regard, the employer's legitimate interests in conducting his business and employing and in retaining the best personnel available cannot be unjustifiably impaired. Thus, it cannot change the present rule which holds that just or good cause for the discharge of an employee at will or the giving of reasons therefore are not required. In addition the exception must guard against a potential flood of unwarranted disputes and litigation that might result from such a doctrine, based on vague notions of public policy. Hence, if there is to be such an exception to the at-will employment rule, it must be tightly circumscribed so as to apply only in cases involving truly significant matters of clear and well-defined public policy and substantial violations thereof. If it is to be established at all, its development must be on a case-to-case basis.

What are some of the "truly significant matters of clear and well-defined public policy" that justify making exceptions to the doctrine of employment at will? A partial answer to this question is provided by a number of court cases decided in recent years. These cases are almost exclusively from state courts, since employment is largely under the jurisdiction of individual states. For this reason, the legal rights of employees vary considerably from one state to another. From the moral point of view, however, it can be claimed that employees (morally) ought to have these rights, whether or not they are guaranteed by law.

First, employees ought not to be subject to demotion, discipline, or discharge for refusing to violate the law. If anything is contrary to public policy, it is a doctrine that permits employers to use the threat of dismissal to force an employee to commit illegal acts. In a 1959 California case, *Petermann* v. *International Brotherhood of Teamsters*, Petermann, the business manager for a local of the Teamsters union, was fired by the union after he refused an order to commit perjury before an investigative committee of the state legislature.[27] The California Court of Appeals held that in order to make the law against perjury effective, some restriction had to be placed on an employer's right of discharge.

In another case from California, a retail sales representative for the Atlantic Richfield Company (ARCO) named Tameny claimed that he had been dismissed for his refusal to cooperate in an illegal price-fixing scheme involving ARCO and independent service stations in his territory. An appellate court decided the case by invoking the tradition of employment at will:

> At an earlier time it was axiomatic that an employee at will was engaged in his occupation wholly at the pleasure of his employer and was subject to discharge at any time for any reason, irrespective of motive. . . . We think the axiom is still the law and has continuing vitality.[28]

However, the California Supreme Court overturned the lower court's decision and argued that an employer's right of discharge does not include the right to force an employee to commit a crime:

> . . . [A]n employer's authority over its employee does not include the right to demand that the employee commit a criminal act to further its interests, and an employer may not coerce compliance with such unlawful directions by discharging an employee who refuses to follow such an order. An employer engaging in such conduct violates a basic duty imposed by law upon all employers. . . .[29]

In a rather different case, an employee was dismissed for being away from work to serve on a jury.[30] Although jury duty is a legal obligation for the persons selected, the court in Oregon did not find that the employer was prevented by any statute from dismissing the employee. Nevertheless, the court ruled in favor of the employee on the grounds that the discharge was for "a socially undesirable motive" that tended to "thwart" the jury system:

> The community's interest in having its citizens serve on jury duty was so important that an employer who interfered with that interest by discharging an employee who served on a jury would be required to compensate the employee for damages suffered.

Second, employers ought not to prevent employees from the full benefit of their legal rights and entitlements relating to employment. The legislation creating many employee rights include antiretaliation provisions, so there is no need for the courts to create a separate public policy exception. Thus, the National Labor Relations Act and the Occupational Safety and Health Act, among others, not only forbid retaliation but provide for legal remedies. In many instances, employees have been dismissed for filing workers' compensation claims for benefits that are guaranteed as a matter of right for injuries suffered on the job. In *Frampton* v. *Central Indiana Gas Company*, an employee named Frampton suffered a permanent 30 percent loss of capacity in one arm in a job-related accident. Although her employer paid all her medical bills and continued her salary while she was unable to work, she was not told that she was entitled to additional compensation from a state program. When she filed a claim a year and a half later, she was fired. The court ruled that she was wrongfully discharged for seeking compensation to which she was legally entitled. "When an employee is discharged solely for exercising a statutorily conferred right," the court held, "an exception to the general rule [of employment at will] must be recognized."[31]

Aside from public policy, the courts have made exceptions under two other conditions. One is the existence of an *implied contract* and the other is the presence of *bad faith and malice.*

An Implied Contract to Continued Employment

In some instances, prospective employees are given assurances in job interviews that dismissal is only for cause, that attempts are made to work through any problems before the company resorts to dismissal, and that due process is followed in all cases. These assurances are conveyed in other instances by employee manuals, policy statements, personnel guidelines and procedures, and other company documents. The claim that an implied contract exists as a result of different kinds of assurances makes an appeal not to a utilitarian justification based on public policy but to the law of contracts. Employee suits have not always been successful, however, as witness the following case.

Walton L. Weiner was hired away from his job at Prentice Hall with promises of secure employment.[32] He was told in a preemployment interview that it was the policy at McGraw-Hill not to dismiss an employee without just cause, and the company's personnel handbook contained a procedure for help in overcoming any problem with an employee's performance. When he was summarily fired after eight years at McGraw-Hill, without just cause and without following the prescribed procedure, he sued his employer for breach of contract. However, the court ruled against Weiner's claim that the company's verbal and written assurances constituted an implied contract. The personnel handbook, for example, was not itself a contract, since it did not spell out the terms of employment, such as salary and duration, and it could be modified at any time by the company. In a dissenting opinion, however, one judge asserted:

... I cannot agree that an employee handbook on personnel policies and procedures is a corporate illusion, "full of sound ... signifying nothing." The application form presented to the employee which required his signature prior to the employment, stated that employment would be subject to handbook rules. An employee should be able to rely thereon, perhaps to his detriment. The employer should be estopped from acting other than with respect thereto.

In two Michigan cases that were decided together, *Toussaint* v. *Blue Cross and Blue Shield of Michigan* and *Ebling* v. *Masco Corporation*, the plaintiffs were given assurances of job security by their employers as long as they performed satisfactorily.[33] Charles Toussaint testified that he was told by his employer that he would be with the company until the mandatory retirement age of 65 "as long as I did my job." The supervisory manual at Blue Cross and Blue Shield stipulated that employees could be dismissed only for just cause and that specific disciplinary proceedings were to be used. The court found that his supervisor, in asking him to resign, had not observed these provisions in the manual. Furthermore, the court held:

While an employer need not establish personnel policies or practices, where an employer chooses to establish such policies and practices and makes them known to its employees, the employment relation is presumably enhanced.

The employer secures an orderly, cooperative and loyal work force, and the employee the peace of mind associated with job security and the conviction that he will be treated fairly.

Walter Ebling was given similar assurances of job security at the Masco Corporation as long as he performed satisfactorily, and he testified that he was told that he could be discharged only for just cause and after a review of the case by the company's executive vice-president. Ebling claimed that he was discharged merely to prevent him from exercising a stock option that had greatly appreciated in value. The Michigan Supreme Court held that the oral assurances and the company manual create a commitment on the part of the employer with regard to the terms of employment and thus constitute an implied contract.

Bad Faith and Malice

Even without an implied contract, a commonly accepted principle in business is acting in good faith. This concept is applied widely as both a moral and a legal requirement in collective bargaining, contract negotiations, consumer relations, and indeed virtually all commercial dealings. The Uniform Commercial Code, for example, requires that all sales be in good faith, which is defined as "honesty in fact and the

observance of reasonable commercial standards of fair dealing in trade."
And the UCC also holds that an "unconscionable" sales contract is unen-
forceable. Although the same requirements have not commonly been
applied by the courts to the employment relation, there are good moral
reasons for doing so.

An example of conspicuous *bad* faith is the case of a twenty-five-
year veteran employee of the National Cash Register Company, named
Fortune, who was dismissed the next business day after he had secured
an order for $5 million worth of equipment to be delivered over the
next four years. The court found that the dismissal was motivated by a
desire to deprive Fortune of the very substantial commission he would
receive as the equipment was sold. The Massachusetts court held that
Fortune had an implied contract with his employers and stated that:

> . . . in every contract there is an implied covenant that neither party shall
> do anything which will have the effect of destroying or injuring the right
> of the other party to receive the fruits of the contract, which means that
> in every contract there exists an implied covenant of good faith and fair
> dealing.[34]

A California court issued a similar ruling in the case of *Cleary* v.
American Airlines.[35] Cleary claimed that his dismissal, after eighteen years
of satisfactory service, was based on a false accusation of work rule
violations and was not in accord with the company's personnel policies.
In agreeing with Cleary, the court held that the dismissal was contrary
to the "implied-in-law covenant of good faith and fair dealing contained
in all covenants." At about the same time, a court in New York ruled in
favor of an employee who was fired after thirteen years of service for
no reason except to deprive him of his pension benefits which would be
vested in two more years.[36] Although New York State law had no provision for wrongful discharge, the court held that the employer's action
"smacks of the unconscionable."

Conclusion

This discussion of unjust dismissal is of vital importance for all
employees and not just those unfortunate enough to be fired without
cause. The reason is that the pivotal doctrine of employment at will
pervades the whole employer-employee relation. To be an at-will employee is to be at all times subject to the power of an employer to grant
or deny something that is essential for our well-being, namely, a job.
The alternative is not necessarily a lifetime guarantee of employment
but an assurance that we will be treated fairly.

Employment at will is, fortunately, an idea whose time is past,
although it still retains a strong hold in the laws of many states. The

main supports, historically, have been property rights and the right of contract, which we have examined in depth. These arguments have been rebutted not by denying these rights but by showing their limits. In particular, the imbalance that exists between employer and employee makes a mockery of the idea that the rights of both are being preserved. When employers can dismiss at will, legitimate property rights of employees and the right of employees to contract freely are severely eroded.

The present-day debate revolves mainly around utilitarian issues.[37] To what extent is the welfare of society advanced by preserving or limiting the traditional prerogatives of employers? Employers typically favor employment at will not because they want to fire without cause but because they would rather avoid the need to account for their personnel decisions in court and face the possibility of stiff punitive awards. Even advocates of greater employee protection recognize the dangers of the courts becoming too deeply involved in business decison-making.

NOTES

1. *Monge* v. *Beebe Rubber Company*, 114 N.H. 130 (1974).
2. *Comerford* v. *International Harvester Co.*, 235 Ala. 376 (1938).
3. H.G. WOOD, *A Treatise on the Law of Master and Servant* (Albany: John D. Parsons, Jr., 1877), 134. Cited by PATRICIA H. WERHANE, *Persons, Rights, and Corporations* (Englewood Cliffs, NJ: Prentice Hall, 1985), 82.
4. *Paine* v. *Western & A.R.R.*, 81 Tenn. 507, 519–20 (1884).
5. 198 U.S. 45, 25 S.Ct. 539 (1905).
6. *West Coast Hotel* v. *Parrish*, 300 U.S. 379 (1937).
7. In a landmark decision, *Nebbia* v. *New York*, 291 U.S. 502 (1934), the Supreme Court had previously ruled that states have the power to regulate business—and thereby limit the property rights of owners—for the sake of the public welfare. The decision in *West Coast Hotel* thus extends the precedent of *Nebbia*, which concerned the setting of prices, to matters of employment.
8. PHILIP J. LEVINE, "Towards a Property Right in Employment," *Buffalo Law Review*, 22 (1973), 1084.
9. C. B. MACPHERSON, "Human Rights as Property Rights," *Dissent*, 24 (Winter 1977), 72.
10. MACPHERSON, "Human Rights as Property Rights," 74.
11. MORRIS R. COHEN, "Property and Sovereignty," in *Law and the Social Order* (New York: Harcourt, Brace and Co., 1933), 47.
12. For discussions of a job as property, see BARBARA A. LEE, "Something Akin to a Property Right: Protections for Employee Job Security," *Business and Professional Ethics Journal*, 8 (Fall 1989), 63–81; and WILLIAM B. GOULD, IV, "The Idea of the Job as Property in Contemporary America: The Legal and

Collective Bargaining Framework," *Brigham Young Law Review* (1986), 885–918.

13. *Perry et al.* v. *Sindermann*, 408 U.S. 593 (1971). See also *Arnett* v. *Kennedy*, 416 U.S. 134 (1974); *Cleveland Board of Education* v. *Loudermill*, 470 U.S. 532 (1985); and *Foley* v. *Interactive Data Corporation*, 47 Cal.3rd 654, 254 Cal. Rptr. 211 (1988).

14. COHEN, "Property and Sovereignty," 45.

15. R. H. TAWNEY, *The Acquisitive Society* (New York: Harcourt, Brace & World, 1920), 53–54.

16. CHARLES A. REICH, "The New Property," *Yale Law Review*, 73 (1964), 733.

17. *Leis* v. *Flynt*, 439 U.S. 438 (1979). There is at least one writer, though, who believes that the due process clause when combined with all the protective legislation which applies to private employment can be interpreted to make interests in a job a form of property so that employees can be protected against unjust discharge. See CORNELIUS J. PECK, "Unjust Discharges from Employment: A Necessary Change in the Law," *Ohio State Law Journal*, 40 (1979), 1–49. This view remains untested in the courts, however.

18. *Adair* v. *United States*, 208 U.S. 161, 28 S.Ct. 277 (1907).

19. *Coppage* v. *Kansas*, 26 U.S. 1, 35 S.Ct. 240 (1914).

20. CHARLES FRIED, *Contracts As Promises: A Theory of Contractual Obligation* (Cambridge: Harvard University Press, 1981), 17.

21. For a discussion of these restrictions, see ANTHONY T. KRONMAN, "Contract Law and Distributive Justice," *The Yale Law Journal*, 89 (1980), 472–97.

22. The argument developed here is largely derived from ADINA SCHWARTZ, "Autonomy in the Workplace," in TOM REGAN, ed., *Just Business: New Introductory Essay in Business Ethics* (New York: Random House, 1984), 129–66.

23. SCHWARTZ, "Autonomy in the Workplace," 151.

24. SCHWARTZ, "Autonomy in the Workplace," 150.

25. *Harless* v. *First National Bank in Fairmont*, 246 S.E. 2d 270 (1978).

26. *Pierce* v. *Ortho Pharmaceutical*, 84 N.J. 58, 417 A. 2d 505 (1980).

27. *Petermann* v. *International Brotherhood of Teamsters*, 174 Cal.App. 2d 184, 344 P.2d 25 (1959).

28. *Tameny* v. *Atlantic Richfield Co.*, 152 Cal.Rptr. 52 (1979).

29. *Tameny* v. *Atlantic Richfield Co.*, 27 Cal.3d 167, 164 Cal.Rptr. 839 (1980).

30. *Nees* v. *Hocks*, 272 Or. 210, 536 P.2d 512 (1975).

31. *Frampton* v. *Central Indiana Gas Company*, 260 Ind. 249, 297 N.E. 2d 425 (1973). In addition, see *Kelsay* v. *Motorola*, 74 Ill. 2d 172, 384 N.E. 2d 353 (1978); *Sventko* v. *Kroger Co.*, 69 Mich. App. 644, 245 N.W. 2d 151 (1976).

32. *Weiner* v. *McGraw-Hill*, 83 A.D. 2d 810 (1981).

33. *Toussaint* v. *Blue Cross and Blue Shield of Michigan* and *Ebling* v. *Masco Corporation*, 408 Mich. 579, 272 N.W. 2d 880 (1980).

34. *Fortune* v. *National Cash Register Company*, 364 N.E. 2d 1251 (1977).

35. *Cleary* v. *American Airlines*, 168 Cal. Rptr. 722 (1980).

36. *Savodnick* v. *Korvettes, Inc.*, 488 F. Supp. 822 (1980).

37. One exception is provided by RICHARD A. EPSTEIN, who argues for retaining contract theory as a basis for the employee relation. See "In Defense of Contract at Will," *The University of Chicago Law Review*, 51 (1984), 947–82.

CHAPTER ELEVEN
Ethical Issues in Advertising

Advertising pervades our lives. It is impossible to read a newspaper or magazine, watch a television show, or travel the streets of our cities without being bombarded by commercial messages. Although some ads may be irritating or offensive, the better efforts of Madison Avenue provide a certain amount of entertainment. We also derive benefit from information about products and from the boost that advertising gives to the economy as a whole. On the other side of the fence, companies with products or services to sell regard advertising as a valuable, indeed indispensable marketing tool. Approximately 2 percent of the gross national product is currently devoted to advertising. So whether we like it or not, advertising is a large and essential part of the American way of doing business.

A typical definition of advertising, from a marketing text, is that it is "a paid form of nonpersonal communication about an organization and/or its products that is transmitted to a target audience through a mass medium."[1] So defined, advertising is only one kind of promotional activity. The others are *publicity* (press releases and other public relations efforts that do not involve the purchase of air time or space in the mass media), *sales promotion* (contests, coupons, free samples, and so on, which are not, strictly speaking, forms of communication), and *personal selling* by shop clerks and telephone solicitors (which, of course, is not impersonal and also does not take place through a mass medium). Although most advertising is for a product or a service, some of it is devoted to enhancing the image of a corporation or advancing some issue or cause. Thus, a distinction is commonly made between product advertising on the one hand and corporate or advocacy advertising on the other.[2]

Advertising is widely criticized. Exaggerated claims and outright falsehoods are the most obvious targets for complaints, followed closely by the lack of taste, irritating repetition, and offensive character of many ads. More recently, questions have been raised about the morality of specific kinds of advertising, such as advertising for alcohol and tobacco products, and the extensive advertising aimed at children. Particular ads are also faulted for their use of excessive sex or violence or for presenting negative stereotypes of certain groups, such as blacks, American workers, and the elderly.[3]

More subtle are the complaints of some critics about the role advertising plays in creating a culture of consumerism. Advertising encourages people not only to buy more and more but also to believe that their most basic needs and desires can be satisfied by things that can be bought. The goals and aspirations of consumers thus come to be defined in materialistic terms. Christopher Lasch claims, for example, that advertising "serves not so much to advertise products as to promote consumption as a way of life."[4] Also part of a consumer culture is the extension of a "market mentality" into all aspects of life.

Other criticisms of advertising are directed against its alleged effects on language and thought in our society. Robert Heilbroner maintains, for example:

> 'Have a nice day' and 'We're Am-mer-ican Airlines, doing what we do best!' are more than trivial irritants. They are instances of a process that empties communication of its content . . . [and] destroys credence in the written or spoken word.[5]

The anthropologist Jules Henry argues that the ability of people to think logically is impaired when ads proclaim that a particular brand of razor blade "rides on liquid ball bearings" or that a nail polish of a certain color is "sizzling on your finger tips (And on your toes, goodness knows)."[6]

Some economists charge that advertising is wasteful and inefficient. In their view, advertising is a largely nonproductive activity that stifles competition and leads to monopoly conditions. A few economists also charge that advertising appeals to the emotions and manipulates the needs and desires of consumers, even to the extent of creating wants, thereby hindering the ability of consumers to make rational choices.

Finally, there is great concern about the potential of advertising for behavior control. In 1957, Vance Packard frightened Americans with his bestselling book *The Hidden Persuaders*, which revealed how advertisers were turning to motivational research to discover the subconscious factors that influence human action. A pioneer in this area, Dr. Ernest Dichter, declared in 1941 that advertising agencies were "one of the most advanced laboratories in psychology" and that a successful advertiser "manipulates human motivations and desires and develops a need for goods with which the public has at one time been unfamiliar—perhaps even undesirous of purchasing."[7] The key to success in advertising, according to Dr. Dichter, is to appeal to feelings "deep in the psychological recesses of the mind" and to discover the right psychological "hook."[8]

These objections to advertising have led to calls for regulation. Deceptive advertising is already subject to control by the Federal Trade Commission (FTC), which has the power to order firms to stop certain advertising practices and, in some instances, to correct the harm done.[9] Many questions arise, however, about the definition of deception in advertising and about the burden of proof an advertiser has for claims made in an ad. Is it deceptive to advertise a pain reliever as superior to competing products, for example, when the active ingredient in all of them is ordinary aspirin?[10] Or how much proof does a company need to support the claim that a product is effective in preventing colds?[11]

The regulation of advertising—both government regulation and voluntary self-regulation—involves a number of substantial ethical issues. Among them is whether regulation hampers competition by preventing price comparisons and keeping rivals out of the market (which is the opposite of the economists' argument that unregulated advertising is anticompetitive) and whether government regulation of advertising violates the First Amendment right of free speech. Some opponents of government regulation argue that as long as the products are legal, as is the case with cigarettes and liquor, manufacturers have a right to advertise them without restrictions.

This chapter examines the ethical objections to advertising and, in particular, the arguments that advertising is wasteful and inefficient and that it uses unacceptable means of persuasion and control. The problem of defining deceptive advertising is also considered, along with the issues involved in regulating advertising.

THE ECONOMIC ANALYSIS OF ADVERTISING

An analysis of the economic impact of advertising is relevant to the ethics of advertising for two reasons. First, from a utilitarian point of view, it is necessary to take into account the effect of advertising on the welfare of society as a whole. If advertising is a waste of resources and an anticompetitive practice, as some economists claim, then there are strong utilitarian grounds for opposing it. Second, if a free market economy is justified on utilitarian or other grounds, then advertising is morally objectionable to the extent that it interferes with the efficient operation of a free market. For both utilitarians and advocates of free market capitalism, then, economic analysis has a bearing on the question of whether advertising is morally justified.

Unfortunately, there is sharp disagreement among economists on the effects of advertising. Many defenders of advertising regard it as an important source of information for market transactions and a legitimate form of nonprice competition. In spite of considerable research, no resolution of the controversy seems to be near. Still, we can examine the arguments on both sides and make some tentative judgments. The overall conclusion to be drawn is that although advertising has some economic benefits in a free market economy, there are limits to the amount and kind of morally permissible advertising.

The Charge That Advertising Is Wasteful

The charge that advertising is wasteful is based on the assumption that advertising adds nothing to the value of consumer products and diverts resources from the production of more valuable goods and services. The money spent on advertising, according to critics, does not result in any new products people can consume; it is used only to persuade people to consume products already available, many of which they do not need and would otherwise not desire. Since the value of a product, in economic terms, resides in its ability to satisfy people's needs and desires, more value could be created by eliminating advertising and using those resources, which are now wasted, on things that could provide more satisfaction.

Advertising automobiles, for example, does not improve their quality or safety. Without the extra cost of advertising, cars could be sold more cheaply or else made better for the same price. Or the money saved by not advertising automobiles could be used to purchase other consumer goods or applied to pressing social problems, such as poverty and education. Even greater savings would be realized if people were not persuaded by advertising to buy higher priced luxury cars with more power than they can use.

Especially wasteful are defensive advertising strategies designed to maintain or enlarge a company's market share. Strategies of this kind often seek to foster brand loyalty by creating illusory differences between products. Many smokers are fiercely loyal to a particular brand of cigarettes, for example, even though blind tests reveal that they often cannot tell one brand from another. Not only are smokers deceived into believing that their favorite brand is superior in some way to the others, but the cost of the advertising that makes this deception possible is passed along to them in the form of higher prices.

Defenses to the Charge of Wastefulness

Defenders of advertising reply to this charge by arguing that the assumption of the critics is flawed. A product cannot satisfy a need or a desire until it is purchased by a consumer, and advertising facilitates the process of consumer choice by providing information. Through advertising, the argument goes, buyers of automobiles, for example, are given the information they need to find the model that best suits them; and with better informed consumers, manufacturers are able to offer consumers a larger number of models with options that more closely fit consumer tastes. The result is an increase in the satisfaction of the needs and desires of consumers and hence an increase in the value of products. To the objection that smokers often cannot taste the difference between brands, defenders reply that smokers who prefer one brand of cigarettes to another are buying, according to economists, a certain image in addition to the taste. And as long as this image satisfies a desire, it too contributes to the value of the product.

Critics respond that the informational content of advertising is minimal and not really a benefit to consumers. Much automobile advertising, for example, consists of nonrational appeals to a desire for status or the thrill of driving fast. The small amount of information provided by such advertising typically reinforces these appeals by stressing luxury features or the power of the engine. Rarely do advertisements for automobiles offer information that permits consumers to make cost comparisons of different makes or judgments about their relative safety. The amount of information in advertisements, moreover, could be conveyed to consumers by much more economical means.

Even advertising designed to foster brand loyalty is defended by some economists. Although some of the differences between brands are illusory, brand identification makes significant product differentiation possible, with the result that consumers have more choices. Brand loyalty also facilitates mass-merchandizing, which lowers the per unit cost of goods, thereby benefiting consumers with lower prices. Consumers who are satisfied from past experience with a certain brand save time while shopping and avoid the risk of experiencing dissatisfaction with unknown brands.

A noted defender of advertising, the economist Phillip Nelson, argues that the amount of advertising for brand-name products is itself a kind of information.[12] The bestselling brands, he argues, are the ones consumers are generally satisfied with and purchase repeatedly. Because these brands are bestsellers, the manufacturers have an incentive to advertise them more heavily. The reason is that, other things being equal, each dollar spent advertising a product that consumers are more likely to buy will bring a greater return than a dollar spent advertising a less popular product. "Simply put," Nelson says, "it pays to advertise winners. It does not pay to advertise losers. In consequence, the brands that are advertised the most heavily are more likely to be winners."[13] A consumer can pick out the best products, therefore, by looking for those with the most advertising.

This argument assumes that being a bestselling product is, first, an indicator of value and, second, a cause and not an effect of heavy advertising. The bestseller list, for example, is not a reliable guide for book-lovers. The reason is that a bestseller is apt to cater to mass tastes, whereas book-lovers tend to prefer books with more limited appeal. In books, tastes differ widely, and where this is true, advertising will not indicate value. Where people want the same things from a product, though, a history of repeat purchases is generally significant. Possible exceptions are cases involving indistinguishable products, such as soaps and detergents, where heavy advertising is more likely to be a cause of their popularity rather than vice versa. A long list of advertising failures shows that no amount of advertising can sell a poor product. However, the amount of advertising is also a reflection of the resources that companies have available. A large, profitable company with an inferior product can afford to spend more on advertising than a small, struggling company with a superior product. Thus, advertising can be used to give large, successful companies a competitive edge.

Advertising is further defended on the grounds that even if some resources are wasted, the overall effect is to create an expanding market with more plentiful and cheaper consumer goods and an increasing number of higher paying jobs. There is no guarantee, moreover, that the resources currently devoted to advertising would be utilized more efficiently for other purposes, especially in a surplus economy. Finally, since advertising is only one of many methods of marketing, it is likely that some of the money saved by cutting back on advertising would still be spent on other marketing methods, some of which are less efficient than advertising.[14]

The Charge That Advertising Is Inefficient

The basis of the second charge—that advertising interferes with the efficient operation of a free market—is that advertising enables large firms with well-established brand-name products to create and maintain monopoly conditions.[15] Massive advertising campaigns by industry leaders serve not only to protect their market share but also to prevent the entry of new and smaller firms into the market. Brand loyalty and artificial product differentiation, which advertising makes possible, tend toward the same end.

In 1970, for example, the Federal Trade Commission issued a report, *Influence of Market Structure on Profit Performance of Food Manufacturing Companies*, accusing the major cereal manufacturers of monopolizing the ready-to-eat breakfast cereal market, in part by the extensive use of advertising.[16] The advertising budgets of the "Big Four"—Kellogg, General Mills, General Foods, and Quaker Oats—which had 91 percent of the market, averaged 18 percent of annual sales, according to the report. (The average for the food industry is 5.3 percent.)[17] Such a high proportion of advertising to sales could not be justified, the FTC claimed, by the return on the amount spent and was designed to keep competitors out of the market. Similarly, the proliferation of new brands by these companies (150 between 1950 and 1970) had the intended effect of stifling competition by outsiders.

Heavy advertising obviously raises the price of products, since the cost is passed along to the consumer. The FTC estimated, for example, that the price of ready-to-eat cereals would be between 15 and 25 percent lower with more reasonable levels of advertising. In addition, the effect of monopoly is to reduce competition, so that manufacturers are able to raise prices above what fully competitive market conditions would allow. Advertising also encourages nonprice competition, thus enabling the members of the Big Four to compete with each other by increasing their advertising budgets rather than reducing prices. Possible savings to consumers, then, are diverted to other uses.

Defenses to the Charge of Inefficiency

The defenders of advertising hold that advertising does not promote monopoly but in fact fosters competition.[18] If the critics are right, then there should be a positive correlation between the extent of monopoly and the amount of advertising as a percentage of sales and a negative correlation with the rate of product turnover. That is, firms in more concentrated industries should devote a higher proportion of revenues to advertising and introduce fewer new products. But no such patterns have been found. Further, advertising facilitates rather than bars market entry, according to the defenders, since it enables firms to inform the public about new products. Some evidence for this view is provided by studies showing that new products are more intensively advertised than old ones.

In addition, there is some theoretical and empirical support for the conclusion that advertising has the effect of lowering prices instead of raising them. Theoretically, advertising should lower prices by reducing the per unit cost of products (because of increased volume) and the sales cost (that is, the cost of making a sale to a customer). Prices should also fall when advertising enables consumers to make price comparisons. The strongest support for this latter proposition comes from a well-known study by the economist Lee Bentham, who found that prices for eye examinations and eyeglasses in states that regulated advertising were almost double those in states with fewer restrictions.[19] Similar results have been obtained from studies of the prescription drug industry.[20]

Finally, defenders reply to the charge that advertising encourages nonprice competition by pointing out that there are many legitimate forms of competition. Instead of reducing prices, for example, manufacturers can offer a higher quality product at the same price—or spend more on advertising. Under competitive conditions, therefore, the decision to lower prices, raise quality, or advertise would be determined by whatever strategy produces the greatest profit. The market, therefore, encourages advertising only as long as it promotes efficiency, and firms that engage in inefficient advertising will be penalized with lower profits. The economist Yale Brozen also argues that if a shared monopoly existed in the cereal industry, as the FTC claimed, then the major firms would be expected to cut advertising in order to raise profits. So the high level of advertising by the Big Four reflects vigorous competition.[21]

Conclusion

In conclusion, the defenders have sufficiently strong arguments for maintaining that advertising has a legitimate role to play in a free market economy, especially when ads contain substantial information that enables consumers to make rational economic choices. The information-providing function of advertising is a weak foundation for building a justification, though, since advertising is a relatively inefficient means for providing consumers with information. Moreover, only ads that are primarily informative, such as classified ads in the newspaper or entries in the yellow pages, could be justified by such an argument. Of course, no advertising that is justified in this way could be deceptive or misleading.

However, providing consumers with information is not the purpose of advertising; it is, rather, to stimulate consumer demand. Although increased consumer demand provides benefits, such as more choices and lower prices, the major beneficiary is still the businesses that advertise. A drawback, therefore, is that the defenders' case is built on the benefits of advertising to consumers and the public at large, but decisions about advertising are made by companies with a view to their own welfare. There is some reason to question whether the welfare of consumers is always well served by such an arrangement. Certainly, benefit to consumers is not the driving force behind advertising, and there is an element of duplicity in arguments for advertising that (misleadingly) suggest that it is all done with the consumer in mind.

At bottom, the economic arguments justifying advertising are utilitarian in character; they appeal to the contribution advertising supposedly makes to the welfare of all members of society. If this is, indeed, the justification of advertising, then it can plausibly be maintained that, on balance, advertising does more good than harm and that the advertising we now have is better than no advertising at all. A utilitarian would insist, however, that advertising be done in a way that best promotes the well-being of society as a whole, and *that* would entail a very different kind of advertising than we have at present.

PERSUASION AND BEHAVIOR CONTROL

Vance Packard's revelations in *The Hidden Persuaders* were disturbing thirty years ago because of the possibility that advertisers have means of influence that we are powerless to resist. It is now fashionable to scoff at extreme claims about the potential of advertising for behavior control. We know that advertising and propaganda—advertising's political cousin—have limited power to change people's basic attitudes. Still, there is evidence that the techniques of modern advertising are reasonably successful in playing on natural human desires for security, acceptance, self-esteem, and the like so as to influence consumer choices. Constant exposure to advertising in general is bound to have some cumulative psychological effect in creating a consumer society.

Although there is no consensus on the extent of the power of advertising to persuade, there is no disputing the fact that this power is substantial. The major difference between critics of advertising and defenders is whether there is anything morally objectionable about the use of this power. What, if anything, is wrong with using the methods of Madison Avenue to bring about changes in consumer behavior? There are two closely related answers to this question. One is given primarily by economists and the other, by philosophers. Both of these answers contend that certain kinds of advertising cross the boundary between legitimate persuasion and unacceptable forms of behavior control.

The Dependence Effect

The economist John Kenneth Galbraith coined the term *dependence effect* to describe the fact that present-day industrial production is concerned not merely with turning out goods to satisfy the wants of consumers but also with creating the wants themselves. He has written:

> As a society becomes increasingly affluent, wants are increasingly created by the process by which they are satisfied. This may operate passively.

> Increases in consumption . . . act by suggestion or emulation to create wants. Or producers may proceed actively to create wants through advertising and salesmanship. Wants thus come to depend on output.[22]

The dependence effect, in turn, is a consequence of the increasingly planned nature of the American economy. New products with a proven consumer demand, such as a pain reliever, require advertising only for the purpose of competing with products already available. But the introduction of an unfamiliar product, such as (at one time) mouthwash, must be preceded by a campaign designed to ensure a receptive market. People who never before worried about "bad breath" now need to be made to feel that they have a problem that only gargling with mouthwash will solve.

The main significance of the dependence effect lies in the challenge it poses to a fundamental tenet of economic theory, which is that production is justified because it satisfies consumer demand. The defense offered by corporate leaders when they are criticized for applying their immense resources to seemingly nonessential consumer goods while ignoring pressing needs is, "We only give the public what it wants." These words are a hollow, self-serving excuse if, as Galbraith and others claim, these same corporations have a good deal to do with determining what the public wants. David Braybrooke has written, for example:

> The automobile companies have shaped the public's ideas about safety, and hence the wants related to safety: negatively, by suppressing information about the dangers of the cars that they produce; and positively, by extolling speed, and selling cars on the basis of power. Half a century of dilation on speed, power, and thrills have fostered and intensified wants that now seem questionable to many; and those who have the wants, without now questioning them, might be brought to revise them by perceiving the interested part that the automobile companies have played in instilling them.[23]

More technically, economic theory presupposes: (1) that the value of goods arises from their role in satisfying the needs and desires of consumers, and (2) that consumers themselves are the best judges of what will best satisfy their needs and desires. (This latter assumption is known as the principle of consumer sovereignty.) It follows that the optimal satisfaction of everyone's needs and desires will be achieved by allowing individuals to express their preferences in a free market. Producers of goods, therefore, do not need to ask whether people would be better off with more books and fewer television sets, since this question is best answered by the free choices of individual consumers.

Galbraith contends that there is a flaw in this argument:

> If the individual's wants are to be urgent they must be original with himself. They cannot be urgent if they must be contrived for him. And above all they must not be contrived by the process of production by which they are satisfied. For this means that the whole case for the urgency of production, based on the urgency of wants, falls to the ground. One cannot defend production as satisfying wants if that production creates the wants. . . . Production only fills a void that it has itself created.[24]

Furthermore, if Galbraith is right about the dependence effect, one cannot argue for the production of more goods on the grounds that the members of society will be better off. "The higher level of production," Galbraith says, "has, merely, a higher level of want creation, necessitating a higher level of want satisfaction."[25]

The significance of the dependence effect is not confined wholly to economic theory. The creation of wants, aided by advertising, is responsible for a conspicuous feature of American society, in Galbraith's view; namely, the imbalance between the private production of consumer goods and the level of public services. When advertising instills a strong desire for products that can be packaged and sold for a profit by a business firm but not for services—such as road maintenance, recreational areas, public health, police protection, and education—that are typically provided by government, the inevitable result is an abundance of the former and a dearth of the latter.

What Wants Are Worth Satisfying?

Galbraith's criticism of advertising has not gone unchallenged. The dependence effect, in Galbraith's formulation, involves a distinction between wants that originate in a person and those that are created by outside forces. F. A. von Hayek has pointed out that almost all wants beyond the most primitive needs for food, shelter, and sex are the result of cultural influences.[26] Thus, desires for art, music, and literature are no less *created* than desires for any consumer product. The creation of the former desires, moreover, is due in part to efforts by painters, composers, and novelists to earn a living. It is a complete non sequitur, therefore, to hold that wants that are created by the forces that also satisfy them are less urgent or important for that reason.

The point that Galbraith is trying to make is that some wants are more worth satisfying than others. What Hayek convincingly demonstrates is that the worth of a want cannot depend on its *source*—that is, on whether it originates within a person or is created by outside forces. A distinction between wants of greater and lesser worth, therefore, cannot be made in the way Galbraith proposes. It may still be possible, however, to rescue Galbraith's point—and with it, his criticism of advertising—by drawing the distinction in another way.

If some wants are more worth satisfying than others, then we need a criterion for making such a distinction. Alan H. Goldman suggests two ways in which a criterion for the worth of wants could be established.[27] One is by positing some ideal or hierarchy of ideals that expresses a conception of human excellence. According to a criterion of this kind, desires for aesthetic enjoyment and intellectual activity might be judged better than those for the accumulation of wealth. The major difficulty with this approach, however, is that people are likely to disagree on the appropriate ideals and their relative order, and there is no easy means for settling such disagreements to everyone's satisfaction. (Galbraith dryly observes, "Wealth is not without its advantages and the case to the contrary, although it has often been made, has never proved widely persuasive."[28])

A second way to establish a criterion for the worth of different wants, Goldman suggests, is by judging whether any given desire is *rational* for the person holding it. Rational desires are more worthy of fulfillment than irrational ones, if indeed irrational desires ought to be fulfilled at all. The success of this criterion depends obviously on developing an account of what makes one desire rational and another irrational.

An Account of Rational Desire

In one account, rationality is a matter of the suitability of a desire for achieving some end or purpose. More precisely, according to Goldman, a desire is *irrational*:

> . . . if (a) the object is desired as a means to something else but is unsuitable for that purpose; or if (b) fulfillment of that desire blocks the satisfaction of other desires that the individual would acknowledge as more important on the individual's own scale of values; or if (c) the costs of fulfilling that desire outweigh the satisfaction to be derived, again for the individual in question.[29]

Consider the desires that advertising creates for expensive brands of liquor or designer clothing by appealing to people's yearning for status. Real status is achieved by accomplishing something in life—or, less democratically, by being fortunate in the circumstances of birth. It is unlikely, in the absence of advertising, that the choice of a drink to serve guests and the name on the label of a garment—worn on the outside for all to see!—would even be thought of as a possible means for obtaining status. And any clear-headed person should see the absurdity of thinking that status could be achieved effectively by such means. These desires are irrational, according to the conditions set forth above, for reason (a): They are unsuitable for the intended purpose.

A defender of advertising can reply that people do not really believe (irrationally) that they are "buying" status in making certain consumer purchases. Rather, advertising has succeeded in surrounding some products with an aura of status, so that people derive a certain satisfaction from purchasing and using those products. Even people who know that there is no difference among vodkas, for example (by law, vodka can contain no flavoring ingredients and must consist solely of water and alcohol), may "feel" something by buying an expensive brand. If this particular "feeling" is what people want—and not status—then buying a heavily advertised, expensive brand of vodka might be a suitable means. In that case, the desire would not be irrational.

Consumer behavior suggests, however, that people really do make certain purchases because they want status and that they recognize subconsciously the irrationality of some of their desires. Vance Packard reported that in the 1950s people expressed reluctance to buy small cars because they were less safe. Research showed that a process of rationalization was taking place. What worried people was not physical safety but psychological safety; they feared that small cars would make them look small in the eyes of neighbors.[30] People wanted large cars for reasons of status but disguised their true motivation as a concern for safety. Today, many ads for luxury cars stress safety so that buyers can assure themselves of the rationality of their decisions, even though status is uppermost in their minds. (The headline of one ad asks, "How important is the elegance of Chrysler Fifth Avenue if it can't protect you in an emergency?")

A more convincing example, perhaps, is the appeal of much of the advertising for cigarettes directed at women. Studies have shown that many women equate smoking with thinness. Consequently, models in the ads are strikingly thin, and some brands of cigarettes are made with a long, thin shape, with such names as Virginia Slims. The desire that these ads create is irrational on all three of Goldman's grounds. Smoking has little to do with thinness and is certainly not a very effective means for achieving it. Assuming that a woman values health above thinness, smoking blocks the realization of a value that is more important for her. Finally, the costs of fulfilling a desire for thinness by smoking more than outweigh the satisfaction to be derived from being thin.

One final example: Advertising for instant coffee often attempts to create an aura of luxury and refinement. The subtle aim, according to some observers, is to reassure anxious consumers. To promote instant coffee for its convenience would be to stress the very factor users feel guilty about. They do not want to be reminded that they are too lazy to prepare freshly brewed coffee.

The second way of establishing a criterion is more satisfactory than the first. The conditions for rationality, unlike the ideal of human excellence, provide reasonably objective grounds for distinguishing between desires that are worth satisfying and those that are not. The resulting conclusion—that advertising is justified only to the extent that it creates rational desires—is compatible with a free market system that assumes that economic agents are rational. The main drawback is that, except for a few extreme examples, such as cigarette advertising that appeals to the desire of women for thinness, it is difficult to determine where to draw the line. Defenders of advertising can plausibly maintain that there is nothing irrational about wanting to buy an expensive brand of vodka, for example, or designer clothes because of an association with status.

There is a third way of establishing a criterion for judging desires, which also employs the concept of rationality. Instead of focusing on the content of desires, however, this approach is concerned with how desires come about. Rational desires are those that are formed by a person who is being rational. Or, irrational desires are those that are created by means that do not allow people to exercise their rationality. This third way is the same as the answer of some philosophers to the question of what is wrong with using the power of modern advertising to persuade consumers. So let us turn to this matter now.

Rational Persuasion

The main concern of philosophers with advertising is whether the influence it exerts on consumers is consistent with a respect for personal freedom or autonomy. Persuasion is a broad category that ranges from the laudable (such as guidance by parents and teachers) to the sinister (psychoactive drugs, psychosurgery, and torture, for example). Advertising does not involve such extreme methods, of course. Still advertising that cynically exploits deep-seated emotions or short-circuits logical thought processes can be criticized on the ground that it wrongfully deprives people of a certain amount of freedom in the making of consumer choices.

An advertising technique that might be faulted for this reason is subliminal communication. There is a story, possibly apocryphal, of an experiment in which a movie theater in New Jersey boosted sales of ice cream by flashing split-second messages on the screen during the regular showing of a film.[31] Several other studies have reported a decrease in shoplifting in department stores when exhortations against stealing were mixed with the background music being piped over speakers.[32] A related form of unconscious, if not subliminal, communication is the conspicuous placement of brand-name products in movies, a practice known as *product placement.*[33]

Although many people believe that subliminal communication is a commonly used technique in advertising,[34] there is little evidence to establish either its frequency or its effectiveness.[35] It might seem scarcely worth exploring the ethical issues in subliminal communication, therefore, except for the help it provides in understanding the concept of rational persuasion, which is relevant to the ethical evaluation of advertising generally.

What Is Wrong with Subliminal Ads?

The ethical argument against the use of subliminal communication in advertising—assuming that it is effective in influencing consumer behavior—is quite simple. Richard T. DeGeorge expressed it in the following way:

> Subliminal advertising is manipulative because it acts on us without our knowledge, and hence without our consent. If an ad appears on TV, we can tune it out or change stations if we do not want to be subject to it. If an ad appears in a magazine, we are not forced to look at it. In either case, if we do choose to look and listen, we can consciously evaluate what we see and hear. We can, if we wish, take a critical stance toward the advertisement. All of this is impossible with subliminal advertising, because we are unaware that we are being subjected to the message. The advertiser is imposing his message on us without our knowledge and consent.[36]

A similar argument can be made against product placement. Because moviegoers are unaware that advertising is being directed at them, they may not be prepared to evaluate it critically. Ads in newspapers and magazines and on television are clearly identified as such, so that we can separate them from news, entertainment, and other elements and treat them accordingly. Plugs in movies, under the guise of entertainment, catch us unawares, without our critical faculties at work, so to speak. We are not able to subject them to the same scrutiny as other ads because we do not recognize them for what they are.[37]

In both of these arguments, the main complaint is that certain advertising techniques—namely, subliminal communication and product placement—do not allow people to use their capacity for critical evaluation. The significance of this capacity lies in the role that it plays in freedom of choice. In the view of many philosophers, a choice is free to the extent that a person makes it on the basis of reasons that are considered by that person to be good reasons for acting. Freedom, in this view, is compatible with persuasion, but only as long as the techniques used do not undermine the ability of people to evaluate reasons for or against a course of action.

One kind of persuasion that enables people to evaluate reasons is rational argument. Advertising does not compare favorably with the dialogues of Plato as a model of reasoned discourse, but there is some argumentation in advertising, especially in the print media. Ads that cite good reasons for buying a product (by showing its uses, for example) or preferring one product over another (such as low cost or better quality) make a rational appeal to consumers and permit them to evaluate the reasons and decide for themselves. Ads of this kind may still be objectionable on other grounds, however. The claim that a low-tar cigarette is safer than other brands, for example, accompanied by data to back it up, makes a rational appeal to health-conscious smokers. But as long as ads are truthful and do not mislead—that is, as long as they contain respectable arguments—they cannot be faulted for depriving consumers of freedom. What makes an ad misleading is, of course, a critical issue. An ad can be deceptive for leaving out certain information, and some critics charge that ads that make an implied health claim for a patently unhealthy product are inherently deceptive. (These matters are discussed in the next section.)

Most attempts at persuasion, including those that involve rational argument, make some emotional or other nonrational appeal. A suitor is unlikely to win the heart of his beloved with logical arguments alone; a romantic setting with candlelight and soft music improves the chances of success. Courtroom lawyers do not rely solely on strong legal arguments to win cases but also on their ability to play on the feelings of jurors.[38] Similarly, good advertising appeals on many levels; it is aesthetically pleasing, intellectually stimulating, and often humorous or heartwarming. In all these examples, both rational and nonrational elements are combined for greater effect than could be achieved by using one element alone. In none of them, however, is a person necessarily being deprived of freedom of choice.

Persuasion and Freedom of Choice

What kind of persuasion, then, would deprive a person of freedom of choice? One possibility put forth by several philosophers is that it is nonrational persuasion that a person could not reasonably be expected to resist.[39] This is a very promising approach, but more needs to be said about what constitutes nonrational persuasion and what a person can reasonably be expected to resist. The dividing line between rational and nonrational persuasion is not easy to draw and may turn out in the end to presuppose some account of rational desire. A person may be rationally persuaded by ads that demonstrate the effectiveness of a brand of deodorant, for example. But does the ad make a rational appeal if the desire for a deodorant itself rests on an irrational association with social acceptability or sexual attractiveness?

Even more difficult, though, is drawing the line between resistible and irresistible influences. Stanley I. Benn holds that one test is whether people can be aware of what is happening to them.[40] By this test, he suggests, subliminal communication is probably objectionable because it operates subconsciously. Other possibilities include political propaganda in a closed society that suppresses all contrary views and advertising directed at children, who have not formed the capacity for critical judgment. Beyond these obvious cases, however, the test is not specific enough to be useful. How much do people have to be able to know, for example, about what is happening to them?

For the test suggested by Benn to be accepted, more psychological research would have to be done into the effects of advertising and other forms of mass communication in order to say with any assurance what people can and cannot resist. We would also need a better understanding of the motivation for choices that are generally considered to be free.[41] If, as psychologists such as B. F. Skinner maintain, our choices are the result of operant conditioning, then freedom is an illusion and the reasons that we give are mere rationalizations. Even if this extreme position is mistaken, probably more of our choices are shaped by outside forces than we would like to admit.

Finally, it may be that an adequate criterion must consider the *ends* for which techniques of persuasion are used and not merely the techniques themselves, considered as *means*. Public health programs employing slick Madison Avenue campaigns, for example, are not usually thought to be objectionable. But if ads to induce people to smoke and antismoking ads both employ the same nonrational techniques of persuasion—including some that people cannot reasonably be expected to resist—then the moral difference between them cannot be solely a matter of the morality of the means. Although some techniques, such as subliminal communication, may be morally unacceptable means no matter how worthy the end, most of the techniques of advertisers can be put to morally acceptable uses. However, if the morality of advertising depends, at least in part, on the ends for which certain techniques are used, then the third criterion is incomplete, and it may be necessary to supplement it with some ideal of human excellence (the first criterion) or a conception of rational desire (the second criterion).

Conclusion

The concerns of economists and philosophers—the former with the creation of wants and the latter with the threat to freedom or autonomy—pose significant challenges to the morality of advertising. Although sweeping charges against advertising as a general practice are unwarranted, there is still an undeniable potential for behavior control that requires advertisers to act in a responsible manner. The major difficulty is finding a precise way of determining what constitutes responsible use of the persuasive power of advertising. Benn's proposal that advertising is morally objectionable when it uses nonrational forms of persuasion which we are unable to resist is sufficient to rule out certain kinds of ads and raise questions about others. However, this criterion is concerned with the ability of people to resist the effects of individual ads but not the barrage of commercial messages that we encounter every day. Even if all ads are resistible individually, it does not follow that even the most rational of us can remain unaffected by the sheer volume of ads around us.

DECEPTIVE ADVERTISING

COLDS-CATCHING SEASON IS HERE AGAIN! NOTHING CAN COLD-PROOF YOU—BUT LISTERINE ANTISEPTIC GIVES YOU A FIGHTING CHANCE! FOR FEWER COLDS, MILDER COLDS, TRY THIS:

GET PLENTY OF REST.

WATCH YOUR DIET.

GARGLE TWICE A DAY WITH FULL-STRENGTH LISTERINE.

FIGHT BACK WITH LISTERINE ANTISEPTIC. GARGLE TWICE A DAY—STARTING NOW—BEFORE YOU GET A COLD. YOU MAY FIND THE COLDS YOU DO GET WILL BE MILDER, LESS SEVERE. THAT'S WHY MORE PEOPLE USE LISTERINE DURING THE COLDS-CATCHING SEASON THAN ANY OTHER ORAL ANTISEPTIC. WHY DON'T YOU?

TESTS OVER A 12-YEAR PERIOD PROVED THAT PEOPLE WHO GARGLE WITH LISTERINE TWICE A DAY HAD FEWER COLDS, MILDER COLDS THAN THOSE WHO DID NOT. HAVE YOUR FAMILY TRY IT.

These are a few of the claims made in print advertising for Listerine Antiseptic that the Federal Trade Commission found deceptive.[42] In a 1975 ruling, the FTC ordered the Warner-Lambert Company, the manufacturer of Listerine, to stop representing, either directly or by implication, that the product would prevent or cure colds or have any effect on the severity of colds.

In support of its position, the FTC relied on medical experts, who testified that colds are infections caused by a virus inhaled through the nose and that no substance has been shown to have any effect on the frequency of colds or their duration or severity. Also, the claim that Listerine "kills millions of germs on contact" is of no medical significance, since bacteria do not cause colds; and the area gargling reaches, namely, the throat, is not the site of the infection. The FTC did not dispute the claim that gargling with Listerine relieves the discomfort of a sore throat. But this effect is achieved by removing accumulated debris from the forward part of the throat, and gargling with any warm liquid is just as effective.

Warner-Lambert executives vigorously disputed the findings of the FTC. First, they denied that the company advertised that Listerine cured colds or by itself prevented colds or sore throats. Rather, they claimed that use of Listerine in conjunction with proper diet and rest resulted in fewer, less severe colds. Second, the executives maintained that the company backed up its claims with substantial evidence and that this evidence had been misunderstood or ignored by the FTC. At issue were two clinical studies. One, the Reddish test, was conducted between 1932 and 1942 with 2,500 subjects drawn from the company's own work force. The second study involved more than 4,000 students at St. Barnabas elementary school who were tested over a four-year period, from 1967 to 1971. Both the Reddish test and the St. Barnabas study purportedly showed that the subjects who gargled with Listerine had less severe colds, and the results of the Reddish test also showed that they had fewer colds that lasted a shorter period of time.

What Is Deception?

Whether the ads for Listerine are deceptive is not easy to determine. The main source of the difficulty is the concept of deception itself, which does not have a clear, settled meaning. As a first approximation, something is deceptive if it has a tendency to deceive. In this definition, the deceptiveness of an ad does not depend solely on the truth or falsity of the claims made in it but also on the impact the ad has on the people who see or hear it. It is possible for advertising to contain false claims without being deceptive and for advertising to be deceptive without containing any false claims.

A patently false claim—for a hair restorer, for example—might not actually deceive anyone or even have the potential to do so. Furthermore, there are other advertising claims that are false if taken literally but are commonly regarded as harmless exaggerations or bits of puffery.[43] Every razor blade, for example, gives the closest, most comfortable shave; every tire, the smoothest, safest ride; and every pain reliever, the quickest, gentlest relief. Few people are deceived by such hyperbole—or, apparently, bothered by the logical inconsistency of two different brands both being the safest or the gentlest. Even if no one is deceived, however, it does not follow that such claims are not objectionable for other reasons, such as the debasement of the language, which Heilbroner has cited.

Similarly, we are not misled by the claims that Avis tries harder (the latest version is "We're trying harder than ever") or that Gallo releases no wine before its time. Expressions such as these are usually regarded not as serious claims to truth but as suggestive rhetorical devices. Some ad copy, furthermore, has no determinate meaning at all and cannot be characterized as either true or false. Examples are pointless comparisons, such as claims that a cleaner is new and improved or 50 percent more effective, and inane jingles such as "Things go better with Coke" and "Chevrolet—the Heartbeat of America."

Some writers even defend the literal falsehoods and meaningless babble of advertising as legitimate and even socially desirable. Perhaps the best known of these defenders is Theodore Levitt, who compares advertising to poetry:

> Like advertising, poetry's purpose is to influence an audience; to affect its perceptions and sensibilities; perhaps even to change its mind. . . . [P]oetry's intent is to convince and seduce. In the service of that intent, it employs without guilt or fear of criticism all the arcane tools of distortion that the literary mind can devise. Keats does not offer a truthful engineering description of his Grecian urn. He offers, instead, . . . a lyrical, exaggerated, distorted, and palpably false description. And he is thoroughly applauded for it, as are all other artists, in whatever medium, who do precisely this same thing successfully.
>
> Commerce, it can be said without apology, takes essentially the same liberties with reality and literality as the artist, except that commerce calls its creations advertising. . . . As with art, the purpose is to influence the audience by creating illusions, symbols, and implications that promise more than pure functionality. . . .[44]

In order to see that true claims can still be deceptive, consider an ad for Anacin that prompted a complaint by the FTC in 1973. The ad asserted that Anacin has a unique pain-killing formula that is superior to all other nonprescription analgesics. Anacin is composed of two active ingredients, aspirin (400 milligrams) and caffeine (32.5 milligrams), but the sole pain-relieving component is aspirin. Aspirin itself is unique—if indeed it makes any sense to describe a chemical compound in this way—and at the time, aspirin was superior to any other pain-reliever available without a prescription. Therefore, it is literally true that Anacin contains a unique and superior pain-killing formula: aspirin. The impression that the ad conveyed, however, was that only Anacin has this superior pain-relieving ingredient (false) and that consequently Anacin itself is superior to competing brands of analgesics containing aspirin (also false).

The basis of the FTC complaint, therefore, was not that the claims made for Anacin are literally false but that they gave rise to, or were likely to give rise to, false beliefs in the minds of consumers. Similarly, ads for Listerine never stated that gargling with the product by itself actually prevents or cures colds. Some ads even caution that nothing can "cold-proof" a person. Still, many readers of the phrases "fewer colds, milder colds" and "fighting chance" undoubtedly drew this inference, and the wording seems to have been intended to produce this effect.

Ads for Anacin also claimed that it causes less frequent side effects. The position of the FTC is that the deceptiveness of this claim does not depend solely on whether it is true or false but also on whether the manufacturer, American Home Products, had sufficient evidence to back it up. That is, unsupported claims that turn out to be true are still deceptive, since, in the words of the court, "a consumer is entitled to assume that the appropriate verification has been performed." Even if Anacin does cause less frequent side effects, the consumer is deceived by being led to believe that there is evidence for the claim when there is not. In order to make comparative claims of superiority that are nondeceptive, therefore, drug companies have a responsibility to conduct scientifically valid clinical studies.

In a more recent case, Bristol-Myers Squibb was ordered to stop advertising that its product Aspirin-Free Excedrin was more effective than Tylenol, made by Johnson & Johnson. Both contain 500 milligrams of the pain-reliever acetaminophen, but Aspirin-Free Excedrin also contains 65 milligrams of caffeine, which Bristol-Myers claims enhances the effectiveness of the product. A judge ruled that this claim has not been substantiated, however, and so cannot be made in advertising.[45]

Even clinical studies may not be sufficient, however. Executives of Warner-Lambert contended that the two studies supported the claims made in ads for Listerine. But the administrative law judge who decided the FTC complaint found the studies to be seriously flawed. The Reddish test was conducted by investigators who were already convinced of the effectiveness of Listerine, and the subjects were mainly Listerine employees, who had an interest in securing favorable results. The subjects were also allowed to choose their group, with the result that subjects who thought that gargling was effective in treating a cold would be more likely to join the test group. Both studies lacked a true placebo. Some subjects in the control groups gargled with tap water or, in the St. Barnabas study, with an amber-colored liquid without the medicinal taste of Listerine. Further bias was thus introduced by the fact that members of each group knew whether they were receiving treatment for a cold. These sources of bias are all the more serious in view of the need to rely on subjective evaluations of the severity of cold symptoms. Also, the examining doctor in the St. Barnabas study was not properly "blinded," since it was possible to tell from their breath which students had gargled with Listerine.

Whether a claim is deceptive, therefore, depends, in some cases, on the strength of the evidence for it. Even if claims are true and supported by some evidence, they are still deceptive if the amount of evidence is less than consumers, viewing an ad, would reasonably be led to expect. Consequently, the resolution of some disputes over the deceptiveness of a claim in an ad depend ultimately on the judgment of experts in scientific methodology.

A More Precise Definition of Deception

The rough definition of deception that has been developed so far is not adequate, either for increasing our understanding of the ethical issues in deceptive advertising or for enforcing a legal prohibition against it. Unfortunately, the FTC has yet to offer a precise legal definition, and none of the attempts by marketing theorists and others to define deception in advertising has been entirely successful.

A frequently cited definition, offered by David M. Gardner, is as follows:

> If an advertisement (or advertising campaign) leaves the consumer with an impressions(s) and/or belief(s) different from what would normally be expected if the consumer had reasonable knowledge, and that impression(s) and/or belief(s) is factually untrue or potentially misleading, then deception is said to exist.[46]

In this definition, deception occurs if after being exposed to an ad a consumer has impressions or beliefs that do not constitute reasonable knowledge and those impressions or beliefs are false or misleading.[47] A number of objections can be raised against this definition.

First, an ad is not deceptive merely for failing to ensure that a consumer has reasonable knowledge.[48] Otherwise, a person who believes that brushing every day eliminates the need for occasional visits to the dentist would be deceived by a toothpaste ad that (truthfully) promoted the benefits of daily brushing without suggesting in the least that users could skip regular dental checkups. Yet, in Gardner's definition such an ad would be deceptive, since the belief that the person is left with is different from that which the person would be expected to have if the person had reasonable knowledge and the belief is false.

Second, the definition counts any ad as deceptive that leaves a person with unreasonable knowledge without regard for whether the fault lies with the ad or with the person. Ivan Preston recounts the story of an irate customer who failed to catch the joke in an ad for a novelty beer, Olde Frothingslosh, that proclaimed it to be the only beer with the foam on the bottom.[49] The customer was dissuaded from taking legal action by a lawyer who pointed out that the FTC does not consider an ad to be deceptive if it fools only a few extremely gullible people. That is, in deciding whether an ad is deceptive, the FTC considers *who* would be misled by an ad. Would it be misleading to any reasonable consumer or only to one who is extremely ignorant?

Consider, for example, whether it is deceptive for Clairol to advertise a dye that will "color hair permanently."[50] Most people know that hair grows, and so only a few, rather ignorant people are likely to be duped into believing that dyeing will never again be necessary. It is even less likely that many people would mistake a slogan used at one time for Ipana toothpaste—"the Smile of Beauty"—for a claim that the product straightens crooked teeth.[51] Both of these cases date from the 1940s, at which time a very literal-minded FTC generally enforced an ignorant consumer standard. Accordingly, these ads were found by the commission to be deceptive. Similar rulings would probably not be made today.

However, the FTC was called upon recently to make a ruling in a case against the Ford Motor Company in which data on a mileage test were accompanied by the following qualification:

> You yourself might actually average less, or for that matter more. Because mileage varies according to maintenance, equipment, total weight, driving habits and road conditions. And no two drivers, even cars, are exactly the same.[52]

Would a reasonably intelligent, well-informed person reading this carefully qualified claim conclude that the data given in the advertisement described the mileage for an *average* driver? The FTC, employing the more restrictive reasonable consumer standard, decided that it did and asked Ford for substantiation.

Third, there is the problem of what constitutes reasonable knowledge. Presumably this means the knowledge that is needed to make rational consumer choices. That is, the false impressions or beliefs conveyed by an ad must be "material" in the sense that they are likely to affect people's purchasing decisions to their detriment. An ad that gives people mistaken information about geography or literature is not for that reason alone deceptive. However, the knowledge needed for making rational consumer choices is an uncertain standard for determining whether deception exists. People always have less than perfect information, and no amount of advertising can clear away all the false impressions and beliefs that they have or, for that matter, avoid creating new ones. Gardner's definition cannot be used to determine whether an ad is deceptive, therefore, without specifying some standard of reasonable knowledge.

Patching Up the Definition

Several suggestions have been made for patching up this analysis of deception. One possible response to the first objection is to say that deception occurs only if the false impressions or beliefs are in some way *caused* by the ad in question.[53] But this is too strong. An ad would probably be considered deceptive if it reinforced or took advantage of an already existing false belief. Another ad for Listerine, for example, reads, "STRONG STUFF," no doubt to remind consumers of the medicinal claims planted in their minds by previous advertising. Also, advertisers did not create the link in the minds of some women between smoking and thinness but merely discovered and took advantage of it. Such appeals in cigarette advertising could still be regarded as deceptive.

An attempt might be made to overcome the second objection by specifying that the consumers in question are intelligent, knowledgeable adults; that is, the rational consumer standard could be built right into the definition. Thomas L. Carson, Richard E. Wokutch, and James E. Cox, Jr., point out that this is inadequate, since the resulting definition does not apply to deceptive advertising to children. They have proposed instead the following definition of deception:

> An advertisement is deceptive if it causes a significant percentage of potential consumers (i.e., those at whom it is directed or whose consumption behavior is likely to be influenced by it) to have false beliefs about the product.[54]

What constitutes a "significant percentage" remains to be specified, but this is not a serious problem. More crucial is the fact that this definition employs a causal analysis of deception, which has already been shown to be inadequate. Furthermore, any false belief about a product that is caused by an ad is sufficient, according to the revised definition, to make it deceptive. Both definitions, therefore, are vulnerable to the third objection.

In order to see the problem more fully, consider health claims in food advertising. The word *natural,* which usually means the absence of artificial ingredients, evokes images of wholesomeness in the minds of consumers. Yet many food products advertised as natural contain unhealthy concentrations of fat and sugar and are deficient in vitamins and minerals.[55] In response to concerns about refined sugar, some manufacturers are switching to more natural-sounding brown sugar and honey, despite the fact that from a nutritional point of view all sugar provides the same empty calories. The makers of some brands of peanut butter advertise their products as cholesterol free even though cholesterol is present only in animal fats, so no brand of peanut butter contains any cholesterol.

Is it deceptive for food advertising to make use of terms such as *natural, sugar free,* and *no cholesterol?* In Gardner's definition, the answer to this question depends on what people with reasonable knowledge know, a matter which is by no means easy to determine.[56] In the revised definition, the answer depends only on whether the use of these terms causes a substantial percentage of potential consumers to have false beliefs about the product. Again, allowance needs to be made for ads that do not create but merely take advantage of the false beliefs of consumers, and the false beliefs need to be limited to those relevant to consumer choice.

A Final Definition

The root of the problem is that deception in advertising is a normative concept. Consequently, it cannot be adequately expressed by purely factual definitions of the kind considered so far. A more satisfactory definition, therefore, is the following:

> Deception occurs when a false belief, which an advertisement either creates or takes advantage of, substantially interferes with the ability of people to make rational consumer choices.

Advertising is not intended to produce knowledgeable consumers, and so it should not be faulted for every failure to do so. Also, not every false belief is of such importance that consumers should be protected from it. But there is still a certain standard of rational consumer behavior, and advertising is deceptive when it achieves its effect by false beliefs that prevent consumers from attaining this standard.

In this definition, deception in advertising is one form of illegitimate persuasion of the kind examined in the previous section. The objection to subliminal advertising and some other persuasive techniques is that they keep people from being able to evaluate the reasons for or against a course of action, thereby depriving them of a certain amount of freedom. Outright lies in advertising, along with more subtle deceptive claims, similarly constitute morally objectionable forms of behavior control.

One shortcoming of this definition is that the concept of a rational consumer choice is left undefined. Any definition of deception is unavoidably normative, however, which is to say that deception must be defined in terms of some other concept that embodies a standard of right and wrong. We have already seen that a purely factual definition cannot work. Any adequate definition, therefore, will contain at least one undefined normative term. The virtue of this definition is that it shows the relation between the ethical objections to behavior control, discussed in the last section, and deception, the subject of this section.

Whether an ad *substantially interferes* with the ability of people to make rational consumer choices assumes some view of what choices they would make if they were not influenced by an ad. Advertisers have no responsibility to ensure that people make rational consumer choices. But when their ads lead people to make choices they would not have made otherwise, they bear some responsibility. Since the aim of advertising is precisely to change (or reinforce) behavior so that people make different choices than they would otherwise, advertisers almost always bear this responsibility. Advertising is laudable to the extent that is enables consumers to make rational choices, but it is objectionable when the result is to interfere with this ability. Not all interference warrants the same degree of concern, however, and the notion of substantial interference sets a threshold beyond which advertising ought not to go.

At least two factors are relevant to the notion of substantial interference. One is the ability of consumers to protect themselves and make rational choices despite advertising that creates or takes advantage of false beliefs. Thus, claims that are easily verified or not taken seriously by consumers are not necessarily deceptive. The second factor is the seriousness of the choice that consumers make. False beliefs that affect the choices we make about our health or financial affairs are of greater concern than false beliefs that bear on inconsequential purchases. Claims in life insurance advertising, for example, ought to be held to a higher standard than those for chewing gum.

Both of these factors can be observed in two cases involving the Campbell Soup Company. Campbell ran afoul of the FTC in 1970 when they ran television ads showing a bowl of vegetable soup chock-full of solids.[57] This effect was achieved by placing clear-glass marbles on the bottom of the bowl to hold the solids near the surface. How does this case differ from one in which clear-plastic cubes are used instead of real ice in ads for cold drinks? In each case, false beliefs are created in consumers' minds. The false beliefs that viewers have about the contents of a glass of iced tea as a result of using plastic cubes have no bearing on a decision to purchase the product (an iced tea mix, for example), whereas a decision to purchase a can of Campbell's vegetable soup can definitely be influenced by the false belief created by the glass marbles. Consumers who buy the soup in the belief that the bowl at home will look like the one in the ad will be disappointed, but not the consumers who buy the iced tea mix. The ads have the potential, therefore, to interfere in the ability of consumers to make rational choices. Whether the interference is substantial is open to question, however. Consumers are able to verify the contents of Campbell's vegetable soup for themselves, and the stakes are relatively low. (A possible reply is that the ads create an impression of "richness" of Campbell soups, which is not eradicated by the consumer's own experience with them.)

In 1991, the Campbell Soup Company was charged again by the FTC for ads stressing the low-fat, low-cholesterol content of some of its soups and linking these qualities to a reduced risk of heart disease.[58] The soups in question have reduced amounts of fat and cholesterol, but the ads failed to mention that they are high in sodium, which increases the risk of some forms of heart disease. In the FTC's judgment, Campbell was implying that their soup could be part of a diet that reduces heart disease, while at the same time refusing to tell consumers how much sodium the soups contain or that salt should be avoided by people concerned about heart disease. Consumers who are unaware of the salt content of canned soups might purchase Campbell products as part of a diet aimed at reducing the risk of heart disease. In so doing, they would be better off buying these products than high-salt soups that are also high in fat and cholesterol. But health-conscious consumers who are aware of the salt content might well make different, more rational consumer purchases instead.

Although these ads may not directly cause consumers to have false beliefs about certain Campbell products, the campaign depends for its success on consumer ignorance about the salt content of its soups and the link between salt and heart disease and thus takes advantage of this fact. Whether Campbell would have an obligation to reveal the sodium content of its soups if it did not make health claims is debatable, but having made claims designed to lead people concerned about heart disease to buy their products, Campbell definitely has such an obligation. (Campbell eventually agreed to reveal the sodium content in ads for soups with more than 500 milligrams of sodium in an eight-ounce serving.[59]) The health claims made on behalf of some Campbell soups also involve the two factors that are a part of *substantial interference*. The salt content of a soup, unlike the amount of vegetable solids, cannot be easily verified by consumers, and the decisions consumers make to protect their health are of great importance. Accordingly, the FTC rigorously scrutinizes health claims in ads and holds them to a higher standard.

Conclusion

The evaluation of advertising in this chapter proceeds on several levels. Charges that advertising is inefficient and manipulative are concerned primarily with advertising as a general practice or with certain advertising techniques. The charge of deception in advertising is directed, by contrast, at the content of specific advertisements and, in particular, the claims made or implied by them. One principle for evaluating advertising is utilitarian. Are we better or worse off with advertising? Does advertising as a practice or do individual ads promote or diminish the welfare of society as a whole? Both manipulative and deceptive advertising are objectionable, according to utilitarianism, for the reason that they harm consumers. A second principle, which ties together the latter two charges, is one based on the Kantian theme of rationality. Consumers ought to be free to make choices that best satisfy their desires. The process of creating desires, which Galbraith calls the dependence effect, can be objected to not only because it prevents the realization of our other desires (a utilitarian reason) but also because it interferes with our ability to act on rational desires (a Kantian reason). The concept of deception, we have seen, assumes that consumers ought to be free to make rational consumer choices. Although advertisers may have no obligation to ensure that we make such choices, they have a negative duty not to create or take advantage of false beliefs that interfere significantly with our ability to make rational consumer choices.

NOTES

1. WILLIAM M. PRIDE and O. C. FERRELL, *Marketing: Basic Concepts and Decisions*, 4th ed. (Boston: Houghton Mifflin, 1985), 332.
2. See H. L. DARLING, "How Companies Are Using Corporate Advertising," *Public Relations Journal*, 31 (November 1975), 26–29; W. S. SACHS, "Corporate Advertising: Ends, Means, Problems," *Public Relations Journal*, 37 (November 1981), 14–17; and S. PRAKASH SETHI, "Institutional/Image Advertising and Idea/Issue Advertising as Marketing Tools: Some Public Policy Issues," *Journal of Marketing*, 47 (January 1983), 68–78.
3. See for example, RONALD HUMPHREY and HOWARD SCHUMAN, "The Portrayal of Blacks in Magazine Advertisements: 1950–1982," *Public Opinion Quarterly*, 48 (1984), 551–63; JAMES U. McNEAL, "Advertising's Disparagement of American Workers," *Business Horizons* (January–February 1983), 7–12; and BRIAN KVASNICKA, BARBARA BEYMER, and RICHARD M. PERLOFF, "Portrayals of the Elderly in Magazine Advertisements," *Journalism Quarterly*, 59 (1982), 656–58.
4. CHRISTOPHER LASCH, *The Culture of Narcissism* (New York: W. W. Norton, 1978), 72.
5. ROBERT HEILBRONER, "The Supply Side Fad," *New York Review of Books*, June 11, 1981, 40.
6. JULES HENRY, *Culture Against Man* (New York: Random House, 1963), 46–48.
7. VANCE PACKARD, *The Hidden Persuaders* (New York: David McKay, 1957), 20–21.
8. PACKARD, *The Hidden Persuaders*, 25.
9. The FTC also has the authority to regulate "unfair" advertising as well as unfair trade practices generally. The meaning of unfairness in advertising has never been clearly defined, however. See DOROTHY COHEN, "Unfairness in Advertising Revisited," *Journal of Marketing*, 46 (Winter 1982), 73–80.
10. This is the question in *American Home Products* v. *FTC*, 695 F.2d 681 (1982).
11. *In the Matter of Warner-Lambert, Federal Trade Commission Decisions*, 86 (July 1, 1975, to December 31, 1975).
12. See PHILLIP NELSON, "Advertising and Ethics," in RICHARD T. DeGEORGE and JOSEPH A. PICHLER, eds., *Ethics, Free Enterprise, and Public Policy* (New York: Oxford University Press, 1978), 187–98.
13. NELSON, "Advertising and Ethics," 190.
14. These points are made in JULES BACKMAN, "Is Advertising Wasteful?" *Journal of Marketing*, 32 (January 1968), 2–8.

15. The foremost advocates of this view are EDWARD CHAMBERLAIN, *The Theory of Monopolistic Competition* (Cambridge: Harvard University Press, 1933); NICHOLAS H. KALDOR, "The Economic Aspects of Advertising," *The Review of Economic Studies*, 18 (1950–51), 1–27; and WILLIAM S. COMANOR and THOMAS A. WILSON, *Advertising and Market Power* (Cambridge: Harvard University Press, 1975).

16. Material on this case is taken from EARL A. MOLANDER, "Marketing Ready-to-Eat Breakfast Cereals at the Kellogg Company," in *Responsive Capitalism: Case Studies in Corporate Social Responsibility* (New York: McGraw-Hill, 1980), 128–43.

17. DONALD TULL and LYNN KAHLE, *Marketing Management* (New York: Macmillan, 1990), 498.

18. The main defenders of advertising against the charge of being an anticompetitive practice are LESTER G. TELSER and YALE BROZEN. See TELSER, "Advertising and Competition," *Journal of Political Economy*, 72 (1964), 537–62; "Some Aspects of the Economics of Advertising," *Journal of Business* (April 1968), 166–73; and BROZEN, "Advertising, the Consumer and Inflation," in JOHN S. WRIGHT and JOHN E. MERTES, eds., *Advertising's Role in Society* (St. Paul: West Publishing Co., 1974), 86–92. For a survey of the literature, see JAMES M. FERGUSON, *Advertising and Competition: Theory and Measurement* (Cambridge: Ballinger, 1974).

19. LEE BENTHAM, "The Effect of Advertising on the Price of Eyeglasses," *Journal of Law and Economics*, 15 (1972), 337–52. See also ROBERT L. STEINER, "Does Advertising Lower Consumer Prices?" *Journal of Marketing*, 37 (October 1973), 19–26.

20. See KEITH B. LEFFLER, "Persuasion or Information? The Economics of Prescription Drug Advertising," *Journal of Law and Economics*, 24 (1981), 45–74.

21. BROZEN, "Advertising, the Consumer and Inflation," 90. One defect in this argument is that advertising currently enjoys a preferential tax status, so that it is more profitable for firms to advertise than to cut prices. In order for free market forces to allocate resources efficiently, advertising would have to be treated like any other expenditure for tax purposes, a move that manufacturers and the advertising industry vigorously oppose.

22. JOHN KENNETH GALBRAITH, *The Affluent Society* (New York: Houghton Mifflin, 1958), 128.

23. DAVID BRAYBROOKE, "Skepticism of Wants, and Certain Subversive Effects of Corporations on American Values," in SIDNEY HOOK, ed., *Human Values and Economic Policy* (New York: New York University Press, 1967), 229.

24. GALBRAITH, *The Affluent Society*, 124–25.

25. GALBRAITH, *The Affluent Society*, 128.

26. F. A. VON HAYEK, "The *Non Sequitur* of the 'Dependence Effect,'" *Southern Economic Journal*, 27 (April 1961), 346–48. Similar points are made in THEODORE LEVITT, "The Morality (?) of Advertising," *Harvard Business Review*, 48 (July–August 1970), 84–92.

27. ALAN H. GOLDMAN, "Ethical Issues in Advertising," in TOM REGAN, ed., *Just Business: New Introductory Essays in Business Ethics* (New York: Random House, 1984), 256–58. Much of the following discussion is indebted to this article.

28. GALBRAITH, *The Affluent Society*, 13.

29. GOLDMAN, "Ethical Issues in Advertising," 257.

30. PACKARD, *The Hidden Persuaders*, 110.
31. Cited in PACKARD, *The Hidden Persuaders*, 35.
32. For one example, see "Secret Voices: Messages That Manipulate," *Time*, September 10, 1979, 71.
33. See MICHAEL SCHUDSON, *Advertising, The Uneasy Persuasion: Its Dubious Impact on Society* (New York: Basic Books, 1984), 102–3.
34. See RALPH NORMAN HABER, "Public Attitudes Regarding Subliminal Advertising," *Public Opinion Quarterly*, 23 (1959), 291–93; and ERIC J. ZANOT, J. DAVID PINCUS, and E. JOSEPH LAMP, "Public Perceptions of Subliminal Advertising," *Journal of Advertising*, 12 (1983), 39–45.
35. A researcher who claims to find evidence for both the frequency and effectiveness of subliminal advertising is WILSON BRIAN KEY, who has written three books, *Subliminal Seduction* (Englewood Cliffs, NJ: Prentice Hall, 1974); *Media Sexploitation* (Englewood Cliffs, NJ: Prentice Hall, 1976); and *The Clam-Plate Orgy and Other Subliminal Techniques for Manipulating Your Behavior* (Englewood Cliffs, NJ: Prentice Hall, 1980). A generally negative appraisal of the effectiveness of the technique is offered in N. F. DIXON, *Subliminal Perception* (London: McGraw-Hill, 1971). For evidence specifically on advertising, see STEPHEN G. GEORGE and LUTHER B. JENNINGS, "Effect of Subliminal Stimuli on Consumer Behavior: Negative Evidence," *Perceptual and Motor Skills*, 41 (1975), 847–54; DEL I. HAWKINS, "The Effects of Subliminal Stimulation on Drive Level and Brand Preference," *Journal of Marketing Research*, 8, (1970) 322–26; and TIMOTHY E. MOORE, "Subliminal Advertising: What You See Is What You Get," *Journal of Marketing*, 46 (Spring 1982), 38–47.
36. RICHARD T. DEGEORGE, *Business Ethics*, 3rd ed. (New York: Macmillan, 1990), 232.
37. This is not the only grounds for objecting to product placement. Critics also cite the element of deception and the corrupting effect of product placement on the artistic integrity of movies.
38. Although this practice is generally accepted as legitimate persuasion, an interesting issue is posed by the increasing use of market research in jury selection and the formation of legal strategy. If lawyers start adopting the techniques of advertisers, then they could open themselves up to many of the same criticisms. See SCOTT M. SMITH, "Marketing Research and Corporate Litigation . . . Where Is the Balance of Ethical Justice?" *Journal of Business Ethics*, 3 (1984), 185–94.
39. This criterion is advanced by STANLEY I. BENN, "Freedom and Persuasion," *Australasian Journal of Philosophy*, 45 (1967), 267.
40. BENN, "Freedom and Persuasion," 269.
41. This point is made in GOLDMAN, "Ethical Issues in Advertising," 251.
42. *In the Matter of Warner-Lambert*. For case studies, see "The FTC and Listerine Antiseptic," *Harvard Business School*; and "Listerine Antiseptic, Colds, and Sore Throats," in TOM L. BEAUCHAMP, ed., *Case Studies in Business, Society, and Ethics*, 2nd ed. (Englewood Cliffs, NJ: Prentice Hall, 1989), 77–86.
43. For a thorough study of puffery, see IVAN L. PRESTON, *The Great American Blow-Up: Puffery in Advertising and Selling* (Madison: University of Wisconsin Press, 1975).

44. LEVITT, "The Morality (?) of Advertising," 85.
45. WADE LAMPERT and AMY DOCKSER MARCUS, "Judge Blocks an Excedrin Ad Campaign," *The Wall Street Journal*, December 18, 1990, p. B10.
46. DAVID M. GARDNER, "Deception in Advertising: A Conceptual Approach," *Journal of Marketing*, 39 (January 1975), 40–46.
47. This definition is open to several different interpretations. See THOMAS L. CARSON, RICHARD E. WOKUTCH, and JAMES E. COX, JR., "An Ethical Analysis of Deception in Advertising," *Journal of Business Ethics*, 4 (1985), 103, note 6.
48. This point is made in CARSON, WOKUTCH, and COX, "An Ethical Analysis of Deception in Advertising," 94–95.
49. IVAN L. PRESTON, "Reasonable or Ignorant Consumer? How the FTC Decides," *Journal of Consumer Affairs*, 8 (1974), 132.
50. *Gelb* v. *FTC*, 144 F.2d 580 (2d Cir. 1944).
51. 47 FTC 162 (1949).
52. Cited in JAMES C. MILLER, "Why FTC Curbs Are Needed," *Advertising Age*, March 22, 1982, 83.
53. CARSON, WOKUTCH, and COX respond in this way. They assert, "in order to count as deceptive an ad must be the cause of one's misinformation or lack of reasonable knowledge." "An Ethical Analysis of Deception in Advertising," 95.
54. CARSON, WOKUTCH, and COX, "Deceptive Advertising," 96.
55. See BONNIE LIEBMAN, "Nouveau Junk Food: Consumers Swallow the Back-to-Nature Bunk," *Business and Society Review*, 51 (Fall 1984), 47–51.
56. Gardner is aware of this problem and proposes a solution as part of a technique for measuring deception. Using what he calls the normative belief technique, "adequately informed consumers," which he defines as those who have the opportunity to acquire extensive information about a product, agree on an "optimal" set of functional attributes for a product. Research can then reveal the extent to which the beliefs of a wide range of consumers deviate from the beliefs of adequately informed consumers regarding the set of functional attributes. This technique does not solve the problem, however, since everything still depends on how much "adequately informed consumers" know—and also on what is an acceptable deviation—which is presumably determined, again, by "adequately informed consumers." See GARDNER, "Deception in Advertising," 44–45.
57. *Campbell Soup*, 77 FTC 664 (1970).
58. See JEANNE SADDLER, "Campbell Soup Will Change Ads to Settle Charges," *The Wall Street Journal*, April 9, 1991, p. B6.
59. "F.T.C. in Accord with Campbell," *The New York Times*, April 10, 1991, sec. 4, p. 4.

CHAPTER TWELVE

Marketing and Product Safety

When the Firestone Tire and Rubber Company began receiving complaints in 1972 about tread separation on the new Firestone 500 steel-belted radial tire, the cause was quickly identified as an "adhesion problem" resulting from a failure of the rubber to bond firmly to the wire cord in the belt.[1] A quality control specialist reported that in one of the company's own tests, "the rubber peeled cleanly from the wire." In an attempt to improve adhesion, Firestone altered the composition of the rubber by adding the chemical Resorcinol. The new material was in use at all the company's plants by the end of 1973, but the tire failures continued. Later, the problem was thought to be due to the presence of moisture in the rubber compound. The installation of equipment for an expensive "dry technology" method was completed in 1977, but this change also failed to solve the problem.

All the while, Firestone was having difficulty with the companies it supplied and its own dealers. General Motors and Ford, the major buyers of the 500 for the original equipment market, were expressing increasing dissatisfaction with the frequency of blowouts, and Firestone feared being cut off as a supplier to the Detroit giants. The company was also receiving complaints from retailers who sold the tire under their own brand name. The Atlas Tire Company dropped the Firestone 500 from their line, and Montgomery Ward successfully demanded a secret $500,000 payment in 1976 to compensate the company for excessive adjustment and replacement costs. Surveys of Firestone dealers found that the number of warranty claims by owners of defective 500s was continuing to rise.

Pressure also came from the federal government. The National Highway Traffic Safety Administration (NHTSA), under prodding by the Center for Auto Safety, a consumer interest group founded by Ralph Nader in 1970, began an investigation into the safety of steel-belted radial tires. NHTSA conducted a survey of owners of new cars equipped with radial tires and found an overwhelming number of complaints against the Firestone 500. Claiming that the survey was statistically invalid (a point NHTSA eventually conceded), the company went to court and succeeded in obtaining a restraining order against publication. But the results were leaked to the news media by the Center for Auto Safety on April 2, 1978. In May and June 1978, a congressional subcommittee began public hearings on the safety problems of the 500. When John Floberg, vice-president and general counsel of Firestone, attempted to defend the company before the subcommittee, he found himself being denounced by the chair of the committee for "merchandising accidents, death, and destruction."

Unfavorable news coverage added to Firestone's woes. Although the company was reported to have discontinued production of the 500 in 1976, a story in the *Miami Herald* in May 1978 revealed that Firestone had actually phased out production of the troubled tire over a period of eighteen months, so that the last 500 came off the assembly line in April 1978. In the same month, other newspaper stories reported that Firestone was selling the 500 in some southeastern states at half price in an apparent effort to dump the remaining stock. The crowning blow came from a front-page story in the Sunday, July 23, edition of the local Akron *Beacon Journal*, which carried the headline "FIRESTONE KNEW OF BAD TIRES." Based on a 1975 company report that the newspaper obtained from an anonymous inside source known as "Deep Tread," the story reported how 26 of 46 tires (more than 56 percent) failed a required Department of Transportation high-speed test.

By 1978, more than 14,000 tire failures had been attributed to the Firestone 500, resulting in 41 deaths and at least 65 injuries. The company was faced with 250 civil suits by individuals and several class action suits. Throughout the controversy, Firestone executives continued to deny that the 500 was significantly less safe than other steel-belted radials on the market. But on October 20, 1978, the company announced a massive voluntary recall that had been worked out with the Department of Transportation, affecting approximately ten million tires. The cost of the recall was estimated by Firestone to be as much as $135 million after taxes, and the company expected to have a loss for the fiscal year 1978.

The Firestone 500 case illustrates some of the ethical problems that marketers face. The initial decision to produce a steel-belted radial was dictated by trends in the highly competitive tire industry. After the introduction of the new product by foreign companies in the late 1960s, the race was on to capture the market, especially in sales of original equipment tires to Detroit. In order to win the race, Firestone took a few shortcuts. These included modifying existing plants rather than building new facilities with equipment especially designed for radial tire production and going ahead with an unproven technology before all the problems were worked out. With a very narrow profit margin on tires (approximately 10 percent before taxes), the amount that Firestone could spend on developing a safer product was limited.

A number of ethically questionable decisions were made after the introduction of the Firestone 500 in response to the wide range of problems that developed as the hazards of the tire became apparent. Giving adequate consideration to ethical issues in the midst of a crisis is not easy. As the Firestone case shows, the need to have a competitive product, to maintain customer relations, to protect the company from legal liability, and to operate in a complex regulatory environment will often lead managers to overlook the ethical aspects of marketing decisions or to give them a lower priority. Because of inadequate information and lack of time, there is also a tendency to react to events in a defensive manner rather than to take positive steps to resolve problems in an ethically responsible manner.[2]

Ethical issues in marketing are not confined to product safety. Virtually all aspects of marketing—from the development of new products to pricing, promotion, and sales—raise ethical questions for which there are no easy answers. This chapter begins with an examination of two competing theories on the role of marketing, in an attempt to develop a framework for understanding the justification of marketing and the basis for the ethical obligations of people engaged in marketing activities. Among the questions that an adequate theory must answer are, What specific rights do buyers and sellers have in market transactions? And what role should the needs and desires of consumers play in making marketing decisions? The rise of the consumer movement since the 1960s has brought these questions to the forefront of public discussion and has forced American corporations to address them as never before.

This theoretical discussion is followed by a brief look at some of the major problem areas in marketing ethics. These include problems in packaging and labeling, the use of deceptive and manipulative sales techniques, and anticompetitive practices, such as price fixing and price discrimination. Of course, these areas of marketing are heavily regulated, so that many unethical marketing practices are specifically prohibited by law. We need to look, therefore, at the ethical justification for consumer protection legislation and other legal restrictions on marketing activities.

Of the many ethical issues involved in product safety, none is more controversial than the responsibility of manufacturers to compensate people who suffer some financial loss or physical injury as a result of defective products. Many observers believe that recent changes in product liability law tip the balance too heavily in favor of consumers and impose an unfair burden on corporations. However, liability suits are an important source of protection for consumers. Not only does the prospect of having to pay compensation for product-related accidents provide a strong incentive for manufacturers to protect consumers against injury, but if accidents do occur, compensating the victims is usually the only way to rectify the wrong that has been done. The remainder of this chapter is devoted, therefore, to examining three rival theories concerning the responsibility of manufacturers for product safety.

ETHICAL ISSUES IN MARKETING

Marketing, according to one often cited definition, "consists of the performance of business activities that direct the flow of goods and services from producer to consumer or user."[3] Within this broad characterization, there are a number of distinct functions, including product development, distribution, pricing, promotion, and sales. Although many of the activities of marketers are relatively free of ethical problems, others have drawn extensive criticism and spawned, in some instances, organized consumer opposition that challenges the prevailing philosophy of marketing in American corporations.

Consumerism and the Marketing Concept

Beginning in the early sixties, the public was stirred to action by books such as *Silent Spring*, by Rachel Carson,[4] which detailed the disastrous effects of pesticides on the environment; Jessica Mitford's scathing critique of sales practices in the funeral industry, *The American Way of Death*;[5] and perhaps the best known of all, *Unsafe at Any Speed*, by Ralph Nader, which criticized General Motors for a callous disregard of safety, especially in the design of the Chevrolet Corvair.[6]

Many politicians at the local, state, and national levels championed the consumer movement, including President John F. Kennedy, who in 1962 proclaimed a four-point bill of rights for consumers: the right to safety, the right to be informed, the right to choose, and the right to be heard. The result of this political backing was a period of legislative activity that saw passage of the Fair Packaging and Labeling Act (1966),

Truth-in-Lending Act (1968), Child Protection and Toy Safety Act (1969), Consumer Product Safety Act (1972), and the Magnuson-Moss Warranty Act (1975). The media also seized on consumerism and spread it with front-page coverage of graphic events, such as grocery store boycotts by enraged shoppers.

The consumer movement arose in spite of the fact that business has long operated with a marketing approach that focuses on consumer satisfaction. The guiding principle in marketing, commonly called the *marketing concept*, stresses that in order to succeed, producers need to begin with an understanding of the needs and desires of consumers and proceed from there to develop and deliver the appropriate goods and services.[7] All the activities of a firm must be integrated into the effort of satisfying consumers, and this effort must be ongoing to ensure that consumers remain satisfied long after the sale.

Ironically, the main targets of consumerism were not small behind-the-times companies but the largest and most progressive corporations that had most fully implemented the marketing concept. This fact prompted *Business Week* to observe that "In the broadest sense, consumerism can be defined as the bankruptcy of what business schools have been calling the 'marketing concept.' "[8] Peter F. Drucker used even stronger language, describing consumerism as "the shame of the total marketing concept."[9] In the view of such critics, the marketing concept itself is faulty and in need of replacement.[10]

Defenders of the marketing concept respond that the goals of consumerism are achieved by making the consumer central to all marketing decisions. There is no need for producers to recognize an expanded list of consumer rights, since it is in their own interest to pay close attention to what consumers want. As long as they obey the law, corporations can continue to operate with only one object in mind, to make a profit, since producers can make a profit only by understanding and satisfying the needs and desires of consumers. Flouting consumer rights is a sure prescription for business failure.

Consumer Rights

Some of the disagreements between marketers and their critics is due to different understandings of the rights of consumers. Traditionally, producers, as sellers, are regarded as having the following rights in a free market system:

1. The right to make decisions regarding the products offered for sale, such as their design and style.
2. The right to set the price for products and all other terms of sale, including warranties.

3. The right to determine how products will be made available to consumers (that is, the right to make decisions about distribution).
4. The right to promote products in any way that they choose, including the use of any truthful advertising message.

These rights are limited by the usual rules of fair market exchanges. Thus, products must be as represented; producers must live up to the terms of the sales agreement; and advertising and other information about products must not be deceptive. Except for these restrictions, however, producers are free to operate pretty much as they please.

Consumers, on the other hand, are traditionally recognized as having only the right not to buy a product that is offered for sale. The opportunity for consumers to satisfy their needs and desires is thus restricted to a "veto" option. If the goods that consumers want are provided by producers, then all is well, but the rights of consumers are not violated if producers fail for any reason to provide consumers with goods they desire. Moreover, the burden of protecting the interests of consumers falls primarily on consumers themselves. In particular, they have the responsibility for acquiring the information needed to make rational choices. The number one rule in market exchanges is thus caveat emptor, or buyer beware.

The consumer movement holds that the right not to buy provides inadequate opportunities for consumers to satisfy their needs and desires. Also, the burden of protecting their own interests is too heavy for consumers to bear, especially in view of the unequal relation between buyers and sellers in present-day markets. In a "David and Goliath" struggle, with giant corporations wielding the immense power of modern marketing tools, individual consumers, armed only with a veto option and limited knowledge, have little chance. Consumer advocates contend, therefore, that the rights outlined by President Kennedy need to be added to the list of the rights of buyers. These rights include:

1. The right to be protected from harmful products.
2. The right to be provided with adequate information about products.
3. The right to be offered a choice that includes the products that consumers truly want.
4. The right to have a voice in the making of major marketing decisions.

The first two of these rights are now embodied to some extent in consumer protection legislation. The Consumer Product Safety Act, for example, created an independent regulatory body, the Consumer Product Safety Commission, which has the power to issue standards, require warnings, and even ban dangerous products entirely. The Fair Packaging and Labeling Act requires that containers disclose the ingredients of the product, the amount, and other pertinent information, including nutritional content in the case of food. The Magnuson-Moss Warranty

Act specifies the information and the minimum conditions that must be included in a full warranty and requires that all warranties be written in comprehensible language. The latter two rights, especially the right to a voice, have not been addressed by the law and remain unrealized goals of the consumer movement.

Packaging and Labeling

Some problems of the right to be informed are revealed by a closer look at the law on packaging and labeling. Consumers need a certain amount of information to make rational choices, and often this information is not easily obtained. A consumer buying apples, for example, can easily check their condition and compare them with other fruit on display. But consider the plight of a consumer comparing two brands of canned apple pie filling or attempting to determine the value of a frozen apple pie in a sealed, opaque cardboard box. Without information on the label, consumers have no practical means for determining the quantity of apples in the filling or the size of the frozen pie. They also cannot easily determine the ingredients used, the nutritional content, or the length of time the product has been sitting on the grocer's shelf or in the freezer case.

Certainly, the more information consumers have, the better they can protect themselves in the marketplace. The ethical question, though, is, how much information is a manufacturer obligated to provide? And to what extent are consumers responsible for informing themselves about the products for sale?

The Fair Packaging and Labeling Act was passed by Congress in 1966 with the aim of enabling consumers to make meaningful value comparisons. Specifically, the act requires that each package list the identity of the product; the name and location of the manufacturer, packer, or distributor; the net quantity; and, as appropriate, the number of servings, applications, and so on. There are detailed requirements for many specific kinds of products in the Fair Packaging and Labeling Act and other statutes. The labels on food products must list the ingredients in order of quantity, for example. However, manufacturers are not required to include the amounts of each ingredient, so that it is generally not possible to compare the amount of apples in two different brands of canned apple pie filling. Diet-conscious consumers might want to know what kind of fat is used in the crust of the apple pie, but this information also need not be included.

Manufacturers offer a number of reasons for not providing more information. A detailed listing of amounts of ingredients might jeopardize recipes that are trade secrets; listing the kind of fat would prevent them from switching ingredients to take advantage of changes in the relative prices of, say, soybean and palm oil; product-dating is often misunderstood by consumers, who reject older products that are still good; and packaging has to be designed with many considerations in mind in addition to revealing the contents. It must be easy to fill, protect goods in transit, prevent spoilage, and so on. Therefore, the objective of the Fair Packaging and Labeling Act, manufacturers argue, needs to be balanced against a number of practical constraints.

Pricing

The question of how much information sellers are obligated to provide arises not only in packaging and labeling but also in pricing. The proliferation of products at different prices makes it difficult for consumers to compare even those from the same manufacturer. Price codes that can be understood only by sales personnel put consumers at a disadvantage. The use of a universal product code (UPC) that can be machine read has raised concern about the accuracy of posted prices, and some retailers attempt to reduce costs by not marking prices on individual packages. As a result, some local and state governments now require retailers to mark the price on each product, and the FTC has investigated the accuracy of the price posted on products. The A&P grocery store chain, for example, entered into a agreement with the FTC to reduce the number of discrepancies between the posted price and the price charged at the checkout counter to an "acceptable level."[11] With improvements in scanning and greater consumer acceptance, this issue has largely died away.

Also, some products have hidden costs. The price of tires, for example, often excludes mounting, balancing, extended warranties, and other extras, which are often mentioned to consumers after a decision has been made to buy (a sales technique know as "low-balling"). Consumers cannot compare two air conditioners without knowing the cost of operating them, since a cheaper but less efficient air conditioner can cost more in the long run. Manufacturers of electrical household appliances are now required by law, therefore, to disclose the amount of energy used in a year and the range of energy consumption for products of the same kind. Similarly, light bulbs must list the average life and the amount of light produced. Comparisons are facilitated by standard units for measuring the relevant factors. Thus, tires are required by federal law to be graded with a tread-wear index and an A, B, or C rating for traction, and insulating materials have an R-value that enables consumers to compare different grades of insulation.

The Obligation to Provide Information

What is the justification for the Fair Packaging and Labeling Act and various statutes governing price displays, disclosure of hidden costs, and standardized units of measurement? Consumer protection legislation of this kind seems, at first glance, to run counter to classical economic theory. In a free market system, buyers bear the primary burden of informing themselves about the products offered for sale. Generally, sellers are not obligated to provide complete information but only to avoid misrepresentation, although buyers are entitled to rely on any representations that are made and to make minimal assumptions about the quality of goods and their suitability. These are referred to in law as implied warranties of merchantability and fitness for use. However, beyond the obligations to be truthful and fulfill warranties, both expressed and implied, caveat emptor is the rule of the marketplace.

An alternative rule that underlies much consumer protection legislation is that manufacturers have an obligation to provide relevant information that consumers cannot reasonably obtain for themselves. The rationale for abandoning caveat emptor is that in a modern industrial economy, with technologically advanced products that are developed, manufactured, and marketed with all the expertise at the command of large corporations, it is impossible for consumers to acquire sufficient information to protect themselves in the marketplace. A division of the burden on buyers and sellers that might have been appropriate to an earlier age is impractical, therefore, under present-day economic conditions. Because manufacturers already have the information or, at least access to it, and because they make the key decisions regarding product development, packaging and labeling, and so on, it is more cost effective to place the burden of providing information on them.

Deceptive and Manipulative Marketing Practices

Deception in marketing is similar to deception in advertising, discussed in the previous chapter. Roughly, marketing practices are deceptive when consumers are led to hold false beliefs about a product. Examples of some common deceptive pricing and sales practices are markdowns from a "suggested retail price" for products that are seldom if ever sold at that price, "cents off" labeling and "introductory offers" that incorrectly purport to offer a savings, and bogus clearance sales in which inferior goods are brought in especially for the sale. In these cases, consumers are led to believe that the prices represent a substantial reduction when, in fact, they do not. Packaging and labeling are deceptive when the size or shape of a container, a picture or description, or the use of terms such as *economy size* and *new and improved* mislead consumers in some significant way. Warranties that cannot be easily understood by the average consumer are also deceptive. And, of course, advertising, provides fertile ground for deceiving consumers.

Manipulation is generally distinguished from deception, in that it typically involves no false or misleading claims. Instead, it consists of taking advantage of consumer psychology to make a sale. More precisely, manipulation is noncoercively shaping the alternatives open to people or their perception of those alternatives so that they are effectively deprived of a choice.[12] Examples of harmless forms of manipulation with full disclosure (and hence no deception) include multiple pricing, such as "3 for $1" and "buy two, get one free," and odd-even pricing, $2.99 instead of $3.00. When customers are accustomed to paying a certain price for a product, such as a candy bar, manufacturers often reduce the amount in order to maintain the same price, a practice known as customary pricing. Customary pricing can also be deceptive, however, when consumers fail to notice the change. In 1991, the size of one popular brand of tuna, for example, was reduced without any fanfare from the industry standard of 6½ ounces to 6⅛, a nearly invisible 5.8 percent price increase.[13]

A more objectionable form of manipulation is "bait and switch," a generally illegal practice in which a customer is lured into a store by an advertisement for a low-cost item and then sold a higher priced version. If the low-cost item is not available, then deception has been used, but often the "bait" is available but of such low quality that customers are easily "switched" to a higher priced product. "Bait and switch" is manipulative not only because consumers are tricked into entering the store but because they enter in a frame of mind to buy as a result of the apparent bargain in the "bait." Having already decided to buy and not merely look, they are more receptive to a sales pitch for a different product.

Manipulation can also take place, with or without deception, by people who are skilled in using high-pressure sales techniques. The sales force of one encyclopedia company used deception to gain entry to the homes of prospects by claiming to be conducting advertising research (the questionnaires were thrown away afterward). Another company offered to place a set of encyclopedias "free" provided the family bought a yearly supplement for a certain number of years at a price that exceeded the cost of the encyclopedia set alone. According to the testimony of one trainee for *Collier's Encyclopedia*:

> The salesmen have to memorize patter carefully devised to wear down most prospects within 30 minutes. Every statement, gesture, smile is carefully prescribed and designed to make the family feel inferior (Collier's instructs its salesmen to sit on a chair higher than the prospective buyer's) and also to play on young suburbanites' desire for status and recognition.[14]

Although the companies involved have agreed to stop using these deceptive practices, subtle psychological manipulation is not easily regulated and still persists. Some groups of people are more vulnerable to manipulation than others, most notably children and the poor.[15] Special care needs to be taken, therefore, in marketing aimed at those groups.

The moral case against deceptive and manipulative marketing needs little explanation, since it rests on the requirement that markets be free of force and fraud. The difficult ethical questions in this area concern the definition of deception and manipulation and the dividing line between acceptable and unacceptable marketing practices. Virtually all companies that market to children, for example, concede the special vulnerability of this group but vigorously deny that their own marketing practices are deceptive or manipulative. Personal selling requires an understanding of consumer psychology and skill in using persuasive techniques. When does effective selling, however, cross the line and become ethically objectionable manipulation?

For drawing the line on deceptive marketing practices, we can use the definition of deception developed in the preceding chapter on advertising. Deception involves creating or taking advantage of false beliefs that significantly interfere with the ability of consumers to make rational choices. The same notion of rational choice can be used to distinguish between effective selling and manipulation. Successful sales personnel are often adept at "sizing up" customers' preferences, for example, and steering them toward suitable goods. Such an understanding of consumer psychology still leaves consumers free to make a rational choice in a way that "bait and switch" does not. In the latter case, consumers who are unaware of what is happening to them are led to make choices they would not make otherwise.

Market Research

Some of the objections to deceptive and manipulative marketing practices apply to the area of market research, which also raises questions about privacy of the kind discussed in Chapter 7. Corporations engage in a great amount of systematic information-gathering about consumers to aid them in developing new products and planning marketing strategies. Data are collected using all the techniques of social science research, including in-depth surveys, field studies, and controlled laboratory experiments.

One set of problems for marketing research conducted by outside agencies concerns the relation between researchers and clients, including integrity in undertaking research assignments and honesty in interpreting data and presenting results.[16] Another set concerns the treatment of research subjects or respondents. These include manipulating persons into participating in research projects, deceiving them about the purpose of a study, and invading their privacy by the use, for example, of one-way mirrors during interviews.[17] An especially blatant form of misconduct in marketing research is the use of surveys and other research tools to make a sales pitch or to generate a list of sales prospects. This is a practice known as *sugging*, from the acronym for selling under the guise of marketing research.

A further threat to privacy comes from the use of research data in the growing field of database marketing, in which retailers, through credit card records and information derived from universal product codes, are able to construct detailed profiles of individual customers and develop tailor-made products or marketing offers. It is no longer necessary to have a mainframe computer for these kinds of tasks; a small desktop PC will do. In April 1990, Lotus Development Corporation announced that it would market a compact disk, called *Lotus Marketplace: Households*, containing the names, addresses, demographic data, and information on the purchasing habits of 120 million Americans, thus giving small businesses with PCs access to the same computerized information large corporations have long used. The announcement aroused a storm of protest about the invasion of consumers' privacy, however, and the project was shelved.[18]

Although market research is a legitimate activity for marketers, care must be taken to ensure that surveys and other instruments are not used to deceive or manipulate test subjects or consumers generally. And safeguards are needed to protect the privacy of all concerned.

Anticompetitive Marketing Practices

Most of the unethical marketing practices that come under the heading of being anticompetitive are also illegal as a result of the major antitrust statutes; namely, the Sherman Act (1890), the Clayton Act (1914), the Federal Trade Commission Act (1914), and the Robinson-Patman Act (1936). Many states also have antitrust statutes that prohibit the same practices. Our task, therefore, is largely to sketch the ethical arguments for prohibiting certain anticompetitive marketing practices and to note some questions about these arguments.

The major anticompetitive marketing practices are

1. Price-fixing. Price-fixing is an agreement among two or more companies operating in the same market to sell goods at a set price. Such an agreement is contrary to the usual practice, whereby prices are set in a free market by arm's-length transactions. Most commonly, price-fixing is *horizontal*, among different sellers at the same level of distribution, but price-fixing can also be *vertical*, when it occurs between buyers and sellers at different levels. An agreement between the manufacturer, a wholesaler, and retailers in transactions involving the same goods is an example. Price-fixing occurs not only when there is an explicit agreement among competitors to charge similar prices but also when the same result is achieved by other means. Among these are the exchange of price information among competitors, a tacit agreement to follow an industry standard (parallel-pricing) or the lead of a dominant seller (price leadership), and a situation in which one company effectively controls the prices of competitors (administered price). Market allocation, in which competitors agree not to compete in certain geographical areas or to seek the business of certain buyers or agree to limit their volume, is also a form of price-fixing.

2. Resale price maintenance. This is a practice whereby products are sold on the condition that they be resold at a price fixed by the manufacturer or distributor. Resale price maintenance is thus a form of vertical price-fixing, as described above. There are various reasons for imposing resale price maintenance on retailers, including fostering a prestige image, enabling a larger number of retailers to carry a product, and providing an adequate margin for promotion or service. As a form of price-fixing, resale price maintenance prevents prices from being set by the forces of a competitive market.

3. Price discrimination. Sellers engage in price discrimination when they charge different prices or offer different terms of sale for goods of the same kind to different buyers. Often this occurs when buyers are located in different geographical regions or vary in size or their access to other sellers. Thus, a seller who gives a discount to large buyers solely by virtue of their size is guilty of discriminating against small buyers.

4. Reciprocal dealing, tying arrangements, and exclusive dealing. Reciprocal dealing involves a sale in which the seller is required to buy something in return, as when an office supply firm agrees to buy a computer system only on the condition that the computer firm agrees to purchase supplies from the office supply firm. A tying arrangement exists when one product is sold on the condition that the buyer purchase another product as well. An example of a tying arrangement is an automotive supply firm that requires as a condition for selling tires to a service station that the buyer also purchase batteries from the seller. In an exclusive dealing agreement, a seller provides a product—a brand of sportswear, for example—on the condition that the buyer not handle competing brands.

The law on anticompetitive practices is extremely complex and makes numerous exceptions. Some of these practices are strictly illegal—such as price-fixing, market allocation, and tying arrangements (so-called per se violations)—but sellers can defend themselves against a charge of price discrimination, for example, by showing that the difference in price is justified as a cost of doing business, as a good faith attempt to meet competition, or as a promotional discount that is available to all similar buyers. Also, legal restrictions on resale price agreements can be skirted by the right of any company not to do business with another. Thus, the law permits a manufacturer to "punish" a retailer for selling below a suggested retail price simply by refusing to sell to that retailer (a tactic known as *Colgating* after a court case vindicating the Colgate Company),[19] although care must be taken that the action does not constitute a concerted effort by two or more manufacturers to retaliate.[20] For a fuller discussion of the law on these practices, consult any standard business law text.

The overall ethical objection to these practices is that they are not fair forms of competition. In particular, anticompetitive practices distort prices by preventing the market from serving as a mechanism for setting prices fairly. The question, "What is a fair price?" has long been debated without any satisfactory answer. However, a price arrived at by mutual agreement under competitive conditions at arm's length is generally considered to be fair. Classical economic theory assumes that competitive markets are characterized by a number of buyers and sellers who are free to enter or leave the market at any time and by largely undifferentiated products that buyers are willing to substitute one for another. Under such conditions, the forces of supply and demand ensure not only that resources are used efficiently (the greatest output for the least input) but that goods are fairly priced.

A more specific objection to horizontal price-fixing is that it leads to monopoly. Where there is a single seller of a product, the forces of supply and demand no longer work and the monopolist is free to manipulate the supply to obtain a higher price than could be achieved under conditions of perfect competition. The primary objective of antitrust legislation, therefore, is to prevent the formation of monopolies, which are clearly incompatible with the operation of a free market. Horizontal price-fixing in its many forms and market allocation permit the creation of monopoly conditions, despite the existence of many sellers, since they act in concert and thus become, in effect, one. If the leading manufacturers of electrical supplies, for example, meet in hotel rooms and agree on prices, then they act as a single seller, thereby creating an artificial monopoly.[21] An agreement to allocate markets achieves the same result, since each seller becomes a monopolist in a certain geographical area or among a select group of buyers.

The main argument against price discrimination and other so-called "predatory" practices is not that they *constitute* monopolies in the manner of price-fixing but that they *facilitate* the creation of monopolies by enabling sellers to eliminate competition. Even when monopoly is not the result, price discrimination enables stronger sellers to inflict harm on weaker competitors and thereby gain an additional advantage. Generally, the lower prices offered to some buyers in cases of price discrimination are based not on any competitive advantage except the sheer size that enables the company to endure a loss that cannot be endured by others. The immediate aim is not to gain some good for the company but to inflict harm on competitors.

A number of early cases were prosecuted under the provision in the Sherman Act against restraint of trade in interstate commerce. If a large national oil company, for example, is permitted to offer lower prices in a few geographical regions, thereby forcing smaller, local companies out of business, then the large company is left in a monopoly position and can raise prices at will to recoup the losses from underselling. This, of course, was a favored tactic of the Standard Oil Company, which around the turn of the century achieved and maintained control over more than 80 percent of the nation's refining capacity.[22] About the same time, the American Tobacco Company attempted to achieve a monopoly by selling their brands at less than cost in local markets to drive out competitors.[23] Price discrimination can be practiced not only by sellers but by large buyers. The law specifically forbidding price discrimination, the Robinson-Patman Act, prevents large buyers, such as chain stores, from demanding and receiving preferential treatment from manufacturers and wholesalers to the detriment of smaller buyers.

Opinion is sharply divided on whether price discrimination actually lessens competition and whether it should be prevented.[24] Price is a legitimate competitive tool that enables firms to take advantage of efficiencies of scale and to respond flexibly to differences in market conditions. It is difficult to distinguish between predatory pricing that attempts to clobber the competition and honest efforts to offer greater value in an attempt to gain market share, albeit at the expense of competitors. Moreover, some economists argue that predatory pricing is generally not advantageous even in the long run because would-be monopolists cannot ordinarily recoup the losses of undercutting the competition.[25]

The remaining practices—resale price maintenance, reciprocal dealing, tying arrangements, and exclusive dealing—are objectionable for the reason that they result in market transactions that are less efficient than they would be otherwise. They do not necessarily lead to monopoly, but they still distort the market mechanism for setting prices. The assumption of the courts is that there would be no need for reciprocal dealing, tying arrangements, or exclusive dealing agreements if any of the exchanges involved would be made under perfectly competitive conditions. The need for the automotive supply firm to insist that buyers of tires also purchase batteries would not exist if the batteries represented as great a value as the tires. The fact that a tying arrangement exists is prima facie evidence that service stations would not buy the batteries if they were given the chance to buy the two products separately. Similarly, an exclusive dealing agreement would not be necessary if the retailer would handle only one line of sportswear given the opportunity to choose.

Conclusion

The ethical issues in marketing are extremely diverse. Packaging and labeling is a moral minefield of questions about what information manufacturers have an obligation to provide and consumers a right to expect. Deception and manipulation are major issues in packaging and labeling as well as in pricing, personal selling, and market research. Market research also raises concerns about consumer privacy, especially in view of the vast amount of information on individuals available to marketers. Finally, the area of anticompetitive practices, which deals primarily with pricing, involves fundamental notions of fair competition as well as highly technical questions about requirements for a free market economy. None of these issues is unique to marketing; they are all discussed elsewhere in this book under other headings. But marketing is an especially rich field for ethical exploration, since the issues are so many and varied.

THEORIES OF PRODUCT LIABILITY

Three theories are commonly used to determine the responsibility of manufacturers to compensate the victims of accidents caused by defective products.[26] Each of them appeals to a different ground for its ethical justification; and as legal doctrines, they each have a different source in the law.

THE DUE CARE THEORY

This theory holds that manufacturers ought to exercise *due care*. Their obligation is to take all reasonable precautions to ensure that products they put on the market are free of defects likely to cause harm. According to this theory, manufacturers are liable for damages only when they fail to carry out this obligation and so are at fault in some way. One ethical justification for this view is the Aristotelian principle of corrective justice: Something is owed by a person who inflicts a wrongful harm upon another. By failing to exercise due care, a manufacturer is acting wrongly and hence ought to pay compensation to anyone who is injured as a result.

The legal expression of this theory is the view in the law of torts that persons are liable for acts of negligence. Negligence is defined in the *Second Restatement of Torts* (Section 282) as "conduct which falls below the standard established by law for the protection of others against unreasonable risk of harm." The usual standard established by law is the care that a "reasonable person" would exercise in a given situation.

Accordingly, a reckless driver is negligent (since a reasonable person would not drive recklessly), and the driver can be legally required to pay compensation to the victims of any accident caused by the negligent behavior.[27] In the case of persons with superior skill or knowledge, the standard is higher. A manufacturer can be assumed to know more than the average person about the product and, hence, can be legally required to exercise a greater degree of care.

The standard of due care for manufacturers or other persons involved in the sale of a product to a consumer, including wholesalers and retailers, covers a wide variety of activities. Among them are

1. Design. The product ought to be designed in accord with government and industry standards to be safe under all foreseeable conditions, including possible misuse by the consumer. A toy with small parts, for example, that a child could choke on, or a toy that could easily be broken by a child to reveal sharp edges is badly designed. Similarly, due care is not taken in the design of a crib or a play pen with slats or other openings in which a child's head could become wedged. Many manufacturers have a design review board, composed of a variety of experts within the company, to evaluate the design of products, and some companies also submit designs to outside consulting firms, such as the Underwriter's Laboratory for electrical products.

2. Materials. The materials specified in the design should also meet government and industry standards and be of sufficient strength and durability to stand up under all reasonable use. Testing should be done to ensure that the materials withstand ordinary wear and tear and do not weaken with age, stress, extremes of temperature, or other forces. The wiring in an appliance is substandard, for example, if the insulation cracks or peels, posing a risk of electrical shock.

3. Production. Due care should be taken in fabricating parts to specifications and assembling them correctly, so that parts are not put in the wrong way or left out. Screws, rivets, welds, and other ways of fastening parts should be properly used, and so on. Defects due to faulty construction can be avoided, in part, by giving adequate training to employees and creating conditions that allow them to do their job properly. Fast assembly lines, for example, are an invitation to defects in workmanship.

4. Quality control. Manufacturers should have a systematic program to inspect products between operations or at the end to ensure that they are of sufficient quality in both materials and construction. Inspections may be done either by trained personnel or by machines. In some programs every product is inspected, whereas in others inspection is done of samples taken at intervals. Records should be maintained of all quality control inspections, and the inspectors themselves should be evaluated for effectiveness.

5. Packaging, labeling, and warnings. The product should be packaged so as to avoid any damage in transit, and the packaging and handling of perishable food stuffs, for example, should not create any new hazard. Since products often come in packages that prevent customers from making a thorough inspection before purchase, manufacturers have an even greater obligation to ensure the quality of the design, materials, and workmanship. Also, the labels and any inserts should include instructions for correct use and adequate warnings in language easily understood by users. Warnings that enable consumers to understand a hazard are more effective. Thus, a label warning of an electrical shock is better than one that simply warns against touching a part.

6. Notification. Finally, the manufacturers of some products should have a system of notifying consumers of hazards that only become apparent later. Automobile manufacturers, for example, maintain lists of buyers, who can be notified of recalls by mail; and appliances, electronic equipment, and the like frequently contain cards for a buyer to return, giving the name and address. Some companies have toll-free numbers, so that customers may ask questions. And recalls, warnings, and other safety messages are often conveyed by paid notices in the media.

The Problem of Misuse

One question that arises in the due care theory is whether manufacturers have an obligation to ensure that a product is safe to use as intended or to anticipate all the conditions under which injury could occur. The driver of a 1963 Chevrolet Corvair, for example, was severely injured in a head-on collision when the steering column struck him in the head. In the model of the car he was driving, the steering column was a rigid shaft that extended to the front end of the car, thus forming a spear aimed directly at the driver. Although this design did not cause the accident, the victim claimed that his injuries were greater as a result of it. General Motors contended that its cars were intended to be used for driving on streets and highways and not for colliding with other objects. Consequently, they had no obligation to make them safe for this latter purpose. A U.S. court of appeals held, however, that due care includes "a duty to design the product so that it will fairly meet any emergency of use which can reasonably be anticipated."[28]

This duty also extends to foreseeable misuse by the consumer. The owner's manual for the 1976 Mercury Cougar, for example, explicitly stated that the original equipment Goodyear tires should not be used "for continuous driving over 90 miles per hour."[29] A U.S. court of appeals determined that the tread separation on the right rear tire of a Cougar being driven in excess of 100 miles per hour was not the result of any flaw in the tire. However, the Ford Motor Company should have known that a car designed for high performance and marketed with an appeal to youthful drivers would occasionally be driven at speeds above the safe operating level of the tires. Accordingly, Ford should have warned owners of the Cougar more effectively or else equipped the car with better tires.

Some courts have held companies responsible not only for foreseeable misuse but also for misuse that is actively encouraged in the marketing of a product.[30] General Motors, for example, marketed the Pontiac Firebird Trans Am by entering specially reinforced models in racing competitions and by featuring the car in crash scenes in "antihero scofflaw" motion pictures. A promotion film that had spliced together stunt scenes from these movies was used for promotions in dealers' showrooms. In a suit brought on behalf of the driver of a 1978 Trans Am who was injured when the car went out of control while traveling more than 100 miles per hour, the court found for the plaintiff by invoking a doctrine of "invited misuse."[31]

What Is Due Care?

The major difficulty with the due care theory is establishing what constitutes due care. Manufacturers have an obligation to take precautions that are more stringent than the "reasonable person" standard, but no means exist for determining exactly how far the obligation of manufacturers extends. The courts have developed a flexible standard derived from Justice Learned Hand's famous formulation of the negligence rule.[32] In this rule, negligence involves the interplay of three factors: (1) the probability of harm, (2) the severity of the harm, and (3) the burden of protecting against the harm. Thus, manufacturers have a greater obligation to protect consumers when injury in an accident is more likely to occur, when the injury is apt to be greater, and when the cost of avoiding injury is relatively minor. These are relevant factors in formulating a standard of due care, but they are not sufficient by themselves to decide every case.

Some standards for design, materials, inspection, packaging, and the like have evolved through long experience and are now incorporated into engineering practice and government regulations. These comprise the minimum standards of due care. However, they also reflect the scientific knowledge and technology at a given time and fail to impose an obligation to guard against hazards that are discovered later. Whether asbestos companies exercised due care, for example, is a case in point.

The manufacture of asbestos products and the instructions for their use in the 1930s and later conformed to industry and government standards. The asbestos companies claim that the danger of asbestos exposure was not known until the 1960s, at which time they instituted changes to make handling asbestos safer. (Critics of the asbestos companies maintain that substantial evidence of the dangers of asbestos was available earlier.) This so-called "state-of-the-art" defense—in which a company contends that it exercised due care as defined by the scientific knowledge and technology at the time—was flatly rejected by the New Jersey Supreme Court decision in *Bashada* v. *Johns-Manville Products Corp.* in 1982.[33] The court reasoned that Johns-Manville ought to have made a greater attempt to discover the hazards of asbestos. In the words of the court:

> Fairness suggests that manufacturers not be excused from liability because their prior inadequate investment in safety rendered the hazards of their products unknowable.

As a legal doctrine, the due care theory is difficult to apply. The focus of the theory is on the *conduct* of the manufacturer rather than on the *condition* of the product. So the mere fact that a product is defective is not sufficient for holding that a manufacturer has failed in an obligation of due care; some knowledge is needed about specific acts that a manufacturer performed or failed to perform. Lawsuits based on the theory thus require proof of negligence, which the victims of accidents caused by defective products are often not able to provide. In addition, common law allows for two defenses under the due care theory: contributory negligence and assumption of risk. Just as a manufacturer has an obligation to act responsibly, so too does a consumer. Similarly, if consumers know the dangers posed by a product and use it anyway, then to some extent they assume responsibility for any injury that results. The ethical basis for these defenses is the same Aristotelian principle of compensatory justice that underlies the due care theory. When consumers do not exercise due care in their use of a product, therefore, or when they are fully aware of the hazards of products and use them anyway, the fault for injury falls on them as well as on the manufacturer. For these reasons, the due care theory is rarely used today in product liability cases. There are easier ways for injured consumers to secure compensation.

THE CONTRACTUAL THEORY

A second theory is that the responsibility of manufacturers for harm resulting from defective products is that specified in a sales *contract*. The relation between buyer and seller is viewed in this theory as a contractual relation, which is subject to the terms of a contract, either implicit or explicit. An explicit written or verbal contract is legally enforceable, of course. In the absence of an explicit contract, there are still certain understandings between the two parties that are revealed by their behavior. This fact is recognized by the Uniform Commercial Code (UCC), Section 2-204(1), which states that:

> A contract for sale of goods may be made in any manner sufficient to show agreement, including conduct by both parties which recognizes the existence of such a contract.

One of the usual understandings is that a product is of an acceptable level of quality and fit for the purpose for which it is ordinarily used. These implicit contractual provisions are part of what is described in Section 2-314 of the UCC as an *implied warranty of merchantability.* Manufacturers have both a moral and a legal obligation, therefore, by virtue of their contractual relation, to offer only products free from dangerous defects. A person who buys a new automobile, for example, is entitled to assume that it will perform as expected and that nothing in the design makes it especially hazardous in the event of an accident.

There is also an *implied warranty of fitness* for a particular purpose when the buyer is relying on the seller's expertise in the selection of the product. In addition, an *express warranty* is created, according to Section 2-313 of the UCC, as follows:

> Any affirmation of fact or promise made by the seller to the buyer which relates to the goods and becomes part of the basis of the bargain creates an express warranty that the goods shall conform to the affirmation or promise.

The notion of an affirmation is very broad and includes any description or illustration on a package or any model or demonstration of the product being used in a certain way. Thus, there is an implied warranty of fitness for a particular purpose that a drill bit is safe to use with concrete if the seller knows that is the purpose which the buyer has in mind, and an express warranty exists if drilling concrete is one of the uses listed on the packaging or pictured in any way.

The ethical basis for the contractual theory is fairness in commercial dealings. Agreements to buy or sell a product are fair only when they are entered into freely by the contracting parties. Freedom in such agreements entails, among other things, that both buyers and sellers have adequate information about the product in question. Consumers know that the use of many products involves some danger, and they voluntarily assume the risk when the nature and extent of the hazards are revealed to them. Manufacturers may not take unfair advantage of consumers by exposing them to the risk of harm from hazards that are not disclosed. Selling a product that the manufacturer knows to be dangerous, without informing consumers, is a form of deception, since crucial information is either suppressed or misrepresented. Even when the manufacturer is unaware of a defect, the cost of any accident caused by a defective product still ought to be borne by the manufacturer, since the product was sold with the understanding that it posed no hazards except those already revealed to consumers.

Legal action for compensation based on the contractual theory is generally a suit for breach of contract under contract law. Manufacturers have an obligation to comply with the contractual terms of any sales agreement. And these terms include not only those in any written warranty but also those in all warranties, express or implied.

Objections to the Contractual Theory

One objection to the contractual theory is that the understandings in a sales agreement, which are the basis for implied and express warranties, are not very precise. Whether a product is of an acceptable level of quality or is fit for the purpose for which it is ordinarily used is an extremely vague standard. In practice, the theory leaves consumers with little protection, except for grossly defective products and products for which the manufacturer makes explicit claims that constitute express warranties.

Second, a sales agreement may consist of a written contract with language that sharply limits the right of an injured consumer to be compensated. If buyers and sellers are both free to contract on mutually agreeable terms, then the sales agreement can explicitly disclaim all warranties, express or implied. Section 2-316 of the Uniform Commercial Code provides for the exclusion or modification of an implied warranty of merchantability as long as (1) the buyer's attention is drawn to the fact that no warranty is being given, with expressions such as "with all faults" or "as is"; (2) the buyer has the opportunity to examine the goods; and (3) the defect is one that can be detected on examination. If a consumer signs a contract with limiting language or explicit disclaimers, then, according to the contractual theory, the terms of that contract are binding.

Both of these objections are illustrated in the classic court case in warranty law *Henningsen* v. *Bloomfield Motors, Inc.*[34] Claus Henningsen purchased a new 1955 Plymouth Plaza "6" Club Sedan for use by his wife, Helen. Ten days after taking delivery of the car from a Chrysler dealer in Bloomfield, New Jersey, Mrs. Henningsen was returning home to Keansburg from a trip to Asbury Park, traveling around 20 miles per hour on a smooth road, when she heard a loud noise under the hood and felt something crack. The steering wheel spun in her hands as the car veered sharply to the right and crashed into a brick wall. Mrs. Henningsen was injured and the vehicle was declared a total wreck by the insurer. At the time of the accident, the odometer registered only 468 miles.

In the sales contract signed by Mr. Henningsen, the Chrysler Corporation offered to replace defective parts for ninety days after the sale or until the car had been driven 4,000 miles, whichever occurred first, "if the part is sent to the factory, transportation charges prepaid, and if examination discloses to its satisfaction that the part is defective." The contract further stipulated that the obligation of the manufacturer under this warranty is limited to the replacement of defective parts, which is "in lieu of all other warranties, expressed or implied, and all other obligations or liabilities on its part." By this language, liability for personal injuries was also excluded in the contract.

The question, as framed by the court, is simple:

> In return for the delusive remedy of replacement of defective parts at the factory, the buyer is said to have accepted the exclusion of the maker's liability for personal injuries arising from the breach of warranty, and to have agreed to the elimination of any other express or implied warranty. An instinctively felt sense of justice cries out against such a sharp bargain. But does the doctrine that a person is bound by his signed agreement, in the absence of fraud, stand in the way of any relief?

In giving an answer, the court decided that considerations of justice have greater force than an otherwise valid contract.

Among the factors cited in the court's decision are:

1. There is a gross inequality of bargaining power between consumers and manufacturers. Virtually all American cars at the time were sold using a standardized form written by the Automobile Manufacturers Association, which the dealer was prohibited from altering. Due to the lack of competition among manufacturers with respect to warranties, consumers had no choice but to buy a car on the manufacturer's terms—or else do without, which is not a genuine alternative in a society where an automobile is a necessity. Hence, consumers did not have freedom of choice in any significant sense, and manufacturers were not offering consumers what they truly wanted. Consumers would most likely prefer to buy cars with better warranties.

2. Consumers are also at a profound disadvantage in their ability to examine an automobile and determine its fitness for use. They are forced to rely, for the most part, on the expertise of the manufacturer and the dealer to ensure that a car is free of defects. Further, the relevant paragraphs in the contract itself were among the hardest to read, and there was nothing in them to draw the reader's attention. "In fact," the court observed, "a studied and concentrated effort would have to be made to read them."

The significance of these factors lies in their incompatibility with the central assumptions in the theory of contracts. According to Manuel G. Velasquez:

> The contractual theory assumes that buyers and sellers are equally skilled at evaluating the quality of a product and that buyers are able to adequately protect their interests against the seller. This is the assumption built into the requirement that contracts must be freely and knowingly entered into: Both parties must know what they are doing and neither must be coerced into doing it. This equality between buyer and seller that the contractual theory assumes, derives from the laissez-faire ideology that accompanied the historical development of contract theory. Classical laissez-faire ideology held that the economy's markets are competitive and that in competitive markets the consumer's bargaining power is equal to that of the seller. Competition forces the seller to offer the consumer as good or better terms than the consumer could get from other competing sellers, so the consumer has the power to threaten to take his or her business to other sellers. Because of this equality between buyer and seller, it was fair that each be allowed to try to out-bargain the other and unfair to place restrictions on either.[35]

However, the relation between consumers and manufacturers in present-day markets is seldom one of equality. And without equality, the contractual theory cannot be applied in matters of product safety.

STRICT LIABILITY

A third theory, now gaining wider acceptance in the courts, holds that manufacturers are responsible for all harm resulting from a dangerously defective product even when due care has been exercised and all contracts observed. In this view, which is known in law as *strict liability*, a manufacturer need not be negligent nor be bound by any implied or express warranty to have responsibility. The mere fact that a product is put into the hands of consumers in a defective condition that poses an unreasonable risk is sufficient for holding the manufacturer liable.

A more precise account of the theory of strict liability is given in Section 402A of the second *Restatement of Torts* as follows:

> **1.** One who sells any product in a defective condition unreasonably dangerous to the user or consumer or to his property is subject to liability for physical harm thereby caused to the ultimate user or consumer, or to his property, if (a) the seller is engaged in the business of selling such a product, and (b) it is expected to and does reach the user or consumer without substantial change in the condition in which it is sold.
> **2.** The rule stated in Subsection (1) applies although (a) the seller has exercised all possible care in the preparation and sale of his products, and

(b) the user or consumer has not bought the product from or entered into any contractual relation with the seller.

The provision of 2(b) addresses an important legal issue in both the due care and the contract theories. Generally, lawsuits under either theory have required that the victim of an accident be in a direct contractual relation with the manufacturer. This relation is known in law as *privity.* Suppose an accident is caused by a defective part that is sold to a manufacturer by a supplier, and the finished product is sold to a wholesaler, who sells it to a retailer. The consumer, under a requirement of privity, can sue only the retailer, who can sue the wholesaler, who in turn can sue the manufacturer, and so on.

The requirement of privity developed as a way of placing reasonable limits on liability, since the consequences of actions extend indefinitely. In a simpler age when goods were often bought directly from the maker, this rule made sense. With the advent of mass production, however, most goods pass through many hands on the way to the ultimate consumer, and the requirement of a direct contractual relation greatly restricts the ability of consumers to collect compensation from manufacturers. In the landmark case *MacPherson* v. *Buick Motor Company* (1916), the New York State Court of Appeals ruled that privity was not necessary when there is negligence.[36] And negligence was present, according to the decision, since the defect in the wooden wheel supplied by another manufacturer should have been detected during the assembly of the car. The Buick Motor Company, in other words, owed a duty of "care and vigilance" to the owner of the car and all others who could be injured as a result of the defective wheel.

The main blow to privity in the contractual theory came in *Baxter* v. *Ford Motor Company* (1934).[37] The Supreme Court of Washington held that a driver who was injured by flying glass when a pebble struck the windshield had a right to compensation because all Ford cars were advertised as having a Triplex shatterproof glass—"so made that it will not fly or shatter under the hardest impact." One ad continued:

> This is an important safety factor because it eliminates the dangers of flying glass—the cause of most of the injuries in automobile accidents. In these days of crowded, heavy traffic, the use of this Triplex glass is an absolute necessity. Its extra margin of safety is something that every motorist should look for in the purchase of a car—especially where there are women and children.

Because the truth of these claims could not be easily determined by an ordinary person, buyers have a right to rely on representations made by the Ford Motor Company. Hence, the wording of advertisements such as this one creates a warranty, in the view of the court, even without a direct contractual relation. The requirement of privity was also rejected in the *Henningsen* decision.

Strict Liability as a Legal Doctrine

Strict liability as a legal doctrine did not make much headway in the courts until 1963, when the California State Supreme Court ruled in *Greenman* v. *Yuba Power Products*.[38] The relevant facts are that for Christmas 1955, Mr. Greenman's wife gave him a multipurpose power tool, called a Shopsmith, that could be used as a saw, a drill, and a lathe. Two years later, while using the machine as a lathe to make a chalice, the piece of wood he was turning flew out of the machine and struck him on the forehead. Expert witnesses testified that some of the screws used to hold parts of the machine together were too weak to withstand the vibration. As a result, the tailstock was allowed to move, releasing the piece of wood that was being turned on the lathe.

The court declined to consider whether Yuba Power Products was negligent in the design and construction of the Shopsmith or whether it breached any warranties, either express or implied. The only relevant consideration, according to the decision, was the fact that the tool was unsafe to use in the intended way. Specifically, the court held:

> To establish the manufacturer's liability it was sufficient that the plaintiff proved that he was injured using the Shopsmith in a way it was intended to be used as a result of a defect in design and manufacture of which plaintiff was not aware that made the Shopsmith unsafe for its intended use.

Section 402A was formulated a year later in 1964. Since that time, all fifty states and the District of Columbia have adopted the doctrine of strict liability as expressed in the second *Restatement of Torts*, although it is mixed with elements of the other two theories in many jurisdictions.

The wording of Section 402A raises two questions of definition. What is a "defective condition"? And what does it mean to say that a product is "unreasonably dangerous"? Generally, a product is in a defective condition either when it is unsuitable for use as it is intended to be used or there is some misuse that can reasonably be foreseen and steps are not taken to prevent it. A ladder that cannot withstand the weight of an ordinary user is an example of the first kind of defect; a ladder without a label warning the user against stepping too high is an example of the second. A defect in a product can include a wide range of problems—from poor design and manufacture to inadequate instructions or warnings.

The definition of "unreasonably dangerous" that is offered in a comment on Section 402A is, "The article sold must be dangerous to an extent beyond that which would be contemplated by the ordinary consumer who purchases it, with the ordinary knowledge common to the community as to its characteristics." A product is not unreasonably dangerous, in this definition, merely because it is capable of causing serious injury to a user; otherwise, any power lawn mower would be labeled as such. However, a lawn mower that was so designed that fuel in the tank leaked on a grade, creating a fire hazard, would be unreasonably dangerous, since this is not a possibility that the ordinary user would anticipate.

This definition is inadequate, however, since it implies that a product is not unreasonably dangerous if most consumers are fully aware of the risks it poses. All power lawn mowers are now required by federal law to be equipped with a "kill switch," which stops the engine when the handle is released. Although the danger of removing debris while the blade is in motion or of slipping on a steep hill are obvious to any user, a machine without a "kill switch" is (arguably) unreasonably dangerous.

The Ethical Arguments for Strict Liability

The ethical arguments for strict liability rest on the two distinct grounds of efficiency and equity. One argument is purely utilitarian and justifies strict liability for securing the greatest amount of protection for consumers at the lowest cost. The second argument is that strict liability is the fairest way of distributing the costs involved in the manufacture and use of products.

Both of these arguments recognize that there is a certain cost in attempting to prevent accidents and in dealing with the consequences of accidents that do occur. Preventing accidents requires that manufacturers expend greater resources on product safety. Consumers must also expend resources to avoid accidents by learning how to select safe products and how to use them correctly. Insofar as manufacturers avoid the cost of reducing accidents and turn out defective products, this cost is passed along to consumers who pay for the injuries that result. A manufacturer may save money, for example, by using a cheaper grade of steel in a hammer, but a user who suffers the loss of an eye when the head chips ends up paying instead. When product safety is viewed as a matter of cost, two questions arise: (1) How can the total cost to both manufacturers and consumers be reduced to the lowest possible level? (2) How should the cost be distributed between manufacturers and consumers?

The *efficiency argument* holds, in the words of one advocate, that "responsibility be fixed wherever it will most effectively reduce the hazards to life and health inherent in defective products that reach the market."[39] By this principle, manufacturers ought to bear this responsibility, since they possess greater expertise than consumers about all aspects of product safety. They also make most of the key decisions about how products are designed, constructed, inspected, and so on. By giving manufacturers a powerful incentive to use the advantages of their position to ensure that the products they turn out are free of dangerous defects, strict liability protects consumers at a relatively low cost. The alternatives, which include placing primary responsibility on government and consumers, involve comparatively higher costs.

Further, the activity of manufacturers imposes a cost on society as a result of product-related accidents. The cost of accidents is thus an *externality*, which should be internalized as much as possible in order for the market to operate efficiently. Strict liability, according to the efficiency argument, is an effective means for internalizing the cost of the injuries to consumers that are caused by defective products. Strict liability is also an effective means, insofar as efficiency is achieved by distributing the cost of accidents broadly, since manufacturers are in a position to pass the cost along to consumers in the form of higher prices.

The principle involved in the *equity argument* is expressed by Richard A. Epstein as follows: "the defendant who captures the entire benefit of his own activities should . . . also bear its entire costs."[40] Insofar as manufacturers are the beneficiaries of their profit-making activity, it is only fair, according to this principle, that they be forced to bear the cost—which includes the cost of the injuries to consumers as a result of defective products. Much of the benefit of a manufacturer's activity is shared by consumers, however. But they also share the cost of compensating the victims of accidents through higher prices, and it is also just that they do so insofar as they reap some benefit. The distribution of the cost of compensating the victims of product-related injuries is fair, then, if this cost is distributed among all who benefit in the proportion that they benefit, so that it is not borne disproportionately by accident victims.

The Problem of Fault

The major stumbling block to the acceptance of strict liability is that the theory ignores the element of fault, which is a fundamental condition for owing compensation on the Aristotelian conception of compensatory justice.[41] We all benefit from automotive travel, for example, but we can justly be required to pay only for accidents that are our fault. Any system of liability that makes us pay for the accidents of others is unjust—or so it seems. Similarly, it is unjust to hold manufacturers liable to pay large sums to people who are injured by defective products in the absence of negligence or a contractual obligation to compensate. And it is equally unjust to force consumers indirectly to pay through higher prices the settlements in product liability suits.

The response of some advocates of strict liability is that it is not unjust to require those who are faultless to pay the cost of an activity *if everyone benefits by the use of an alternative method of paying compensation.* After all, the victims of accidents caused by defective products are not necessarily at fault either, and everyone is potentially a victim who deserves to be compensated for injuries received from defective products. Thus, those who "pay" under a system of strict liability are also protected. If a system of strict liability is in fact more efficient than any alternative scheme, then the total cost to society of ensuring that the victims of product-related accidents are compensated is less. This fact alone does not guarantee that the savings will be shared by everyone. But if manufacturers were not held strictly liable for the injuries caused by defective products, then they would take fewer precautions. As a result, everyone would have to spend more, to protect themselves—by taking more care in the selection of products, by using them more carefully, and perhaps by taking out insurance policies—and to make up the losses they suffer in product-related accidents where no one is at fault. In either case, the lower prices that consumers pay for products under a negligence system based on the due care theory would not be sufficient to offset the higher cost of insurance, medical care, and so on.

Under a system of strict liability, consumers give up a right they have in the due care theory—namely, the right not to be forced to contribute to the compensation of accident victims when they (the consumers) are not at fault. Prices are also higher under a strict liability system in order to cover the cost of paying compensation. But consumers gain more than they lose by not being required to spend money protecting themselves and making up their own losses. They also acquire a new right: the right to be compensated for injuries from defective products without regard to fault. Thus, everyone is better off under a strict liability system than under a negligence system.

Critics reject many key assumptions in the two arguments for strict liability. Product liability covers many different kinds of accidents, and the most efficient or equitable system for one kind may not be efficient or equitable for another. Careful studies need to be made of the consequences of competing theories for each kind of accident. Insofar as efficiency and equity are incompatible, decisions must be made about how to handle the efficiency/equity tradeoff. Some proposals for reform have recommended strict liability for defects in construction and a negligence system for design defects, for example.[42]

Moreover, the "deep pockets" view, which holds that corporations are able to distribute the burden of strict liability to consumers effortlessly, is not always true. Multimillion-dollar awards in product liability suits and the high cost of insurance premiums place a heavy burden on manufacturers, driving some out of business and hindering the ability of others to compete. The principal beneficiary of the suits is the legal profession. According to a study conducted by the Rand Corporation, for every one dollar received by accident victims in product liability suits, two dollars are spent for legal services.[43] Other complaints of critics are that the threat of liability suits stifles innovation, since new and untested products are more likely to be defective, and that a patchwork of state laws with differing theories and standards creates uncertainty for manufacturers. For these reasons, many business leaders have pressed for uniform product liability laws, upper limits on awards, and other steps to ease the impact of product liability on manufacturers.

Conclusion

Which theory of liability is applied by the courts is of immense importance to manufacturers and consumers. Although this is a matter to be decided, in part, by legal and political considerations, there are also important ethical issues in the debate. The theories rest on different ethical foundations. The due care theory is based on the Aristotelian principle of compensatory justice; the contractual theory, on freedom of contract; and strict liability, largely on utilitarian considerations. Each one embodies something we consider morally fundamental, and yet the three theories are ultimately incompatible. The contractual theory is the least satisfactory because of the power of manufacturers to write warranties and other agreements to their own advantage and to offer them to consumers on a "take it or leave it" basis. The main shortcoming of the due care theory is the difficulty of deciding what constitutes due care and whether it was exercised. Strict liability, despite the absence of fault, is arguably the best theory. It provides a powerful incentive for manufacturers to take extreme precautions and creates a workable legal framework for compensating consumers who are injured by defective products. For strict liability to be just, however, the costs have to be properly distributed, so that they are fair to all parties.

NOTES

1. Material on this case is taken from *Corporation v. Environment: The Case of the Firestone 500 Radial*, Sloan School of Management, MIT; and "Managing Product Safety: The Firestone 500," Harvard Business School. The case is also described in MANUEL G. VELASQUEZ, *Business Ethics: Concepts and Cases*, 2nd ed. (Englewood Cliffs, NJ: Prentice Hall, 1988), 269–71.
2. For a discussion of this point, see ELIZABETH GATEWOOD and ARCHIE B. CARROLL, "The Anatomy of Corporate Social Response: The Rely, Firestone 500, and Pinto Cases," *Business Horizons*, 24 (September–October 1981), 9–16.
3. *Marketing Definitions: A Glossary of Marketing Terms* (Chicago: American Marketing Association, 1960), 15.
4. RACHEL CARSON, *Silent Spring* (Boston: Houghton Mifflin, 1962).

5. JESSICA MITFORD, *The American Way of Death* (New York: Simon & Schuster, 1963).

6. RALPH NADER, *Unsafe at Any Speed* (New York: Brossman, 1965).

7. An explanation of the marketing concept can be found in any standard marketing textbook. The origin of the concept is commonly attributed to J. B. MCKITTERICK, "What Is the Marketing Management Concept?" in FRANK M. BASS, ed., *The Frontiers of Marketing Thought and Science* (Chicago: American Marketing Association 1958), 71–82. See also A. P. FELTON "Making the Marketing Concept Work," *Harvard Business Review*, 37 (July–August 1959), 55–65.

8. "Business Responds to Consumerism," *Business Week*, September 6, 1969, p. 95.

9. PETER F. DRUCKER, "The Shame of Marketing," *Marketing/Communications*, August 1969, p. 60.

10. For further criticism of the marketing concept, see LESLIE M. DAWSON, "The Human Concept: New Philosophy of Business," *Business Horizons*, 12 (December 1969), 29–38; MARTIN L. BELL and C. WILLIAM EMORY, "The Faltering Market Concept," *Journal of Marketing*, 35 (October 1971), 37–42; PHILIP KOTLER, "What Consumerism Means for Marketers," *Harvard Business Review*, 50 (May–June 1972), 48–57; ROGER C. BENNETT and ROBERT G. COOPER, "Beyond the Marketing Concept," *Business Horizons*, 22 (June 1979), 76–83; PETER C. RIESZ, "Revenge of the Marketing Concept," *Business Horizons*, 23 (June 1980), 49–53; LESLIE M. DAWSON, "Marketing for Human Needs," *Business Horizons*, 23 (June 1980), 72–82; ROGER C. BENNETT and ROBERT G. COOPER, "The Misuse of Marketing: An American Tragedy," *Business Horizons*, 24 (November–December 1981), 36–48.

11. *Great A & P Co., Inc.*, 85 F.T.C. 601 (1975).

12. See TOM L. BEAUCHAMP, "Manipulative Advertising," in TOM L. BEAUCHAMP and NORMAN E. BOWIE, eds. *Ethical Theory and Business*, 3rd ed. (Englewood Cliffs, NJ: Prentice Hall, 1988), 425.

13. JOHN B. HINGE, "Critics Call Cuts in Package Size Deceptive Move," *The Wall Street Journal*, February 5, 1991 p. B1.

14. ERIC GELLER, "Selling Encyclopedias," in DAVID SANFORD, *Hot War on the Consumer* (New York: Pitman, 1969), 135.

15. Manipulative sales practices that exploit the poor are well documented in DAVID CAPLOVITZ, *The Poor Pay More* (New York: The Free Press, 1963) and the report by the National Advisory Commission on Civil Disorders, better known as the Kerner Commission, in 1968. Another study is ALAN R. ANDREASEN, *The Disadvantaged Consumer* (New York: The Free Press, 1975).

16. See, for example, LEO BOGART, "The Researcher's Dilemma," *Journal of Marketing*, 26 (January 1962), 6–11; A. B. BLANKENSHIP, "Some Aspects of Ethics in Marketing Research," *Journal of Marketing Research*, 1 (May 1964), 26–31; SHELBY D. HUNT, LAWRENCE B. CHONKO, and JAMES B. WILCOX, "Ethical Problems of Market Researchers," *Journal of Marketing Research*, 21 (1984), 309–24.

17. See ALICE M. TYBOUT and GERALD ZALTMAN, "Ethics in Marketing Research: Their Practical Relevance," *Journal of Marketing Research*, 11 (November 1974), 357–68; KENNETH C. SCHNEIDER, "Subject and Respondent

Abuse in Marketing Research," *MSU Business Topics*, Spring 1977, 13–20; and DEL I. HAWKINS, "The Impact of Sponsor Identification and Direct Disclosure on Respondent Rights on the Quantity and Quality of Mail Survey Data," *Journal of Business*, 52 (1979), 577–90.

18. See JOHN R. WILKE, "Lotus Product Spurs Fears About Privacy," *The Wall Street Journal*, November 13, 1990, p. B1; and MICHAEL W. MILLER, "Lotus Is Likely to Abandon Consumer-Data Project," *The Wall Street Journal*, January 23 1991, p. B1.

19. *United States* v. *Colgate & Company*, 250 U.S. 300 (1919).

20. See, for example, *United States* v. *Parke, Davis, & Co.*, 362 U.S. 29 (1960).

21. There have been two large-scale price-fixing conspiracies in the last half century, one among electrical equipment manufacturers around 1960 and a second among folding box manufacturers in the late 1970s. On the first, see RICHARD A. SMITH, "The Incredible Electrical Conspiracy," *Fortune*, Part I (April 1961) and Part II (May 1961). An insightful discussion of the factors that lead companies to engage in such conspiracies is JEFFREY SONNENFELD and PAUL R. LAWRENCE, "Why Do Companies Succumb to Price Fixing?" *Harvard Business Review*, 56 (July–August 1978), 145–57.

22. *Standard Oil Company New Jersey* v. *U.S.*, 221 U.S. 1 (1911).

23. *U.S.* v. *American Tobacco Company*, 221 U.S. 106 (1911).

24. See JOHN S. MCGEE, "Predatory Price Cutting: The Standard Oil (N.J.) Case," *Journal of Law and Economics*, 1 (1958), 137–69; PHILIP AREEDA and DONALD F. TURNER, "Predatory Pricing and Related Practices under Section 2 of the Sherman Act," *Harvard Law Review*, 88 (1975), 720–32; and OLIVER E. WILLIAMSON, "Predatory Pricing: A Strategic and Welfare Analysis," *Yale Law Journal*, 87 (1977), 284–340.

25. See B. S. YAMEY, "Predatory Price Cutting: Notes and Comments," *Journal of Law and Economics*, 15 (1972), 129–47.

26. For the sake of simplicity, the discussion in this section focuses only on manufacturers, but a responsibility for product safety extends to wholesalers, distributors, franchisers, and retailers, among others, although their responsibility is generally less than that of manufacturers.

27. The conditions under which a negligent act is a cause of injury to another person (known in law as *proximate* cause) are complicated. See any standard textbook on business law for an explanation.

28. *Larsen* v. *General Motors Corporation*, 391 F.2d 495 (8th Cir. 1968).

29. *LeBouef* v. *Goodyear Tire and Rubber Co.*, 623 F.2d 985 (5th Cir. 1980).

30. See ED TIMMERMAN and BRAD REID, "The Doctrine of Invited Misuse: A Societal Response to Marketing Promotion," *Journal of Macromarketing*, 4 (Fall 1984), 40–48.

31. *Commercial National Bank of Little Rock, Guardian of the Estate of Jo Ann Fitzsimmons* v. *General Motors Corporation*, U.S. Dist. Ct. E.D.Ark., No. LR-C-79-168 (1979).

32. *United States* v. *Carroll Towing Co.*, 159 F.2d 169 (2d Cir. 1947).

33. *Bashada* v. *Johns-Manville Products Corp.*, 90 N.J. 191, 447 A.2d 539 (1982). The "state-of-the-art" defense has been accepted in other cases. See, for example, *Boatland of Houston, Inc.* v. *Bailey*, 609 S.W.2d 743 (Tex. 1980). For an overview, see JORDAN H. LEIBMAN, "The Manufacturer's Responsibility to

Warn Product Users of Unknowable Dangers," *American Business Law Journal*, 21 (1984), 403–38.

34. *Henningsen* v. *Bloomfield Motors, Inc. and Chrysler Corporation*, 161 A.2d 69 (1960).
35. VELASQUEZ, *Business Ethics*, 282.
36. *MacPherson* v. *Buick Motor Company*, 217 N.Y. 382 (1916).
37. *Baxter* v. *Ford Motor Co.*, 168 Wash. 456, 12 P.2d 409 (1932); 179 Wash. 123, 35 P.2d 1090 (1934).
38. *Greenman* v. *Yuba Power Products*, 59 Cal. 2d 57, 377 P. 2d 897, 27 Cal. Rptr. 697 (1963). The theory was enunciated nineteen years earlier in *Escola* v. *Coca-Cola Bottling Co.*, 24 Cal. 2d 453, 150 P. 2d 436 (1944).
39. *Escola* v. *Coca-Cola Bottling Co.*
40. RICHARD A. EPSTEIN, *Modern Products Liability Law* (Westport, CT: Quorum Books, 1980), 27. Epstein holds, however, that this principle has limited application in product liability cases.
41. GEORGE P. FLETCHER, "Fairness and Utility in Tort Theory," *Harvard Law Review*, 85 (1972), 537–73; RICHARD A. EPSTEIN, "A Theory of Strict Liability," *Journal of Legal Studies*, 2 (1973), 151–204; and JULES L. COLEMAN, "The Morality of Strict Tort Liability," *William and Mary Law Review*, 18 (1976), 259–586. RICHARD POSNER argues that the Aristotelian principle of compensatory justice in a negligence system, correctly understood, is the same as the principle of efficiency that underlies strict liability. See "A Theory of Negligence," *Journal of Legal Studies*, 1 (1972), 29–96; and "The Concept of Corrective Justice in Recent Theories of Tort Law," *Journal of Legal Studies*, 10 (1981), 187–206.
42. This proposal was contained in S. 44, an unsuccessful bill introduced in the 98th Congress.
43. Cited in STEPHEN M. SETTLE and SHARON SPIGELMYER, *Product Liability: A Multibillion-Dollar Dilemma* (New York: American Management Association, 1984), 10.

CHAPTER THIRTEEN
Occupational Health and Safety

Benzene is a colorless, vaporous liquid widely used as a solvent in the printing, rubber, paint, and dry-cleaning industries. It is a raw material or an intermediate product in the synthesis of many chemicals and a constituent of many petroleum products. Benzene is also highly toxic. Contact with the skin causes irritation and blistering, and the consequences of breathing benzene vapors in high concentrations include headache, fatigue, dizziness, convulsions, and even death from paralysis of the nervous system. The most serious effects of benzene exposure result from damage to the blood-cell-forming system of the bone marrow. Victims of benzene poisoning experience a variety of blood disorders that often lead to debilitating aplastic anemia and potentially fatal infections. Chronic exposure to high levels of benzene has also been linked to leukemia.

Before the dangers of benzene were known, the exposure of workers was routine. According to a study done in 1939, three printing plants in New York City, employing 350 men, used about fifty thousand gallons of benzene a month, mostly as an ink solvent.[1] The workers were exposed to fumes from open troughs of ink on the printing presses, from accidental spills on the floor, and from ink drying on the paper. Benzene was also used to clean the machines, and workers cleaned themselves with it at the end of the day. An examination of 332 workers found that 130 of them had benzene poisoning in varying degrees, and further tests on a group of 102 workers revealed 22 severe cases, including 6 requiring hospitalization. The use of benzene in printing has long since been discontinued, but it was replaced at first with methanol, also known as wood alcohol, and carbon tetrachloride, both of which damage the central nervous system and internal organs, including the liver and kidneys. Methanol can also produce blindness.

Because of the toxicity of benzene, a permissible exposure limit (PEL) of 10 parts per million (ppm) was set by the Occupational Safety and Health Administration (OSHA), the federal regulatory body created in 1970 to protect Americans from workplace hazards. The assumption that exposure below the level of 10 ppm is safe was challenged in 1977 when a disproportionate number of leukemia deaths occurred at two rubber pliofilm plants in Ohio.[2] On the evidence contained in a report by the National Institute for Occupational Safety and Health (NIOSH), OSHA declared benzene to be a leukemia-causing agent and issued an emergency temporary standard ordering that the PEL for benzene in most work sites be reduced to 1 ppm until a hearing could be conducted on setting a new limit. OSHA was acting under a section of the law that requires the PEL for a known carcinogen (cancer-causing agent) to be set at the lowest technologically feasible level that will not impair the viability of the industries being regulated.

In the resulting uproar, the American Petroleum Institute, a trade association of domestic oil companies, contended that the evidence linking benzene to leukemia was not conclusive and that the exposure standard should take into account the cost of compliance. Previous studies had documented the incidence of leukemia only at exposures above 25 ppm. One study of exposure below 10 ppm, conducted by Dow Chemical Company, found three leukemia deaths in a group of 594 workers, where 0.2 deaths would be expected, but it was impossible to rule out other causes, since the workers who developed leukemia had been exposed to other carcinogens during their careers. OSHA was unable to demonstrate, therefore, that exposure to benzene below the level of 10 ppm had ever caused leukemia.

According to OSHA figures, complying with the 1 ppm standard would require companies to spend approximately $266 million in capital improvements, $187 million to $205 million in first-year operating costs, and $34 million in recurring annual costs. The burden would be least in the rubber industry, where two thirds of the workers exposed to benzene are employed. The petroleum-refining industry, by contrast, would be required to incur $24 million in capital costs and $600,000 in first-year operating expenses. The cost of protecting 300 petroleum refinery workers would be $82,000 each, compared with a cost of only $1,390 per worker in the rubber industry.

No one questions the hazards posed by benzene and the necessity to limit the exposure of workers. Workers have a right to be protected from excessive exposure to toxic chemicals in the workplace. It may be asked, however, whether a reduction to the lowest technologically feasible level is justified, especially in view of the lack of conclusive evidence of the hazards at low levels of exposure. Also, should the cost of complying with the reduced standard be a factor in determining the acceptable level of safety in the workplace?

These are some of the questions that are posed by the benzene case. Other cases raise questions about the right of employees to be given information about the workplace hazards to which they are exposed and their right to refuse to perform dangerous work without fear of dismissal or other reprisals. An especially difficult kind of case is posed by the fact that certain jobs pose a health threat to the fetus of a pregnant woman and to the reproductive capacities of both men and women. Some pregnant women and women of child-bearing age are demanding the right to transfer out of jobs thought to pose reproductive hazards. On the other hand, employers who exclude pregnant women or women of child-bearing age from certain jobs because of reproductive hazards are open to charges of illegal sexual discrimination, especially when they do not show an equal concern for the reproductive risk to men.

This chapter is concerned with determining how questions about the rights of workers in matters of occupational health and safety ought to be answered. At issue in these questions is not only the obligation of employers with respect to the rights of workers but also the justification for government regulation of the workplace, especially by the Occupational Safety and Health Administration. As a result, many of the questions discussed in this chapter deal with specific regulatory programs and policies, which are the subject of intense controversy.

THE SCOPE OF THE PROBLEM

Many Americans live with the possibility of serious injury and death every working day. For some workers, the threat comes from a major industrial accident, such as the collapse of a mine or a refinery explosion, or from widespread exposure to a hazardous substance, such as asbestos, which is estimated to have caused more than 350,000 cancer deaths since 1940.[3] The greatest toll on the work force is exacted, however, by little publicized injuries to individual workers, some of which are gradual, such as hearing loss from constant noise or nerve damage from repetitive motions. Some of the leading causes of death, such as heart disease, cancer, and respiratory conditions, are thought to be job-related, although causal connections are often difficult to make.

Even stress on the job is now being recognized as a workplace hazard that is responsible for headaches, back and chest pains, stomach ailments, and a variety of emotional disorders.

The Distinction Between Health and Safety

Although the term *safety* is often used to encompass all workplace hazards, it is useful to make a distinction between *safety* and *health*.[4] Safety hazards generally involve loss of limbs, burns, broken bones, electrical shocks, cuts, sprains, bruises, and impairment of sight or hearing. These injuries are usually the result of sudden and often violent events involving industrial equipment or the physical environment of the workplace. Examples include coming into contact with moving parts of machinery or electrical lines, getting hit by falling objects or flying debris, chemical spills and explosions, fires, and falls from great heights.

Health hazards are factors in the workplace that cause illnesses and other conditions which develop over a lifetime of exposure. Many diseases associated with specific occupations have long been known. In 1567, Paracelsus identified pneumoconiosis, or black lung disease, in a book entitled *Miners' Sickness and Other Miners' Diseases*. Silicosis, or the "white plague," has traditionally been associated with stone cutters. Other well-known occupational diseases are caisson disease among divers, cataracts in glass blowers, skin cancer among chimney sweeps, and phosphorus poisoning in match makers. Mercury poisoning, once common among felt workers, produces tremors, known as "the hatters' shakes," and delusions and hallucinations that gave rise to the phrase "mad as a hatter."

In the modern workplace, most occupational health problems result from routine exposure to hazardous substances. Among these substances are fine particles, such as asbestos, which causes asbestiosis, and cotton dust, which causes byssinosis; heavy metals, such as lead, cadmium, and beryllium; gases, including chlorine, ozone, sulphur dioxide, carbon monoxide, hydrogen sulfide, and hydrogen cyanide, which damage the lungs and often cause neurological problems; solvents, such as benzene, carbon tetrachloride, and carbon disulfide; and certain classes of chemicals, especially phenols, ketones, and epoxies. Pesticides pose a serious threat to agricultural workers and radiation is an occupational hazard to X-ray technicians and workers in the nuclear industry.

Because occupationally related diseases result from long-term exposure and not from identifiable events on the job, employers have generally not been held liable for them, and they have not, until recently, been recognized in workers' compensation programs. The fact that the onset of many diseases occurs years after the initial exposure—thirty or forty years in the case of asbestos—hides the causal connection. The links are further obscured by a multiplicity of causes. The textile industry, for example, claims that byssinosis among its workers results from their own decision to smoke and not from inhaling cotton dust on the job.[5] Lack of knowledge, especially about cancer, adds to the difficulty of establishing causal connections.

Regulation of Occupational Health and Safety

Prior to the passage of the Occupational Safety and Health Act (OSH Act) in 1970, government regulation of occupational health and safety was almost entirely the province of the states. Understaffed and underfunded, the agencies charged with protecting workers in most states were not very effective.[6] Only a small percentage of workers in many states were even under the jurisdiction of regulatory agencies; often, powerful economic interests were able to influence their activities. Because the agencies lacked the resources to set standards for exposure to hazardous substances, they relied heavily on private standard-setting organizations and the industries themselves. The emphasis in most states was on education and training, and prosecutions for violations were rare. State regulatory agencies were also concerned almost exclusively with safety rather than with health.

States still play a major role in occupational health and safety through workers' compensation systems, but in 1970, primary responsibility for the regulation of working conditions passed to the federal government. The "general duty clause" of the OSH Act requires employers "to furnish to each of his employees employment and a place of employment which are free from recognized hazards that are causing or are likely to cause death or serious injury."[7] In addition, employers have a specific duty to comply with all the occupational safety and health standards that OSHA is empowered to make. Employees also have a duty, under Section 5(b), to "comply with occupational safety and health standards and all rules, regulations, and orders issued pursuant to this Act which are applicable to his own actions and conduct." OSHA regulates occupational health and safety primarily by issuing and enforcing standards, which are commonly enforced by workplace inspections. Examples of standards are permissible exposure limits (PELs) for toxic substances and specifications for equipment and facilities, such as guards on saws and the height and strength of railings.

THE RIGHT TO A SAFE AND HEALTHY WORKPLACE

At first glance, the right of employees to a safe and healthy workplace might seem to be too obvious to need any justification. This right—and the corresponding obligation of employers to provide working conditions free of recognized hazards—appears to follow from a more fundamental right—namely, the right of survival. Patricia H. Werhane writes, for example, "Dangerous working conditions threaten the very existence of employees and cannot be countenanced when they are avoidable." Without this right, she argues, all other rights lose their significance.[8] Some other writers base a right to a safe and healthy workplace on the Kantian ground that persons ought to be treated as ends rather than as means. Mark MacCarthy has described this view as follows:

> People have rights that protect them from others who would enslave them or otherwise use them for their own purposes. In bringing this idea to bear on the problem of occupational safety, many people have thought that workers have an inalienable right to earn their living free from the ravages of job-caused death, disease, and injury.[9]

Congress, in passing the OSH Act granting the right to all employees of a safe and healthy workplace, was apparently relying on a cost-benefit analysis, balancing the cost to industry with the savings to the economy as a whole. Congress, in other words, appears to have been employing essentially utilitarian reasoning. Regardless of the ethical reasoning used, though, workers have an undeniable right not to be injured or killed on the job.

It is not clear, though, what specific protection workers are entitled to or what specific obligations employers have with respect to occupational health and safety. One position, recognized in common law, is that workers have a right to be protected against harm resulting directly from the actions of employers where the employer is at fault in some way. Consider the case of the owner of a drilling company in Los Angeles who had a 23-year-old worker lowered into a 33-foot-deep, 18-inch-wide hole that was being dug for an elevator shaft.[10] No test was made of the air at the bottom of the hole, and while he was being lowered, the worker began to have difficulty breathing. Rescue workers were hampered by the lack of shoring, and the worker died before he could be pulled to the surface. The owner of the drilling company was convicted of manslaughter, sentenced to 45 days in jail, and ordered to pay $12,000 in compensation to the family of the victim. A prosecutor in the Los Angeles County district attorney's office explained the decision to bring criminal charges with the words, "Our opinion is you can't risk somebody's life to save a few bucks. That's the bottom line."

Few people would hesitate to say that the owner of the company in this case violated an employee's rights by recklessly endangering his life. In most workplace accidents, however, employers can defend themselves against the charge of violating the rights of workers with two arguments. One is that their actions were not the *direct cause* of the death or injury, and the other is that the worker *voluntarily assumed the risk*. These defenses are considered in turn.

The Notion of a Direct Cause

Two factors enable employers to deny that their actions are a direct cause of an accident in the workplace.[11] One factor is that industrial accidents are typically caused by a combination of factors, frequently including the actions of workers themselves. When there is such a multiplicity of causes, it is difficult to assign responsibility to any one person.[12] The legal treatment of industrial accidents in the United States incorporates this factor by recognizing two common-law defenses for employers: that a workplace accident was caused in part by (1) lack of care on the part of the employee (the doctrine of "contributory negligence") or by (2) the negligence of co-workers (the "fellow-servant rule"). As long as employers are not negligent in meeting minimal obligations, they are not generally held liable for deaths or injuries resulting from industrial accidents.

The second factor is that it is often not practical to reduce the probability of harm any further. It is reasonable to hold an employer responsible for the incidence of cancer in workers who are exposed to high levels of a known carcinogen, especially when the exposure is avoidable. But a small number of cancer deaths can be statistically predicted to result from very low exposure levels to some widely used chemicals. Is it reasonable to hold employers responsible when workers contract cancer from exposure to carcinogens at levels that are considered to pose only a slight risk? The so-called Delaney amendment, for example, forbids the use of any food additive found to cause cancer.[13] Such an absolute prohibition is practicable for food additives, since substitutes are usually readily available. But when union and public-interest groups petitioned OSHA in 1972 to set zero tolerance levels for ten powerful carcinogens, the agency refused on the ground that workers should be protected from carcinogens "to the maximum extent practicable *consistent with continued use*."[14] The position of OSHA, apparently, was that it is unreasonable to forego the benefit of useful chemicals when there are no ready substitutes and the probability of cancer can be kept low by strict controls. This is also the position of philosopher Alan Gewirth, who argues that the right of persons not to have cancer inflicted on them is not absolute. He concluded, "Whether the use of or exposure to some substance should be prohibited should depend on the degree to which it poses the risk of cancer. . . . If the risks are very slight . . . and if no substitutes are available, then use of it may be permitted, subject to stringent safeguards."[15]

The Benzene Case

This issue arose again in 1977 in the benzene case discussed in the introduction to this chapter. The main legal issue faced by the Supreme Court is the authority of the Secretary of Labor under the OSH Act to set standards. An "occupational safety and health standard" is defined in Section 3(8) of the OSH Act as "a standard which requires conditions, or the adoption or use of one or more practices, means, methods, operations, or processes, reasonably necessary or appropriate to provide safe or healthful employment and places of employment." And Section 6(b)(5) states:

> The Secretary, in promulgating standards dealing with toxic materials or harmful physical agents under this subsection, shall set the standard which most adequately assures, to the extent feasible, on the basis of the best available evidence, that no employee will suffer material impairment of health or functional capacity even if such employee has regular exposure to the hazard dealt with by such standard for the period of his working life. Development of standards under this subsection shall be based upon research, demonstrations, experiments, and such other information as may be appropriate. In addition to the attainment of the highest degree of health and safety protection for the employee, other considerations shall be the latest available scientific data in the field, the feasibility of the standards, and experience gained under this and other health and safety laws.

Two specific issues raised by the language of the OSH Act are (1) What is meant by "to the extent feasible"? Should all technologically possible steps be taken? Or should some consideration be given to the economic burden on employers? Should the agency, in determining what is "reasonably necessary and appropriate," also weigh costs and benefits? (2) What amount of evidence is required? To what extent should the agency be required to provide valid scientific studies to prove that a standard addresses a genuine problem and will, in fact, achieve the intended result? On the one hand, the power to set emergency standards on the basis of flimsy evidence that turns out later not to warrant action exposes businesses to the possibility of heavy and unpredictable expenses. On the other hand, adequate scientific research is very costly and time-consuming. Lack of funding for research and the time lag between suspicion and proof that a substance is carcinogenic, for example, could result in the needless deaths of many workers. A high level of proof exposes workers to preventable harm, therefore, but at the price of a possibly unnecessary cost to employers. Where does the balance lie?

A plurality of justices agreed with a lower court opinion that OSHA does not have "unbridled discretion to adopt standards designed to create absolutely risk-free workplaces regardless of the cost." But no consensus was achieved on how the level of risk is to be determined and, in particular, whether OSHA is required to use cost-benefit analysis in setting standards. By a bare majority, though, the Supreme Court struck down the 1 ppm standard because the agency was unable to prove that exposure to benzene below concentrations of 10 ppm is harmful. Ample evidence existed at the time to justify a 10 ppm standard, but little evidence indicated that a lower standard would achieve any additional benefits. The Court's answer to the second question, then, is that a rather high level of proof is needed to impose a highly restrictive standard.

In a subsequent case, however, the Court ruled that OSHA is not required to take cost into account but only technological feasibility. The case, *American Textile Manufacturers Institute Inc.* v. *Raymond J. Donovan, Secretary of Labor*, concerned an established standard for cotton dust, which is the primary cause of byssinosis, or "brown lung," disease. The evidence linking cotton dust to byssinosis was not in dispute, but OSHA relied on cost-benefit studies that the agency itself admitted underestimated the cost of compliance. The reason given for not requiring OSHA to consider costs and benefits is that Congress in passing the OSH Act had already made a cost-benefit analysis.[16] According to the majority opinion:

> Not only does the legislative history confirm that Congress meant "feasible" rather than "cost-benefit" when it used the former term, but it also shows that Congress understood that the Act would create substantial costs for employers, yet intended to impose such costs when necessary to create a safe and healthful working environment. . . . Indeed Congress thought that the *financial costs* of health and safety problems in the workplace were as large as or larger than the *financial costs* of eliminating these problems.

Cost-benefit analysis is the proper instrument for striking a balance on issues of worker health and safety, in other words, but this instrument was used by Congress as a justification for empowering OSHA to set standards without regard for costs. OSHA, therefore, should base its decisions solely on technological feasibility.

As a postscript to the benzene case, OSHA announced in March 1986 a new standard based on subsequent research. The new standard, which took effect in February 1988, set a permissible exposure limit of 1 ppm for an eight-hour workday, with a short-term limit of 5 ppm. By this time, however, improvements in equipment and the monitoring of airborne pollutants required by the Environmental Protection Agency (EPA) had already reduced the level of exposure to benzene close to the 1 ppm standard. Consequently, the initial capital expenditures for meeting the new standard were considerably less than in 1977, ten years earlier, when the controversy first erupted.

The Voluntary Assumption of Risk

A further common-law defense is that employees voluntarily assume the risk inherent in work. Some jobs, such as coal mining, construction, longshoring, and meatpacking, are well-known for their high accident rates, and yet some individuals freely choose these lines of work, even when safer employment is available. The risk itself is sometimes part of the allure, but more often the fact that hazardous jobs offer a wage premium in order to compensate for the greater risk leads workers to prefer them to less hazardous, less well-paying jobs. Like people who choose to engage in risky recreational activities, such as mountain-climbing, workers in hazardous occupations, according to the argument, knowingly accept the risk in return for benefits that cannot be obtained without it. Injury and even death are part of the price they may have to pay. And except when an employer or a fellow employee is negligent in some way, workers who have chosen to work under dangerous conditions have no one to blame but themselves.

A related argument is that occupational health and safety ought not to be regulated because it interferes with the freedom of individuals to choose the kind of work that they want to perform. Workers who prefer the higher wages of hazardous work ought to be free to accept such employment, and those with a greater aversion to risk ought to be free to choose other kinds of employment or to bargain for more safety, presumably with lower pay. To deny workers this freedom of choice is to treat them as persons incapable of looking after their own welfare.[17] W. Kip Viscusi, who served as a consultant to OSHA during the Reagan administration, adds an extra twist by arguing that programs designed to keep workers from being maimed and killed on the job are a form of class oppression. He has written:

> Efforts to promote present risk regulations on the basis that they enhance worker rights are certainly misguided. Uniform standards do not enlarge worker choices; they deprive workers of the opportunity to select the job most appropriate to their own risk preferences. The actual "rights" issue involved is whether those in upper income groups have a right to impose their job risk preferences on the poor.[18]

The argument that employees assume the risk of work can be challenged on several grounds. First, workers need to possess a sufficient amount of information about the hazards involved. They cannot be said to assume the risk of performing dangerous work when they do not know what the risks are. Also, they cannot exercise the right to bargain for safer working conditions without access to the relevant information. Yet, employers have generally been reluctant to notify workers or their bargaining agents of dangerous conditions or to release documents in their possession. Oftentimes, hazards in the workplace are not known by the employer or the employee until after the harm has been done. In order for employers to be relieved of responsibility for injury or death in the workplace, though, it is necessary that employees have adequate information *at the time they make a choice.*

Second, the choice of employees must be truly free. When workers are forced to perform dangerous work for lack of acceptable alternatives, they cannot be said to assume the risk. For many people with few skills and limited mobility in economically depressed areas, the only work available is often in a local slaughterhouse or textile mill, where they run great risks. Whether they are coerced into accepting work of this kind is a controversial question. Individuals are free in one sense to accept or decline whatever employment is available, but the alternatives of unemployment or work at poverty level wages may be so unacceptable that people lack freedom of choice in any significant sense.

Risk and Coercion

In order to determine whether workers assume the risk of employment by their free choice, we need some account of the concept of coercion. A paradigm example is the mugger who says with a gun in hand, "Your money or your life." The "choice" offered by the mugger contains an undesirable set of alternatives that are imposed on the victim by a threat of dire consequences. A standard analysis of coercion that is suggested by this example involves two elements: (1) getting a person to choose an alternative that he or she does not want, and (2) issuing a threat to make the person worse off if he or she does not choose that alternative.

Consider the case of an employer who offers a worker who already holds a satisfactory job higher wages in return for taking on new duties involving a greater amount of risk.[19] The employer's offer is not coercive because there is no threat involved. The worker may welcome the offer, but declining it leaves the worker still in possession of an acceptable position. Is an employer acting like a mugger, however, when the offer of higher pay for more dangerous work is accompanied by the threat of dismissal? Is "Do this hazardous work or be fired!" like or unlike the "choice" offered by the mugger? The question is even more difficult when the only "threat" is not to hire a person. Is it coercive to say, "Accept this dangerous job or stay unemployed!" since the alternative of remaining out of work leaves the person in exactly the same position as before? Remaining unemployed, moreover, is unlike getting fired, in that it is not something that an employer inflicts on a person.

In order to answer these questions, the standard analysis of coercion needs to be supplemented by an account of what it means to issue a threat. A threat involves a stated intention of making a person worse off in some way. To fire a person from a job is usually to make that person worse off, but we would not say that an employer is coercing a worker by threatening dismissal for failure to perform the normal duties of a job. Similarly, we would not say that an employer is making a threat in not hiring a person who refuses to carry out the same normal duties. A person who turns down a job because the office is not provided with air conditioning, for example, is not being made worse off by the employer. So why would we say that a person who chooses to remain unemployed rather than work in a coal mine that lacks adequate ventilation is being coerced?

The answer of some philosophers is that providing employees with air conditioning is not morally required; however, maintaining a safe mine is. Whether a threat is coercive because it would make a person worse off can be determined only if there is some base line that answers the question, worse off compared to what? Robert Nozick gives an example of an abusive slave owner who offers not to give a slave his daily beating if the slave will perform some disagreeable task the slave owner wants done.[20] Even though the slave might welcome the offer, it is still coercive, since the daily beating involves treating the slave in an immoral manner. For Nozick and others, what is *morally required* is the relevant base line for determining whether a person would be made worse off by a threatened course of action.[21]

It follows from this analysis that coercion is an inherently ethical concept that can be applied only after determining what is morally required in a given situation.[22] As a result, the argument that the assumption of risk by employees relieves employers of responsibility involves circular reasoning. Employers are freed from responsibility for workplace injuries on the ground that workers assume the risk of employment only if workers are not coerced into accepting hazardous work. But whether workers are coerced depends on the right of employees to a safe and healthy workplace—and the obligation of employers to provide it.

Conclusion

In conclusion, the right of employees to a safe and healthy workplace cannot be justified merely by appealing to a right not to be injured or killed. The weakness of this argument lies in the difficulty of determining the extent to which employers are *responsible* for the harm that workers suffer as a result of occupational injuries and diseases. The argument applies only to dangers that are directly caused by the actions of employers; however, industrial accidents result from many causes, including the actions of co-workers and the affected workers themselves.

The responsibility of employers is also problematical when the probability of harm from their actions is low. Moreover, the responsibility of employers is reduced insofar as employees voluntarily assume the risk inherent in employment. Whether the choice to accept hazardous work is voluntary, though, depends in part on difficult questions about the concept of coercion, which, on one standard analysis, can be applied only after the rights of employees in matters of occupational health and safety have been determined.

THE RIGHT TO KNOW ABOUT AND REFUSE HAZARDOUS WORK

The Whirlpool Corporation operates a plant in Marion, Ohio, for the assembly of household appliances.[23] Components for the appliances are carried throughout the plant by an elaborate system of overhead conveyors. To protect workers from the objects that occasionally fall from the conveyors, a huge wire mesh screen was installed approximately twenty feet above the floor. The screen is attached to an angle-iron frame suspended from the ceiling of the building. Maintenance employees at the plant spend several hours every week retrieving fallen objects from the screen. Their job also includes replacing paper that is spread on the screen to catch dripping grease from the conveyors, and occasionally they do maintenance work on the conveyors themselves. Workers are usually able to stand on the frame to perform these tasks, but occasionally it is necessary to step onto the screen.

In 1973, several workers fell partway through the screen, and one worker fell completely through to the floor of the plant below but survived. Afterward, Whirlpool began replacing the screen with heavier wire mesh, but on June 28, 1974, a maintenance employee fell to his death through a portion of the screen that had not been replaced. The company responded by making additional repairs and forbidding employees to stand on the angle-iron frame or step onto the screen. An alternative method for retrieving objects was devised using hooks.

Two maintenance employees at the Marion plant, Virgil Deemer and Thomas Cornwell, were still not satisfied. On July 7, 1974, they met with the maintenance supervisor at the plant to express their concern about the safety of the screen. At a meeting two days later with the plant safety director, they requested the name, address, and telephone number of a representative in the local office of the Occupational Safety and Health Administration. The safety director warned the men that they "had better stop and think about what they were doing," but he gave them the requested information. Deemer called the OSHA representative later that day to discuss the problem.

When Deemer and Cornwell reported for the night shift at 10:45 PM the next day, July 10, they were ordered by the foreman to perform routine maintenance duties above an old section of the screen. They refused, claiming that the work was unsafe; whereupon the foreman ordered the two employees to punch out. In addition to losing wages for the six hours they did not work that night, Deemer and Cornwell received written reprimands, which were placed in their personnel files.

This case illustrates a cruel dilemma faced by many American workers. If they stay on the job and perform hazardous work, then they risk serious injury and even death. On the other hand, if they refuse to work as directed, then they risk disciplinary action, which can include loss of wages, unfavorable evaluation, demotion, and dismissal. Many people believe that it is unjust for workers to be put into the position of having to choose between safety and their job. Rather, employees ought to be able to refuse orders to perform hazardous work without fear of suffering adverse consequences.

Even worse are situations in which workers face hazards of which they are unaware. Kept in the dark about dangers lurking in the workplace, employees have no reason to refuse hazardous work and are unable to take other steps to protect themselves.

Features of the Right to Know and Refuse

The right to refuse hazardous work is different from a right to a safe and healthy workplace. If it is unsafe to work above the old screen, as Deemer and Cornwell contended, then their right to a safe and healthy workplace was violated. A right to refuse hazardous work, however, is only one of several alternatives that workers have for securing the right to a safe and healthy workplace. Victims of racial or sexual discrimination, for example, also suffer a violation of their rights, but it does not follow that they have a right to disobey orders or to walk off the job in an effort to avoid discrimination. Other means are available for ending discrimination and for receiving compensation for the harm done. The same is true for the right to a safe and healthy workplace.

The right to know is actually an aggregation of several rights. Thomas O. McGarity classifies these rights by the correlative duties that they impose on employers. These are (1) the duty to *reveal* information already possessed; (2) the duty to *communicate* information about hazards through labeling, written communications, and training programs; (3) the duty to *seek out* existing information from the scientific literature and other sources; and (4) the duty to *produce* new information (for example, through animal testing) relevant to employee health.[24] Advocates of the right of workers to know need to specify which of these particular rights are included in their claim.

Disagreement also arises over questions about what information workers have a right to know and which workers have a right to know it. In particular, does the information that employers have a duty to reveal include information about the past exposure of workers to hazardous substances? And do employers have a duty to notify past as well as present employees? The issue at stake in these questions is a part of the "right to know" controversy commonly called *worker notification.*

The main argument for denying workers a right to refuse hazardous work is that such a right conflicts with the obligation of employees to obey all reasonable directives from an employer. An order for a worker to perform some especially dangerous task may not be reasonable, however. The foreman in the Whirlpool case, for example, was acting contrary to a company rule forbidding workers to step on the screen. Still, a common-law principle is that employees should obey even an improper order and file a grievance afterward, if a grievance procedure is in place, or seek whatever other recourse is available. The rationale for this principle is that employees may be mistaken about whether an order is proper, and chaos would result if employees could stop work until the question is decided. It is better for workers to obey now and correct any violation of their rights later.

The fatal flaw in this argument is that later may be too late. The right to a safe and healthy workplace, unlike the right not to be discriminated against, can effectively provide protection for workers only if violations of the right are prevented in the first place. Debilitating injury and death cannot be corrected later; neither can workers and their families ever be adequately compensated for a loss of this kind. The right to refuse hazardous work, therefore, is necessary for the existence of the right to a safe and healthy workplace.

The Justification for Refusing Hazardous Work

A right to a safe and healthy workplace is empty unless workers have a right in some circumstances to refuse hazardous work, but there is a tremendous amount of controversy over what these circumstances are. In the Whirlpool case, the Supreme Court cited two factors as relevant for justifying a refusal to work. These are (1) that the employee reasonably believes that the working conditions pose an imminent risk of death or serious injury, and (2) that the employee has reason to believe that the risk cannot be avoided by any less disruptive course of action. Employees have a right to refuse hazardous work, in other words, only as a last resort—when it is not possible to bring unsafe working conditions to the attention of the employer or to request an OSHA inspection. Also, the hazards that employees believe to exist must involve a high degree of risk of serious harm. Refusing to work because of a slight chance of minor injury is less likely to be justified. The fact that a number of workers had already fallen through the screen at the

Whirlpool plant, for example, and that one had been killed strengthens the claim that the two employees had a right to refuse their foreman's order to step onto it.

The pivotal question, of course, is the proper standard for a reasonable belief. How much evidence should employees be required to have in order to be justified in refusing to work? Or should the relevant standard be the actual existence of a workplace hazard rather than the belief of employees, no matter how reasonable? A minimal requirement, which has been insisted on by the courts, is that employees act in *good faith*. Generally, acting in good faith means that employees have an honest belief that a hazard exists and that their only intention is to protect themselves from the hazard. The "good faith" requirement serves primarily to exclude refusals based on deliberately false charges of unsafe working conditions or on sabotage by employees. Whether a refusal is in good faith does not depend on the reasonableness or correctness of the employees' beliefs about the hazards in the workplace. Thus, employees who refuse an order to fill a tank with a dangerous chemical in the mistaken but sincere belief that a valve is faulty are acting in good faith, but employees who use the same excuse to conduct a work stoppage for other reasons are not acting in good faith, even if it should turn out that the valve is faulty.

Three standards are commonly used for determining whether good faith refusals are justified. One is the *subjective* standard, which requires only that employees have evidence that they sincerely regard as sufficient for their belief that a hazard exists or which most workers in their situation would regard as sufficient. At the opposite extreme is the *objective* standard. This standard requires evidence that experts regard as sufficient to establish the existence of a hazard. In between these two is the *reasonable person* standard, which requires that the evidence be strong enough to persuade a reasonable person that a hazard exists.

The subjective standard provides the greatest protection for worker health and safety. Employees cannot be expected to have full knowledge of the hazards facing them in the workplace. They may not be told what chemicals they are using, for example, or what exposure levels are safe for these chemicals. Safe exposure levels for the chemicals may not even have been scientifically determined. Employees may also not have the means at the moment to measure the levels to which they are exposed. Yet, the objective standard forces employees to bear the consequences if their beliefs about the hazards present in the workplace cannot be substantiated. The reasonable person standard is less exacting, since it requires only that employees exercise reasonable judgment. Still, this standard places a strong burden of proof on workers who have to make a quick assessment under difficult circumstances. A wrong decision can result in the loss of a job or possibly the loss of a worker's life.

On the other hand, the subjective standard allows employees to make decisions that are ordinarily the province of management. Usually management is better informed about hazards in the workplace, along with other aspects of the work to be performed, and so their judgment should generally prevail. To allow workers to shut down production on the basis of unsubstantiated beliefs, and thereby to substitute their uninformed judgment for that of management, is likely to result in many costly mistakes. The subjective standard creates no incentive for workers to be cautious in refusing hazardous work because the cost is borne solely by the company. The reasonable person standard, therefore, which places a moderate burden of proof on employees, is perhaps the best balance of the competing considerations.

The Justification of a Right to Know

Unlike the right to refuse hazardous work, the right to know about workplace hazards is not necessary for the right to a safe and healthy workplace. This latter right is fully protected as long as employers succeed in ridding the workplace of significant hazards. Some argue that the right to know is still an effective, if not an absolutely essential, means for securing the right to a safe and healthy workplace. Others maintain, however, that the right to know is not dependent for its justification on the right to a safe and healthy workplace; that is, even employees who are adequately protected by their employers against occupational injury and disease still have a right to be told what substances they are handling, what dangers it poses, what precautions to take, and so on.

The most common argument for the right to know is one based on autonomy. This argument begins with the premise that autonomous individuals are those who are able to exercise free choice in matters that affect their welfare most deeply.[25] Sometimes this premise is expressed by saying that autonomous individuals are those who are able to *participate* in decision making about these matters. One matter that profoundly affects the welfare of workers is the amount of risk that they assume in the course of earning a living. Autonomy requires, therefore, that workers be free to avoid hazardous work, if they so choose, or have the opportunity to accept greater risks in return for higher pay, if that is their choice. In order to choose freely, however, or to participate in decision making, it is necessary to possess relevant information. And in the matter of risk assumption, the relevant information includes knowledge of the hazards present in the workplace. Workers can be autonomous, therefore, only if they have a right to know.

In response, employers maintain that they can protect workers from hazards more effectively than workers can themselves without informing workers of the nature of those hazards. Such a paternalistic concern, even when it is sincere and well-founded, is incompatible, however, with a respect for the autonomy of workers. A similar argument is sometimes used to justify paternalism in the doctor-patient relation. For a doctor to conceal information from a patient even in cases where exclusive reliance on the doctor's greater training and experience would result in better medical care is now generally regarded as unjustified. If paternalism is morally unacceptable in the doctor-patient relation, where doctors have an obligation to act in the patient's interest, then it is all the more suspect in the employer-employee relation, where employers have no such obligation.[26]

Although autonomy is a value, it does not follow that employers have an obligation to further it in their dealings with employees. The autonomy of buyers in market transactions is also increased by having more information, but the sellers of a product are not generally required to provide this information except when concealment constitutes fraud.[27] The gain of autonomy for employers must be balanced, moreover, against the not inconsiderable cost to employers of implementing a "right to know" policy in the workplace. In addition to the direct cost of assembling information, attaching warning labels, training workers, and so on, there are also indirect costs. Employees who are aware of the risk they are taking are more likely to demand higher wages or else safer working conditions. They are more likely to avail themselves of workers' compensation benefits and to sue employers over occupational injury and disease. Finally, companies are concerned about the loss of valuable trade secrets that could occur from informing workers about the hazards of certain substances.

An alternative to a right to know policy that respects the autonomy of both parties is to allow bargaining over information. Thomas O. McGarity has described this alternative in the following way:

> Because acquiring information costs money, employees desiring information about workplace risks should be willing to pay the employer (in reduced wages) or someone else to produce or gather the relevant information. A straightforward economic analysis would suggest that employees would be willing to pay for health and safety information up to the point at which the value in wage negotiations of the last piece of information purchased equaled the cost of that additional information.[28]

Although promising in theory, this alternative is not practical. It creates a disincentive for employers, who possess most of the information, to yield any of it without some concession by employees, even when it could be provided at little or no cost. Bargaining is feasible for large unions with expertise in safety matters, but reliance on it would leave members of other unions and nonunionized workers without adequate means of protection. In the absence of a market for information, neither employers nor employees would have a basis for determining the value of information in advance of negotiations. Finally, there are costs associated with using the bargaining process to decide any matter—what economists call "transaction costs"—and these are apt to be quite high in negotiations over safety issues. It is unlikely, therefore, that either autonomy or worker health and safety would be well-served by the alternative of bargaining over matters of occupational health and safety.

Utilitarian Arguments for a Right to Know

There are two arguments for the right to know as a means to greater worker health and safety. Both are broadly utilitarian in character. One argument is based on the plausible assumption that workers who are aware of hazards in the workplace will be better equipped to protect themselves. Warning labels or rules requiring protective clothing and respirators are more likely to be effective when workers fully appreciate the nature and extent of the risks they are taking. Also, merely revealing information about hazardous substances in the workplace is not apt to be effective without extensive training in the procedures for handling them safely and responding to accidents. Finally, workers who are aware of the consequences of exposure to hazardous substances will also be more likely to spot symptoms of occupational diseases and seek early treatment.

The second utilitarian argument is offered by economists who hold that overall welfare is best achieved by allowing market forces to determine the level of acceptable risk. In a free market, wages are determined in part by the willingness of workers to accept risks in return for wages. Employers can attract a sufficient supply of workers to perform hazardous work either by spending money to make the workplace safer, thereby reducing the risks, or by increasing wages to compensate workers for the greater risks. The choice is determined by the marginal utility of each kind of investment. Thus, an employer will make the workplace safer up to the point that the last dollar spent equals the increase in wages that would otherwise be required to induce workers to accept the risks. At that point, workers indicate their preference for accepting the remaining risks rather than foregoing a loss of wages in return for a safer workplace.

Unlike the autonomy argument, in which workers bargain over risk information, this argument proposes that workers bargain over the tradeoff between risks and wages. In order for a free market to determine this tradeoff in a way that achieves overall welfare, it is necessary for workers to have a sufficient amount of information about the hazard in the workplace. Thomas O. McGarity has expressed this point as follows:

A crucial component of the free market model of wage and risk determination is its assumption that workers are fully informed about the risks that they face as they bargain over wages. To the extent that risks are unknown to employees, they will undervalue overall workplace risks in wage negotiations. The result will be lower wages and an inadequate incentive to employers to install health and safety devices. In addition, to the extent that employees can avoid risks by taking action, uninformed employees will fail to do so. Society will then underinvest in wages and risk prevention, and overall societal wealth will decline. Moreover, a humane society is not likely to require diseased or injured workers to suffer without proper medical attention. In many cases, society will pick up the tab. . . .[29]

Although these two utilitarian arguments provide strong support for the right to know, they are both open to the objection that there might be more efficient means, such as more extensive OSHA regulation, for securing the goal of worker health and safety. Could the resources devoted to complying with a right to know law, for example, be better spent on formulating and enforcing more stringent standards on permissible exposure limits and on developing technologies to achieve these standards? And could the cost of producing, gathering, and disseminating information be better borne by a government agency than individual employers? These are difficult empirical questions for which conclusive evidence is largely lacking.

The Problem of Trade Secrets

One issue that remains to be addressed is the protection of trade secrets. Occasionally, information about the chemical composition of the substances used in industrial processes cannot be disclosed to workers without compromising the ability of a company to maintain a legally protected trade secret. When this is the case, is it justifiable to place limits on the right to know? These two rights—the right of workers to know about the hazards of substances that they use and the right of employers to maintain trade secrets—are not wholly incompatible, however. So it may be possible to implement the right to know in a way that maximizes the amount of information available to workers while at the same time minimizing the risk of exposing trade secrets.

Before limiting the right of employees to know, we need to be sure, first, that a genuine trade secret is involved and that it cannot be protected by any less restrictive means, such as obtaining a patent. Also, employers do not have a right to conceal *all* information connected with a trade secret but only the portion that cannot be revealed without jeopardy. Even when an employer is justified in not disclosing the chemical identity of a critical ingredient in a formula or a process, for example, there may be no justification for not providing workers with information about some of the physical characteristics and special hazards of that ingredient. Finally, information can sometimes be revealed in ways that preserve secrecy. It might be possible, for example, to reveal information about hazardous substances to union representatives or to the employees' own private physicians under a pledge of confidentiality without endangering valuable trade secrets.

THE PROBLEM OF REPRODUCTIVE HAZARDS

Hazardous substances pose a threat not only to workers but to their offspring. Pregnant women who are exposed to certain chemicals in the workplace run an increased risk of spontaneous abortion, miscarriage, and stillbirth, and they are more likely to produce children with birth defects. One common workplace substance that is know to damage the reproductive capacity of women and inflict harm on a fetus in the womb is lead, a fact that caused Johnson Controls, Inc., to consider the problem of lead exposure among its women employees.[30]

Based in Milwaukee, Wisconsin, Johnson Controls is the largest manufacturer of automobile batteries for the United States replacement market. In 1977, the company informed women in the lead battery division of the hazards of lead and asked them to sign a statement that they had been told of the risks of having a child while exposed to lead in the workplace. Between 1979 and 1983, however, eight women with blood lead levels in excess of 30 micrograms per deciliter became pregnant. In response, the company changed its policy in 1982 to exclude fertile women from all jobs where lead is present. Specifically, the policy stated:

> It is [Johnson Controls'] policy that women who are pregnant or who are capable of bearing children will not be placed into jobs involving lead exposure or which could expose them to lead through the exercise of job bidding, bumping, transfer or promotion rights.

The policy defined women "capable of bearing children" as "all women except those whose inability to bear children is medically documented."

In April 1984, a class action suit was filed, charging that Johnson Controls' fetal protection policy violated the Title VII prohibition against sex discrimination. The policy is discriminatory, the employees complained, because it singled out fertile women for exclusion, when evidence indicates that lead also poses a hazard to the reproductive capacities of men as well. Among the employees suing were a women who had chosen to be sterilized in order to keep her job, a 50-year-old divorcée who had been forced to accept a demotion because of the policy, and a man who had requested a leave of absence in order to reduce his blood lead level before becoming a father.

The problem of reproductive hazards puts companies such as Johnson Controls in a very difficult position. On the one hand, fetal protection policies are open to the charge of being discriminatory because they limit the job opportunities of fertile women while ignoring the substantial evidence of risk to men. Employees also claim that the policies are adopted by employers as a quick and cheap alternative to cleaning up the workplace. On the other hand, employers have a responsibility not to inflict harm, and this obligation extends, presumably, to the fetus of a pregnant employee. Asking employees to sign waivers releasing a company from responsibility is no solution, however, because employees cannot waive the right of their future children to sue for prenatal injuries. Employers seem to face a choice, therefore, between discriminating against their female employees and allowing fetuses to be harmed, with potentially ruinous consequences for the company.

The Issue of Who Decides

A number of employers have resolved this dilemma by adopting fetal protection policies similar to that of Johnson Controls. However, many women are claiming the right to decide for themselves whether to work at jobs that involve reproductive risks. Although they have a strong maternal interest in the health of an unborn child, they are also concerned about their own economic well-being and want to be free to choose the level of risk to themselves and their offspring that they feel is appropriate. Ronald Bayer has observed that these responses to the problem of reproductive hazards involve a reversal of the usual positions of employers and employees:

> Typically, workers and their representatives have pressed management for the most extensive reductions in exposure levels to toxic substances. Further, they have argued that uncertainty requires the most cautious assumptions about the possibility of harmful consequences. Corporations have responded by arguing that a risk-free environment is chimerical and that uncertainty requires a willingness to tolerate levels of exposure that have not been proven harmful. Yet in relation to reproductive hazards, and especially fetal danger, it is labor that has tended to view with some skepticism the data on potential risk. Corporations, on the other hand, have adopted an almost alarmist posture.[31]

This reversal is not hard to understand. Protecting unborn children from harmful chemicals in the workplace and coping with the consequences of occupationally related birth defects involve substantial costs. The struggle between employers and employees is over who will exercise the choice about assuming the risk of reproductive hazards and who will bear the burden of responsibility. Fetal protection policies are adopted by corporate managers who assume the right to make crucial decisions about how the fetus of an employee will be protected. The cost of these decisions is borne largely by women, however, who find that their economic opportunities are sharply limited. According to estimates by the federal government in 1980, at least 100,000 jobs were closed to women because of fetal protection policies already in place,[32] and as many as 20 million jobs would be closed if women were excluded from all work involving reproductive hazards.[33] The women most affected by the reduction in the number of jobs available are those with the fewest skills and the least education, who are already near the bottom of the economic ladder. Because they bear the heavy cost, women argue that they should be the ones to make the decisions involved in protecting their own offspring.

Are Women Forced to Undergo Sterilization?

The debate over fetal protection policies takes on a tragic dimension when women undergo sterilization for fear of losing a job. When five women were laid off by the Allied Chemical Company in 1977 because of concern for fetal damage by a substance known as Fluorocarbon 22, two of them underwent surgical sterilization in order to return to work. Shortly afterward, the company determined that Fluorocarbon 22 posed no threat to a developing fetus, so the women's loss of fertility was needless.[34] When the American Cyanamid Company announced the adoption of a fetal protection policy at a plant in Willow Island, West Virginia, in 1978, five women between the ages of 26 and 43 submitted to sterilization in order to retain jobs that involved exposure to lead chromate, an ingredient of paint pigments. Two years later, American Cyanamid stopped producing paint pigments because of a decreased demand for the lead-based product.[35]

Certainly, no person, man or woman, should be put in the position of having to choose between holding a job and being able to bear children unless there is no acceptable alternative. Employers insist that they do not encourage women to take the drastic step of undergoing sterilization. But they also maintain that they have no control over such an intimate decision by employees or women seeking employment and that there is no reason to exclude women who undergo sterilization from jobs involving exposure to reproductive hazards. According to critics of fetal protection policies, however, companies that exclude fertile women from such jobs effectively force sterilization on those who have no other satisfactory employment opportunities. The problem is one of intentions versus results. Although there is no intention to force women to become sterile, they create situations that have precisely this result.

Issues in the Charge of Sex Discrimination

Whether employers have a right to adopt fetal protection policies depends in part on whether excluding fertile women from certain jobs is a form of sex discrimination. The point at issue is not whether women are vulnerable to reproductive hazards (they certainly are) but whether men are vulnerable as well. If they are, then it is discriminatory for employers to adopt a policy that applies only to women and not to men. In order to evaluate the scientific evidence, it is necessary to understand more about the nature of reproductive hazards.

Substances harmful to a fetus are of three kinds. First, there are *fetotoxins*. These are toxic substances that affect a fetus in the same way that they affect an adult, although a fetus, because of the smaller size, may be harmed by exposure to substances below the permissible limits for adults. *Teratogens*, the second kind of substances, interfere with the normal development of the fetus *in utero*. These may pose no danger to a fully developed person outside the womb. Finally, some substances are *mutagens*, which damage genetic material before conception. The effects of fetotoxins, teratogens, and mutagens are similar. They include spontaneous abortion, miscarriage, stillbirth, and congenital defects. Some defects, such as deformities, are visible at birth, whereas others may be latent conditions that manifest themselves later, as in the case of childhood cancers.

Fetotoxins and teratogens (many substances are both) must be transmitted to the fetus through the mother. This can occur, however, when the father is exposed to a hazardous substance in the workplace. Studies show that the nonworking wives of men exposed to lead, beryllium, benzene, vinyl chloride, and anesthetic gases, for example, have higher than normal rates of miscarriage. Children of fathers exposed to asbestos and benzene are shown in studies to have a greater incidence of cancer. The most likely explanation for these correlations is that the hazardous substances are brought home on the father's body or on his clothing and other belongings.

The main reproductive hazard to men is posed by mutagenic substances, since these are capable of altering the chromosomal structure of both the ovum and the sperm. Although the mutagenic effect of many suspected substances is not firmly established, some researchers theorize that most teratogens are also mutagens and that there is a strong connection between the three phenomena: teratogenesis, mutagenesis, and carcinogenesis (that is, the development of cancers). The reason is that all three operate on the cellular level by altering the DNA molecule.[36] If these relationships exist, then virtually any substance that poses a reproductive hazard to a woman is also hazardous to the reproductive capacity of a man and ultimately the health of a fetus.

The research on reproductive hazards, although inconclusive, suggests that fetal harm can result when either parent is exposed to hazardous substances. If that is in fact the case, then fetal protection policies should apply to both sexes. Wendy W. Williams, argues:

> There is simply no basis for resolving doubts about the evidence by applying a policy to women but not to men on the unsubstantiated generalization that the fetus is placed at greatest risk by workplace exposure of the pregnant woman. Indeed, the limited scientific evidence available requires that doubts about the evidence be resolved in favor of an assumption of equal jeopardy.[37]

Fetal protection policies are also discriminatory if they are applied only to women who occupy traditionally male jobs and not to women in female-dominated lines of work where the hazard is just as great. Some critics charge that fetal protection policies have been used to discriminate by reinforcing job segregation through their selective application to women with jobs in areas formerly dominated by men, while the reproductive risks to other women have been ignored.

American Cyanamid, for example, identified five substances in use at the Willow Island plant as suspected fetotoxins and notified twenty-three women in production jobs that they were exposed to reproductive hazards and would be transferred if they became pregnant. However, the fetal protection policy was applied only to the nine women who held comparatively high paying jobs in the paint pigments department, which had formerly been reserved for men. Barbara Cantwell, one of the four women who submitted to sterilization in order to retain her job, remarked, "I smelled harassment when the problem was suddenly narrowed to the area where women worked."[38]

Among the women in traditionally female lines of work who are exposed to reproductive hazards are nurses in operating rooms, who have twice as many miscarriages as other women because of anesthetic gases; female X-ray technicians, who are twice as likely to bear defective children; and women who work in dry-cleaning operations, where petroleum-based solvents are used.[39] Yet there has been no movement in the industries employing these women to implement fetal protection policies similar to those in the male-dominated chemical, petroleum, and heavy manufacturing industries.

Defenses to the Charge of Sex Discrimination

Distinctions based on sex are not always discriminatory. They are morally permissible if they have an adequate justification, and Title VII of the 1964 Civil Rights Act recognizes this by allowing employers two defenses. These are the claims that a sex-based policy serves a proper business purpose (the business necessity defense) and that a person's sex is a bona fide occupational qualification (the BFOQ defense). A bona fide occupational qualification is defined as a qualification "reasonably necessary to the normal operation" of a business. As we saw in Chapter 8 on discrimination, this exception has been narrowly limited by the courts. The business necessity defense is less stringent. Generally, an employer must establish that a policy is essential for achieving a proper business objective in a safe and efficient manner and that the objective cannot reasonably be achieved by less discriminatory means.

The lower courts ruled that the fetal protection policy adopted by Johnson Controls was permissible under Title VII. The Court of Appeals for the Seventh Circuit held that the policy passed a three-step business necessity defense because the company had established: (1) there is a substantial risk to a fetus, (2) this risk occurs only through women, and (3) there is no less discriminatory alternative. Although not required to do so, the court addressed the question of whether sex is a BFOQ in this case and concluded that it is. The crucial phrase in the BFOQ defense "reasonably necessary for the normal operation" of a business has been interpreted by the courts to include "ethical, legal, and business concerns about the effects of an employer's activities on third parties." Simply put, a qualification is a BFOQ if it is necessary for conducting business without greatly endangering other people. Under this interpretation, the courts had ruled that age was a BFOQ for being an airline flight engineer because the safety of passengers depended on that person's performance.[40] By the same line of reasoning, sex is a BFOQ because a woman working in a battery factory is liable to expose a third party—namely, a fetus—to harm.

The U.S. Supreme Court in a landmark 9–0 decision overruled the lower courts and held Johnson Controls' fetal protection policy to be discriminatory in violation of Title VII. The policy is discriminatory for the reason that it excludes women based only on their childbearing capacity and ignores the risk to men. Thus, the policy does not protect "effectively and equally" the offspring of all employees. Further, the Court ruled that sex is not a BFOQ in this case. All evidence indicates that fertile and even pregnant women are as capable of manufacturing batteries as anyone else. According to the majority opinion, the claim that the safety of third parties ought to be taken into consideration is inapplicable because this exception concerns only the ability of an employee to perform a job in a safe manner, and a fetus, in this case, is not endangered by the manner in which the job is performed. The workers at Johnson Controls, in other words, are not manufacturing batteries in ways that are unsafe for children. "No one can disregard the possibility of injury to future children," the opinion states, but the BFOQ defense "is not so broad that it transforms this deep social concern into an essential aspect of batterymaking."[41]

Remaining Issues

The decision in *Johnson Controls* clearly establishes that fetal protection policies constitute illegal sex discrimination, and the ruling is a victory for working women. It gives women the right not to have their job opportunities limited because of their ability to conceive and bear children. Still, two important issues remain. One is how to balance this right with the desirable social goal of fetal protection. The other is whether the right established in *Johnson Controls* conflicts with another desirable goal, namely, protecting corporations against liability in the event that a person is harmed before birth from exposure to reproductive hazards in the workplace.

The ruling in *Johnson Controls* does not leave the unborn without protection. In the words of the Court, "Decisions about the welfare of future children must be left to the parents who conceive, bear, support, and raise them rather than to the employers who hire those parents." There is little reason to believe that employees are any less concerned than employers about the well-being of their offspring. Indeed, they have a far more compelling interest. This is not to say that some parents-to-be (both men and women) will not continue to choose work that exposes them to reproductive hazards. However, they, rather than their employer, will be making the crucial decision about the reasonableness of that choice. Employees may decide—all things considered—that the risk is worth the price. Parents also choose where to live with their children, thereby deciding whether they can afford to live farther away from sources of pollution and other hazards. Because parents in our society make choices in other matters that bear on the welfare of their children, why should an exception be made in the case of reproductive hazards? What is unfortunate is that any parents are required to choose between making a living and protecting their children.

Whether the *Johnson Controls* ruling exposes corporations to heavy tort liability is an open question. The view expressed in the majority opinion is that the prospect is "remote at best," provided that employers: (1) fully inform employees of the risks they face and (2) do not act negligently. If employees are to make rational choices in cases of exposure to reproductive hazards, then they must have sufficient information, which employers have an obligation to provide. Employers can protect themselves from suits by cleaning up the workplace and reducing the risk as much as possible. The issue of tort liability, then, is hypothetical but nonetheless important for that reason.

NOTES

1. MAY MEYERS, *et al.*, "Benzene (benzol) Poisoning in the Rotogravure Printing in New York City," *Journal of Industrial Hygiene and Toxicology* (October 1939),

395–420. The study is cited in JOSEPH A. PAGE and MARY-WIN O'BRIEN, *Bitter Wages* (New York: Grossman, 1973), 37–38.

2. The details in this case are contained in *Industrial Union Dept., AFL-CIO v. American Petroleum Institute*, 448 U.S. 607 (1980).

3. The estimate is made in W. J. NICHOLSON, "Failure to Regulate—Asbestos: A Lethal Legacy," U.S. Congress, Committee of Government Operations, 1980.

4. Much of the following description of health and safety problems is adapted from NICHOLAS ASKOUNES ASHFORD, *Crisis in the Workplace: Occupational Disease and Injury* (Cambridge: MIT Press, 1976), chap. 3.

5. For a review of the controversy that discredits the industry claim, see ROBERT H. HALL, "The Truth about Brown Lung," *Business and Society Review*, 40 (Winter 1981), 15–20.

6. For a critical assessment of state efforts, see PAGE and O'BRIEN, *Bitter Wages*, 69–85.

7. Sec. 5(a)(1). This clause is the subject of much legal analysis. See RICHARD S. MORLEY, "The General Duty Clause of the Occupational Safety and Health Act of 1970," *Harvard Law Review*, 86 (1973), 988–1005.

8. PATRICIA H. WERHANE, *Persons, Rights, and Corporations* (Englewood Cliffs, NJ: Prentice Hall, 1985), 132.

9. MARK MACCARTHY, "A Review of Some Normative and Conceptual Issues in Occupational Safety and Health," *Environmental Affairs*, 9 (1981), 782–83.

10. The case is related in STEPHEN G. MINTER, "Are Prosecutors Stepping in Where OSHA Fears to Tread?" *Occupational Hazards*, 49 (September 1987), 101–2.

11. These two factors are discussed by Alan Gewirth, who cites them as exceptions to his claim that persons have a right not to have cancer inflicted on them by the actions of others. See ALAN GEWIRTH, "Human Rights and the Prevention of Cancer," in *Human Rights: Essays on Justification and Applications* (Chicago: University of Chicago Press, 1982), 181–96. For an evaluation, see ERIC VON MAGNUS, "Rights and Risks," *Journal of Business Ethics*, 2 (February 1983), 23–26.

12. See H.L.A. HART and A. M. HONORE, *Causation in the Law* (Oxford: Oxford University Press, 1959), 64–76.

13. U.S. Code 21, 348(c)(3).

14. *Federal Register*, vol. 39, no. 20 (January 29, 1974), 3758. Emphasis added.

15. GEWIRTH, "Human Rights and the Prevention of Cancer," 189.

16. *American Textile Manufacturers Institute Inc. v. Raymond J. Donovan, Secretary of Labor*, 452 U.S. 490 (1981).

17. For an argument of this kind, see TIBOR R. MACHAN, "Human Rights, Workers' Rights, and the Right to Occupational Safety," in GERTRUDE EZORSKY, ed., *Moral Rights in the Workplace* (Albany: State University of New York Press, 1987), 45–50.

18. W. KIP VISCUSI, *Risk by Choice* (Cambridge: Harvard University Press, 1983), 80.

19. The following argument is adapted from NORMAN DANIELS, "Does OSHA Protect Too Much?" in EZORSKY, *Moral Rights in the Workplace*, 51–60.

20. ROBERT NOZICK, "Coercion," in SIDNEY MORGENBESSER, PATRICK SUPPES,

and MORTON WHITE, eds., *Philosophy, Science and Method* (New York: St. Martin's Press, 1969), 440–72.

21. In considering whether a person voluntarily chooses undesirable work when all of the alternatives are even worse as a result of the actions of other people, Nozick says that the answer "depends upon whether these others had the right to act as they did." ROBERT NOZICK, *Anarchy, State, and Utopia* (New York: Basic Books, 1974), 262.

22. Some philosophers have attempted to give a morally neutral analysis of coercion that involves no assumptions about what is morally required. See DAVID ZIMMERMAN, "Coercive Wage Offers," *Philosophy and Public Affairs*, 10 (1981), 121–45.

23. Information on this case is contained in *Whirlpool Corporation* v. *Marshall*, 445 U.S. 1 (1980).

24. THOMAS O. MCGARITY, "The New OSHA Rules and the Worker's Right to Know," *The Hastings Center Report*, 14 (August 1984), 38–39.

25. For a version of this argument see MCGARITY, "The New OSHA Rules and the Worker's Right to Know." Much of the following discussion of the autonomy argument is adapted from this article.

26. This point is made in RUTH R. FADEN and TOM L. BEAUCHAMP, "The Right to Risk Information and the Right to Refuse Health Hazards in the Workplace," in TOM L. BEAUCHAMP and NORMAN E. BOWIE, eds., *Ethical Theory and Business*, 3rd ed. (Englewood Cliffs, NJ: Prentice Hall, 1988), 228.

27. This exception suggests a further argument for the right to know based on fairness. Employers who knowingly place workers at risk are taking unfair advantage of the workers' ignorance. See MCGARITY, "The New OSHA Rules and the Worker's Right to Know," 40.

28. MCGARITY, "The New OSHA Rules and the Worker's Right to Know," 40.

29. MCGARITY, "The New OSHA Rules and the Worker's Right to Know," 41.

30. *United Automobile Workers, et al.* v. *Johnson Controls, Inc.*, U.S. Supreme Court, No. 89–1215. See also LINDA GREENHOUSE, "Court Backs Right of Women to Jobs with Health Risks," *The New York Times*, March 21, 1991, sec. 1, p. 1; and STEPHEN WERMIEL, "Justices Bar 'Fetal Protection' Policies," *The Wall Street Journal*, March 21, 1991, p. B1.

31. RONALD BAYER, "Women, Work, and Reproductive Hazards," *The Hastings Center Report*, 12 (October 1982), 18.

32. WENDY W. WILLIAMS, "Firing the Woman to Protect the Fetus: The Reconciliation of Fetal Protection with Employment Opportunity Goals under Title VII," *The Georgetown Law Journal*, 69 (1981), 647.

33. Equal Employment Opportunity Commission and Office of Federal Contract Compliance Programs, "Interpretive Guidelines on Employment Discrimination and Reproductive Hazards," *Federal Register* (February 1, 1980), 7514.

34. GAIL BRONSON, "Issue of Fetal Damage Stirs Women Workers at Chemical Plants," *The Wall Street Journal*, February 9 1979, p. A1.

35. "Company and Union in Dispute as Women Undergo Sterilization," *The New York Times*, January 4, 1979, sec. 1, p. 1; "4 Women Assert Jobs Were Linked to Sterilization," *The New York Times*, January 5, 1979, sec. 1, p. 1; PHILIP SHABECOFF, "Job Threats to Workers' Fertility Emerging as Civil Liberties

Issue," *The New York Times*, January 15, 1979, sec. 1, p. 1; and BRONSON, "Issue of Fetal Damage Stirs Women Workers at Chemical Plants."

36. See WILLIAMS, "Firing the Woman to Protect the Fetus," 659–60.

37. WILLIAMS, "Firing the Woman to Protect the Fetus," 663.

38. Cited in BRONSON, "Issue of Fetal Damage Stirs Women Workers at Chemical Plants."

39. These examples are cited in LOIS VANDERWAERDT, "Resolving the Conflict between Hazardous Substances in the Workplace and Equal Employment Opportunity," *American Business Law Journal*, 21 (1983), 172–73.

40. *Western Airlines v. Criswell*, 472 U.S. 400 (1985).

41. The Supreme Court did not consider the business necessity defense, since only the BFOQ defense was held to be applicable in this case. The reason is that the fetal protection policy adopted by Johnson Controls was considered by the court to be "facial" discrimination, which is to say that a distinction was made explicitly on the basis of sex, and "facial" discrimination requires the more demanding BFOQ defense rather than the weaker business necessity defense.

CHAPTER FOURTEEN
Corporate Social Responsibility

Although corporations are primarily business organizations, run for the benefit of shareholders, they have a wide-ranging set of responsibilities—to their own employees and customers, to the communities in which they are located, and to society at large. Most corporations recognize these responsibilities and make a serious effort to fulfill them. Often, these responsibilities are set out in formal statements, such as the document from the Campbell Soup Company entitled *Our Principles*.

Corporations do not always succeed in fulfilling the responsibilities they acknowledge, and disagreements inevitably arise over the responsibilities of corporations in particular situations. In spite of the written declaration of Campbell Soup "to protect the environment and natural resources around us," the company has been charged on numerous occasions with illegal dumping of grease and vegetable wastes into municipal sewage systems and local rivers at plants in New Jersey, Delaware, Pennsylvania, Ohio, Illinois, and Arkansas.[1] Still, these are lapses that the company has moved to correct.

Campbell Soup is justifiably proud of its record of involvement in the more than 100 communities in which it has operations. In fiscal year 1987, the company contributed $3,652,000 (on net earnings before taxes of $417,900,000) to support educational institutions, civic organizations, health and human service programs, youth activities, and arts and cul-

OUR PRINCIPLES

We are a Company committed to quality and excellence in everything we do.

Our first responsibility is to the people who buy and use our products and services. We are dedicated to providing them with superior quality and value.

Our wholesale and retail customers provide the link to our consumers. We are dedicated to giving these customers outstanding service by providing products they need when they need them. Our customers are expected to make a fair profit on our products.

We believe in our commitment to employees who are, each of them, individuals with dignity and merit. It is our employees—individually and together—who make us strong. It is our constant goal to provide fair compensation as well as orderly and safe working conditions.

Employees are encouraged to express their views and opinions—and management is encouraged to listen and respond. We place special value on innovation . . . the results of which will be our common reward. We are dedicated to equal opportunity for employment, development and advancement for those qualified. We must provide competent management with integrity whose actions are just and ethical.

Our suppliers contribute significantly to the quality and value that goes into our products and services. We must be selective in choosing outstanding suppliers—and treat them with respect, courtesy and fairness.

We believe in being good neighbors. We are dedicated to making our communities better and supporting causes consistent with their importance to the good of the community. We must strive to protect the environment and natural resources around us.

Our final responsibility is to our shareholders. Pioneering new technologies, creating new products and penetrating new markets are activities which require investment of resources; thus, both our present and our future products and services must be sufficiently profitable to generate funds to insure growth . . . while providing reasonable returns to our shareholders.

Campbell Soup Company

tural affairs.[2] One charitable program aroused unexpected opposition, however. Under the Labels for Education program, launched in 1974, children were able to buy audiovisual and sports equipment for their schools by collecting labels from soup cans and other Campbell products. Although many schools that were starved for funds benefited from this program, critics charged that the increased sales for Campbell Soup offset much of the cost of the program, thus making it a relatively cheap promotional tool. Research by the Committee on Corporate Responsibility showed that savings from buying less expensive cans of soup would have more than paid for the "free" equipment provided by Campbell Soup.[3] And another consumer interest group, The Educational Products Information Exchange Institute, questioned the appropriateness of a corporation's becoming involved in the classroom. They argued that "children are in school to learn, not to engage in helping increase the ingestion of soup and beans in the community."[4]

One of the most difficult periods in the history of the Campbell Soup Company occurred in late 1985.[5] An Ohio-based group fighting for increased wages and improved living and working conditions for migrant farmworkers was threatening to disrupt the annual shareholders' meeting with a demonstration that would have greatly embarrassed company executives. Since 1979, the company had been the target of a nationwide boycott of its products, instigated by a group known as the Farm Labor Organizing Committee (FLOC). Under the dynamic leadership of Baldemar Velasquez, FLOC gained support for the boycott from the major Protestant and Catholic church organizations in Ohio and from many influential national groups. In July 1983, about 100 members and supporters of FLOC marched 560 miles from FLOC headquarters in Toledo, Ohio, to the headquarters of the Campbell Soup Company in Camden, New Jersey, to dramatize the boycott and to press their demand for a labor contract.

At the urging of the National Council of Churches, which had been persuaded by FLOC to intervene in the dispute, representatives from the two sides sat down and negotiated an agreement that set up procedures for conducting elections to determine whether the farmworkers wanted to be represented by FLOC. The agreement was signed in May 1985, and the voting took place in September, during the first month of the tomato harvest. The election process broke down, however, amid allegations by FLOC of unfair labor practices, including charges that the growers brought in local laborers on the day of the election and prevented some migrant farmworkers from voting. The possibility now existed that the National Council of Churches would support the boycott, a move that would generate considerable adverse publicity for Campbell Soup. And FLOC's plan to stage a demonstration at the upcoming shareholders' meeting would create additional bad press.

The plight of the migrant farmworkers is truly deplorable. Many live in crowded camps, without electricity, fresh drinking water, or adequate toilets. Poor nutrition, communicable diseases, and constant exposure to pesticides result in a high infant mortality rate and a life expectancy twenty-five years below the average. FLOC claimed that laborers received an average hourly wage of less than $2.00, although Campbell Soup disputed this figure and insisted they were paid at least the minimum wage of $3.35 an hour. In addition, migrant farmworkers generally lack health insurance and the other benefits that most American workers take for granted.

Still, R. Gordon McGovern, the president and CEO of the Campbell Soup Company believed that the company had done all it could under the circumstances. When the National Labor Relations Act was passed in 1935, giving most workers the right to organize and engage in collective bargaining, farm laborers were deliberately excluded. So the company was under no legal obligation to recognize the existence of FLOC. The migrant farmworkers, moreover, were not Campbell employees but were hired by independent growers, who held contracts with the company to devote a specified number of acres to tomatoes that were sold to the company at a fixed rate. Executives of Campbell Soup did not believe that they had a right to negotiate over the heads of the growers or to dictate to the growers how they should treat their employees.

FLOC decided to launch a campaign against Campbell Soup in the belief that the price the company set for tomatoes did not allow enough profit margin for the growers to increase wages and improve working conditions even if they wanted to. FLOC disregarded the claim that Campbell Soup did not employ the migrant farmworkers, since the company provided seedlings to the growers and dictated how they were to be raised and picked. In response to a strike organized by FLOC in 1978, the company ordered the growers to switch to mechanical harvesters. Thus, the control that Campbell Soup exercised over the growers was greater than that normally exercised by a company over suppliers. The high visibility of the company and its carefully cultivated reputation also made it vulnerable to attack and contributed to FLOC's decision to make Campbell Soup the target of its campaign.

The charge of allowing child labor was one that deeply stung company officials. The basis of the accusation was a 1983 ruling by a federal district court that a pickle grower, who employed workers on a piece-rate basis, had no legal obligation to prevent children from working alongside their parents in the fields, since the workers, in the view of the court, are independent, self-employed contractors.[6] Although Campbell Soup also markets pickles through its Vlasic subsidiary, the company contended that the decision did not apply to tomato pickers, who are paid hourly rates because of the different method of harvesting tomatoes. The company denied, moreover, that it approved of children helping their parents in the tomato fields. In fact, Campbell Soup created the post of Ombudsman for Migrant Affairs in part to promote the availability of day-care facilities and to ensure that children of migrant farmworkers attend classes during the school year.

Campbell Soup took other steps to improve the living conditions of the workers who picked tomatoes. After the passage of an Ohio law upgrading the minimum standards for migrant housing, the duties of the ombudsman were expanded to include inspection of facilities on farms with company contracts. The company also offered to finance half the cost of new housing and to provide low-interest loans for the balance. In addition, a pilot health care project was started. Campbell executives refused to budge, however, on FLOC's main demand for union recognition and a labor contract.

In February 1986, a revolutionary three-way agreement was signed by FLOC, the Campbell Soup Company, and representatives of the growers.[7] Workers in the tomato fields were guaranteed an hourly wage of $4.50 under the terms of the three-year agreement, and they could earn up to $9.00 an hour in the peak season when they would be paid by the amount they picked. The agreement also provided for improved living and working conditions and some health care benefits. Baldemar Velasquez exclaimed, "We have an approach that is the future of farm-labor organizing." The growers benefited as much as the laborers from the agreement because they were guaranteed a market for their tomatoes over the life of the agreement. Campbell asserted that growers would be able to offset the higher labor costs through improved production techniques, leading to higher yields. Executives of the Campbell Soup Company expressed satisfaction with the agreement, although Ray Page, vice-president for corporate relations, remarked, "It took us a long time to reach this point."

What are the responsibilities of Campbell Soup for the welfare of the migrant farmworkers who harvest the tomatoes at farms under contract with the company? Any responsibilities that the company has with respect to this group are in addition to those it has to the growers, its own employees, and Campbell shareholders, among others. What is the proper balance among these different responsibilities? There are no easy answers to such questions, but some help can be obtained from the theories of corporate social responsibility examined in this chapter. These range from a very restricted position—that corporations have no social responsibility beyond making a profit—to the position that corporations ought to assume a more active role in addressing major social problems. Several preliminary matters must be addressed first, though, beginning with the concept of responsibility itself.

THE MEANING OF CORPORATE SOCIAL RESPONSIBILITY

The concept of corporate social responsibility originated in the 1950s, as American corporations rapidly increased in size and power. And the concept continued to figure prominently in public debate during the sixties and seventies as the nation confronted pressing social problems such as poverty, unemployment, race relations, urban blight, and pollution.[8] Corporate social responsibility became a rallying cry for diverse groups demanding change in American business.

Economic and Legal Responsibilities

All accounts of corporate social responsibility recognize that business firms have not one but many different kinds of responsibility, including economic and legal responsibilities. Corporations have an *economic* responsibility to produce goods and services and to provide jobs and good wages to the work force while earning a profit. Economic responsibility also includes the obligation to seek out supplies of raw materials, to discover new resources and technological improvements, and to develop new products. By fulfilling these roles, corporations will increase the economic well-being of society and ensure the survival and growth of the organization.

In addition, business firms have certain *legal* responsibilities. One of these is to act as a fiduciary, managing the assets of a corporation in the interests of shareholders and distributing the profits to them as dividends. The immense body of commercial law provides an essential framework for business activity. Corporations also have legal responsibilities to employees, customers, suppliers, and other parties. The legal responsibilities of business, which are created by legislatures, regulatory agencies, and the courts, are constantly increasing, largely in response to greater societal expectations.

Going Beyond Economic and Legal Responsibilities

The concept of corporate social responsibility is often expressed as the voluntary assumption of responsibilities that go beyond the purely economic and legal responsibilities of business firms.[9] More specifically, social responsibility, according to some accounts, is the selection of corporate goals and the evaluation of outcomes not solely by the criteria of profitability and organizational well-being but by ethical standards or judgments of social desirability. The exercise of social responsibility, in this view, must be consistent with the corporate objective of earning a satisfactory level of profit, but it implies a willingness to forego a certain measure of profit in order to achieve noneconomic ends.

Archie B. Carroll views social responsibility as a four-stage continuum.[10] Beyond economic and legal responsibilities lie ethical responsibilities, which are "additional behaviors and activities that are not necessarily codified into law but nevertheless are expected of business by society's members."[11] At the far end of the continuum are discretionary responsibilities. These are responsibilities "about which society has no clear-cut message for business."

These roles are purely voluntary, and the decision to assume them is guided only by a business's desire to engage in social roles not mandated, not required by law, and not even generally expected of business in an ethical sense.[12]

The social responsibility of corporations, in Carroll's view, encompasses all four of these sets of responsibilities.

In 1971, the Committee for Economic Development issued an influential report that characterized corporate social responsibility in a similar fashion but without an explicit mention of legal responsibilities. The responsibilities of corporations are described in this report as consisting of three concentric circles.

The *inner circle* includes the clear-cut basic responsibilities for the efficient execution of the economic function—products, jobs, and economic growth.

The *intermediate circle* encompasses responsibility to exercise this economic function with a sensitive awareness of changing social values and priorities: for example, with respect to environmental conservation; hiring and relations with employees; and more rigorous expectations of customers for information, fair treatment, and protection from injury.

The *outer circle* outlines newly emerging and still amorphous responsibilities that business should assume to become more broadly involved in actively improving the social environment. Society is beginning to turn to corporations for help with major social problems such as poverty and urban blight. This is not so much because the public considers business singularly responsible for creating these problems, but because it feels large corporations possess considerable resources and skills that could make a critical difference in solving these problems.[13]

A different kind of approach is developed by S. Prakash Sethi. He notes that social responsibility is a relative concept: What is only a vague ideal at one point in time or in one culture may be a definite legal requirement at another point in time or in another culture. One criterion that permits comparisons at different points in time or across cultures is the *legitimacy* of corporate activity. Legitimacy, in turn, is the extent to which this activity meets the expectations of the members of society. In most of the advanced nations of the world, fulfilling traditional economic and legal responsibilities is no longer regarded as sufficient for legitimizing the activity of large corporations. That is, operating efficiently and within the law (which Sethi calls "social obligation") is not enough; corporations are now expected to do more. Corporate social responsibility can thus be defined as "bringing corporate behavior up to a level where it is congruent with the prevailing social norms, values, and expectations of performance."[14] Sethi has written:

Social responsibility does not require a radical departure from the usual nature of corporate activities or the normal pattern of corporate behavior. It is simply a step ahead of its time—before the new social expectations are codified into legal requirements.[15]

Examples of Social Responsibility

Although there are some important differences between the accounts of the concept of corporate social responsibility offered by these writers, there is general agreement on the types of corporate activities that show social responsibility. Among these are

1. Choosing to operate on an ethical level that is higher than what the law requires.
2. Making contributions to civic and charitable organizations and nonprofit institutions.
3. Providing benefits for employees and improving the quality of life in the workplace beyond economic and legal requirements.
4. Taking advantage of an economic opportunity that is judged to be less profitable but more socially desirable than some alternatives.
5. Using corporate resources to operate a program that addresses some major social problem.

There are countless examples of activities of these types.[16]

1. Many companies have codes of ethics that are more than rules for employee behavior or public relations devices. The best of them, such as Johnson & Johnson's "Our Credo" and the beliefs of Borg-Warner "To Reach beyond the Minimal," set forth very high standards of conduct that are consciously applied in the corporate decision-making process.

2. Most corporations practice some form of philanthropy, and the largest often have a company foundation to channel gifts to worthy causes. Although few corporate contributions exceed one percent of pretax profits, the Dayton Hudson Corporation, a Minneapolis-based retailer, has given 5 percent every year since 1946.

3. Virtually all corporations recognize the importance of good employee relations and worker satisfaction, and many have exemplary benefit packages and "quality of work life" (QWL) programs. Lincoln Electric, in Cleveland, Ohio, a maker of welding equipment and supplies, has long been known for worker participation in decision-making and for generous bonuses that often equal the base salary. Workers are guaranteed job security after one year, and no one has been laid off since 1949. During slow periods, all employees work fewer hours.

4. Examples of decisions based more on social than economic factors include the following: In 1975, when scientists first suggested that fluorocarbons from aerosol cans were damaging the ozone layer, Johnson Wax voluntarily withdrew all products containing fluorocarbons from the market, years before a ban was issued by the FDA, despite some loss of sales and criticism from other manufacturers. The Reynolds Metal Company constructed a $1 million addition to a plant in Alabama to recycle aluminum cans in 1981, before it became profitable to do so. And in the late 1960s, Control Data Corporation decided to tackle the problem of racial tensions by locating a new plant in a predominantly black area of Minneapolis-St. Paul. The CEO of Control Data, William Norris, was willing to wait three years for the new plant to match the productivity of other CDC plants.

5. Many companies have set up programs to address such social problems as hunger (Pillsbury), adult literacy (the B. Dalton bookstore chain), low-income housing (Aetna Life and Casualty), and minority-owned businesses (Control Data). This list, of course, is only a small sampling.

Although these activities are all beyond the economic and legal responsibilities of corporations and may involve some sacrifice of profit, they are not necessarily antithetical to corporate interests and even the long-term profitability of a corporation. Some corporate philanthropy, such as a contribution that makes the community in which a company is located a better place to live and work, results in direct benefits. And the "goodwill" that socially responsible activities create makes it easier for corporations to conduct their business.

It should come as no surprise, then, that some of the most successful corporations are also among the most socially responsible. They are led by executives who see that even the narrow economic and legal responsibilities of corporations cannot be fulfilled without the articulation of noneconomic values to guide corporate decision-making and the adoption of nontraditional business activities that satisfy the demands of diverse constituencies.

Responsibility and Responsiveness

The concept of social responsibility focuses on specific acts that corporations are obligated to perform. Another important aspect of corporate performance in areas of social concern is the *responsiveness* of corporations—that is, the ability of corporations to respond in a socially responsible manner to new challenges.[17] William C. Frederick wrote:

> Corporate social responsiveness refers to the capacity of a corporation to respond to social pressures. The literal act of responding, or of achieving a generally responsive posture, to society is the focus.[18]

The emphasis of corporate social responsiveness, in other words, is on the *process* of responding or the readiness to respond, rather than on the *content* of an actual response.

An analogy is, a *responsible* motorist is one who stops to offer whatever aid is available to another motorist in distress; but a *responsive* motorist is one who carries a flashlight, tools, battery cables, and so on and is prepared to offer effective aid. Similarly, a socially responsive corporation uses its resources to anticipate social issues and develop policies, programs, and other means of dealing with them. The management of social issues in a socially responsive corporation is integrated into the strategic planning process, instead of being handled as an ad hoc reaction to specific crises.[19] Many sophisticated techniques for social responsiveness are available to corporations, including social forecasting, the social audit, social marketing, public relations campaigns, and political lobbying.

A danger of the concept of corporate social responsiveness is that it contains no normative standards for the use of the powerful techniques available to corporations for anticipating and dealing with social issues.[20] The likelihood is high that a corporation threatened by emerging social forces will marshall its immense resources in a way that protects the corporation rather than promotes socially desirable change. As a result, some writers have expressed the need for another concept, beyond corporate social responsibility and corporate social responsiveness. Such a concept needs to include specific ethical principles to guide corporate decision-making and to serve as a measure of corporate social performance.[21]

THE CLASSICAL VIEW

By now, the idea that corporations have an obligation to be socially responsible is so widely held, even among business leaders themselves, that it may seem pointless to bring it into question. The movement toward greater corporate social responsibility is not without its critics, however.

Some contend that corporate social responsibility is altogether a pernicious idea. The well-known conservative economist Milton Friedman writes, "Few trends could so thoroughly undermine the very foundations of our free society as the acceptance by corporate officials of a social responsibility other than making as much money for their stockholders as possible."[22] At the other extreme are critics who would like corporations to be more socially responsible but are mistrustful. They consider talk about corporate social responsibility to be a public relations ploy designed to legitimize the role of corporations in present-day American society and to divert attention away from the destructive social consequences of corporate activity.

Even those who are more favorably disposed to the idea have reservations about the ability of corporations, especially as they are currently structured, to respond effectively to social issues. Businesses are single purpose institutions, conceived, organized, and managed solely in order to engage in economic activity. As such, they lack the resources and the expertise for solving major social problems. And some add that they lack the legitimacy as well. Corporate executives are not elected officials with a mandate from the American people to apply the resources under their control to just any ends that they deem worthwhile.

Furthermore, the idea that corporations should be more socially responsible fails to give adequate ethical guidance to the executives who must decide which causes to pursue and how much to commit to them. This problem is especially acute in view of the fact that all choices involve tradeoffs. A program to increase minority employment, for example, might reduce efficiency, thereby keeping the corporation from fulfilling obligations to shareholders and perhaps its other employees, while raising prices for consumers. Or such a program might be adopted at the expense of achieving a greater reduction in the amount of pollution, which creates a conflict with another demand that is made on corporations in the name of social responsibility. Corporations committed to exercising greater social responsibility need more specific moral rules or principles to give them reasons for acting in one way rather than another. As William C. Frederick observes, " 'Doing good' is generally admirable but one must have some moral basis for doing so."[23]

The major alternative to the concept of corporate social responsibility in recent American history is what is often called the *classical view* of corporate social responsibility. This view, which prevailed in the nineteenth century, is still very influential today, especially among economists. It is expressed by James W. McKie in three basic propositions:

1. Economic behavior is separate and distinct from other types of behavior, and business organizations are distinct from other organizations, even though the same individuals may be involved in business and nonbusiness affairs. Business organizations do not serve the same goals as other organizations in a pluralistic society.
2. The primary criteria of business performance are economic efficiency and growth in production of goods and services, including improvements in technology and innovations in goods and services.
3. The primary goal and motivating force for business organizations is profit. The firm attempts to make as large a profit as it can, thereby maintaining its efficiency and taking advantage of available opportunities to innovate and contribute to growth.[24]

Friedman's Statement of the Classical View

Perhaps the best-known exponent of the classical view is Milton Friedman, who writes in *Capitalism and Freedom*:

> The view has been gaining widespread acceptance that corporate officials . . . have a "social responsibility" that goes beyond serving the interest of their stockholders. . . . This view shows a fundamental misconception of the character and nature of a free economy. In such an economy, there is one and only one social responsibility of business—to use its resources and engage in activities designed to increase its profits so long as it stays within the rules of the game, which is to say, engages in open and free competition, without deception or fraud. . . . It is the responsibility of the rest of us to establish a framework of law such that an individual pursuing his own interest is, to quote Adam Smith . . . , "led by an invisible hand to promote an end which was no part of his intention. Nor is it always the worse for society that it was no part of it. By pursuing his own interest, he frequently promotes that of the society more effectually than when he really intends to promote it. I have never known much good done by those who affected to trade for the public good."[25]

Friedman's main argument for the classical view is that corporate executives, when they are acting in their official capacity and not as private persons, are agents of the stockholders of the corporation. As such, executives of a corporation have an obligation to make decisions in the interests of the stockholders, who are ultimately their employers. He has asked:

> What does it mean to say that the corporate executive has a "social responsibility" in his capacity as businessman? If this statement is not pure rhetoric, it must mean that he is to act in some way that is not in the interest of his employers. For example, that he is to refrain from increasing the price of the product in order to contribute to the social objective of preventing inflation, even though a price increase would be in the best interests of the corporation. Or that he is to make expenditures on reducing pollution beyond the amount that is in the best interests of the corporation or that is required by law in order to contribute to the social objective of improving the environment. Or that, at the expense of corporate profits, he is to hire "hardcore" unemployed instead of better qualified available workmen to contribute to the social objective of reducing poverty.
>
> In each of these cases, the corporate executive would be spending someone else's money for a general social interest. Insofar as his actions in accord with his "social responsibility" reduce returns to stockholders, he is spending their money. Insofar as his actions raise the price to customers, he is spending the customers' money. Insofar as his actions lower the wages of some employees, he is spending their money.[26]

When corporate executives act in the way Friedman describes, they take on a role of imposing taxes and spending the proceeds that properly belongs only to elected officials. They become, in effect, civil servants who are selected by the stockholders of private business firms. According to Friedman:

On grounds of political principle, it is intolerable that such civil servants . . . should be selected as they are now. If they are to be civil servants, then they must be selected through a political process. If they are to impose taxes and make expenditures to foster "social" objectives, then political machinery must be set up to guide the assessment of taxes and to determine through a political process the objectives to be served.[27]

Some Features of the Classical View

The classical view does not sanction an unrestrained pursuit of profit. Friedman himself acknowledges that business must observe certain essential limitations on permissible conduct, which he describes as the "rules of the game." Presumably, he would also grant the necessity of government with limited powers for setting and enforcing rules. Business activity requires, in other words, a minimal state—Nozick's "nightwatchman" state—in order to prevent anti-competitive practices and to enforce the basics of commercial law. Friedman recognizes, further, that many supposed socially responsible actions are really disguised forms of self-interest. Contributions to schools, hospitals, community organizations, cultural groups, and the like are compatible with the classical view insofar as corporations receive indirect benefits from the contributions. All Friedman asks is that corporations recognize these as effective means for making a profit and not as philanthropic activities.

In addition, holders of the classical view generally admit the legitimacy of three other functions of government that place limits on business activity.[28] First, business activity generates many *externalities*, that is, social harms, such as worker injury, which result indirectly from the operation of business firms. In order to prevent these harms or to correct them after they occur, it is proper for government to act—by requiring safer working conditions, for example, or by taxing employers to fund workers' compensation programs.[29] Second, the operation of a free market economy results in considerable *inequalities* in the distribution of income and wealth. Insofar as it is desirable as a matter of public policy to reduce these inequalities, it is appropriate for government to undertake the task by such means as progressive taxation and redistribution schemes. It is the job of government, in other words, and not business, to manage the equity/efficiency tradeoff.[30] Third, free markets are prone to *instability* that manifests itself in inflation, recessions, unemployment, and other economic ills. Individual firms are too small to have much effect on the economy as a whole, and so government must step in and use its powers of taxation, public expenditure, control of the money supply, and the like to make the economy more stable.

The classical view is compatible, then, with some intervention in business activity by government in order to secure the public welfare. The important point to recognize is that the restraints are almost entirely *external*. The primary burden for ensuring that corporations act in a way that is generally beneficial rests on society as a whole, which is charged by Friedman with the task of creating a framework of law that allows business firms to operate solely in their self-interest. The classical theory, therefore, does not permit corporations to *act* in a socially irresponsible manner; it only relieves them of the need to *think* about matters of social responsibility. In a well-ordered society, corporations attend to business while government and other institutions fulfill their proper roles.

CRITICISM OF THE CLASSICAL VIEW

Business activity, in the classical view, is justified partly on the ground that it secures the well-being of society as a whole. The crux of this argument is the efficacy of Adam Smith's invisible hand in harmonizing self-interested behavior to secure an end that is not a part of anyone's intention. The argument also depends on the ability of the rest of society to create the conditions necessary for the invisible hand to operate and to deal with the problems of externalities, inequalities, and instability, without the aid of business. Generally, the classical view is accepted by those who have great faith in free markets, whereas it is rejected by those who are more skeptical. The debate over the workings of the invisible hand cannot be settled here (it is examined at some length in Chapter 4), but there are substantial problems with the classical view.

The Moral Minimum of the Market

First, the classical view does not adequately appreciate the extent to which social responsibility is required by free markets. Holders of this view recognize that a certain level of ethical conduct is necessary for the invisible hand to operate, or indeed for business activity to take place at all. Milton Friedman speaks of the "rules of the game," by which he means "open and free competition, without deception or fraud." And Theodore Levitt, in his article "The Dangers of Social Responsibility," says that, aside from seeking material gain, business has only one responsibility, and that is "to obey the elementary canons of everyday face-to-face civility (honesty, good faith, and so on)."[31] The "rules of the game" and "face-to-face civility" impose not inconsequential contraints on business. Presumably, the prohibition against deception and fraud obligates corporations to deal fairly with employees, customers, and the public and to avoid sharp sales practices, misleading advertising, and the like. Honesty and good faith, moreover, are important elements in the concept of corporate social responsibility.

Several writers find fault with Levitt's concept of social responsibility, in particular. John G. Simon, Charles W. Powers, and Jon P. Gunnemann have argued:

> . . . Levitt presents the reader with a choice between, on the one hand, getting involved in the management of society . . . and, on the other hand, fulfilling the profit-making function. But such a choice excludes another meaning of corporate responsibility: the making of profits in such a way as to minimize social injury. Levitt at no point considers the possibility that business activity may at times injure others and that it may be necessary to regulate the social consequences of one's business activities accordingly.[32]

They appeal in their argument to an important distinction in both law and morality between *negative injunctions* and *affirmative duties*. Although not all corporations have an affirmative duty to take on specific tasks, such as cleaning up the environment, all are under a negative injunction to prevent pollution from occurring and to correct any environmental damage that results from their own activities. For both individuals and corporations, the negative injunction to prevent injury is a moral minimum.

For some holders of the classical view, the minimum level of conduct is what the law requires. If corporations recognize no obligation to adhere to a standard of conduct higher than the legal minimum, however, then they leave themselves open to intervention by outside forces, including pressure from special interest groups and regulation by government. One of the major reasons advanced for corporations to exercise greater social responsibility is to avoid such external interference. By "internalizing" the expectations of society, corporations retain control over decision making and avoid the costs associated with government regulation. This is a purely self-interested argument, but there are good reasons to believe that the public welfare is also better served when corporations voluntarily adopt a higher level of conduct. Keith Davis has argued, for example:

> This view [that corporations ought to assume greater social responsibility] is . . . consistent with existing political philosophy, which attempts to keep power as decentralized as possible in a democratic system. Further, this view is consistent with organizational theory, which holds that decision making should be kept as near as possible to the point where an operating problem occurs. For these reasons, if the businessman by his own socially responsible behavior can prevent the government from introducing new restrictions, it can be argued that he probably is accomplishing a public good, as well as his own private good.[33]

Power and Responsibility

A second objection is that corporations have become so large and powerful that they are not effectively restrained by market forces and government regulation. Some self-imposed restraint in the form of a voluntary assumption of greater social responsibility is necessary, therefore, for corporate activity to secure the public welfare.

The classical view developed in the nineteenth century when most business firms were small and limited in resources, so that corporate activity posed little threat to the welfare of individuals. Corporations had little need at that time to be concerned with anything besides making a profit. With the rise of corporations to a dominant position in American society, however, has come the need to exercise their immense power responsibly. Keith Davis expressed this point succinctly in the proposition: *"social responsibility arises from social power."*[34] He also cited what he calls the Iron Law of Responsibility: "In the long run, those who do not use power in a manner which society considers responsible will tend to lose it."[35] The need for greater social responsibility by corporations, then, is an inevitable result of their increasing size and influence in American society.

Holders of the classical theory argue in reply that precisely because of the immense power of corporations, it would be dangerous to unleash it from the discipline of the market in order to achieve vaguely defined social goals.[36] Kenneth E. Goodpaster and John B. Matthews, Jr., concede that this is a matter for serious concern but argue in response:

> What seems not to be appreciated is the fact that power affects when it is used as well as when it is not used. A decision by [a corporation] . . . not to exercise its economic influence according to "non-economic" criteria is inevitably a moral decision and just as inevitably affects the community. The issue in the end is not whether corporations (and other organizations) should be "unleashed" to exert moral force in our society but rather how critically and self-consciously they should choose to do so.[37]

A related objection is that business already has enough power, so that the pursuit of social goals by corporations would result in an excessive concentration of power. Such a concentration would threaten the division of power that is required for a pluralistic society and also weaken the effectiveness of other institutions that are better suited for solving social problems.[38] If corporations already have too much power, then it follows that they should not take on any new responsibilities that add to that power. But it also follows that they should be all the more concerned to use the power they have responsibly. Exercising greater social responsibility, moreover, does not alway add to the power of corporations, and it is possible for responsible corporate activity to enhance pluralism and strengthen other institutions in society. The support of education by corporations and contributions to civic organizations are obvious examples.

Giving a Helping Hand to Government

Third, the classical view assumes that business provides for the economic well-being of the members of a society, whereas noneconomic goals are best left to government and the other noneconomic institutions of society. In particular, the classical view relies on government, rather than corporations, to deal with the externalities of business activity, considerations of equality, and the task of stabilizing the economy. This sharp distinction between the proper spheres of activity for business and government is justified by utilitarianism on grounds of efficiency. Although certain noneconomic goals are better left to government, it does not follow that corporations have *no* responsibility to provide a helping hand. Corporations have an obligation, for reasons of efficiency, to make whatever contributions are consistent with their role in society as primarily economic institutions.

Corporations cannot attempt to solve every social problem, of course. Some criteria are needed for distinguishing those situations in which corporations have an obligation to pursue noneconomic goals. John G. Simon, Charles W. Powers, and Jon P. Gunnemann, propose the following four criteria.[39]

1. *The urgency of the need*
2. *The proximity of a corporation to the need*
3. *The capability of a corporation to respond effectively*
4. *The likelihood that the need will not be met unless a corporation acts*

In general, a corporation has an obligation to address social problems that involve more substantial threats to the well-being of large numbers of people, that are close at hand and related in some way to the corporation's activity, that the corporation has the resources and expertise to solve, and that would likely persist without some action by the corporation.

By these criteria, the Campbell Soup Company had a responsibility to help alleviate the plight of migrant farmworkers in Ohio, despite the lack of a direct relation. The need was certainly urgent. Although not located in close geographical proximity, the company occupied a prominent position in the tomato growing industry, and the actions of the company bore directly on the situation of the farmworkers. Campbell Soup also had the capability of improving the conditions of the migrant laborers, and because of their pivotal role as a large buyer that contracted with many growers, only Campbell was in a position to bring about the three-way agreement which emerged. If Campbell had not acted, then it is unlikely that the need would have been met. Thus, all four of the criteria set out above are met in the Campbell Soup case.

THE "TAXATION" ARGUMENT

The classical view is not based solely on utilitarian considerations of well-being but also on the property rights of shareholders. This latter justification underlies Friedman's argument that managers in exercising corporate social responsibility are spending someone else's money and taking on a role that properly belongs to elected officials. Investors, according to the "taxation" argument, entrust their money to the managers of corporations in the expectation that it will be put to the most productive use, with the profits returned to the shareholders in the form of dividends. Spending money to pursue social ends is thus a form of taxation without any authority.

Many things are wrong with the "taxation" argument. Even if we accept the main assumption of the argument—that managers have an obligation to operate a corporation in the interests of the legal owners and those of no one else—it does not follow that a corporation has no other obligations that are a part of its social responsibility. A strong case can be made, moreover, for rejecting the underlying assumption of the "taxation" argument. Although shareholders have well-defined legal rights, which are different from those of other members of society, many people have both moral and legal claims that compete with those of investors.

The Question of Means

First, managers of a corporation do not have an obligation to earn the greatest amount of profit for shareholders without regard for the means used. A taxi driver hired to take a passenger to the airport as fast as possible, for example, is not obligated to break traffic laws and endanger everyone else on the road. Similarly, money spent on product safety or pollution control may reduce the potential return to shareholders, but the alternative is to conduct business in a way that threatens the well-being of others in society. Doing business in South Africa might represent the best investment opportunity for a corporation, but would the managers of that corporation be remiss in their duty to the owners if they refused on moral grounds to support a system of apartheid? Friedman would insist, of course, that managers carry out their responsibility to shareholders within the "rules of the game," but the moral obligation of managers to be sensitive to the social impact of their actions is more extensive than the minimal restraints listed by Friedman.

Taking a Long-Term View

Second, the obligation of managers is not merely to secure the maximum return but also to preserve the equity invested in a corporation. Securing the maximum return for shareholders consistent with the preservation of invested capital requires managers to take a long-term view that considers the stability and growth of the corporation. For corporations to survive, they must satisfy the legitimate expectations of society and serve the purposes for which they have been created. And among the factors that contribute to the viability of corporations are socially responsible investments in employee and consumer relations and in the local community. Friedman admits the legitimacy of acts of social responsibility as long as they are ultimately in the self-interest of the corporation. The main area of disagreement between proponents and critics of social responsibility is, how much socially responsible behavior is in a corporation's long-term self-interest?

What Are the Interests of Shareholders?

A third objection is that instead of being profligate with the shareholders' money, managers are often more profit-minded than the shareholders themselves. The interests of shareholders are not narrowly economic; corporations are generally expected by their owners to pursue some socially desirable ends. Shareholders are also consumers, environmentalists, and citizens in communities; consequently, they are affected when corporations fail to act responsibly. In fact, they may be morally opposed to some activities of a corporation and would like to bring about changes. One writer contends that "there are conventionally motivated investors who have an interest in the social characteristics of their portfolios *as well as* dividends and capital gains."[40]

If this is so, then managers who exercise social responsibility are not "taxing" shareholders and spending the money contrary to their interests but quite the opposite; managers who do *not* act in a socially responsible manner are using the money of shareholders in ways that are against the interests of their shareholders. A Friedmanite response is, if shareholders want certain social goals, let them use their dividends for that purpose. However, it may be more efficient for corporations to expend funds on environmental protection, for example, than for shareholders to spend the same amount in dividends for the same purpose. Also, corporations do not strive to make the maximum amount of profit. They must make enough profit to attract sufficient capital from investors, of course, but the decision to declare a certain dividend is generally made by balancing several competing goals, of which the interests of shareholders is only one.

The Property Rights of Shareholders

Fourth, even if shareholders have an interest only in the largest possible profit, they are not owners of a corporation in a sense that entitles them to use their property for their own ends or that obligates a manager to whom that property is entrusted to operate in the interest of the owner. That is, the concept of a right to property on which the "taxation" argument depends does not apply to ownership in a corporation and hence does not support the conclusion that Friedman attempts to draw from it. This objection requires an extended argument that can be sketched in the following way.

The concept of a property right that is presupposed by the "taxation" argument is illustrated by an example used in a business ethics textbook to explain Friedman's position:

> Suppose I had a million dollars to start a business. After getting the business on its feet, I hired you to run it and retired to Florida to golf and enjoy myself. When I returned and asked you for an accounting, you told me there were no profits because the people of the community needed recreational facilities and you took whatever surplus cash there was and donated it to their cause. Is that what I hired you for? Of course not. You were hired to make money for me.[41]

In this example, the business is the property of the owner in much the same way that a piece of land or an automobile is owned by a person. It can be used for any desired end, and by entrusting the business to a manager, that person is obligated to use the property for the end dictated by the owner. The question is, is this the kind of property right held by the shareholders of a corporation?

If shareholders were truly the owners of a corporation, as the "taxation" argument assumes, then they would have a right to set that corporation's direction, including, if they wished, socially desirable goals. Corporations are created and maintained, however, for purposes that are carefully defined in their charters. Shareholders who "buy" part of a corporation by purchasing stock acquire a set of rights that includes a claim on earnings and a right to vote on certain matters, but shareholders have very limited power to determine the overall course of corporate activity.

To cite just one example, SEC Rule 14a-8(c) allows a corporation to refuse a request for shareholder action on proposals that are concerned with "ordinary business operations" or that are submitted primarily for the purpose of promoting "general economic, political, racial, religious, social or similar causes." These two conditions would seem to rule out most initiatives by shareholders who want the corporations they "own" to be more socially responsible.[42] Besides, most shareholder initiatives at annual meetings are defeated overwhelmingly.

Marvin A. Chirelstein points out, moreover, that managers are legally permitted to ignore even a majority vote on a proposal to reduce the profitability of a corporation as long as some shareholders object. Decisions to abandon a profitable opportunity (or to replace corporate assets with property of lesser value) are known in law as "acts of waste," and such acts cannot be undertaken unless every shareholder agrees. The law assumes, in other words, that corporations are designed to increase shareholder wealth, so that a majority cannot impose a loss on an unwilling minority, no matter how worthy the cause or how small the minority.[43] In general, shareholders have little alternative but to accept the profit-making end of corporate activity and the means chosen by management to achieve that end. To say that corporations ought to be run in the interests of shareholders, therefore, is to say nothing more than that they ought to make a profit. Talk about the interests of shareholders is superfluous.

The "taxation" argument thus misconceives the relation between managers and shareholders of a publicly held corporation. Shareholders do not entrust their property to managers with the understanding that the managers will use it in the interests of the shareholders. Rather, corporations are institutions created by law with a charter that specifies the goals to be pursued. Persons who purchase shares of a corporation and thereby become the legal owners have a right to expect only that a corporation will be operated in accord with its charter, not in accord with the interests of the individual shareholders. Friedman's argument yields the desired result in the case of a sole proprietorship of the kind described in the example of the person who retires to Florida to play golf and entrusts his business to a manager. It is a mistake, however, to extrapolate from this example to a publicly held corporation such as General Motors or IBM.

Conclusion

For these reasons, then, the "taxation" argument in support of the classical view of corporate social responsibility is not very compelling. Although the property rights of shareholders place some limits on what businesses can justifiably do to address major social concerns, they do not yield the very narrowly circumscribed view of Friedman and others. The taxation argument assumes that the money which corporations spend for socially desirable goals rightly belongs to shareholders as the owners. An alternative view is that this money is spent by corporations in order to realize the purposes for which they have been created by society. And although one end is the making of a profit for shareholders, another is to operate in a socially responsible manner.

THE MANAGERIAL AND STAKEHOLDER VIEWS

The classical view has seldom been adopted in its pure form by the managers of American corporations. In practice, it has been modified by two important concepts, namely, those of *philanthropy* and *trusteeship*. The result is what is sometimes called the *managerial view* of corporate responsibility.[44] In addition to their traditional economic role, corporations have, in this view, the tasks of providing support for worthy causes and of guarding society's resources. This view found increasing favor in the 1920s and the 1930s as a result of a number of historical forces, including the increasing size of corporations, the dispersal of ownership, and the separation between ownership and management.[45]

Corporate Philanthropy

Philanthropy has traditionally been an obligation of individuals and nonprofit organizations such as churches, hospitals, and social welfare agencies. In a famous 1889 article entitled simply "Wealth," Andrew Carnegie popularized the idea that successful business leaders have a responsibility to distribute their riches in ways "best calculated to produce the most beneficial results for the community."[46] Carnegie set an example by contributing generously for libraries, parks, concert halls, and other public facilities. However, the magnitude of social problems in the early decades of the twentieth century exceeded the capacities of even the wealthiest individuals, and organizations turned increasingly to business for contributions. Corporations responded with funds for the Community Chest movement, YMCAs, Red Cross, and a host of other projects.[47]

Although the classical theory permits giving that confers an indirect benefit on a corporation, the concept of corporate philanthropy is based on the recognition of an obligation to serve society without any anticipated return. The argument for holding that corporations have such an obligation is based largely on the idea of corporate citizenship. An illustration is provided by H. Brewster Atwater, Jr., chairman and CEO of General Mills, who has written:

> Corporations are classed as citizens under U.S. law, and they enjoy both the privileges and duties of citizenship. This broad concept of corporate citizenship may stem from the view that no citizen can prosper in an unhealthy society. And one of the important duties of each citizen, whether a corporation or an individual, is to work in a multitude of ways for the betterment of society.[48]

The Concept of Trusteeship

The concept of trusteeship—or stewardship, as it is sometimes called—derives from the biblical precept that human beings are not the owners of the earth; rather, it belongs to God, who has entrusted it to people currently living for the benefit of all. Consequently, we have an obligation to use the bounty of creation wisely and to preserve it for future generations. Business leaders, who have command over vast productive and natural resources on which the welfare of workers and the rest of society depends, have a special responsibility to act as trustees or stewards of this accumulated wealth. Unlike the concept of philanthropy, which involves charitable giving out of the earnings of a corporation, trusteeship entails an obligation concerning the total resources of a corporation. In the words of one writer, "It is not the surplus which constitutes the special trust, it is everything the owner owns."[49]

The concept of trusteeship leads corporate managers to be more than profit maximizers for the benefit of shareholders and to take the interests of a diverse constituency into account. According to Robert Hay and Ed Gray:

> The . . . trusteeship manager recognizes that self-interest plays a large role in his actions, but he also recognizes the interest of those people who contribute to his organization—customers, employees, suppliers, owners, creditors, government, and community. He thus operates from self-interest plus the interest of other groups. . . . He is a profit satisficer; that is, he balances the profits of the owners and the organization with the wages for employees, taxes for the government, interest for the creditors, and so forth. Money is important to him, but so are people, because his values tell him that satisfying people's needs is a better goal than just making money.
>
> In balancing the needs of the various contributors to the organization, the trusteeship manager deals with the customers as the chief providers of revenue to the firm. . . . He views employees as having certain rights which must be recognized; they are more than a mere commodity to be traded in the marketplace. His accountability as a manager is to owners as well as customers, employees, suppliers, creditors, government, and the community.[50]

The Managerial View and Social Responsibility

The managerial view, then, with the concepts of philanthropy and trusteeship, is much broader than the classical view, but it is still more limited than the present-day understanding of the social responsibility of corporations to take an active role in addressing major social problems. The concept of trusteeship, in particular, although often acknowledged by business leaders, has not served historically as a meaningful guide for the exercise of corporate social responsibility. Trusteeship is usually interpreted as maintaining a corporation as a going concern, which is compatible with plant closings that devastate communities, strip mining and logging that despoil the environment, and so on.

The concept of philanthropy is similarly inadequate. Although corporations are an important source of support for nonprofit organizations, a very small portion of corporate wealth is actually devoted to charitable giving. The average philanthropic contribution for American corporations has long hovered around 1 percent.[51] Charitable giving, moreover, is concerned with the disposition of the earnings of a corporation and not with the way in which it conducts day-to-day operations. But social responsibility is reflected in all that a corporation does and so cannot be confined to a department of corporate philanthropy.

The Stakeholder Theory

A third concept that goes beyond philanthropy and trusteeship and enlarges the managerial view is that of a *stakeholder*. Instead of serving only the interests of shareholders or stockholders, corporations are operated for the benefit of all those who have a stake in the enterprise, including employees, customers, suppliers, and the local community. A stakeholder is variously defined as "those groups who are vital to the survival and success of the corporation"[52] and as "any group or individual who can affect or is affected by the achievement of the organization's objectives."[53] Although the relation of shareholders, as the owners of a corporation, is different from that of employees, consumers, and so on, all of these constituencies are integral to the operation of a corporation.

From the fact that there are stakeholders, however, nothing follows about whether corporations have a moral obligation to take their interests into account. Holders of the classical view of social responsibility are perfectly aware that employees, customers, suppliers, and the general public are important to the operation of a corporation. What they deny is the idea that corporations are morally obligated to undertake some actions or refrain from others merely because of the impact on the interests of these groups. Corporations have an obligation to respect the rights of each stakeholder group, but these rights are limited, in the classical view, to the rights of parties in market exchanges, which is to say, the "rules of the game."

To the extent that employees, consumers, and others have a more extensive set of rights that are now recognized in law, corporations have an obligation to act with a regard for the interests of stakeholders in many matters. If employees have a right to a safe and healthy workplace, for example, and consumers have a right to products that are not likely to cause serious injury, then corporations are obligated to take the welfare of these groups into account in making decisions about work routines, product design, and so on. The stakeholder view, then, does not consist merely of the fact that there are many groups besides shareholders who have a stake in a corporation. It has inescapable normative implications about the obligation of corporations to take the interests of other groups into account.

Some writers reject the stakeholder view on the ground that the interests of all groups other than shareholders constitute *constraints* on corporate activities in pursuit of the goal of making a profit rather than *goals* themselves. Igor Ansoff, for example, in his classic 1965 book *Corporate Strategy* contends that "responsibilities" and "objectives" are not the same; the former are obligations that limit the achievement of the main objectives of a firm.[54] The stakeholder view, then, confuses the responsibilities of a corporation (which include the obligations to stakeholder groups) with its objectives (one of which is to operate at a profit).

Kenneth E. Goodpaster has criticized the stakeholder view from another direction.[55] Although conceding that corporations have genuine obligations toward various stakeholders which are not merely constraints, Goodpaster insists that the obligations to shareholders are different in kind. The obligation of a manager to the shareholders is that of a *fiduciary*, who is bound to conserve and utilize the assets of the corporation in the interests of these owners. The obligations of managers to employees, customers, and others is morally significant, but they are nonfiduciary obligations. The effect of treating the obligations to shareholders and stakeholders alike is, according to Goodpaster, to obscure an important distinction.

Goodpaster makes an important point, but we also need to keep two other things in mind. First, the stakeholder theory does not deny the obvious fact that the obligations of managers are different for every stakeholder group, but it stresses that they also have a certain commonality. A complete development of a stakeholder theory of the corporation would involve, therefore, a description of the obligations of managers to each stakeholder group—what they have in common as well as how they differ.

Second, although shareholders are legally the owners of a corporation, the corporation itself is a legal entity with interests recognized in law that are not necessarily identical with those of the shareholders. Part of the justification of our system of corporate governance is a version of Adam Smith's "invisible hand" argument, to the effect that stockholders in promoting their own interests will also promote the interests of the corporation, as well as those of society as a whole. For a manager to place special emphasis on serving the interests of shareholders *directly* can be viewed, then, as a way of *indirectly* serving the interests of other stakeholder groups. The creation of a special fiduciary relation between managers and shareholders is designed, in other words, to benefit everyone alike.

A more crucial objection to the stakeholder view is its shortcomings as an action guide for business. Even managers committed to honoring obligations to all stakeholders will find that the stakeholder theory leaves many questions unanswered. The major difficulties are explained by Thomas Donaldson as follows:

> No serious attempt has been made by defenders of the model to devise a principle for making trade-offs between the interests of shareholders, suppliers, employees, consumers, members of the general public, or anyone else who might qualify as a stakeholder. But it is here that the toughest problems of ethics usually emerge. The stakeholder model implies that IBM ought not merely serve the interests of shareholders; it implies that it should do more than focus on maximal return on investment while neglecting the interests of the general public. But we are left wondering how to weigh and balance the interests at stake. Consider the issue of whether

IBM should sell its computers to the Chilean government when it believes the government will use the computers to track down and torture political dissidents. Or consider whether the U.S.-based USG Corporation should pay lower wages to nonwhite South African workers . . . if it believes it will benefit stockholders to do so. Here it is of little help to note that the interests of Chilean dissidents and of South African nonwhites are relevant to corporate decision making. What we need to know is just *how* relevant they are.[56]

Donaldson also notes that the responsibility of corporations to stakeholders cannot be determined by a simple utilitarian calculation, since the claims of some groups have greater weight than those of others. If, on the other hand, the stakeholder view involves respecting rights, then corporations have no obligation to be concerned with the interests of any group beyond observing an absolute minimum level of conduct. That is, USG should not discriminate by paying nonwhite workers less but would have no obligation to be concerned about their welfare.

Despite these objections, the stakeholder theory remains a very promising version of the managerial view. The concept of a stakeholder is a valuable device for identifying and organizing the multitude of obligations that corporations have to different groups. At the present time, however, the theory is only a framework to help us get started on the very difficult task of deciding exactly what obligations of corporations come under the heading of corporate social responsibility.

Conclusion

The aim of this chapter has been to answer some very practical questions, such as the responsibility of the Campbell Soup Company for the plight of migrant farmworkers in Ohio. In order to do this, however, we are led, of necessity, to consider fundamental issues about the nature and purpose of a corporation. These theoretical matters must be addressed first before we can hope to settle any practical questions about the social responsibility of corporations.

At the center of the debate over corporate social responsibility are two competing positions. One views the modern corporation as a social enterprise, an institution created by society to provide us with goods and services, as well as the means to secure a livelihood. Although recognizing the limited economic purpose of corporations, this position still measures success by the extent to which corporations contribute to the welfare of the whole of society. Questions about the social responsibility of corporations are to be settled ultimately by utilitarian considerations.

The other position holds that corporations are forms of property created by individuals in the exercise of their property rights. Not only shareholders, who are the legal owners of a corporation, but employees and consumers, as well as the owners of other businesses, exercise their property rights by entering into the myriad relations that constitute the activity of a corporation. The social responsibility of corporations is properly judged, in this view, in terms of their success in respecting the property rights of all concerned.

These two positions are not wholly incompatible and often lead to similar results in practice. The reason is that corporations cannot exist without satisfying the expectations of society, and these often include a responsiveness to pressing social problems. However, companies such as Campbell, which regards itself as having the social responsibility expressed in the statement *Our Principles*, will respond to problems differently from one that takes another view. The differences may be subtle and hard to detect, but they are of the utmost importance.

NOTES

1. JIM TERRY, "Campbell Soup in Hot Water with Organized Labor," *Business and Society Review*, 46 (Summer 1983), 37–38.
2. "Distribution of Campbell Soup Contributions Fiscal 1987," company document.
3. TERRY, "Campbell Soup in Hot Water with Organized Labor," 39.
4. TERRY, "Campbell Soup in Hot Water with Organized Labor," 39.
5. Information on this case is taken from "Campbell Soup Company," The Wharton School of the University of Pennsylvania.
6. *Brandel* v. *United States*, U.S. District Court, Western District of Michigan, Southern Division, 83–1228.
7. KEITH SCHNEIDER, "Campbell Soup Accord Ends a Decade of Strife," *The New York Times*, February 24, 1986, sec. 2, p. 7.
8. For a comprehensive account of the historical development of the concept of corporate social responsibility, see MORRELL HEALD, *The Social Responsibilities of Business: Company and Community, 1900–1960* (Cleveland: Case Western Reserve University Press, 1970). Brief accounts are given in CLARENCE C. WALTON, *Corporate Social Responsibilities* (Belmont, CA: Wadsworth, 1967), 21–53; and JAMES W. McKIE, "Changing Views," in McKIE, ed. *Social Responsibility and the Business Predicament* (Washington, DC: The Brookings Institution, 1974), 17–40.
9. JOSEPH W. McGUIRE, *Business and Society* (New York: McGraw-Hill, 1963), 144. For the point that the assumption of responsibility must be voluntary, see HENRY MANNE and HENRY C. WALLICH, *The Modern Corporation and Social Responsibility* (Washington, DC: American Enterprise Institute for Public Policy Research, 1972), 5.
10. ARCHIE B. CARROLL, "A Three-Dimensional Conceptual Model of Corporate Performance," *Academy of Management Review*, 4 (1979), 497–505.
11. CARROLL, "A Three-Dimensional Conceptual Model of Corporate Performance," 500.

12. CARROLL, "A Three-Dimensional Conceptual Model of Corporate Perform-ance," 500.

13. *Social Responsibilities of Business Corporations* (New York: Committee for Eco-nomic Development, 1971), 15.

14. S. PRAKASH SETHI, "Dimensions of Corporate Social Performance: An Ana-lytical Framework for Measurement and Analysis," *California Management Review*, 17 (Spring 1975), 62. Emphasis in original omitted.

15. SETHI, "Dimensions of Corporate Social Performance," 62.

16. For a good survey of socially responsible corporate activities, from which many of the following examples are taken, see TAD TULEJA, *Beyond the Bottom Line: How Business Leaders are Turning Principles into Profits* (New York: Facts on File, 1985).

17. The concept of corporate social responsiveness is developed in ROBERT W. ACKERMAN and RAYMOND A. BAUER, *Corporate Social Responsiveness: The Mod-ern Dilemma* (Reston, VA: Reston, 1976). See also, SETHI, "Dimensions of Corporate Social Performance"; and CARROLL, "A Three-Dimensional Model of Corporate Performance."

18. From an unpublished paper, quoted in CARROLL, "A Three-Dimensional Model of Corporate Performance," 501.

19. For a discussion of the integration of responsiveness into the strategic plan-ning process, see R. EDWARD FREEMAN and DANIEL R. GILBERT, JR., *Corpo-rate Strategy and the Search for Ethics* (Englewood Cliffs, NJ: Prentice Hall, 1988).

20. This point is made by WILLIAM C. FREDERICK, "Toward CSR3: Why Ethical Analysis Is Indispensable and Unavoidable in Corporate Affairs," *California Management Review*, 28 (1986), 131–32.

21. Frederick, in "Toward CSR3," proposes as a third concept, beyond corporate social responsibility (CSR1) and corporate social responsiveness (CSR2), CSR3, which is corporate social rectitude. Also see EDWIN M. EPSTEIN, "The Corporate Social Policy Process: Beyond Business Ethics, Corporate Social Responsibility, and Corporate Social Responsiveness," *California Management Review*, 29 (Spring 1987), 99–114, in which corporate social policy is pro-posed as a fourth concept that unifies and integrates the others in a way that can be implemented in business practice.

22. MILTON FRIEDMAN, *Capitalism and Freedom* (Chicago: University of Chicago Press, 1962), 133.

23. WILLIAM C. FREDERICK, "Theories of Corporate Social Performance," in S. PRAKASH SETHI and CECILIA M. FALBE, *Business and Society: Dimensions of Conflict and Cooperation* (Lexington, MA: Lexington Books, 1987), 147.

24. MCKIE, "Changing Views," 18–19.

25. FRIEDMAN, *Capitalism and Freedom*, 133. The quotation of Adam Smith is from *The Wealth of Nations*, Book IV, Chapter II. This famous paragraph concludes: "It is an affectation, indeed, not very common among merchants, and very few words need be employed in dissuading them from it."

26. MILTON FRIEDMAN, "The Social Responsibility of Business Is to Increase Its Profits," *New York Times Magazine*, September 13, 1970, 33.

27. FRIEDMAN, "The Social Responsibility of Business Is to Increase Its Profits," 122.

28. See, for example, RICHARD MUSGRAVE, *The Theory of Public Finance* (New

York: McGraw-Hill, 1959), in which the three functions of securing efficiency (which includes considerations of externalities), equity, and stability properly belong to government.

29. Holders of the classical view generally favor market solutions over government action in the belief that many externalities result from a lack, rather than an excess, of free market forces and that regulation is often ineffective. Still, they usually admit the principle that government regulation is appropriate in some instances to deal with externalities.

30. For an explanation and discussion of this concept, see ARTHUR M. OKUN, *Equality and Efficiency: The Big Tradeoff* (Washington, DC: The Brookings Institution, 1975).

31. THEODORE LEVITT, "The Dangers of Social Responsibility," *Harvard Business Review*, 36 (September–October 1958), 49.

32. JOHN G. SIMON, CHARLES W. POWERS, and JON P. GUNNEMANN, "The Responsibilities of Corporations and Their Owners," in *The Ethical Investor: Universities and Corporate Responsibility* (New Haven: Yale University Press, 1972), 16–17.

33. KEITH DAVIS, "The Case for and against Business Assumption of Social Responsibilities," *Academy of Management Journal*, 16 (June 1973), 314.

34. KEITH DAVIS, "Five Propositions for Social Responsibility," *Business Horizons*, 18 (June 1975), 20. Italics in the original.

35. KEITH DAVIS and ROBERT L. BLOMSTROM, *Business and Society: Environment and Responsibility*, 3rd ed. (New York: McGraw-Hill, 1975), 50.

36. This objection is formulated in KENNETH E. GOODPASTER and JOHN B. MATTHEWS, JR., "Can a Corporation Have a Conscience?" *Harvard Business Review*, 60 (January–February 1982), 139–40.

37. GOODPASTER and MATTHEWS, "Can a Corporation Have a Conscience?" 140.

38. These points are made in DAVIS, "The Case for and against Assumption of Social Responsibilities," 320. Ironically, another argument is that the assumption of greater social responsibility would weaken the power of corporations by diverting their resources from their most productive use, with the result that they would not be able to fulfill either their economic or social role well. The inconsistency of these arguments has not prevented some critics from using both.

39. SIMON, POWERS, and GUNNEMANN, "The Responsibilities of Corporations and Their Owners."

40. MARVIN A. CHIRELSTEIN, "Corporate Law Reform," in MCKIE, *Social Responsibility and the Business Predicament*, 55.

41. NORMAN E. BOWIE and RONALD F. DUSKA, *Business Ethics*, 2nd ed. (Englewood Cliffs, NJ: Prentice Hall, 1990), 24.

42. These conditions have been weakened somewhat to allow for dissident resolutions. See *Medical Committee for Human Rights v. Securities and Exchange Commission*, 432 F.2d 659 (D.C. Cir. 1970), in which an antiwar group won the right to submit a resolution protesting the production of Napalm to the shareholders of Dow Chemical Company.

43. CHIRELSTEIN, "Corporate Law Reform," 60–61.

44. The terms "classical view" and "managerial view" are adapted from MCKIE, "Changing Views." McKie uses the term "managerial view," however, to denote a view that reached full development in the present-day conception of

corporate social responsibility. The division developed here corresponds more closely to the three phases distinguished in ROBERT HAY and ED GRAY, "Social Responsibilities of Business Managers," *Academy of Management Journal*, 17 (March 1974), 135–43.

45. These developments are described in the classic work by A. A. BERLE, JR., and GARDNER MEANS, *The Modern Corporation and Private Property* (New York: Macmillan, 1932).

46. ANDREW CARNEGIE, "Wealth," *North American Review* (June 1889).

47. For a detailed history of corporate philanthropy, and especially the Community Chest movement, see HEALD, *The Social Responsibilities of Business*. A brief survey is given in BARRY D. KARL, "Corporate Philanthropy: Historical Background," in *Corporate Philanthropy* (Washington, DC: Council on Foundations, 1982), 132–35. A more general history of philanthropy in the United States is provided by ROBERT H. BREMMER, *American Philanthropy* (Chicago: University of Chicago Press, 1960).

48. H. BREWSTER ATWATER, JR., "The Corporation as Good Citizen," in *Corporate Philanthropy*, 17.

49. WILLIAM J. BYRON, "Christianity and Capitalism," *Review of Social Economy*, 40 (1982), 316.

50. HAY and GRAY, "Social Responsibilities of Business Managers," 139.

51. For a compilation of current data, see KATHARINE TROY, "Statistical Analysis of Corporate Philanthropy," in *Corporate Philanthropy*, 136–48. A thorough but dated study is F. EMERSON ANDREWS, *Philanthropic Giving* (New York: Russell Sage Foundation, 1950).

52. WILLIAM M. EVAN and R. EDWARD FREEMAN, "A Stakeholder Theory of the Modern Corporation: Kantian Capitalism," in TOM L. BEAUCHAMP and NORMAN E. BOWIE, eds., *Ethical Theory and Business*, 3rd ed. (Englewood Cliffs, NJ: Prentice Hall, 1988), 100. See also R. EDWARD FREEMAN and D. REED, "Stockholders and Stakeholders: A New Perspective on Corporate Governance," in C. HUIZINGA, ed., *Corporate Governance: A Definitive Exploration of the Issues* (Los Angeles: UCLA Extension Press, 1983).

53. R. EDWARD FREEMAN, *Strategic Management: A Stakeholder Approach* (Boston: Pitman, 1984), 46. This book provides a useful discussion of the history of the stakeholder concept and the literature on it.

54. IGOR ANSOFF, *Corporate Strategy* (New York: McGraw-Hill, 1965), 38.

55. KENNETH E. GOODPASTER, "Business Ethics and Stakeholder Analysis," *Business Ethics Quarterly*, 1 (1991), 53–73.

56. THOMAS DONALDSON, *The Ethics of International Business* (New York: Oxford University Press, 1989), 45–46. Donaldson notes that USG has been scrupulous not to discriminate in the wages it pays in South Africa.

CHAPTER FIFTEEN

Ethics in International Business

The record shows that when U.S. enterprises operate in less developed countries, there is a very high probability that they will be charged from some quarters with various serious failings in terms of social responsibility.[1]

—RAYMOND VERNON

Although many firms engage in business abroad, most of the ethical issues in this area arise for the *transnational corporation*, or TNC, which is generally defined as a firm that has a *direct investment* in two or more countries.[2] The forms that foreign direct investment take vary enormously. Usually, though, there is full or partial ownership of affiliates in other countries which are subject to some degree of control from the parent corporation. In some instances, the owners and managers of a TNC are from the home country exclusively; in others, the owners and managers of a firm include people of many different nationalities.

The emergence of TNCs in the second half of the twentieth century has had a profound effect on developed and undeveloped countries alike. Their wealth and power have given rise to concern about the impact on local economies in both home and host countries and about the capacity of governments, even in such countries as the United States, to regulate them effectively.[3] The controversy over transnationals extends beyond their responsibility in less developed countries to include policy prescriptions for national governments in dealing with TNCs and the obligations of the developed countries to share their wealth with the poorer countries of the world. Although important, these are largely political matters that cannot be examined here.

Our concern in this chapter is rather with the moral obligations of managers of transnationals and other firms in dealing with difficult issues, such as those raised by the marketing of pharmaceuticals in the third world. This area, where TNCs have been extensively criticized, is examined first to illustrate the many problems encountered in international business. The main task, though, is to develop an ethical framework for determining the appropriate standards for the different situations in which managers of TNCs find themselves. The framework developed in this chapter is then applied to the problem of risk management in a third world country, looking specifically at the Bhopal tragedy.

MARKETING PHARMACEUTICALS IN THE THIRD WORLD

The pharmaceutical industry, more than any other, has been criticized for its activities abroad. Although prescription and over-the-counter drugs have done much to alleviate suffering and increase the well-being of people around the globe, the major drug companies are also faulted for many of their practices.

Different Instructions

One of the most heavily criticized practices is promoting drugs in the third world with more indications for their use and fewer warnings about side effects than in developed countries. The following are some typical examples.

Diarrhea is a mild inconvenience in developed countries, but it is a life-threatening condition in the third world and the major killer of children under the age of three.[4] One treatment for diarrhea is Lomotil, marketed by G. D. Searle. This drug does not treat the underlying causes of diarrhea, however, but merely relieves the symptoms by producing constipation. Consequently, the World Health Organization (WHO) has declared Lomotil to be of "no value" in the treatment of diarrhea and a waste of time and money.[5] The drug is also dangerous for young children and should not be prescribed to children under the age of two.[6] But Searle has recommended the drug for diarrhea in children as young as one year in Indonesia and in infants between three and six months in Hong Kong, Thailand, the Philippines, and Central America.[7]

Anabolic steroids are a group of synthetic male sex hormones with a reputation of stimulating appetite, increasing body weight, strengthening bones, and generally improving athletic ability. They are too dangerous to be taken for such trivial purposes, however, since their side effects include stunted growth, abnormal sexual development, and liver damage. Anabolic steroids have been found safe and effective only for the treatment of pituitary dwarfism, some forms of anemia, and osteoporosis. In some Latin American countries, however, the instructions accompanying Winstrol, the anabolic steroid stanozol, marketed by Winthrop Products, a division of Sterling Drug, recommended the drug for appetite loss, malnutrition, and retarded growth.[8] An advertisement in a Mexican medical journal in 1972 showed a healthy looking boy about seven years old and recommended Winstrol Compound (Winstrol fortified with vitamins and iron) "if he complains of poor appetite, fatigue, or weight loss."[9]

Chloramphenicol, marketed by Parke-Davis under the brand name of Chloromycetin, is a highly effective drug for treating severe life-threatening infections, such a typhoid fever. In a few susceptible people, however, the drug can cause a frequently fatal form of aplastic anemia. Accordingly, the *Physicians' Desk Reference* states, "It must not be used in the treatment of trivial infections or where it is not indicated, as in colds, influenza, infections of the throat, or as a prophylactic agent to prevent bacterial infections." WHO has repeatedly issued warnings against indiscriminate use of this drug.[10] Physicians are advised to conduct frequent blood studies, so that treatment can be halted at the first sign of side effects.[11] Parke-Davis claims to have standardized labeling worldwide,[12] but some instances of more extensive indications and fewer warnings have been uncovered in Central and South America, Indonesia, and the Philippines.[13] In Mexico and Central America, for example, Chloromycetin has been indicated for tonsillitis, urinary tract infections, bacterial pneumonia, and undulant fever, among other conditions, and it has been sold without the warnings given to doctors in the United States to conduct blood studies every two days.[14]

Drug Dumping

Another charge against pharmaceutical firms is that they engage in *drug dumping*, the practice of selling abroad drugs which have not been approved or for which approval has been withdrawn in the country where they are manufactured. Combination antibiotics (two or more drugs in a fixed ratio) have been removed from the U.S. market as a result of findings by the FDA that the drugs can interfere with each other and that the fixed ratios prevent doctors from prescribing the proper dose for each patient. Combination antibiotics are still marketed in most developing countries, however, and even command premium prices.[15] Perhaps the most controversial allegation of drug dumping concerns Depo-Provera, an injected contraceptive that protects women against pregnancy for three months or more. In the early 1970s, the FDA refused to approve Depo-Provera because tests conducted since 1965 showed that it can cause extended and even permanent infertility and possible breast tumors and cervical cancer. All the time, Upjohn was promoting this contraceptive outside the United States with no warnings about its side effects.[16] American companies are forbidden by the Food, Drug, and Cosmetic Act of 1938 to export drugs not approved for use in the United States,[17] but many means are available for evading this restriction. Upjohn, for example, was able to manufacture Depo-Provera legally by shifting production to plants in Belgium.[18]

Problems With Pricing

Drug companies are further charged with placing higher prices on some products and lower prices on others in the third world for no apparent reason except what the market will bear.[19] In *Global Reach*, Richard J. Barnet and Ronald E. Muller cite a study showing that the prices for the tranquilizers Valium and Librium in Columbia were, respectively, 82 and 65 times higher than the standard charges elsewhere.[20] *Transfer pricing*, the means by which companies charge their own subsidiaries for goods, makes it possible for transnationals to bypass laws designed to keep profits from being taken out of a country or to limit the taxes paid on profits earned in any given country. This is accomplished by importing raw materials and partially finished products at very low prices into countries with favorable tax and profit repatriation laws and then exporting them to subsidiaries in the third world at artificially high prices so that virtually no profit is recorded there.[21]

Another criticism of the pharmaceutical industry is that the price paid for drugs in third world countries includes the costs of research and development, but priority is commonly given by transnationals to drugs for the treatment of health problems in developed first world countries. Consequently, people suffering from tropical diseases are forced to pay the research and development costs of drugs for cancer therapy, for example, while little or no money goes into the search for drugs to cure sleeping sickness.[22] An apparent exception that only proves the rule is the discovery by Marion Merrell Dow of a new drug, Ornidyl, for the treatment of sleeping sickness. This important discovery was made accidentally, however, by researchers trying to develop a drug for treating cancer.[23]

Free Samples and Bribery

A common practice in the third world is to provide physicians with free samples, which are then sold to patients for extra income. The effect is not only to create a subtle form of bribery (since doctors are encouraged to prescribe a given brand in order to continue the flow of free samples) but also to increase the sale of unneeded drugs by encouraging doctors to unload their stocks on patients. Some doctors are bribed by less subtle means, including free trips, lavish entertainment, and cash payments.[24] In addition, representatives of the major pharmaceutical firms encourage the use of branded drugs in the third world rather than cheaper generics, and extensive advertising prompts people to engage in self-medication and to buy all manner of useless pills and tonics.

DEVELOPING AN ETHICAL FRAMEWORK

The crux of the charges against the activities of drug companies abroad is that they adopt a double standard, doing in less developed third world countries what would be regarded as wrong if done in the developed first world. "The moral failure of the transnationals," according to one critic, "lies in their willingness to settle for much lower standards than at home."[25] However, many of the practices just described are legal in the countries in question and are not considered to be unethical by local standards.

The marketing of pharmaceuticals in the third world illustrates a quandary faced by all transnational corporations; namely, deciding which standards of ethics to follow. Should TNCs be bound by the laws and prevailing morality of the home country and, in the case of American corporations, act everywhere as they do in the United States? Should they follow the practices of the host country and adopt the adage, "When in Rome, do as the Romans do"? Or are there special ethical standards that apply when business is conducted across national boundaries? And if so, what are the standards appropriate for international business?

Unfortunately, there are no easy answers to these questions. In some cases, the standards contained in American law and morality ought to be observed beyond our borders; in other cases, there is no moral obligation to do so. Similarly, it is morally permissible for managers of TNCs to follow local practice and "do as the Romans do" in some situations but not others. And even if there are special ethical standards for international business, they cannot be applied without taking into account differences in cultures and value systems, the levels of economic development, and the social and political structures of the foreign countries in which TNCs operate. The existence of special standards, in other words, does not require us to act in the same way in all parts of the world, regardless of the situation. Local circumstances must always be taken into consideration in conducting business abroad.

"No Double Standards!"

Let us consider, first, the position taken by some critics of TNCs: that business ought to be conducted in the same way the world over with no double standards. In particular, United States corporations ought to observe domestic law and a single code of conduct in their dealings everywhere. This position might be expressed as, "When in Rome or anywhere else, do as you would at home."[26] A little reflection suffices to show that this high level of conduct is not morally required of TNCs in all instances and that they should not be faulted for every departure from home country standards in doing business abroad. Good reasons can be advanced to show that different practices in different parts of the world are, in some instances, morally justified.

First, the conditions prevailing in other parts of the world are different in some morally relevant respects from those in the United States and other developed countries. If Rome is a significantly different place, then standards that are appropriate at home do not necessarily apply there. Drug laws in the developed would, for example, are very stringent, reflecting greater affluence and better overall health. The standards embodied in these laws are not always appropriate in poorer, less developed countries with fewer medical resources and more severe health problems.

In the United States, the risk of prescribing an antidiarrheal drug such as Lomotil to children is not worth taking. But a physician in Central America, where children frequently die of untreated diarrhea, might evaluate the risk differently. Similarly, the effectiveness of Chloromycetin for massive infections might offset the possibility of aplastic anemia in a country where some people would die without the drug. A missionary in Bolivia who spoke with doctors about the extentive use of chloramphenicol (the generic name for Chloromycetin) reported: "The response was that in the States, because of our better state of general health, we could afford to have the luxury of saving that drug for rare cases. Here, the people's general health is so poor that one must make an all out attack on illness."[27]

Second, some aspects of American law and practice reflect incidental features of our situation, so that not all United States standards express universal moral requirements.[28] The fact that a drug has not been approved in the home country of a transnational or has been withdrawn from the market does not automatically mean that it is unsafe or ineffective. A drug for a tropical disease might never have been submitted for approval, since there is no market for it in the country where it is manufactured. Other drugs might not be approved because of concerns that are unfounded or open to question.

The FDA acted conservatively in refusing approval for Depo-Provera, for example; many countries of Western Europe and Canada, with equally strict drug testing requirements, permit the use of this drug as a last resort contraceptive. In borderline cases, there is room for legitimate debate between competent, well-intentioned persons about the correctness of FDA decisions. Also, the approval of drugs in the United States is a lengthy process. Companies convinced of the safety of a drug might be justified in rushing it to market in countries where it is legally permitted, while waiting for approval at home, especially if there is a pressing need abroad.

Third, many factors in other countries, especially in the third world, are beyond the control of TNCs, and they often have little choice but to adapt to local conditions—if they are going to do business at all. This position can perhaps be expressed as, "We do not entirely agree with the Romans, but we sometimes find it necessary to do things their way." For example, physicians in the third world often prefer to prescribe multiple drugs for a single ailment. Hence, the demand for combination antibiotics. Although this practice is disapproved by the American medical community, extending the United States ban on such drugs to the rest of the world is unlikely to bring about any significant change. If combination antibiotics were not sold, many doctors would continue to issue prescriptions for several different drugs to be taken simultaneously, very possibly in the wrong proportions.

As another example, consider the ethics of marketing prescription drugs directly to consumers. Deep opposition to this practice exists in the United States, and drug companies are severely criticized for ad campaigns that appeal to patients over the heads of physicians. In much of the third world, however, self-medication is a deeply ingrained practice, since many people are too poor to consult a doctor, if, indeed, one is available. And many drugs that are available only by prescription in the United States are freely dispensed by pharmacists in the third world—and even by street corner vendors. Under these conditions, drug companies contend that advertising cannot be effective if it is aimed only at physicians. Drug companies are accused, however, of encouraging self-medication and inducing the population to spend scarce resources on pills, tonics, and other medications when they have so many more pressing needs.

"When in Rome . . ."

The opposite extreme—that the only guide for business conduct abroad is what is legally and morally accepted in any given country where a TNC operates—is equally untenable. "When in Rome do as the Romans do" cannot be followed without exception. In order to see this, however, we need to distinguish at least three different arguments that are used to support this position. These correspond to the objections to the first position just examined and can be sketched briefly as follows:

1. There really are morally relevant differences. The justification for holding a double standard and marketing a drug in a host country that is not approved at home, for example, is that the conditions that prevail in the country are different in morally relevant respects.

2. The people affected have a right to decide. Where different standards exist, the right of a host country to determine which to apply should be respected. The primary responsibility for setting standards properly rests on the government and the people of the country in which business is being conducted.

3. There is no other way of doing business. Where local conditions require that corporations engage in certain practices as a condition of doing business, then those practices are justified. This is a version of the argument, "We do not entirely agree with the Romans, but we sometimes find it necessary to do things their way."

The first argument presupposes the existence of general principles of justification, such as the utilitarian principle that justifies practices in terms of their consequences for benefit and harm. As a result, it is possible that no ultimate conflict exists in some cases of apparent double standards; whatever principles are employed simply justify different practices when conditions are different in morally relevant respects. Many of the criticisms directed against TNCs fail to recognize the extent to which the practices in host countries are capable of being justified by the same principles that justify different practices at home. We have already noted some of the relevant differences that might justify different marketing practices for prescription drugs, but there are many other cases that illustrate the point.

Consider whether a double standard is involved, for example, when TNCs pay wages in less developed countries that are a fraction of those in the developed world. One possible position is that although there are vast differences in the actual wages paid by a TNC in the United States and, say, Mexico, the disparity is not unjust *if the same mechanism for setting wages is employed in both cases.* Thus, the wage paid to a worker in the third world must provide a decent standard of living in that country and be arrived at by a process of fair bargaining that fully respects workers as human beings. In order for these conditions to be satisfied, unions might also be necessary to ensure that workers are adequately represented.[29] What is morally objectionable about the wages paid by many TNCs in the third world, then, is not that they are lower than those in the home country but that they are imposed on workers in violation of their rights.

How far this argument is able to justify the use of different standards in host and home countries is a matter for speculation. Although a few of the marketing practices for which the pharmaceutical industry is criticized can perhaps be justified in this manner, it is difficult to believe that the differences between countries are sufficient to justify extensive double standards. A serious effort by TNCs to apply the ethical principles underlying home country standards to the varying conditions they encounter in different parts of the world would be a welcome development—and one that would result, most likely, in many changes in current marketing practices.

Abiding by Local Standards

The argument, "The people affected have a right to decide" is not a form of ethical relativism. Just because physicians in some less developed countries routinely sell free samples does not make the practice right. Even when the practice is legal in the country in question and condoned by the local medical community, the indirect payment provided by the sale of free samples that makes it possible for drug companies to bribe physicians can still be branded as morally wrong. The argument is rather an expression of respect for the right of people to govern their own affairs. Imposing the standards of a developed first world country in the third world is criticized by some as a form of "ethical imperialism."[30]

Although there is some merit in this argument, it cannot be accepted without considerable qualification. A respect for the right of people to set their own standards does not automatically justify corporations in inflicting grave harm on innocent people, for example, or violating basic human rights. In deciding whether to employ a practice that is regarded as wrong at home but is legal and apparently approved in a host country, a number of factors must be considered.

First, some countries, especially those in the third world, lack the *capacity* to regulate effectively the activities of transnational corporations within their own borders. The governments of these countries are, in many instances, no less committed than those in the United States and Western Europe to protecting their people against harm from prescription and over-the-counter drugs, but they do not always have the resources—the money, skilled personnel, and institutions—to accomplish the task.

The law in Nigeria, for example, prohibits the marketing of any drug in a way that is "false, or misleading, or is likely to create a wrong impression as to its quality, character, value, composition, merit, or safety."[31] Such a law cannot be effective, however, without an agency such as the FDA to acquire information about the vast number of drugs that enter the country and issue detailed guidelines for their use. Such steps can also be thwarted by powerful transnationals. One Nigerian has complained:

> . . . [W]e have a proposed new drug reviewed by a committee of experts—many of them highly competent people trained in England, Canada, and the United States. They review all the evidence, both that submitted by the company and that published in the best scientific journals. They may

decide that the proposed drug is not safe or not effective enough, and they reject the application. But then the company goes to court with all its expensive legal talent. It files suit. And sometimes our recommendation is overruled.[32]

Second, some countries with the capacity to regulate transnationals lack the necessary *will*. Often, the local medical community and powerful segments of the population benefit from the unethical marketing practices of the giant drug companies and willingly permit and even encourage their use. TNCs, through the exercise of economic power, including payments to government officials, frequently are able to influence regulatory measures. Third world governments also have to be cautious about offending powerful economic interests in countries of the developed world on which they depend for aid. The absence of laws against unethical marketing practices is sometimes part of a pattern of oppression that exists within the country itself. Drug companies are taking advantage of the immorality of others, therefore, when they use certain practices in third world countries with corrupt governments and elites.

In order for the argument, "The people affected have a right to decide" to justify the adoption of different standards, it is necessary to ask whether the standard in a host country, if it is lower than that at home, truly represents the considered judgment of the people in question. Does it reflect the decision that they would make if they had both the capacity to protect their own interests effectively and the means for expressing their collective will? A genuine respect for the right of people to determine which standards to apply in their own country requires a careful and sympathetic consideration of what people would do under certain hypothetical conditions rather than what is actually expressed in the law, conventional morality, and commonly accepted practices.

As in the case of the first argument, it is difficult to speculate on the consequences of applying this one to the broad range of situations faced by TNCs. There is little reason to believe, however, that people in less developed countries, if consulted, would approve the marketing of drugs with more indications and fewer warnings than are provided in the United States, or that they would approve the dumping of drugs that are not permitted to be prescribed in the United States, and so on. The common contention that bribery and other forms of corruption are accepted in the third world often proves to be unfounded. Although common in some countries, these practices are, nevertheless, deeply resented by the bulk of the population and often regretted even by many who stand to benefit. Revelations of official corruption have led to the downfall of more than one government, thus indicating that bribery is not approved in those countries.

The Need to "Go Along"

The final argument, "There is no other way of doing business," like the other two, has some merit. As long as they have a right to operate abroad, corporations ought to be permitted to do what is necessary for the conduct of business—within limits, of course. American firms with contracts for projects in the Middle East, for example, have complied in many instances with requests not to station women and Jewish employees in those countries. Although discrimination of this kind is morally repugnant, it is (arguably) morally permissible when the alternative is to risk losing business in the Arab world. Attempts have been made to justify the practice on the ground that American corporations are forced to go along.

A more complicated case is provided by the Arab boycott of Israel, which was begun by the countries of the Arab League in 1945.[33] In order to avoid blacklisting that would bar them from doing business with participating Arab countries, many prominent American transnationals cooperated by avoiding investment in Israel. Other U.S. corporations, however, refused to cooperate with the boycott for ethical reasons. An executive of RCA declared, for example:

> We're a worldwide communications company that has done business with China and Rumania, and we'd like to do business with the Arabs. But we are not going to end relations with Israel to get an Arab contract. This is a moral issue that we feel strongly about.[34]

(The position taken by RCA is now required by law. An amendment to the Export Administration Act, signed into law in June 1977 over vigorous objections by segments of the business community, prohibits American corporations from cooperating with the Arab boycott against Israel.)

As with the other arguments, "There is no other way of doing business" cannot be accepted without some qualifications. First, the alternative is seldom to cease doing business; rather, the claim that a practice is "necessary" often means merely that it is the most profitable way of doing business. Drug companies might lose some business by refusing to market combination antibiotics, for example, but the amount is not likely to be substantial, especially if the changeover is accompanied by a promotional effort to educate doctors about the proper use of drugs. Similarly, direct marketing is less likely to be objectionable if advertising is used to educate consumers about drugs in a way that genuinely contributes to their well-being instead of the profit of the transnationals. The Arab embargo against Israel greatly complicated the problems of doing business in the Middle East, but some companies were able to avoid cooperating with the boycott and still have business relations with Arab countries.

Second, there are some situations in which a company is morally obligated to withdraw if there is no other way to do business. At one time, any company with plants and other production facilities in South Africa was required by law to observe the rigid segregation imposed by apartheid. Some critics held at the time that if the only alternative to participating in racial oppression is to cease all operations there, then the latter is the morally preferable course of action. Subsequently, the South African government allowed U.S. subsidiaries to integrate their work force and abide by the so-called Sullivan Code, which bars discrimination in employment.

However, the Sullivan Code does not address the charge that American firms are still contributing by their presence to the survival of a country that systematically violates the rights of its own people. Also, critics charge that some of the products sold in South Africa contribute to the maintenance of apartheid. Several computer companies in the United States, including IBM, for example, were accused of selling equipment that enabled the South African police to enforce the hated passbook and to keep track of dissidents. American banks have also been criticized for making loans that help to preserve the economic stability of the present white regime. These critics contend that such involvement in an immoral system cannot be justified and that the only moral course is to cease doing business there.

Defenders point out in reply that American companies provide high-paying jobs for blacks in South Africa and that their presence encourages a gradual process of liberalization. If they were to withdraw, the condition of the oppressed majority would, most likely, not be improved and pressure on the government to make reforms would be eased. The main consequence would probably be that other foreign investors and white South Africans would take the place of the departing American firms with worse consequences.

The difficulty with both of the qualifications just discussed lies in finding the appropriate cutoff points. When is conforming to the local way of doing things absolutely necessary and when is it a matter of convenience or mere profitability? When is it morally permissible for a corporation to remain in a country such as South Africa and when is a corporation morally obligated to withdraw? Answering these questions requires a careful consideration of the hard realities of the situation and the possibility of justifying each practice. The argument, "There is no other way of doing business," therefore, does not settle the matter in any given case but only serves as a starting point for further ethical inquiry.

Special Standards for International Business

Our results so far have been largely negative. The two extreme positions—"When in Rome, do as the Romans do" and "When in Rome or anywhere else, do as you would at home"—are both inadequate guides in international business. However, the discussion of these positions suggests some principles that can be used to make decisions in difficult cases. These principles recognize that the world of the TNC requires a slightly different approach to issues than the one appropriate to a corporation operating wholly within a single nation state. This is so for several reasons besides those already mentioned.

First, some of the conditions that create a social responsibility for corporations in a country such as the United States are absent elsewhere. The basis for many of the obligations of American corporations to employees, consumers, and the public at large lies in the extensive powers and privileges that we have conferred upon them. Their responsibility to society rests, in other words, on an implicit "social contract," and that contract does exist to the same degree when corporations operate abroad. The role of TNCs is often limited to marketing goods produced elsewhere, participating in joint ventures with local companies, and so on. Thus, they are not full-fledged "corporate citizens" of a host country, so to speak, but are more like guests. Hence, they have less reason to exhibit the good citizenship that we expect of domestic corporations, although they should still be good "corporate guests."

Second, the lack of effective international law with comprehensive multinational agreements, codes of conduct, and the like creates a less regulated, more competitive environment for international business. One benefit of a legal system is a uniform system of enforceable rules that provides a level playing field for all firms. Business competition within a single country with an extensive set of laws is thus like an athletic competition. International business, by contrast, is more akin to war, which cannot be conducted by the detailed rules of a boxing match, for example. Even war is bound by moral limits, however, such as the concept of a just war and rules such as the Geneva Conventions.

Because of these features of international business, it is not appropriate to hold that TNCs have all the same obligations abroad that they have at home and to use the same principles of justification to determine the extent of their obligations in foreign operations. Still, there is a minimal set of obligations that every corporation is morally bound to observe no matter where the activity takes place. An ethical framework for international business consists in part, then, of the moral minimum for corporations operating abroad.

Minimal and Maximal Duties

Thomas Donaldson suggests that we distinguish the minimal and maximal duties of corporations and come to some agreement about the former. A maximal duty or obligation, he says, is one whose fulfillment would be "praiseworthy but not absolutely mandatory," whereas a minimal duty is one such that "the persistent failure to observe [it] would deprive the corporation of its moral right to exist."[35] The requests of third world countries for help in improving living conditions and developing the local economy, although often expressed as demands for justice, are, in Donaldson's view, pleas for a kind of "corporate philanthropy" that is, at best, a maximal duty and not a moral minimum.[36] Further impoverishing a people or violating a fundamental human right, such as employing child labor, is, by contrast, a failure to observe minimal obligations that apply to all business enterprises.

What principles might serve to justify the minimal duties or obligations of corporations engaged in international business? Two have been proposed. One is the principle of *negative harm*, which holds that in their dealings abroad, corporations have an obligation not to add substantially to the deprivation and suffering of people.[37] The utilitarian injunction to produce the greatest possible benefit to people creates a set of maximal obligations of TNCs, but a concern with consequences can take a number of progressively weaker forms that include preventing harm and merely avoiding the infliction of harm. William K. Frankena distinguishes four versions of an obligation of beneficence: (1) One ought not to inflict evil or harm, (2) one ought to prevent evil or harm, (3) one ought to remove evil, and (4) one ought to do or promote good.[38] The negative-harm principle, which is the weakest form, is (arguably) a moral minimum, so that regardless of what other obligations corporations have in foreign operations, they have this one. The only morally justified exceptions to the obligation not to inflict substantial harm on a people are to avoid violating an important right of some kind or to produce a greater benefit in the long run.

A second principle, proposed by Thomas Donaldson, is that corporations have an obligation to respect certain rights; namely, those that ought to be recognized as *fundamental international rights*.[39] TNCs are not obligated to extend all the rights of United States citizens to people everywhere in the world, but there are certain basic rights that no person or institution, including a corporation, is morally permitted to violate. Fundamental international rights are roughly the same as *natural* or *human* rights, discussed in Chapter 3, and some of these are given explicit recognition in documents ranging from general statements, such as the United Nations Universal Declaration of Human Rights, to the very specific, such as the World Health Organization (WHO) Code of Marketing Breast Milk Substitutes.

Of course, the main problem with a principle to respect fundamental international rights (or fundamental rights, for short) is specifying the rights in question. Even undeniable human rights that create an obligation for some person or institution, such as the government of a country, are not always relevant to a transnational corporation. Everyone has a right to subsistence, for example, but TNCs may be under no obligation to feed the hungry in a country where it operates. It has an obligation, however, not to contribute directly to starvation by, say, converting cultivated land to the production of an export crop. To deal with these complications, Donaldson says that a right must meet the following conditions:

1. The right must protect something of very great importance.
2. The right must be subject to substantial and recurrent threats.
3. The obligations and burdens imposed by the right must be (a) affordable and (b) distributed fairly.[40]

The "fairness-affordability" criterion, expressed in condition 3, serves to relieve corporations of an obligation to do what is beyond its resources and more than its fair share.

Although a more extensive list could perhaps be justified by Donaldson's conditions, he suggests the following as a moral minimum:

1. The right to freedom of physical movement.
2. The right to ownership of property.
3. The right to freedom from torture.
4. The right to a fair trial.
5. The right to nondiscriminatory treatment.
6. The right to physical security.
7. The right to freedom of speech and association.
8. The right to minimal education.
9. The right to political participation.
10. The right to subsistence.[41]

Sample applications of these rights, according to Donaldson, include: failing to provide safety equipment, such as goggles, to protect employees from obvious hazards (the right to physical security); using coercive tactics to prevent workers from organizing (the right to freedom of speech and association); employing child labor (the right to minimal education); and bribing government officials to violate their duty or seeking to overthrow democratically elected governments.[42]

THE TRAGEDY AT BHOPAL

Shortly after midnight on December 3, 1984, Suman Dey, an engineer on duty at the Union Carbide plant in Bhopal, India, noticed that pressure and temperature gauges for tank E610 had suddenly shot up to their maximum readings.[43] Although the instruments in the control room were considered by employees to be unreliable, Dey was concerned this time. Tank E610 contained more than 40 tons of methyl isocyanate (MIC), and workers at that moment were attempting to find the source of a reported leak. The high readings indicated that the normally refrigerated liquid was turning into a hot gas that could rupture the tank. At 12:40 AM, Dey rushed to the site, where he could hear the rumbling sound of a violent reaction in the tank and feel the intense heat. He ran away in terror just as a six-foot-thick sixty-foot-long slab of concrete covering three partially submerged MIC tanks began to shake and break apart. Then a safety valve on a vent shaft gave way, allowing the dense gas to escape and form a lethal cloud that silently settled on the surrounding area.

Hundreds of thousands of Indians, most of them desperately poor, lived in makeshift hovels around the plant. Some of these people died in their beds, unable to move, as the gas seared their lungs and caused them to suffocate on the fluid that formed. Others were roused from their sleep by the sounds of a growing panic, and finding themselves nauseous, unable to breathe, and temporarily blinded, they began a stampede to flee the danger. Hospitals were filled to overflowing with desperate people seeking relief from searing chest pains and irritated eyes. Morning found corpses spread across the city, as people lay where they fell. Most were victims of the gas, but some were trampled to death in the stampede. By the end of the week, more than 2,000 were known to have died, and the eventual toll is now estimated to exceed 3,500.[44] At least 200,000 other people were injured in the disaster, many permanently.

Like most major industrial accidents, the tragedy at Bhopal was caused by a complex interplay of human, organizational, and technological factors.[45] Mistakes by workers on the scene, along with a series of faulty decisions by the management of Union Carbide, defects in the design of the plant, and equipment failures at the time of the accident, all played a part. A heavy responsibility must be borne, though, by Union Carbide, as the parent company, since the safety standards observed at the Bhopal plant were considerably lower than those at facilities in the United States, such as the plant at Institute, West Virginia, where MIC is also produced.[46]

The role of Union Carbide in this immense human tragedy is complicated, however, by differences encountered in international business. Deliberate exposure of any group to death and injury on this scale would certainly be a failure to fulfill the duty not to inflict harm and also a violation of a fundamental human right, the right to physical security. The issue in this case, though, is not the ethics of practices that have known consequences but of operations that pose a certain level of *risk*, and determining what is an acceptable level of risk varies from one setting to another. Thus, a country with a desperate need to raise food for a growing population might accept a tradeoff that creates a greater risk of an industrial accident in return for more fertilizers and pesticides. Similarly, a government might accept lower safety standards as the price for gaining local control and creating jobs for its own citizens. Transnational corporations might not find it profitable to invest in less developed countries if they were required to install extensive safety equipment or to employ less hazardous technologies. One reason that companies in developed countries go abroad, in fact, is to take advantage of a looser regulatory environment in order to utilize manufacturing methods that are prohibited at home. Finally, risks are sometimes increased by local conditions beyond the control of TNCs. All of these factors were present in the Bhopal case.

The History of the Plant

Founded as a private company in 1934 for the manufacture of batteries, Union Carbide India Limited (UCIL) became a publicly owned corporation in 1955, with the parent company holding 50.8 percent of the stock. UCIL was a largely autonomous unit staffed by Indian managers, although overall direction was provided by Union Carbide, located in Danbury, Connecticut. At the time of the accident, UCIL was the twenty-first largest corporation in India, with about $170 million in revenues. UCIL entered the pesticide market in the 1960s at the urging of the Indian government, which was conducting a campaign to modernize agricultural production as part of the much touted "Green Revolution." The Indian government also pressed UCIL to build a plant in Bhopal, the capital of Madhya Pradesh, since this populous and impoverished state was in desperate need of modernization. An annual rent of 500 rupees (about $40) per acre was offered to encourage UCIL to locate there. The company accepted the offer, and in 1968, the Agricultural Products Division was transferred to a new facility in Bhopal.

At first the Bhopal plant produced fertilizers and pesticides using chemicals imported from other countries, but the Indian government was anxious to become self-sufficient and prodded UCIL to manufacture finished products from scratch. Also, local production created more jobs and added to the country's output. This policy suited the needs of the American parent company. Increased competition in India from other chemical companies combined with a downturn in farmers' use of fertilizers and pesticides put a squeeze on profits, and Union Carbide Corporation was looking for ways to cut costs. Manufacturing its major pesticide, Sevin, from beginning to end at one plant would be a step in this direction. Because of the toxic nature of the ingredients for Sevin, especially MIC, the expansion of the Bhopal plant was opposed by local officials, but their objections were overruled by the national government. The high expectations of Union Carbide and the Indian government for the new plant at Bhopal were never realized, however. In 1984, the Bhopal plant was losing money for the company and was operating at only 40 percent of capacity. At the time of the accident, in fact, Union Carbide was seeking to sell the facility.

The lack of profitability contributed to the low level of safety at the plant. Although it is possible to manufacture Sevin without producing MIC in an intermediate step, the more hazardous process was adopted for reasons of cost. Storing large quantities of MIC is also not necessary if the chemical is manufactured only as needed, but cost considerations led to the adoption of a system of bulk production. The design of the plant did not incorporate the use of multiple gauges, backup safety devices, and automatic shutoffs that were in common use elsewhere. According to a Union Carbide official, the Bhopal plant was built with a manual rather than an automatic safety system at the insistence of the Indian government, since the former created more jobs.[47] Also, because of cutbacks, the number of employees at the Bhopal plant had been sharply reduced, with a resulting decline in maintenance. Lax safety standards, inadequate training in safety procedures, and a rapid turnover of the work force further contributed to problems at the plant.

Causes of the Accident

The immediate cause of the accident was the failure of a maintenance worker to block the line leading to tank E610 during a routine washing of the line with water to remove residue. As a result, water was allowed to enter the tank, where it reacted with the highly volatile contents.[48] Three safety systems on the MIC tanks were simultaneously out of order. A refrigeration unit for cooling the tanks in an emergency had been shut down and the coolant used elsewhere in the plant; a scrubber designed to neutralize escaping MIC vapor with a caustic soda solution was switched to a standby position and could not be activated during the crisis; and a flare tower that burned the gas to render it harmless had been turned off so that a piece of corroded pipe could be replaced. A final emergency procedure, spraying the escaping gas with water, proved ineffective when water from fire hoses could not reach the top of the flare tower where the gas was being vented. In any event, none of these systems was designed to contain the amount of MIC that was actually released in the early hours of December 3.

The human toll of the accident was greatly increased by social, political, and economic conditions in the region where the plant is located. As Paul Shrivastava observes, "Bhopal is a textbook example of a rapidly developing city that sought—and obtained—sophisticated Western-style industrialization without making a commensurate investment in industrial infrastructure or rural development."[49] The emphasis on industrial development at the expense of agriculture drove people from the land into Bhopal. As a result, throngs of people occupied hovels right up to the fence of the plant on land that was largely vacant when Union Carbide first arrived. In an effort to improve living conditions, the city passed a law in 1984 granting ownership to the land that squatters already occupied, thus legalizing slums that should never have been allowed in the first place. The plant was also located about a mile from the train station where hundreds of people died on the night of the tragedy.

Ethically Evaluating Union Carbide's Conduct

Under these circumstances, was Union Carbide morally justified in operating the plant at Bhopal and exposing its workers and the local population to the potential harm that became a reality? This question can be repeated for corporations that manufacture asbestos and other hazardous materials abroad, dump toxic wastes in third world countries, pollute the environment, and, in general, create hazards for people around the globe. The negative harm principle requires us to conduct a risk assessment to ensure that the benefit for the people involved exceeds the harm. Such assessments are routine in evaluating hazards within the United States and other developed countries. Assessing risk in less developed countries is greatly complicated by the difficulty of determining the relative weight that other people place on the various benefits and harms. This is especially true when, as Thomas Donaldson points out, differences in evaluation reflect cultural norms. A Pakistani, for example, might give up some material well-being in order to maintain that country's Moslem heritage.[50]

Another impediment to assessing risk in less developed countries is the lack of a market to provide a monetary measure of the relative weight of benefits and harms. The willingness of American workers to accept more dangerous jobs at higher pay offers some indication of the value placed by people in our society on health and safety. Because of massive unemployment in the third world, combined with grinding poverty and a general ignorance of the hazards of many kinds of work, the low wages accepted do not accurately reflect their scale of values. Decisions by the government of a host country are also not always reliable indicators of a people's weighting of benefits and harms. As we have already observed, governments in the third world are often unable or unwilling to protect their own people effectively, and they all too frequently reflect the interests of only a narrow segment of the population.

One means for conducting a risk assessment in less developed countries with very different cultural traditions is to consider as sympathetically as possible how the people affected evaluate the benefits and harms of adopting a certain standard. Thomas Donaldson calls this the test of *rational empathy*, which he describes as putting ourselves in the shoes of a foreigner:

> To be more specific, it makes sense to consider ourselves and our own culture at a level of economic development relevantly similar to that of the other country. And, if, having done this, we find that *under such hypothetically altered social circumstances* we ourselves would accept the lower risk standards, then it is permissible to adopt the standards that appear inferior.[51]

The shortcomings of this method are obvious. Even a limited empathy requires considerable knowledge of other cultures, and truly putting ourselves in the shoes of people of very different cultural traditions is probably a psychological impossibility, even for those who make a sincere effort. Also, the test of rational empathy offers no protection against the coercion that results from dire economic necessity. Desperately poor people might be better off, all things considered, having a hazardous industry in their midst than doing without the jobs and other benefits it provides. Does this fact justify, however, the use of the most profitable technology consistent with ensuring a marginal benefit to the people affected, especially when a slight reduction in profitability could greatly reduce the risk and increase the benefit of an industry to the local population?

Applying the test of rational empathy to the operation of the Union Carbide plant in Bhopal yields inconclusive results. Lower safety standards in the facility are justified to some extent by the desire of the Indian government to boost the industrial output of the country and provide jobs and needed products. UCIL had not been profitable for several years prior to the accident, and the Bhopal plant, in particular, was a liability to the company, even with the use of less costly (and more hazardous) methods of production. Without cutbacks in staffing and maintenance, it is possible that the plant could not have remained open. When the plant closed for good in 1985, 650 people were thrown out of work and an estimated 1,500 other jobs that were related to the presence of Union Carbide were lost.[52] In addition, the city lost an important source of tax revenue.

Certainly, many mistakes by both Union Carbide and the Indian government made a severe accident more likely. The danger that the plant posed to the local population could have been significantly reduced by inexpensive measures, such as a more adequate warning system for the surrounding area. (A manually activated siren was sounded thirty minutes after the release of the gas and was switched off after a few minutes.) If the alternative had been to increase the level of safety to the point that the plant would no longer be profitable to operate, however, it is possible, given India's relative economic underdevelopment, that the benefits of a less safe plant would be sufficient to justify the risk posed by its continued operation.

Objections to the Negative Harm Principle

Some philosophers contend that the negative harm principle, as just applied to the Bhopal case, is misconceived. The obligation of a corporation such as Union Carbide is not merely to assess risk in terms of benefit and harm but to avoid inflicting harm (period), or at least to avoid inflicting certain *prohibited harms* except with the consent of the persons involved.[53] The negative harm principle, in other words, is not a weak version of utilitarianism ("Do more good than evil") but is more akin to Donaldson's right to physical security. Specifically, people have a right not to be harmed in certain prohibited ways without their consent. This interpretation of the negative harm principle is widely accepted in medical ethics, which holds that a doctor has no right to treat a patient, even for his or her own good, without that person's informed consent.

In this interpretation, Union Carbide would not be justified in operating a hazardous plant merely because the people of Bhopal would accept the risk if they were fully informed (this is what the test of rational empathy seeks to establish), but rather that the company has an obligation to inform workers and residents of the dangers they face, so that they can make an informed choice. This interpretation of the negative harm principle directs our attention not only to the safety standards adopted by Union Carbide at the Bhopal plant but also to the way the company treats the people concerned. Revealing the hazards posed by the plant shows respect for the people of Bhopal and enables them to exercise greater control over their lives.

A major problem of this interpretation of the negative harm principle is specifying the class of prohibited harms. Which harms do people have a right to be informed about? Henry Shue proposes six criteria for distinguishing harms that may not be imposed without the consent of those who will suffer them. According to these criteria, prohibited harms are those that result from a decision that:

> ... (1) may lead to *bodily damage*, (2) that is *serious* and (3) *irreversible*, in circumstances in which the damage is also (4) *unavoidably undetectable* to the person actually suffering it, (5) *unavoidably unpredictable* for the people who may potentially suffer it, and (6) *very likely* to occur.[54]

These criteria reflect the view that people have a right to protect themselves against serious irreversible bodily damage, such as permanently impaired lung capacity and blindness (which afflict the victims of Bhopal today). This is especially true when the source of the hazard is a leak in a tank, for example, that people cannot observe themselves, when they have no way of predicting a leak, and when the probability of a leak is quite high. Although each one of these criteria is subject to some uncertainty (how high must the probability be, for example?), they are all satisfied by the Bhopal case.

Compensating the Victims of the Tragedy

The justification of Union Carbide's operation of the plant in Bhopal is not the only issue raised by the case. The response of the company in the aftermath of the tragedy provides a revealing study of the responsibility of an American corporation to compensate the victims of an accident in a faraway place. Initially, Union Carbide, denied that it had any obligation to pay, since it was merely a 51 percent shareholder in Union Carbide India Limited. The company's position was that UCIL bore sole legal liability. Extensive litigation then followed. In April 1985, Union Carbide agreed to pay $5 million for interim relief ordered by a U.S. federal court, but a similar order from a court in the state of Madhya Pradesh in January 1988 to provide $270 million in relief was fought by Union Carbide until the amount was reduced to $190 million.

A $3.3 billion suit by the Indian government, acting on behalf of all the victims of Bhopal, was transferred by a U.S. judge to India, and in February 1989, more than five years after the accident, the Indian Supreme Court ordered Union Carbide to pay $470 million in compensation.[55] In the settlement, blame for the accident was not fixed and all criminal charges against Union Carbide and its executives were dropped. (The CEO, Warren Anderson, was arrested upon arriving in India immediately after the accident and later a charge of homicide was lodged against him.) The amount of compensation is about $940 for each of 500,000 claimants.

The Aftermath

The American parent company was deeply affected by the whole episode.[56] Coping with the crisis became a full-time job for many top executives, and the barrage of criticism from around the world caused employee morale to suffer. In its weakened state, Union Carbide became the target of a takeover bid by GAF Corporation. To protect itself, Union Carbide adopted a $4.3 billion recapitalization plan that required the company to sell off its consumer products division that marketed such household name items as Prestone antifreeze, Eveready batteries, and Glad Bags, and to slash its work force by more than half. Union Carbide is now a financially secure but much smaller company. Its reputation has been tarnished, however, and any time the company proposes to build a new plant anywhere in the world, the memory of Bhopal will be rekindled.

Conclusion

The passage from Raymond Vernon that begins this chapter has been amply borne out. Operating abroad, especially in the third world, creates dilemmas that lead to charges of serious ethical failings. Transnational corporations generally recognize a social responsibility and attempt to fulfill their responsibilities everywhere they are located. The major cause of occasional failures to act responsibly is not the lack of effort but the diversity of political and legal systems around the world and differences in economic development. Foreign operations give rise to challenges—and also create opportunities for misconduct—that simply do not exist for purely domestic enterprises.

One quandary facing all TNCs is deciding which standards to follow. We have seen that neither of the two extreme positions is satisfactory. The familiar adage, "When in Rome, do as the Romans do" and the opposite, "When in Rome or anywhere else, do as you would at home" are both inadequate guides. The standards of American business practice have been developed for a specific set of conditions and reflect certain choices that we have made as a society. Other, equally justified standards are possible, and some may be more appropriate for the particular circumstances of a third world country. Merely following accepted practices of a country or abiding by the law is no defense, however, when the conduct in question is unethical by any justified standard.

Some guidance is provided by the notion of a moral minimum that specifies a list of minimal obligations or duties for corporations engaged in international business. Two principles, in particular, yield such a list; namely, the principle of negative harm and the principle of respect for fundamental rights. These principles do not escape entirely the difficulties that plague the two positions "When in Rome, do as the Romans do" and "When in Rome or anywhere else, do as you would at home." Still, the two principles under discussion provide a framework for evaluating practices that is capable of yielding reasonably well-supported conclusions in a wide variety of situations. These principles are superceded, of course, by international agreements developed by such bodies as the United Nations, the International Labour Organization, and the Organization for Economic Cooperation and Development. As codes of conduct for transnationals become more detailed and comprehensive, the need for special principles of international business will, it is hoped, diminish.

NOTES

1. RAYMOND VERNON, "Foreign Operations," in JAMES W. MCKIE, ed., *Social Responsibility and the Business Predicament* (Washington, DC: The Brookings Institution, 1974), 287.
2. Some sources, including the United Nations, prefer the term *transnational*

instead of the more common *multinational* to emphasize the fact that the corporations in question are usually not owned and operated by people in many nations but are more commonly legally chartered in one country and conduct business across national boundaries. See *Transnational Corporations and Developing Countries: New Policies for a Changing World Economy* (New York: Committee for Economic Development, 1981), 15.

3. A critical view of TNCs is presented in RICHARD J. BARNET and RONALD E. MULLER, *Global Reach: The Power of the Multinational Corporations* (New York: Simon & Schuster, 1974). More approving of transnationals are two books by RAYMOND VERNON, *Sovereignty at Bay* (New York: Basic Books, 1971) and *Storm over the Multinationals* (Cambridge: Harvard University Press, 1977). A study focusing on the United States is C. FRED BERGSTEN, THOMAS HORST, and THEODORE H. MORAN, *American Multinationals and American Interests* (Washington, DC: The Brookings Institution, 1978).

4. CHARLES MEDAWAR and BARBARA FREESE, "Drug Multinationals in the Third World," *Business and Society Review*, 38 (Summer 1981), 23. See also CHARLES MEDAWAR and BARBARA FREESE, *Drug Diplomacy* (London: Social Audit, 1982).

5. MEDAWAR and FREESE, "Drug Multinationals in the Third World," 23.

6. MILTON SILVERMAN, PHILIP R. LEE, and MIA LYDECKER, *Prescriptions for Death: The Drugging of the Third World* (Berkeley and Los Angeles: University of California Press, 1982), 59.

7. MEDAWAR and FREESE, "Drug Multinationals in the Third World," 23; SILVERMAN, LEE, and LYDECKER, *Prescriptions for Death*, 59.

8. RALPH J. LEDOGAR, *Hungry for Profits: U.S. and Drug Multinationals in Latin America* (New York: IDOC/North America, 1975), 28–29.

9. *The Medical Letter: A Non-profit Publication on Drugs and Therapeutics*, vol. 15, no. 6 (March 16, 1973), 28. A spokesperson for Sterling Drug described this advertisement as a one-time mistake that is not typical of the company's marketing of Winstrol. Both the advertisement and the company response are cited in LEDOGAR, *Hungry for Profits*, 28.

10. MILTON SILVERMAN, *The Drugging of the Americas* (Berkeley and Los Angeles: University of California Press, 1976), 9.

11. SILVERMAN, LEE, and LYDECKER, *Prescriptions for Death*, 21.

12. LEDOGAR, *Hungry for Profits*, 48–49.

13. SILVERMAN, *The Drugging of the Americas*, 13; and SILVERMAN, LEE, and LYDECKER, *Prescriptions for Death*, 28.

14. SILVERMAN, *The Drugging of the Americas*, 13–15.

15. SILVERMAN, LEE, and LYDECKER *Prescriptions for Death*, 37–39.

16. LEDOGAR, *Hungry for Profits*, 37–39.

17. This act was amended in 1986 to allow the export of certain nonapproved drugs, such as drugs for the treatment of diseases not found in the United States.

18. SILVERMAN, LEE, and LYDECKER, *Prescriptions for Death*, 136.

19. SILVERMAN, LEE, and LYDECKER, *Prescriptions for Death*, 98. See also MILTON SILVERMAN and PHILIP R. LEE, *Pills, Profits, and Politics* (Berkeley and Los Angeles: University of California Press, 1976), 178–81.

20. BARNET and MULLER, *Global Reach*, 158.

21. BARNET and MULLER, *Global Reach*, 158.
22. SILVERMAN, LEE, and LYDECKER, *Prescriptions for Death*, 98–100.
23. "FDA Clears Drug to Cure African Sleeping Sickness," *The Wall Street Journal*, November 30 1990, p. B7.
24. See SILVERMAN, LEE, and LYDECKER, *Prescriptions for Death*, chap. 5.
25. JOHN BRAITHWAITE, *Corporate Crime in the Pharmaceutical Industry* (London: Routledge and Kegan Paul, 1984), 246.
26. NORMAN E. BOWIE, "The Moral Obligations of Multinational Corporations," in STEVEN LUPER-FOY, ed., *Problems of International Justice* (Boulder, CO: Westview Press, 1987), 97.
27. Quoted in LEDOGAR, *Hungry for Profits*, 46–47.
28. This point is made by RICHARD T. DEGEORGE, "Ethical Dilemmas for Multinational Enterprise," in W. MICHAEL HOFFMAN, ANN E. LANGE, and DAVID A. FREDO, eds., *Ethics and the Multinational Enterprise* (Lanham, MD: University Press of America, 1986), 40.
29. For an argument of this kind, see HENRY SHUE, "Transnational Transgressions," in TOM REGAN, *Just Business: New Introductory Essays in Business Ethics* (New York: Random House, 1984), 271–91.
30. See, for example, JACK BERMAN, "Should Companies Export Ethics?" *The New York Times*, September 2, 1973, sec. 3, p. 12.
31. SILVERMAN, LEE, and LYDECKER, *Prescriptions for Death*, 116.
32. SILVERMAN, LEE, and LYDECKER, *Prescriptions for Death*, 111.
33. For a history of the Arab boycott, see DAN S. CHILL, *The Arab Boycott of Israel* (New York: Praeger, 1976).
34. WALTER GUZZARDI, JR., "That Curious Barrier on the Arab Frontier," *Fortune*, July 1975, 170.
35. THOMAS DONALDSON, *The Ethics of International Business* (New York: Oxford University Press, 1989), 62.
36. DONALDSON, *The Ethics of International Business*, 63.
37. For an application of the negative harm principle to business in South Africa, see PATRICIA H. WERHANE, "Moral Justifications for Doing Business in South Africa," in HOFFMAN, LANGE, and FREDO, *Ethics and the Multinational Enterprise*, 435–42. The principle is applied to hazardous wastes and technology in HENRY SHUE, "Exporting Hazards," in PETER G. BROWN and HENRY SHUE, eds., *Boundaries: National Autonomy and Its Limits* (Totowa, NJ: Rowman and Littlefield, 1981), 107–45.
38. WILLIAM K. FRANKENA, *Ethics*, 2nd ed. (Englewood Cliffs, NJ: Prentice Hall, 1973), 47.
39. DONALDSON, *The Ethics of International Business*, chap. 5.
40. DONALDSON, *The Ethics of International Business*, 75–76.
41. DONALDSON, *The Ethics of International Business*, 81.
42. DONALDSON. *The Ethics of International Business*, 87–89.
43. Detailed accounts of the accident at Bhopal are provided in DAN KURZMAN, *A Killing Wind: Inside Union Carbide and the Bhopal Catastrophe* (New York: McGraw-Hill, 1987); and PAUL SHRIVASTAVA, *Bhopal: Anatomy of a Crisis* (Cambridge: Ballinger, 1987).
44. See SANJOY HAZARIKA, "Bhopal Payments Set at $470 Million for Union Carbide," *The New York Times*, February 15, 1989, sec. 4, p. 30.

45. For a discussion of this so-called HOT analysis, see SHRIVASTAVA, *Bhopal*, 48–57.

46. This double standard was admitted by Union Carbide CEO Warren Anderson. See STUART DIAMOND, "Warren Anderson: A Public Crisis, A Personal Ordeal," *The New York Times*, May 19, 1985, sec. 3, p. 1.

47. KURZMAN, *A Killing Wind*, 25.

48. Union Carbide has contended that water was pumped into the tank by a disgruntled employee, but this charge has never been substiantiated. For details, see KURZMAN, *A Killing Wind*, 185–89.

49. SHRIVASTAVA, *Bhopal*, 57.

50. DONALDSON, *The Ethics of International Business*, 113.

51. DONALDSON, *The Ethics of International Business*, 124.

52. SHRIVASTAVA, *Bhopal*, 72.

53. This is the position of Henry Shue, in SHUE "Exporting Hazards," 122.

54. SHUE, "Exporting Hazards," 124.

55. HAZARIKA, "Bhopal Payments Set at $470 Million for Union Carbide."

56. See JONATHAN P. HICKS, "After the Disaster, Carbide is Rebuilt," *The New York Times*, February 15, 1989, sec. 4, p. 3.

Index

X